ENGAGING CHINA

A NANCY BERNKOPF TUCKER AND WARREN I. COHEN BOOK
ON AMERICAN-EAST ASIAN RELATIONS

NANCY BERNKOPF TUCKER
and WARREN I. COHEN
Books on American-East Asian Relations

A NANCY BERNKOPF TUCKER AND WARREN I. COHEN BOOK
ON AMERICAN–EAST ASIAN RELATIONS

Edited by Thomas J. Christensen
Mark Philip Bradley
Rosemary Foot

Michael J. Green, *By More Than Providence: Grand Strategy and American Power in the Asia Pacific Since 1783*

Jeanne Guillemin, *Hidden Atrocities: Japanese Germ Warfare and American Obstruction of Justice at the Tokyo Trial*

Andrew B. Kennedy, *The Conflicted Superpower: America's Collaboration with China and India in Global Innovation*

Nancy Bernkopf Tucker was a historian of American diplomacy whose work focused on American–East Asian relations. She published seven books, including the prize-winning *Uncertain Friendships: Taiwan, Hong Kong, and the United States, 1945–1992*. Her articles and essays appeared in countless journals and anthologies, including the *American Historical Review*, *Diplomatic History*, *Foreign Affairs*, and the *Journal of American History*. In addition to teaching at Colgate and Georgetown (where she was the first woman to be awarded tenure in the School of Foreign Service), she served on the China desk of the Department of State and in the American embassy in Beijing. When the Office of the Director of National Intelligence was created, she was chosen to serve as the first assistant deputy director of national intelligence for analytic integrity and standards and ombudsman, and she was awarded the National Intelligence Medal of Achievement in 2007. To honor her, in 2012 the Woodrow Wilson International Center for Scholars established an annual Nancy Bernkopf Tucker Memorial Lecture on U.S.–East Asian Relations.

Warren I. Cohen is university distinguished professor emeritus at Michigan State University and the University of Maryland, Baltimore County, and a senior scholar in the Asia Program of the Woodrow Wilson Center. He has written thirteen books and edited eight others. He served as a line officer in the U.S. Pacific Fleet, editor of *Diplomatic History*, president of the Society for Historians of American Foreign Relations, and chairman of the Department of State Advisory Committee on Historical Diplomatic Documentation. In addition to scholarly publications, he has written for the *Atlantic*, the *Baltimore Sun*, the *Christian Science Monitor*, *Dissent*, *Foreign Affairs*, the *International Herald Tribune*, the *Los Angeles Times*, the *Nation*, the *New York Times*, the *Times Literary Supplement*, and the *Washington Post*. He has also been a consultant on Chinese affairs to various government organizations.

ENGAGING CHINA

—⚬⚭⚬—

Fifty Years of
Sino-American Relations

EDITED BY

ANNE F. THURSTON

Columbia University Press

New York

Columbia University Press
Publishers Since 1893
New York   Chichester, West Sussex
cup.columbia.edu

Library of Congress Cataloging-in-Publication Data
Names: Thurston, Anne F., editor.
Title: Engaging China : fifty years of Sino-American relations / edited by
Anne F. Thurston.
Other titles: Fifty years of Sino-American relations
Description: New York : Columbia University Press, [2021] |
Includes bibliographical references and index.
Identifiers: LCCN 2021001762 (print) | LCCN 2021001763 (ebook) |
ISBN 9780231201285 (hardback) | ISBN 9780231201292 (trade paperback) |
ISBN 9780231554022 (ebook)
Subjects: LCSH: United States—Foreign relations—China. | China—
Foreign relations—United States. | China—Foreign relations—1976– |
United States—Foreign relations—1945–1989. | United States—Foreign
relations—1989–
Classification: LCC E183.8.C6 E54 2021 (print) | LCC E183.8.C6 (ebook) |
DDC 327.73051—dc23
LC record available at https://lccn.loc.gov/2021001762
LC ebook record available at https://lccn.loc.gov/2021001763

Cover image: Mao and Nixon in 1972.
Credit: Photo © Leonard de Selva / Bridgeman Images
Cover design: Lisa Hamm

To David M. (Mike) Lampton
With gratitude, admiration, and respect
For your lifetime of contributions to the China field

CONTENTS

ENGAGING CHINA

PART I

THE MAKING AND UNMAKING OF THE U.S.-CHINA RELATIONSHIP

CHAPTER 1

ENGAGING CHINA

Fifty Years of Sino-American Relations

ANNE F. THURSTON

fter Mao Zedong stood on the Gate of Heavenly Peace on October 1, 1949, and declared the establishment of the People's Republic of China (PRC), the United States refused to recognize the new Chinese government.[1] America had supported Chiang Kai-shek and the Nationalist Party in China's long civil war and continued to recognize the Nationalists even after they fled to Taiwan. Within months, the United States and Communist China were at war on the Korean Peninsula. When the armistice was signed in July 1953, the United States was still in the grip of a virulent strain of anticommunism. Any suggestion of engagement with China ran the risk of being labeled treasonous. A number of China specialists thought to be sympathetic to the Chinese Communist Party, including academics and government civil servants, lost their jobs during those years.[2]

Not until the mid-1960s did glimmers of change appear. In 1966, an influential and diverse group of American philanthropists and leading China specialists convened to establish the National Committee on U.S.-China Relations as a nongovernmental vehicle for exploring the possibility of ending the mutual estrangement between China and the United States. John D. Rockefeller, one of the founders, noted that American thinking about China during this period was so dominated by fear that "many regarded it as virtually treasonable to even raise the question of rethinking China policy."[3]

Months later, in October 1967, a year before his successful bid for the presidency, the private citizen and staunch anticommunist Richard Nixon published a seminal article in *Foreign Affairs* that labeled Red China a clear and present danger and argued that the world could not be safe until China changed. The way to do this, Nixon said, was to persuade China that its interests could best be served only by accepting the basic rules of international civility. He wanted to pull China back into the world community not as the epicenter of world revolution but as a great and progressing nation. China, he said, "cannot be left forever outside the family of nations, there to nurture its fantasies, cherish its hates and threaten its neighbors."[4]

The article foreshadowed Nixon's later overture to China. In February 1972, Richard Nixon, as president of the United States, made his historic visit to Beijing to meet with Chinese Communist Party Chairman Mao Zedong. And seven years later, on January 1, 1979, U.S. President Jimmy Carter formally established diplomatic relations with the People's Republic of China, an event that was followed soon thereafter by a much applauded visit to the United States by China's newly resurrected and powerful leader, Deng Xiaoping. The age of engagement had begun.

And now it may be at an end.

This book examines almost fifty years of U.S. engagement with China and asks four basic questions: What happened? What went right? What went wrong? And where do we go from here? The idea for the book originated at a conference held at the Wingspread Conference Center in Racine, Wisconsin, in November 2018, titled "Five Decades of U.S. Engagement with China: What Have We Learned?" The contributors are some of the leading China specialists in the United States and the world. All have played a role, often significant, in engaging China. Some are academics, others have been leaders of nongovernmental organizations, and some have been in the government and diplomatic service.

The intellectual starting point of the book is that American engagement with China has been complex, multifaceted, and multilayered and can be understood only historically over time, at a variety of levels, and from a variety of disciplinary and substantive perspectives. John Garver's chapter 3, on the history of engagement, takes the longest view. For more than a century, he argues, the core element of American foreign policy toward China was the facilitation of China's national quest for wealth and power, and he describes why and how, now that China has become strong, that long-standing policy of mutual cooperation and friendship has come to an end. Other chapters focus on nongovernmental exchanges. Whereas the media generally report on the government-to-government side of the relationship and much of Washington focuses on issues of security, many of the richest and most productive exchanges have taken place out of the limelight at subnational and nongovernmental (and hence also less political) levels. These nongovernmental exchanges have not only operated substantive, productive programs with Americans and Chinese working side by side, they have also served to maintain stability on the ground when relations at higher levels threatened to go off course. Thus, in addition to addressing the overall U.S.-China relationship (in chapters 2, 3, 13, and 14 by Fingar, Garver, Lieberthal and Thornton, and Lampton, respectively), the book includes chapters on Chinese and American perceptions and misperceptions (Madsen, chapter 5), academic relationships and exchanges (Daly, chapter 10), cooperation in the area of health (Huang, chapter 9), the role of American nongovernmental organizations (Bullock, chapter 8), the state of the China field (Mertha, chapter 4), economics (Naughton, chapter 7), trade and finance (Allen, chapter 6), issues concerning China's geographic periphery (Carla Freeman, chapter 12), and the military (Chas Freeman, chapter 11).

Most—probably all—of the volume's authors would agree that engagement with China has been a net positive good. Engagement opened the doors for China's participation in the international system, encouraging it to become, in Robert Zoellick's words, a responsible stakeholder, not just adjusting to the international rules developed over the last century but joining to address the challenges of the new century.[5] As a participant in that system, China became a member of the UN Security Council, the World Trade Organization, the International Monetary Fund, and the World Bank. It became a signatory to the Treaty on the Non-Proliferation of Nuclear Weapons in 1992 and to the Comprehensive Nuclear-Test-Ban Treaty in 1996, and signed on to the Paris Climate Agreement in 2016. Between 2000 and 2018, China supported 182 of 190 UN Security Council resolutions imposing sanctions on states violating international rules. It is the second largest funder of the UN and has deployed, under UN auspices, some 2,500 peacekeepers to various parts of the world.[6] Engagement helped bring about a new era of peace in East Asia, which in turn stoked China's unprecedentedly rapid economic growth, fueling social change and economic betterment throughout Asia and beyond. Even many Americans who do not believe that China has become the hoped-for responsible stakeholder would concede that the PRC has demonstrated a willingness to contribute meaningfully and responsibly on issues where the interests of both sides have converged, including, for instance, climate change, the Iran nuclear deal, and sanctions against North Korea.[7] Although Beijing's record remains far from perfect from the American perspective, it is nonetheless a vast improvement over the preengagement period.

Not even the most enthusiastic proponents of engagement would say that the relationship has not been fraught with problems. The contributors to this volume know from experience that the U.S.-China relationship has never been simple or easy, and they are also clear-headed realists. The challenges have been frequent and sometimes perilous. Misperceptions, misunderstandings, and genuine frictions born of divergent interests and values have been endless. Richard Madsen devotes chapter 5 to those misperceptions. The most egregious and untoward challenges to the relationship have come from both sides and include China's violent military suppression of citizen protests in Beijing and other parts of China in June 1989, its missile launches in the Taiwan Strait in the mid-1990s, the accidental and lethal bombing by U.S. NATO forces of China's Belgrade embassy in 1999, and the 2001 EP-3 incident, when an American reconnaissance aircraft and a Chinese fighter jet collided, killing the Chinese pilot and forcing the American plane to land without permission on Hainan Island. All of these incidents, covered in chapter 11 by Chas Freeman, threatened to derail the relationship and had a cumulative toll on the underlying strategic foundation of bilateral ties. This volume thus details not only the accomplishments of engagement but also the blunders, mistakes, misunderstandings, frustrations, and sometimes the well-earned distrust.

The importance of the U.S.-China relationship—and the implications of its potential failure—cannot be overstated. In the early twenty-first century, as the rise of China became an inescapable fact, most American foreign policy specialists came to regard bilateral ties with China as the most important interstate relationship of the era. The corollary to that recognition was that, therefore, we had better get China right. As one study introducing the challenges of a rising China put it:

> As the 21st century unfurls, the stakes have never been higher for getting U.S. policy toward China right. The direction that China and U.S.-China relations take will define the strategic future of the world for years to come. No relationship matters more—for better or for worse—in resolving the enduring challenges of our time, maintaining stability among great powers, sustaining global economic growth, stemming dangerous weapons proliferation, countering terrorism, and confronting new transnational threats of infectious disease, environmental degradation, international crime, and failing states.[8]

A 2010 study of American public opinion toward China concluded that the American people were both relatively well informed about the changes that had taken place in China in recent decades and concerned about how those changes might affect their own lives and work.[9] Whatever those concerns, however, the American public generally accepted the policy of engagement that had guided every president from Nixon to Obama. The mainstream popular presumption was that relations between the two countries were generally mutually beneficial and would continue to improve, particularly if the Chinese economy kept growing and its government continued to move in the direction of permitting greater openness and personal freedoms. Most would not have disputed President Obama's mantra that the relationship between the United States and China is the most important bilateral relationship of the twenty-first century or taken exception to his repeated declarations that he welcomed China's rise.[10] Getting China right was assumed to be difficult because understanding and communicating with China requires considerable training and expertise and because our political systems and values are so different. Sometimes our fundamental interests simply clash.

Over time, different constituencies with different interests developed, and popular views of China diversified. The business community was long the most enthusiastic champion of engagement, whereas human rights groups often expressed concern that the U.S. government was not doing enough to push China on human rights issues. And when the success of China's burgeoning new industries contributed to employment declines in American manufacturing, a phenomenon Barry Naughton describes in his chapter on economics, union representatives of displaced American workers spoke out to decry China's role in the loss of American jobs and castigate American firms for offshoring.

Within this increasingly diversified panorama of interests, China was sometimes painted in extremes. The popular fear of a China threat is not new. And the question of whither China has long been staple fare of China watching. The early 2000s, somewhat contradictorily, entertained both a China threat school of thought and a China collapse school of thought. The China threat school saw Chinese communism and American democracy as fundamentally incompatible, rejected the possibility that China's trade with the West could have any democratizing effect, and concluded that the China threat could only be met by a renewed commitment to democracy and a strengthening of American military power.[11] The China collapse school argued that without a major change in Chinese leadership, the combination of a failing economy, massive unemployment, corruption within the government, and the reforms that China would have to adopt after joining the World Trade Organization would lead to a collapse of the Chinese economy and government within ten years.[12] Revised and updated versions of these contending views continue to this day, and some are presented by sophisticated and erudite scholars. Speculations about China's future still include predictions of both a coming upheaval and crack-up, on the one hand,[13] and the possibility, on the other, that Xi Jinping's vision of the Chinese dream, with its illiberal politics, military buildup, Wolf Warrior ethos, and often exaggerated notions of American decline, will not only precipitate decades of unresolved tensions between the two countries but also perhaps lead to war.[14] The possibility of war is often given credence under the rubric of the Thucydides Trap, whereby a new rising power emerges to challenge an older, now defensive, great power.

President Obama repeatedly expressed his view that the U.S.-China relationship was the most important bilateral relationship of the twenty-first century and continued to avow that he welcomed China's rise, but he never actually declared China a friend. The idea of a partnership with China was toxic in Washington politics. Indeed, President Obama made clear that he intended the United States—and not countries like China—to continue making the rules for the world economy.[15] The number of misunderstandings, misperceptions, and disagreements grew as the relationship became more complex. Some of these were engendered by China's growing economic might as the world's second largest economy and its perception of Obama's pivot to Asia as an effort to contain China's rise. On the American side, legitimate issues related to intellectual property theft, forced technology transfers, and Made in China 2025 continued to fester. China's industrial policies did not sit easily with American aspirations for a level playing field in international trade and finance. China's new activism on the international stage, such as the ambitious Belt and Road Initiative launched in 2013 and Beijing's establishment of the Asian Infrastructure Investment Bank in 2016, were seen by some not as China assuming the role of a responsible stakeholder but as an effort by Beijing to rewrite the global rules of engagement and reshape Asia's economic geography to shut out the United States. Tensions continued to build throughout Obama's presidency.[16]

But U.S.-China relations took a sudden, precipitous turn for the worse when the strongman rule of Xi Jinping in Beijing came up against the assumption of the American presidency by Donald Trump. At the end of 2017 and the beginning of 2018, the Trump administration submitted its *National Security Strategy* to Congress, and the Department of Defense made public its new *National Defense Strategy*, signed by then Secretary of Defense James Mattis.[17] Although the *National Security Strategy* called for continued cooperation with China, it also asserted that "China and Russia challenge American power, influence and interests, attempting to erode American security and prosperity. They are determined to make economies less free and less fair, to grow their militaries, and to control information and data to repress their societies and expand their influence."[18] The *National Defense Strategy* lamented the erosion in America's competitive military advantage and declared the central challenge to U.S. prosperity and security to be "the reemergence of long-term, strategic competition by . . . revisionist powers."[19] Both documents labeled China and Russia revisionist powers, accusing them of undermining the international order by exploiting its benefits while simultaneously undercutting its principles. China was accused of using predatory economics to intimidate its neighbors and militarizing features in the South China Sea.[20] Between Russia and China, China was characterized as the greater threat.

A speech to the Hudson Institute in October 2018 by Vice President Mike Pence both echoed the *National Defense Strategy* report and carried the allegations against China still further:

> Beijing is employing a whole-of-government approach to advance its influence and benefit its interests. It's employing this power in more proactive and coercive ways to interfere in the domestic policies of this country and to interfere in the politics of the United States. . . . The Chinese Communist Party is rewarding or coercing American businesses, movie studios, universities, think

tanks, scholars, journalists, and local, state and federal officials. . . . And worst of all, China has initiated an unprecedented effort to influence American public opinion, the 2018 elections, and the environment leading into the 2020 presidential elections.[21]

A year later, on October 24, 2019, Vice President Pence declared that the United States wanted practical cooperation and engagement with China, but engagement in a manner consistent with fairness, mutual respect, and the international rules of commerce. He presented a litany of Chinese offenses, from the arrest of Christian ministers and the destruction of Christian churches, to the treatment of Uighur Muslims in Xinjiang, numerous cases of intellectual property theft, the vast amount of Chinese fentanyl flooding across American borders causing thousands of deaths every year, and the militarization of the South China Sea. These accusations, by and large, were both true and legitimate cause for American concern.

The U.S. government closed the Chinese consulate in Houston soon thereafter, alleging that its offices served as a base for Chinese spies and intellectual property theft.[22] China, in turn, retaliated by closing the American consulate in Chengdu. During July 2020, in order to publicize the content of the updated Strategic Approach to the People's Republic of China, Secretary of State Pompeo sent several of the administration's top officials out to deliver a series of major speeches on China to select audiences in such venues as the Hudson Institute, the Gerald R. Ford Presidential Museum, and the Nixon Presidential Library. Filled with rhetoric reminiscent of the darkest days of the Cold War, the starting point of those speeches was that the greatest failure of American foreign policy since the 1930s has been to engage China on the premise that as China developed, it would become a responsible stakeholder, more open economically and politically, and generally more like us.[23] Instead, Director Christopher Wray of the FBI alleged that China is engaged in a whole of state effort to become the world's only superpower by any means necessary.[24] The goal of the Chinese Communist Party under Xi Jinping, according to National Security Advisor Robert O'Brien, is to remake the world according to the Chinese Communist Party. According to O'Brien, the Chinese Communist Party has already gained leverage over individual Americans by "collecting your most intimate data, your words, your actions, your purchases, your whereabouts, your health records, your social media posts, your texts, and they are mapping your network of friends and acquaintances."[25] Many American companies, according to Attorney General William Barr, have already succumbed to China's influence. Hollywood is alleged to be so successfully under China's spell that American movie directors censor to China's satisfaction without even being asked.[26] According to Attorney General Barr, some leaders of American corporations are so under China's sway that they should be registered as agents for a foreign government. And big American tech companies even helped build the Great Firewall of China.[27]

Secretary of State Pompeo delivered the penultimate speech in the series, describing his role as detailing for the American people what the China threat means for our economy, for our liberty, and indeed for the future of free democracies around the world. If we want to have a free twenty-first century, and not the Chinese century of which Xi Jinping dreams, he said, the old paradigm of blind engagement with China simply won't get it done. Quoting from Nixon's article in *Foreign Affairs*, he declared that freedom-loving nations of the world must induce China to change, just as President Nixon wanted. He alleged that Communist China is already within our borders, that some Chinese coming to the United States ostensibly as students are in fact here to steal our intellectual property and take it back to their country, and that if we don't act now . . . our children's children may be at the mercy of the Chinese Communist Party.[28]

Thus, the United States officially came to see China as a major threat although labeled a strategic competitor rather than an outright enemy. Public opinion polls reflect the change. A survey conducted by the Pew Research Center in March 2020 found the highest percentage of negative views toward China since its polling began in 2005. Two-thirds of those polled had a negative view of China, and 90 percent viewed China as a threat. More than 70 percent viewed China's president and party general secretary Xi Jinping unfavorably. Party differences were significant, with Republicans consistently viewing China more unfavorably than Democrats on all dimensions.[29] The particular issues of most concern to the respondents were China's impact on the global environment (61 percent), the possibility of further cyberattacks from China (57 percent), the trade deficit (49 percent), and the loss of jobs to China (52 percent). A Gallup poll conducted in February 2020 similarly found that only 33 percent of those polled had a favorable opinion of China, 1 percent lower than a poll conducted soon after the military opened fire against protesters in Beijing in 1989.[30]

Washington pundits are fond of finding areas of consensus in the country's notoriously polarized capital city. And indeed, some see a new Washington consensus on the question of China that regards much of the PRC's behavior as deeply problematic and hence requiring a more forceful response[31] on the part of the United States. What that response should be, however, remains problematic.[32] A multitude of think tanks, task forces, working groups, and assorted China specialists, including some contributors to this volume, have presented thoughtful, balanced, and well-researched proposals.[33] A number of sober-minded China specialists, including Richard Madsen in this volume, have suggested that the United States needs first to get its own house in order before the U.S.-China relationship goes too far astray. This would mean launching a new domestic revitalization effort that would include seriously addressing and seeking to resolve the divisions that have driven us as a people apart and undermined our day-to-day practice of democracy at home and our national effectiveness abroad. Before America can be united and at peace at home and influential and respected abroad, we must address long-standing problems of health, education, and infrastructure. Only then can the United States resume its role as a global leader, reembracing its allies in Europe, Asia, and the Pacific and becoming actively useful to nations on the road to development. This goal seems consistent with the goals of the new Biden administration.

∗ ∗ ∗

In the meantime two divergent schools of thought, almost at polar extremes, seem to have emerged in Washington over the issue of China. These views can be discerned in two different open letters to the White House and Congress.

In early July 2019, the *Washington Post* published an open letter to President Trump and members of Congress titled "China Is Not an Enemy." It was signed by some 100 people, including leading China specialists from both the academic and foreign policy communities. The letter was not uncritical of China. It expressed deep concern about China's recent international and domestic behavior, including increased domestic repression, increased state control over private firms, failure to live up to trade commitments, and its generally more assertive foreign policy. But it also expressed deep concern about the growing deterioration in bilateral ties, arguing that the growing rift was not in the best U.S. or global interests and asserting that Washington's response was contributing to the continuing deterioration of relations and that Washington therefore also bore responsibility. The letter took direct exception to official statements labeling China an economic enemy and an existential national security threat. It offered seven propositions for a more effective American policy toward China. Among the organizers of this open letter were several contributors to this volume. Among the signatories were several more.[34]

But then came another open letter to President Trump, titled "Stay the Course on China." This letter, more in keeping with the Trump administration policy as articulated by Secretary of State Pompeo, asserted that the ambitions of the Chinese communists are antithetical to those of America and declared that the past forty years of engagement have contributed to the incremental erosion of U.S. national security. The letter alleged that over the past forty years of Sino-American relations, many American foreign policy experts did not accurately assess the PRC's intentions or attributed the Chinese Communist Party's reprehensible conduct to the difficulties of governing a country of 1.3 billion people. "American policymakers were told time and again by these adherents of the China engagement school that the PRC would become a responsible stakeholder once a sufficient level of economic modernization was achieved," the letter states. "This did not happen and cannot so long as the CCP rules China."[35] This letter was also signed by some one hundred individuals.[36]

The differences between the two letters are stark. The first letter is evidence that it is possible to be critical of China while still believing in engagement. It did not place all the blame for declining relations on China, arguing instead that the United States bears some of the responsibility. It presented a set of suggestions designed to ameliorate the dispute, inveighing against treating China as an enemy, arguing that with a correct balance of competition and cooperation, those Chinese leaders who still want to play a constructive role in the world would be strengthened, and insisting on the need to work together with other nations and international organizations. The second letter asserts that China is not and never has been a peaceful regime and that it uses its economic and military force to bully and intimidate others. It concludes both that American policymakers got China wrong and that American goals with China cannot be achieved so long as the Chinese Communist Party is in power. The implication is that regime change is a prerequisite to a productive relationship between the two countries.[37]

Washington thus seems to contain two apparently irreconcilable camps. In one camp are those who have long seen value in engagement with China and danger in the recent rift and would prefer engagement to continue even if in an attenuated form. In the other camp are those who see China as an existential threat.

The first camp has been outspoken about the perils ahead if the relationship continues its decline. The *New York Times* columnist Thomas Friedman wrote that:

> It is impossible to exaggerate what a dangerous cliff the U.S. and China are perched on today. If the current trade dispute tips over into a full-blown economic war . . . the world as we've known it for the last four decades is going to be replaced with something much uglier, less prosperous, less stable and less able to meet global challenges like climate change and cyber crime, that are barreling down on us now.[38]

Even the ordinarily restrained Henry Kissinger, whose secret trip from Pakistan to China on behalf of President Nixon in July 1971 began the process of engagement, sounded an alarm. Before a gathering of supporters of the National Committee on U.S.-China Relations, Kissinger argued that conflict between the United States and China will be inevitable and result in a catastrophic outcome that will be worse than world wars unless the two countries settle their differences.[39]

The second camp now has a small cottage industry devoted to the twin propositions that America got China wrong and (therefore) that engagement was a failure.

The most consequential and controversial opening salvo contending that somebody got China wrong was a 2018 article in *Foreign Affairs* by Kurt Campbell, who was assistant secretary of state for East Asian and Pacific affairs from 2009 to 2013, and Ely Ratner, who was deputy national security advisor to Vice President Joseph Biden from 2015 to 2017.[40] They argue that since Nixon's 1967 article in *Foreign Affairs* calling for a rapprochement with China, "the assumption that deepening commercial, diplomatic, and cultural ties would transform China's internal development and external behavior has been a bedrock of U.S. strategy." But all sides erred, they say, including "free traders and financiers who foresaw inevitable and increasing openness in China, integrationists who argued that Beijing's ambitions would be tamed by greater interaction with the international community, and hawks who believed that China's power would be abated by perpetual American primacy." But nothing, they argue, has swayed China as predicted. "Washington now faces its most dynamic and formidable competition in modern history. Getting this challenge right will require doing away with the hopeful thinking that has long characterized the United States' approach to China."[41]

Response to the Campbell/Ratner argument has been considerable. The Brookings Institution's Jeffery Bader points out that engagement was never undertaken as a favor to China but because it was judged to be in the interest of the United States, an argument also made by Thomas Fingar in this volume. As a result of engagement, Bader argues, Soviet expansionism was stopped and the USSR ultimately collapsed; peace came to Asia, where 350,000 people had died in wars the half century before; Taiwan has prospered both economically and politically; China is spectacularly prosperous; and Americans from widely different professions and interests have benefitted from people-to-people interactions. The dramatic expansion of trade between the two countries, from almost nothing to billions of dollars a year, has also been a significant accomplishment, Bader asserts, as has the cap on new weapons of mass destruction.[42]

Robert Zoellick has also pushed back forcefully, by arguing that those who blithely assume that U.S. cooperation with China did not produce results are flat wrong and that those who assume that China has been more a disrupter than a constructive actor are misleading themselves.[43] Harvard's Alastair Iain Johnston argues that the goals of the American policy of engagement were never as expansive as what those who have declared the policy a failure say they were—i.e., to promote a Chinese commitment to the U.S.-dominated liberal international order and to liberalize, even democratize, China's political system. To Johnston, the very concept of a U.S.-dominated liberal order is both exaggerated and oversimplified, and the assertion that the earlier engagers believed that engagement would lead inexorably to political liberalization and democratization is a bad caricature of what they were really saying. He credits the Dalai Lama with perhaps the most accurate assessment of engagement.

In 1997, when asked whether engagement with China had failed, the Tibetan spiritual leader responded that engagement cannot be regarded as "a complete failure. The situation is more complicated."[44]

The situation is indeed more complicated, as the chapters in this book attest. Getting China right remains particularly important and challenging in light of the increasingly assertive, authoritarian stance of China's current leadership, the unpredictable and ever-changing bombast of the recent the American administration, and the consequent erosion of America's moral authority abroad. But well-informed, thoughtful China specialists in both academia and think tanks and including the contributors to this volume, continue to produce analyses that avoid extremes and take a middle ground. The experience with and knowledge of China possessed by the group of China specialists assembled for this volume is genuinely formidable.

Many had their first on-the-ground introduction to China in the mid to late 1970s and early 1980s and were witness to the transformations that began at that time. Several went even earlier. Chas Freeman was the first. He was the lead American interpreter during Nixon's 1972 visit. Kenneth Lieberthal had just arrived for his first visit to Beijing in July 1976 and was fast asleep when he was startled awake by the tremors of the massive Tangshan earthquake that killed hundreds of thousands of Chinese citizens and literally shook Mao's regime just months before the chairman's death. David Lampton took his first trip to China shortly after Mao's death in September 1976 and was in Shanghai, ten days into the visit, when citizens of that city first learned that a shadowy disciple of Mao named Hua Guofeng had been appointed to the position held by the deceased party chairman and that two gangs of four, one based in Beijing, the other in Shanghai, had just been overthrown. The reaction he witnessed from the citizens of Shanghai, Lampton told me, was "like I imagine the liberation of Paris to have been after the Nazis."

The China encountered by those who first visited in the 1970s and early 1980s, still recovering from the ravages of Mao, was a far cry from the China of today. The Beijing Hotel, at seventeen stories, was the tallest building in China's capital city. Villages, as seen from the window of a bus in rural areas outside the major cities, looked pretty much as they had a century or two before: rude earthen huts, cooking fires fueled by straw, mule-drawn wooden carts piled high with cabbages, no machines, an occasional light bulb or two, and a few bicycles. Rural China was painfully poor. Many farmers were destitute.

In the cities, everyone dressed in the same dark trousers or skirts and the same white shirts. There were three types of hairstyles, one for men, one for women, and pigtails for young girls who had yet to reach adulthood. Foreigners were segregated from ordinary Chinese, who were not allowed into the hotels where perplexed foreigners were housed in isolation from the citizens of the country they had come to visit. The foreigners shopped in Friendship Stores where Chinese were not allowed and where purchases were paid for not in the official Chinese currency, the renminbi, but in a special foreign exchange currency bought with U.S. dollars (and other hard currencies) that could be used only by foreigners and only to buy goods in Friendship Stores and hotels open only to foreigners. Real conversation was almost nonexistent. People spoke like the pages of the *People's Daily*. All the news was good. The famine of the Great Leap Forward, during which tens of millions died, did not exist. The violence and breakdown of social norms during the Cultural Revolution were left unspoken. The brief introduction and tea that began every meeting with the foreigner inevitably included a recognition that China had had some troubles, due entirely to the Gang of Four. But since the overthrow of the gang, everyone agreed, the situation had continued to improve day by day, which indeed it had.

Then suddenly the country came alive. Deng Xiaoping's ascension to power at the Third Plenary Session of the Eleventh Central Committee in December 1978 signaled the end of the disastrous Mao era and the beginning of major political and economic reforms designed to make the political system more functionally specialized, data driven, and responsive. A number of the contributors to this volume were firsthand witnesses. The late Richard Baum (whose contribution to the China field is covered more fully in the chapter by Andrew Mertha) has described the *fang* (letting go) and *shou* (tightening up) cycles that began with the Democracy Wall movement of 1978–1979 and continued to the end of the 1980s.[45] As Baum wrote, it was a time of experimentation and innovation.[46] Important new political and economic reforms were introduced. The system of lifetime tenure for party and government leaders was being abolished. A new election law mandated direct popular elections of delegates to local peoples congresses at and below the level of the county with more candidates than seats and selection through secret ballots.[47] Universities also held elections of student leaders, which caused an international stir when the university administrators at Peking University and Hunan Teachers College voided the elections in their schools when the outspoken commitment to democratic reform expressed by the victorious candidates proved more than even a newly liberalized political atmosphere could bear.[48]

That decade-plus was a time of tremendous ferment, an outpouring of political and social energy, and continual, head-spinning letting go and tightening up. In December 1978, Wei Jingsheng posted his first big character poster on Beijing's Democracy Wall calling for a fifth modernization—democracy.[49] Some three months later, he put up another poster declaring Deng Xiaoping a new dictator. Wei was arrested and spent fourteen and a half years of his fifteen-year sentence in prison, only to be rearrested and sentenced to four more years following his release.[50]

At the same time, thousands, perhaps tens of thousands, of scholars and writers who had been persecuted during the Cultural Revolution, sent to the countryside or labor reform camps, or to the so-called May Seventh Cadre Schools, were returning to China's cities, reemerging to resume their academic and writing careers. In April 1979, China sent the first delegation of social scientists and humanists to visit the United States since before 1949. Headed by vice president of the Chinese Academy of Social Sciences and former ambassador to the European Union, Huan Xiang, the delegation included China's preeminent sociologist/anthropologist Fei Xiaotong, acclaimed novelist and literary critic Qian Zhongxu, and onetime Christian minister Zhao Fusan. Many on the delegation had only recently been rehabilitated and returned to their previous place of work.[51] Several had studied in the West before the establishment of the PRC and were able to reconnect with old American friends, some of whom had become distinguished scholars of China, including, for instance, Harvard's grandfather of China studies, John King Fairbank and his wife Wilma.

It was a time of soul searching. As China's intellectuals were rehabilitated and writers took up their pens once more, stories of violence and persecution and abuse that never made the pages of the *People's Daily* began to appear. Writers such as Liu Binyan, exiled first during the Anti-Rightist Campaign of 1957 and then again with the outbreak of the Cultural Revolution, reemerged to write a new form of critical literature called *baogao wenxue*, or reportage literature, stories of the abuse of power by Communist Party cadres directed against ordinary, upstanding Chinese citizens. One of his most popular pieces was "People or Monsters?" The monsters were the corrupt party officials who, Liu wrote, still dominated at all levels of society.[52] Others wrote *shanghen wenxue*, literature of the wounded, tales of persecution and violence and retribution during the Cultural Revolution. Ba Jin, one of China's preeminent twentieth-century writers, wrote elegantly and movingly of the agonizing guilt he continued to feel for the death of his wife, who had been persecuted just for being his wife and who, because she was his wife, was not able to get medical care when she was seriously ill.[53] Indeed, during the Cultural Revolution, Mao had regularly denied medical treatment to high-ranking officials he had attacked, including the former president Liu Shaoqi and Premier Zhou Enlai, both of whom died, at least in part, as a result.[54]

Churches, mosques, and temples, closed for decades, began to reopen. Chinese began to take part in religious activities.[55] Soon, some individual Chinese felt safe enough to pour out their souls to foreigners. The history of China since 1949, as told to Americans by individual Chinese, was harrowing. American journalists in particular began to write about the abuses that had occurred under Mao.[56] And so did some academics.[57] By December of 1986, astrophysicist Fang Lizhi, then vice president of China's Hefei-based University of Science and Technology, had gained fame for the speeches he was giving at various universities across the country with titles like "Democracy, Reform, and Modernization." Fang called for complete Westernization and full democracy in China, even while admitting that "our understanding of democracy is so inadequate that we can barely even discuss it."[58] He told of his experience as a visiting scholar at Princeton University's Institute for Advanced Study early in 1986 during which he had received a mailing from the local congressional representative in the district where he was staying. The representative explained what bills were coming up before Congress and how he had voted on various issues. He solicited his constituents' opinions and suggestions. Fang was impressed that in what the Chinese government insisted on labeling a false democracy, his opinions were actively sought, whereas in China, which claimed to be a true democracy, he knew nothing about his supposed representative and had never been asked his views.[59]

Then, when the winter of 1986–87 saw a series of protests by university students, the liberal-minded Party General Secretary Hu Yaobang was removed from office. Liu Binyan and Fang Lizhi were expelled from the Communist Party. A new clampdown had begun.

But still the liberal critics raised their voices. Su Xiaokang's six-part, highly controversial television series, *Heshang*, often translated as *River Elegy*, was shown twice in the second half of 1988. Nothing on official Chinese television before or since has matched the depth and breadth of *Heshang*'s criticisms. The documentary's attack on traditional Chinese culture was reminiscent of the May Fourth Movement of 1919, arguing that Chinese culture was incapable of bringing the country into the modern world. *Heshang* saw socialism as a failure and praised the culture of the West. It mocked traditional Chinese icons such as the Yellow River, hallowed as the source of China's early civilization, and the allegedly two-thousand-year-old Great Wall that had never succeeded in keeping intruders out but was successful in locking the Chinese people in, unaware and ignorant.[60] The documentary gained wide acclaim within China, including among educated, disaffected university students. The new General Party Secretary Zhao Ziyang is said to have praised it and perhaps even to have given a copy to Singapore's Lee Kuan Yew.

Where for decades the Chinese public had only the eight officially designated revolutionary operas as entertainment, Cui Jian introduced Chinese-style rock to China's restive young. Shocking new films such as Zhang Yimou's *Red Sorghum*, with scenes of rape, drunkenness, murder, and gut-wrenching violence, played to packed houses, and some movie theaters stayed open and full twenty-four hours a day.

In short, the China encountered by China specialists in the early years of reform and opening was no rising power. It was restive, angry, open, and full of spunk. The country's transformation was in the Chinese air we breathed. David Lampton recalls a meeting with Zhao Ziyang in January 1984 and being struck by the youth and dynamism of the leader's aides and by the premier's repeated invitation for them to respond to the foreigners' questions before he weighed in.[61]

In January 1989, Fang Lizhi wrote an open letter to Deng Xiaoping noting that 1989 was the fortieth anniversary of the founding of the PRC, the seventieth anniversary of the May Fourth Movement, and the two-hundredth anniversary of the French Revolution. He thought the time was ripe for a decree of amnesty for China's political prisoners, including Wei Jingsheng. Fang's open letter was followed by another similar letter signed by thirty-three of China's most prominent writers. Their letter was followed by another, signed by forty-two prominent academics, including twenty-seven of China's leading scientists.[62] Then, on April 15, 1989, Hu Yaobang, the popular deposed party secretary general, suddenly died of a heart attack. The university students of Beijing took to the streets, first to mourn his death and then to protest against the Chinese government, calling for democracy, freedom, and a crackdown on corruption, and demanding that several leaders, with Premier Li Peng at the top of the list, step down. The fact that inflation at the time was running above 20 percent only added fuel to the fire.

The protests continued for weeks and spread to cities and county seats across China. On May 13, some three thousand students occupied Tiananmen Square in the very heart of Beijing and began a hunger strike. Supporters joined them in the square. Days later, the capital city was filled with the sound of ambulance sirens as student after hunger-striking student fainted from lack of food. Rock star Cui Jian's "Nothing to My Name," which can be interpreted both as a love song of despair and a cry of youthful alienation from the Chinese Communist Party, became the anthem of the protesters. Cui Jian himself went to the square to meet with the protesters and perform his song. When Soviet party chief Mikhail Gorbachev arrived on May 15 for the first state visit of a Soviet leader in decades, officially marking the end of the Sino-Soviet dispute, the square was still full of protesting students, some of whom carried banners hailing Gorbachev as the ambassador of democracy. It is said the students tried to invite the Soviet leader to join them in the square. The grand opening ceremony scheduled to take place in the square had to be cancelled, deeply humiliating the Chinese leadership. The official meetings took place inside the Great Hall of the People, even as, on May 16 and 18, a million of Beijing's citizens marched to Tiananmen Square in support of the hunger-striking protesters.[63]

As the students continued their protests, an event that would culminate in earthshaking geopolitical change was taking place inside the Great Hall of the People. When Mikhail Gorbachev shook hands with China's leaders—from Deng Xiaoping to Zhao Ziyang, Li Peng, and Yang Shangkun—the decades of enmity between the two countries were over. The Soviet Union was no longer China's enemy. And the underlying strategic rationale for the U.S.-China relationship was seriously undermined. The initial basis of that relationship had been a marriage of convenience directed at a common enemy, the Soviet Union. That rationale evaporated when China's former enemy became, albeit cautiously, a new friend.

On May 19, the day after Gorbachev's departure, Premier Li Peng declared martial law, and still the citizens of Beijing marched to Tiananmen Square in protest. And then, on the night of June 3, the army finally marched in. Many citizens of Beijing were killed, and many more were injured. Similar, though smaller, incidents occurred the length and breadth of China.[64] And Zhao Ziyang was purged, never to appear in public again.[65]

Tiananmen was a watershed in U.S.-China relations. For the first decade after normalization, the two sides had essentially followed the dictum put forth by Chinese Premier Zhou Enlai not to interfere in the internal affairs of the other, to "find common ground while reserving our minor differences" and not let different ideologies come between us.[66] The promotion of democracy and protection of the human rights of Chinese citizens were not tenets of American policy.

But events in China during the spring of 1989 made ignoring the differences difficult, indeed impossible. The Chinese people had not needed American influence or help or prodding to begin demanding more democracy for themselves. The sight of millions of Chinese students and citizens demonstrating not only in Beijing but in cities and towns across the country and the popular support those demonstrations clearly received from ordinary Chinese people were surely a surprise to the American public. But China's violent military response was a shock. It meant that the Chinese government was willing to kill its own citizens, its own children, in order to maintain its power. From the American side, it meant that issues of human rights in China could no longer be ignored. And Americans' previously positive view of China and the Chinese government evaporated overnight.[67]

The American government, in particular the American president, George H. W. Bush, was in a quandary. The question was how to promote a kinder, gentler Chinese government without being accused of interfering in China's internal affairs. George H. W. Bush was the only American president ever to have substantial political experience with China prior to taking office.[68] In 1974–1975, as relations between the two countries had improved but prior to the establishment of full diplomatic relations, Bush had served as head of the Liaison Office in Beijing, where he and his wife Barbara had endeared themselves to the citizens of the city by exploring China's capital by bicycle, unescorted.[69] Although repulsed by the military suppression in Beijing, Bush, as president, was determined to keep the relationship on track in so far as possible, even as Congress and the American public clamored for some form of retribution for the Chinese military's violent suppression of peaceful protesters. President

Bush soon announced a set of punitive measures, including the suspension of all government-to-government sales and commercial exports of weapons and police equipment to China, a suspension of high-level official visits between the two countries, and an indefinite extension of visas for Chinese students already studying in the United States. A few weeks later, Bush secretly sent two personal envoys, National Security Council Advisor Brent Scowcroft and Deputy Secretary of State Lawrence Eagleburger, to meet with the Chinese leadership in Beijing. Barely a month had passed since the crackdown.

When the two envoys met with Deng Xiaoping, the Chinese leader described the turmoil in Beijing as an earthshaking event and insisted that the demonstrations were a counterrevolutionary rebellion with the aim of overthrowing the PRC and its socialist system. Deng saw the angry response of the American Congress in particular as a threat. "Indeed," Deng said, "Sino-US relations are in a very delicate state and you can even say they are in a dangerous state. Such actions are leading to the breakup of the relationship."[70]

President Bush was worried about China moving closer to the Soviet Union and needed a new rationale to continue the relationship. He found it in the renewal of trade. "I didn't want to punish the Chinese people for the acts of their government," George Bush wrote in his memoir with Scowcroft. "I believed that the commercial contacts between our countries had helped lead to the quest for more freedom. If people have commercial incentives, whether it's in China or in other totalitarian systems, the move to democracy becomes inexorable. For this reason I wanted to avoid cutting off the entire commercial relationship."[71]

Bush did not explain exactly how commerce made democracy inexorable. But James Lilley, who had become the U.S. ambassador to China just as the protests of 1989 were beginning and was the first person President Bush called when learning of the military suppression in Beijing, comes close to spelling it out. James Lilley was born in Qingdao, China, where his father was a salesman with John D. Rockefeller's Standard Oil Company. He lived there until he was eight years old. Back in the United States, in his last year at Yale, Lilley was recruited into the CIA. In July 1973, after some twenty years with the CIA in Asia, he became the first CIA station chief in China. Only three months earlier, his Yale classmate, friend, and fellow CIA recruit, Jack Downey, had been released after twenty years in a Chinese prison. In 1952, in the midst of the Korean War, Downey had been one of two survivors when a CIA aircraft sent to pick up a Chinese agent on the ground had been shot down over Manchuria. Downey and his fellow survivor, Richard Fecteau, had been tried and convicted as spies.[72] Jim Lilley was a man of few illusions. He adamantly believed that more contact between the United States and China could and would foster democracy and human rights. He also insisted that other issues, such as trade and weapons proliferation, had to be part of the bundle of issues to be pursued.

He, like Bush, saw the evolution of democracy through the lens of American involvement in China's developing economy. Wrote Lilley in 1994:

> Through encouraging broadened American involvement in China's economy, the United States fosters democratic forces and enhances human rights. Rapid economic growth and joint ventures have done more to improve the human rights situation in South China than innumerable threats, demarches, and unilaterally imposed conditions. . . . To be faithful to American principles, the Clinton administration must keep up the pressure on China to take specific steps to improve the lot of its people. In order to be effective, though, that pressure has to be part of an over-all plan. It cannot be driven by any single-issue constituency that ignores other important issues such as trade, weapons proliferation, and mutual cultural expansion. That mixture is ultimately the means to foster democracy and human rights in China.[73]

China has never again been as vibrantly open and free as in the weeks leading up to the Tiananmen massacre. Paradoxically, though, although many have seen post-Tiananmen relations as something of a nadir in the bilateral relationship, new opportunities for unofficial, nongovernmental organizations (NGOs) came into bloom soon after, as Mary Bullock describes so well in her chapter. Not only did the Chinese government publicly encourage Americans to return to China to see for themselves that everything was back to normal, but Chinese government officials were also soon encouraging foreign participation in an experiment being conducted in the Chinese countryside—competitive elections for village leaders. Order had been breaking down in many rural areas, and the number of popular protests there had been growing. The Chinese leadership hoped to relegitimize the party in rural areas by allowing local leaders to be popularly elected by the villagers themselves. Because they had the know-how and experience in getting things done, many, if not most, of the newly elected village leaders were members of the Communist Party.

The United Nations Development Programme and the European Union set up programs providing materials and trainings for village elections, and several American NGOs also introduced programs—the Ford Foundation, the International Republican Institute, the Asia Foundation, and the Carter Center. In 2001, former president Jimmy Carter himself traveled to China to witness a village election firsthand. Carter was cautiously optimistic in his assessment of the elections, noting that villagers had more authority over their own lives and encouraging China's leaders to extend them to higher levels but realistic about whether that would happen during Premier Zhu Rongji's term in office.[74] Foreigners involved in such programs were fully aware that they had no guarantee of success and that any form of Chinese democracy would look different from democracies in the West. Americans working on the ground in China knew that any hidden hopes of making the Chinese more like us would, for the time being at least, likely go unfulfilled. But foreign supporters of China's village elections also knew that the path to democracy in Taiwan had begun at the local level, only gradually working upward. There was a sense that even minor, imperfect political reforms were better than none, that competitive elections at the local level would be an improvement over appointments from above, and that, as some Chinese said, "you cannot not try." Trying and failing was better than not trying at all.[75] And, most importantly, the seeds of democracy were being sown.

As Lieberthal and Thornton note in their chapter, successive American presidents came to see helping China alleviate its enormous challenges as both in the American national interest and a moral imperative in its own right. In the best-case scenario, helping China would surely include promoting a democratic form of government. But few saw democracy as inevitable, and most surely knew that any such political evolution was likely to be tumultuous and would take time—a long time. In the interim, China could be commended for lifting hundreds of millions of people out of poverty, vastly improving ordinary citizens' standard of living, greatly improving and expanding educational opportunities, providing new possibilities to travel abroad, and allowing the marvels of the Internet even behind the Great Chinese Firewall. Chinese people are incomparably better off today than they were when Nixon made his first trip to China or when diplomatic relations were established in 1979.

So, yes, some Americans with deep involvement in China hoped that, over the long term, China would become more democratic and open. They also believed that greater person-to-person contact between Chinese and Americans would likely lead to a more open China. But they were still realists.

And the relationship between economic development and the emergence of democracy cannot be dismissed out of hand. Some still postulate, going back to Seymour Martin Lipset's 1959 "Some Social Requisites of Democracy," that there is a correlation between economic development and the emergence of democracy, although the precise causal relationships are hard to establish. Lipset saw industrialization, wealth, urbanization, and education as indicators of economic development.[76] To the extent that expansion of trade produces economic growth and development, long-term economic development gives rise to a substantial middle class, and a strong and vibrant middle class begins to demand more responsive, predictable, and responsible governance, new possibilities for liberalization begin to emerge, not necessarily because people are demanding democracy per se but because they want better governance to protect what they believe is theirs. But such a process takes time, often generations, and democracy sometimes arrives only after the passing of the dictator under whose rule the country came to prosper. Such was the case in Spain following the death of Franco.[77]

The World Bank credits China with having lifted more than 850 million people out of poverty since the reform period began in 1978. But its per capita income of $10,410 is still only about a sixth that of the United States ($65,760). Estimates are that about 373 million Chinese, a number significantly larger than the population of the United States, still live below the upper-middle income poverty line of $5.50 a day.[78] And although China's level of urbanization is high (60 percent), 40 percent of the population, some 556 million people, still live in rural areas, where their incomes remain far below those who live in cities. Within China's largest cities, a substantial portion of the population are migrants, working in low-wage jobs without an urban *hukou* (household registration), and hence deprived of urban benefits available to those with *hukou* such as state-supported education and health insurance. Instead, they are consigned to remain an underprivileged, potentially disgruntled underclass.

Some look to China's growing middle class as a force for democratization. Indeed, Chinese described as middle class have protested vocally, and sometimes successfully, over issues affecting their lives, such as factory pollution threatening the environment, official corruption that threatens their pocketbooks, poisoned baby formulas that might kill their children, and contaminated food that threatens their health. But such protests remain limited in scope and remain a daunting challenge to organize. Moreover, the real size and nature of China's middle class are so unclear that one report describes it as "something of a mystic entity."[79] Official Chinese government figures put the size of the middle class at around 400 million and define a middle-class household as one making the exchange rate equivalent in yuan of between US$3,640 and US$36,400 a year.[80] While consumption is often seen as both a conspicuous feature of the middle-class lifestyle and a driver of economic growth, the consumption capabilities of many in China's middle class are currently hampered by high levels of housing debt, taxes, educational fees, the cost of medical care, and the support they provide for their elders. Moreover, a substantial percentage of the middle class are government workers, direct beneficiaries of government policies, and thus generally less inclined to push for democratic reforms.[81] The time may not yet be ripe for the mystic entity of the Chinese middle class to play the role ascribed to it by modernization theory.

U.S.-China relations are now at what many people believe to be their lowest level since the establishment of diplomatic relations. David M. Lampton, in whose honor this book was conceived, to whom it is dedicated, and whose entire adult life has been devoted to the cause of engagement, warned in 2015 that relations between China and the United States were reaching the tipping point between engagement and adversity.[82] That point has been reached. Lampton concludes this volume by declaring engagement as we knew it dead and writing a eulogy in its praise. The decline of engagement began sometime before Xi Jinping's assumption of power in late 2012 and early 2013.

Cooperative efforts at the nongovernmental level had begun to slide as early as 2005, which was the last year the Carter Center observed village elections.[83]

One early signal of a clampdown on Chinese citizens was the promulgation in April 2013 of Xi Jinping's Document No. 9 inveighing against embracing such challenges to China's officially prescribed norms as Western constitutional democracy, universal values, civil society, neoliberalism, Western-style journalism, historical nihilism, and any questioning of China's reform and opening.[84] That Central Committee directive cowed many liberal-minded Chinese, although some have dared to mock it as well. The new law governing foreign NGOs in China, which came into effect in early 2017, is the most telling indication of the Chinese government's determination to keep tight control over foreign NGO activity in China. The new law transferred jurisdiction over foreign NGOs from the Ministry of Civil Affairs to the Public Security Bureau. As Thomas Kellogg describes in stark detail, the new law is based on the premise that "foreign NGOs should be viewed with suspicion, that they are guilty until proven innocent, akin to public enemies, second-class citizens, or criminal suspects."[85] Maintaining many of the nongovernmental programs that had long underpinned the relationship when things went wrong and that saw Chinese and Americans working cooperatively together toward common goals has become not only difficult but increasingly impossible. Many, if not most, American NGOs have pulled out of China altogether. Cooperation on issues of health, as detailed by Yanzhong Huang in his chapter, had long been one of the most successful facets of the relationship, saving literally millions of lives. Now that collaboration has collapsed in shambles. Of the approximately 130 American NGOs that had been registered by June 2020, most are apolitical professional associations.

The relationship has continued to decline with the onset of the COVID-19 pandemic, which began as this book was already in manuscript form. Although China initially tried to cover up the virus and failed to take measures that could have prevented its spread both within China and abroad, the mutual, often false, recriminations that flew back and forth between China and the United States, even as the scope of the pandemic continued to expand, brought discredit to the leadership of both countries. On May 20, 2020, the White House sent to Congress a new and updated version of the administration's *National Security Strategy* of December 2017.[86] Titled *United States Strategic Approach to the People's Republic of China*, the document asserted that U.S. engagement with China since 1979 was premised largely on the hope that engagement would spur both an economic and political opening of China and lead to its emergence as a constructive and responsible global stakeholder and a more open and liberal society. It declares that the policy failed. It further argues that China's expanding use of economic, political, and military power not only harms vital American interests but also undermines the sovereignty and dignity of countries and individuals around the world. The Trump administration was therefore willing to tolerate more bilateral friction in order to protect the vital interests of the United States. At the same time, the new strategy averred a deep and abiding respect for the Chinese people.[87]

The time to be optimistic about the possibility of China's future evolution in a more democratic direction or an improvement in U.S.-China relations has not yet come. In his chapter, Richard Madsen wisely admonishes us to be wary of the proposition that China will come to democracy through some inevitable process of modernization, reminding us that, for the foreseeable future, China will combine a successful, dynamic economy with a repressive authoritarian state. We must deal with China on those terms. David Lampton similarly warns that this period of diminishing engagement is apt to be a long one and that the best we might hope for in the interim is to minimize the deterioration and try to build a better foundation for a more productive future.

But all is not gloom and doom. We know that behind the curtain that has descended across China, quieting the voices of those who would speak out in favor of reform and liberalization, are countless numbers of Chinese who will come forth when the time is ripe. History is not over, as several in this volume have noted. And occasionally the curtain opens to a pleasant surprise. Messages of optimism get out. One such missive appeared on a popular English-language, China-related online newsletter as this book was in its final stages of editing and review. The Chinese author is a longtime grassroots activist who has worked for many years to promote competitive elections at the county and village levels. The successes he has witnessed in his work on the ground have led him to be optimistic about the development of democracy in his country. He sees China on the trajectory posited by the modernization theory he likely learned while a student in the United States more than four decades ago. He believes that as China has continued to grow wealthier, and as its citizens have become more educated and urbanized, they are taking more of an interest in politics and beginning to demand more government protection of their rights and interests. He notes that during the four decades of reform, relative openness, and foreign engagement, the Chinese people learned about freedom, the rule of law, human rights, and civil society. They learned that democracy is better than tyranny. They have not stopped believing in freedom and democracy. "We have achieved many goals, such as industrialization, urbanization, and the spread of modern knowledge everywhere," he writes. He states that China's interaction with other governments, international organizations, civil society organizations, scholars, and media has had a deep effect. He believes that China is in the last stage before democracy can be achieved. He believes that the current retrenchment cannot last.[88] The author was a student of David Lampton's when Lampton was a young professor at Ohio State University.

I have been reminded often in editing this book of the late John King Fairbank. "Things change," he was fond of saying. "They always do." Most American China specialists did not get China wrong. China changed. And so did the United States. And both will change again. As this book nears it final production, the United States is undergoing a major change with Joseph Biden's assumption of the presidency, bringing hope for a more reasonable, rational, and evidence-based policy toward China. In the long run, even the possibility of a future democratization of China cannot be ruled out. I see China's thirst for democracy like the plague bacillus in Camus's classic novel, *The Plague*—never dying or disappearing for good but lying dormant for years and years, hiding away until the time is finally ripe.[89] If Xi Jinping's dream for the rejuvenation of China really materializes, and China becomes a moderately well-off society by the one hundredth anniversary of the establishment of the Chinese Communist Party in 2021 and a fully developed nation by the one hundredth anniversary of the establishment of the PRC in 2049, the social requisites of democracy will have been well and fully met. By then, the seeds of Chinese democracy may well be ripe.

NOTES

My thanks to David M. Lampton, Andrew Mertha, Andrew J. Nathan, Madelyn Ross, Stephen Wesley, and two anonymous reviewers for their comments and suggestions on this chapter.

1. For a much fuller description of U.S. reasons for not recognizing China, see Nancy Bernkopf Tucker, *Patterns in the Dust: Chinese-American Relations and the Recognition Controversy, 1949–1950* (New York: Columbia University Press, 1983). See also Michael M. Gunter, "US Refusal to Recognize China (1949–1979)," *Cappadocia Journal of Area Studies* 2, no. 1 (June 2020): 35, http://dx.doi.org/10.38154/cjas.

2. See chapter 4, by Andrew Mertha, for the tribulations of China specialists.

3. See Mary Brown Bullock in chapter 8 for the founding of the National Committee and of John D. Rockefeller's role in it.

4. Richard M. Nixon, "Asia After Viet Nam," *Foreign Affairs* 46, no. 1 (October 1967): 111–25.

5. Robert B. Zoellick, "Whither China? From Membership to Responsibility: Remarks to the National Committee on U.S. China Relations," September 21, 2005, https://2001-2009 .state.gov/s/d/former/zoellick/rem/53682.htm.

6. Robert B. Zoellick, "Can America and China Be Stakeholders?" Carnegie Endowment for International Peace (speech, U.S.-China Business Council, December 4, 2019), https://carnegieendowment.org/2019/12/04/can-america-and-china-be-stakeholders -pub-80510.

7. See Judah Grunstein, "The U.S. Should Base Its China Strategy on Competitive Cooperation, Not Containment," *World Politics Review*, April 17, 2019, https://www .worldpoliticsreview.com/articles/27765/the-u-s-should-base-its-china-strategy-on -competitive-cooperation-not-containment.

8. C. Fred Bergsten, Bates Gill, Nicholas R. Lardy, and Derek Mitchell, eds., *China: The Balance Sheet; What the World Needs to Know About the Emerging Superpower* (New York: Public Affairs, 2006), 1.

9. See Benjamin I. Page and Tao Xie, *Living with the Dragon: How the American Public Views the Rise of China* (New York: Columbia University Press, 2010).

10. See Cheng Li, "Assessing U.S.-China Relations Under the Obama Administration," August 30, 2016, https://www.brookings.edu/opinions/assessing-u-s-chna-relations -under-the-obama-administration.

11. See Bill Gertz, *The China Threat: How the People's Republic Targets America* (Washington, DC: Regnery, 2000), xii–xiv.

12. See Gordon G. Chang, *The Coming Collapse of China* (New York: Random House, 2001), xviii–xx.

13. Minxin Pei and David Shambaugh are two examples. See Minxin Pei, "China's Coming Upheaval: Competition, the Coronavirus, and the Weakness of Xi Jinping," *Foreign Affairs*, April 3, 2020, https://www.foreignaffairs.com/articles/united-states/2020-04-03 /chinas-coming-upheaval; and David Shambaugh, "The Coming Chinese Crackup," the *Wall Street Journal*, March 6, 2015.

14. See, for instance, Denny Roy and Brad Glosserman, "The Coming Crisis in US-China Relations," *PacNet*, no. 23, March 26, 2018.

15. David M. Lampton, "The Tipping Point: Can We Amplify What We Have in Common?" *Horizons*, no. 4 (Summer 2015), https://www.cirsd.org/en/horizons/horizons-summer -2015--issue-no4/the-tipping-point---can-we-amplify-what-we-have-in-common-.

16. See Li, "Reassessing U.S.-China Relations."

17. Donald J. Trump, *National Security Strategy of the United States of America* (Washington, DC: The White House, December 2017); Jim Mattis, *Summary of the 2018 National Defense Strategy of the United States of America: Sharpening the American Military's Competitive Edge* (Washington, DC: Department of Defense, 2018).

18. Trump, *National Security Strategy*, 2.

19. Mattis,*National Defense Strategy*, 2.

20. Mattis, *National Defense Strategy*, 1.

21. Michael Pence, "Remarks by Vice President Pence on the Administration's Policy Toward China" (speech, Hudson Institute, Washington, DC, October 4, 2018), https://www .hudson.org/events/1610-vice-president-mike-pence-s-remarks-on-the-administration -s-policy-towards-china102018. In reality, the implementation of this harsh official policy was often at odds with public pronouncements about China. President Trump publicly touted China's President Xi Jinping as his good friend, congratulated China on seventy years of communist rule, and called for China to investigate his political rivals.

22. Michael R. Pompeo, "Communist China and the Free World's Future" (speech, Richard Nixon Presidential Library and Museum, Yorba Linda, CA, July 23, 2020), https://www .state.gov/communist-china-and-the-free-worlds-future.

23. Robert O'Brien, "Stronger America, Safer America" (speech, Arizona Commerce Authority, Phoenix, AZ, June 24, 2020).

24. Christopher Wray, "The Threat Posed by the Chinese Government and the Chinese Communist Party to the Economic and National Security of the United States" (speech, Hudson Institute, Washington, DC, July 7, 2020), https://www.fbi.gov/news/speeches /the-threat-posed-by-the-chinese-government-and-the-chinese-communist-party-to -the-economic-and-national-security-of-the-united-states.

25. O'Brien, "Stronger America."

26. This accusation has considerable merit. See James Tager, *Made in Hollywood, Censored by Beijing* (New York: PEN America, 2020).

27. William P. Barr, "Attorney General William P. Barr Delivers Remarks on China Policy at the Gerald R. Ford Presidential Museum" (speech, Gerald R. Ford Presidential Museum,

Grand Rapids, MI, July 16, 2020), https://www.justice.gov/opa/speech/attorney-general
-william-p-barr-delivers-remarks-china-policy-gerald-r-ford-presidential.

28. Pompeo, "Communist China."

29. Kat Devlin, Laura Silver, and Christine Huang, "U.S. Views of China Increasingly
Negative Amid Coronavirus Outbreak," April 21, 2020, https://www.pewresearch.org
/global/2020/04/21/u-s-views-of-china-increasingly-negative-amid-coronavirus
-outbreak/. See also "US Public's Opinion of China Hits 20-Year Low, Gallup Poll Says,"
South China Morning Post, March 3, 2020, https://www.scmp.com/news/china/diplomacy
/article/3064730/us-publics-opinion-china-hits-20-year-low-gallup-poll-says.

30. "US Public's Opinion of China Hits 20-Year Low."

31. Zack Cooper and Annie Kowalewski, "The New Washington Consensus," The Asian
Forum, American Enterprise Institute, December 21, 2018, http://www.theasanforum
.org/the-new-washington-consensus/.

32. Hal Brands and Zack Cooper, "After the Responsible Stakeholder, What? Debating
America's China Strategy," *Texas National Security Review* 2, no. 2 (2019): 1, http://dx
.doi.org/10.26153/tsw/1943.

33. For a smattering of these recommendations, see Brands and Cooper, "After the Responsible Stakeholder, What?"; David Dollar et al., "Avoiding War: Containment, Competition,
and Cooperation in US-China Relations," November 2017, https://www.brookings.edu
/research/avoiding-war-containment-competition-and-cooperation-in-u-s-china-relations/;
Kelly Magsamen and Melanie Hart, "Here's What a Progressive China Strategy Would
Look Like: Trump's Trade War Won't Put Washington on Strong Footing to Compete with Beijing," *Foreign Policy*, May 10, 2019, https://foreignpolicy.com/2019/05/10
/heres-what-a-progressive-china-strategy-would-look-like/; Melanie Hart and Kelly
Magsamen, "Limit, Leverage and Competition: a New Strategy on China," Center for
American Progress, April 3, 2019, https://www.americanprogress.org/issues/security
/reports/2019/04/03/468136/limit-leverage-compete-new-strategy-china/; Evan S.
Medeiros, "U.S.-China Relations and Its Impact on National Security and Intelligence
in a Post-COVID World" (statement before the House Permanent Select Committee on
Intelligence, Washington, DC, July 1, 2020), https://www.brookings.edu/testimonies/u-s
-china-relations-and-its-impact-on-national-security-and-intelligence-in-a-post
-covid-world/; Orville Schell and Susan Shirk, "US Policy Toward China: Recommendations for a New Administration Task Force Report," Asia Society and 21st Century China
Center, UC San Diego, February 2017, https://asiasociety.org/files/US-China_Task_
Force_Report_FINAL.pdf; Orville Schell and Susan Shirk, "Course Correction: Toward
an Effective and Sustainable China Policy," Asia Society Center on U.S.-China Relations,
February 2019, https://asiasociety.org/sites/default/files/inline-files/CourseCorrection
_FINAL_2.7.19_1.pdf; Ashley J. Tellis, Alison Szalwinski, and Michael Wills, eds.,
"U.S.-China Competition for Global Influence," in *Strategic Asia 2020* (Washington, DC:
The National Bureau of Asian Research, January 2020); Larry Diamond and Orville
Schell, *China's Influence and American Interests: Promoting Constructive Vigilance* (Stan-
ford, CA: Hoover Institution 2019), publication no. 702. See also the testimony to the
House Intelligence Committee at House Intelligence, "U.S.-China Relations and Its
Impact on National Security and Intelligence in a Post-COVID World," July 1, 2020,
video, https://www.youtube.com/watch?v=x-WdgL9N9dQ&feature=youtu.be.

34. See M. Taylor Fravel et al., "China Is Not an Enemy," *Washington Post*, July 3, 2019, https:
//www.washingtonpost.com/opinions/making-china-a-us-enemy-is-counterproductive
/2019/07/02/647d49d0-9bfa-11e9-b27f-ed2942f73d70_story.html?utm_term=.3e7418355996.
For more analysis of this letter, see Ali Wyne, "Beyond Hawks and Doves: A Better Way

to Debate U.S.-China Policy," *ChinaFile*, September 18, 2019, https://www.chinafile.com /reporting-opinion/viewpoint/beyond-hawks-and-doves.

35. See "Stay the Course on China: An Open Letter to Donald Trump," *Journal of Political Risk*, July 18, 2019, http://www.jpolrisk.com/stay-the-course-on-china-an-open-letter -to-president-trump.

36. Note that more signatures were added to both letters following their publication.

37. For another article calling for regime change in China, see Joseph Bosco, "US Engagement Has Failed in China," *Taipei Times*, September 21, 2018.

38. Thomas L. Friedman, "Trump and Xi Can Both Win the Trade War," the *New York Times*, August 28, 2019, A23.

39. Jodi Xu Klein, "Henry Kissinger Warns of 'Catastrophic' Conflict Unless China and U.S. Settle Their Differences," *South China Morning Post*, November 15, 2019, https:// www.scmp.com/news/china/diplomacy/article/3037870/kissinger-warns-us-and -china-their-conflicts-will-be.

40. Kurt M. Campbell and Ely Ratner, "The China Reckoning: How Beijing Defied American Expectations," *Foreign Affairs* 97, no. 2 (March/April 2018): 60–71.

41. Campbell and Ratner, "The China Reckoning," 60–61, 70.

42. See Jeffrey Bader, "U.S.-China Relations: Is It Time to End the Engagement?" Brookings Institution Policy Brief, September 2018, https://www.brookings.edu/research/u-s -china-relations-is-it-time-to-end-the-engagement/; and Jack Zhang, "The State of US-China Policy: Three Questions with Jeffrey Bader," September 4, 2019, https://chinafocus .ucsd.edu/2019/09/04/the-state-of-us-china-policy-3-questions-with-jeffery-bader/.

43. Robert B. Zoellick, "Can America and China Be Stakeholders?" U.S.-China Business Council, December 4, 2019, https://carnegieendowment.org/2019/12/04/can-america -and-china-be-stakeholders-pub-80510.

44. Alastair Iain Johnston, "The Failures of the 'Failure of Engagement' with China," the *Washington Quarterly* 42, no. 2 (Summer 2019): 99–114.

45. Richard Baum, *Burying Mao: Chinese Politics in the Age of Deng Xiaoping* (Princeton, NJ: Princeton University Press, 1994), 5–23.

46. Baum, *Burying Mao*, 95.

47. Baum, *Burying Mao*, 85.

48. Baum, *Burying Mao*, 108–9.

49. See Wei Jingsheng, ed., "The Fifth Modernization: Democracy," in *The Courage to Stand Alone: Letters from Prison and Other Writings* (New York: Viking Penguin, 1997), 201–12.

50. Wei was released from his second sentence in November 1997 on medical parole and was given political asylum in the United States, where he still lives today.

51. See Anne F. Thurston, "New Opportunities for Research in China," in *Items* (New York: Social Science Research Council) 33, no. 2 (June 1979): 13–25.

52. Liu Binyan, "People or Monsters?" in *People or Monsters and Other Stories and Reportage from China After Mao*, ed. Perry Link (Bloomington, IN: Indiana University Press, 1983), 11–69.

53. See Anne F. Thurston, *Enemies of the People: The Ordeal of China's Intellectuals in China's Great Cultural Revolution* (New York: Knopf, 1987), 232.

54. For a description of Liu Shaoqi's death, see Thurston, *Enemies of the People*, 151–53.

55. On Christmas Eve of 1981, when I attended the Catholic High Mass being celebrated in the Nantang Cathedral that traces its history back to the Italian Jesuit Matteo Ricci, the cathedral was filled to overflowing. Hundreds of worshippers were crowded together in the large courtyard outside, while the cathedral itself was so packed that pews were filled to overflowing, the congregation filled the aisles and the choir loft, and children sat atop their fathers' shoulders.

56. For three of the earliest, see Roger Garside, *Coming Alive: China After Mao* (New York: McGraw-Hill, 1981); Richard Bernstein, *From the Center of the Earth: The Search for the Truth About China* (Boston: Little Brown, 1982); and Fox Butterfield, *China: Alive in the Bitter Sea* (New York: Bantam-Dell, 1983).

57. See Thurston, *Enemies of the People.*

58. See Fang Lizhi, *Bringing Down the Great Wall: Writings on Science, Culture, and Democracy in China* (New York: Norton, 1990), 166.

59. Fang, *Bringing Down the Great Wall*, 108–9.

60. For a translation of *Heshang*, see Su Xiaokang and Wang Luxiang, *Deathsong of the River: A Reader's Guide to the Chinese TV Series, Heshang*, trans. Richard W. Bodman and Pin P. Wan (Ithaca, NY: Cornell University Press, 1991), 91–223.

61. Personal communication with author.

62. Fang, *Bringing Down the Great Wall*, 242–44, 305–9.

63. The documentary film *The Gate of Heavenly Peace* by Carma Hinton is an excellent, now classic, depiction of the events in Beijing.

64. I was in Beijing from May 3 to May 29, 1989, and led a group of Americans on a cruise up the Yangtze from Wuhan to Chongqing. The city of Wuhan was closed because of protests, and every village and town we saw or visited along the river and its tributaries was also having protests. Chongqing, too, was closed when we arrived, on June 4 and protests were still going on when we left several days later.

65. See Andrew J. Nathan and Perry Link, *Tiananmen Papers: The Chinese Leadership's Decision to Use Force Against Their Own People—In Their Own Words* (New York: Public Affairs, 2001), 175–223; and Zhao Ziyang, *Prisoner of the State: The Secret Journal of Premier Zhao Ziyang* (New York: Simon and Schuster, 2009). Liu Binyan had gone to Harvard University as a visiting scholar in 1988 and was still there when the protests broke out in China. He never returned to China and died in New Jersey in 2005. Fang Lizhi was in China in the spring of 1989 and sought refuge in the American embassy in Beijing after the June 4 massacre. Upon his exit from the embassy a year later, he went to England and then to the United States, first to Princeton where he had done research at the Institute for Advanced Study in 1986 and then to the University of Arizona where he became a professor of physics. Fang died in 2012.

66. George Bush and Brent Scowcroft, *A World Transformed* (New York: Vintage, 1999), 176.

67. David M. Lampton, *Same Bed, Different Dreams: Managing U.S.-China Relations, 1989-2000* (Berkeley: University of California Press, 2001), 385.

68. Herbert Hoover, however, had been a mining engineer in northern China before becoming president. I am grateful to David Lampton for pointing this out to me.

69. David Lampton also points out that Bush played tennis and knew a who's who of China's elite. In the conversations I used to have with the old men who walked their birds early in the morning in Ritan Park near the American embassy, I was told stories of them having often seen Bush running and walking in the park. They considered him something of a friend.

70. Bush and Scowcroft, *A World Transformed*, 106.

71. Bush and Scowcroft, *A World Transformed*, 89.

72. This story is taken from the transcript of a Voice of America interview I conducted with Lilley in 1998, pp. 3–17. See also James R. Lilley and Jeffrey Lilley, *China Hand: Nine Decades of Adventure, Espionage, and Diplomacy in Asia* (New York: Public Affairs, 2004).

73. James Lilley, "Freedom Through Trade," *Foreign Policy* 94 (Spring 1994): 37–42.

74. Martin Fackler, "Chinese Village Voting Wins Praise, Yahoo News, September 5, 2001, http://dailynews.yahoo.com/h/ap/20010905/wl/china_carter_1

75. For a discussion of what foreigners expected of village elections at the time, see Anne F. Thurston, *Muddling Toward Democracy: Political Change in Grassroots China* (Washington, DC: United States Institute of Peace, 1998), iii–iv.

76. Seymour Martin Lipset, "Some Social Requisites of Democracy: Economic Development and Political Legitimacy," the *American Political Science Review* 53, no. 1 (March 1959): 71, For a study of the puzzle of China's middle class that draws on Lipset's analysis, see Andrew J. Nathan, "The Puzzle of the Chinese Middle Class," *Journal of Democracy* 27, no. 2 (April 2016): 5–19.

77. Daniel Treisman, "Economic Development Promotes Democracy, but There's a Catch," *Washington Post*, December 29, 2014, https://www.washingtonpost.com/news/monkey-cage/wp/2014/12/29/economic-development-promotes-democracy-but-theres-a-catch/.

78. "The World Bank in China," the World Bank, https://www.worldbank.org/en/country/china/overview.

79. Zhou Xin, "The Question Mark Hanging Over China's 400 Million-Strong Middle Class," October 13, 2018, https://scmp.com/economy/china-economy/article/2168177/question-mark-hanging-over-chinas-400-million-strong-middle-class.

80. Melissa Cyril, "China's Middle Class in 5 Simple Questions," February 13, 2019, https://www.china-briefing.com/news/chinas-middle-class-5-questions-answered/.

81. Zhou, "The Question Mark."

82. Lampton, "The Tipping Point."

83. See chapter 8 by Mary Bullock in this volume.

84. ChinaFile. http://www.chinafile.com/sites/default/files/assets/images/article/featured/73604126.jpg.

85. See Thomas E. Kellogg, "The Foreign NGO Law and the Closing of China," in *Authoritarian Legality in Asia: Formation, Development, and Transition*, eds. Weitseng Chen and Hualing Fu (New York: Cambridge University Press, 2020), 132–33.

86. Trump, *National Security Strategy*.

87. National Security Council, "United States Strategic Approach to the People's Republic of China," May 20, 2020, https://www.whitehouse.gov/articles/united-states-strategic-approach-to-the-peoples-republic-of-china/.

88. Although this article has been published both in English and Chinese and is available both in the United States and China, out of perhaps an abundance of caution, I am refraining from revealing the author's identity.

89. Albert Camus, *The Plague*, trans. Stuart Gilbert (New York: Modern Library, 1948), 278.

CHAPTER 2

THE LOGIC AND EFFICACY OF ENGAGEMENT

Objectives, Assumptions, and Impacts

THOMAS FINGAR

The Soviet Union was often mocked for rewriting history to better align with later priorities and power relationships, and the People's Republic of China (PRC) is justly criticized for selective amnesia and mythologizing and airbrushing key parts of its own history.[1] The current American narrative on U.S. engagement with China may be less egregious than Soviet and Chinese revisionism, but it similarly reconstructs and distorts the past in order to discredit the objectives, instruments, and impacts of China policy from Nixon through Obama. To be sure, what I have characterized as a single policy was reassessed and tweaked many times by Republican and Democratic administrations, but irrespective of party or whether the administration was liberal or conservative, and despite major changes in China and the international situation, the fundamental policy of engagement remained remarkably stable. That stability cannot be explained away by assertions of ineptitude and inertia. The policy remained stable because it protected American interests, helped achieve American goals, and facilitated society-to-society interactions that, over time, constrained the ability of governments to change the enabling policies.

No policy is perfect or can persist without timely adjustments to reflect changed circumstances, and that is certainly true of engagement. But the stability of the logic and goals of engagement is noteworthy, especially when compared to the magnitude of changes in China, the international system, and American domestic politics over the past fifty years. Before heeding or parroting calls to discard engagement in favor of decoupling, containment, and confrontation, American officials and others now inclined to deride engagement as nothing more than a naïve, foolhardy, and failed attempt to remake China in America's image must replace caricatures with a more accurate understanding of what the policy was—and was not—intended to achieve.[2]

America's China policy is neither conceived nor executed in a vacuum. The United States is a global actor with global interests. Relations with China are one of those interests, but during most of the past fifty years, China has been less central to American foreign policy than many other places and problems.[3] China, like most other countries, believes that its concerns and relationship with the United States are more salient to the president and other top officials than they are—most of the time.[4] The same is generally true of academics and others who study China (or any other country) and its relationship with the United States. They overestimate the centrality of "their" country and impute anything that can be construed as affecting that country as the primary objective of that action or policy. Often, this is not the case. I point this out because understanding how relations with China fit into and were shaped by higher priority U.S. interests elsewhere on the globe is essential for understanding the logic of engagement and some of the reasons for its stability over time. Other sources of stability derive from the nature of the American system and the limited scope of our federalist system that empowers, but has only limited ability to control, individuals, interest groups, and lower levels of government.

U.S. reengagement with China began some fifty years ago with the lead-up to Henry Kissinger's secret trip in 1971 and Richard Nixon's historic visit the following year. This initiated a process of rapprochement with limited but important goals and expectations. The primary motivation on both sides was to exploit "enemy of my enemy might be my friend" possibilities to counter the perceived threat to each from the Soviet Union. This was a classic manifestation of realist balancing tactics that neither assumed nor sought dramatically closer relations or political change. Little was required beyond rhetorical and symbolic adjustments sufficient to make Moscow uncertain about whether and how the United States and China might respond to Soviet aggression.[5] The approach was pure realpolitik with no transformational objectives or expectations.[6] It produced an axis of convenience not an alliance.[7] The amount and scope of interaction between American and Chinese governments, institutions, and individuals were extremely limited. Beijing wanted it that way, and Washington recognized that pressing for more would reveal the limited scope of U.S.-China cooperation and jeopardize the illusion of partnership needed to deter the Soviet Union.

When rapprochement began, and throughout the period of normalization, the primary objective of the slightly warmer relationship was to enhance U.S. and Chinese security. Normalization was both a process and a goal. The process involved building trust and removing obstacles; the goal was the establishment of a normal relationship (i.e., cooperative with full diplomatic relations).[8] Virtually all official statements and scholarly commentary on the new relationship focused narrowly on its geostrategic importance. There was very little speculation about the potential for economic, people-to-people, or other forms of interaction, probably because such possibilities seemed remote and unnecessary to achieve security objectives as they were defined at the time. Both sides achieved their primary objective of complicating Moscow's strategic calculus with Nixon's visit and issuance of the Shanghai Communiqué on February 27, 1972.[9]

The Shanghai Communiqué paved the way for the exchange of a small number of quasi-official delegations and individual visits, but essentially no one envisioned deeper or broader engagement until the issues that impeded the establishment of formal diplomatic relations were resolved. The list of critical impediments includes Mao's deep suspicion of the United States, Watergate, and domestic politics in both countries.[10] Until 1978, however, the primary obstacle was that Beijing did not want broader or deeper engagement and was therefore unwilling to make policy changes necessary to elicit greater interest in Washington.

Genesis of Engagement

The U.S. relationship with China changed fundamentally in late 1978 after Beijing abandoned Mao's quest for revolutionary (and autarkic) development in favor of the Asian Tiger model of export-led growth. It made this shift after the Carter administration signaled that, if China adopted policies now subsumed under the rubric of reform and opening, the United States would enable and assist the international dimensions of the new strategy.[11] The two developments were inextricably linked; the new strategy, widely but too narrowly credited to Deng Xiaoping, could not go forward without U.S. cooperation, but the United States would have little incentive to assist China if Beijing did not open the door to trade, investment, and people-to-people contacts. Deng's professed willingness to open China to the outside world offered the first opportunity in three decades, and perhaps the best opportunity ever, to achieve long-standing American security, commercial, and missionary goals.[12] Engagement was both the process and the product of efforts to achieve those objectives.

Carter's decision to support Deng's reform and opening strategy was rooted in the same realpolitik calculus that motivated Nixon and Kissinger, but it was also shaped by his personal commitment to religious freedom, boyhood experiences in Plains, Georgia, and his first peek at China when his naval ship visited Qingdao in the late 1940s. The international situation was essentially the same as it had been in the early 1970s. The Soviet Union still posed an existential threat to the United States and its free world allies in the Cold War competition, and this threat was expected to continue indefinitely.[13] By late 1977, it was clear that Chinese politics and policy were in flux, that Mao's successors (Mao died in September 1976) were determined if not desperate to rebuild the economy and restore party legitimacy, and that Beijing needed the implied deterrence of Moscow that more intimate ties with Washington would provide.[14] This concatenation of factors created new opportunities for the United States, but with so much in flux, it might also degrade the axis of convenience initiated by Nixon and Mao. Washington was as eager to preserve what it had as it was to explore and expand new possibilities.

Deng Xiaoping's reform and opening created those possibilities. Deng's emphasis on modernization, development, and economic growth created commercial opportunities for American firms, but it also offered the prospect of making China a more capable strategic partner. Stated another way, if China was going to be our partner in the seemingly never-ending struggle with the Soviet bloc, it would be better for China to be a strong partner. There were clear realpolitik reasons to assist China's modernization, but they were not the only reasons for doing so.

The United States is a capitalist and commercial nation, and American firms have sought access to the fabled "China market" since being shut out of British markets after gaining independence.[15] Too weak to force China to open its markets in the nineteenth century, the United States sought and obtained limited access by piggybacking on the gains secured by Britain and France after the Opium War (1840–1842) and the Arrow War (1856–1860). The situation was very different in 1978 when U.S. economic strength and technical preeminence put American firms in a favorable position to take advantage of new commercial opportunities in China. Their position was made even more favorable by the fact that Beijing needed U.S. acquiescence, if not active support, to gain access to the markets, capital, and technology of other developed nations, virtually all of which were behind a wall of export controls and trade prohibitions in the U.S.-led free world. In addition, Beijing needed the quasi security partnership with the United States to deter the Soviet Union (and the United States) while cutting defense expenditures in order to focus on domestic development.

Reform and opening also created new possibilities for people-to-people contacts. In the nineteenth century, this was largely a missionary goal that began with a narrow focus on conversion to Christianity but soon broadened to include education, health care, and, in the twentieth century, human and civil rights.[16] There was (and is) an element of hubris involved, but there are also significant elements of compassion for others and conviction that, by simply being themselves, Americans provide a positive role model that is corrosive to authoritarian regimes and behaviors,[17] as chapters 8 and 9 in this volume make clear. This type of interaction acquired special symbolic significance during the run-up to the conjoined announcements of reform and opening and the exchange of diplomatic recognition in December 1978.[18]

The most important sticking point was disagreement over the nature of U.S. relations with Taiwan after switching formal diplomatic recognition to the PRC. That issue was not resolved—finessed—until Carter persuaded Beijing that the United States was prepared to assist Deng's modernization-based strategy of development. The arrival in Beijing of a delegation of government scientists headed by White House science advisor Frank Press in August 1978 was a key step in doing so. This was the most senior science delegation ever sent to another country by the United States. Its message, both symbolic and explicit, was that the United States was prepared to support Beijing's science-based developmental strategy.[19] Another step was confirmation that the United States was willing to accept hundreds, even thousands, of Chinese students wishing to study in American universities as long as they were admitted through regular channels and were not the financial responsibility of the U.S. government. This was in stark contrast to the handful of students exchanged, under very restrictive conditions, between the United States and the Soviet Union, which required individually negotiated one-for-one student/researcher swaps.[20]

All three dimensions of engagement (security, commerce, and people-to-people contact) were expected to help keep China on the U.S.-led side of the Cold War divide, to make China a stronger and more capable partner, and to facilitate mutually beneficial economic relationships that would add resilience to the relationship by reinforcing the security pillar and giving more individuals and institutions a stake in the relationship. The envisioned interactions were purposive and to a degree instrumental, but they were not carefully integrated components of grand strategy, in part because, once unleashed, American society follows its own dreams, impulses, and interests. It is now common to describe engagement as a bold (or naïve and failed) American strategy to achieve regime change in China and to view individual relationships as elements of a detailed blueprint for change. It was none of those things. To evaluate the efficacy, strengths, and weaknesses of engagement, the starting point must be what the approach—or strategy—actually attempted to do. That, in turn, requires proper understanding of the circumstances in which it evolved.

Engagement did not spring full grown from the head of Jimmy Carter, his anti-Soviet national security advisor Zbigniew Brzezinski, or a bureaucratic version of Medusa; it emerged and evolved in an iterative process that was influenced more by events and experience than by theories of development and international relations. Although, in retrospect, the components can be fitted together in ways that have the appearance of a strategy or grand design, they did not start out that way. As noted earlier, the most significant shaping factor was the Cold War and the desire to prevent Beijing from realigning with Moscow or drifting into a diplomatic spoiler and international troublemaker role, not least in the developing world. Binding China more tightly to the United States and the free world was an important—often the most important—objective of U.S. policy. By the late 1970s, Washington had learned many lessons germane to that objective.

Washington's Cold War strategy relied on asymmetries that required the United States to accept a disproportionate defense burden and accorded greater access to U.S. markets, technologies, and other benefits than it received or demanded from its allies.[21] This strategy was judged to have accelerated the recovery and subsequent growth of allied economies and increased their industrial capabilities in ways that could be used for collective defense. This strengthened the alliance as a whole, enhanced deterrence, and made the United States more secure. It also made the allies more prosperous and able to purchase more goods and services from American firms. It produced win-win results in both the security and the economic arenas. Less concretely, development and prosperity seem also to have contributed to support for democratic systems and the liberal values they professed—at home and in the liberal, rules-based, international order.

As China's new strategy to achieve rapid growth became clearer, the United States had to decide whether to adopt a variant of containment that aimed to keep China poor and weak by denying access to U.S. and allied economic resources or to extend to China benefits that had heretofore been reserved for formal allies. As noted earlier, the decision to assist China's modernization was made, in part, to retain the quasi security partnership by demonstrating support rather than indifference or opposition. Lessons learned earlier in the Cold War provided a preemptive answer to the question of whether granting asymmetric benefits to China (with or without demanding political change) would be advantageous to the United States. That answer was yes. The decision was also influenced by considerations about what policies our allies would support over time.

The choice to allow—and subsequently to facilitate—commercial interactions on essentially the same terms as were accorded to U.S. allies was a policy decision with many subcomponents. One important component involved relaxing export control restrictions applied to China so that Chinese and American firms seeking to operate in China could gain access to controlled technologies.[22] Decisions about whether and how to engage were made by the private sector. American and U.S.-based multinational firms had learned from their engagement with Europe, Japan, Taiwan, and Korea that expansion into overseas markets could take many forms and yield higher profits. Their eager response transformed engagement from a government policy into a multifaceted bundle of interdependent relationships that operated largely in the nongovernmental arena. It also created an increasingly large and powerful constituency with the incentive and ability to demand stable policies and stability in the overarching U.S.-China relationship. These developments both reinforced Washington's intent and constrained the scope of future government actions. One consequence was extraordinary continuity in U.S. policy toward China from one administration to the next, often despite harsh criticism of engagement during presidential campaigns, as described in chapter 13 by Lieberthal and Thornton. Rather quickly, society-to-society dimensions of the relationship became as significant as—or more significant than—the government-to-government relationship that made them possible.

Another Cold War lesson, albeit one that was only beginning to be recognized in the late 1970s, involved the transformative effects of modernization and economic growth. The prime examples of this transformation were Taiwan and South Korea. Both had been—and in the late 1970s still were—authoritarian regimes. Their achievements after adopting export-led growth strategies were models for Deng and his colleagues. Unable to admit that they wanted to learn from Taiwan, they referred instead to a Japanese path of development. The modernization-driven political transformations in the Republic of Korea and Taiwan later became cautionary tales for China's leaders and encouraging examples for supporters of engagement.

What happened in the Republic of Korea and Taiwan did not prove that modernization would quickly or inevitably transform the party-state in China, but it did challenge assertions that modernization would inevitably strengthen and prolong communist party rule on the mainland. The argument at the time, at least as I remember it, was not whether or how quickly modernization would yield regime change and democracy, but whether U.S. assistance to China's quest for modernity would foolishly strengthen the communist state. Both Marxism and modernization theory argued that economic growth and modernization were necessary prerequisites for transition to a viable democratic state, but the real-world examples of Taiwan, Korea, and, somewhat misleadingly, Japan were more influential than social science theories.

An important but seldom noted dimension of engagement was the (re) establishment of institutional and individual ties. The U.S. federal government paved the way by relaxing or removing restrictions. Beijing gradually did the same, but the primary drivers of increased institutional and individual interactions came from the "private sector." The reason I put the phrase private sector in quotation marks is that virtually all institutional actors in the PRC were—and still are—components of the party-state. But when universities, municipal governments, lawyers, doctors, or musicians responded to or reached out to counterparts, they acted more like interest or associational groups than agents of the central government. In other words, they had or obtained a "license" to interact with American counterparts. The governments in Washington and Beijing made this possible but did not directly control what happened. To be sure, Beijing was warier and monitored the interactions more closely than did

Washington, but the vast majority of such interactions were not tightly con-trolled and the degree of central control diminished over time. This changed, primarily on the Chinese side, after 2008, but during most of the forty-year engagement era, there was considerable room for initiative and inventive forms of interaction.

On the American side, this process was intentional but not controlled, and in that respect, it was consistent with normal American practice with respect to interactions between individuals and institutions in the United States and allied nations. What made it intentional was a policy decision to eschew the kinds of controls imposed (and enforced) by containment policies applied to the Soviet Union and its allies. This reflected, in part, recognition that the containment policies intended to deny Moscow and its partner regimes the benefits of inter-action with Americans that might alleviate the regimes' inherent weaknesses and prolong their survival also precluded the corrosive and transformational effects of interaction with Americans.

Unleashing the transformative power of American people and practices did not require—and could not have been achieved with—micromanagement by the federal government. All Washington had to do was get out of the way. Although there were some in the early 1980s who argued that simply unleash-ing Americans to interact with Chinese counterparts was a bad or risky idea, such arguments did not gain much traction. That probably was not the case in Beijing, where suspicion of American motives and methods ran deep and the ability to maintain control was greater. The slow pace at which individual relationships developed and evolved was largely attributable to this suspicion. Suspicion remained high and intensified for a while after Tiananmen before abating again for almost two decades.[23]

The U.S. decision to allow extensive engagement by individuals and pri-vate entities was part of a broader strategy to add resilience to the new rela-tionship by forging numerous official and unofficial ties. These ties would link national governments (e.g., ministries and departments, bureaus with compa-rable responsibilities, and agencies with similar missions), administrative units (states, provinces, and cities), educational institutions, professional associa-tions, and myriad other interests and constituencies. The underlying logic was simple but important: the greater the number and scope of relationships and interests, the larger the array of constituencies with a stake in the relationship and the easier it would be to prevent disagreements in one arena from derailing the overall relationship. I do not know whether Beijing ever shared this objec-tive but doubt that it did.

Modes of engagement were not discussed in detail. Precisely how American firms would interact with state-owned and private enterprises, how scientists and medical professionals might collaborate, and how myriad other concrete forms of engagement would take place were to be worked out through a process of experimentation and problem-solving. There was no master plan or blue-print on either side. Beijing, in essence, applied the approach described as "crossing the river by feeling the stones." This cautious step-by-step approach precluded the need for protracted and contentious debate among top leaders and between Beijing and the United States and other partners in the developed world. Taking small steps allowed both sides to identify and solve problems, gain experience and confidence, and avoid the risks of attempting too much at the same time.

Americans would have preferred to move more quickly but were constrained by Chinese caution. This difference was partly cultural. Americans are always in a hurry and confident that any problems can be resolved on the fly. Chinese worry more about the consequences of failure and the perils of entrapment. But American impatience and Chinese caution reflected more than cultural differences. Chinese policies had changed so often and so much during the preceding thirty years that Washington was eager to lock in the promise and possibilities of reform and opening as quickly as possible. Deng was already seventy-four years old, and no one could be confident that his policies would continue if he became incapacitated or died.[24] Rather than base engagement and its favorable possibilities on the health of one or a few leaders, American policy makers wanted to demonstrate quickly the benefits that would flow to China if it implemented the reform and opening strategy. Beijing saw American eagerness as intended to ensnare China in arrangements that would create dependence and constrain freedom of action. This judgment was not entirely wrong.

The American desire to lock in reform and opening was complemented by confidence that enabling the PRC to participate in the rules-based order that had evolved on the free world side of the Cold War divide would ensnare Beijing in that system by providing benefits that made it increasingly costly to withdraw.[25] To characterize this as a strategy of entrapment would go too far, but there was a clear expectation that Chinese would increasingly understand that they could achieve the goals of reform and opening (e.g., wealth, power, security, influence) more quickly by working with and within the U.S.-led liberal order than by dropping out or limiting compliance with the rules and norms that enabled the system to work as well as it does. This expectation was based on the behavior of other nations that grew and modernized within the free world order and on the imputed and observed pragmatism of Chinese actors. We know, through engagement, that more than a few Chinese shared many of these objectives and expectations.

Engagement was not limited to interaction with the United States and American entities. As anticipated, China immediately sought to mitigate and hedge against the vulnerability and risks of dependence on the United States by using engagement with other developed countries to counterbalance U.S. leverage. Rather than seeing Beijing's effort to counterbalance U.S. economic leverage by engaging with Japan and European countries as a problem, Washington viewed it positively. Engagement with other free world nations would—and did—accelerate China's development as a stronger (and hopefully long-term) partner in the Cold War, alleviate Beijing's fear of entrapment by the United States, and demonstrate that Washington was not the only partner championing the advantages of the rules-based system.[26]

Beijing may have hoped to play U.S. allies off against the United States or one another in order to obtain terms more favorable to China, but it soon discovered that all of its free world partners subscribed to essentially the same view of the system from which they benefitted and were unwilling to jeopardize their own interests by violating its norms. Competition among firms located in different capitalist countries enabled the PRC to take advantage of market-based competition, but its ability to exploit political differences proved far more limited. Nevertheless, the ability to develop and use various forms of engagement with U.S. allies did mitigate Chinese fears of U.S. hegemony and intentions and thereby reduced ideological opposition and reluctance to sustain the reform process. It also exposed Chinese individuals and institutions to the views and operating styles of people from other democratic systems who shared many values with American citizens. This enhanced the corrosive and influential effects of engagement with Americans.

Evolution of Engagement

The explication of engagement presented in the previous section exaggerates the coherence and conscious design of what was in fact an evolutionary and iterative process that, in retrospect, appears to be a more coherent strategy than it was. Like all policies, it was a product of the time and conditions in which it evolved. The most important factor in that context was the Cold War and the expectation that it would continue indefinitely. The starting point for understanding what came to be called engagement is that it was a tactical move to keep China on the free world side of the bipolar world and a response to perceived possibilities generated by the shift from a quest for revolutionary autarky to pursuit of export-led growth. Additional shaping factors included expectations derived from the evolution of other nations that modernized by working within the liberal order and the perceived opportunity to achieve long-standing American security, commercial, and missionary objectives.

Events and decisions in China provided the necessary prerequisite for adoption of engagement policies by the United States. Engagement was a response to possibilities and opportunities, not an initiative to change China. The current narrative on U.S.-China relations largely ignores its security-based origins but asks, implicitly or explicitly, why engagement continued despite major changes in the international situation and in Chinese behavior. These are reasonable questions that must be addressed in order to understand what engagement is and why it has proven so durable.

Given engagement's origins in the Cold War rivalry with the Soviet Union, why did it persist after the demise of the USSR and the bipolar world? The admittedly overly simplified answer is that it persisted as a result of a combination of uncertainty, inertia, constituent demands, and the downsides of alternative approaches. With benefit of hindsight, we can confidently assert that the Soviet Union ceased to exist in December 1991. But at the time of its demise, and for almost a decade thereafter, there was considerable fear that it was not really dead and might be reincarnated from the chaos of Yeltsin's Russia. In response to uncertainty, the Clinton administration hedged. One part of the hedging strategy was to preserve the security partnership with China.[27] Despite Tiananmen and China's pullback from modes of engagement that had evolved during the previous decade, it was prudent to maintain the quasi-formal security arrangement with China at least until the situation in Russia became clearer and more stable. Vladimir Putin brought stability and greater clarity about Russian capabilities and intentions, including interest in resurrecting the appearance, though not the reality, of what was once called the strategic triangle of relations among Washington, Moscow and Beijing.[28] In this international context and despite China's military buildup and increasingly assertive behavior, it remained prudent for the United States to maintain a reasonably good security relationship with China.

Inertia also played a role. By the time the Cold War was recognized to be truly over, engagement had been evolving for two decades. The policies that made it possible were well understood by career professionals in Washington, and the most senior officials in successive administrations were preoccupied with other issues. For Clinton, it was the Balkans, the Middle East, and North Korea; for George W. Bush, it was terrorism, Afghanistan, and Iraq. Obama had to contend with the Great Recession, the Middle East, and attempts to end the wars in Afghanistan and Iraq. Engineering a fundamental change in U.S. foreign policy is a major undertaking. None of these presidents was willing—or, given their priorities, able—to attempt major changes in U.S. policies toward China. Indeed, in several of these crises, Beijing's stance in the United Nations and other international organizations was an important consideration. There were issues to be sure, and they became more obvious and more frustrating by the year, but they were treated as manageable problems in a bilateral relationship that, overall, was working reasonably well. For almost two decades, policy toward China was treated as an example of, "If it ain't broke, don't fix it." Moreover, the policy was well understood, largely uncontested, and implemented primarily by nongovernmental actors; thus, it required only minimal time and attention from the president and top cabinet officials. Attempting to make the relationship better was repeatedly judged to be more trouble than it was worth. And, given globalization and the competitive economic relationships among America and its allies, no one wanted to forego the immediate economic gains for the uncertainties that more conflict with Beijing would bring.

The third source of continuity was the collective influence of important nongovernmental beneficiaries and defenders of engagement. The most influential of these constituencies was the business community. As noted earlier, one of the primary reasons the United States responded positively to Deng's reform and opening strategy was that it appeared to offer significant possibilities for market access and people-to-people interaction. By the time the dust had settled after the collapse of the Soviet Union, American business was heavily committed to China. Investments made over almost two decades were paying off, many firms had important Chinese nodes in production and supply chains, and the domestic market was beginning to open. Becoming established in China had been a long and difficult process, but it was beginning to yield results—profits. Ironically, it was the business community that had the most complaints about Chinese behavior (e.g., theft of intellectual property, failure to honor World Trade Organization [WTO] and other treaty commitments, coerced transfers of technology), but it was this constituency that became the strongest and most effective voice demanding continuity in U.S. China policy. Its voice was heard because firms and business executives provide a disproportionate share of the funding for American political campaigns.[29] Making money is not the only objective or concern of American businesses in China, but for most, most of the time, earnings trump traditional security concerns and violations of human rights, academic freedom, and other soft issues.

Business is the largest and best-organized constituency with a stake in engagement, but there are many others. The restoration of diplomatic relations and possibilities inherent in reform and opening opened the way to the reestablishment of academic, medical, and other professional ties that had been severed during the Maoist era. As all the other chapters in this volume show, individuals and institutions on both sides of the Pacific were prepared, even eager, to restore collaborative relationships, some dating from the late nineteenth and early twentieth centuries. Many had grown out of missionary activities to bring enlightenment (Christianity, education, medical care, rule of law, etc.) to the Chinese people and reflected then-common manifestations of cultural superiority and religious zeal. Vestiges of such thinking doubtless continue to exist, but it seems fair to say that religious motivations have been complemented if not supplanted by humanist concerns about fellow human beings.

Motivations changed with the passage of time and the forces of modernization, globalization, and social evolution. No one conceived of engagement as a return to halcyon days of yore when Americans (and other Westerners) had a moral obligation to bring enlightenment to the Chinese people. In its place was a complementarity of interests in which the Chinese government had elevated rapid modernization to the status of a national priority, Chinese institutions and individuals were eager to contribute to that effort, and American counterparts were willing to help. The motivations of individuals and institutions differed, but unlike in the nineteenth century when American efforts to "help" China were often resisted or resented, the period of engagement had participants on both sides who were eager to cooperate.

In China, modernization was defined by the party as an urgent need. This created opportunities and incentives to establish and reestablish ties linking any and (almost) all entities that could contribute to that effort. Beijing was wary of unmanaged contacts and what it called the danger of "spiritual pollution," but it was willing to accept the risks in order to achieve rapid development and economic growth. Their willingness was based on conviction that it was only a matter of time until the perfidious Americans pulled the plug and reverted to what Beijing characterized as containment designed to constrain China's rise. Americans were also interested in speed, albeit for different reasons. Some feared that the opening to the outside world would be as transitory as policies adopted in the Maoist period and were eager to establish ties and demonstrate concrete benefits in hope of forestalling another reversal of policy. Other ties were based on long-severed relationships between aging Americans and Chinese. For both personal and purposive reasons, they were in a hurry to build on past friendships and experience. Others had instrumental motivations. For example, if China was to attract foreign investment, it would be necessary to put in place at least a rudimentary legal framework and mechanisms to transfer funds and transport goods. Both sides were eager to get started and to use initial achievements to justify and impel transformation of the country and people suffering from Mao's disastrous policies.

Engagement as Description of Reality

Although often characterized as strategy, it is more accurate to describe engagement as the reality created by Deng's decision to open China to the outside world and Carter's decision to seize the opportunity that offered to achieve long-standing American goals. To the extent that it was a strategy, it envisioned but could not mandate establishment of multiple relationships between Chinese and American entities. For reasons summarized earlier, the opening led to steady increases in the number, scope, variety, and depth of interconnected and interdependent relationships involving multiple interests and constituencies. Beijing is warier of these relationships than is Washington, but both see them as channels of information and agents of change. For Beijing, that is worrisome because these relationships are seen as instruments of an imputed American intention to achieve peaceful transformation, regime change, or color revolution. Washington sees them as largely autonomous relationships that contribute to the attainment of U.S. security and developmental objectives but operate largely without government guidance or control. In the current American political environment, such porous relations are seen as channels by which Beijing gains national capabilities at U.S. expense.

The result of these cultural and systemic differences is that Beijing has greater ability and incentive to manage the vehicles and interactions that constitute engagement than does Washington. The nature of the U.S. system and extra-governmental origins and interests of the actors on the U.S. side of the equation constrain Washington's ability to use or limit their interactions with Chinese counterparts. This fact poses a significant obstacle to implementation of calls to curtail engagement and decouple from China. On the U.S. side, engagement is the fact and substance of actions by myriad independent actors, each of which is a legitimate (and sometimes powerful) constituency in the American political process. It would be very hard for any U.S. administration to curtail engagement even if it wanted to. Although this chapter does not look closely at the Chinese side, it is worth asserting that forty years of engagement have made it significantly and increasingly costly for Beijing to rupture relationships. That, it should be recalled, was one of the Carter administration's original objectives, and in that respect, engagement has succeeded.

Engagement is an elastic concept that subsumes elements of the U.S. strategy to reengage with China, the products of contact and development of relationships between numerous and disparate American and Chinese entities, and constellations of political actors and interests on both sides with incentives and abilities to defend their stakes in the U.S.-China relationship. Over the past four decades, U.S. constituencies have repeatedly and effectively defended their interests and pressed for stability and predictability in U.S. policy toward China. China—or more explicitly, an exaggerated and demonized caricature of China—has been a whipping boy in every presidential campaign since relations were normalized in 1979. But no matter how intense the rhetoric (e.g., Clinton's "butchers of Beijing"), U.S. China policy remained fundamentally the same. Preoccupation with other issues and recurring decisions not to complicate the pursuit of higher-priority objectives by taking steps that would worsen relations with China account, in part, for this stability. But policy continuity was also the product of pressure brought to bear by the multiple interests with a stake in engagement. To a considerable degree, engagement had become a reality operating substantially outside the scope of U.S. government control.

What Has Changed?

U.S. policy and the modalities of engagement remained remarkably stable from 1979 until Obama's second term but changed markedly during the Trump administration. What accounts for the change? Some point to the ascension of Xi Jinping and the inauguration of Donald Trump and ascribe the deterioration of relations to the personalities and policy preferences of these individuals and their administrations, implicitly suggesting that if one or both had not come to power when they did, the U.S.-China relationship would have continued to evolve along more or less the same post-Nixon trajectory.[30] I find such explanations unsatisfactory because they ignore or minimize the importance of context and the cumulative consequences of engagement.

As in the early 1970s, the late 1970s, and the 1990s, U.S. China policy in the second decade of the twentieth century has been shaped by the international situation and national security priorities. The policy adjustments and revalidations made during the first three periods were strongly influenced by the Cold War and a conceptual framework that continued to give priority to uncertainty about Russian intentions. By 2001, the perceived threat from Russia was declining and China's then decade-long military buildup had put it on the U.S. security radar, but the 9/11 terrorist attacks moved terrorism to the top of the U.S. security agenda. China and Russia were immediately seen as potentially helpful partners in what came to be called the "war on terror." Other concerns about the domestic policies and military programs of Russia and China were subordinated to cooperation in meeting the immediate and alarming terrorist threat. One can argue, in retrospect, that the Bush administration exaggerated that threat and neglected other important and pressing problems, but the fact is that combatting terror took precedence over concern about China's military modernization. The logic of keeping China on our side de facto mandated deferral of action to alleviate problems in the relationship and, thus, continuation of engagement.

Fixation on the terrorist threat was waning as the decade drew to a close, and national security officials began to pay more attention to cumulative changes in Chinese military capabilities with the potential, later realized, to change the security situation in the western Pacific. This was occurring in the context of inevitable retrenchment after a decade of war and the need to replace equipment developed for the Cold War with new weapons and missions for the post–Cold War era. Determining what to build and how to deploy it required judgments about the capabilities of prospective enemies—not just today, but ten to twenty years into the future. China's new capabilities and imputed intentions provided a rationale both for continued high defense expenditures and for an emphasis on naval and air power. One consequence of this somewhat technical debate about the type of military needed for the future was broader public discussion of China's military capabilities and intentions, increased congressional testimony explaining new threats and military needs, and descriptions of China in public national security documents that Beijing interpreted as hostile.[31] In short, events had come together in a way that created a classic security dilemma in which the actions of one side are perceived to require a defensive response by the other, and an action-reaction spiral evolved that included a widening array of economic, technological, and other arenas. At present, the stage of these developments is that both sides have a more negative view of each other than at any time since the immediate post-Tiananmen period.

The economic context also changed in significant ways. China's sustained and rapid growth after it was admitted to the WTO in 2001 is often cited by Chinese as proving that they have a better system and by critics of engagement as proof that it was dangerously foolish of the United States to have agreed to China's admission before it had actually met more of the formal requirements.[32] This is not the place to address those issues; the point I want to make here is that the period from 2001 to 2011 was one of spectacular growth that underpins Chinese and foreign perceptions and projections of its rise to major, and perhaps great, power status.[33] The era of miracle growth is now over, but the size and composition of China's economy coming out of that period are such that it is no longer prudent—or, given the interests of key constituencies, possible— to ignore the impact of its blatant disregard for international norms, treaty commitments, bilateral agreements, and commercial contracts. If Malawi or Uruguay acted as China has and does, it would be unfortunate and unfair, but it would not have much of an impact on American and other foreign firms and workers. China's enormous size compounds the impact and importance of its deviant economic behavior. What could be overlooked at earlier stages of China's development and in much smaller economies can no longer be ignored.

Engagement deliberately and effectively facilitated China's rise in order to make it a stronger partner, more prosperous country, and more tightly enmeshed in the rules-based order. In the process of doing so, it spawned thousands, and perhaps tens of thousands, of economic ties that endured because they were currently or prospectively profitable to all partners. Along the way, American businesses accommodated or accepted Chinese behaviors as the necessary price of securing a place in the Chinese market and/or production chains. As China's economy grew, the untoward behaviors became more consequential. They also became more visible to U.S. government observers and public intellectuals who increasingly asked whether Washington should do something.[34] Until roughly the second half of the second Obama administration, the answer, from the business community, was, "No. This is a business problem that we can handle. Do not make it harder to solve by politicizing it."[35]

Business leaders may have overestimated their ability to change the behavior of Chinese entities, many of whom acted with the backing of or direction from the party-state. They may also have overestimated the likelihood that Chinese counterparts would recognize that it was in their (and China's) long-term interest to shed practices that were tolerable for companies and countries at an earlier stage of development but counterproductive in more advanced economies. If that was their assumption or calculation, it proved wrong. During Obama's second term, the business community, which as noted earlier had long been the most forceful and effective advocate of stability in American policy toward

China, reversed its position. Long-festering problems had become worse and more costly, and businesses (like many other constituencies) had grown weary of promises from Beijing to finally do things (like comply with commitments made at the time of WTO accession) that it had promised many times before.[36] Now the business community argued, in effect, that businesses alone could not solve the problems without jeopardizing their own substantial interests and that Washington should step in and use its leverage to solve the problems for all American (and by extension, other foreign) firms. This made it imperative for whoever was elected in 2016 to challenge and attempt to change Chinese practices that were now widely perceived to be unfair and unacceptable. Many American allies shared these concerns. They complained but were more reluctant to confront Beijing.

Conditions also have changed in the third or catchall category of engagement that subsumes academic contacts, nongovernmental organization (NGO) activities, and myriad professional and other groups. The trigger for that change, I argue, is the retreat from reforms and liberalization of contacts between Chinese and foreign counterparts that has occurred since the latter part of the Hu Jintao administration and took very concrete form in 2016 when the new law on foreign NGO activities in China moved oversight of foreign NGOs from the Ministry of Civil Affairs to the Ministry of Public Security.[37] Many attribute this retreat and the attendant tightening of controls and restrictions on both Chinese and their foreign partners to Xi personally.[38] I think it is more a reflection of top-level concern about the potential for instability resulting from the slowing of growth, fear that instability will lead to economic disruptions that undermine performance-based legitimacy, and conviction that the danger of social disturbances is exacerbated by contacts with Americans and other foreigners suspected of acting as instruments of imputed American policies to engineer a color revolution in the PRC.[39] In other words, there is both a domestic rationale for Beijing's intensifying efforts to restrict and control the actions of civil society and other potential vehicles of organized dissent and an international rationale for restricting people-to-people dimensions of engagement. Regardless of the precise allocation of blame for Beijing's crackdown, the net effect has been to alienate more or less every constituency in the United States that had formerly championed and benefitted from engagement. In the current sour context, defending engagement is often perceived as equivalent to defending the regime in Beijing and its offensive behaviors.

Has Engagement Failed?

Critics of U.S. engagement with China contend that it foolishly helped to create an economic juggernaut that threatens to overtake the United States and that it allowed China to exploit asymmetric opportunities and American naivete by acting in ways that were unfair and at times illegal. They also assert that foolhardy U.S. policies enabled China to acquire—legally or through legerdemain—technologies that contribute to its military buildup and ability to surveil and thus control Chinese society and that engagement has strengthened the party-state and enhanced its ability to manipulate opinion in China and the United States.[40] The greatest mistake of all, according to critics of engagement, was to believe that engagement would lead to transformation of the regime in Beijing from authoritarian party-state into American-style democracy. The tag line, implicit or otherwise, is, "How could Washington have been so foolish, naïve, and oblivious to American security and economic interests?"

Such charges mischaracterize the objectives of engagement, ignore the contexts of its origin and evolution, and blithely glide over the fact that the policy was reexamined and sustained by six presidents and ten administrations (two additional presidents and three more administrations if one starts the clock with Nixon's rapprochement). Were all of those administrations, Republican and Democrat, liberal and conservative, equally naïve and myopic? Could none of them see at the time the risks and downsides of engagement that seem so clear in retrospect to proponents of the "engagement failed" school? What alternative policies could or should the United States have pursued in order to achieve a different outcome, and why would the alternative approach have succeeded where the actual one failed? Without convincing answers to these and related questions, it is hard to regard the critics' disparagement of engagement and its practitioners as justifying proposals to decouple and mount a whole of government and whole of society effort to contain and constrain China. More fundamentally, who among America's traditional allies would follow Washington along such a road?

Rather than faulting engagement for failing to achieve an objective (transformation of China's party-state into a liberal democracy) that those (including me) involved at its inception or subsequent reassessments do not remember setting or discussing, the remainder of this chapter summarizes briefly what engagement did achieve.[41] As argued earlier, the initial and principal objective was to enhance American security by complicating Moscow's strategic calculus. The transition from rapprochement to engagement that occurred in late 1978 (symbolized by the establishment of formal diplomatic relations) coincided with the apogee of Soviet power and assertiveness. Its intent was to strengthen deterrence and further reduce the danger of nuclear war and Soviet attack on the United States and its allies. The deepening of the U.S.-China relationship and the clear intent of the United States to support China's developmental efforts probably were not decisive factors in deterring Soviet aggression or the demise of the Soviet Union (remember Moscow invaded Afghanistan shortly after normalization), but they certainly were contributing factors. Engagement probably also played a role in mitigating Beijing's fear of U.S. aggression and deferring the military buildup that Deng had paused in order to devote more resources to development and persuade Washington and its developed country allies (principally Japan) that aiding China's quest for modernization would not, at least not immediately, endanger their own security.

Quantifying the contribution of engagement to the avoidance of conflict between China and the United States, China and Taiwan, or China and Japan is impossible. But it is objectively the case that there have been no major conflicts in East Asia since the Vietnam War. Perhaps that was simply a matter of luck, but during the preceding fifty years, the United States was massively involved in the Pacific theater of World War II, the Korean War, and the Vietnam War and risked war with China in the 1954 and 1958 Taiwan Strait Crises. Whether engagement caused Beijing to withhold support for a second Democratic People's Republic of Korea (DPRK) attack on the Republic of Korea is impossible to determine, but the attack did not happen. It is at least plausible that the DPRK's doubts about the reliability of its ally in Beijing after rapprochement and engagement with the United States had a restraining influence.[42]

In addition to the avoidance of conflict in East Asia that enabled it to become the fastest-growing and most dynamic region in the world, engagement with China gave Washington a freer hand to operate militarily in other parts of the world. This was the inverse of what engagement did to Moscow. Because Washington did not have to worry about China, it was less constrained when undertaking military operations in the First Gulf War, the Balkans, Afghanistan, and Iraq. Many (including myself) question the wisdom of the Iraq misadventure, but the fact remains that Washington benefitted from China's support or abstentions in the UN Security Council and did not have to worry that Beijing might attempt to take advantage of U.S. preoccupation in other parts of the world.

The economic arena is the one most often cited to prove the folly of engagement, often with the implication or assertion that China's economic rise was detrimental to the United States. The evidence indicates otherwise. When engagement began in 1978, the U.S. share of the global economy was 27 percent, a figure pretty close to its pre–World War II average. Forty years later, after China's miracle growth, the rise (and fall) of Japan's economy, the incorporation of central European states into the European Union, and rapid growth in India, Africa, and elsewhere, the U.S. share has fallen, but only to 23.9 percent (2018).[43] Considering that the U.S. share of world population declined over this period from 5.2 to 4.3 percent, on a per capita basis, we play a larger role than we did before engagement.[44]

Economic engagement was expected to increase prosperity in China *and* the United States. In the period of post–World War II economic reconstruction, that is what happened in countries allied with the United States and able to take advantage of the asymmetric opportunities offered by U.S. policies to foster growth and participation in the rules-based order. That is what happened in China as well. Per capita GDP in China rose from $156 in 1978 to $9,771 in 2018. During that same period, per capita GDP in the United States rose from $10,565 to $62,794.[45] We have a distribution problem in the United States (and so does China), but that is not the fault of engagement. Critics of engagement often point to the transfer of jobs from the United States to China, sometimes asserting that the jobs were stolen by the PRC. It is hard to blame the decline in U.S. factory jobs on theft by China when the decisions to move manufacturing were made by mostly U.S.-based boards of directors honoring their fiduciary responsibility to shareholders (including American pension funds and 401K investors) to maintain or increase profits. Moreover, study after study has shown that more jobs have been lost to automation than to movement outside the United States and that the increase in trade with China and many other countries has created more high-paying jobs in transportation, warehousing, insurance, and other industries than have been lost in manufacturing.[46] That is no consolation to workers displaced by factory closures and towns deprived of important sources of tax revenue, but the failure of U.S. governments at the federal and state levels to implement effective transition measures is not the fault of Beijing or engagement.

When engagement began, China was party to almost no international organizations or control regimes (outside of the UN system). Beijing still proclaimed adherence to the Maoist principle that China would not be bound by any international arrangements that it had not helped to establish and would not be bound by rules that it had not agreed to at the time they were established. Forty years later, China is an active participant in more than 150 international regimes including the Treaty on the Non-Proliferation of Nuclear Weapons (NPT), the WTO, and UN peacekeeping operations, as other contributors to this volume also note. Though its acquiescence and acceptance of the rules-based order have been grudging and slow, it now accepts and contributes to this order because it understands that, most of the time, it is in China's interest to do so.[47] Stated another way, China increasingly acts as a responsible stakeholder in the international system. Beijing understandably insists that being a stakeholder entitles China to a voice in decisions affecting the control regime and China's interests. That is a much better situation than existed previously. Illustrative examples include China's improved proliferation behavior after joining the NPT and other control regimes, its participation in negotiation of the Joint Comprehensive Plan of Action limiting Iranian nuclear activity, and its endorsement of the Responsibility to Protect (R2P), which requires international action when a country cannot or will not protect its own people.[48] This position is diametrically opposite to the preengagement PRC position on sovereignty and nonintervention.

The list of examples could be expanded to include cooperation on climate change, the incorporation of international standards into the operating guidelines of the Chinese-led Asian Infrastructure Investment Bank, and many other developments noted in other chapters of this book. The bottom line is that engagement has contributed to peace and prosperity in Asia, helped to make China a better place and more responsible international actor, contributed to the prosperity of American citizens, and made China and Chinese people more active contributors to efforts to meet transnational challenges. Most wish that China had not retreated from reforms adopted before the rise of Xi Jinping and that it will return to the reformist and ultimately transformative policies from which it has retreated out of fear of the implications for the party-state and ruling elite. However, as other contributors to this book point out, history has not ended, and China, like other countries, will continue to evolve. It is far too soon to declare engagement a failed policy that must be replaced by its opposite, which would be a variant of containment. Those who believe engagement a failure must articulate what policies would have produced better results and what should have been done instead at each of the junctures where circumstances changed and American policy makers reviewed the bidding and decided to retain the goals and methods of engagement. They also must explain how to deal with the business community and many other constituencies with a stake in engagement. Being unhappy about Beijing's current behavior and constraints on interaction with Americans is not at all the same as being supportive of proposals to abandon the approach that has served the United States, China, the region, and the global system remarkably well.

NOTES

1. See, for example, Robert Conquest, *Reflections on a Ravaged Century* (New York: Norton, 2001); and Louisa Lim, "Rewriting History in the People's Republic of Amnesia and Beyond," The Conversation, May 28, 2018, http://theconversation.com /rewriting-history-in-the-peoples-republic-of-amnesia-and-beyond-90014.
2. Examples include Kurt M. Campbell and Ely Ratner, "The China Reckoning: How Beijing Defied American Expectations," *Foreign Affairs* 97, no. 2 (March/April 2018): 60–70; and Ben Weingarten, "Is It Time for America to Begin Decoupling from Communist China?" *The Federalist*, October 22, 2019, https://thefederalist.com/2019/10/22 /is-it-time-for-america-to-begin-decoupling-from-communist-china/.
3. Surveys of American history and the memoirs of most secretaries of state devote only limited attention to China. See, for example, Warren I. Cohen, *The New Cambridge History of American Foreign Relations, Volume 4: Challenges to American Primacy, 1945–the Present* (Cambridge: Cambridge University Press, 2013); and George P. Shultz, *Triumph and Turmoil: My Years as Secretary of State* (New York: Scribner, 2010).
4. This situation changed during the Trump administration when China became more central to decisions on a wide range of issues.

5. See Henry Kissinger, *The White House Years* (Boston: Little, Brown, 1979), 1087–1096.

6. See, for example, John Bew, *Realpolitik: A History* (Oxford: Oxford University Press, 2016).

7. The term *axis of convenience* is borrowed from Bobo Lo, *Axis of Convenience: Moscow, Beijing, and the New Geopolitics* (Washington, DC: Brookings Institution Press, 2008).

8. See William C. Kirby, Robert S. Ross, and Gong Li, eds., *Normalization of US-China Relations: An International History* (Cambridge, MA: Harvard University East Asia Center, 2007).

9. The text of the communique is available in Office of the Historian, "Document 203," in *Foreign Relations of the United States, 1969–1976, Volume XVII, China, 1969–1972* (Washington, DC: U.S. Department of State, 1972), https://history.state.gov /historicaldocuments/frus1969-76v17/d203.

10. See, for example, Harry Harding, *A Fragile Relationship: The United States and China Since 1972* (Washington, DC: The Brookings Institution, 1992).

11. Harding, *Fragile Relationship*.

12. See, for example, Michael Green, *By More Than Providence: Grand Strategy and American Power in the Asia-Pacific Since 1783* (New York: Columbia University Press, 2017).

13. See Michel Oksenberg, "Reconsiderations: A Decade of Sino-American Relations," *Foreign Affairs* 61, no. 1 (Fall 1982): 175–95.

14. See, for example, Ezra F. Vogel, *Deng Xiaoping and the Transformation of China* (Cambridge, MA: Harvard University Press, 2011).

15. See, for example, Thomas J. McCormick, *China Market: America's Quest for Informal Empire, 1893–1901* (New York: Quadrangle Books, 1967); and Green, *By More Than Providence*.

16. See Paul A. Varg, *Missionaries, Chinese, and Diplomats: The American Protestant Missionary Movement in China 1890–1952* (Princeton, NJ: Princeton University Press, 1958).

17. Benjamin I. Page with Marshall M. Bouton, *The Foreign Policy Disconnect: What Americans Want from Our Leaders but Don't Get* (Chicago: University of Chicago Press, 2008).

18. Vogel, *Deng Xiaoping*.

19. See Bernard Gwertzman, "Top Government Science Mission Being Sent to China Next Week," *New York Times*, June 28, 1978, https://www.nytimes.com/1978/06/28/archives /top-government-science-mission-being-sent-to-china-next-week-carter.html.

20. The government-to-government agreement reestablishing student exchanges was not signed until December 19, 1978, but the "trial balloon" template agreement between Stanford University and the Chinese Academy of Sciences was concluded in October, and the first students arrived on the Stanford campus on November 12, 1978. See Thomas Fingar, "Negotiating Scholarly Exchanges: The Stanford Experience," *Contemporary China* 3, no. 4 (Winter 1979).

21. See Thomas Fingar, "American Foreign Policy in Transition: From Cold War Consensus to Controversy and Confusion," *Contemporary American Studies Review* 2, no. 1 (2018): 70–83 (in Chinese); English text available at https://aparc.fsi.stanford.edu/publication /american-foreign-policy-transition-cold-war-consensus-controversy-and-confusion.

22. See, for example, Elizabeth M. Nimmo, "United States Policy Regarding the Transfer of Technology to the People's Republic of China," *Northwestern Journal of International Law and Business* 6, no. 1 (Spring 1984): 249–84; and U.S. Congress, Office of Technology Transfer, *Technology Transfer to China* (Washington, DC: U.S. Government Printing Office, July 1987).

23. Suspicion of American malign intent reasserted itself in the latter half of the 2000–2010 decade when reform slowed and then transitioned to an accelerating rollback of policies that allowed deepening contact between Chinese and Americans.

24. Indeed, the policies were challenged by Chinese "liberals" in the Democracy Wall movement (1979) and, a decade later, by Chinese "conservatives" in the aftermath of Tiananmen.

25. For a general treatise on the low costs of entry and high costs of exit from the liberal order, see G. John Ikenberry, *Liberal Leviathan: The Origins, Crisis, and Transformation of the American World Order* (Princeton, NJ: Princeton University Press, 2011).

26. See Thomas Fingar, "Sources and Shapers of China's Foreign Policy," in *Fateful Decisions: Choices That Will Shape China's Future*, eds. Thomas Fingar and Jean C. Oi (Stanford, CA: Stanford University Press, 2020), 225–46.

27. To hedge against uncertainty, including uncertainty about China, the United States bolstered its alliances and Obama launched his strategy to "rebalance" Asia. See, for example, Green, *By More Than Providence*; Kurt M. Campbell, *The Pivot: The Future of American Statecraft in Asia* (New York: Twelve, 2016); and Aaron L. Friedberg, *A Contest for Supremacy: China, America, and the Struggle for Mastery in Asia* (New York: W.W. Norton, 2011).

28. See, for example, Robert S. Ross, ed., *China, the United States, and the Soviet Union: Tripolarity and Policymaking in the Cold War* (Abington, UK: Routledge, 1993).

29. See Mark Green, *Selling Out: How Big Corporate Money Buys Elections, Rams Through Legislation, and Betrays Our Democracy* (New York: Regan Books, 2013).

30. See, for example, Elizabeth C. Economy, *The Third Revolution: Xi Jinping and the New Chinese State* (Oxford: Oxford University Press, 2018); and Michael H. Fuchs, "How to Lose Friends and Strain Alliances: Washington's Partners Aren't Buying Its China Policy," *Foreign Affairs*, March 12, 2020, https://www.foreignaffairs.com/articles/china/2020-03-12/how-lose-friends-and-strain-alliances.

31. See, for example, Daniel R. Coates, "Statement for the Record: Worldwide Threat Assessment of the US Intelligence Community," Senate Select Committee on Intelligence, January 29, 2019, https://www.dni.gov/index.php/newsroom/congressional-testimonies/item/1947-statement-for-the-record-worldwide-threat-assessment-of-the-us-intelligence-community; and Donald J. Trump, *National Security Strategy of the United States of America* (Washington, DC: The White House, December 2017), https://www.whitehouse.gov/wp-content/uploads/2017/12/NSS-Final-12-18-2017-0905-2.pdf.

32. See Office of the United States Trade Representative, *Findings of the Investigation Into China's Acts, Policies, and Practices Related to Technology Transfer, Intellectual Property, and Innovation Under Section 301 of the Trade Act of 1974* (Washington, DC: The White House, March 22, 2018), https://ustr.gov/sites/default/files/Section%20301%20FINAL.PDF; and Philip Levy, "Was Letting China Into the WTO a Mistake? Why There Were Not Better Alternatives," *Foreign Affairs*, April 2, 2018, https://www.foreignaffairs.com/articles/china/2018-04-02/was-letting-china-wto-mistake.

33. See, for example, Susan L. Shirk, *China: Fragile Superpower* (Oxford: Oxford University Press, 2007); and David Shambaugh, *China Goes Global: The Partial Power* (Oxford: Oxford University Press, 2013).

34. The shift in business attitudes can be tracked by comparing the annual Business Climate Survey results released by the American Chamber of Commerce in China and the Annual Member Survey results of the US-China Business Council.

35. This is not an actual quotation; I have put it in quotes to characterize the views expressed by executives in American firms operating in China. See, for example,

Laura Sullivan and Cat Schuknecht, "As China Hacked, US Business Turned a Blind Eye," *NPR*, April 12, 2019, https://www.npr.org/2019/04/12/711779130/as-china-hacked-u-s-businesses-turned-a-blind-eye.

36. See, for example, "When It Comes to China, Foreign Investors Are Getting 'Promise Fatigue,'" *Fortune*, September 18, 2017, https://fortune.com/2017/09/18/china-politburo-reforms-foreign-investment/.

37. On the slowing of reform under Hu Jintao, see, for example, Ian Johnson, "China's Lost Decade," *New York Review of Books*, September 17, 2012, https://www.nybooks.com/articles/2012/09/27/chinas-lost-decade/. On the nongovernmental organization law, see Edward Wong, "Clampdown in China Restricts 7,000 Foreign Organizations," *New York Times*, April 28, 2016, https://www.nytimes.com/2016/04/29/world/asia/china-foreign-ngo-law.html.

38. See, for example, Economy, *The Third Revolution*; and "China's Xi Tightens Ideological Control in Universities," *Reuters*, December 29, 2014, https://www.reuters.com/article/us-china-universities-idUSKBN0K70TI20141229.

39. See Thomas Fingar and Jean C. Oi, "China's Challenges: Now It Gets Much Harder," *The Washington Quarterly* 43, no. 1 (March 2020): 67–84.

40. Office of the United States Trade Representative, *Findings of the Investigation*; "Confronting the China Threat," FBI News, February 6, 2020, https://www.fbi.gov/news/stories/wray-addresses-china-threat-at-doj-conference-020620; and Larry Diamond and Orville Schell, eds., *China's Influence and American Interests: Promoting Constructive Vigilance* (Stanford, CA: Hoover Institution, 2019).

41. See comments by J. Stapleton Roy and by Thomas Christianson and Patricia Kim, in Wang Jisi et al., "Did America Get China Wrong: The Engagement Debate," *Foreign Affairs* 97, no. 4 (July/August 2018): 185–90, https://www.foreignaffairs.com/articles/china/2018-06-14/did-america-get-china-wrong.

42. See Don Oberdorfer and Robert Carlin, *The Two Koreas: A Contemporary History*, rev. 2nd ed. (New York: Basic Books, 2014).

43. The U.S. share of the world economy is calculated using World Bank data, available at https://data.worldbank.org/indicator/NY.GDP.MKTP.CD?locations=US-CN-1W.

44. The U.S. share of the world population is calculated from World Bank data, available at https://data.worldbank.org/indicator/SP.POP.TOTL?locations=US-CN-1W.

45. GDP per capita figures are in current U.S. dollars and are taken from World Bank data, available at https://data.worldbank.org/indicator/NY.GDP.PCAP.CD?locations=CN-US.

46. See Federica Cocco, "Most US Manufacturing Jobs Lost to Technology, Not Trade," *Financial Times*, December 2, 2016, https://www.ft.com/content/dec677c0-b7e6-11e6-ba85-95d1533d9a62.

47. See Ann Kent, *Beyond Compliance: China, International Organizations, and Global Security* (Stanford, CA: Stanford University Press, 2007).

48. See, for example, Evan Medeiros, *Reluctant Restraint: The Evolution of China's Nonproliferation Policies and Practices, 1980–2004* (Stanford, CA: Stanford University Press, 2007); and Courtney J. Fung, *China and the Responsibility to Protect: From Opposition to Advocacy* (Washington, DC: U.S. Institute of Peace, 2016).

CHAPTER 3

MISMANAGING CHINA'S RISE

The South China Sea Dispute and the Transformation of Sino-American Relations from Strategic Partners to Strategic Rivals

JOHN W. GARVER

For well over a century, with one notable twenty-year-long exception, a core element of American policy toward China was the facilitation of China's national quest for wealth and power (*fu guo, qiang bing*). From the Qing dynasty to Chiang Kai-shek's Nationalist government and the post-Mao communist period, American foreign policy supported China's efforts at economic, political, and (sometimes) military development. As the leading China historian Warren Cohen has noted, the twenty years of Sino-American confrontation between 1950 and 1971 were a "great aberration" from a much longer period of friendship.[1] The broad pattern of Sino-American relations, Cohen tells us, was mutually beneficial cooperation. America's traditional China policy was to help China become strong. The reality, however, was that China was weak.

When Deng Xiaoping assumed the reins of power in 1978, two years after the death of Mao, he confronted the reality of China's weakness head on, instituting a successful (and U.S.-supported) development push centered around abandoning the deeply flawed Soviet-style planned economy imposed on China in the 1950s, while carefully nourishing a diplomacy of what might be called "strategic humility" to persuade the American leadership that China did not aspire to confront or replace the United States. So rapidly did China's economy grow that its national power will soon approximate that of the United States. And now that China is strong, the long-standing policy of mutual cooperation and friendship with the United States has come to an end. This chapter seeks to understand both how and why, beginning around 2012–2018, U.S.-China relations became so tense and adversarial, to describe the ongoing nature of the disputes with particular attention to China's seizure of the South China Sea, to explain Washington's determination to maintain its policy of freedom of navigation, and finally, to offer suggestions for prudent changes in U.S. China policy in the new era of strategic rivalry between the two countries.

In brief, the substantial change in the aggregate national power of the United States and the People's Republic of China (PRC) that occurred between 1978, when China's opening and reform began, and 2012, when a new leadership team headed by Xi Jinping took over, led China to adopt a more assertive, more confrontational, less risk-adverse foreign policy designed to shape China's international environment to comport more fully with Xi's aspiration of the "great rejuvenation of the Chinese nation."

The most dangerous manifestation of the newly conflictual relationship is the ongoing dispute over sovereignty in the South China Sea. One important target of Xi's vision of rejuvenated national greatness has been in the maritime realm, where a new, modern, and potent Chinese navy, the People's Liberation Army Navy (PLAN), has been used to grow China's military influence over a wide swath of the western Pacific Ocean within what Chinese analysts call the first and second island chains. Within this broader maritime context, China's struggle for control of the South China Sea has become an area of intense geopolitical rivalry between China and the United States.

A number of factors in addition to maritime rivalry contributed to the increasingly acute tension in U.S.-PRC relations in the years after 2010. But the maritime territorial disputes in the South China Sea have generated the most acute and dangerous conflict.

The Chinese navy's influence inclines toward robust efforts to establish and defend Chinese control over the South China Sea.[2] The PLAN views itself as the guardian of China's territorial core interests against encroachment by the small Southeast Asian states egged on by the United States and Japan. Following the thinking of Alfred Thayer Mahan around 1900 on the role of sea power in world history, the PLAN also views its ability to obtain global ranging sea power as a prerequisite for China's rise as a leading nation of the world.[3] From the Chinese navy's perspective, securing full control over the South China Sea opens the door to securing Chinese sea lines of communication in the Indian Ocean, establishing a defense line at the first and then the second island chains, and finally, allowing the Chinese navy to range the oceans of the world freely as a fully rejuvenated great power.

The United States has viewed China's hard-edged campaign to establish control over the South China Sea as a challenge to the U.S.-sponsored post-1945 order in East and Southeast Asia. Under the Trump administration, U.S. policy progressively hardened, culminating in top-level strategy statements issued in December 2017 and January 2018 and a speech by Vice President Pence on

TABLE 3.1 Periods of U.S.-China Strategic Partnership

1898–1922	United States supports the Open Door policy and opposes carving the melon	Success: enshrined in 1922 Nine-Power Treaty
1931–1948	United States supports China against Japanese aggression and restores China as new policeman of Greater East Asia	Cairo Declaration, UN O enshrine China's paramount position
1949–1971	Confrontation with United States and then with United States and USSR	Twenty-year great aberration
1972–1989	Strategic partnership against USSR	Successful: USSR ends in 1991
1992–2013	Post–Cold War search for continued strategic partnership	U.S. offer of responsible stakeholder
2013–2020	Strategic rivalry with United States for preeminence in Asia	Break with Deng's doctrine of strategic humility

October 4, 2018. Quoting from the National Security Strategy of December 2017, Pence declared this a new era of great power competition and argued that China wants "nothing more than to push the United States of America from the Western Pacific and attempt to prevent us from coming to the aid of our allies."[4] Official American policy has thus changed from being supportive of China's rise as a strong and prosperous state to treating China as an adversarial great power attempting to undermine the United States and seeking ultimately to replace it as the dominant power in Asia. The long-standing American policy of friendship with China is at an end.

Table 3.1 summarizes the structure of the argument regarding the shifting pattern of geopolitical rivalry between China and the United States that will be presented in this chapter.

America's Traditional Policy of Support for China's Rise

Long-standing U.S. policy, beginning as early as the 1880s, sought to facilitate China's efforts to become prosperous and strong. U.S. policy makers generally saw support for a strong China both as a means of serving immediate

U.S. interests and, later, as a way of co-opting China to support the international political-economic system established and upheld by the United States after 1945. American leaders and mainstream public opinion expected that a China that had grown prosperous and strong with American support would become, in the often-noted words of U.S. deputy secretary of state Robert Zoellick in 2005, a responsible stakeholder willing to partner with the United States to uphold the rules-bound and open international order to the benefit of both countries.

American support did, in fact, help China become prosperous and strong. But the result of U.S. policy is not what the United States expected. Contrary to American hopes and expectations, a now-strong China is using its great power to challenge U.S. military dominance in the western Pacific. China aspires to create a security zone extending out to what it calls the first and second island chains. Such a maritime security zone would, essentially, replace American naval dominance in the western Pacific, a dominance won by tough fighting against the Imperial Japanese Navy in 1941–1945. Understanding this long tradition of U.S. support for China's rise is useful in understanding the American sense of betrayal and disappointment now feeding the debate over what American policy should be.

Support for China's quest for national wealth and power was a core element of the U.S. China policy for over a century. Beginning as early as the 1880s, American representatives articulated this policy in terms of American benevolence toward China, although such benevolence also served the important U.S. interest in preventing China from joining any hostile coalition or empire to dominate the Asian landmass.

By the 1880s, the United States was already well established as the world's leading industrial power and had turned to China as a lucrative market for its exports. But with the defeat of Qing China by Japan in 1895, the great powers, led by Japan, Germany, and Russia, began carving out spheres of influence inside the crumbling Chinese empire. American leaders feared that the division of China into spheres of influence could hamper the growth of U.S. exports to China. Some American diplomats, focused more on maintaining American power than commercial gain, also saw China as a potential check on the growth of Japanese and/or Russian power in Northeast Asia. Consequently, in 1899 (the year after Hawaii, Guam, and the Philippines were annexed by the United States) and 1900, the United States issued two Open Door Notes addressed to the various treaty powers and calling on them to respect China's sovereignty and abstain from measures that could diminish China's territorial or administrative integrity. The door to commercial opportunity in China should be open to all powers equally, the notes insisted.

The apparent benevolence of U.S. policy was tempered in reality by a strong strain of racism that was manifested in 1882 and 1902 by federal laws severely limiting Chinese immigration to the United States—bans not fully lifted until 1943. Such expressions of American racism had a deep impact on Chinese attitudes toward the United States, but China's national leaders nonetheless tended to see the United States as more supportive than other leading powers of its efforts to fend off aggression and hold China together.[5] And China often used the America card as leverage against the more aggressive powers.

World War I provided Japan an opportunity to further expand its influence in China. In 1915, with the Western powers engrossed in mutual slaughter in Europe and the new Republic of China (established in 1912) trying desperately to establish its authority, Tokyo secretly presented the struggling Chinese government a set of twenty-one demands meant to turn China into a satellite of Japan. When American diplomats learned of the plot, the resulting American pressure forced Tokyo to back away from the more onerous demands. Then, in August 1917, China entered the war on the side of the Allies, expecting that the victorious Allied coalition would strengthen China's position at the postwar peace conference, securing, at a minimum, the reversion to China of German holdings in Shandong.

The emergence of Japan as the most vigorous challenger to the Open Door policy during World War I strengthened the geopolitical basis of cooperation between China and the United States. Washington's support for Chinese sovereignty and independence took a new and expanded form after the war. Whereas the original Open Door Notes had been unilateral American communications to various powers, in 1922, Washington succeeded in translating the principles of the Open Door Notes into a multilateral Nine-Power Treaty. The new treaty pledged the signatory powers, including Japan, to safeguard the "rights and interests of China," "respect the sovereignty, the independence, and the territorial and administrative integrity of China," and "provide the fullest and most unembarrassed opportunity to China to develop and maintain for herself an effective and stable government."[6] China's diplomats considered this treaty, pushed through with U.S. support, a major gain, substantially strengthening China's position vis-à-vis Britain and Japan.

The Nine-Power Treaty became the primary legal basis for American opposition to Japan's aggression in China.[7] When Japan seized Manchuria in 1931–1932, Washington declared the move a clear violation of the treaty and refused to recognize the Japanese seizure.[8] Disagreement between Japan and the United States over China's status deepened steadily throughout the 1930s. China was the core issue in dispute between the two countries during the intense final nine months of negotiations leading to the attack on Pearl Harbor. It is fair to say that the war that began between the United States and Japan in December 1941 was, to a considerable degree, a war over the status of China. Was China to be fully independent and sovereign or under the tutelage of Japan?

At the same time, by 1941, convergent Chinese and U.S. interests had brought the two countries into full (though not formal) alliance. Over time, this alliance led to the legal extinction of extraterritoriality,[9] the return of Taiwan to China as per the Cairo Declaration of 1943, the return of Manchuria to China as per the Yalta agreement of early 1945, and a permanent, veto-holding seat for China on the Security Council of the newly established United Nations.

During this period, President Roosevelt's core strategic objective with respect to China was to make a strong China the major power in Asia, replacing imperial Japan as the policeman of Asia and checking the advance of the Soviet Union. Roosevelt's policies were solidly rooted in the Open Door Notes and the Nine-Power Treaty.

China's representatives fully welcomed U.S. support. Several colorful postage stamps, shown in Figure 3.1 and issued in 1945, commemorated the signing of the new treaties ending extraterritoriality. Providing evidence of China's official stance toward the United States at the time, the Stature of Liberty, symbol of the United States, radiates her benevolent light across China. The map of China includes Taiwan, Manchuria, Mongolia, and large swaths of northern Myanmar and northeastern India.

3.1 Republic of China postage stamp issued in 1945 on the second anniversary of signing the equal treaties ending extraterritoriality.

The prospect of civil war in China after Japan's surrender was a challenge to the American vision of China as a stabilizing policeman of Asia able to check further Soviet advance.[10] Despite the efforts of George Marshal, one of America's most prestigious generals, to negotiate a power-sharing agreement between the Nationalists and the Communists, and despite significant military aid to the Nationalists, the best Trumann could do was to keep U.S. military forces from being involved in the Nationalist-Communist fighting and limit further appropriation of American funds to rearm the crumbling Nationalist armies.

In late 1948, following the Communist victory at Huaihai in northwestern Jiangsu, the prospect of a complete Communist victory forced a back-to-basics rethinking of U.S. China policy. The result was a decision to court Chinese Titoism, meaning a China ruled by the Chinese Communist Party and led by Mao Zedong that was nonetheless motivated by such deep nationalist aspirations that conflict with the Soviet Union was inevitable.[11] From the American standpoint, the United States and China still shared many common interests and had a long tradition of cooperation. But China and the USSR had deep conflicts of interest, including the Soviet Union's special rights in Manchuria as demanded by Stalin at Yalta, the issue of Xinjiang where Soviet control had been eliminated only in 1943–1944, and Mongolia.[12] The American strategy was to disengage from the defeated Guomindang regime, let the dust of China's civil war settle, and court China's new communist but still deeply nationalistic regime. Within a few years, the American planners reasoned, an acceptable relationship might be worked out between the United States and communist-ruled China.[13]

The Chinese Communist Party leaders understood the American offer. The U.S. moves were plain enough. But the communist response was not encouraging. The American consul in Shenyang, Angus Ward, had been ordered by Washington to remain in place and seek regular, working relations with the new Chinese authorities now governing the city. After a week of practical cooperation between U.S. diplomats in Shenyang and People's Liberation Army (PLA) authorities in the city, the Shenyang consulate was taken over and closed down by the PLA. Communications equipment was seized, and Ward was arrested and held prisoner for over a year, all in violation of normal and treaty-based diplomatic immunity. Yet Truman's bid for a new modus vivendi with the PRC did not change.

The response to Truman's overture by the newly established PRC was to sign, in February 1950, a thirty-year treaty of military alliance with the Soviet Union. China's new communist leaders saw the U.S. bid as an attempt to split the socialist camp (which indeed it was) and rejected it in favor of full alliance with the Soviet Union.[14] Full Chinese membership in the Soviet camp also mandated Mao's approval of Kim Il Sung's war to take over South Korea. That decision led, in turn, to full-scale war with the United States and (even more enduring) the transformation of the psychology of the Sino-American relation-ship from one of mutual goodwill to one of intense mutual hatred.

Thus began the twenty-plus-year period of the great aberration from the long tradition of Sino-American cooperation described by Warren Cohen. The result of Beijing's dual decisions of military alliance with Moscow and support for Kim Il Sung's attempted military conquest of South Korea was two decades of intense confrontation between China and the United States—two wars (in Korea and Vietnam), mutual fear and hatred, and mutual injury by all means short of outright homeland-to-homeland war. This sad period may also serve as warning of what might happen as a result of choices by a now-strong China and an America increasingly apprehensive about its shrinking share of global economic wherewithal.

By 1969, however, the premise that had governed American policy makers in 1949—that Chinese nationalism was so strong that conflict with the Soviet Union was inevitable—was proving true. China had come to see the Soviet Union as an enemy. At the strategic core of the revival of Sino-American cooperation gener-ated by Mao and Nixon, Zhou Enlai, and Henry Kissinger were parallel interests in countering Soviet expansionism. Thus, during the Sino-Soviet border war of 1969, Washington rejected Soviet solicitation of U.S. approval for a preemptive military strike against China's nuclear facilities—a possibility that the Kennedy and Johnson administrations had themselves considered earlier and rejected! The United States also dropped its earlier opposition to other nations establish-ing diplomatic ties with the PRC, thus leading to an avalanche of expanding diplomatic ties between China and countries around the world. The PRC took over, without U.S. objection and with tacit U.S. support, China's seat on the UN Security Council. Soon Washington gave tacit approval for sales of sophisti-cated weapons systems to China by its European allies. And the United States displayed an understanding attitude when the PLA seized the Paracel Islands from South Vietnam in 1974 and again when the Chinese army taught Vietnam a lesson in 1979. The U.S. objective in all these moves was a traditional one—to promote the strengthening of China in order to contain inroads by another for-eign power, in this case the Soviet Union.

Mao surely never envisioned a deep engagement of China with global cap-italist markets, but his policy of cooperation with the United States gave post-humous legitimacy to Deng Xiaoping's embrace of much-expanded economic cooperation with the United States. In effect, Deng poured economic wine into the bottles of strategic cooperation forged by Mao and Nixon. After 1978, the United States was immensely helpful to China in its new drive for wealth and power. Washington quickly granted China most favored nation status (later renamed normal trade relations), a move that made possible substantial reduc-tions in U.S. tariffs, thus greatly facilitating China's early push to expand its exports. Washington also granted China large quotas for export of its textiles to the United States. And with U.S. support, China was granted full membership in the World Bank and International Monetary Fund (IMF) in 1980 and was granted generous special drawing rights in 2006. Over the ensuing decades, China became a major recipient of World Bank lending.

The United States also cooperated with Beijing in arranging the stable return of Hong Kong to Chinese control in 1997. This was immensely helpful to Beijing's economic drive. Early in China's post-1978 development drive, Hong Kong had emerged as the leading source of foreign investment to China. Hong Kong's sophisticated marketing, financial, logistic, and other service capabilities meshed with the cheap labor, land, and industrial resources of Guangdong province to become the engine of southern China's rapid industrialization and globalization. The Hong Kong–Guangdong nexus became a key driver of China's emergence as a leading exporter of the world. Hong Kong also provided a door into China for ethnic Chinese capital from Southeast Asia and (before the opening of cross-strait relations circa 1990) Taiwan.

The process of Hong Kong's reversion was extremely unpredictable. Uncertainty could have resulted in a major flight of capital. Middle-class professionals, many of whom had relatives and investments in immigration-friendly, English-speaking countries, might flee. Property and stock values could collapse. The United States could have easily found ways to wreck Hong Kong's reversion under the rubric of Deng's one country, two systems. But it did not.

Perhaps most important of all, in late 2001, Washington agreed to China's entry into the World Trade Organization (WTO), with the United States agreeing to lengthy periods during which China would be entitled to use protectionist measures to shelter its infant industries.

The Easy Wisdom of Retrospection

China's integration into the global market economy has made it prosperous and strong, but the course China has chosen is not the one U.S. policy makers had imagined. It is easy to look back and write different historical scripts producing different outcomes in Sino-American relations and declare some alternate outcome preferable to the one that actually transpired. With this in mind, one may ask whether and to what extent U.S. cooperation with China actually served U.S. security interests. In this analysis, the defeat of both Japan's and the Soviet Union's successive quests for hegemony over Asia comported well with long-term U.S. security against powerful and ambitious antidemocratic states. A number of alternate histories were possible. Had the United States not partnered with China against Japan, but instead allowed Japan to successfully break China into a series of Tokyo-oriented satellite states, then eliminated the Western colonial presence of the White Powers in Southeast Asia,[15] pushed the U.S. defense frontier eastward to Hawaii, and organized the New Order in Asia in partnership with a German-led New Order in Europe and the Middle East—all of these constituting core Japanese objectives by 1941—the situation confronting the United States by a Japan-ordered Asia could have been dire. Similarly, had the USSR intervened successfully in the early 1970s to support the Chinese Communist Party's healthy Marxist-Leninist forces (i.e., Mao's opponents within the Chinese Communist Party) and then followed up on Hanoi's 1975 defeat of the United States in Indochina[16] by aggressively supporting Marxist proxy forces in Africa and Central America with the support of a new, blue-water Soviet navy, the rejuvenation of U.S. anti-Soviet containment under Ronald Reagan might never have occurred. Instead, a United States chastened by defeat in Vietnam might have retreated to its default tradition of isolation. The relatively benign international situation the United States faced by 1990 could have been very different. Soviet hegemony, like Japanese hegemony over Asia, could have shaped a far darker vista for the United States. A strong China was a key reason why history tilted events toward a U.S.-favored and against a Moscow-supported outcome.

Similarly, in terms of values, conditions propitious for the emergence of liberal democracy for the nations of East and Southeast Asia, from Japan through the Philippines to Indonesia, could have been replaced by conditions shaped instead by imperial Japan or the Soviet Union. The emergence of first East Asia and then Southeast Asia as leading growth centers of the global economy benefited U.S. businesses and U.S. consumers. Japan's concept of a New Order in Asia and Moscow's vision of a socialist community of states were antithetical to the U.S. vision of open global markets. China's gradual integration after 1978, with U.S. support, into this open global economy was a central part of the U.S. effort to cooperate with China by making it wealthy and strong, while simultaneously making American businesses and consumers more prosperous. It may be too soon to declare engagement with China a failure because it produced a strong but ultimately antagonistic Chinese stance toward the U.S. role in Asia. Radical swings in policy are not unknown in China, and China may again embrace cooperation and partnership with the United States, perhaps especially as the costs of adversarial rivalry with the United States and its partners become apparent.

Weak China Becomes Strong and Challenges the United States[17]

American's century-long hope for China—that as China grew prosperous and strong with U.S. help and support it would choose to operate within the international order established and upheld by the United States—has not come to pass. China has not assumed the role of a responsible stakeholder. As noted in the previous section, America's traditional policy was to help China become strong because the reality was that China was weak. However, this is no longer the case. A mid-2018 study by Australia's Lowy Institute comparing the power capabilities of 114 states ranked the United States as still the most powerful state

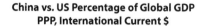

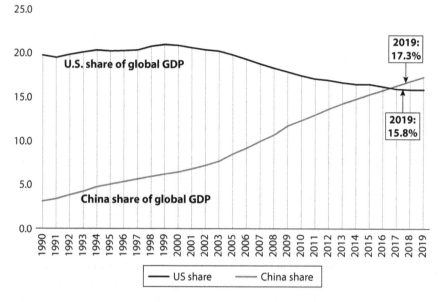

3.2 Percentage of global GDP in China versus the United States (in purchasing power parity [PPP] terms; World Bank calculations).

Source: World Bank Data Bank.

with a ranking of 85.[18] But China was close behind and closing in rapidly, with a ranking of 75.5, a ranking well above the major powers of Japan and India, with rankings of 42.1 and 41.5, respectively. The Lowy Institute study assigned 20 percent weight each to economic and military capabilities, but also factored in amorphous variables such as allies and quality of diplomacy.[19]

Two other means are often used to measure national power—a country's GDP as a percentage of global economic production and the possession of a strong blue-water navy. Figure 3.2 shows that by the first measure China surpassed the United States in 2016, and by 2019, China accounted for 17.3 percent of global GDP, whereas the United States accounted for 15.8 percent.

The construction and deployment of a large, powerful, modern, blue-water navy has also been one of the most important dimensions of China's rise. As Ambassador Chas Freeman explains in chapter 11 of this volume, in 1998, following the face-off in the Taiwan Strait two years earlier, China's leaders decided to construct a modern and powerful fleet that could credibly deter or, failing that, defeat the United States in a war over Taiwan. The new naval capabilities were to be in place by 2008, roughly corresponding to the Chinese navy's intensified operations in the South China Sea in 2010.

The decision to acquire a modern navy was of profound importance. Over its long history, China has rarely been a naval power. The United States, on the other hand, has been an ocean-going maritime state since its inception in the late eighteenth century. Prior to China's post-1998 effort to construct a modern navy, a sort of geopolitical division of Chinese and American spheres of influence developed to help stabilize that relationship. The United States would dominate in the maritime sphere, and China would control the continent. The new reality is that China has become a major naval power, steadily expanding into maritime, air, and outer space, which were previously dominated by the United States—a process similar to Germany's construction of the High Seas Fleet to challenge Britain's Royal Navy in the decades leading up to World War I.

China's new navy has gotten very good, very fast. A detailed study by the RAND Corporation in 2015 compared the capabilities of U.S. and Chinese navies in ten critical areas within the context of a hypothetical U.S.-PRC war over Taiwan or the South China Sea.[20] The RAND report concluded that in most areas—long-distance precision strike, air defense, air superiority, space and antispace, cyber, electronic warfare, and submarine and antisubmarine— the United States still enjoyed superiority. But the margin of U.S. superiority was rapidly diminishing. Any U.S. victory in the imagined war would be very close. In the crucial area of attacking and destroying surface ships, the PLAN was already superior to the United States. According to Chinese navy doctrine, U.S. warships approaching Taiwan were to be attacked simultaneously from multiple vectors by missiles launched by submarines, aircraft including missile-armed helicopters, ultramodern ballistic missiles, and several classes of Chinese surface warships. The defenses of U.S. warships would simply be overwhelmed.

China's embrace of global sea power means that the United States faces a true maritime peer competitor for the first time since confronting the Imperial Japanese Navy in 1940.[21] U.S. domination of the global seas, including those of the western Pacific, has been a central component of U.S. global dominance since 1945. Indeed, support for freedom of the seas has been a core U.S. interest since, quite literally, the birth of the United States as an independent republic.[22]

Today, the United States finds itself engaged in an increasingly intense quantitative and qualitative naval arms race with China, focused on the question of freedom of navigation in the South China Sea. A key concern of the United States is that China has begun using its increasing naval power to revise the existing oceanic order. China, now strong, is apparently set on an old, well-trodden road of territorial expansion via military coercion. But securing control over disputed bits of maritime territory is only Beijing's proximate objective. The longer-term purpose seems to be to secure recognition of China's primacy in Asia, restoring the rightful, natural *tianxia* order before China's Century of National Humiliation.[23] Chinese primacy in Asia could then serve as an essential stepping stone for a contest with the United State for world leadership.

The Chinese elite decisions that led to China's seizure of the South China Sea trace to assessments by the leadership of China's growing comprehensive national strength relative to that of the United States. As noted earlier, when Deng Xiaoping became China's paramount leader in 1978, he was well aware of China's technological backwardness. He concluded that a focused development drive extended over several decades would be necessary to modernize. A key component of that drive would be to draw deeply on the advanced technologies of the Western countries. To achieve that, a nonconfrontational, amicable relationship with the United States would be necessary. China would thus avoid confrontation with the United States if at all possible and seek to convince the United States that China was not, and would not become, a hostile power. This is the origin of the policy of strategic humility. Deng's frequently conciliatory approaches were sometimes challenged (for example, by senior PLA leaders to Deng's low-keyed responses to U.S. sale of F-16 aircraft to Taiwan prior to the 1992 U.S. presidential election),[24] but by and large, the policy of strategic humility served to stabilize the U.S.-China relationship.

Reassessment of Deng's humble approach began not long after his death in 1997, with the onset of the Asian financial crisis the same year. During that financial crisis, a number of Asia's leading Western-linked economies (Thailand, South Korea, and Indonesia) faced collapsing currency values as a result of unsustainable levels of debt. Beijing responded to the crisis by not devaluing the renminbi, a non-action that helped stabilize the exports of debt-stricken economies. The U.S. response, in contrast, was widely seen as lethargic and inadequate. Then the massive flow of capital into China that began with China's accession to the WTO in late 2001 fueled the rapid emergence of China as a leading global manufacturer of labor-intensive goods. In 2008, another financial crisis and deep economic recession befell the Western economies, producing the deepest and longest-lasting economic crisis since the 1930s. China responded with massive public works programs, building highways, high-speed railways, fiber-optic cable systems, vast housing complexes—and a new navy. As China's economy boomed, Western economies struggled with high unemployment and slow growth. In the political sphere, the successful conduct of the 2008 international Olympic Games in Beijing showcased China's rapid development for the whole world to see and went a long way in countering the moral stigma the Chinese government had suffered from the Beijing massacre of 1989.

By 2009, theoretical journals published by the Communist Party began to assert that China was now strong enough to cast Deng's line of strategic humility aside.[25] Instead, China should begin using its growing strength more vigorously to shape the international environment to conform to China's interests as a true great power and be more willing to use its greater power to challenge U.S. moves that injured China's interests.

These impulses were apparent in China's policies in the South China Sea under Hu Jintao, China's paramount leader from 2002 to 2012. But it was Xi Jinping who elevated the more assertive nationalist approach to the center of his rule, laying out a vision of China as one of the world's leading powers, with a world-class military able to fight and win wars and active across both the Pacific and Indian Oceans. In this way, China would resume its position as the dominant power in Asia prior to the long period of national humiliation, the position China had enjoyed for millennia before its defeat in the first Opium War of 1839–1842. The One Belt, One Road program (later renamed the Belt and Road Initiative) was a major aspect of Xi's drive for rejuvenated national stature. The establishment of China's control over the South China Sea was another.

China's Response to the Multilateral Order of Freedom of Navigation

China had no role in shaping the maritime/oceanic regime it confronted as it began integrating itself into the global community after 1978. The basic structure of that system traced to the practices of European maritime powers of the fifteenth century that embraced revolutionary designs of hull and sail to produce ships that could carry large volumes of cargo speedily across even the wildest of the world's oceans. These maritime powers—Spain, Holland, England, and France—saw their advantage in keeping the world's oceans open to their growing trade. This led to the principle of freedom of navigation. Vessels of nations joining the compact to uphold this legal principle were to identify their ships by their national flags and forego a short list of forbidden practices—seizure of vessels and cargos of declared neutral ships in time of war, piracy, and, later, trafficking in slaves. A corollary was the idea that coastal states had sovereign jurisdiction over only a narrow belt of territorial sea, originally set by the two-nautical-mile range of a cannon shot. Beyond that limit lay the high seas, open to the free movement of all.

China's nonparticipation in crafting the early modern maritime regime is remarkable. Prior to the European eruption that brought European ships to Asia in the late fifteenth century, there was a robust, centuries-old monsoon trade carrying the same sort of Chinese goods to the West that Dutch and English ships carried later—silk, porcelain, tea—through the South China Sea, across the Indian Ocean, to the eastern Mediterranean. This monsoon trade used junks of very different hull and sail design suited to an annual circuit powered by strong and predictable winds. China and its high-value products were a key supplier in this monsoon system. The Asian monsoon trade system and the early modern European maritime system paralleled each other well into the nineteenth century. China was pivotal in both systems, but China's government seldom encouraged that trade or concerned itself with trade affairs beyond the country's borders. Even in 1792 when Britain sent a high-level delegation to China to persuade China to enter the European-led trade system, China declined.[26] It was the multiple wars imposed on China by European powers during China's Century of National Humiliation that compelled China to enter the global economy organized around Western principles—including the freedom of navigation.

With its liberation from Western modernity in 1949, China turned sharply away from participation in the Western system of trade in favor of Soviet-style socialism.[27] When it then reengaged Western-defined modernity in 1978, China was emerging from a period of national seclusion under Mao as profound as its isolation under Emperor Qianlong (reign 1735–1796).

At the same time China was a continental inward-looking power, the United States, from the very inception of the republic, embraced freedom of navigation. Understanding this is important, because this proposition brings into question Chinese assertions and beliefs that U.S. objections to China's claims in the South China Sea derive from a desire to contain, encircle, or weaken China. In fact, U.S. concern for freedom of navigation traces to 1776 when "cutting off our Trade with all parts of the World" and impressing U.S. sailors on the high seas into service in the British navy were among the reasons for rebellion enumerated in the Declaration of Independence. Upholding freedom of navigation figured in America's War of 1812 and in pirate-suppression actions in the Mediterranean—remembered in the U.S. Marine Corps anthem even today as "the shores of Tripoli." As Britain and the United States maneuvered toward rapprochement in the late nineteenth century, common support for freedom of navigation was an important element of the Anglo-American strategic partnership. Germany's violation of freedom of navigation by resort to unrestricted submarine warfare against neutral American ships was a major factor in the U.S. entry into World War I in 1914.[28] Washington's successful demand at the 1922 Washington Naval Conference that Britain terminate its 1902 alliance with Japan was predicated on a U.S. desire to ensure that the 1902 treaty not stand in the way of Anglo-American cooperation in countering Japan's growing naval activity in the South Pacific after Japan's acquisition of Germany's pre–World War I holdings in that region. The New Order announced in the Tripartite Treaty of Germany, Japan, and Italy in 1940 envisioned redistribution of the world's oceans, with the three signatory countries awarded primacy over the great seas surrounding their new continental realms. Britain and the United States went to war to thwart the Axis New Order and worked closely in the postwar period to uphold and advance freedom of navigation in such fora as the United Nations Convention on the Law of the Sea (UNCLOS).

By the 1960s, numerous developments indicated that major revision and codification of the law of the sea were necessary. The globe-spanning colonial empires had collapsed, producing large numbers of new claimants to sovereignty including claims to large areas of the sea. Many of the new states were small and weak and looked to international law formulated through UN processes as protection against the actions of large and more powerful states.[29] More powerful states, including the Soviet Union and the United States, wanted to protect the traditional rights of great powers. Overfishing and environmental pollution were increasing and needed to be addressed. New technologies had emerged and promised expanded mining of sea floor energy and mineral resources. Conflicting claims were rife, with many based on long histories of use of nearby seas. Sorting out contending historical claims would be difficult and probably unworkable. The need for a UN-driven multilateral effort to revise the global oceanic order was apparent. The effort began in 1973 and was completed in 1982.

China, having entered the UN only in 1971, took little part in the UNCLOS negotiations. Its diplomatic apparatus had been shattered by the Cultural Revolution. Yet China signed UNCLOS in 1982 when it was opened for signature, and again upon ratification in 2006. On both occasions, China issued statements putting China's view of contentious issues on record.

China had three main differences with UNCLOS. The first difference was the role of history in determining claims to sovereignty. The second was determining the scope of a coastal country's sovereignty over a two-hundred-nautical-mile exclusive economic zone (EEZ). Was control limited to management of economic resources, or did the coastal state have full sovereignty within the EEZ? And finally, did littoral states have the right to regulate and deny innocent passage of warships of other states through its territorial sea, including the EEZ?

China claims the South China Sea as an historic sea that has long been under China's control and administration. According to this claim, Chinese boats have long exploited the fish, coral, and pearls of these waters. Chinese commercial junks participating in the monsoon trade called at some islands. So, too, did occasional official ships—most prominently Zheng He's fleets of the early fifteenth century. Chinese navigational maps showed the location of South China Seas islands. A series of nine dashed lines around the circumference of the South China Sea on a 1947 map published by an agency of the Republic (*not* the People's Republic) of China illustrated China's claim in the South China Sea. That map depicted roughly 90 percent of the South China Sea as belonging to China. Although the Chinese government has never formally stated exactly what those dashed lines mean, the implication is that all the waters, seafloors, reefs, shoals, and rocks within those dashes were China's sovereign territory. In Beijing's view, China's usage of the South China Sea antedated and exceeded in frequency and scope that of any other claimant state. Because the map antedates UNCLOS, it should be grandfathered under UNCLOS, according to Beijing.

Figure 3.3 illustrates the system put in place by China in the South China Sea.

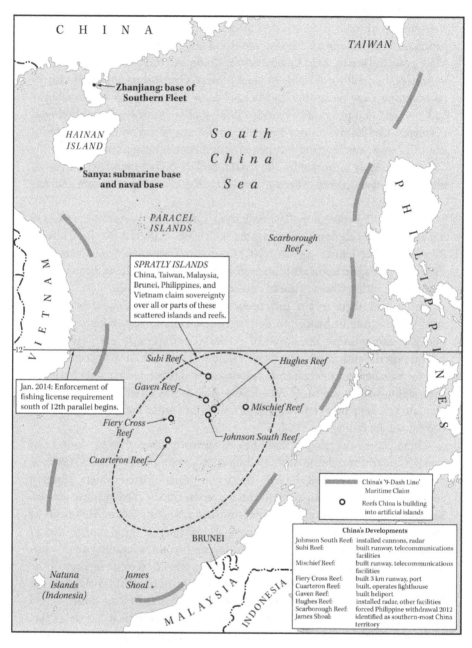

3.3 China's military-administrative system in the South China Sea.

Source: John Garver, *China's Quest: The History of the Foreign Relations of the People's Republic of China*, paperback ed. (New York: Oxford University Press, 2018), 777.

Many other states involved in territorial disputes in the South China Sea and elsewhere have relied on ostensibly historical arguments, using such evidence as medieval maps, journals, and diaries. Sorting out these contending historical claims would have been a long and difficult process. Even if final judgments about the antiquity and/or authority of battling maps could be made, parties would still feel aggrieved. To cut the Gordian knot of contending allegedly historical evidence, UNCLOS used a clear geographic principle that could put to rest the tangled historical claims of coastal countries. A continental baseline connecting protuberances of the continental coastline was established, and distance from this baseline then established a relatively narrow belt of territorial sea (finally set at twelve nautical miles) over which littoral states enjoyed full sovereignty. Thus, Beijing's claim that China owned and had full sovereignty over the South China Sea as an historic sea flatly contradicted the central purpose of UNCLOS.

Regarding the scope of a coastal state's control within the two-hundred-nautical-mile EEZ, a PRC signing statement (a document giving a signatory's understanding of a specific controversial issue), issued in June 1996 when China formally ratified the UNCLOS treaty, stated the PRC "shall enjoy sovereign rights and jurisdiction over an exclusive economic zone of 200 nautical miles."[30] The UNCLOS treaty dealing with the two-hundred-mile-wide EEZ stipulates that sovereign rights within the EEZ were "for the purpose of exploring, exploiting and managing the natural resources" of the EEZ.

Regarding innocent passage, UNCLOS provided that warships of a state may pass through the territorial sea of a coastal state as long as that transit does not militarily threaten the coastal state. However, China's 1996 signing statement stated that this right of innocent passage "shall not prejudice the right of a coastal state to request in accordance with its laws and regulations, a foreign State to obtain advance approval from or give prior notification . . . for the passage of its warships through the territorial sea of the coastal state."[31]

The United States, a sea-faring nation long before it became a great power, followed its traditional policy of support for broad freedom of navigation. China, without the tradition of a sea-faring maritime state but with strong memories of national humiliation at the hands of sea-faring imperialist powers, favored greater restriction on the movement of warships of big powers. Perhaps Beijing, early in the UNCLOS process and after China's long isolation from the United States and most of the international community, did not understand the depth of Washington's devotion to freedom of the seas.[32] When China found itself facing the Philippines, Vietnam, and others in debate over the division of the South China Sea, Beijing came quickly to the conclusion that the United States was attempting to contain, encircle, or weaken China. As positions on UNCLOS and the South China Sea were clarified, Beijing dug in to defend its unilateralist position, while almost all the Southeast Asian countries sharpened their multilateral opposition to Beijing's go-it-alone approach. (Cambodia and Laos generally aligned with China over these issues.) As alignment of most ASEAN countries with the United States and against China emerged, Beijing concluded that nefarious U.S. instigation stood behind Southeast Asian challenges to China's just claims to the South China Sea. Beijing trumped its rivals by resorting to force majeure to bring the islands and waters of that sea under the protection of China's now powerful navy.

China Seizes the South China Sea

The common dictionary meaning of the word *seizure* is to take something into possession by force or legal process. This seems to be an apt term describing China's military occupation by force majeure and subsequent administration of the waters and maritime features lying within Beijing's nine-dash line. Thus defined, China's seizure of the South China Sea raises a question for the United States, Asian allies of the United States, and indeed all countries of the world. Is this how China will behave as it grows still stronger?

China's use of its enhanced military power to seize control over the South China Sea has, more than any other factor, challenged the East Asian state order established and upheld by U.S. power. Through use of systematic, albeit nonlethal coercion, China has transformed a large and extremely important part of the global high seas beyond the sovereignty of any state and open to the free navigation of all into China's territorial sea. Through its seizure of the South China Sea, China has transformed itself into a resident power in Southeast Asia—a fact with profound geopolitical implications.

China's construction of a modern blue-water navy did not, in and of itself, qualify China as a peer competitor of the United States. It was, rather, the particular way in which China used its new naval power in the seas of the western Pacific, and especially in the South China Sea, that brought China and the United States into direct confrontation. China has used its growing naval power to establish sovereign control over western Pacific seas that the United States has long viewed as part of the global high seas beyond the sovereign jurisdiction of any state. Stated simply, China has, at least in the South China Sea, used its growing power to expand its territorial control.

Until about 2010, only very limited Chinese moves gave substance to China's claim to the Spratly Islands, the more southernly portion of the South China Sea. After Chinese forces seized Fiery Cross Shoal from Vietnamese forces in 1988, pylons were driven into the seafloor of several features in the Spratly Islands. Small but multifloor concrete buildings were built atop the pylons. These were very modest structures and without heavy weapons.[33] They did, however, establish a permanent Chinese presence in the South China Sea, giving substance to China's previously nominal claim. Starting in 2010 and accelerating greatly after Xi Jinping took power in late 2012, China took vigorous measures to bring the length and breadth of that sea under Chinese administrative and military control.

Artificial islands were built by large-scale dredging. Sand was siphoned from nearby seafloor and piled atop reefs and shoals. Well-sheltered harbors with fairly deep berths were dug. Large rocks and interlocking concrete structures designed to give greater solidity to the new islands were brought in from the mainland by barge. By 2017, seven new islands with a combined land area of thirteen square kilometers were near completion. These man-made islands were spacious enough to accommodate lengthy airplane landing strips. As China's island-construction efforts intensified, ASEAN countries called for China to eschew militarization of the new artificial islands. Beijing denied any such intention, but once the new islands were ready, they were turned into military platforms, complete with airplane landing strips (if they were large enough), helicopter pads, revetted airplane hangars, hardened munitions and fuel storage facilities, barracks and other buildings, coastal defense artillery, radar, satellite download, telecommunications, electronic warfare gear, and antiair and antiship missiles. Together, these new, man-made islands constituted a network of unsinkable, albeit immobile, aircraft carriers. Large and recently built roll-on, roll-off vehicle transport ships brought in armored vehicles and troops. As new facilities were completed, Chinese civilian airlines practiced surging personnel to the new bases. Chinese vessels followed a division of labor designed to rebut charges of Chinese militarization of the South China Sea conflict. Ostensibly civilian fishing boats of the maritime militia were on the front line of challenging the noncompliant activities of non-Chinese ships. If necessary, larger but still civilian ships of the Chinese Coast Guard or Maritime Enforcement Service would move in. Typically, just over the horizon, PLAN warships exercised escalation deterrence through their overwhelming numbers and size.

The frequency of PLAN deployments to the South China Sea increased as the new man-made islands came into operation. As the capabilities of PLAN warships grew, China began enforcing compliance with administrative regulations. In January 2014, China Maritime Enforcement ships began demanding that foreign fishing vessels operating south of the twelfth parallel have a permit issued by the Hainan government on pain of an $82,000 fine and forfeiture of the vessel's catch.[34] Non-Chinese fishing boats without the requisite China-issued documents were forced to abandon the sea. Harassment by Chinese fishing trawlers helped persuade non-Chinese boats to quit the area. Chinese boats would cut across fishing nets and lines of non-Chinese trawlers and ram non-Chinese fishing boats. Sometimes Chinese maritime militia boats would swarm around non-Chinese ships, making continued operation impossible.

All these activities were accompanied by loudspeakers demanding that the foreign ship leave Chinese territory immediately.

Wooden-hulled maritime militia ships were steadily replaced by larger, steel-hulled ships better able to ram smaller, wooden-hulled non-Chinese fishing boats. Vessels of the Chinese Coast Guard with primary authority for enforcing Chinese regulations also grew in size. New Chinese Coast Guard ships were armed with high-pressure water hoses mounted high on the ship and powerful enough to shatter window glass or pump water down the smokestacks of non-Chinese vessels. Swarms of Chinese maritime militia fishing boats, under military command and with military communications and GPS equipment aboard, often coordinated with Coast Guard ships in harassing non-Chinese vessels, civilian and military. The Chinese naval base at Sanya on the southern coast of Hainan Island was enlarged and renovated to serve as a home port for warships on South China Sea duty.

As noted earlier, China's island building took place under the protection of PLAN warships hovering nearby. Typically, when Chinese maritime militia or Coast Guard ships engaged in confrontations with non-Chinese vessels in the South China Sea, Chinese navy warships (corvettes, frigates, or destroyers) hovered just over the horizon. This served as a sort of escalation control, deterring China's rival from escalating by firing on the nonmilitary Chinese vessels on the front line of struggle against alleged violation of China's sovereignty.[35] China's tactics resulted in few (if any) deaths but were clearly coercive, constituting what the U.S. Navy called "gray zone" tactics lying between noncoercive negotiations on the one hand and lethal coercion on the other.[36] The completion of the new islands in the Spratlys supported and facilitated these gray zone coercive efforts.

By late 2018, the South China Sea was effectively under Chinese control. In July 2016, the international Permanent Court of Arbitration based in The Hague had ruled against China's claim to the South China Sea as an historic sea. China rejected both the jurisdiction of the Permanent Court of Arbitration and the wisdom of the court's finding. China's efforts to create an integrated military system over the South China Sea did not slow.

The United States refused to recognize China's seizure of the South China Sea and occasionally ordered U.S. warships to conduct freedom of navigation operations (FONOPs) in which American ships sometimes passed within the twelve-mile limit of these islands. These FONOPs underlined Washington's determination to uphold provisions of UNCLOS that specified that artificial, man-made islands were not entitled to an encircling territorial sea.

The U.S. Navy is powerful and confident enough that it could conduct such Freedom of Navigation Operations. The navies of the rival Southeast Asian claimants to the Spratlys, in contrast, are miniscule and in no position physically to oppose China's island-building activities. A major thrust of U.S. policy during the Trump administration was to persuade the regional powers of Japan, Australia, and India to join U.S. Freedom of Navigation Operations in the South China Sea.

Another dimension of Beijing's effort to impose a new maritime order in the western Pacific involves Chinese efforts to compel the United States to suspend intelligence-gathering operations within China's two-hundred-nautical-mile EEZ. Typically, these operations entailed electronic recording by U.S. ships or airplanes for later analysis of the specific sounds and electromagnetic emissions of Chinese warships, airplanes, and ground facilities. The mission of the USS *Impeccable* in March 2009, for example, included the collection of sonar data on a new class of Chinese nuclear missile submarine based in a recently detected underground submarine base at Sanya on Hainan Island. In effect, these U.S. intelligence collection operations were preparing the battleground for a possible maritime clash between the U.S. and Chinese navies.

The South China Sea as a Strategic Corridor

In seizing the South China Sea, China took control of one of the world's most important strategic maritime corridors. Whereas the contemporary role of the South China Sea as a corridor for energy and merchandise trade is well understood, the role of the South China Sea in regional geopolitics is less well understood. In fact, control of the South China Sea has been a high-value objective esteemed by state players of great power politics. *China's seizure and establishment of control over the South China Sea entailed seizure of a sea lane long seen as vital by the United States.* The geography of the South China Sea has repeatedly become entangled with an American quest to prevent any power from achieving hegemony over Greater East Asia. Simply stated, the United States has repeatedly exerted great national effort, even to the extent of war, to prevent another power from achieving hegemony over Greater East Asia. It was this historically important maritime corridor that China seized between 2010 and 2018.

The Significance of China's Seizure of the South China Sea

The development of the Chinese navy's antisubmarine surveillance and targeting networks using China's seven new islands in the South China Sea will strengthen PLAN's ability to seal off the southern approaches to Taiwan in the event of an antiaccess, area denial war with the United States over Taiwan. Utilization of the South China Sea man-made islands for electronic maritime monitoring and overhead protection of Chinese ships moving south will cut approximately in half the unprotected distance a Chinese fleet venturing into the Andaman Sea would have to transit before reaching putative supply points on Myanmar's Arakan coast and logistic nodes there linking northward to Kunming. When married with new high-speed Belt and Road highways and rail lines linking Indian Ocean logistic posts such as Kyaukpyu on Myanmar's Arakan coast, Gwadar in Pakistan, or Hambantota in Sri Lanka, the PLAN will become far more capable of sustaining complex combat operations as far as the western Indian Ocean—not against the United States, perhaps, but against a regional rival such as India.

Transformation of the South China Sea from part of the global high seas to a Chinese territorial sea will bring Chinese power closer to India in a way not too dissimilar from the transformation of Tibet from a de facto buffer zone between India and China to an integral part of China and platform for projection of Chinese military power. India will come under greater Chinese pressure.

Settlement of territorial disputes over the South China Sea on China's terms, backed by force majeure, will entail far more than disposition of a particular tiny piece of reef or sea. Specifically, it will speak to how the global oceanic regime in the era of China's ascendency will be determined. Will it be by decisions of Beijing backed up by superior and assertive Chinese force, or by multilateral negotiations among countries on equal standing and without threat of resort to military force? In other words, how will China exercise its new ascendency? Like an emperor of the Ming or Qing dynasty? Or like the United States during its post–World War II primacy?

The UNCLOS process offers a good example of a liberal order. China's South China Sea policies suggest preference both for a far narrower purview for freedom of navigation and for a more hierarchical order, with China at the apex as in the days of Emperor Qianlong.

China's seizure of the South China Sea speaks to the position of the disputants within a hierarchal order. Settlement of China's territorial conflicts with Vietnam, Japan, and India on Chinese terms and by superior Chinese military power implies submission to China in a new, hierarchical Asian state order. Such an order would bear a strong resemblance to the tributary system that Chinese believe ordered Asia for thousands of years, with China's Son of Heaven emperor at the apex exercising universal celestial authority over all other lesser states arrayed at various ranks below the Chinese emperor. Is this what Xi Jinping really means by the dream of great rejuvenation of the Chinese nation?

The political implications of Chinese ownership of the South China Sea are significant. If, per China's nine-dash line, China's territory extends to just eighty-three kilometers (forty-five nautical miles) from the coast of the Malaysian state of Sarawak, China will have become a Southeast Asian country. The substantial oceanic buffer that historically helped separate China from Southeast Asia will have disappeared. China's military forces will be much closer, permanently, to

Southeast Asia. Vietnam, historically the Southeast Asian country most willing to challenge China, will find that its sea lines of communication must transit China's maritime territories, in addition to having lost to China the larger part of the maritime resources lying off its long eastern coast. Indonesian officials have noted the conspicuous gap between two dashes of the nine-dash line just north of Indonesia's Natuna Island. Indonesia's two-hundred-mile EEZ derives from a Natuna baseline that overlaps with China's claim based on the nine-dash line. Jakarta has asked Beijing to formally declare where, in China's view, the boundary between Indonesia's Natuna and China's maritime territory lies.

Consideration of the future role of Southeast Asia's ethnic Chinese in the emerging era of strong China is also important. Seventy-six percent of Singapore's population are ethnic Chinese. That city was expelled from the initial Malaysian federation in 1965 because ethnic Malay leaders of Malaysia feared domination by the city's economically powerful Chinese. Singapore lies just beyond the bottom of Beijing's nine-dash line. About 24 percent Sarawak's population (in eastern Malaysia) is ethnic Chinese, who also happen to dominate that Malaysian state's commerce. As Lee Kuan Yew explained in his memoir, during the period of postcolonial state formation, questions of Chinese ethnic identity were very much in play.[37] Might that again be the case as China rises in power and authority? How different would a strong Chinese response be to future anti-Chinese pogroms in a Southeast Asian country—perhaps something like the anti-Chinese pogroms that erupted in 1998 as Indonesia transited from military rule to democracy?

Might China Return to a More Multipolar, Nonhegemonic Course?

The possibility still remains that China may return to the more prudent policy approach of Deng Xiaoping. Holding open an invitation for China to take such a course should be an element of U.S. China policy.[38] The debate in China over confrontation with the United States has been continual since June 1989, and although only the broad contours are apparent, that debate continues today.[39] Sagacious Chinese leaders have been well aware of China's propensity toward nationalistic hubris. Li Shenzhi, one of China's leading liberal public intellectuals and a key advisor of Deng Xiaoping regarding PRC-U.S. relations, wrote the following shortly before his death in 2003.

Recent years . . . have seen the appearance of some extreme [Chinese] nationalists who think that the United States is too dominant in the world and too overbearing and aggressive toward China . . . they want China to say no to the United States. They question Deng Xiaoping's two main goals of "peace and development" and criticize the Chinese government's foreign policies as being too weak. This tendency requires our attention. China is a big country with an area a little larger than that of the United States, but with the largest population and longest history in the world. A national mentality of self-importance has been deeply rooted in people's minds as a result of over five decades of propaganda. . . . This extreme nationalism has a market in China. . . . If we allow it to evolve freely, it may put the future of the nation at risk. This should be brought to everyone's attention.[40]

The pitfalls for Xi Jinping's more assertive foreign policy are apparent. Asian countries frightened by China's new coercive unilateralism in the South China Sea and drive for primacy in Asia have drawn together and into deepening alignment with Japan, India, and Australia. Xi's bold push for primacy in Asia is leading Asian countries to strengthen military capabilities. Countries seduced by blandishments of easy money via partnership in China's Belt and Road Initiative projects are increasingly speaking out and looking more skeptically at China's offers, including Malaysia, Pakistan, Sri Lanka, and the Maldives, among others. China's diplomatic leverage with Washington may be strengthened through closer association with Vladimir Putin's Russia, but China tarnishes its reputation as a responsible stakeholder through an axis with Russia supporting Putin's armed aggression against the Ukraine.

Wise Chinese voices are certain to point out the progress China has made through partnership with the United States and how much China lost the last time it divorced itself from the United States in 1949–1950. The question is whether a Chinese renunciation of a quest for hegemony in the Asia-Pacific region that was acceptable to a weak China in 1972 will continue to be acceptable to the strong China of today. An open, multipolar order would need to encompass other ambitious and proud Asian nations—Japan, India, and Australia—as well as mid-range powers such as Vietnam, Thailand, and Indonesia. A Chinese push for hegemony over the Indo-Pacific region will push many of these countries into alignment with one another, with the United States, and against a Chinese quest for hegemony. The harder China pushes to establish its primacy over Asia, the greater will be the resistance to China's efforts.

As Ambassador Chas Freeman has noted in chapter 11 of this volume, imperialism generates its own anti-imperialist antibodies. If China chooses to pursue hegemony over the Asia-Pacific region, as it now seems to be doing, it will find itself on a path of confrontation—and probably war. If, on the other hand, China magnanimously cedes to Japan, India, Australia, and other regional powers seats and a voice in a new multipolar "concert of Asia" within which a China-U.S. group of two helps stabilize and guide, China might accomplish a peaceful rise, positioning itself at the center of an open system of regional power. Along this path, a risen China might look like the great Tang dynasty.[41]

The 1972 U.S.-PRC joint communiqué might be used to mutually renounce a quest for hegemony in Asia. The 1972 communiqué stipulated that "neither [China nor the United States] should seek hegemony in the Asia-Pacific region and each is opposed to efforts by any other country or group of countries to establish such hegemony." In effect, China and the United States envisioned a multipolar international order in Greater Asia, with no power—China, the United States, or the Soviet Union—seeking or exercising hegemony. Might the antihegemony principle of 1972 serve as a framework for the 2020s?

The contradiction between China's long list of territorial claims and aspirations of Asian primacy on the one hand and the U.S. interest in preventing hegemony over Asia by a single power or combination of powers on the other is deep and highly dangerous. Such a contradiction could lead to another Sino-American war. An abiding American idea has been that rule over vast swaths of Greater East Asia by a single antidemocratic power or combination of powers would yield an unacceptably grave threat to American security and global interests. The United States would use the full range of national power, war included in extremis, to prevent this.

Against the long list of China's historical and territorial grievances, a question must be asked: Could appeasement of China's demands be a viable solution for the United States? Appeasement can be defined, in the case at hand, as deliberately and systematically conceding to China a privileged strategic space in East Asia in order to avoid a war in which China tried to take such a sphere by force and the United States tried to deny it. Lyle Goldstein, professor at the U.S. Navy War College, argues cogently that China's desire for such a sphere is virtually inevitable, that a China-U.S. war would be a catastrophe, and that a policy of appeasement undertaken early (while the United States is still stronger relative to China) and via a process of negotiated, issue-by-issue compromise has a good chance of success.[42]

The key criticism of a strategy of appeasement is that it would allow China to become dominant in Asia, eventually presenting the United States with a combination of power that would threaten the United States. A long-standing principle of U.S. strategy—indeed, one of the reasons why the United States supported the emergence of a strong China—was to prevent the domination of Greater Asia by a single power or coalition of powers because such awesome power could threaten the United States.

But the questions must be asked: Would China become sated if its demands regarding the South China Sea and the first island chain were conceded by Washington, with U.S. partnerships with South Korea, Japan, Taiwan, the Philippines, and others being adjusted accordingly? Or would the satisfaction of China's demands feed Chinese ambition and confirm for Chinese nationalists the utility of further demands to redress ancient grievances?

No one, probably not even members of the Chinese Communist Party Politburo, can say when China will be satisfied by territorial concessions reversing perceived injuries of China's traumatic experience in the nineteenth and twentieth centuries. My own guesstimate is that China's ambitions and aims will be grand and wide ranging, will grow with China's capabilities, and will not be easily satisfied. It also seems likely that the fewer the obstacles to Chinese expansion qua national rejuvenation, the further China will advance. China's appetite might well grow with the eating.

A combination of engagement and dissuasion via military preparedness seems the most prudent response to the current turning point in U.S.-China relations. The key question here is really a Chinese question, for China and its people to address and answer: Does China want to dominate Asia as its imperial dynasties once did, or will it grant equal status and voice to other nations of Asia? The United States cannot answer this question for China, but the United States can and should voice its views on this core question, especially because the Chinese people cannot now openly and freely discuss the issue themselves. Through engagement with China, the United States should explain to China's leaders and citizens the sense of American disappointment at China's use of coercive military force (even that of the sublethal gray zone type) unilaterally, in violation of the UN's solemn UNCLOS, to take control of a highly important maritime corridor, the South China Sea. U.S. representatives should reprise the long-standing American diplomatic tradition of support for China's rise as a positive, stabilizing element of the world order. Support for research into the various ways the United States has facilitated China's rise would be helpful if conveyed in a tone of sad disappointment, rather than anger or strident belligerency. A review of the origins and unfortunate consequences of China's 1950 decision to divorce the United States would be useful. The United States should not be stingy in recognizing China's positive contributions to world affairs, including especially Chinese efforts that dovetail with American efforts. China's positive roles in Iraqi reconstruction, Afghanistan stabilization, and the Iran nuclear agreement of 2015 are examples. U.S. public diplomacy could usefully convey these and similar themes. The key theme should be a hope that China will use its growing power in harmony with other weaker countries, not unilaterally to dominate them as Japan did in the 1930s.[43]

Identification of antihegemony as an organizing principle for an Asia being reshaped by China's rise could be useful. Because this term was invented by China and offered by China to the United States in 1972, China can claim authorship. Nonhegemony would also offer a convenient way to structure discussion of norms and rules for an emerging Asia. Presumably, a nonhegemonic Asian order would be multipolar, with all significant powers—certainly Japan, India, Australia, and Indonesia—having a voice. An engaged United States might debate with China what constitutes unacceptable (i.e., hegemonic) military coercion, when to resort to economic sanctions, or what defines interference in internal affairs, with China's neighbors seeking to shape those principles to comport with their own security interests.

Open expression of concern by China's Asian neighbors about possible Chinese hegemony should be encouraged. Examples include the openly critical comments in June 2015 by Philippine president Benigno Aquino comparing China's claims in the South China Sea to Nazi Germany's 1938 seizure of Czechoslovakia's Sudetenland, and Malaysian president Mahathir Mohamad's comments in August 2018 about the unsustainable levels of debt that came with ambitious railway and pipeline projects that were part of China's Belt and Road Initiative. Whether the Chinese are able to see themselves as their Asian neighbors see them is by no means clear, and there is a strong Chinese tendency to attribute comments critical of China to a hostile United States. Increased Asian candor in discussing China's policies should be encouraged. If China hears the unvarnished view of China's tendencies toward hegemony, it may recalibrate.

Europe and Russia could play important roles in nudging China to foreswear a quest for hegemony over Asia and accept an open, multipolar, nonhegemonic Asia. Dialogue with both of those entities about the security implications of China's rise would be useful. Also useful would be another UNCLOS conference centered on China's rise and the law of the sea addressing the new era of China's ascendancy and questions related to freedom of navigation and historic seas."] All sides would benefit from hearing China's views on these issues, and it would benefit China to hear the views of other countries about China's policies. This might be a good way to meet China halfway, especially if that is the alternative to war.

NOTES

1. Warren I. Cohen calls the period from 1950 to 1970 a "great aberration" to the broader century-long period of China-U.S. partnership. Warren Cohen, *America's Response to China*, 5th ed. (New York: Columbia University Press, 2010).

2. See Isaac B. Kardon and Phillip Saunders, "Reconsidering the PLA as an Interest Group," in *PLA Influence on China's National Security Policymaking*, eds. Phillip Saunders and Andrew Scobell, editors (Stanford, CA: Stanford University Press, 2015), 33–57.

3. For PLAN's embrace of Mahanism, see James R. Holmes and Toshi Yoshihara, *Chinese Naval Strategy in the 21st Century: The Turn to Mahan* (London: Routledge, 2008).

4. Michael Pence, "Remarks by Vice President Pence on the Administration's Policy Toward China" (speech, Hudson Institute, Washington, DC, October 4, 2018), https://www.hudson.org/events/1610-vice-president-mike-pence-s-remarks-on-the-administration-s-policy-towards-china102018.

5. Michael H. Hunt, *The Making of a Special Relationship: The United States and China to 1914* (New York: Columbia University Press, 1983).

6. William L. Tung, *V. K. Wellington Koo and China's Wartime Diplomacy* (New York: St. John's University, 1977), 141–45.

7. John W. Garver, "China," in *The Origins of World War Two: The Debate Continues*, eds. Robert Boyce and Joseph A. Maiolo (London: Palgrave, 2003), 190–203.

8. For more on this "nonrecognition," see Christopher Thorne, *The Limits of Foreign Policy: The West, the League and the Far Eastern Crisis of 1931–1933* (New York: Putnam, 1972).

9. Wesley R. Fishel, *The End of Extraterritoriality in China* (Berkeley: University of California Press, 1952).

10. At Yalta, Roosevelt granted Stalin restoration of special rights in Manchuria that had been lost by Russia after its 1905 defeat by Japan.

11. Yugoslav's Tito broke with the USSR to ally with the West in 1948.

12. For Stalin's extortion of privileges from China, see John W. Garver, *Chinese-Soviet Relations, 1937–1945: The Diplomacy of Chinese Nationalism* (New York: Oxford University Press, 1988).

13. John Lewis Gaddis, "The American 'Wedge' Strategy, 1949–1955," in *Sino-American Relations, 1945–1599: A Joint Reassessment of a Critical Decade*, eds. Harry Harding and Yuan Ming (Wilmington, DE: SR Books, 1989), 157–83; David Allan Mayers, *Cracking the Monolith: U.S. Policy Against the Sino-Soviet Alliance, 1949–1955* (Baton Rouge: Louisiana State University Press, 1986).

14. Niu Jun, *From Yan'an to the World: The Origins and Development of Chinese Communist Foreign Policy* (Norwalk, CT: Eastbridge, 2005), 316–43. I explore this critical Chinese decision in John W. Garver, *China's Quest: The History of the Foreign Relations of the People's Republic of China* (New York: Oxford University Press, 2016).

15. For the racialist categories employed by both Japan and the United States, see John W. Dower, *War Without Mercy: Race and Power in the Pacific War* (New York: W.W. Norton, 1986); and Robeson Taj Frazier, *The East Is Black: Cold War China in the Black Radical Imagination* (Durham, NC: Duke University Press, 2015).

16. A peace agreement signed in January 1973 led to the withdrawal of U.S. combat forces from Vietnam, whereas in June of the same year, Congress mandated cutoff of funding for any military operations in, over, or off the coast of Indochina. The funding cutoff abandoned U.S. South Vietnamese allies to their fate, which turned out to be utter defeat by Hanoi's conventional forces in April 1975.

17. An antimainstream school of analysis represented by Bill Gertz, Edward Timperlake, William Triplett, Steven Mosher, and Michael Pillsbury tended to view Chinese "friendship" toward the United States as strategic deception and U.S. support of China's rise as an immense blunder.

18. Mitsuru Obe, "Redrawing the Power Map: New Index Shows That China Is Gaining Fast on the US," *Nikkei Asian Review* 14–20 (May 2018): 42.

19. Thomas J. Christensen, *The China Challenge: Shaping the Choices of a Rising Power* (New York: W.W. Norton, 2013). Christensen points out that the United States still outmatches China in alliances, innovation, science and technology, and appeal of way of life. He concludes that China is still far from catching up and the United States should recognize this reality and act more self-confidently.

20. See Eric Heginbotham et al., *The U.S.-China Military Scorecard: Forces, Geography, and the Evolving Balance of Power 1996–2017* (Santa Monica, CA: Rand, 2015).

21. Neither Nazi Germany nor the USSR was a strong naval power. Both powers relied primarily on sea denial via submarines, leaving the U.S. Navy and its British Empire allies to dominate the sea lines of communication that carried global commerce.

22. The terms *freedom of the seas* and *freedom of navigation* are used interchangeably in this chapter.

23. Fei-ling Wang, *The China Order: Centralia, World Empire, and the Nature of Chinese Power* (Albany: State University of New York, 2017).

24. See John Garver, *Face Off: China, the United States, and Taiwan's Democratization* (Seattle: University of Washington Press, 2011), 51–66.

25. Garver, *China's Quest*, 664–66.

26. Alain Peyrefitte, *The Immobile Empire* (New York: Alfred A. Knopf, 1992).

27. Garver, *China's Quest*, 19–55.

28. Under international law, a declaration of neutrality—such as the U.S. government gave in 1914—protected the ships of the neutral country against interference by a belligerent state.

29. See Robert H. Jackson, *Quasi-states: Sovereignty, International Relations and the Third World* (New York: Cambridge University Press, 1993).

30. United Nations, "China, Signing Statement, in Declarations Made Upon Signature, Ratification, Accession or Succession, Division for Ocean Affairs and the Law of the Sea, Oceans and the Law of the Sea, United Nations," April 10, 2013, http://www.un.org /depts/convention/convention-agreements/convention_declar . . .

31. United Nations, "China, Signing Statement."]

32. Recent U.S. freedom of navigation operations include Gulf of Sidra (Libya), Gibraltar, Hormoz, and Malacca; see Maritime Security and Navigation, U.S. Department of State, https://www.state.gov/e/locns/opa/maritimesecurity.

33. For China's early push to the Spratly Islands, see John Garver, "China's Push Through the South China Sea: The Interaction of National and Bureaucratic Interests," *China Quarterly* 132 (December 1992): 999–1028.

34. Han Yong, "Making Up the Rules," *Newschina*, April 1, 2018, 44–46.

35. Ryan D. Martinson, *Echelon Defense: The Role of Sea Power in Chinese Maritime Dispute Strategy, Study No. 15* (Newport, RI: China Maritime Studies Institute, U.S. Navy War College, February 2018).

36. "China's Maritime Gray Zone Operations" (conference, China Maritime Studies Institute, U.S. Navy War College, Newport, RI, May 2–3, 2017).

37. Lee Kuan Yew, *The Singapore Story: Memories of Lee Kuan Yew* (Singapore: Prentice Hall, 1999). See also Garth Alexander, *The Invisible China: The Overseas Chinese and he Politics of Southeast Asia* (New York: Macmillan, 1973).

38. David Lampton noted that U.S. China policy across seven presidential administrations constituted a balance between engagement, which sought to draw the PRC into interdependent international systems that benefited China and for which China would develop a sense of shared responsibility, and confrontation, by which the United States sought to retard China's movement up the state power hierarchy through use of hard power. David Lampton, "Paradigm Lost: The Demise of 'Weak China,' " *The National Interest* 81 (September 2005): 73–80

39. Regarding China's perpetual debate over U.S. policy, see Garver, *China's Quest*, 2018 ed., 639–78.

40. Li Shenzhi, "On the Diplomacy of the People's Republic of China," in *Selected Writings of Li Shenzhi*, eds. Ilse Tebbetts and Libby Kingseed (Dayton, OH: Kettering Foundation Press, 2010), 35–152, 149.

41. Mark Edward Lewis, *China's Cosmopolitan Empire, the Tang Dynasty* (Cambridge, MA: Harvard University Press, 2009).

42. Lyle J. Goldstein, *Meeting China Halfway: How to Defuse the Emerging US-China Rivalry* (Washington, DC: Georgetown University Press, 2015).

43. For Japan's choice between unilateralism and multilateralism in the 1930s, see Akira Iriye, *After Imperialism: The Search for a New Order in the Far East, 1921–1931* (Chicago: Imprint Publishers, 1990).

PART II

THINKING ABOUT HOW
WE THINK ABOUT CHINA

CHAPTER 4

A HALF CENTURY OF ENGAGEMENT

The Study of China and the Role of the China
Scholar Community[1]

ANDREW MERTHA

One of the chief beneficiaries of—and contributors to—the era
of U.S. engagement with China is the community of American
China scholars. The resurgence of China scholarship that set
the stage for engagement rose from the ashes of the McCarthy period, when
sinologists were often met with suspicion and hostility. The careers of such
China experts as Owen Lattimore, John Service, and John Paton Davies were
abruptly curtailed, and a generation of China expertise was sacrificed at the
altar of the who-lost-China debate.[2] In an echo of the past, engagement with
China has once again become something of a dirty word. In the United States,
the growing bipartisan consensus that China has become stronger, more assertive, and more authoritarian has dampened earlier enthusiasm for sustained
interaction. Chinese students are coming under increasing suspicion of stealing
secrets to strengthen the People's Republic of China (PRC) at the expense of
U.S. interests.[3] Visas are now being used as a political tool, not only in China
(where this has always been the case) but also in the United States.[4] The FBI
is making the rounds to warn U.S. citizens and professionals about the insid-
ious ways in which China is infiltrating the United States in order to weaken
American competitiveness.[5] And some China hands have become jaundiced in
their views of Chinese motivations and intentions.

China's illiberal behavior has made disillusion easier. Opportunities and
access that had been taken for granted by American China scholars during the
period of engagement have disappeared under Xi Jinping. The frigid political
climate that has accompanied Xi's rise to power and his tightening of party

and coercive control has challenged our ability to understand what is actually happening in China. China's rise, particularly in the wake of the global financial crisis and the tarnishing of the liberal international economic order, has driven nationalist sentiment in China. This has, in turn, been reinforced by the PRC's muscular behavior in the South China Sea and, more recently, in Hong Kong.[6] Beijing's actions in Xinjiang have been deeply disturbing.[7] And China's forays into soft power—mobilizing its own citizens abroad through a more open united front (whole of society) strategy and seeking to generate a positive international image to compete with the West—have only complicated engagement and increased suspicion on all sides.[8]

One of the more problematic narratives that has arisen amid the debate over what to do about China is that the China studies community somehow got China wrong. This narrative often assumes that the community has been of one voice in advocating engagement as a way of encouraging China to move in the direction of political liberalization and eventually democratization.[9] A version of this story has been articulated at the highest levels of the U.S. government:

> Look, the President has done his level best to correct 40 years of appeasement of China. . . . For an awful long time there was this theory that if we just were nice to China that their system would change and the Chinese Communist Party would begin to behave in ways that were consistent with the things that were of a benefit to America.[10]

Not only does this play into one of the most deeply held suspicions of leftist Chinese authorities—that engagement has been little more than a Trojan horse, the perennial Chinese preoccupation with peaceful evolution (*heping yanbian*) going back to John Foster Dulles—but it is also empirically inaccurate and historically untrue, as other chapters in this volume similarly demonstrate.[11] Very few serious scholars of China were motivated by this objective, and the majority did not see it as a likely outcome.[12] Rather, most serious China scholars are animated by a different overarching goal: a thirst for knowledge contributing to deeper understanding that would be mutually beneficial for our two peoples, regardless of what form of government our respective countries might take.

Indeed, stepping back from the fray, the current state of bilateral relations actually supports and reinforces the case for engagement. The present downturn is precisely what happens when the infrastructure for engagement is drawn down and hollowed out within an environment of runaway nationalism (in China), intense politicization (on both sides), and administrative incompetence (predominantly within the Trump administration). The correct premise is not that engagement makes problems within the bilateral relationship go away; rather, it is that this vital relationship is immensely challenging at even the very best of times, and engagement is what keeps it from spiraling out of control. When engagement is dropped from the equation, nothing can prevent a race to the bottom like the one in which we find ourselves today.

In my view, the bilateral political relationship between our two countries is best served by depoliticizing the actual nodes of engagement—in this case, those that allow meaningful scholarship to take place. Regardless of whether their relations are friendly or adversarial, neither side benefits from curtailing knowledge about the other. Closing off channels of scholarship and mutual understanding can lead to misperceptions and potentially destabilizing political outcomes, the dangers of which far outweigh the perceived benefits of micromanaging these nodes of contact in the shortsighted belief that one side will gain a tactical advantage over the other.

To underscore the mutual and iterative benefits of engagement, this chapter documents what we have learned (and how we learned it) in the period from 1971 to 2020. I begin with a history of the accumulation of knowledge going back to the 1960s and conclude with five profoundly important advances in our understanding made possible by engagement, as well as two areas that have suffered during this same period. I begin with the baseline of the state of the field in the 1960s, when Pekingology and the reading of the figurative and literal tea leaves were among the few intellectual resources available to members of the China-watching community and policy makers who relied on them.

How Did We Know What We Knew Back Then?

To ascertain what we have learned as a field from the era of engagement, we must look at the period immediately before engagement as a benchmark. The figures of that generation—among them Lucian Pye, A. Doak Barnett, John King Fairbank, and Robert Scalapino—stood out in at least two ways. First, they differed from their predecessors in that their contributions were not bound by the all-consuming urge to change China.[13] Second, they were responsible for training the generation that came of age at the eve of the engagement era, some of whom are contributors to this volume. The question that drives this section is: *How in the world did these individuals learn so much about China when they had so little real contact with it?*

Part of the answer is that they were themselves products of China.[14] Many of these scholars, journalists, and government employees came from missionary, business, and other families that had lived in China for decades or had considerable professional experience there, especially in the military during the Second World War. Additionally, these individuals and many of their students were exceptional people whose deep knowledge of China was matched by their intelligence, drive, and ability to withstand discomfort as well as accept often significant risks to their own careers and livelihoods. They were often fiercely entrepreneurial and bureaucratically savvy. Perhaps the most important reason we knew what we knew back then (and know what we know now) has to do with the sheer intelligence, diligence, and enthusiasm these individuals had to create from scratch a critical mass of scholars committed to the study of China. They were helped in their effort by great American philanthropies, several of which had long histories in China, such as the Rockefeller and Luce foundations, and, later on, Ford.

Second, greater China continued to exist as a key node not simply for language study but as a rich environment to understand and appreciate Chinese cultural norms—from *guanxi* to bureaucratic practices to the everyday exercise of power—that could provide essential, if indirect, understandings of the kind of interactions that sometimes lay just under the layer of Maoist conformity and the engineering of the new socialist man. Richard Solomon relied to no small degree on surveys conducted in Taiwan for his classic study of Chinese political culture.[15] And, of course, intelligence on the PRC was diligently collected by Taiwanese government agencies and foreign analysists in Hong Kong (the location of the largest American consulate in the world at the time). Sometimes, a lucky scholar simply stumbled upon a gold mine. While studying in Taiwan in the mid-1960s, a quick-thinking Richard Baum suggested that he help a young assistant librarian in what was known as the "dirty books room" of the Institute of International Relations translate a stack of soiled, water-damaged documents marked *top secret*. These turned out to be important Communist Party directives bookending the just-completed Socialist Education Movement. Moreover, Baum's careful reading of these documents uncovered a split at the very top of the Chinese leadership that would subsequently lead to the purge of Liu Shaoqi and Deng Xiaoping and the instigation of the Great Proletarian Cultural Revolution. Eventually, Baum teamed up with a young Frederick Teiwes (then a doctoral candidate and now one of the luminaries of archival-based scholarship on Chinese politics) to further analyze these documents. Their collaboration resulted in a Berkeley monograph, *Ssu-Ch'ing: The Socialist Education Movement of 1962–1966*, which to this day remains an essential piece of scholarship on Mao-era Chinese politics.[16]

Third, sources like the CIA-funded Foreign Broadcast Information Service (FBIS), which monitored broadcast media in the PRC, became publicly available and provided an important thread for keeping abreast of developments behind the bamboo curtain. FBIS continued to be an invaluable resource for understanding the twists and turns in China's official media at the national and local levels well into the 1990s.[17] Another source, the U.S. Joint Publications Research Service (JPRS), published reports on a broader sweep of Chinese society and made use of an even larger number of sources. The *Selections from the Chinese Mainland Press* (SCMP) and *Selections from Chinese Main-land Magazines* (SCMM) provided translations of Cultural Revolution materials, including Red Guard documents and local newspapers, as well as other media. In addition, the U.S. consulate in Hong Kong allowed access to its Daily Appearance Tracking Data set of all Chinese leaders (in the form of a card file kept in a vault).[18]

Perhaps the most important single resource on contemporary China, one that signaled the shift from the pre-engagement period and has informed China scholarship from the beginning of the engagement period onward, is the Universities Service Centre (USC) in Hong Kong. The USC served as ground zero for much of the research on China through the 1970s and the collection, now at a different venue, continues to serve as a staging ground for scholarship to this very day.[19] It is difficult to overestimate the importance of the USC or to imagine what the state of China scholarship would be today in its absence. The USC brought together several generations of some of the titans of the field, then developing the knowledge and expertise that would eventually shape the study of China. These included Michel Oksenberg, Ezra Vogel, Steven Goldstein, Andrew Walder, Mike Lampton, Susan Shirk, Martin Whyte, and Kenneth Lieberthal. In the words of Mike Lampton, "it was an intergenerational hothouse," which was "a wonderful experience for a young person."

The idea for the USC was conceived in the late 1950s by Lucian Pye and Bill Marvel, both of whom recognized that universities were extremely nervous about sponsoring the study of contemporary China (as distinct from Chinese history, language, and literature) in the wake of McCarthyism and the purge of China expertise throughout the U.S. government. In addition, there was a growing rivalry between the two main China centers at the time, one on the East Coast (at Harvard, under John King Fairbank) and the other on the West Coast (at the University of Washington under George Taylor). Their competition grew out of disagreements between Fairbank and Taylor dating from their work together at the Office of War Information during the Second World War. Even then, the U.S. China studies field was undeniably polarized. Hong Kong, although not exactly neutral ground—as the mid- to late 1960s would dramatically illustrate—was nonetheless somewhat more hospitable than the United States (although the Social Science Research Council and the American Council of Learned Societies were supporting nascent programs at the time, while the National Defense Education Act and the Ford Foundation offered four-year awards for language and graduate study—underscoring that Hong Kong was certainly less systematically biased than Taiwan). The USC was, if you will, a safe space for the study of Chinese politics.

Another place where one could undertake the careful reading of official pronouncements trickling out of China was the Union Research Institute (URI), which shared its English- and Chinese-language press clippings with the USC.[20]

These were worth their weight in gold. As Simon Leys[21], who served as the Belgian cultural attaché in Beijing in 1972, wrote:

> Sometimes, in all innocence, the woman at the market stall where you buy your pound of apples or the cobbler who has repaired your shoes will absent-mindedly give you your goods wrapped in a taboo old [local] newspaper; needless to say, the dirty and crumpled sheets are then smoothed over lovingly by China-watchers, who pass them around with trembling hands, deeply excited, and after being multi-photocopied they end of up in the black market in Hong Kong, where various research institutes outbid themselves to get them.[22]

This task was eventually taken over by the USC as the URI began to decline in the mid-1960s and, combined with the USC's growing collection of books and periodicals, led the USC to become the one-stop shop for archived data sources on contemporary China.[23]

Meanwhile, a small army of interviewees shuttled between Western academics eager to learn from them. The interviewers had to be careful about the veracity of such sources, since the twenty Hong Kong dollars per hour the refugees received for their interviews were not exactly an incentive to stick to the facts. Two of the most entrepreneurial sources—but also among the most knowledgeable—were the "Yangs" (fondly recalled as "Xiao Yang" and "Lao Yang"). The Yangs were important informants for "the vast majority of scholarly books, articles, and PhD dissertations written about China during the Cultural Revolution decade, 1966–1976," recounted Richard Baum, with tongue only half in cheek. In fact, people like Sai-cheung Yeung ("Lao Yang") were instrumental in providing data necessary for the work of such scholars as Michel Oksenberg, Ronald Montaperto, and David Lampton (who even credited him in his monograph, *Paths to Power*).[24] These informants became research assistants as well, helping scholars like Ezra Vogel, Michel Oksenberg, Susan Shirk, B. Michael Frolic, Steven Goldstein, Jerome Cohen, Suzanne Pepper, John Dolfin, and a host of others in their work.

Four factors contributed to the unique environment of the USC. The first was the configuration of disciplines represented by these young scholars: political science, economics, anthropology, sociology, journalism, history, and law, as well as some of the humanities. The USC provided the opportunity for these scholars to analyze the complex organizations and developments within China as truly interdisciplinary area specialists. Second, the USC was international in the makeup of individual scholars among its ranks and was therefore able to push back against tendencies toward what Ezra Vogel called "American chauvinism" in the study of China. Third, unlike the rigid pecking-order system in most university departments, the USC created an environment where no hierarchy existed—an extremely liberating experience for young China scholars at the time. Finally, during its initial stages, the USC was unparalleled in its ability to attract prime sources of information on the otherwise closed book that was mainland China. Chief among them were the refugees who fled the PRC, beginning in earnest in 1962, and who (reluctantly at first) provided personal accounts of local politics and everyday life in Maoist China.[25]

It was at the USC, for example, that Doak Barnett interviewed the former cadres who formed the basis of his classic *Cadres, Bureaucracy, and Political Power in Communist China*.[26] Barnett's volume is invaluable even today in providing a structural roadmap for the party-state system in China, bringing in such diverse but essential elements as inside versus outside cadres, party life, indoctrination, and guest houses and canteens, alongside such bread-and-butter concepts as staffing, formal supervision, organization and appointments, and document flows. Nonetheless, Vogel is unflinching in describing the challenges that this community faced in their role as scholars of contemporary China:

> It is now hard to recapture the scale of our ignorance about mainland China when the USC opened its doors, and the naïve excitement as we listened with bated breath to the latest traveler or refugee from China or to government officials from various countries who had access to sources of information that we did not. We did not even know China's simple organizational charts. We were just beginning to understand the operation of political campaigns, the structure of communes, neighborhoods, *danwei* [organizational units] and work points.[27]

In addition to the foundational work done by Barnett, Vogel, and others, this period witnessed a shift from, to paraphrase Donald Rumsfeld, "not knowing what we don't know" to getting a handle on "knowing what we don't know." This was the state of the field at the dawn of the era of engagement.

The Opening to China and the Schism of the Vietnam War

Despite the careful scholarship being undertaken in Taiwan and Hong Kong at a time when Americans were unable to visit the PRC and in the growing number of U.S. China centers entering the fray (Columbia, Michigan, Stanford, and Berkeley, for instance), the actual, on-the-ground impressions of the earliest Western scholars in China betrayed the limits of what could be gleaned from the outside looking in. Those lucky few who were allowed into China, like the first delegation of the Committee of Concerned Asian Scholars in 1971, were often presented with a stage-managed experience—including a secretly planned flat tire somewhere in the countryside after which local peasants would magically appear with a spare and change the tire—that only further confirmed their bias as "friends of China." These highly choreographed tours were "always superbly organized, anything that might be unpredictable, unexpected, spontaneous, or improvised [was] ruthlessly eliminated."[28] Edward Friedman, skeptical by nature and armed with the advice of social anthropologist Fei Xiaotong to "learn to see the invisible," was nonetheless unknowingly drawn into researching Chinese Potemkin villages (in this case, Wugong village in Raoyang County), convinced that he had "beaten the system." Subsequently humbled when he checked his notes against the clippings at URI ("a critical reading of the URI files was more revealing than the prior two months in China"), his response was to redouble his efforts at finding the truths hidden in the "invisible" on subsequent trips.[29] This was in 1978.

Early forays into China often left researchers on more extreme ends of the political spectrum. On the one hand were those who became caught up in the propaganda of the regime, allowing the seductive images from such officially produced magazines as *China Reconstructs* and *China Pictorial* to color what they were being presented in situ in China. On the other were those who felt a sense of betrayal at being so easily (and, in retrospect, obviously) duped by the Chinese authorities. Jonathan Mirsky went "from Mao fan to counterrevolutionary in 48 hours" when, the day after he visited a model Chinese work unit in Guangdong, he came upon the same unit the next morning on an unaccompanied walk. He was invited in for *bai kaishui* (literally "white hot water," which substituted for tea when the host was too poor to afford tea) by a worker whose living conditions and attitude toward the state completely contradicted the rosy, carefully orchestrated experience of the workers he had met the day before. The cold, even hostile reception Mirsky received from his Chinese handlers in response to his transgression further removed the scales from his eyes, confirmed four years later when one of his guides told him, "we wanted to put rings in your noses, and you helped us put them there."[30]

In short, officially arranged visits to the PRC were not particularly propitious for careful, disinterested analyses of the country, and the different and contradictory experiences of those early visitors also served to open up profound cleavages and divisions among students of Asia that threatened to upend the China studies community.

By 1968, the Vietnam War was polarizing American society. Among scholars of Asia, such polarization led to a schism in which those on the left often allowed their political biases to shape their approaches to China. This led them not only to ask questions and pursue topics that might not have otherwise been undertaken—Mark Selden's classic *The Yenan Way in Revolutionary China* is the apogee of this line of research[31]—but also spurred many to adopt an attitude toward China lacking the minimum academic standard of skepticism. One fiery revolutionary is reputed to have tried to swim to a North Vietnamese vessel anchored in Hong Kong's harbor as a show of his support, but he never quite got there.[32]

For some, the rosy view of late Maoism engendered prescriptive possibilities for the social upheavals then taking place in the United States.[33] The Committee of Concerned Asian Scholars (CCAS) was one manifestation of this preoccupation, and it led to a split within the growing field of Asia scholarship. The result was a growing number of pitched scholarly and even ideological battles on the one hand and a multidimensional richness in Asia scholarship on the other, the likes of which continues to the present day in the journal *Critical Asian Studies*.[34]

This growing cleavage reached its nadir in 1971 when former Kennedy administration national security adviser McGeorge Bundy, then the president of the Ford Foundation, which was a major funder of USC, was invited to lunch at the USC in Hong Kong.

> When Bundy was introduced to the assembled scholars in the center's lunchroom, a CCAS spokesman . . . rose to his feet to read a prepared statement [detailing Bundy's alleged war crimes]. . . . Thereupon he and the other CCAS members silently and in unison turned over their lunch plates. Displayed on each overturned dish was the famous photo of a naked young Vietnamese girl who had been napalmed by US forces.[35]

The incident created a schism within the China community that took decades to heal. Apparently Bundy never mentioned the incident to his colleagues at Ford, and the Centre's funding from the foundation continued for a number of years.

Less known were important differences within CCAS in members' motivations and approaches to scholarship. While the more revolutionary strand felt that the American system itself was immoral, another group had come to oppose the war for different reasons. This reformist constituency of the CCAS was made up of people who had served in the U.S. military (Mike Lampton and Thomas Fingar; Terry Lautz had actually been deployed to Vietnam) or had joined the Peace Corps (Halsey Beemer). They believed the Vietnam War was a tragic mistake and the result of profound ignorance about Asia. They saw their scholarship as a mission to educate decision makers in order to avoid such monumental errors in the future.

As China moved away from the Cultural Revolution, attitudes about it changed across the spectrum. Overseas leftists felt betrayed by the geopolitical (and subsequently *capitalist*) path China was taking, while the establishment view shifted 180 degrees from negative to positive (as it would again, in the opposite direction, following Tiananmen in 1989[36]) as images broadcast before and after Nixon's February 1972 visit to China saturated the media.[37] But even while public opinion about China in the United States was shifting, opportunities for China watchers to glean any meaningful insight into unofficial China remained limited and challenging, notwithstanding academic delegations under the auspices of the Committee on Scholarly Communication with the People's Republic of China.

One record of China at the time, fiercely negative, nonetheless transcended some of the more knee-jerk (positive or negative) reactions of other contemporary works and remains a dark but compelling commentary on late Maoist China. Simon Leys's *Chinese Shadows* underscored the limits of what could be garnered from everyday experiences—"in the end, one learns most from the repetition of certain silences, the recurrence of a certain reticence about several points."[38] As Leys was at pains to admit, he could only guess at what lay behind the gray conformity of the local cadres that controlled the universe for ordinary Chinese (and foreigners living inside the walled compounds of Beijing's diplomatic ghettos). More measured, but only slightly less critical, were the accounts that emerged in the thaw after the establishment of diplomatic relations between the United States and China, which led to American journalists taking up posts in Beijing for the first time since 1949. Roger Garside's *Coming Alive: China After Mao* and Fox Butterfield's *China: Alive in the Bitter Sea* are good examples of how journalists experienced China in those early years following normalization.[39] Unfortunately, Butterfield's failure to protect his sources foreshadowed the challenges of conducting field research within an extremely politicized setting and the moral imperative of protecting informants.

The Era of Access, 1979–2008

In 2002, Andrew Walder looked back on the strides made by China studies since 1979 and identified areas where China scholarship had made advances so significant that it no longer resembled that of the earlier era described in the previous section. The first of these had to do with the newfound access to information brought on by a remarkable expansion of domestic research opportunities. As restrictions on publications were relaxed in the PRC, scholars "eventually found themselves buried in an avalanche of new newspapers and periodicals, books, and published regulations, and the trickle of more valuable 'internal' documents and books also grew to a steady stream," overloading the dockets of scholars and East Asia librarians.[40]

Second, research opportunities available to American scholars within China grew apace. Individual scholars were gradually permitted to undertake language study and conduct fieldwork in China.[41] Initially, these opportunities were heavily regulated by the Chinese authorities and far more structured than they would be a decade or so hence.

The Committee on Scholarly Communication with the People's Republic of China, sponsored jointly by the National Academy of Sciences, the Social Science Research Council, and the American Council of Learned Societies, began exchanges in the fall of 1979, initially sending only language students.

Shortly thereafter, the committee sought to place researchers with universities and academies of social science; within two years, scholars were sent to China for field research, and there followed a long struggle to gain research access to archives and villages.

These new opportunities were not without incident. The case of anthropologist Steven Mosher represented both what was possible as well as what was spectacularly ill-advised. The Committee for Scholarly Communication with the People's Republic of China and the Social Science Research Council's Joint Committee on Contemporary China had lobbied hard for the first contingent of American researchers in China to include an anthropologist conducting research in a Chinese village. That anthropologist was Stanford PhD candidate Mosher. Mosher's work in rural Guangdong shifted from dispassionate scholarship to activist research as he witnessed firsthand the draconian enforcement of the one-child policy. Subsequently charged with being a spy and expelled from the PRC, his actions led to a moratorium on rural field research for several years. Stanford University's collective decision not to award Mosher a PhD was based on charges of academic dishonesty and exposing his sources to retaliation and elicited countercharges that Stanford was folding in the face of Chinese pressure (a theme that has returned in present-day discourse). The episode, taken as a whole, underscored a fundamental tension that would emerge within the China studies field. One camp sought to objectively describe and analyze what was going on in China (and would be roundly criticized by Mosher and others for discounting human rights abuses). The other embraced a kind of activist scholarship that was reminiscent of the CCAS but now firmly opposed the Chinese line instead of accepting it at face value.[42]

Yet as access widened, it became increasingly difficult to ignore the quality of life endured by the overwhelming majority of Chinese, which often bordered on the horrific. According to one colleague, who is anything but an anti-China activist:

> The biggest thing I learned from studying the history of the party and from talking to people in China is how cruel the party can be to its own people. Although this leads to a lot of grumbling and dissatisfaction and even fear among party cadres, most also feel that they don't have any alternatives to the party. They don't see an alternative either in China's political system or in their own career trajectories. This has led to stability in the party's rule. However, this also means that the moment that people within the party can see an alternative, the continuation of CCP rule will be very fragile.[43]

How to process all of this without falling into the traps of apologia, cultural relativism, or critical analysis is a fine line that China scholars walk to this day.

Nonetheless, by the end of the 1980s, in-country scholarship was becoming the norm. During this time, the field grew more functionally and spatially specialized, as well as focused on a wider range of issue areas (agriculture, health care, education, etc.). Certain individuals ventured beyond Beijing in their selection of primary field sites and contributed greatly to our understanding of China by undertaking arguably more arduous research in the provinces. There, challenges like unfamiliarity with foreigners and nonadherence to educational policies aimed at foreign researchers were tempered by curiosity and local conditions that allowed for central directives to be overlooked or even quietly challenged.

While this was occurring, risk-acceptant and forward-thinking universities all over China were seeking to establish programs with their foreign counterparts, sponsoring language and other study programs, joint research, and university-to-university exchanges. Some of these operated under the aegis of state-to-state relationships, such as that between Ohio and Hubei province. These programs expanded the universe of personal relationships that foreign scholars, up to that point, had been singularly ill-equipped to establish and nurture themselves. This was one of the primary results of the Luce Foundation's U.S.-China Cooperative Research Program, which funded forty-nine joint projects during the late 1980s and into the 1990s. These informal norms, in turn, created professional relationships that blossomed into friendships—perhaps the most important single element providing those on the outside a window through which to understand the functioning of the Chinese state and its shaping of Chinese society. Often the most profound eureka moments were, in retrospect, the most straightforward and prosaic:

> A rather obvious and saccharine but nonetheless important take-away would be that when one gets to interact and talk directly with Chinese people, be they party officials or noodle-shop owners or sheep-herders, it is fairly easy to find common ground even about political issues that seem to divide the US and China. In some ways, the best versions of American and Chinese culture are complementary: we respect and enjoy different aspects of each other.[44]

But, as Harry Harding notes, this was also a time of sober reassessment of our most basic assumptions about China. In no small part, this was a corrective to much of the euphoria that followed in the wake of the 1972 Nixon visit, as well as lingering misconceptions of Chinese reality that took official narratives of equality, unity, and meaningful political participation at their word. Harding provides a particularly egregious example:

> In the mid-1970s, Joel Fort, a celebrity psychiatrist from San Francisco, could win ardent applause from a student audience at Stanford by proclaiming that there was no rape or premarital sex in China and that was so because Chinese youth, unlike their American counterparts, sublimated their libidinal energies toward service to the nation.[45]

Part of this reassessment emerged from questioning earlier conclusions about China that were, on their face, ridiculous. But much had to do with the fact that the scholars emerging in the 1980s were spending more time in China than had their predecessors. They coexisted with the journalists and businesspeople whose perspectives broke sharply with the prevailing wisdom. Extended exposure to Chinese realities contributed to frustration over restrictions on interacting with Chinese friends and colleagues and recognition of the inefficiencies and immovability of the vast bureaucracy upon which so much depended.[46] These were a fact of life for China's citizens, and they soon became part of foreign scholars' experiences in China and informed their research.

And then came 1989. The crackdown and subsequent shift in the U.S. narrative—from being overly credulous (pandas and the Great Wall) to painting all of China with a single, negative brush (butchers of Beijing)—changed some of the parameters for access. Surprisingly, though, it did not close China off to research entirely. In fact, the period bookended by Tiananmen and the 1995–1996 Taiwan Strait Crisis witnessed some of the most penetrating new research to be done in China: "jointly planned and administered sample surveys or field research projects, in which Chinese and foreign researchers jointly analyze and publish the resulting data . . . [on] political participation and political attitudes, rural household incomes, health and nutrition, mate choice and marriage patterns, social stratification and mobility, and other subjects."[47] These, too, were not without incident. When the first round of data to be gleaned from the Four-County Survey was embargoed in China, the U.S. administrators of the study argued to the Chinese that they had approved the questions. The Chinese authorities responded with "yes, but we didn't approve the answers."[48]

Another feature of this era, alluded to earlier, was the dramatic influx of Chinese students coming to study in American universities. Chinese politics—long the domain of white men and a few white women—was expanded quantitatively and qualitatively not simply through collaboration with Chinese scholars in China but by students from the PRC in the United States, some of whom stayed on and built their careers in U.S. colleges, universities, and think tanks, a phenomenon described in detail by Robert Daly in his contribution to this volume. Walder writes of these students:

> From the first few graduate students to arrive in the [late 1970s and] early 1980s, the PRC graduate student has become an important fixture in social science departments across these three fields [political science, economics, and sociology]. This is an immense and seemingly inexhaustible national pool of talent; its impact on such fields as physics and chemistry is already legendary in this country. The effect has not been so dramatic in the social sciences, but the impact is highly magnified in the study of contemporary China.[49]

Indeed, this flood of new talent required us to update our conception of the area specialist. As Walder writes, many of these students eschewed that label and have acted as a force for mainstreaming the study of China within their respective social science disciplines:

> From our area studies perspective, we would have expected such students to excel at intensive documentary research of the kind we commonly practiced ourselves, enjoying a massive linguistic advantage. Instead, students from China gravitated quickly to models that predominated in the core of the disciplines: theoretically engaged empirical research, often highly mathematical and statistical in orientation. . . . This single-minded dedication to disciplinary canons has served these students well in the competition for elite faculty positions during the past 15 years. Near the end of the 1980s it was becoming apparent that students from China were out-competing students trained in the traditional "area studies" approach in the job market. In the 1990s, the most highly coveted jobs in Political Science—Yale, Princeton, Chicago, Duke, and Michigan—have been filled by PhDs who came originally from China. In sociology, students from the PRC have been offered similar entry-level jobs at Harvard, Chicago, Cornell, Duke, Minnesota, Michigan, and California-Irvine.[50]

As this implies, one of the greatest changes in the field has been a shift in the grounding of the study of China from a tribalist outlier in the social science disciplines to a subfield that is rightly seen as a peer to the more traditional subfields in economics, sociology, and especially political science.[51] When asked point blank what it is that these Chinese scholars bring to the China field that is different from their non-Chinese counterparts—besides native language skills, contextualized knowledge, and excellent professional and social networks—the best answer I can give is: *nothing*. That is to say, when one looks at the work by Yasheng Huang, Cheng Li, or Wang Yuhua, to name just three, there is nothing Chinese about it; rather, it is the sheer superiority of their scholarship and its power to move the subfield of Chinese politics forward that matter.

This is not simply a result of the changing demographics of the China field; it is also a result of ongoing changes in China itself. The 1980s provided an unprecedented sociopolitical experiment in state transformation. This began with the politics of early reform (changing ownership patterns in agriculture and rural industry) and extended through the first significant challenges faced by China's reformers (industrial reform and early privatization). At the same time, how Chinese society responded to and absorbed these changes, and through them asserted individual and group agency, altered Chinese state behavior in ways earlier scholarship was unable to capture.

The heady 1990s and early 2000s saw a further retreat by the state from interfering with the work of foreign scholars. The type of engagement that was possible at this time was extraordinary compared to what had been possible in the not-so-recent past as well as the immediate future. American China scholars were able to make themselves sufficiently invisible to become participant-observers of factory floors,[52] enforcement against illegal market activity,[53] legal proceedings,[54] informal employment markets for laid-off workers,[55] and retail outlets in state-owned department stores[56]; one even worked undercover as a karaoke hostess.[57] These undercover approaches were enhanced by increasingly sophisticated survey techniques made possible by technological improvements in data collection and analysis as well as the cumulative formal and informal institutionalization of access made possible by years of collaboration.

This golden era is encapsulated by an exchange I had with some local officials during an alcohol-soaked lunch in the Sino–North Korean border town of Dandong in the fall of 2004. I was traveling with a family whose patriarch was a provincial-level official on a working vacation. We had rented a boat to take us to the North Korean shore and visited the one-and-a-half bridges that spanned the Yalu River, the older of which had been bombed by U.S. planes during the Korean War. The expanse from the middle of the river to the North Korean shore was completely destroyed, earning it the moniker of the "Yalu River Broken Bridge" (*Yalu Jiang Duan Qiao*). During lunch, one of the local cadres at our table staggered over to me and mumbled in my ear, reeking of liquor.

"What country are you from?"
Oh, God, here it comes, I thought. "The United States."
"Do you see those two bridges?"
I looked down from our perch in the rooftop restaurant. "Yes," I ventured cautiously.
"Do you know why one of those bridges is only half standing?" he wheezed.
I nodded, dreading what was coming next.
"You Americans blew up that bridge. You Americans. Americans . . ."
I waited for the other shoe to drop.
"I *respect* you Americans!"
What? I looked up in shock.

He said it again; there was no mistaking it, *wo peifu nimen Meiguo ren!* He continued, "You Americans flew in and blew up the Korean side of the bridge and left the Chinese side standing, all with 1950s technology. You Americans!" And he flashed the thumbs up sign.

Overtaken by the moment and clearly off-balance, I raised my glass and shouted, "*Meidizhuyi wansui!*" ("Long live American imperialism!")

Before I could realize the magnitude of my faux pas, everyone at our table—my cadre friend, his family members, and all the local cadres who had joined us—immediately stood up, raised their glasses, and roared, "Long live American imperialism!"

In that moment, all differences melted away, the multilayered insider irony of what we were saying was clearly understood by all, and the subversive absurdity of the moment was equally relished around the table.

Sadly, this was not to last.

The Downturn, 2008–2020

Beginning around 2006, access to people, publications, and data in China began to slowly diminish. This was partly due to the color revolutions unfolding elsewhere in the world. Suspicion was deepened by leftist dissatisfaction with developments in China deemed antithetical to Marxism.[58] The Chinese state was becoming increasingly anxious about its ability to maintain control in an era of rapidly evolving communication facilitated by smart phones and the Internet. Although this process had started a few years before, everything seemed to converge in 2008. As China prepared for the Beijing Olympics in September of that year, two events provided the parameters for what would be the increasingly mixed environment for China studies in the decade after 2008. The Tibetan protests in March became a lightning rod for anti-Chinese activism worldwide, nationalistic reaction among the Chinese inside and outside China, and Beijing's perennial suspicion of foreign influence. Two months later, in May, and aided by the fortuitous presence of an NPR crew working on a project in Chengdu, the world was able to follow the devastation wrought by the Sichuan earthquake in real time—including the state's attempts to simultaneously control the narrative and scramble to help its victims.[59] Genuine sympathy for the latter and positive reporting on the mobilization of Chinese society to assist in the recovery were contrasted with stories on the shoddy construction of schools and other infrastructure that led to the unnecessary deaths of scores of schoolchildren in Dujiangyan and outlying counties.[60]

The period since 2008 has witnessed a general restriction of scholarly access and a closing-off of critical nodes of contact between foreign researchers and the Chinese state, epitomized by the promulgation of the infamous "Communiqué on the Current State of the Ideological Sphere" (commonly referred to as "Document 9") and accelerated by the rise of Xi Jinping.[61] China has not returned to the pre-1979 period, let alone the pre-engagement era, but it has become increasingly difficult to undertake the type of research that had been done in the recent past. This has reinforced the tendency within the social science disciplines and the academic job market to force China scholars to perform increasingly niche research and rely on a more arm's-length approach than had previously been the norm. Although some of these scholars still make somewhat intrepid, risk-embracing forays into studying the Chinese body politic, these are quickly becoming the exception. A few scholars have responded to this narrowing of access to China by adjusting their research approach to be more comparative in scope. For instance, David Lampton and two colleagues have done an eight-nation study of Chinese rail building, Maria Repnikova has taken a deep dive to look at how Chinese soft power unfolds in Africa, and I have extended my own field sites into Cambodia to document China's foreign assistance to the Khmer Rouge.[62]

For the most part, we are seeing fewer and fewer opportunities to conduct field interviews, access data sources we used to take for granted, and invest in networks of sources and associates that had been nurtured for decades. Even more alarmingly, the generation of China scholars currently being minted is confronted with truncated fieldwork opportunities and limitation of access. The inevitably from-a-distance nature of what research is still possible reinforces the tone as well as the content of the discourse that emerges from it. Our knowledge base risks becoming increasingly brittle, bereft of the nuance and subtleties central to our understanding of the Chinese state. It is therefore reasonable to conclude that we are witnessing a historical bookend for the engagement era in the China studies field as well as in the political and economic spheres.

What Have We Learned in the Era of Engagement?

So, what have we learned? The short answer is both more than we could have possibly imagined and less than we would like to think. It is humbling to consider the extent of what we knew at the dawn of engagement and how much of what we have subsequently learned is largely a fleshing out of those initial insights. Articulated in the 1960s and early 1970s, these understandings continue to inform China scholarship into the present, despite trends within the academy to supersede them and evolutionary changes in China that coexist alongside or build upon these earlier-documented forms of statecraft.

From Structure to Process: Examining the Makeup of the Party-State

A. Doak Barnett's masterful mapping of the Chinese government and party bureaucracy remains a Rosetta stone for those who study China's political institutions. Going through its index, substituting *pinyin* for Wade-Giles, the reader is struck by the number of terms and phrases that continue to be the vocabulary of Chinese cadres themselves as well as those who study them.

Yet such a description, while representing an extraordinary step forward in our knowledge of the Chinese state structure, tells us less about how it functions in the everyday governance of the country.

Extending the work of Barnett are Lieberthal and Oksenberg in their path-breaking book, *Policy Making in China*, and Lampton's earlier work on policy making and implementation.[63] Collectively referred to as "fragmented authoritarianism," the framework that emerged from their scholarship moved Barnett's descriptive findings and demonstrated how cadres and other bureaucrats in China contributed to a policy making process characterized by bargaining and negotiated outcomes, in which the eventual contours of a given policy reflect the interests of the implementation agents at the expense of the policy making bodies' original intentions.

The work of Lieberthal and Oksenberg in particular demonstrated the newfound availability of data sources that the denizens of the USC could only dream about.[64] *Policy Making in China* was itself the continuation of a study commissioned by the U.S. Department of Energy that allowed an unprecedented degree of access at all levels of the political system to the two scholars and was made possible by the steadily maturing strands of engagement between the United States and China.[65]

A generation later, this framework remained the standard lens through which to understand policy making and implementation in China, but was updated to include the early signs of (subsequently reversed) political liberalization, in which nonstate actors as well as those within the state that did not necessarily have a political mandate to encroach upon a given policy area nonetheless did, altering not only the outcomes of implementation but also the actual shape and scope of the policy itself. Initially drawn from studies of China's hydropower policy, these updates were extended to other policy areas, including international trade, heath care and tobacco regulation, and civil-military relations.[66] The ability to undertake the shoe-leather field research necessary to uncover this evolution in policy making was possible because by the mid-2000s, one could undertake off-the-grid research through freedom of movement within China and informal networks of individuals embedded within the policy sphere. The chief constraints were time, research funds, the individual researcher's threshold for discomfort, and accumulated connections and trust earned with informants.

More recent work on other aspects of China's policy making, particularly on coordinating mechanisms like leading groups (*lingdao xiaozu*) and government–Chinese Communist Party (CCP) relations, have developed Barnett's work even further.[67] As a result, we have a much clearer understanding of how the wheels on the Chinese Leviathan actually move and can make sense of why and how the various constituent parts of the Chinese state combine to make or undermine a given policy area.

Increased access has also let us look more closely at the CCP itself. Descriptive accounts like those of John Burns have been extended and deepened over the past four decades. Susan Shirk's groundbreaking work on the early reform era applied principal-agent theory to the relationship between the CCP and the government.[68] Dan Lynch's research on the impact of marketization on thought work showed that the CCP was not simply a collection of "sinister keepers of the ideological flame."[69] Charlotte Lee has extended this to the party schools themselves, demonstrating how cadre training has literally been internationalized and underscoring the important point that CCP officials serve crucial civil service functions.[70] David Shambaugh has documented how the party has undertaken substantial efforts to remake itself in a domestic and global environment of change.[71] Victor Shih and Cheng Li have dusted off the focus on factional politics to show that the CCP is anything but a monolith.[72] And Christian Sorace has reinvigorated the pioneering work of Franz Schurmann to illustrate that ideology and organization continue to remain alive and well—and in tension with one another.[73] Indeed, the promotion incentives facing party cadres, research spearheaded by Yasheng Huang in the 1990s, have become a facet of much of the current work explaining outcomes that could only be hinted at by the earlier scholarship of Barnett.[74]

There has likewise been an extraordinarily deep dive into Chinese military studies. Historical approaches weave the military history of the CCP into current practices. Other studies look at the evolution of the People's Liberation Army over time, from training for Maoist "people's war," to becoming commercialized in the 1980s and 1990s, to developing into the world-class military it is today.[75] There is a great deal of technical work that is important to comprehending the empirics of military development, procurement, and deployment. Our understanding of the military's relations with the CCP has been incalculably helped by the early work of Ellis Joffe, Michael Swaine, and others.[76]

The fact that the Chinese Leninist state operates differently from that of the Soviet Union provides important clues as to the fault lines and pressure points that underlie governance, control, and the management of propaganda and communications in the PRC. This has important comparative and policy implications. To cite one dramatic example, the debacle of de-Baathification during the second Gulf War could have been avoided, and history might have been very different, if the lessons learned by China scholars of how one-party states function—that party membership is not simply the domain of the true believers and keepers of the ideological flame but also a meritocratic ladder for the best and the brightest to ascend to the top of their fields—had been applied by policy makers in rebuilding Iraq.[77]

The Richness of State-Society Relations

Perhaps the most dramatic expansion of our knowledge about China in the past quarter century derives from studies of state-society relations.

As Elizabeth Perry cogently argues, the first generation of China scholarship used the USSR as the major comparison case to China, the second generation drew inordinately from American conceptual approaches, and the third generation was "too drawn to European exemplars." That is, the paradigm by which to leverage our understanding of where the state ended and society began was that of the seventeenth- and eighteenth-century European concept of civil society. This approach received a particular boost in the wake of the student protests that preceded the 1989 crackdown. Perry herself questioned the utility of such an approach because "the economic trends characteristic of modern Europe never really took hold" in China.[78]

Rather than overreliance on the civil society concept, much of the work on state-society relations in China that began to emerge in the 1990s embraced a more inductive approach. One of the prominent themes in personal accounts of China watchers' first direct exposure to China is the relentless degree to which China's own citizens were shaped by the politics that ruled over them. The ubiquity of the work unit (*danwei*) and household registration (*hukou*) systems from the Mao era through the 1980s made it difficult to determine where the state ended and society began. The protests in 1989 led to soul-searching on how this type of mobilization could have existed outside of approved state channels. Trying to force onto the study of Chinese politics the lessons learned from the fall of communism in Eastern Europe and the Soviet Union ended up at a dead end. But as the *danwei* system itself became increasingly relaxed and the itinerant Chinese workforce grew to 150 million and beyond, traditional ways of conceptualizing social organization could not capture what was happening in China.

The fact that individual Chinese citizens were no longer tied to their work units led to a vast range of studies on organization outside of the state. Dorothy Solinger's work on migrant workers was timely and groundbreaking.[79] Jean Oi's research on rural industry coincided with a revolution in government-workplace relations after which the relationship between state and society could no longer be captured by the traditional role of the state.[80] Scott Kennedy's investigation of lobbying groups and the publications by Jessica Teets and Timothy Hildebrandt on nongovernmental organizations shed light on an extremely complex network of individuals alternatively being coopted by and pushing back against the state.[81] Scholarship by Anita Chan, Ching Kwan Lee, Mary Gallagher, and Diana Fu has revealed the factory floor as a venue for transformative change, drawing on Walder's classic study of workplace politics.[82] Kellee Tsai's trailblazing work on unofficial banking and finance would have been impossible without her granular field research and would have left all sorts of unknowns in place as far as our understanding of China's ubiquitous, yet often invisible, informal finance ecosystem is concerned.[83] Studies by Barry Naughton and Edward Steinfeld, among many others, have opened wide windows into the inner workings of state-owned enterprises and the ways in which they have evolved.[84] They were able to do so because of the remarkable access they had to the factories they studied. More recent work on local people's congresses, village elections, mayor's mailboxes, and petitions and letters have expanded the use of survey techniques, Internet scraping, and dogged local field and archival research to tell us much about how the state works with its citizens.[85] And work on local enforcement in China—too many to cite here—shows us the sometimes unbridgeable gulf between how things are perceived to occur in the capital and how they actually play out throughout the continent-sized country.

Case studies of counties like Zouping[86] or rich longitudinal studies like those undertaken by Ralph Thaxton[87] have allowed other scholars to understand the political microclimates of individual locales in China and to use local eccentricities to test their own abilities to generalize as well as contextualize the subjects of their study. Localized but broader studies by scholars like Kevin O'Brien and Lianjiang Li have provided key links between these microsites and more generalizable conclusions.[88]

The Heterogeneity of China

During his first meeting with Mao, Richard Nixon told the Chairman that "you have changed the world," to which Mao responded, "I have only been able to change a few places in the vicinity of Peking."[89] While a graduate student at Michigan, a professor there told me of an infamous (and likely deliberately provocative) comment he attributed to Michel Oksenberg that "to understand Chinese politics, you don't have to look outside of Beijing." Whether that was ever the case, it certainly is not today. The four decades of engagement have demonstrated this beyond any doubt, and Oksenberg himself embodied this change in thinking and in access when he became the "honorary mayor of Zouping" by fostering intensive research on local governance there.[90]

Ezra Vogel's classic *Canton Under Communism* and the work of Chan, Madsen, and Unger on the various iterations of *Chen Village* were early indications there was much to learn outside of Beijing.[91] However, it is no accident that these studies relied substantially on émigrés to Hong Kong, most of whom were from Guangdong. Beginning in the 1980s, scholars were able to travel to a growing list of cities that were no longer off-limits and witness for themselves the ways in which coastal and interior provinces differed from one another. The city of Wuhan, for example, became a major field site for Mike Lampton and Dorothy Solinger. Minority politics became increasingly variegated as scholars gained access to Yunnan as well as Tibet, Xinjiang, and other autonomous regions. Researchers there were able to gain insights into the different models of local statecraft that governed these areas and the diverse experiences of various minority groups.[92] It is impossible to understand why Beijing implements the policies it does—and why these policies are often so misguided or realized in the *breach*—without understanding Beijing *and* these outlying areas. Historical and cultural attributes, as well as experiences over contested border inter- and intrastate areas, also raised questions about modes of state penetration as well as reactions to them.

When policies linking enormous areas of China required cooperation among two or more political units (be they provinces, prefectures, or counties), a focus on Beijing provided the observer with little, if any, insight or predictive power over outcomes. What was taken as gospel in Beijing was not the case in Heilongjiang or Guizhou. Sometimes this was idiosyncratic, sometimes due to a set of measurable indicators—but regardless, it was a reality that required our understanding and attention.[93] Early studies on the Three Gorges Dam project, extending into current work on infrastructure like high-speed rail,[94] can only be undertaken with this preoccupation in mind. Indeed, the very question about what Chinese state capacity really is can only be examined by thinking of the Chinese body politic as a whole.

This is even more relevant given the current state of globalization. As China embarks on its Belt and Road Initiative (BRI), it is not simply the national-level state-owned enterprises that are on the front lines. The vast majority of foreign direct investment is being done by subnational corporations and the local governments in which they are embedded, lifting the veil and suggesting the fault lines in this little-understood but globally significant policy turn.[95]

Even studies of nationalism benefit from looking at variation in different parts of China. After the 1999 U.S. bombing of the Chinese embassy in Belgrade, it was safe to say that all Chinese were up in arms about the event, but the ways in which protests against the United States unfolded in Beijing, Shenyang, Shanghai, Guangzhou, and Chengdu told us as much about local politics as they did about national policies.[96] Similarly, what people often miss about the significance of the 1989 protests is that they occurred in *every major city* in China. This was a national phenomenon, not simply one that took place in front of the cameras in Tiananmen Square. Moreover, each local government handled the crisis differently—Shanghai, Chengdu, Changchun, and Chongqing being prime examples—which had important local and national ramifications.[97]

The Cyclical Importance of History

It is a cliché to talk about the resonance of history to the ways in which Chinese look at their place in the world. But in addition to the nationalistic uses of Chinese history to explain Chinese backwardness or suspicion of the outside world, history remains instructive.

For example, by going back in time, we can see how patterns of elation, enthusiasm, and subsequent disappointment actually go back as far as contact between the United States and China itself. John Pomfret's *The Beautiful Country and the Middle Kingdom* describes this cycle particularly well.[98] It underscores the fact that what we observe in the relationship at any point in history has already occurred, often many times, and thus decreases the sense of crisis we might be fueling at that moment. It also lays bare the important fact that the U.S.-China relationship is one that has endured over time. It may be, as Harding has argued, "a fragile relationship," but it is not as fragile as we might think, and history is replete with lessons on how to improve upon it.[99]

Jeremy Wallace has also raised an important point: engagement, well into its fourth decade, allows us to revisit some of the earlier works on China in order to mine their conclusions as secondary data from which to demonstrate change and continuity.[100] This gives the study of China a longitudinal dimension that contains a multitude of lessons, insights, and policy recommendations.

History is useful at a somewhat "meta" level as well. For many, the things that initially attracted them to China, but got lost along the way as China evolved over this period, have come back with a vengeance. For example, the ways in which China's leaders shaped Marxism to suit Chinese conditions (quite apart from the empty sloganeering of, say, "socialism with Chinese characteristics") or how Chinese society was mobilized for political campaigns during the Mao era lost their bearings during the late 1990s and early 2000s. They are, however, making a comeback and have been captured by a new generation of young scholars (and reenergized some older ones) eager to dust off these concepts and engage them in fascinating new ways.[101] Furthermore, these can be deployed in comparisons with governance structures, social movements, and the power of ideas to help us understand them in non-China contexts.[102]

... And Two Things We Have Unlearned About China

Despite the extraordinary trove of knowledge and scholarship made possible over these forty years of engagement, there are at least two areas that have been somewhat undermined by the richness of data and institutionalized incentives within the scholarly profession: "Pekingology" and our ability to understand and analyze China as a singular unit of analysis.

Pekingology

Perhaps not surprisingly, given the sheer amount of information that is now available on China, one of the analytical tools that has been dulled during this time period is the ability to read between the lines in those areas for which there is little information—the political "black boxes," such as succession, national security decision making, and deeper intraparty deliberations. A handful of China watchers (Joseph Fewsmith, Alice Lyman Miller, and Cheng Li, for example) serve as invaluable resources into making sense of contemporary Chinese court politics. But the type of approach that is required is one that is often supplanted by the more available and less frustratingly muddy data that can be used to follow other scholarly lines of inquiry, while neglecting this more difficult parsing of elite politics. It is perhaps ironic, then, that as China continues to close itself off to direct access to individuals and documents for foreign researchers, these Pekingological tools might make a comeback—necessitating a shift in scholarship that the current incentives in academia do not favor.[103]

"China," Unmodified

Finally, when one looks back at the scholarship of the 1980s—Harding, Lieberthal, Oksenberg, Lampton, and, more recently, David Shambaugh[104]—especially among those scholars with one foot in (or aspirations to join) the policy world, one is struck by the extraordinary skills they demonstrated in aggregating their vast amounts of knowledge to describe and analyze China as a whole. Of course, they were able to go into detail and focus on particular aspects of China as the situation saw fit, but they were also capable of corralling all they knew into one big picture. Many scholars today are at a disadvantage in following this model. Part of the problem is that these earlier scholars made it look *easy*, thereby masking their own talents in accomplishing this difficult task. Another part of the problem is that we are now aware of so many more moving parts that such an aggregation poses a greater challenge than it did in, say, 1985.[105] Nevertheless, it is an important skill to master, both in terms of where our own specific areas of knowledge fit in, but also as a vehicle for communicating as public intellectuals outside the rarified halls of China scholarship. One way to think about this is that everybody in China is bilingual: they speak *Putonghua* and they speak their local *fangyan*. Those of us in the China field need to aspire to do the same with regard to our knowledge of China.

✳ ✳ ✳

A little knowledge can be a dangerous thing. I have argued that under the era of engagement, we have learned a tremendous amount about China. The political constraints that are emerging in both China and the United States threaten to curtail this important mission. There is a tendency to divide people with strong opinions about China into two camps: the "panda huggers" (or the "red team") and the "dragon slayers" (or the "blue team"). These are biases that have been mercifully exiled to the periphery of the China studies field but are increasingly being mainstreamed as labels to differentiate one group from the other. Commitment to engagement is increasingly seen as a characteristic weakness of the panda huggers. This is a dangerous distinction, not simply because it marginalizes a group of people whose collective body of work has expanded the universe of knowledge about China in ways that would have been unimaginable at the time of Nixon's 1972 visit. It is also dangerous because, regardless of whether one sees China as a threat, a nuanced understanding of the People's Republic is absolutely necessary in the pursuit of policies that are beneficial to the United States. In *The Godfather Part II*, Michael Corleone warns us, "Keep your friends close, but your enemies closer." The China hawks may well wish to consider this—and, in doing so, inevitably secure a better appreciation for China's complexity, complicating the good and softening the bad.

NOTES

1. I would like to thank David M. (Mike) Lampton, Terry Lautz, Anne Thurston, Stan Rosen, Madelyn Ross, and Ezra Vogel for comments on earlier drafts of this chapter and Huang Yufan for his editorial assistance. I want to thank all the participants at the November 2018 Wingspread conference (Five Decades of U.S. Engagement with China: What Have We Learned?) for sharing their experiences and insights accumulated over the past half century. All remaining errors are mine.

2. Lynne Joiner, *Honorable Survivor: Mao's China, McCarthy's America and the Persecution of John S. Service* (Annapolis, MD: Naval Institute Press, 2009).

3. Zachary Cohen and Alex Marquardt, "US Intelligence Warns China Is Using Student Spies to Steal Secrets," CNN, February 1, 2019, https://www.cnn.com/2019/02/01/politics/us-intelligence-chinese-student-espionage/index.html.

4. Jane Perlez, "F.B.I. Bars Some China Scholars from Visiting U.S. over Spying Fears," *New York Times*, April 14, 2019, https://www.nytimes.com/2019/04/14/world/asia/china-academics-fbi-visa-bans.html.

5. Ellen Nakashima, "Top FBI Official Warns of Strategic Threat from China Through Economic and Other Forms of Espionage," *Washington Post*, December 12, 2018, https://www.washingtonpost.com/world/national-security/top-fbi-official-warns-of-strategic-threat-from-china-through-economic-and-other-forms-of-espionage/2018/12/12/38067ee2-fe36-11e8-83c0-b06139e540e5_story.html.

6. Peter S. Goodman and Jane Perlez, "Money and Muscle Pave China's Way to Global Power," *New York Times*, November 25, 2018, https://www.nytimes.com/interactive/2018/11/25/world/asia/china-world-power.html.

7. Adrian Zenz, "'Thoroughly Reforming Them Towards a Healthy Heart Attitude': China's Political Re-education Campaign in Xinjiang," *Central Asian Survey* 38, no. 1 (2018): 102–28.

8. Rosen et al. argue that China is more interested in influence; that is, having target countries refrain from undertaking certain actions rather than saying—or believing—positive things about China. See Rosen et al. (forthcoming).

9. Amy Zegart, "Decades of Being Wrong About China Should Teach Us Something," *The Atlantic*, June 8, 2019, https://www.theatlantic.com/ideas/archive/2019/06/30-years-after-tiananmen-us-doesnt-get-china/591310/.

10. "Secretary Michael R. Pompeo with Shannon Bream of Fox News," U.S. Department of State, April 29, 2020, https://www.state.gov/secretary-michael-r-pompeo-with-shannon-bream-of-fox-news/.

11. Jude Blanchett, *China's New Red Guards: The Return of Radicalism and the Rebirth of Mao Zedong* (New York: Oxford University Press, 2019).

12. Bruce Gilley did seem captivated by it; see Bruce Gilley, *China's Democratic Future: How It Will Happen and Where It Will Lead* (New York: Columbia University Press, 2005).

13. Jonathan Spence, *To Change China: Western Advisors in China* (Boston: Little, Brown, 1969); James C. Thompson, *While China Faced West: American Reformers in Nationalist China, 1928–1937* (Cambridge, MA: Harvard University Press, 1969); James C. Thompson, *While China Faced West: American Reformers in Nationalist China, 1928–1937* (Cambridge, MA: Harvard University Press, 1969).

14. James R. Lilley and Jeffrey Lilley, *China Hands: Nine Decades of Adventure, Espionage, and Diplomacy in Asia* (New York: Public Affairs, 2005).

15. Richard H. Solomon, *Mao's Revolution and Chinese Political Culture* (Berkeley: University of California Press, 1971).

16. Richard Baum, *China Watcher: Confessions of a Peking Tom* (Seattle: University of Washington Press, 2010), 22–28; Richard Baum and Frederick C. Teiwes, *Ssu-Ch'ing: The Socialist Education Movement of 1962–1966* (Berkeley: Center for Chinese Studies, University of California, 1968).

17. "Foreign Broadcast Information Service," Wikipedia, May 13, 2019, https://en.wikipedia.org/wiki/Foreign_Broadcast_Information_Service.

18. This file showed the movements of individual Chinese leaders and when they all converged in a single place at the same time. High-level meetings, which today receive open media coverage, were secret back then and required detective work to uncover.

19. Few Western scholars still use the collection. Most visitors are from mainland China. In 2015, the USC lost access to *neibu* (internal) materials from the mainland, thus decreasing the value of the library for some, although it remains an extraordinary resource.

20. Ezra Vogel, "The First Forty Years of the University Services Centre for China Studies," *The China Journal* 53 (January 2005): 13.

21. The nom de plume for Pierre Ryckmans.

22. Simon Leys, *Chinese Shadows* (New York: Viking Press, 1977), 172.

23. To get a sense of the extraordinary variety of materials and collections that were identified at this time, see Peter Berton and Eugene Wu, *Contemporary China: A Research Guide*, ed. Howard Koch Jr. (Stanford, CA: Hoover Institution, 1967). See also Gordon A. Bennett, "Hong Kong and Taiwan Sources for Research Into the Cultural Revolution Period," *China Quarterly* 36 (October-December 1968): 133–37; and Kenneth Lieberthal, "The Evolution of the China Field in Political Science," in *Contemporary Chinese Politics: New Sources, Methods, and Field Strategies*, eds. Allen Carlson et al. (New York: Cambridge University Press, 2010), 268–70.

24. David M. Lampton, *Paths to Power: Elite Mobility in Contemporary China* (Ann Arbor: Michigan Monographs in China Studies, 1986), 55.

25. Vogel, "The First Forty Years," 1–7.

26. A. Doak Barnett and Ezra F. Vogel, *Cadres, Bureaucracy, and Political Power in Communist China. With a Contribution by Ezra Vogel* (New York: Columbia University Press, 1967) and Baum, *China Watcher*, 236.

27. Vogel, "The First Forty Years," 4.

28. Leys, *Chinese Shadows*, 2

29. Edward Friedman, "Finding the Truth About Rural China," in *My First Trip to China: Scholars, Diplomats and Journalists Reflect on their First Encounters with China*, ed. Liu Kin-ming (Hong Kong: Hong Kong University Press, 2012), 29, 32.

30. Jonathan Mirsky, "From Mao Fan to Counter-Revolutionary in 48 Hours," in *My First Trip to China: Scholars, Diplomats and Journalists Reflect on their First Encounters with China*, ed. Liu Kin-ming (Hong Kong: Hong Kong University Press, 2012), 28.

31. Mark Selden, *The Yenan Way in Revolutionary China* (Cambridge, MA: Harvard University Press, 1974).

32. See Jonathan Mirsky, "Report from the China Sea," New York Review of Books, August 21, 1969.

33. Selden subsequently revised some of his conclusions. See Mark Selden, *China in Revolution: The Yenan Way Revisited* (Armonk, NY: M. E. Sharpe, 1995).

34. Committee of Concerned Asian Scholars, *China!: Inside the People's Republic* (London: Bantam Books, 1972). See also Fabio Lanza, *The End of Concern: Maoist China, Activism, and Asian Studies* (Durham, NC: Duke University Press, 2017).

35. Baum, *China Watcher*, 238.

36. Harold R. Isaacs, *Scratches on Our Minds: American Images of China and India* (London: Routledge, 1980), xxvii–xxxviii.

37. This new direction in China studies deprived them of jobs and tenure, since research done by CCAS advocates such as Chuck Cell, Michael Gatz, Mitch Meisner, and others was based on faulty data they were given. See, for example, Mitch Meisner, "Dazhai: The Mass Line in Practice," *Modern China* 4, no. 1 (1978): 27–62; for overly supportive analyses of Chinese innovations in various fields, see Mitch Meisner, "The Shenyang Transformer Factory—A Profile," *China Quarterly*, no. 52 (1972): 717–37.

38. Leys, *Chinese Shadows*, 145.

39. Roger Garside, *Coming Alive: China After Mao* (New York: New American Library, 1982); Fox Butterfield, *China: Alive in the Bitter Sea* (London: Coronet, 1983).

40. Andrew G. Walder, "The Transformation of Contemporary China Studies, 1977–2002," in *The Politics of Knowledge: Area Studies and the Disciplines*, ed. David L. Szanton (Berkeley: University of California Press, 2002), 314–40.

41. The Inter-University Program for Chinese Language Studies, based at National Taiwan University from the early 1960s until it moved to Beijing in the late 1990s, was extremely important in offering an advanced language curriculum for several generations of China scholars.

42. Steven W. Mosher, *Broken Earth* (New York: Free Press, 1983).

43. Personal communication, June 2019.

44. Personal communication, June 2019.

45. Harry Harding, "From China, with Disdain: New Trends in the Study of China," *Asian Survey* 22, no. 10 (October 1982): 941.

46. Harding, "From China, with Disdain," 949.

47. Walder, "Contemporary China Studies," 330.

48. Comments at a conference celebrating the work of Kenneth Lieberthal in Ann Arbor, Michigan.

49. Walder, "Contemporary China Studies," 330–31.

50. Walder, "Contemporary China Studies," 333.

51. Walder, "Contemporary China Studies," 332–34.

52. Lu Zhang, *Inside China's Automobile Factories: The Politics of Labor and Worker Resistance* (New York: Cambridge University Press, 2015).

53. Martin K. Dimitrov, *Piracy and the State: The Politics of Intellectual Property Rights in China* (Cambridge: Cambridge University Press, 2012); Andrew Mertha, *The Politics of Piracy: Intellectual Property in Contemporary China* (Ithaca, NY: Cornell Paperbacks, 2007).

54. William Hurst, *Ruling Before the Law: The Politics of Legal Regimes in China and Indonesia* (Cambridge: Cambridge University Press, 2018).

55. William Hurst, *The Chinese Worker After Socialism* (Cambridge: Cambridge University Press, 2012).

56. Amy Hanser, *Service Encounters: Class, Gender, and the Market for Social Distinction in Urban China* (Stanford, CA: Stanford University Press, 2008).

57. Tiantian Zheng, *Red Lights: The Lives of Sex Workers in Postsocialist China* (Minneapolis: University of Minnesota Press, 2009).

58. Blanchett, *China's New Red Guards.*

59. Steve Inskeep and Frank Langfitt, "Analysis: Politics of Natural Disaster in China," NPR, May 13, 2008, https://www.npr.org/templates/story/story.php?storyId=90394707.

60. Andrew Jacobs, "Parents' Grief Turns to Rage at Chinese Officials," *New York Times*, May 28, 2008. https://www.nytimes.com/2008/05/28/world/asia/28quake.html.

61. "Document 9: A ChinaFile Translation," *ChinaFile*, October 30, 2015, http://www.chinafile.com/document-9-chinafile-translation.

62. David M. Lampton, Selina Ho, and Cheng-Chwee Kuik, *Rivers of Iron: Railroads and Chinese Power in Southeast Asia* (Berkeley: University of California Press, 2020).

63. David M. Lampton, ed., *Policy Implementation in Post-Mao China* (Berkeley: University of California Press, 1987).

64. For example, Marc Blecher and Gordon White's book, *Micropolitics in Contemporary China: A Technical Unit During and After the Cultural Revolution* (London: Macmillan, 1980), was based on information provided by a *single* interviewee.

65. Kenneth Lieberthal and Michel Oksenberg, *Policy Making in China: Leaders, Structures, and Processes* (Princeton, NJ: Princeton University Press, 1988). See also, Kenneth Lieberthal and Michel Oksenberg, *Bureaucratic Politics and Chinese Energy Development* (Washington, DC: U.S. Department of Commerce, International Trade Administration, 1986).

66. Andrew Mertha, "'Fragmented Authoritarianism 2.0': Political Pluralization in the Chinese Policy Process," *China Quarterly*, no. 200 (2009): 995–1012; Kjeld Erik Brødsgaard, ed., *Chinese Politics as Fragmented Authoritarianism: Earthquakes, Energy and Environment* (London: Routledge Taylor & Francis Group, 2017).

67. Alice Miller, "The CCP Central Committee's Leading Small Groups," *China Leadership Monitor* 26 (2008): 279–303; Christopher K. Johnson, Scott Kennedy, and Mingda Qiu, "Xi's Signature Governance Innovation: The Rise of Leading Small Groups," Center for Strategic and International Studies, October 17, 2017, https://www.csis.org/analysis/xis-signature-governance-innovation-rise-leading-small-groups; Carol Lee Hamrin, "The Party Leadership System," in *Bureaucracy, Politics, and Decision Making in Post-Mao China*, eds. Kenneth G. Lieberthal and David M. Lampton (Berkeley: University of California Press, 1992), 95–124.

68. Susan L. Shirk, *The Political Logic of Economic Reform in China* (Berkeley: University of California Press, 1993).

69. Daniel C. Lynch, *After the Propaganda State: Media, Politics, and "Thought Work" in Reformed China* (Stanford, CA: Stanford University Press, 1999).

70. Charlotte P. Lee, *Training the Party: Party Adaptation and Elite Training in Reform-Era China* (Cambridge: Cambridge University Press, 2018).

71. David L. Shambaugh, *China's Communist Party: Atrophy and Adaptation* (Berkeley: University of California Press, 2008).

72. Victor C. Shih, *Factions and Finance in China: Elite Conflict and Inflation* (Cambridge: Cambridge University Press, 2009); Cheng Li, *Chinese Politics in the Xi Jinping Era: Reassessing Collective Leadership* (Washington, DC: Brookings Institution Press, 2016).

73. Christian P. Sorace, *Shaken Authority: China's Communist Party and the 2008 Sichuan Earthquake* (Ithaca, NY: Cornell University Press, 2017).

74. Yasheng Huang, *Inflation and Investment Controls in China: The Political Economy of Central Local Relations During the Reform Era* (Cambridge: Cambridge University Press, 1999).

75. Xuezhi Guo, *China's Security State: Philosophy, Evolution, and Politics* (Cambridge: Cambridge University Press, 2012).

76. Michael D. Swaine, *The Military and Political Succession in China: Leadership, Institutions, Beliefs* (Santa Monica, CA: RAND, 1992); and Ellis Joffe, *The Chinese Army After Mao* (Cambridge, MA: Harvard University Press, 1987). See also, inter alia, Alastair I. Johnston, *Cultural Realism: Strategic Culture and Grand Strategy in Chinese History* (Princeton, NJ: Princeton University Press, 1995); Xuezhi Guo, *China's Security State: Philosophy, Evolution, and Politics* (Cambridge: Cambridge University Press, 2012); David L. Shambaugh, *Modernizing China's Military: Progress, Problems, and Prospects* (Berkeley: University of California Press, 2002); M. Taylor Fravel, *Strong Borders, Secure Nation: Cooperation and Conflict in China's Territorial Disputes* (Princeton, NJ: Princeton University Press, 2008); Oriana Skylar Mastro, *The Costs of Conversation: Obstacles to Peace Talks in Wartime* (Ithaca, NY: Cornell University Press, 2019); James C. Mulvenon, *Soldiers of Fortune: The Rise and Fall of the Chinese Military-Business Complex, 1978–1998* (Armonk, NY: M.E. Sharpe, 2001).

77. Thomas E. Ricks, *Fiasco: The American Military Adventure in Iraq, 2003 to 2005* (New York: Penguin Books, 2006).

78. Elizabeth Perry, "Trends in the Study of Chinese Politics: State-Society Relations," *China Quarterly*, no. 139 (September 1994): 709.

79. Dorothy J. Solinger, *Contesting Citizenship in Urban China: Peasant Migrants, the State, and the Logic of the Market* (Berkeley: University of California Press, 1999).

80. Jean Chun Oi, *State and Peasant in Contemporary China: The Political Economy of Village Government* (Berkeley: University of California Press, 1989).

81. Scott Kennedy, *The Business of Lobbying in China* (Cambridge, MA: Harvard University Press, 2005); Jessica C. Teets, *Civil Society Under Authoritarianism: The China Model* (Cambridge: Cambridge University Press, 2014); Timothy Hildebrandt, *Social Organizations and the Authoritarian State in China* (Cambridge: Cambridge University Press, 2013).

82. Anita Chan, *China's Workers Under Assault: The Exploitation of Labor in a Globalizing Economy* (Armonk, NY: M.E. Sharpe, 2001); Ching Kwan Lee, *Against the Law: Labor Protests in China's Rustbelt and Sunbelt* (Berkeley: University of California Press, 2007); Mary Elizabeth Gallagher, *Contagious Capitalism: Globalization and the Politics of Labor in China* (Princeton, NJ: Princeton University Press, 2005); Diana Fu, *Mobilizing Without the Masses: Control and Contention in China* (Cambridge: Cambridge University Press, 2018).

83. Kellee S. Tsai, *Back-Alley Banking: Private Entrepreneurs in China* (Ithaca, NY: Cornell University Press, 2002).

84. Barry Naughton, *Growing Out of the Plan: Chinese Economic Reform, 1978–1993* (New York: Cambridge University Press, 1995); Edward S. Steinfeld, *Forging Reform in China: The Fate of State-Owned Industry* (Cambridge: Cambridge University Press, 1998).

85. Melanie Manion, "When Communist Party Candidates Can Lose, Who Wins? Assessing the Role of Local People's Congresses in the Selection of Leaders in China," *China Quarterly* 195 (September 2008): 607–30; Anne F. Thurston, *Muddling Toward Democracy: Political Change in Grass Roots China* (Washington, DC: U.S. Institute of Peace, 1998); Gregory Distelhorst and Yue Hou, "Constituency Service Under Nondemocratic Rule: Evidence from China," *Journal of Politics* 79, no. 3 (2017): 1024–40; and Carl F. Minzner, "*Xinfang*: An Alternative to Formal Chinese Legal Institutions," *Stanford Journal of International Law* 42 (2006): 103–79.

86. Andrew G. Walder, *Zouping in Transition: The Process of Reform in Rural North China* (Cambridge, MA: Harvard University Press, 1998); see also Marc J. Blecher and Vivienne Shue, *Tethered Deer: Government and Economy in a Chinese County* (Stanford, CA: Stanford University Press, 1996).

87. Ralph Thaxton, *Catastrophe and Contention in Rural China: Mao's Great Leap Forward Famine and the Origins of Righteous Resistance in Da Fo Village* (Cambridge: Cambridge University Press, 2008); Ralph Thaxton, *Force and Contention in Contemporary China: Memory and Resistance in the Long Shadow of the Catastrophic Past* (New York: Cambridge University Press, 2016).

88. Kevin J. O'Brien and Lianjiang Li, *Rightful Resistance in Rural China* (Cambridge: Cambridge University Press, 2006).

89. Henry Kissinger, *White House Years* (Boston: Little, Brown, 1979), 1063.

90. Conversation with Michel Oksenberg, May 1998. See, for example, Andrew G. Walder, *Zouping in Transition: The Process of Reform in Rural North China* (Cambridge, MA: Harvard University Press, 1998).

91. Ezra F. Vogel, *Canton Under Communism: Programs and Politics in a Provincial Capital, 1949–1968* (Cambridge, MA: Harvard University Press, 1969); Anita Chan, Richard Madsen, and Jonathan Unger, *Chen Village: Revolution to Globalization*, 3rd ed. (Berkeley: University of California Press, 2009).

92. Emily T. Yeh, *Taming Tibet: Landscape Transformation and the Gift of Chinese Development* (Ithaca, NY: Cornell University Press, 2013); Gardner Bovingdon, *The Uyghurs: Strangers in Their Own Land* (New York: Columbia University Press, 2010); James A. Millward, *Violent Separatism in Xinjiang: A Critical Assessment* (Washington, DC: East-West Center Washington, 2004).

93. For example, local decision makers had to know which central policies were the crucial ones and which targets they had to meet. See Stanley Rosen, "Restoring Key Secondary Schools in Post-Mao China: The Politics of Competition and Educational Quality," in *Policy Implementation in Post-Mao China*, ed. David M. Lampton (Berkeley: University of California Press, 1987), 321–53.

94. Lampton et al., *Rivers of Iron*.

95. Min Ye, *The Belt Road and Beyond: State-Mobilized Globalization in China: 1998–2018* (New York: Cambridge University Press, 2020).

96. Peter Hays Gries, *China's New Nationalism: Pride, Politics, and Diplomacy* (Berkeley: University of California Press, 2004).

97. Michel Oksenberg, Lawrence R. Sullivan, and Marc Lambert, *Beijing Spring, 1989: Confrontation and Conflict: The Basic Documents* (Armonk, NY: M.E. Sharpe, 1990); Louisa Lim, *The People's Republic of Amnesia: Tiananmen Revisited* (New York: Oxford University Press, 2015); Jay Lieberman, *A Democracy Movement Journal: Changchun, China 1989* (CreateSpace, 2015).

98. John Pomfret, *The Beautiful Country and the Middle Kingdom: America and China, 1776 to the Present* (New York: Henry Holt, 2016).

99. Harry Harding, *A Fragile Relationship: The United States and China Since 1972* (Washington, DC: Brookings Institution Press, 1992).

100. Personal communication, August 2019.

101. Elizabeth J. Perry, "Reclaiming the Chinese Revolution," *Journal of Asian Studies* 67, no. 4 (2008): 1147–64; Neil J. Diamant and Xiaocai Feng, "Textual Anxiety: Reading (and Misreading) the Draft Constitution in China, 1954," *Journal of Cold War Studies* 20, no. 3 (2018): 153–79; Mark W. Frazier, *Socialist Insecurity: Pensions and the Politics of Uneven Development in China* (Ithaca, NY: Cornell University Press, 2010).

102. Christian P. Sorace, Ivan Franceschini, and Nicholas Loubere, eds., *Afterlives of Chinese Communism: Political Concepts from Mao To Xi* (Acton, Australian Capital Territory: ANU Press, 2019).

103. Roderick MacFarquhar, "On Photographs," *China Quarterly*, no. 46 (1971): 289–307.

104. Harry Harding, *China's Second Revolution: Reform After Mao* (Washington, DC: Brookings Institution, 1987); Kenneth Lieberthal, *Governing China: From Revolution Through Reform* (New York: Norton, 1995).

105. Big-picture takes on China are not generally published in the disciplinary journals scholars need for tenure, promotion, or even to exist in political science departments of any standing. Much of this has to do with the professional incentive structures within the discipline.

CHAPTER 5

THE AMERICAN DREAM AND
THE CHINA DREAM

Unpeaceful Evolutions

RICHARD MADSEN

Stephen K. Bannon, the former chairman of Breitbart News and onetime chief strategist in Donald Trump's White House, has come to believe that the United States is at war with China. The war, he alleges, is first of all an economic war, but also an information war. Not yet, but possibly inevitably, it will become a kinetic war. These wars are the result of the rise of China as a totalitarian, mercantilist system. The rise of this malevolent China has been aided by globalist American elites who rely on their allies in the mainstream media and academia to convince the public that China is not a threat. But ordinary Americans, like those in the upper Midwest, get it. China has caused the hollowing out of their industries and contributed, at least indirectly, Bannon tells us, to the current opioid crisis. The confrontation is on a broad scale and between two different systems. The problem is not merely political but cultural as well. "One thing Chinese fear more than America . . . they fear Christianity more than anything,"[1] Bannon asserts. The United States should ally with strong Christian countries, like Russia, to confront the cultural-political threat from China.[2] One of us is going to be a hegemon in 25 or 30 years, says Bannon. The only acceptable outcome for the United States is total victory. Because of President Trump, America is winning the war.

Although Bannon left the Trump administration after only seven months, he apparently continued to exert considerable informal influence. Clear echoes of his rhetoric (along with the ideas of like-minded conservative think tank leaders such as Michael Pillsbury)[3] appeared in Vice President Pence's speech to the Hudson Institute on October 4, 2018, which was seen by many as the definitive official American statement on U.S.-China relations. "China has sought to advance its strategic interests across the world, with growing intensity and sophistication," Pence says. "Yet previous administrations all but ignored China's actions—and in many cases, they abetted them. But those days are over. Under President Trump's leadership, the United States of America has been defending our interests with renewed American strength."

Pence cited not only China's economic aggression but also military aggression, much of it based on stolen technology from America. He also cited religious repression of Tibetan Buddhists and Uighur Muslims and especially emphasized the problems facing China's Christians—"For China's Christians, these are desperate times, " he claimed. Finally, he warned about China's information warfare: "To that end, Beijing has mobilized covert actors, front groups, and propaganda outlets to shift Americans' perceptions of Chinese politics. As a senior career member of our intelligence community recently told me, what the Russians are doing pales in comparison to what the Chinese are doing across this country." Pence concluded, "These and other actions, taken as a whole, constitute an intensifying effort to shift American public opinion and public policy away from the America First leadership of President Donald Trump. But our message to China's rulers is this: This president will not back down—and the American people will not be swayed."[4]

In the give and take of bureaucratic and interest group politics, coupled with the mercurial personality of President Trump, this hyperbolic rhetoric did not necessarily translate into policy, at least not fully. But the Pence statement does seem to resonate strongly with the real sentiments of Trump's base of supporters, many of whom must feel that Bannon's rhetoric and Pence's speech put into words what they would have liked to say themselves. Pence's words reflect but also help to constitute a vision, a narrative about where America has stood in relation to China and where that relationship is headed. In the present configuration of American power, this way of thinking and feeling about China has gained hegemony, an unavoidable part of the environment for policy discussions even in the Biden administration. Plenty of people disagree with the narrative, of course, but the disagreements convey a defensive tone. The terms of debate are being shaped by the hegemonic rhetoric, which recycles many old themes that have not been prominent since the Cold War.[5]

How did we get to this point? Twenty-five years ago, I published a book called *China and the American Dream*,[6] about how the stories that Americans and Chinese used to frame their understandings of each other had developed over the previous quarter century. The book was an exercise in the comparative sociology of culture—my specialty—tinged with some moral philosophy, which I had also studied. In the interim since the book was published, both China and America have changed, and so have their narratives. Drawing upon themes from that book and using the kind of analysis it contained, my aim here is to reflect on the past twenty-five years since the book was published, first with reference to the development of China in the American Dream and then with reference to America in the China Dream.

American Narratives of China

An underlying assumption in *China and the American Dream*—learned from the philosopher Charles Taylor[7]—was that our understanding of someone else is closely connected with our understanding of ourself. Mutual understanding is a process that shapes self-understandings on both sides. American debates about China have been connected with debates about American identity, and the converse is true for Chinese debates about America. Thus, in the late 1960s, contending American visions of China as a Red Menace or a Troubled Modernizer or a Revolutionary Redeemer were connected to concerns about what kind of society America was or should be.

If, for instance, China was indeed a Red Menace, then the nation needed to mobilize itself for war against an implacable enemy. This could entail curtailing freedom of speech and association and casting suspicion on China experts in academia and government, as in the McCarthy era. It could also justify the expansion of the national security state, along with the Indochina war.

The middle-class and middle-aged academic, religious, and political leaders who organized national discussions on China in the mid-1960s—which led to the establishment of the National Committee on U.S.-China Relations[8]— were concerned about preserving American institutions of representative democracy. These concerns shaped their understanding of China as a Troubled Modernizer that hopefully would settle down eventually to become a society run by rational bureaucrats and, carried along by the inevitable forces of modernization, would finally develop the whole ensemble of liberal modernity: a free market economy, a democratic government, and a culture based on scientific reason and respect for individual rights.

On the other hand, many young adults, especially graduate students in Asian studies at elite universities at the time, were inspired by critiques of their own country's structural racism and militaristic imperialism, suspicious of lies told by political and economic elites, and fearful of being drafted into a senseless war. In organizations like the Committee of Concerned Asian Scholars, which is described in considerable detail in chapter 4 by Andrew Mertha, they helped create an alternative vision of Maoist China as a Revolutionary Redeemer representing the hopes of people aspiring to overthrow the oppressive structures of Western capitalism and imperialism.

These visions of China were expressed in terms of grand narratives, which I call "myths," the term used in the sociology of religion for sacred stories that called for faith and commitment as much as reason. I tried to show how the narrative of China as a Troubled Modernizer became hegemonic in American public life. That doesn't mean that the other narratives ceased to exist. As my colleague and mentor Robert Bellah used to say, nothing is ever lost when it comes to culture. Older narratives about China continued and still had their proponents, but they weren't the hegemonic mainstream (which of course also contained many different voices and interests) and were usually on the defensive against the mainstream position.

At that time, I contended that the Troubled Modernizer narrative became predominant as the result of a confluence of ideas and sentiments from different sources. The evolving ideas of professional China scholars were one source. But despite the conceit of us academics that our ideas are determinative of our society's cultural trends, the ideas that develop in universities and think tanks only become powerfully alive when conjoined with other cultural forces. In the 1960s and 1970s, these included circles of religious believers inspired by, in the case of Catholics, the Second Vatican Council's calls for worldwide cultural dialogue, by the commitment of the National Council of Churches to a broad-based ecumenism, and by evangelical Christians' hopes for new missionary opportunities overseas. They also included business leaders eager to open new markets, artists eager to participate in a confluence of cultures, and of course not least, geopoliticians like Nixon and Kissinger, who saw a rapprochement with China as a key to balancing the influence of the Soviet Union. Adding to this was the media, which was fascinated by the emergence of a big new story about China. These various cultural strands came together and were at least partly fused in Nixon's breakthrough trip to China in February 1972, one of the great media spectacles of that era. The effect is akin to the denouement of a play, when the various strands of a narrative all come together to produce a memorable scene that sears into the imagination the defining message of the story.[9]

The story of China as a Troubled Modernizer, albeit embracing many variants and nuances, gained hegemony as a broadly shared unifying narrative that framed a wide variety of initiatives toward China. After the introduction of Deng Xiaoping's reforms and the normalization of U.S.-China relations in 1979, this narrative became a dominant framework for American engagement with China.

All grand narratives have blind spots, and this one was no exception. The blind spots were exposed with the military crackdown against student demonstrators on June 4, 1989. I initially thought that the narrative would be shattered by that event. But subsequent history convinced me that it was only shaken deeply rather than shattered completely. But we still needed to find new narratives. This did not happen quickly. But now a new narrative—or rather a new version of an old narrative—has finally risen to dominance. It is not the one I would have hoped for. The new/old narrative seems to be a revised version of the old Red Menace narrative—or (though I hate to say it) perhaps the Yellow

Menace narrative, because racism is now such a prominent part of it. Another potential alternative might have been one evolved from the Revolutionary Redeemer narrative, but that was simply not viable.[10]

The Path from the Early 1990s to Now

Predominant, unifying narratives do not just gradually evolve. Different strands of the narrative arising from different institutions and different social strata begin to change, and major changes in the dominant narrative take place when many different strands come together, not through the skilled hand of a playwright, but in response to some widely shared spectacular public event. In all these strands, changing understandings of China are connected with changing concerns about American identity. Let us now review milestones in the paths taken by some of these narrative strands from the early 1990s down to the present day.

Outrage and Optimism: Economic Engagement and Human Rights

During the 1992 presidential election campaign, candidate Bill Clinton denounced President George H. W. Bush for having coddled the Chinese rulers after the brutal crackdown on protesters around Tiananmen Square. But the U.S. presidential campaign took place around the same time as Deng Xiaoping's April 1992 Southern Tour that later spurred the Chinese economy toward renewed marketization and openness to outside investment. The economy began a rapid growth that amazed Western pundits who had assumed that Tiananmen would bring about the end of economic reform. New economic openness brought in new opportunities for American businesses to invest in export processing ventures in China's expanding special economic zones. Economic engagement with China continued apace, only somewhat constrained by the requirement, imposed by Congress after Tiananmen, that China's most favored nation (MFN) trading status had to be renewed every year.

The relocation to China of industries like textiles and furniture caused the collapse of these industries in the American South—especially in North Carolina. But the overall economic effect of trade with China seemed positive. Following Clinton's election to the presidency, the American economy continued to grow. Some concern was expressed about the suppression of human rights in China, especially during the annual congressional debates over MFN, and there was some hand wringing in the mainstream media about China's repressive political system, but the positive economic news predominated. MFN was always renewed.

The luncheon I attended (at the invitation of the National Committee on U.S.-China Relations) for Jiang Zemin at the Beverly Hills Hilton during his state visit in 1997 is an example of the somewhat dissonant prevailing moods. Inside the Hilton, CEOs of Ford, General Motors, General Electric, Boeing, etc., the cream of American industry, sat at the head table, with Rupert Murdoch, the man who brought them all together and organized them to pay for the lunch, sitting in the middle. At the lower tables, where I was, were prominent businessmen and a few women from throughout the West Coast. Outside, on the street in the hot sun, without a ticket to the exclusive event, was my wife, together with a large assemblage of protestors advocating a wide variety of human rights causes. The positive feelings of the well-dressed business and political elites superseded the voices of the scruffy protestors. While China was demonstrating a new form of authoritarian capitalism, American business and political leaders could still hold out hope that increased economic prosperity would eventually lead to increased openness to democracy. And in any case, from their point of view, the economic relationship with China was good for the American economy—and themselves.

Behind this public optimism, however, was an ominous trend: economic inequality in America was accelerating. Real weekly earnings for those in the bottom half of the income distribution were flat, although the decline in incomes for men was balanced by a slight rise in those for women. College degree holders were still seeing modest increases in their incomes, but the only significant increases were for those with a postgraduate education.[11] Meanwhile, returns to capital mainly benefiting the top 1 percent began to take off after 1993 and have positively soared in the 2000s.[12] Economic anxiety was beginning to fester among the working classes, especially among men.

How did this change affect American perceptions of China?

Negative Narratives: Immigration

The 1990s were a time of increasing immigration to the United States, not just from Latin America but from China as well. The Chinese influx was dramatized in 1993, when the *Golden Venture*, a rusty cargo ship whose squalid hold was packed with 286 illegal immigrants from Fujian Province, ran aground near Rockaway Beach in New York City. Ten people drowned while swimming to shore. The rest were detained by the Immigration and Naturalization Service, and most spent years in custody. (Previous immigrants had been treated to catch and release after promises to appear later in immigration court. This was the first time that large numbers of illegal immigrants were subject to prolonged detention—a practice that was taken to a new level by the Trump administration.) The grounding of the *Golden Venture* was a major news story that helped set in motion a narrative strand about a dangerous influx of alien Chinese. In this narrative, China was "not sending its best." These were illegal immigrants of lower-class Chinese pouring into American cities, usually through arrangements made by a well-organized Chinese underworld.[13]

The narrative was based on some facts. The CIA estimated that about 100,000 such Chinese immigrants were arriving every year during the 1990s. (After the 2000s, the numbers of impoverished immigrants slowly decreased as the Chinese economy began to flourish, but as an article in the *New York Times* on October 16, 2018, about the death of a Chinese prostitute in Flushing, Queens, vividly relates, such immigration has certainly not stopped.[14])

But the narrative also went well beyond facts. It included a powerful emotional current based in concern about the changing demographics of America.[15] It drew on fears that supposedly traditional American values were being challenged by cultural diversity and by the critical academics and their elite sponsors who embraced such multiculturalism.

In fact, the influx of illegal Chinese aliens was accompanied by an increasing number of legal immigrants, too—students and visiting scholars, scientists, and entrepreneurs. Besides recent immigrants, the wider Asian American community was becoming more prosperous and more visible. The changes in the American population, especially in major cities, proved upsetting to some American whites. For example, there have been angry objections to the use of Chinese signs in the Los Angeles area of Monterey Park and an attempt to pass an English-only law, though it failed.[16] Some were concerned also about the high percentage of Asian students entering the University of California and other major universities. (On my campus, Asians and Asian Americans constitute almost 50 percent of the student body. Only about 20 percent are white.) For populations whose incomes remained flat, the arrival of visible foreigners could provoke unease, sometimes tending toward outright racism. This fed the narrative strand about a developing threat to American values posed by the presence of Chinese in this country, which gained power because of its resonance with other concerns about all forms of immigration, especially from non-European countries.

Elite Complicity

The narrative was reinforced in the late 1990s by the public scandal of "Chinagate," labeled by the online right-wing *Independent Sentinel* as "the worst scandal in American history."[17] Charlie Trie, a Chinese American restaurant owner in Little Rock, had befriended Bill Clinton when he was governor of Arkansas. In 1996, Trie donated $450,000 to Clinton's legal defense fund and later $220,000 to the Democratic National Committee (DNC). He then sent a letter to Clinton advising him to exercise restraint in confronting

Chinese military exercises against Taiwan. The money seems to have come from a variety of Chinese sources, some funneled through Macau. It was eventually returned, and Trie was convicted of violating campaign finance laws.

A second Chinese businessman named Johnny Chung, who, like Trie, had been born in Taiwan, had managed to ingratiate himself with the Washington elite and made forty-nine separate visits to the White House between 1994 and 1996. He donated $366,000 to the DNC, some of which, it was later discovered, came from persons connected with Chinese military intelligence. The money was eventually returned, and Chung was convicted of financial crimes and violation of campaign finance laws.

John Huang was another fundraiser for the DNC and a frequent visitor to the White House. He raised nearly $3.4 million for the DNC, half of which had to be returned because of questionable sourcing.

Maria Hsia was a Los Angeles–based fundraiser for Vice President Al Gore and a business associate of John Huang. She organized $100,000 in campaign contributions channeled through the Buddhist nuns at the Hsi Lai Temple in Los Angeles, a branch of the Taiwan-based Buddha's Light Mountain. The contributions were later proved illegal.

These cases provoked congressional investigations and received widespread news coverage. One fairly spectacular event was the testimony of a group of exotic-looking Buddhist nuns testifying to Congress that they did not know there was anything wrong with their campaign contributions. The media dubbed this collection of scandals Chinagate and connected them to a series of allegations about Clinton cash.[18]

Thus, another narrative strand was developing, which gained power through its resonance with other spreading concerns, in an era of increasing economic polarization, about the corruptibility of American politics. Sinister rich Chinese were channeling money through easily corrupted American elites for the purpose of swaying American politics in the interests of the Chinese Communists. The Clintons were seen as a prime example of these corrupted elites, although there were certainly others connected with the business and political establishments. Most of the protagonists in these scandals were not recent immigrants but longtime American citizens. Moreover, most were actually from Taiwan with dubious allegiance to Chinese Communism. Their specific political allegiances were overridden by the fact that they were ethnically Chinese. This resonated with the gradual emergence of such racist narratives as the Yellow Menace.

Espionage

These resonances were reinforced by espionage concerns. In 1999, the Cox Committee of the U.S. House of Representatives issued a "Report on U.S.

National Security and Military/Commercial Concerns with the People's Republic of China," alleging that China had acquired design information on America's most advanced nuclear weapons and ballistic missiles. This had been done through some combination of direct espionage, thorough study of unclassified information, and manipulation of help offered by American companies to improve the reliability of commercial satellite launches.[19] The issue took a dramatic turn later that year when Wen-ho Lee, a Taiwanese American scientist at the Los Alamos National Laboratory, was indicted for downloading data about advanced nuclear weapons design and giving it to the Chinese government. He was arrested and held in solitary confinement for nine months. The case was a major item in the press. A typical headline from the *New York Times* was: "China Stole Nuclear Secrets for Bombs, Aides Say." In the end, all charges against Wen-ho Lee were dropped for lack of evidence, except for one of mishandling classified information. The judge in the case issued a strong apology to Lee for the way he had been treated and denounced the government for its abuse of power. In his memoir, *My Country Versus Me*, Lee contended that he had been a victim of racial profiling. He was after all a native Taiwanese, not from the People's Republic of China (PRC), and other non-Chinese scientists had been only lightly disciplined for similar lapses.[20]

But perhaps the dramatic and public indictment of a sinister Asian made a greater public impact than his acquittal. In any case, the following decade witnessed a string of espionage cases involving Asian scientists and engineers, most of them Chinese, but also others of Korean and other Asian ethnicities. All were accused of giving classified defense information to China. Most cases resulted in convictions. While this group did not receive such widespread media notoriety as Wen-ho Lee, their cases nonetheless reinforced the public narrative that, albeit falsely, had begun with Lee: Chinese agents, including Chinese Americans, were infiltrating our scientific establishments to steal secrets for China. And as Mike Pence would later assert, Chinese military might was largely based on stolen technology from America. This narrative strand gained special traction in the American defense community.[21] Once again, it was based on some facts but infused with invidious stereotypes that gave it a powerful emotional charge.

Persecution of Christians

A different narrative strand gained momentum in America's evangelical Protestant community. The 1990s were an exciting time for American Christians concerned about China, especially evangelical Protestants. The Chinese government continued to bar foreign missionaries, but American Christians were engaged in a vigorous business of smuggling Bibles and entering China under the guise of English teachers, business investors, or tourists. Their exploits required some derring-do and made good material for sermons and promotional videos among the extensive Christian broadcasting networks. These stories from the underground inspired devout Christians to donate money to the cause of converting China.

Meanwhile, the growth of evangelical Protestant Christianity in China had been truly spectacular. In 1949, China had less than a million Protestants, and they had been severely persecuted under Mao, particularly during the Cultural Revolution. Since Deng Xiaoping's reforms, the numbers have grown exponentially and now surpass fifty million.[22] Beginning in the early 1980s, the Chinese government allowed the limited reopening of churches, although only under the control of the Protestant Three-Self Patriotic Movement and the Chinese Patriotic Catholic Association—mass association transmission belts from the Communist Party's United Front Work Department. But most of the growth was among unregistered house churches that operated outside the legal framework of the government. Leaders of these churches were regularly subject to arrest.[23]

Coupled with the successful growth of Christianity, the production of Christian martyrs inspired American Christian missionaries to redouble their efforts to make China a Christian nation. Through organizations like the ChinaAid Association, based in Texas and founded by Bob Fu, a student activist turned Christian convert and house church leader, the American media was provided with well-researched reports on the persecution of Chinese Christians and atrocities of forced abortions because of the one-child policy.[24] Fu had gained asylum in the United States with the help of lobbying from the National Association of Evangelicals after having been briefly imprisoned in China for his Christian activities and threatened after his wife became pregnant without getting the proper permission under the one-child policy. Some of these stories made it into the mainstream secular media, but even more circulated through the magazines and cable broadcast media that link together evangelical Christian communities throughout the United States. Similar initiatives were taken by Catholics, notably through the Connecticut-based Cardinal Kung Foundation that broadcast the cause of the underground church that refused to submit to the Chinese Patriotic Catholic Association.[25]

For both Protestants and Catholics, these efforts were seen in some degree as in opposition to liberal Protestants and Catholics and their secular allies and became connected to America's culture wars. Secular human rights organizations like Freedom House advocated for the rights of persecuted Chinese Christians, but the main energy came from evangelical Christians themselves. Thus began another narrative strand: the Chinese people were ripe for the harvest of Christian conversion, but they were being persecuted by an atheist government. The persecution was being ignored and even abetted by liberal secular American elites who were prepared to overlook Chinese atrocities because their interests were somehow aligned with the Chinese government.

Thus, by the year 2000, in different social sectors and from different parts of American political and cultural traditions, several distinct narrative strands telling a story about China as a threat to fundamental American values and interests were developing. The strands arose out of real events and real acts done by some Chinese people and the Chinese government. But they touched different concerns among different sectors of American society. Some were worried that classic American values, based on an Anglo-European tradition, were being challenged by a multiculturalism brought about by invasions of immigrants from the Far East as well as the Global South—people who were "not the best" and were connected with criminal smugglers and dangerous spies. Others worried that basic human rights were being sacrificed for the sake of money and power, not only in China but among political and corporate elites who were benefiting from the rich and powerful in China. Others saw a story about a battle between American Christian values and the Chinese forces of global atheistic secularism. The stories were separate, carried by the media of different communities in the American community of communities and nurtured by face-to-face communication in the voluntary associations of those communities. The narratives carried a vision of China as a dangerous competitor of the United States, but they were coming from different directions and had not coalesced into a hegemonic public narrative.

Fearful Narratives

As noted earlier, such a coalescence often requires some sort of spectacular public event to bring the public narratives together. At the beginning of the new millennium, the downing of the American EP-3 electronic surveillance plane off the coast of Hainan Island was one candidate for such an event. The aircraft was flying in the South China Sea about seventy miles off the coast of Hainan within China's exclusive economic zone, an area in which, according to the United Nations Law of the Sea, the coastal country has exclusive fishing and mining rights but which is open to freedom of navigation. The Chinese government would contend that this freedom of navigation does not extend to vessels conducting electronic spying. Typically, Chinese fighter aircraft closely followed American surveillance aircraft on these missions. On April 1, 2001, a Chinese jet clipped the wing of the EP-3. The Chinese jet crashed and its pilot was killed. The EP-3 was crippled and forced to land at a Chinese military base on Hainan Island, where its crew was taken into custody. Thus began the first major diplomatic struggle of the new George W. Bush administration. Both sides offered angry denunciations of the incident. The American side claimed that the Chinese pilot had been reckless; the Chinese said that the American air-craft had veered into the Chinese jet (and declared the Chinese pilot a national hero) and, besides, the Americans had no right to be there anyway. The Chinese demanded an apology as a precondition to the release of the Americans, lead-ing to controversy within the United States over how far to go in apologiz-ing to China.[26] After much negotiation, the American government issued an ambiguously worded letter expressing "regret and sorrow" but no apology. The Americans were released, and their aircraft was returned dismantled and in pieces. The public anger at China in the United States marked the beginning of a new narrative in which China was seen once more as a hostile adversary.

Six months later, on September 11, 2001, this public discourse about China was drowned out by the attack on the twin towers. For the next nine years, the public narrative that saw China as a national adversary was eclipsed by the Global War on Terrorism. The various anti-China narrative strands that had begun in the 1990s did not coalesce into a larger public narrative.

But the narrative strands continued to develop, now abetted by a background context of increasing popular anxieties about American national identity. First, the United States failed to achieve any clear victory in the War on Terror despite more than a trillion dollars spent and thousands of lives lost. Especially com-pared with the heady days at the end of the Cold War, America's standing in the world appeared to be on the decline. Second, and more subtly, economic polar-ization in the United States steadily increased. After 2003, wealth inequality began a rapid acceleration. By 2008, it had reached a level not seen for almost a hundred years.[27]

Part of the rising inequality came from what economists have been calling the "China shock." In 2000, after a contentious debate, the Clinton administra-tion had succeeded in having Congress grant China permanent normal trade relations status (a better-sounding name than MFN),[28] thus clearing the way for China's accession to the World Trade Organization in 2001. For American busi-ness, the result of this accession was a more stable environment for investment in China, which rapidly accelerated the use of China as a platform for low-cost manufacturing of American products. Major American corporations profited from this arrangement, and American consumers benefited from low-cost products from China. But American workers in many manufacturing indus-tries, especially in the upper Midwest were devastated. The overall American economy grew as the result of the increased China trade but with long-lasting localized effects that most economists had not foreseen, as Barry Naughton describes in some detail in chapter 7. Standard economic theory would have assumed that workers from industries disrupted by such trade relations would find new and perhaps even better jobs in the rising economy made possible by this trade. This assumes that workers who lost their jobs would be willing and able to relocate and get retrained for new jobs. But that did not happen, especially in the old midwestern manufacturing centers. Many communities were plagued by persistent unemployment and social maladies such as drug abuse. The social and economic dysfunction affected the American Dream of upward mobility, which continued to be strong in coastal areas but remained low in Middle America.[29]

The relocation of low-wage manufacturing to China was a contributing cause—economists estimate that about 10 percent of the manufacturing job losses were due to China trade—but there were many other causes, too, including new technologies, tax policies, and a lack of investment in education and social support that could rebuild communities and facilitate transition to new industries. Whatever the relationship with China, wise and humane corporate and political leadership could and should have done much more to mitigate inequality, alleviate the pain of economic dislocation, and preserve the American Dream of upward mobility in a middle-class society. But for many workers in the American heartland, the China shock was vivid and visceral. Many of the newly disadvantaged came to see China as an obvious villain in their plight.

Nonetheless, the various narratives about China continued to develop along their own lines. Leaders of major American financial institutions waxed bullish on China even as they continued to advocate reform of its fiscal system. Henry Paulson, the head of Goldman Sachs who became President Bush's treasury secretary, was a prime example. Having visited China more than seventy times when he was chairman of Goldman Sachs, Paulson had warm relations with top Chinese elites. Although not uncritical, his views on China's reforms were very positive, and he placed strong hope on U.S. engagement with China. During the Bush administration, he initiated and led the U.S.-China Strategic and Economic Dialogue. (However, now he has changed his tune. At the end of 2018, he was warning about an economic iron curtain and an emerging cold war between the United States and China.[30]) The mainstream media, while reporting serious problems in China, especially treatment of dissidents and religious and ethnic minorities, seemed to see U.S.-China relations on balance in a favorable light.

Overall, American opinion toward China seemed cautiously positive. In 2006, 52 percent of Americans reported a favorable opinion of China, whereas only 29 percent reported an unfavorable opinion.[31] But in 2008, a spectacular set of events began to bring different strands of the China narrative together. The first was the Beijing Olympics. From the American point of view, there were controversies leading up to the Olympics, notably the heavy-handed attempts of Chinese security to prevent any disruption of the Olympic torch relay in San Francisco and concerns about whether China would allow free access to journalists and freedom of speech during the games. But the Beijing Olympics were a huge success for China. Its meticulously choreographed opening ceremonies were among the most spectacular ever—impressive evidence that China had arrived as a global great power. Then, only a month later, the American economy collapsed, and a financial meltdown led to the beginning of a long recession, in which millions of middle-class Americans lost their homes as well as their jobs. Most of the global economy collapsed as well, but through massive government stimulus programs, the Chinese economy weathered the worst shocks and recovered quickly. The seeds were sown for a new story about a rising China and an America in decline.

Leaders in the Chinese government may have believed this narrative. By 2009, they were beginning to act more assertively in countering the dominance of the United States and its allies in the South and East China Seas. They also began to change their public ideology about eventually adopting Western norms on human rights. Until the early 2000s, the official line was that China had to attend to people's rights to a good livelihood while protecting social stability before being ready to embrace Western norms of human and political rights.[32] But now as a new nationalism began to develop, the line changed: China would never adopt Western values. Its own values were superior.

The opinion of American intellectual and national security elites began to tip away from China. For economic elites, the theft of intellectual property and stealing of proprietary technology, often through cyber hacking, was an even more important tipping factor. American manufacturing corporations had initially prospered by relocating production facilities to China. But as the Chinese economy grew and the supply of workers from the countryside declined—due partially to smaller family sizes created by coercive birth control policies that went into effect in 1980—labor costs increased. Companies looking for cheap labor began looking elsewhere, to the Philippines, Indonesia, and Bangladesh. Future growth in China would come not from using it as a platform for low-cost manufacturing but through selling it the products of advanced technology. But China was restricting the importation of such technology and, to a disconcerting degree, copying or outright stealing it (and turning some of it into military weapons). A new story line in which China was seen as an unfair, even devious, competitor was in the making.

Thus, an elite narrative was arising to merge with the various popular story lines. Favorable public opinion toward China remained in the 50 percent range for a few years, but by 2012, it began a sharp decline to below 40 percent.

The spectacular event that would finally unite the negative narratives was the rise of Donald Trump. For thirty years, Trump had been complaining that China was taking advantage of America on trade. (He did not have similar complaints about human rights. In 1989, he defended the Tiananmen crackdown.) During his 2016 campaign, he claimed that China was raping American workers. He denounced the Obama administration for being too accommodating to China and its rulers, failing to stop it from stealing American jobs, and failing to stand up to its expansion into the South China Sea. He denounced "crooked

Hillary" and implied that the Clintons (and their allies in the establishment) had sold out American interests for cash from elites around the world, including certainly China. In his inaugural address, he painted a picture of American carnage and proclaimed a nationalistic policy of America First.

His unexpected victory pulled together all the quietly developing China narratives described earlier in this chapter—of people afraid of being displaced by alien immigrants, workers concerned about being sold out to China and angry about the complicity of elites in the betrayal, Christians frustrated with obstacles to proclaiming the Gospel, and finally, some manufacturers worried about having their technology stolen and market access blocked. All of these narratives have received forceful articulation by ideologues like Steve Bannon. They have been echoed in the recent rhetoric of Michael Pence, pursued in the policies advocated by such close Trump advisers as Peter Navarro and Stephen Miller, and encouraged by advice from hawkish Washington think tanks and nationalistic commentators on Fox News. It is a story as much about America as China. Should America be a multicultural society open to constant renewal from immigration, enriched through global economic interdependence and a confluence of global cultures, committed to enough equality to sustain a vigorous middle class and confident enough in its democratic institutions to allow open participation from all kinds of citizens? Or should America become a socially and culturally closed society, standing alone and strong against a hostile world? Should it be like rising Athens or like fearful Sparta?

Chinese Narratives of America

As the Trump administration was developing its narrative of how to "Make America Great Again," Xi Jinping had been presenting his China Dream of the "Great Rejuvenation of the Chinese Nation." While Trump told a tale of American carnage that will be overcome by such efforts as stopping China from taking advantage of us, Xi was recounting a Century of National Humiliation that could be overcome by China asserting itself. The great rejuvenation of the Chinese people will be pursued by the hard work of each of the more than 1.3 billion Chinese people drawing upon the wisdom of five thousand years of Chinese history and unified by a strong Communist Party. This will lead to a prosperous nation with a high standard of living and with military power and cultural prestige that will give it high status among all the nations of the world. This great rejuvenation will not lead China to stand alone but will enable it to play a major constructive role in global governance.[33]

Xi's writings on the China Dream do not have many explicit references to America. An official compendium of Xi's writings includes a joint press conference with President Obama in 2013 in which Xi states that the China Dream "is a dream of peace, development, cooperation, and mutual benefit, and it is closely linked to the dreams of the people of the world, including the United States."[34] The vision evoked by many in the Trump administration, on the other hand, emphasized competition, even war, with China and held that leaders like Obama were dangerously naïve to expect cooperation and mutual benefit.

Xi himself does not make explicit comparisons with the United States, but a Chinese commentator in an official publication contends that the "core of the American Dream is the actualization of personal values. In other words it is the realization of core values advocated by America through individual efforts. . . . Individualism is the ideological foundation and heart and soul of the American Dream, while collectivism is the ideological foundation and soul of the Chinese Dream. The core of the Chinese Dream is to realize the collective or holistic values."[35] The author quotes a former minister of the State Council Information Office: "The American Dream starts with the individual and ends with the state, while the Chinese Dream starts with the state and ends with the individual."[36]

What are the long-term implications of the clash between the official Chinese narrative, carefully organized by the Communist Party's propaganda department, and the hegemonic American narrative arising from the complex social forces discussed earlier? Part of the answer has to do with the status of the official Chinese narrative. As the product of a top-down ideological construction, it is not as resonant with grassroots narratives as the American hegemonic narrative. In my recent book, *The Chinese Pursuit of Happiness*, I and my colleagues argued that there are truly multiple narratives at play in Chinese society.[37] To give just a few examples, there is still widespread commitment to the ideals of a strong extended patriarchal family even as modern pressures make it difficult to sustain such families and younger generations embrace new ideals of individual self-expression and gender equality. There is devotion to professional integrity, even as the government demands that all professions serve the state. There are aspirations to social equality together with eagerness to get rich first.

Does the Xi Jinping official narrative synthesize the many narratives about national identity arising from the many sectors of Chinese society? How have these narratives been shaped by the developing encounter with American society? Let us briefly consider the development of some of these narratives over the past quarter century.

Actualization of Personal Values

After the Tiananmen crackdown, the most articulate leaders of the protests went into exile, to jail, or into hiding. Although some who went into exile wrote memoirs, narratives expressing the hopes and aspirations of those who stayed behind went underground. What did appear visibly on the surface were narratives about self-expression through consumerism, with the gold standard for consumerism being found in the United States, at least in the images of America conveyed through advertising. The exploration of new identities through new forms of eating and entertainment was seen as genuinely liberating.

For example, after a meeting in Wuhan, my Chinese colleagues took me to a lavish new vaudeville show that featured a drag queen. This, my colleagues explained without irony, was "thought liberation." As shown in the work of James Farrer, this liberation extended to many different forms of sexual expression from discos to KTV (karaoke clubs) to massage parlors.[38] It was freedom from the puritanical restrictions of the Mao era.

As Yunxiang Yan shows in his much-cited articles on McDonald's, other forms of liberation came from consuming American fast food.[39] Many Chinese consumers did not actually like the taste of American fast food, but they saw restaurants like McDonald's and Kentucky Fried Chicken as venues for a new kind of social experience, which they identified as American. The experience was one of individual choice and egalitarian relationships. Each individual could choose from a fairly large menu, and the choice was made standing face to face with an employee who was trained to smile at the customer. A variety of tables enabled customers to dine alone or with one or two friends as well as large family groups. Women especially liked the opportunity to eat alone or with some women friends. Dating couples could have heart-to-heart talks over Big Macs and fries. Such public spaces for flexible, egalitarian sociability had not existed in China before. McDonald's was seen as a taste of America but was really a Chinese version of America. In America, McDonald's stands for cheap fast food. In China in the 1990s, McDonald's was not cheap by contemporary living standards, was not fast because diners lingered over their meals for a long time, and was not merely food because the experience was more important than the cuisine. The experience was one of liberation from hierarchical constraints. As Deborah Davis argued in the introduction to her edited book *The Consumer Revolution in Urban China*, "Eating a Big Mac will not bring down a dictator, but it can send a million daily messages that old ways have changed."[40]

Indeed, many of the old ways remained prevalent in ordinary life, but the experience, not just of American fast food and coffee shops like Starbucks, but of American clothing fashions (clothes that were manufactured in Chinese factories), American music, and other forms of pop culture (filtered through Hong Kong or Korea), generated a narrative of beginning to move toward possibilities that existed in America. Newly affluent middle-class Chinese could of course participate more fully in these new possibilities, but even migrant workers could alleviate the hardship of factory work by enjoying at least a taste of the pleasures of the new consumerism.

In this narrative, America stood for a level of private personal freedom that was not yet available in China. One way to realize this freedom was actually to go to America, by getting smuggled there as on the *Golden Venture*, getting a fellowship to study there, or obtaining an EB-5 visa to invest money there. For many, actual life in the Old Gold Mountain (as Chinese call San Francisco) turned out to be disappointingly harsh, but the narrative of immigration to America as a hope for individual freedom has persisted.

Hopes for Professional Integrity

Would this quest for individual freedom lead to efforts to change China in the direction of more political freedom as well? The government clearly hoped not, counting on the quests for freedom wrought by consumerism to be confined to private life. More consequential visions of political change perhaps came from narratives generated by reconstituted professions like law, social science, journalism, and social work. Suppressed during the Maoist era, these professions were being rebuilt in the 1990s with the robust help of such American institutions as the Ford Foundation, with the basic rebuilding mostly completed by the early 2000s. What was crucial was not so much the formal ideology of the professions but the practices cultivated in the training of aspiring lawyers, social scientists, journalists, and social workers.

Lawyers, for example, were introduced to the practice of seeking justice through determining facts in accordance with fairly applied legal procedures. Social scientists learned evidence-based research methods using accurate data. Journalists studied how to construct an accurate story. Social workers sought to help solve the problems of clients by discovering their real needs. In all these cases, professional practice has been hampered by the demands of the state. As one social worker responded when I noted that their agencies all had names like "Happy Communities" and asked how exactly they made people happy, "One thing you should know is that in practice our job is not to make the *laobaixing* (ordinary people) happy but to make the government happy." Nonetheless, he and his colleagues felt that as social workers they actually should be making the *laobaixing* happy, and the tension between government demands and professional practice was making social workers unhappy.[41]

Similar dilemmas are felt by all the socially oriented professions. Their training often leads them toward a narrative of change oriented toward practices realized at least imperfectly in America but frustrated by Chinese constraints. Meanwhile, the Xi Jinping regime is carrying on a campaign to sinicize all professions. Professionals whom I have interviewed are in general happy to indigenize their practices to better fit the concrete needs of their society, but they fear that, in reality, sinicization simply means to follow the dictates of the government. (Sinicization—*zhongguohua*—one of them says, simply means to "do as you're told"—*tinghua*.) Most professionals adapt to the increasing government constraints, but some, like well-known rights lawyers and dissident journalists, have been inspired bravely to uphold their professional ideals.

The American media understandably focuses on such heroic dissidents who have too often paid a severe price for their commitment to seeking truth and justice. Scholars of China would do well to also understand those conflicted professionals who quietly struggle with ambivalence toward the Chinese political system. In the long run, they may be the greater force for social change.

But even when some of their ambivalence arises from training in professional practices coming from America, the actual stories they tell about where their profession and their country is and should be going are fundamentally narratives about China, not America, and they are most powerful when they resonate with themes from Chinese history and culture. In the book *The Chinese Pursuit of Happiness* is an essay by Jay Chen (from Taiwan's Academia Sinica) based on interviews with prominent rights lawyers, dissident journalists, and labor activists. When asked what motivated them on their difficult quests (which they say in the end give them happiness despite the suffering they have caused), many cite not the ideals of Jefferson or Lincoln but the heroes in Chinese tales of the wandering knight as well as Maoist ideals about social equality.[42]

Looking for Faith

A similar argument could be made about the narratives of Chinese Christians, especially the various kinds of evangelical Christians whose numbers have been increasing exponentially (and may now be reaching a plateau). Chinese Christians are widely aware that their faith came from abroad, often from American missionaries, and most are aware of the support (monetary or moral) they may receive from American support groups like ChinaAid. But they see their faith as a universal one, not an American one. (See chapter 8 by Mary Bullock for a discussion of the sinicization of Christianity in China.)

There are many different kinds of Chinese Christians. Some tell an apocalyptic story of a sinful world destined soon to be destroyed with the return of Christ. Others, like the neo-Calvinists most popular among Chinese intellectuals (and propagated by Korean evangelists) tell a story of resolute striving among faithful people to make a better world. Prominent dissidents like Yu Jie—best-selling Christian author and social critic, close friend of Liu Xiaobo, and signatory of Charter 08 who immigrated to the United States in 2012 after a brief imprisonment—have arisen out of this tradition, but they are not representative of the complicated population of Chinese Christians.[43]

In any case, these Christian narratives that may make some connection, even if indirect, to America are embedded in a rich, expanding, religious ecology of Daoists and Buddhists and all kinds of folk religion, including sectarian practices like Falun Gong. Although government calls to sinicization, which basically means subordination to state purposes, are embraced by the officially recognized churches (connected to the Protestant Three-Self Patriotic Movement and the Chinese Patriotic Catholic Association referenced in chapter 8), the unregistered Protestant house churches and underground Catholic churches have long practiced a kind of indigenization from below. All of these generate their own stories of where the Chinese people have been and where they are going, with no reference to America. This religious ecology has at least as much influence on Chinese Christian narratives as anything brought by missionaries from America.[44]

Practically all of the narratives coming from Chinese religious sources, like those coming from more secular sectors of the society, are about hopes for Chinese society with at most only secondary concern about America. But the hopes are different, with some built on reverence for China's ancient traditions, others built on stories of struggles to overcome the Century of National Humiliation, and still others unleashed by the exciting prospects of modernity. Almost all of them look toward a China that can be proud of its place in world history.

Nationalism

Perhaps sensing that a Marxist narrative of history has little relevance to most of the narratives that Chinese people are constructing about their past and future, the Chinese government has been using nationalistic pride as the basis for its legitimacy. This emphasis on nationalism began in the early 2000s, but the Beijing Olympics in 2008 can be seen as its launching point into global awareness. The Beijing Olympics was a spectacular event that could fuse many of these disparate narratives together in a celebration of national pride. The opening ceremonies celebrated traditional culture—Confucianism, Daoism, Buddhism, ancient sages, and heroes. Reform and opening, Karl Marx and Mao Zedong, were not so much as mentioned.

The Chinese government's umbrella of nationalism covers many different narratives that are not necessarily compatible with one another. But perhaps one area of agreement is that the present situation in the United States is not the model for a better Chinese future. The cosmopolitan people I met in Shanghai in 2008 expressed genuine admiration for a society that would allow an African American child of a single mother to become president. But the slowness of America's economic recovery from the financial crash, the eruption of unvarnished racism, and the increasing dysfunction of American politics have diminished America's image as a model to be emulated—even if it has increased in stature as a good place for rich people to launder money or for students to get a prestigious education.

As I argue in the epilogue to the book on the Chinese pursuit of happiness, the Chinese moral order today is characterized by a plurality of narratives of the good life—different values and indeed different moral visions that form a frame of reference for different groups and institutions. This condition of multiple goods and multiple definitions of happiness is common in all complex modern societies, although perhaps particularly so in the United States. What may be distinctive about China is the level of dissonance and tension between the competing visions of the good life. The rapid speed of China's development, along with its traumatic disruptions throughout the twentieth century, have all produced a condition that some scholars of Asia are calling "compressed modernity." In this situation, none of the pluralistic values and the narratives that express them satisfactorily correspond to the rapidly changing social circumstances of today.[45]

The Xi Jinping regime is trying to hold this pluralism together within the integument of a powerful state justified by an official version of the China Dream. When most Americans consider China, they see the integument and they hear the words about the China Dream and use those references as a foil in their debates about their own identity. Most do not see or know how to assess the multiplicity of popular narratives that express many different dreams that stand in tension with Xi's official dream. Better knowledge of this might help to counter or at least complicate the new hegemonic narrative about China as a menacing adversary. Most of the values actually embraced by ordinary Chinese people are not at odds with American values, and many are even worthy of emulation.

The present American confrontational narrative is likely to lead to a defensive hardening by the Chinese state, which could also intensify the suppression of its domestic cultural pluralism. A more nuanced understanding of China arising from the many different sectors of American society might lead to a more nuanced balance of cooperation and competition with the Chinese state and eventually—although one cannot predict this for the near future—an increased openness to the diversity of Chinese dreams. A more open, democratic, equal, and just America might also become a more attractive model for emulation. Chinese narratives about America will always be more about Chinese identity than America. But a more genuinely attractive America might help Chinese to embrace the better angels in their own culture.

Toward New Narratives for a New World

The present hegemonic American narrative of an inevitable economic, informational, and even kinetic war with China is part and parcel of a vision of

America as an ethnonationalist society that needs to purify itself of alien influences, close its borders, and use its power to control its relationship with the
rest of the world. Those who find the narrative abhorrent need to develop alternatives. Here is what, in my view, an alternative that is true to America's best
ideals might look like.

It would first recognize that China is not going to develop democratic institutions through some inevitable process of modernization. For the foreseeable
future, China will combine a successful, dynamic economy with a repressive,
authoritarian state. The fact that democracy is not part of an inevitable process
should also make Americans realize that their own democracy is not a guaranteed outcome of the tide of history. Maintaining democracy requires continuing work from each new generation. What most certainly would further
undermine our own democracy would be the temptation to fight fire with fire,
to confront Chinese dictatorship by becoming dictatorial ourselves.

One part of the work to maintain democracy would include heeding some
of the concerns of the 1960s generation of leftists who, for a while, looked to
Maoist China as a revolutionary redeemer and were concerned that the forces
of unrestrained global capitalism, especially in concert with racism, nationalism, and the arrogance of imperial power, would in the end stifle authentic
freedom.[46] China certainly turned out to be no redeemer, but the concerns
behind the original vision are still valid. Using China as a scapegoat for rising
inequality, the corruption of governments, and the erosion of traditional values
may remain tempting, but in fact, scapegoating China simply avoids taking
responsibly for democratically addressing these problems ourselves.

A constructive relationship with China as a rising power would require
Americans to double down on traditional strengths—democratic openness,
grassroots innovation, and civic participation—while continuing to combat
traditional evils like racism. Insofar as Chinese leaders threaten a world order
that protects the independence of other nations and that enjoins respect for
religious freedom and ethnic dignity, China should be resisted by a coalition of
nations committed to upholding such an order. The resistance would not preclude the use of force if necessary but would mostly be accomplished through
diplomatic pressure. If Americans and other democratic nations manage to
make their values truly attractive—if democratic openness can underpin a sustained and sustainable prosperity and a vibrant cultural creativity—then the
Chinese people may someday want to emulate us again. This would be the outcome of a story that would see a constructive blending of the American Dream
and the China Dream.

I have said that we academics have a conceit that our ideas are determinative. They certainly are not. But we can make a contribution through our
research and teaching, especially if carried out with awareness of the other
cultural forces in which we are embedded.

NOTES

1. Compilation of Bannon quotes, mostly from an interview at CNBC's Delivering Alpha conference, July 18, 2018, https://www.cnbc.com/delivering-alpha-2018/. The sentiments in this interview are typical of many speeches that Bannon has been giving. "One of us is going to be a hegemon" is from an interview with Robert Kuttner, "Steve Bannon, Unrepentant," *American Prospect*, August 16, 2017, https://prospect.org/power/steve-bannon-unrepentant/. "They fear Christianity" quoted from a Breitbart radio show in Benjamin Haas, "Steve Bannon: 'we're going to war in the South China Sea . . . no doubt,'" *South China Morning Post*, February 2, 2017, https://www.scmp.com/news/china/diplomacy-defence/article/2067457/steve-bannon-were-going-war-south-china-sea-no-doubt. "Totalitarian, mercantilist system" from an interview on Australian ABC, *Four Corners*, July 9, 2018, https://www.abc.net.au/4corners/populist-revolution/10196348.

2. Isobel Thompson, "The Sinister History Behind the Right's Putin-mania," *Vanity Fair*, July 20, 2018, https://www.vanityfair.com/news/2018/07/sinister-history-behind-the-rights-putin-mania-steve-bannon-china.

3. Michael Pillsbury, *The Hundred Year Marathon: China's Secret Strategy to Replace America as the Global Superpower* (New York: Henry Holt, 2015).

4. Hudson Institute, "Vice President Mike Pence's Remarks on the Administration's Policy Towards China," October 4, 2018, https://www.hudson.org/events/1610-vice-president-mike-pence-s-remarks-on-the-administration-s-policy-towards-china102018.

5. By hegemonic rhetoric, I mean a dominant frame of reference for public discussion about China. This frame of reference may often be built upon a fundamental narrative about where the U.S.-China relationship has been and where it is going, a narrative that combines both fact and emotion. Such narratives do not necessarily represent a consensus in public opinion, but they shape the way a consensus may or may not get formed. For instance, opinion polls ask whether or not there is a "China threat." They do not ask whether there is a "Canada threat" or "Europe threat." Even if, according to recent polls, only about 40 percent say that China is a "critical threat" (although in a Gallup poll more than an additional 40 percent now say that China is at least an "important threat" economically and militarily), the threat rhetoric sets the terms of opinion formation (Gallup, "China," https://news.gallup.com/poll/1627/china.aspx). The rhetoric about China as at least a potential threat has indeed now become predominant among a large segment of both Republican and Democratic American public elites—those who pay a lot of attention to China and spread their ideas and feelings through public media—although they may not agree upon means and tactics. See Daniel W. Drezner, "The China Gap," *Washington Post*, January 31, 2019, https://www.washington-post.com/outlook/2019/01/31/china-gap/. Although not necessarily shared among the whole spectrum of ordinary American citizens, these rhetorical frameworks probably resonate intellectually and emotionally among the kind of citizens who usually vote in primary elections.

6. Richard Madsen, *China and the American Dream: A Moral Inquiry* (Berkeley: University of California Press, 1995).

7. From many of his writings, but see Charles Taylor, "Democracy, Inclusive and Exclusive," in *Meaning and Modernity: Religion, Polity, and Self*, eds. Richard Madsen et al. (Berkeley: University of California Press, 2002), 181–94, 192–93.

8. Chapter 8 in this book, by Mary Bullock, contains a fuller description of how and why the National Committee on U.S.-China Relations was formed.

9. I am indebted to the playwright Allan Havis for insight into the importance of scènes à faire in dramatic structure.

10. The 1960s New Left never developed a practical vision of how to put their ideals into practice in the context of American politics. The adulation of some Committee of Concerned Asian Scholars (CCAS) members for China also began to wane as the brutality of the Mao Zedong regime came into view and as China itself embarked on quasi-imperialistic aggression by attacking Vietnam in 1979. The CCAS broke apart in that year. Some of the idealistic vision stays alive, however, in the pages of *Critical Asian Studies*, the successor journal to the *Bulletin of Concerned Asian Scholars*, and could become implemented under changing political circumstances.

11. David Autor, "Changes in Real Wage Levels of Full-Time US Workers by Sex and Education, 1963–2012," *Science* 344 (2014): 843–51.

12. Thomas Piketty and Emmanuel Saez, "Income Inequality in the United States, 1913–1998," *Quarterly Journal of Economics* 118, no. 1 (2003): 1–41. Updated data until 2013 are available at http://eml.berkeley.edu/~saez/TabFig2015prel.xls.

13. In addition to the many written articles about the *Golden Venture*, see also the full-length documentary *Golden Venture: A Documentary About the US Immigration Crisis*, directed by Peter Cohn (New York: GoldenVenture, 2006).

14. Dan Berry and Jeffrey E. Singer, "The Case of Jane Doe Ponytail," *New York Times*, October 16, 2018, https://www.nytimes.com/interactive/2018/10/11/nyregion/sex-workers-massage-parlor.html.

15. See Ko-lin Chin, *Smuggled Chinese: Clandestine Immigration to the USA* (Philadelphia: Temple University Press, 1999).

16. The controversy is ongoing. Frank Shyong, "Monterey Park Sign Ordinance Debate Recalls '80s Ethnic Controversy," *Los Angeles Times*, August 3, 2013, https://www.latimes.com/local/la-xpm-2013-aug-03-la-me-english-signs-20130804-story.html.

17. M. Dowling, "Lest We Forget Chinagate, the Most Serious Scandal in US History," *Independent Sentinel*, October 24, 2015, https://www.independentsentinel.com/lest-we-forget-hillarys-china-gate-scandal/.

18. There are numerous media reports on all of this. Most of the information is summarized in Senate Committee on Governmental Affairs, *Summary of the Committee's Findings Relating to the Effort of the People's Republic of China to Influence US Policies and Elections* (Washington, DC: Senate Committee on Governmental Affairs, 1998).

19. Shirley A. Kan, "Congressional Research Service Report to Congress. China's Technology Acquisitions: Cox Committee's Report—Findings, Issues, and Recommendations," June 8, 1999, http://congressionalresearch.com/RL30220/document.php. But as Congressman Spratt of the Cox Committee noted, "It is a reach to say that 'stolen nuclear secrets gave the PRC design information on thermonuclear weapons on a par with our own' " or that Chinese missiles could now become as powerful or accurate as ours.

20. Wen-ho Lee and Helen Zia, *My Country Versus Me: The First-Hand Account by the Los Alamos Scientist Who Was Falsely Accused of Being a Spy* (New York: Hyperion, 2003); Dan Stober and Ian Hoffman, *A Convenient Spy: Wen Ho Lee and the Politics of Nuclear Espionage* (New York: Simon and Schuster, 2002); Notra Trulock, *Code Name Kindred Spirit: Inside the Chinese Nuclear Espionage Scandal* (New York: Encounter Books, 2002).

21. Dallas Boyd, Jeffrey G. Lewis, and Joshua H. Pollack, *Advanced Technology Acquisition Strategies of the People's Republic of China* (Ft. Belvoir, VA: Defense Threat Reduction Agency, Advanced Systems and Concepts Office, Department of Defense, September 2010).

22. It is very difficult to get accurate statistics. The official Chinese press says there are only twenty million, which even many Chinese scholars say is too low. Some U.S.-based

evangelical Christians say there are over one hundred million, which may be based more on hope than reality. The Pew Forum on Religion and Public Life estimates that Protestant Christians constitute around 5 percent of the Chinese population, which would amount to over sixty million. I rely on Pew estimates (conservatively interpreted) here. Pew Research Center, "The Future of World Religions: Population Growth Projections, 2010-2050," April 2, 2015, https://www.pewforum.org/2015/04/02 /religious-projections-2010-2050/.

23. A book that summarizes the relevant information and expresses the hope of evangelical Christians is David Aikman, *Jesus in Beijing: How Christianity Is Transforming China and Changing the Global Balance of Power* (Washington, DC: Regnery, 2003). See also Mary Bullock's chapter (chapter 8) for a fuller discussion of contemporary Christianity in China.

24. ChinaAid, "Bob Fu," https://www.chinaaid.org/p/bob-fu.html.

25. The Cardinal Kung Foundation, Cardinalkungfoundation.org.

26. "Hainan Island Incident," Wikipedia, https://en.wikipedia.org/wiki/Hainan_Island _incident.

27. Piketty and Saez, "Income Inequality in the United States."

28. See chapter 13 by Kenneth Lieberthal and Susan Thornton for a fuller discussion of MFN and its meaning.

29. David H. Autor, David Dorn, and Gordon H. Hanson, "The China Shock: Learning from Labor Market Adjustment to Large Changes in Trade," *Annual Review of Economics* 8, no. 1 (2016): 205-40.

30. Henry M. Paulson Jr. and Michael K. Carroll, *Dealing with China: An Insider Unmasks the New Economic Superpower* (New York: Grand Central Publishing, 2015).

31. Public opinion data from Pew Research Center.

32. Information Office of the State Council of the People's Republic of China, "Human Rights in China," White Paper, November 1991, http://www.china.org.cn/e-white/7 /index.htm. *People's Daily* article in September 2008, rejecting "universal values." The seven forbidden topics in the Communist Party's Document No. 9 of 2013 include discussion of "universal values."

33. Xi Jinping, *The Chinese Dream of the Great Rejuvenation of the Chinese Nation* (Beijing: Foreign Languages Press, 2014).

34. Xi, *The Chinese Dream*, 80-81.

35. Ren Xiaosi, *The Chinese Dream: What It Means for China and the Rest of the World* (Beijing: New World Press, 2013), 56.

36. Ren, *The Chinese Dream*, 54.

37. Becky Hsu and Richard Madsen, eds., *The Chinese Pursuit of Happiness: Anxieties, Hopes, and Moral Tensions in Everyday Life* (Berkeley: University of California Press, 2019).

38. James Farrer, *Opening Up: Youth Sex Culture and Market Reforms in Shanghai* (Chicago: University of Chicago Press, 2002).

39. Yunxiang Yan, "Of Hamburger and Social Space: Consuming McDonald's in Beijing," in *The Consumer Revolution in Urban China*, ed. Deborah S. Davis (Berkeley: University of California Press, 2000), 201-25.

40. Deborah S. Davis, "Introduction," in *The Consumer Revolution in Urban China*, ed. Deborah S. Davis (Berkeley: University of California Press, 2000), 22.

41. Richard Madsen, "Making the People Happy or the Government Happy: Dilemmas of Social Workers in a Morally Pluralistic Society," in *The Chinese Pursuit of Happiness: Anxieties, Hopes, and Moral Tensions in Everyday Life*, eds. Becky Hsu and Richard Madsen (Berkeley: University of California Press, 2019), 110-30.

42. Chih-Jou Jay Chen, "Deriving Happiness from Making Society Better: Chinese Activists Confronting Warring Gods," in *The Chinese Pursuit of Happiness: Anxieties, Hopes, and Moral Tensions in Everyday Life*, eds. Becky Hsu and Richard Madsen (Berkeley: University of California Press, 2019), 131–54.

43. Richard Madsen, "Multiple Meanings of Multiple Christianities," in *Sinicizing Christianity*, ed. Yang-wen Zheng (Leiden, the Netherlands: Brill, 2017).

44. Ian Johnson, *The Souls of China: The Return of Religion After Mao* (New York: Pantheon, 2017).

45. Richard Madsen, "Epilogue," in *The Chinese Pursuit of Happiness: Anxieties, Hopes, and Moral Tensions in Everyday Life*, eds. Becky Hsu and Richard Madsen (Berkeley: University of California Press, 2019), 155–70.

46. Mark Selden, "Reflections on the Committee of Concerned Asian Scholars at Fifty," *Critical Asian Studies* 50, no. 1 (March 2018): 3–15.

CHAPTER 6

U.S.-CHINA RETROSPECTIVE

Forty Years of Commercial Relations

CRAIG ALLEN

I n the past forty years, China has evolved from a poor and backward nation to become both the world's largest manufacturing power and its largest trading nation. This transition has had an enormous impact—both positive and negative—on the American economy, American corporations, and indeed the world. The effect of the interaction between the United States and China through trade and investment and of China's integration into the global economy has been profound, affecting virtually every American company, consumer, and citizen.

The history of commercial relations between the United States and China predates the formal establishment of the United States. Indeed, Britain's taxation of tea from Fujian Province was one of the proximate causes of the American Revolution. The first officially American-flagged sailing vessel, the *Empress of China*, set out for the Chinese port of Canton in February 1784 with a shipment of American ginseng, metals, and animal hides. The American constitution would not be ratified for another four years. After the Opium Wars of 1839–1842 and 1856–1860, both American missionary activity and investment expanded rapidly, as did Chinese emigration to the United States, especially after the Gold Rush of 1849. The two countries cooperated in both World War I and World War II. But virtually all economic exchanges came to a halt with the establishment of the People's Republic of China on October 1, 1949. Only in the 1970s, after a twenty-one-year-long trade embargo, did the United States and China begin to trade on a very small scale in response both to the beginning of limited diplomatic contact and to market forces in both countries.

The National Council for U.S.-China Trade (now the U.S.-China Business Council) was established in 1973 to help facilitate these early trade contacts.[1] Significant economic exchanges did not begin until the advent of formal diplomatic recognition in 1979.[2]

This chapter reviews and assesses the history of the past forty years of commercial relations between the United States and China, focusing primarily on trade and investment. The examination reveals a clear pattern. Since the two countries established diplomatic relations, U.S. trade and investment relations with China have gone through four distinct periods, or cycles, each approximately a decade long and each following a roughly similar pattern. Domestic political and economic developments within China are the main cause of these cycles. Reacting to swings in Chinese economic and political policies, American companies typically begin the cycle with exuberant expectations, leading to rapid growth in trade and investment. This upswing is followed by a period of disenchantment, with a (relative) slowdown in trade and investment. Each of the cycles has been punctuated by diplomatic tensions that are eventually partially resolved through negotiations that reset the overall terms and conditions of the relationship. American companies and consumers have both benefited from and been injured by these dramatic economic and political swings.

This relationship is not mechanistic or deterministic. Within the overall relationship, other important cycles also recur, including U.S. presidential elections every four years and business cycles in both countries. In addition, the dissemination of innovation and new technologies has had profound impacts on both trade and investment.

After analyzing the forces at play through each of these cycles, this chapter concludes by asking whether the repeating pattern of growth followed by disenchantment will continue after the Trump administration and into Biden's. As the Biden administration begins, the United States and China are in an unprecedented and extended phase of disenchantment.

Setting the Stage: Cycle 1: 1979–1989

The first period of renewed trade was an age of boisterous innocence and began with the establishment of diplomatic relations following Deng Xiaoping's 1978 announcement of his new policy of reform and opening, after which China went through a series of tectonic political and economic shifts. The cycle ended abruptly with the Tiananmen Incident of June 4, 1989. This period is roughly contemporaneous with the administrations of Presidents Jimmy Carter and Ronald Reagan and includes Deng Xiaoping's visit to the United States in 1979 and Ronald Reagan's visit to China in 1984.

The Chinese decision to establish diplomatic relations with the United States rested largely on two factors, one externally driven and the other internal. The external motivation was the military threat posed by the Soviet Union on China's northern border and was surely Deng Xiaoping's most important reason for seeking diplomatic relations with the United States and, more broadly, with many other nonsocialist countries. The internal motivation was Deng's realization that in the interim since the establishment of the People's Republic, China had fallen far behind its neighbors and the rest of the world across all dimensions of human and economic development. Deng knew that strengthening Chinese institutions was necessary to ensure sustainable development for one billion Chinese people.

In 1977, in the wake of the Cultural Revolution and following the death of Mao Zedong, Deng had announced a campaign to pursue the Four Modernizations, first articulated by Zhou Enlai as early as 1963. The goal was a rapid upgrading of Chinese industry, agriculture, science and technology, and military defense. Deng also knew that the goal of the Four Modernizations could not be realized without a concomitant policy of reform and opening, of relying on more developed countries to serve the modernization of China, as John Garver further details in chapter 3 of this volume. The Four Modernizations served as a vision and a set of priorities for the structure of China's interaction with the United States and the rest of the world, including Europe and Japan.

With Deng's formal ascension to power at the Third Plenum of the Eleventh Party Congress in December 1978, he had sufficient authority to begin implementing his proposed policies. On January 29, 1979, four weeks after the establishment of diplomatic relations, Deng arrived in Washington, DC, as the honored guest of President Jimmy Carter. The U.S. government and the private business sector both warmly welcomed the establishment of diplomatic relations and Deng Xiaoping's new policies. American industry opened its arms to China's paramount leader. In Atlanta, Henry Ford himself led Deng and his entourage on a tour of the Ford automotive assembly plant. In Houston, Deng inspected facilities of the Hughes Tool Company and visited the Johnson Space Center. In Seattle, Deng's final stop, he toured a Boeing plant that was assembling three 747SP aircraft that had been purchased by the Chinese government.

Throughout Deng's visit, the nexus between national security and business was clear to all. In an interview, Deng could not have been more explicit when he said, "If we really want to be able to place curbs on the polar bear, the only thing is for us to unite."[3] At the same time, American business literally rolled out the red carpet with a performance and reception at the Kennedy Center attended by some fifteen hundred guests.[4]

The Carter administration welcomed the possibility of a rapid expansion of economic relations. In a briefing for American business people, Secretary of State Cyrus Vance argued that important economic benefits would flow from the establishment of economic relations with Beijing. "These include our participation as a regular supplier of agricultural commodities to China, the ability of U.S. exporters to compete on an equal basis with our suppliers, and the resumption of shipping, air, banking, and other normal economic relations with China," he said.[5]

A constant stream of U.S. trade missions and delegations, from a wide range of industries, followed Deng's triumphant visit. The American corporate approach to China in 1979 was reminiscent of the Gold Rush of 1849. American companies hurried into the exciting new market, happy to export anything that the Chinese could pay for with hard currency. Soon, the two sides were signing foreign direct investment agreements in the form of joint ventures between American firms and Chinese ministries or state-owned enterprises (SOEs).

Figure 6.1 details the rapid growth of U.S. exports to China from 1979–1989, whereas Figure 6.2 shows the rise in U.S. direct foreign investment in China over roughly the same period.

As seen in these figures, both U.S. exports to China and U.S. investment in China expanded rapidly from 1979 to 1985. After a period of consolidation in 1986, there was another surge in both trade and investment flows. This surge in the second half of the decade was correlated with a new wave of probusiness reform in China. The late Richard Baum, political science professor at the University of California, Los Angeles, described this well. "In the economic realm, Deng's self-styled 'Second Chinese Revolution' began the year under a full head of steam," he wrote, "with reformers and rich peasants marching forward under the banner, 'a little capitalism isn't necessarily a bad thing.' "[6] As we see repeatedly, internal Chinese domestic dynamics determine the ebb and flow of both American trade and investment.

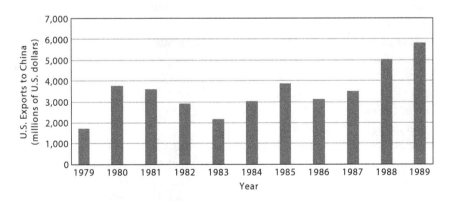

6.1 U.S. exports to China, 1979–1989.

Source: International Monetary Fund.
Category: goods, free on board (FOB).

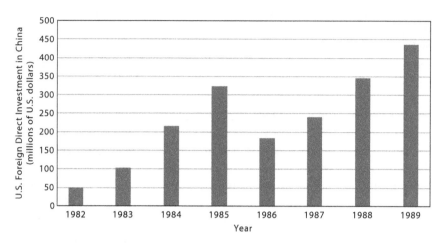

6.2 U.S. foreign direct investment in China, 1982–1989.

Source: U.S. Bureau of Economic Analysis, Department of Commerce.

Note: Balance of payments and direct investment position data on a historical-cost basis (millions of dollars).

Despite the American business community's enthusiastic response to China's opening, the diplomatic and legal issues associated with large-scale trade were daunting. In particular, the American Trade Act of 1974 and the Jackson-Vanik amendment to it served as a brake on bilateral trade and investment until China joined the World Trade Organization in 2001. The original Trade Act was meant to expand U.S. participation in international trade and protect the American worker, while the later Jackson-Vanik amendment denied most favored nation status to countries with nonmarket economies (e.g., socialist countries such as China) that restricted immigration. Most favored nation status (renamed normal trade relations in 1998)[7] could be granted to non-market economies only with presidential approval temporarily waiving the requirements, and the waiver had to be renewed on a yearly basis.[8] In fact, American presidents waived these requirements for China every year from 1979 to 2000—rather routinely for the first ten years, but only with a great annual debate after the Tiananmen tragedy of 1989 that so profoundly affected the entire U.S.-China relationship.[9]

At the same time, other countries and economic entities, particularly those in Northeast Asia, witnessed the U.S.-China rapprochement and also moved successfully to strengthen economic ties with China. As a result, by the mid-1980s, wages for factory workers in places such as Hong Kong, Japan, South Korea, and Taiwan were increasing at a rapid rate. Companies from these Northeast Asian countries and economic entities began to consider moving the more labor-intensive parts of their production processes to China, where workers' wages would be significantly cheaper. But foreign companies wishing to invest in China had no clear legal pathway to establishing operations there.

Deng Xiaoping understood this. He knew that China lacked the legal and economic structures necessary for direct foreign participation in manufacturing, but he also believed that China and Chinese firms could benefit greatly from foreign participation in China's domestic economy. To facilitate market-led growth, Deng put his imprimatur on a policy of selective opening to foreign firms through the introduction of special economic zones (SEZs). In 1980, he oversaw the opening of the first such SEZ in Shenzhen, just across the border from Hong Kong. In Shenzhen, the Chinese central government introduced special tax incentives, simplified approval processes, and allowed flexible management procedures favorable to foreign investors that were not permitted in other parts of the country. For the most part, foreign entities operating in the Shenzhen SEZ concentrated on export processing, with elaborate regulations to ensure that the assembled merchandise did not escape the bonded warehouses and enter China's domestic economy. Products produced in the SEZs' foreign-invested factories could not legally be bought or sold in China.

The Shenzhen SEZ was enormously successful in attracting labor-intensive manufacturing investment, mostly because enthusiastic Hong Kong, Japanese, South Korean, and Taiwanese manufacturers moved the more labor-intensive parts of their production processes there. Chinese SOEs invested beside them. Under this system, Chinese exports to OECD countries, mostly in the form of consumer goods from foreign-invested factories, grew rapidly. The major industries in Shenzhen were electronics, machinery, food processing, construction and building materials, and textiles.[10] Soon the Chinese government gave permission for the establishment of SEZs in other parts of the country, and the number of SEZs began sprouting like mushrooms, although most were still concentrated along the southeastern coast. China quickly became a major exporter of manufactured goods. Within Asia, regional supply chains grew more complex. Asian manufacturers were able to specialize, taking advantage of relatively cheap Chinese labor and expanding production to larger economies of scale.

While Hong Kong, Japanese, South Korean, and Taiwanese companies were successful in Shenzhen and other SEZs, American investment was relatively small as a percentage of total foreign investment. The dominant form of Chinese inbound investment came from what was called the "flock of geese" style of migration from higher labor cost economies in various parts of Northeast Asia to the lower labor cost economies of the SEZs. But the growth of U.S. trade with China was inhibited by both the lack of a regulatory framework outside the SEZs and the foreign exchange certificate (FEC) system controlled by the Bank of China. In place from 1979 to 1995, the FEC system constrained U.S. exports to and investments in China.

The FEC system was not unique to China. It had been a common tool in countries where the national currencies were subject to exchange controls or were not convertible. Under the Chinese system, foreign goods could be bought only with FECs obtained through a Chinese bank and purchased in foreign currency. FECs, in theory at least, could be spent only in businesses serving foreigners and only for foreign goods. Those with access to foreign exchange could purchase otherwise unavailable imported goods. But even with both the desire and the financial wherewithal to purchase foreign goods, private citizens and companies in China had almost no legal access to the foreign exchange necessary to purchase the FEC that would make such purchases possible. The system also penalized foreign exporters wishing to access the China market, who had to accommodate requests for barter trade or other forms of irregular payment systems, such as buying FECs with renminbi at prices far exceeding the official value. Smuggling and other corrupt or illegal practices became common among bureaucrats, trade officials, and others with access to power.

Other profound changes were simultaneously taking place in the Chinese economy. Most important, perhaps, the Chinese government began allowing market pricing for a wide range of products, with food being the most critical example. In Chinese cities, where food had long been rationed and could be purchased only in state-owned stores, small free markets began springing up everywhere as farmers from the surrounding countryside, who had recently returned to family farming after years of living in collectives, brought their produce to the cities to sell. Starting from a very low economic base, China's farmers had been the first to take advantage of economic liberalization by eschewing collectives and reverting to family stewardship of the fields, a return to trusted traditional methods of farming.

In the 1980s, the Chinese government also initiated an enormous drive to encourage domestic investment in urban infrastructure. At the time, the investment was designed to catch up from a decade or more of underinvestment in both real estate and infrastructure during the Cultural Revolution and its aftermath. By the late 1980s, China's urban landscape was beginning to be modernized and reformed, but this process led to supply shortages, corruption, poor-quality buildings, and eventually, rampant inflation in urban areas.

Deng Xiaoping's initial efforts to modernize China through reform and opening were spectacularly successful, leading to the rapid transformation of the country. China's per capita income was only around U.S. $200 a year in 1979, so room for catch-up growth was enormous. Nonetheless, by the second half of the 1980s, the rapid expansion of trade and investment, along with urban infrastructure investment and partial price liberalization, had created conditions that contributed to excessive growth and accelerating inflation. By the end of the 1980s, inflation in China was running at approximately 20 percent. The government, well aware of the consequences of hyperinflation during the unstable civil war period, became concerned about the prospect of a new period of runaway inflation.

By early 1988 and 1989, both high inflation and rampant corruption had also become increasingly obvious to ordinary Chinese people. At that time, in large parts of the Chinese economy, particularly urban real estate, the Communist Party was beginning to experiment with the transition from public to private ownership. Often, such transitions were noncontroversial, as when the long-time occupant of a ministry- or SOE-owned apartment obtained individual ownership of a flat for an affordable price. But at other times, the privatization process was more contentious.

In late 1988 and early 1989, China's central government began to address the problem of inflation by slamming on the economic brakes. One unintended consequence of that effort was a further spike in corruption. For example, while the government had drained liquidity from the banks to reduce frothy economic activity, some real estate developers in places such as Beijing and Shanghai were still able to find the money to continue construction. These were often projects protected by high-ranking officials. While most construction had stopped and unemployed construction workers roamed the streets of Beijing, projects that were protected by high-ranking officials found a way to continue. From the point of view of the average Beijing resident in 1989, inflation, corruption, and unemployment all spiked at the same time, largely as a consequence of urgent government measures to stop inflation.

The Tiananmen Upheaval

This was the economic backdrop that planted the seeds for the popular protests that ultimately led to the Tiananmen Incident of June 4, 1989. Raging inflation, obvious corruption, and a sudden liquidity tightening that precipitated a spike in unemployment were the economic antecedents driving students and others to protest in Tiananmen Square in the weeks following the death of China's deposed general secretary of the party Hu Yaobang on April 15.

The military crackdown on the student protestors in Tiananmen Square on June 4, 1989, was a turning point in modern Chinese history. The crackdown had economic antecedents. The rise in the USSR of Mikhail Gorbachev as the general secretary of the Communist Party and his reform policies of *glasnost* (openness) and *perestroika* (restructuring) had informed the demonstrators. In 1989, Gorbachev paid a visit to Beijing when the student demonstrations were at their height. The public pressure created by the students led to a schism between factions within the Communist Party of China and the abrupt dismissal of Zhao Ziyang as party general secretary and his subsequent replacement by Jiang Zemin. While these economic and political events of 1989 were not directly associated with U.S.-China bilateral relations, they had a profound impact on U.S.-China trade and investment relations.

The U.S. government's stance toward China changed abruptly after June 4. President George H. W. Bush, who had served as head of the Liaison Office in Beijing in 1974–1975, denounced the military's actions in Tiananmen Square, suspended military sales to China, and cut off high-level exchanges between Chinese and American officials. Many members of Congress and the American public thought the president's measures had not gone far enough. Some in the U.S. Congress opposed granting China most favored nation trading status, and the issue remained controversial until China joined the World Trade Organization in 2001.

President Bush's response was reflected in the business community. A number of nongovernmental organizations with close ties to China, including the U.S.-China Business Council, also publicly criticized the military's actions against the demonstrators in Beijing. On June 7, 1989, the board of directors of the council published a resolution stating:

> The members of the U.S.-China Business Council deplore the violent suppression and wanton killing of pro-democracy demonstrators in Beijing and the apparent turning away from the policies of reform and economic liberalization by the government of the People's Republic of China. The commercial and economic relations between the United States and China, so carefully nurtured and developed through the efforts of people on both sides in the past 18 years and so clearly in the overall strategic interest of both our two countries, have been disrupted and could suffer long-term damage. . . . It is critically important to both countries that we preserve the links between us until they can again be expanded. We pledge our support for the effort to rebuild the shattered relationship when that becomes possible and call upon the Chinese government to return to the policy of reform and respect for the legitimate aspirations of the Chinese people for basic human freedoms.[11]

Both American exports to China and U.S. foreign investment in China slowed dramatically in the aftermath of the Tiananmen Incident, with U.S. exports dropping from $58 billion in 1980 to $48 billion in 1990, as seen in Figure 6.3. Total trade growth dropped from 38 percent growth in 1988 to 31 percent in 1989 and to only 13 percent in 1990. U.S. direct investment in China also slowed, as indicated in Figure 6.4, and did not regain significant growth until 1993.

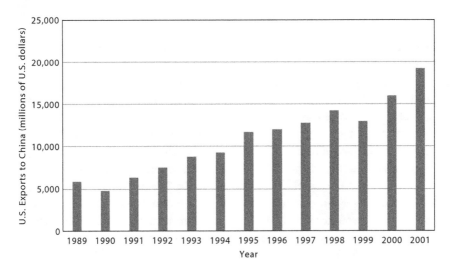

6.3 U.S. exports to China, 1989–2001. Category: goods, free on board (FOB).

Source: International Monetary Fund.

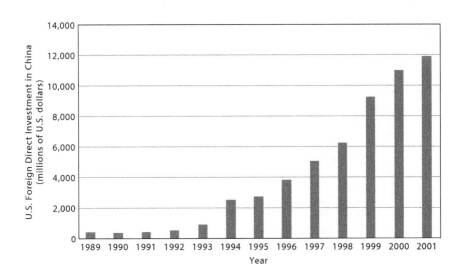

6.4 U.S. foreign direct investment in China, 1989–2001.

Source: U.S. Bureau of Economic Analysis, Department of Commerce.

Note: Balance of payments and direct investment position data on a historical-cost basis (millions of dollars).

Cycle 2: 1989–2001

The second cycle began on June 5, 1989, the day after the military crackdown on protestors in Beijing, and ended on December 11, 2001, when China joined the World Trade Organization. This cycle coincided with the presidencies of George H. W. Bush and Bill Clinton, during which Jiang Zemin served as president of China and general secretary of the Chinese Communist Party.

In 1990 and 1991, U.S.-China trade and investment were stagnant at best, in response to China's domestic political and economic turmoil in the aftermath of Tiananmen. During this period, in Beijing, conservative policy makers within the Communist Party held the upper hand. In January and February 1992, Deng Xiaoping again engineered a tectonic structural shift by his successful execution of a Southern Tour, visiting the reform-minded cities of Guangzhou, Shenzhen, Zhuhai, and Shanghai where the reforms had been launched the previous decade. This visit by the paramount leader turned the tables on the conservative faction and opened a new wave of reform and openness. By the end of 1992, it had become clear in Washington that a substantial shift had again taken place.

In December 1992, after the November presidential election and in the final days of the George H. W. Bush administration, President Bush asked Secretary of Commerce Barbara Franklin to travel to Beijing for an official visit that would clear the way for the resumption of normal diplomatic and business ties for the incoming Clinton administration. The Franklin visit signaled to the American business community that the U.S.-China relationship was about to enter a new, post-Tiananmen phase. China's economy had begun its recovery from the inflation of the late 1980s. With inflation tamed, the economy was poised to expand even more rapidly, and a small but growing urban middle class was beginning to emerge.

But newly elected president Bill Clinton had run his 1992 election campaign with an explicitly strident anti-China message, promising at the Democratic National Convention "an America that will not coddle tyrants, from Baghdad to Beijing."[12]

Clinton's new foreign policy emphasized human rights and democracy, values heralded in the late 1970s by President Jimmy Carter. On May 28, 1993, shortly after taking office, Clinton issued an executive order explicitly tying the next yearly grant of most favored nation (MFN) status to China on its "overall significant progress on human rights,"[13] a condition that Secretary of State Warren Christopher would be called upon to certify. President Clinton was the first to set such a sweeping condition. As noted earlier, China's eligibility for MFN status was subject to the freedom of emigration conditions imposed by the Jackson-Vanik amendment (Section 402) of the Trade Act of 1974, which permits U.S. authorities to grant MFN status to a non–market economy country providing that that country does not restrict emigration. Under U.S. law, the president may either determine that China is in full compliance with the Jackson-Vanik amendment or else waive the requirement of full compliance, as U.S. presidents did with China beginning in 1980.[14]

Disagreement over the advisability of conditioning MFN status on a significant improvement in human rights became a contentious policy that pitted the U.S. business community against those in the Clinton administration who favored conditionality based on human rights improvements. I remember one visit by Department of Commerce Under Secretary Jeffrey Garten to Beijing in 1994, when I was the commercial attaché at the U.S. embassy there. Under Secretary Garten gave a strong human rights–themed speech and then had to face direct criticism by the American business community in Beijing for not being supportive of their efforts to export to an increasingly competitive market.

In March 1994, Secretary of State Warren Christopher also traveled to Beijing on a mission to explore human rights protocols with the Chinese. The secretary met with the American Chamber of Commerce in Beijing, and the tensions over human rights versus trade were on full display in front of the American press. According to the *Los Angeles Times*, "Christopher found himself besieged by business executives, who warned him that U.S. policies linking trade benefits to human rights reform could cost the United States billions of dollars in lost business." Summing up the discontent, one American Chamber of Commerce officer stated, "U.S. policy puts U.S. businesses at a competitive disadvantage."[15]

Over time, the policy of conditioning trade on human rights became more and more difficult to maintain. The tensions between the two priorities were contentious even within the Clinton cabinet. In my role with the Department of Commerce, I remember apparent tensions between Secretary of Commerce Ron Brown and Secretary of State Warren Christopher at cabinet meetings about competing, and incompatible, priorities: American export jobs and human rights in China.

In the end, after vigorous lobbying by the U.S. business community and the president's economic advisors, the president pulled back from conditionality. Secretary of State Christopher admitted that although some progress had been made in emigration and prison labor, no significant progress had been made on other human rights issues. On May 26, 1994, Clinton announced his decision to grant MFN status despite the lack of progress, arguing both that the link between trade and human rights was no longer tenable and that the cause of human rights in China could be better advanced if China were not isolated.[16] President Clinton thus effectively prioritized U.S. exports, American jobs, and economic engagement over human rights. Clinton called his new policy "comprehensive engagement."[17]

The political furor within the United States did not die down following the decision to renew MFN status. Rather, an unending series of political skirmishes ensued between those advocating human rights and those who wished to engage fully in China's booming economy.

While the possibility of setting such an expansive improvement of human rights as a condition for China's receiving MFN status was never seriously proposed again, the issue continued to come up year after year. And the Clinton administration continued to raise the issue of human rights. First Lady Hillary Clinton made history when she attended the United Nations Fourth World Conference on Women in Beijing in 1995, delivering the historic observation that "women's rights are human rights" and directly criticizing the Chinese government for its ongoing abuse of human rights. On the margins of the conference, the first lady had apparently personally witnessed a number of Chinese feminist activists being beaten and dragged away by Chinese security. Incidents like this added to uncertainty in bilateral relations.

During President Jiang Zemin's state visit to the United States in the fall of 1997, President Clinton again brought up the issue of human rights even while stressing the need for a broad and multifaceted relationship. And when President Clinton visited China in June 1998, he raised the issue of Tiananmen in a televised joint press conference with President Jiang, arguing that the Chinese military had been wrong to use force against the protesters. Clinton also encouraged the Chinese leader to begin a dialogue with the exiled Dalai Lama. Clinton's continuing emphasis on democracy and human rights did not sit well with Jiang Zemin.

The Clinton administration's emphasis on human rights also continued to come into conflict with the perceived needs of American business and their opportunities in China throughout much of the Clinton presidency. From the perspective of business, conflicts between the two governments created commercial uncertainty and put American companies at a disadvantage relative to European and Japanese competitors. The annual debate about extending China's MFN status became a painful exercise pitting the U.S. business, agriculture, and foreign policy communities against labor and human rights organizations. This annual debate created uncontrollable political risk and uncertainty for all American companies investing in or doing business with China, as well as those considering it.

In November of 1999, thirteen years after China had first attempted to join the World Trade Organization (WTO), the United States and China signed an agreement paving the way for China's entry.[18] In 2000, the last year of the Clinton administration, both houses of Congress passed legislation that effectively amended the Trade Law of 1974 to provide China with permanent normal trade relations. Requirements that the U.S. government monitor and report on both human rights trends in China and restrictions on labor accompanied the legislation.

The establishment of permanent normal trade relations set the stage for the United States to negotiate the terms under which China would be permitted to join the WTO. In the latter half of 2000 and the first part of 2001, the United States and China had a series of intense negotiations over the protocol of potential WTO accession, which spelled out in detail China's commitments to WTO rules. Several commitments were set forth or clarified at the WTO in Geneva, at a multilateral level rather than as a bilateral exercise.

By the time of China's accession to the WTO, the rate of domestic economic growth within China had declined significantly. Indeed, the growth rate had declined for seven consecutive years. According to official Chinese economic data, economic growth in 1999 was only 7.1 percent. China's economic planners realized that an overhaul of the Chinese economic structure—through the WTO-mandated opening—would be needed for sustainable growth into the future.

President and Party Chairman Jiang Zemin and Premier Zhu Rongji used the WTO as a wedge to effect much-needed reforms to the Chinese economy. Implementation of the WTO protocols would dramatically reduce the power of the Chinese government and SOEs across broad swathes of the Chinese economy, while simultaneously unleashing the entrepreneurial energies of millions of Chinese private companies and profoundly affecting the course of commercial relations between China and the United States.

Cycle 3: 2001–2008

The third period commenced with China's entry into the WTO in 2001 and lasted until the global financial crisis in 2008, which began with the bankruptcy of Lehman Brothers on September 15 of that year. This period coincides almost exactly with the leadership of President George W. Bush and President and General Secretary of the Communist Party Hu Jintao.

China's entry into the WTO in 2001 led, in turn, to another surge in American trade and investment, as part of the rapid increase in the pace of China's integration into the global economy. From 2000 to 2008, as shown in Figure 6.5, American exports to China grew robustly from year to year. At the same time, with many of the legal restraints against U.S. investment removed, in accordance with the WTO accession agreement, American capital also began flowing into China on a much larger scale, as shown by Figure 6.6.

China's entry into the WTO was not just a bilateral phenomenon, of course. Doors were opened to other economies as well, sparking a second wave of investment into factories and other production facilities by Hong Kong, Japanese, South Korean, and Taiwanese investors who had previously operated primarily in SEZs, concentrating on final assembly and exports. Under the WTO, they were able to operate inside China on a much larger scale, moving entire supply chains there and supplying both the Chinese and foreign export markets, including the United States.

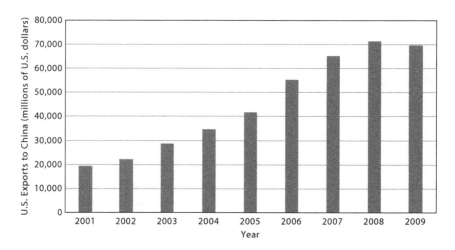

6.5 U.S. exports to China, 2001–2009.

Source: International Monetary Fund.
Category: goods, free on board (FOB).

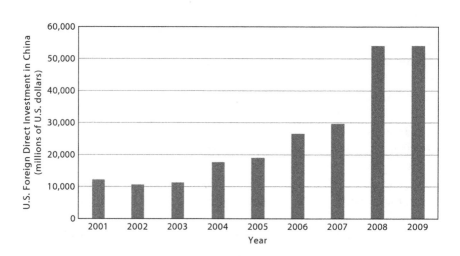

6.6 U.S. foreign direct investment in China, 2001–2009.

Source: U.S. Bureau of Economic Analysis, Department of Commerce.
Note: Balance of payments and direct investment position data on a historical-cost basis (millions of dollars).

The China-based operations of these Hong Kong, Japanese, South Korean, and Taiwanese companies had a number of important competitive advantages. They were able to employ large numbers of relatively well-educated rural migrant workers, especially young women. They had established connections with buyers around the world. They were familiar with global best practices in manufacturing and could produce at world-quality standards. And in China, they were relatively unconstrained by strict enforcement of environmental or labor standards.

Most importantly, many of these East Asian manufacturers were able to produce on an extremely large scale, establishing global economies of scale significantly beyond traditional American manufacturing standards. Factories employing tens of thousands of workers were not unusual. Many of them were more than ten times larger than factories making the same goods in the United States. Similarly, an army of parts, supply, and service companies gradually migrated to China along with the prime contractors. Over time, a vast ecosystem evolved in China's coastal provinces, leading to extremely efficient industrial clusters focused on every manner of consumer and industrial goods.

Not surprisingly, ethnic Chinese from Hong Kong, Singapore, and Taiwan played, and continue to play, a vital role in knitting together these regional and global supply chains. Conglomerates such as Hong Kong–based Li & Fung Limited oversaw huge supply chains of primarily Western brands, assuring massive quantity and improved quality at unbeatable prices. Singaporeans occupied, and still occupy, many senior management positions throughout China's industrial economy. Taiwanese engineers played, and still play, important roles in training and upgrading the skills of factory workers.

One example of this type of industry-cluster development by Taiwanese, Hong Kong, and Korean business people was the furniture industry. In the post-WTO period, large investments were made in the furniture industry in the eastern Pearl River Delta, the Yangtze River Delta, and the Bohai region. These factories often imported hardwoods from the forests of the American Southeast and then manufactured bedroom or dining room furniture for export back to the United States, which in turned forced the closure of many smaller-scale traditional American furniture manufacturing companies in North Carolina and elsewhere.

A number of factors allowed these foreign-invested enterprises in China's furniture export sector to prevail. First, they often enjoyed free or very cheap access to land. Second, Chinese wages in the early 2000s were significantly cheaper than in the United States. Third, the companies had access to cheap American-sourced hardwoods that allowed easy penetration into the North American markets. Fourth, the scale and efficiency of the China-invested foreign enterprises were much greater than in the more craft-oriented factories of the United States. They also enjoyed efficient import and export infrastructure, especially ready access to ports. Finally, American retailers of furniture welcomed the supply competition from China, which provided them with cheap and high-quality goods popular with American customers.

This export juggernaut, for the most part, was not directly supported or directed by China's central government or its many state-owned institutions. Provincial and municipal governments, however, were enthusiastic supporters of foreign direct investment, competing ruthlessly among themselves with promises to potential investors of free land, improved infrastructure, tax breaks, and other types of support.

Governments in import markets around the world, particularly in Europe and North America, responded to the surge in Chinese exports by vigorously using the antidumping and countervailing duty provisions of the WTO. China's trading partners were able to impose high duties on Chinese imports due to China's status in the WTO as a nonmarket economy. Thus, from the mid-2000s until today, Chinese exporters face high duties under either one or both of these legal mechanisms. This imposition of WTO-compatible tariffs by foreign governments forced Chinese manufacturers to focus increasingly on developing domestic markets in China.

Within China's huge and rapidly growing domestic market, imported products initially competed against both joint venture products and products made by domestic Chinese companies. In the early 2000s, there was a clear difference in price and quality between these three production modes: imports and products made by wholly foreign-owned manufacturers stood at the high end, joint venture products dominated the middle, and domestic Chinese products fell at the low end. But this gradually changed as Chinese manufactured goods climbed up the value chain, first by underpricing joint venture competitors and foreign manufacturers and then by systematically improving quality.

The economic model of China's Asian-owned large-scale assembly operations producing for both domestic and foreign consumption proved extremely disruptive for many domestic American companies, as Barry Naughton details so well in chapter 7 of this volume. Some traditional American industries producing such goods as furniture, automotive parts, apparel, footwear, sporting equipment, and consumer electronics could not adapt easily to the tsunami of Chinese exports produced in highly labor-intensive factories. The China price of a particular product became a hurdle that many traditional American manufacturers were not able to overcome. Many American companies that ignored or reacted passively to Chinese competition were simply wiped out.

This process of Schumpeterian creative destruction (the incessant product and process innovation mechanism by which new production units replace outdated ones and thus create productivity growth) was not inevitable or clear-cut. Many companies adapted; many did not. In fact, most economists agree that productivity improvements in American manufacturing were responsible for a far larger share of the American manufacturing job losses than trade with China.

According to the U.S. Bureau of Labor Statistics, "Employment in manufacturing grew to an all-time peak of 19.6 million in June 1979, then declined and never fully recovered to the peak level. In December 2015, manufacturing jobs totaled 12.3 million and accounted for 8.6 percent of all non-farm employment."[19] Total manufacturing employment in the United States as of this writing was 12.56 million.

Indeed, the intricate interplay between productivity gains, foreign direct investment, and trade provides the most powerful engines of globalization and job destruction in the United States. Companies that outsourced the most labor-intensive parts of their production chain and upgraded core competencies in research and design or distribution often triumphed in this more globalized world. The overall output of manufacturing in the United States, even having largely accommodated China's rise, never declined in the aggregate. Indeed, manufacturing productivity and profitability remain healthy to this day.

A very different economic model began to appear during the decade of the 2000s. China began a gradual, but inexorable, process of Chinese industrial domestication beginning at the lower levels of the supply chain and gradually moving up to higher levels of value-added production. Initially, this process was confined largely to the private sector. Over time, however, the Chinese government at all levels ramped up support for more and more production using more and more Chinese content, displacing both imports and joint venture products. Increasingly, when there was a choice between a joint venture product and a more Chinese product, especially if that product was from an SOE, the scales were tipped in favor of the wholly owned Chinese company.

During the era of Jiang Zemin, the Communist Party's policy of allowing a rapidly expanding market economy to lift all boats served China's interests well. The transition from Jiang Zemin to Hu Jintao as general secretary of the Communist Party in 2002, however, saw a conservative backlash against market-oriented, laissez-faire policies in favor of state intervention and the more visible hand of the party. The scales were decidedly tipped in favor of Chinese companies and particularly the SOEs.

Hu Jintao was a relatively weak leader without a strong power base within the party. He was unable to control the party-based special interest groups that clustered around specific SOE-dominated industries, such as energy, telecommunications, construction, railroads, aviation, media, banking, insurance, steel, and aluminum. Over time, the party perfected mechanisms that promoted the welfare of SOEs at the expense of imports and foreign investors in all of the sensitive industries.

Moreover, the party controlled senior personnel appointments to state-owned banks and other financial institutions, the various market regulatory agencies, SOEs, and provincial and municipal governments. In most cases, the most senior person in these industrial networks, in terms of party rank, was the CEO of the SOE, which was also the national champion in that particular industry. Through party networks, the industry regulator would promote the party through nontransparent party channels. Through this mechanism, the party gained greater and greater control over the commanding heights of the Chinese economy. Through their control of SOEs and through favoritism toward state-controlled entities over all privately controlled enterprises, including all foreign companies, the party increasingly asserted (and enriched) itself.

Sometime after 2005, many foreign companies competing with Chinese SOEs began to feel distinctly unwelcome in China. Private sector Chinese companies were also not able to operate on a level playing field with their state-owned competitors. In these circumstances, SOEs—including those owned at the national, provincial, and local levels—were growing into large, complex, and often inefficient operations. In contrast, Chinese private sector companies and foreign-invested enterprises were not treated equally by regulators or by state-owned financial institutions.

On the other hand, this period also saw some nominally private firms that were closely allied with the Chinese Communist Party and the government leap onto the global stage. Companies such as Dalian Wanda (real estate and entertainment), HNA (a conglomerate that grew out of Hainan Airlines and now includes several airlines, hotels, and tourist companies), Huawei (telecommunications), and Anbang (insurance) became global players. Charismatic individual entrepreneurs rooted in the extremely dynamic Chinese private sector headed all these companies. While nominally private, these companies nonetheless received national champion treatment from Chinese banks and regulators.

Not all successful private sector Chinese companies have received such a high degree of support from the Chinese government. In the internet sector, for example, the government set the general parameters for domestic innovation and then allowed private sector Chinese companies to compete freely among themselves—but in a market where foreign competition was highly circumscribed. Thus, Chinese entrepreneurs would study foreign internet companies and their business models and then reproduce them in the Chinese market behind the so-called Great Firewall. Some of these internet companies found it expedient to copy business models from abroad wholesale and then expand rapidly in the domestic hot house environment free from foreign competition. In the internet business, this business model is commonly referred to as "block and copy" or "copy to China."

Many of these Chinese internet companies later became important global-scale enterprises. They were strongly supported by foreign investors, mostly American. By 2019, approximately 1.2 trillion U.S. dollars were invested in Chinese companies on the New York–based NASDAQ. A number of these companies are led by globally respected internet leaders, such as Alibaba's Jack Ma and Tencent's Pony Ma. These companies have themselves become global technology titans, investing in many hundreds of foreign technology companies around the world. At the same time, the ability of American and other foreign firms to engage in the internet business in China remains highly circumscribed. The Chinese national champions—public or private—maintain an effective profit sanctuary in China, which gives them a large competitive advantage globally.

Over time, the Chinese government's role in supporting both public and private sector domestic enterprises over joint venture production or imports became increasingly blatant. Chinese industry regulators rigorously enforced the law against foreign investors but declined to enforce the same laws against Chinese competitors in an equivalent manner. Many foreign companies began to perceive systemic discrimination across multiple dimensions of government regulation: tax, environmental protection, labor, consumer safety, and antitrust.

Cycle 4: 2008–2019

The fourth phase spans the period from the global financial crisis to the early Trump administration. The Chinese government reacted to the global financial crisis of 2008 with a huge fiscal stimulus and enormous investments in domestic infrastructure. On the Chinese side, leadership in this period transitioned from President Hu Jintao to President and General Secretary of the Communist Party Xi Jinping. In the United States, President Barack Obama was succeeded by Donald Trump as president in January 2017.

The global financial crisis that began in 2008 and, more specifically, China's response to that crisis began the next stage of rapid expansion of American exports and investment in China. As the financial crisis spread from the United States to Europe and beyond, the entire global economy was in danger of slipping into recession—or worse, a depression. While the crisis began in American real estate markets, other highly leveraged companies and countries were soon deeply implicated.

As Figures 6.7 and 6.8 show, American exporters benefitted from China's response to the great financial crisis, especially from its massive infrastructure-building campaigns. Exports from the United States increased each year from 2009 to 2015. American companies' financial strength and will to invest in China were reduced, but American firms began to increase their investment in China during the second half of the decade as they recovered from the financial crisis.

At the time of the crisis, the Chinese financial system was not reliant on external financing, and Chinese banks had relatively little exposure to foreign

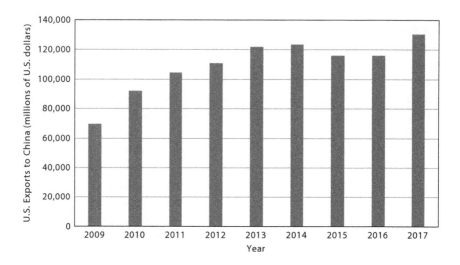

6.7 U.S. exports to China, 2009–2017. Category: goods, free on board (FOB).

Source: International Monetary Fund.

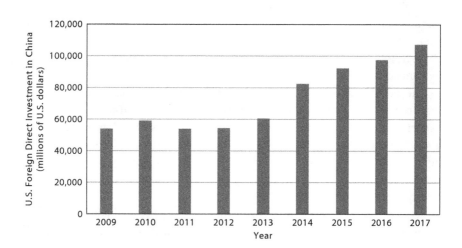

6.8 U.S. foreign direct investment in China, 2009–2017.

Source: U.S. Bureau of Economic Analysis, Department of Commerce.

Note: Balance of payments and direct investment position data on a historical-cost basis (millions of dollars).

risk, such as the collateralized debt obligations that brought down Lehman Brothers. Chinese banks and other financial institutions had invested in U.S. Treasuries and other high-quality dollar-denominated assets. Nonetheless, with bankruptcies roiling global financial markets, they could not avoid indirect consequences such as slowing global growth, decreased exports, and heightened global uncertainty.

In 2009 and 2010, Chinese policy makers responded to the global financial crisis with four main strategies: maintaining the value of the Chinese currency, the renminbi (RMB), while continuing the liberalization of interest rates; dramatically expanding fiscal stimulus through an epic domestic and later foreign infrastructure-building campaign; encouraging expansion of domestic service industries; and expanding subsidies and other types of support for high-technology industries. This suite of policies, each described in more detail in the following sections, was remarkably successful in stabilizing the macroeconomy and contributed both to increased U.S. exports and to the gradual overall recovery of the global economy.

Maintaining the Value of the Renminbi

From 2008 to 2014, the RMB strengthened from 6.8 RMB per U.S. dollar to 6.1 RMB per U.S. dollar. The support of the RMB by the People's Bank of China, the country's central bank, was critical for overall global financial stability. The other countries and economies of the region were able to adjust their exchange rates and expand their exports without the headwind of competing against a depreciated Chinese currency. Further, the Chinese market continued to absorb increasing amounts of all types of imports, especially a huge volume of commodities. From 2010 to 2014, commodity prices soared and energy prices nearly doubled on the strength of Chinese demand.

While maintaining a strong RMB, the People's Bank of China and other financial industry regulators were able to free interest rates gradually but steadily to better reflect market conditions. Working closely with the International Monetary Fund and the World Bank, China slowly liberalized its interest rate policy. Specifically, nonbanks outside of the SOE banking system started to offer consumers and private sector enterprises market-based interest rates for savings accounts and loans.

Infrastructure

In the wake of the financial crisis, China's economic decision makers knew that they would not be able to rely on net exports to grow the economy. Net exports as a percentage of GDP had peaked at 14 percent in 2007 and fell precipitously to −4 percent in 2009. In response, the Chinese government, at virtually all levels, began an enormous fiscal stimulus program by building infrastructure across every sector of the economy. The government approved construction of new subway systems, telecommunications projects, power plants, airports, high-speed railways, and highways. Often, the projects were funded not by the central government, but by municipal or provincial governments with central government approval. SOEs carried out almost all of the construction.

The Service Sector

The Chinese government also endeavored to expand the service sector as rapidly as possible, in part to address the problem of unemployment. The government realized that China's economy was excessively reliant on manufacturing and lacked resilience and a healthy balance between the manufacturing and service sectors.

Moreover, there was enormous pent-up demand from Chinese middle-class consumers for high-quality services of all types. The average Chinese person had become much more conscious of pollution, poor-quality food, and the lack of reliable health care. By and large, the government allowed the private sector to meet these typically middle-class consumption demands. Travel and tourism, entertainment, education, and health care spending all increased rapidly. American service franchises and other consumer brands quickly expanded their presence in China.

High Technology

Partially in response to the global financial crisis, but also as a continuation of previous policies, the Chinese government, mostly through the Ministry of Industry and Information Technology, pursued aggressive techno-nationalistic policies. For example, the government implemented cybersecurity policies to restrict or remove foreign software and hardware from government computer systems. The Chinese government also pushed hard to maximize Chinese influence in the global industrial standards-setting bodies, such as the International Organization for Standardization.

Massive Chinese industrial subsidies poured into technologies of the future, including information technologies, biotechnology, aviation, telecommunications, robotics, semiconductors, and new-energy vehicles. These subsidy programs and funding vehicles took many forms. But they were consistently implemented in a mercantilist manner with a view to minimizing imports, maximizing exports, and gradually moving up the global supply chain. While foreign enterprises were nominally invited to participate in these projects, they would find that the terms and conditions of participation systemically favored local players, especially SOEs.

Over the later part of the Hu Jintao era and the early part of the Xi Jinping era, American companies remained generally optimistic about their continued engagement in China's economic growth. American government and industry observers were especially encouraged by the results of the Third Plenum of the Eighteenth Party Congress in December 2013, where the party pledged to allow the market to play a decisive role in economic decision-making. Many believed that this was a turning point and that Chinese private sector companies and foreign enterprises might finally be able to compete on a level playing field with SOEs in the Chinese domestic market. American exports to and investments in China both rose on the expectation that there would be further market-oriented reform and opening.

By 2015 and 2016, however, President Xi's policies to address the global financial crisis had clearly led to economic distortions. As a result of large investments in infrastructure, debt had expanded rapidly as a percentage of total GDP, reaching 300 percent by 2018. As China's domestic infrastructure splurge began to wind down, in 2013, Xi Jinping announced a new Belt and Road Initiative (BRI) that would give Chinese companies the opportunity to continue building infrastructure in other countries. But the BRI has led to even more debt for both the participating Chinese companies and the recipient states. On the technology front, massive subsidies, epitomized by the Made in China 2025 policy, galvanized foreign opposition and led to increased export and investment controls in OECD counties. By 2017 and 2018, the Chinese economy was clearly overindebted and overextended.

Today, Chinese policies generally show preference for party and state control over the economy at the expense of both Chinese private companies and foreign firms. SOEs are encouraged to expand aggressively both inside and outside of China and are protected from foreign competition inside China by state-owned banks and economic regulators.

By the Nineteenth Party Congress in October 2017, China seemed—at least temporarily—to have reversed the decision of the Eighteenth Party Congress to allow the market to play the decisive role in the economy. Instead, the party, the state, and SOEs were given primacy and allowed every opportunity to expand their remit beyond traditional boundaries. China's Company Law was amended to force SOEs to obey the party committee and require private companies to faithfully follow party dictates. The National Intelligence Law adopted in 2017 requires that Chinese citizens and organizations "support, cooperate with, and collaborate on national intelligence work."[20]

Since the Nineteenth Party Congress in 2017, President Xi has redoubled efforts to expand the Communist Party's ability to control most aspects of political, social, and economic life in China. Sometimes, these efforts have benefitted foreign business. The anticorruption campaign, for example, has significantly reduced the opportunities for corrupt officials to demand bribes from foreign companies. Usually, however, the imposition of the party into the economic sphere has not been welcomed by foreign investors in China. Many companies have been subject to public pressure campaigns to conform with Chinese socialist norms. In part due to rising nationalism, foreign companies also find recruiting and retaining Chinese talent more difficult.

The retreat of market-oriented reforms and the increasing dominance of the party over social institutions has become one of the key issues in the growing crisis in U.S.-China relations. In 2018, U.S. exports slowed, and investment flowing both ways has dropped precipitously. American corporate leaders are becoming unwilling to step forward to defend the bilateral relationship against the backdrop of the Chinese government's increasingly mercantilist policies.

* * *

Although U.S. exports to and investment in China have grown rapidly over the past forty years, reflecting dramatic political and economic changes in China's domestic governance, this expansion has been extremely volatile. There is no certainty that past trends will continue or that we will see another cycle of expansion.

The election of President Donald Trump in 2016 led to a much more confrontational and assertive foreign policy toward China. In the U.S. government's 2017 National Security Strategy and National Defense Strategy, both China and Russia were named as strategic competitors of the United States, as several other contributors to this volume have also noted. The publication of these documents presaged an overall reassessment of the U.S.-China relationship and led to an increase in the competitive aspects of that relationship, along with a reduction in the areas where the two governments collaborate or cooperate.

Director Christopher Wray of the FBI, testifying in front of the Senate in February 2018, summed up the Trump administration's position when he said, "One of the things we're trying to do is view the China threat as not just a whole-of-government threat but a whole-of-society threat on their end, and I think that it's going to take a whole-of-society response by us."[21]

President Trump initially chose to focus on the enormous bilateral trade deficit between the United States and China and blamed his predecessors for allowing China to take advantage of American companies to expand exports and block American imports. Moreover, the Trump administration—unlike all its recent predecessors—preferred a direct and confrontational bilateral approach, rather than using multilateral dispute resolution mechanisms, such as those offered by the WTO, to resolve disagreements.

In 2018, using the national security exceptions allowed under the WTO combined with the Section 301 provisions of the U.S. Trade Law, which allow the president to impose penalties on foreign trading partners engaged in unfair trading practices, the Trump administration levied tariffs on as much as half of Chinese imports. The Chinese government responded with roughly commensurate retaliatory tariffs against American exports. Multiple rounds of bilateral negotiations followed, led by Trade Representative Robert Lighthizer and Secretary of the Treasury Steven Mnuchin from the United States and Vice Premier Liu He from China. Talks focused on issues articulated in the Section 301 submission: forced technology transfer, intellectual property rights, SOEs, subsides, market access, and cyber incursions into U.S. companies for the purpose of commercial gain. In January 2019, the two sides signed a Phase One trade agreement, which brought a temporary halt to additional tariffs but did little to ease the tensions in U.S.-China relations.

Instead, trade disputes broadened significantly to include export controls, technology transfer, and additional investment restrictions imposed by both sides. The U.S. Department of the Treasury was the lead agency implementing expanded import controls. In particular, the U.S. government's comprehensive global campaign against Chinese telecommunications firm Huawei exacerbated the lack of trust between the two sides. Through 2019 and 2020, the U.S. government attempted to restrict technology flows to China by cutting global supply chains to Chinese high-technology firms. China responded by doubling down on plans to invest in its own technology development and homegrown technology companies. A dramatic increase in U.S.-China tensions took place in 2020 as the COVID-19 virus spread around the world. Both sides blamed the other for originating and failing to contain the virus.

The Trump administration's approach to China marks a decisive break with the past. China, as detailed so well in chapter 3 by John Garver, is no longer a poor developing country. Rather, it is a near-peer competitor that challenges the United States across all dimensions of international relations: strategic, economic, trade, ideology, and technology. As such, many believe that some degree of economic decoupling—especially in the national security–sensitive high-technology areas—was to be welcomed.

The Trump administration forced China to the negotiating table to discuss systemic issues that have bedeviled American exporters and investors for some twenty years. Did the Trump administration force Chinese economic decision makers to adhere more closely to their WTO and other commitments? Did the Chinese Communist Party loosen its control over industries dominated by SOEs? Did the party agree to measures to ensure that foreign companies are treated equally? Have subsidies to Chinese national champions been reduced?

Have Chinese techno-nationalism and aggressive industrial policy measures been constrained to conform to OECD norms? Even with a reduction in tension and a measure of goodwill, is it reasonable to expect the vast Chinese bureaucracy to effectively implement any agreement with a foreign country, especially at the local or provincial level?

Whether the U.S.-China bilateral relationship is going through another cyclical change or whether the tension is more structural and long lasting remains to be seen, but the outlook is not positive. Across many dimensions, internal tensions in China seem to be leading to political and economic divergence with the United States, rather than a convergence of the two countries' interests.

In the short term, more tension and volatility seem inevitable. The Biden administration will no doubt encourage China to conform to the system of global norms and participate in the global economy as the responsible stakeholder so many in the world hope it will become. But as David Lampton notes in chapter 14, the conclusion of this volume, decades may pass before the stars are sufficiently aligned to return to a more cooperative and productive relationship.

NOTES

1. The mission of the National Council for U.S.-China Trade and the later U.S.-China Business Council is to promote the U.S.-China commercial relationship for the benefit of its members and the U.S. economy.
2. Mei Renyi and Chen Juebin, "U.S.-China Trade Relations in the 1970s and Hong Kong's Role," in *Bridging the U.S.-China Divide*, ed. Priscilla Roberts (London: Cambridge Scholars Publishing, 2007).
3. Jonathon Steele, "America Puts the Flag Out for Deng," *Guardian*, January 30, 1979, https://www.theguardian.com/world/1979/jan/30/china.usa.
4. "Council Activities," *China Business Review* 6, no. 1 (January–February 1979): 13.
5. "Cabinet Briefing on Trade Implications of Normalization," *China Business Review* 6, no. 1 (January–February 1979): 14.
6. Richard Baum, "China in 1985: The Greening of the Revolution," *Asian Survey* 26, no. 1 (January 1986): 30.
7. See chapter 13 by Kenneth Lieberthal and Susan Thornton for a fuller description of normal trade relations.
8. See Kerry Dumbaugh, "China's Most-Favored-Nation (MFN) Status: Congressional Considerations, 1989–1998," Congressional Research Service, The Library of Congress, August 1998, http://congressionalresearch.com/98-603/document.php.
9. Other outstanding issues that slowed the expansion of commercial ties included the resolution of private and public sector claims on assets and the need for maritime and aviation agreements.
10. Mee Kam Ng and Wing-Shing Tang, "The Role of Planning in the Development of Shenzhen, China: Rhetoric and Realities," *Eurasian Geography and Economics* 45, no. 3 (2004): 190–211.
11. See "Resolution," in Roger W. Sullivan, "A Government in Transition," *China Business Review* (July-August 1989): 9.

12. See Nicholas D. Kristof, "China Worried by Clinton's Linking of Trade to Human Rights," *New York Times*, October 9, 1992, https://www.nytimes.com/1992/10/09/world /china-worried-by-clinton-s-linking-of-trade-to-human-rights.html.

13. These included a halt of exports to the United States made by prison labor, substantial adherence to the free immigration objectives in the Jackson-Vanik amendment, and adherence to the Universal Declaration of Human Rights, which included releasing and accounting for political prisoners, ensuring humane treatment of prisoners, protecting Tibet's religious and cultural heritage, and permitting international radio and television broadcasts into China.

14. Dumbaugh, "China's Most-Favored-Nation (MFN) Status," 1–2.

15. James Mann and Rone Tempest, "U.S., China Trade Embittered Words on Human Rights," *Los Angeles Times*, March 13, 1994, https://www.latimes.com/archives/la-xpm -1994-03-13-mn-33644-story.html.

16. Dumbaugh, "China's Most-Favored-Nation (MFN) Status," 23–26.

17. Dumbaugh, "China's Most-Favored-Nation (MFN) Status," 23.

18. See chapter 13 by Lieberthal and Thornton for further discussion of China's WTO accession.

19. See Steve Goldstein, "U.S. Enjoys Best Manufacturing Growth in the Last 30 Years," MarketWatch, January 21, 2019, https://www.marketwatch.com/story/manufacturing -employment-in-the-us-is-at-the-same-level-of-69-years-ago-2019-01-04; and Bureau of Labor Statistics, "Current Employment Statistics Survey: 100 Years of Employment, Hours, and Earnings," August 2016, https://www.bls.gov/opub/mlr/2016/article/current -employment-statistics-survey-100-years-of-employment-hours-and-earnings.htm.

20. See Murray Scot Tanner, "Beijing's New National Intelligence Law: From Defense to Offense," Lawfare, July 20, 2017, https://www.lawfareblog.com/beijings-new-national -intelligence-law-defense-offense.

21. Christopher Wray, "Remarks at U.S. Senate Select Committee on Intelligence," February 13, 2018, https://www.intelligence.senate.gov/hearings/open-hearing-worldwide -threats-0.

CHAPTER 7

A PERSPECTIVE ON CHINESE ECONOMICS

What Have We Learned? What Did We Fail to Anticipate?

BARRY NAUGHTON

A palpable mood of frustration and disappointment with China is pervasive in the United States today. Inevitably, such an intense reaction triggers reconsiderations of what we thought we knew about China and also recriminations around the possibility that we got things wrong or that they misled us about China.[1] Reconsideration of what we thought we knew about China is certainly positive and desirable; recrimination over what we got wrong, less so. This chapter is largely a reconsideration of what we thought we knew about China, rather than a recrimination, and proceeds in three movements. Each of these sections has a different and contrasting tone, but they are complementary and built on a common structure. Therefore, a musical metaphor seems appropriate. In the first movement, I argue that generally speaking, Western economists got China right. Focused on the possibility that marketization and institutional reforms would unleash China's enormous potential, economists were generally optimistic and on target. This simple point is rather obvious but worth restating. Given the current atmosphere of recrimination, the fact that the economists' optimism was warranted might otherwise slip by without comment.

The second movement argues that most economists (including myself) were simply unable to envision the vastness of the changes associated with China's emergence as an economic superpower. This failure of vision is linked to the failure to foresee the moderate acceleration of China's growth that occurred after 2003 (and up through 2010). Both of these lapses of foresight can be attributed to technological revolutions and global restructurings that accompanied and were intertwined with China's ultimate rise. These were unprecedented and impossible to anticipate. I argue that four of these changes acted as accelerators, both of China's growth and of China's global impact. Incorporating such elements in our retrospective understanding is important, but assigning blame is rather meaningless. Nobody had—or has—a crystal ball. The changes really were unprecedented. In retrospect, however, perhaps we should have spent more time thinking through the implications of structural and global changes that were facilitated by China's emergence and that, in turn, sped up China's arrival.

The third movement is a discussion of what we got wrong. To begin with, we were far too slow to understand the policy changes that took place after 2003. We broadly underestimated the strength of conservative (or leftist) forces within the Communist Party and the possibility that they would take credit for the achievements of reform while hijacking the policy process. This under-estimation, in turn, led us to be slow in recognizing the steps through which reform was drained out of the policy-making process. Practically speaking, from the moment Jiang Zemin and Zhu Rongji stepped down in 2002 and 2003, respectively, intentional economic reform has been feeble and rarely successful. This change clearly predates the global financial crisis (GFC) that began in 2008. Subsequently, the attraction of the American model was profoundly diminished during the GFC, and Chinese policy makers increasingly contrasted the achievements of Chinese policy making during the GFC with American failures. China's turn away from aggressive market-oriented reform was confirmed. Since Xi Jinping's consolidation of power, the commitment to markets as the ultimate drivers of the economy has further declined. The chapter concludes with an examination of several implications of these observations.

First Movement: Foreseeing a Chinese Miracle

Generally speaking, American economists got China right.[2] Dwight Perkins's 1985 lectures at the University of Washington, later published as *China: Asia's Next Economic Giant?*, are a case in point. The lectures were delivered at a time when China's leadership under Zhao Ziyang had firmly embraced radical economic reforms, but before the fundamental outcomes of reform (beyond the agricultural sector) had become visible. While Perkins puts his title in the interrogative, he leaves no doubt that the answer to his question is "yes." To quote from Perkins:

> Japan, South Korea, Taiwan, and others have demonstrated that GNP growth rates of 8 percent a year and even higher are feasible in the post–World War II era.... [Although] China's need to limit food imports ... makes it more difficult

for China to achieve comparable rates of growth in overall productivity . . . on balance [and given that reforms are likely to maintain their momentum] there is every reason to assume that rapid growth in China will continue. Rapid growth in this context means an annual average increase in GNP of 6 to 8 percent over the next decade and a half or more.[3]

And so it happened. Indeed, China's growth rate exceeded Perkins's optimistic forecast, and the rapid growth continued until 2010. What actually happened—gross national product (GNP) growth of 10 percent over the next two decades and a half—certainly surpassed the prediction of Perkins but counts as a confirmation of his basic logic and judgment. Perkins's approach is typical of many economists working at that time: a focus on institutional change; some cautions because of specific difficulties or constraints; optimism; and limited interest in exploring the implications of these optimistic expectations.

Because of their general orientation, economists returned to optimism relatively quickly after the 1989 Tiananmen disaster and the period of backsliding and repression that followed. From Deng Xiaoping's Southern Tour in January 1992 through the Third Plenum of the Fourteenth Party Congress in November 1993, economic policy underwent a profound reorientation, as the Chinese leadership committed the country to just the kind of changes most economists believed in. As a result, at a time when many noneconomists were still profoundly pessimistic about China—when "China Deconstructs" seemed a witty and apposite title for an edited volume of analysis—most economists had already swung back to the side of optimism.[4] As successive waves of profound institutional reforms succeeded one after the other, this feeling of optimism turned into conviction.

When, after 1997, Zhu Rongji finally took on the task of reform of the state sector, which had appeared until then to be the final untouchable interest group, most economists concluded that market-oriented economic reforms would surely carry the day. At about this time, veteran China analyst William Overholt—then ending two decades as a banker in Asia and en route to heading the RAND Corporation's Asia research team—coined a nice phrase: "China is in about as deep a hole as anybody but it is digging itself out faster than anyone else." This statement captures the fact that it was the *policy orientation* that made economists optimistic: stated more broadly, Chinese policy makers were doing difficult things that involved short-term pain in pursuit of long-term benefit. A short-term rise in unemployment was inevitable; insistence on hard budget constraints (bank loans that had to be repaid) required a wrenching change in mentality and operating procedures. In all these cases, the political system was responding rationally to a serious long-term challenge and short-term crisis. Some gave credit to the system, and some to the nature of the policy response, but in any case, the mid- to late 1990s represented a remarkable case of a system taking necessary steps and rising to meet a challenge.

By the time Zhu Rongji stepped down in the spring of 2003, China had clearly turned the corner. The foundations of a market economy had been laid; China had joined the World Trade Organization (WTO), providing some international commitments to reinforce what had been achieved domestically; and the ground had been prepared for a subsequent decade of rapid productivity growth and overall economic growth. Moreover, most of the immediate knock-on effects of dramatic growth quickly became evident. An economically successful China opened up new directions for economic growth, while creating a more diversified, more urban, and more middle-class society. Chinese saw an explosion of capabilities and curiosity about the outside world. In the United States, we benefited from the hundreds of thousands of Chinese students in American universities (370,000 in the 2018–2019 academic year) whose training, hard work, and diversity are a testament to China's success in developing an urban middle class. Overall, popular demands for a better life in China increased and diversified.[5]

Second Movement: What We Didn't Foresee

While economists were generally optimistic about China's potential, China's growth rate was nonetheless slightly (but significantly) faster than most had expected. GDP growth averaged 10 percent per year through 2010, and (most surprisingly) growth was actually slightly higher in the 2000s than it had been in the 1980s and 1990s. In fact, it makes sense to talk of a second takeoff that occurred after 2003–2004, one that was not anticipated by most economists. Large structural forces, both inside China and globally, contributed to China's growth, accelerating the pace of change. These forces were weakly foreseen and rarely incorporated into our analyses. These accelerators allowed the benefits of growth to be realized quickly, but also made the adjustments to China's emergence more difficult. Change was simply too fast.

In retrospect, four dimensions seem especially important among the things that we did not foresee. First, we underestimated the role and importance of the so-called demographic dividend, with the result that our timing was off. Second, we did not foresee (nor could we have foreseen) the impact of the information technology revolution, which was intertwined with China's emergence. Third, we did not understand the impact of the restructuring of the American corporation that took place at about the same time. Fourth, we did not realize that the forces accelerating the pace and impact of China's integration into the world economy would cause significant pain in the American manufacturing heartland.

First, the powerful concept of the demographic dividend was only partially appreciated in the 1980s and 1990s. The demographic dividend refers to a period when the population structure is especially favorable to economic growth. It follows an initial baby boom (which occurred in China in the 1950s and 1960s), and it becomes a dividend when the new generation begins to limit its own fertility. The result is that the labor force increases very quickly while the dependency rate (composed of children and the elderly) declines. The rapid growth of China's labor force in the 1980s was understood at the time primarily as a challenge: How could work be found for all those young people? In fact, employment ultimately expanded rapidly enough to absorb labor force entrants, and the designers of China's one-child policy were not the only ones who overestimated the problem of population growth. Similarly, few envisioned how profound the impact of economic growth and urbanization would be in bringing about voluntary reductions in fertility. At that time, the dramatic reduction in birth rates in Japan, Taiwan, and Korea had begun, but the fact that they would produce total fertility rates far below replacement over the long term had not yet become clear. The speed and thoroughness of the East Asian fertility transition simply had not permeated broader awareness. The rapid fall in Chinese fertility was obscured by bad data and the deeply controversial provisions of the one-child policy. As a result, little attention was paid to the fact that China's demographic situation was becoming increasingly favorable as China entered the twenty-first century. Dependency rates continued to fall, and the economy had absorbed the bulk of the earlier baby boom workers. By the 1990s, as a new generation of parents limited themselves to one or two children, overall labor force growth began to fall. As a result, the ability of the economy to absorb workers from the countryside increased around the turn of the century—and there were plenty of workers available in the countryside.

These demographic factors are essential to understanding what happened in the twenty-first century, but at first, they were invisible. Rural workers had for years been kept in the countryside by the household registration system. Moreover, at the turn of the century, urban unemployment was high, following the shrinkage of the state and urban collective workforces, and it seemed unlikely that much more rural-to-urban migration would be permitted. But as external conditions changed and the effects of WTO membership kicked in, labor demand increased extremely quickly. This change of conditions surprised many (or perhaps it was just that, as conditions improved, we stopped worrying and no longer paid attention). As a result, we didn't foresee that China could take advantage of the final phases of its demographic dividend so decisively after 2003. China lowered barriers to rural-to-urban migration surprisingly quickly and effectively (even without a major change in legal residence categories). Between 2005 and 2010, more than ten million people each year crossed provincial boundaries to take up a new life in the cities. We did not foresee that China could sprint to the end of its demographic dividend period. Most of us were thinking in terms of a gradually slowing growth momentum.[6] In practice, Chinese policy makers were able to defer this structural slowdown until after 2010.

To be sure, this achievement was only possible because labor demand was already growing rapidly and in practice probably required an export-oriented strategy. China had just entered the WTO, and the great China housing boom was also taking off at this time. Both of these important changes in the composition of demand can plausibly be considered consequences of the Zhu Rongji reform period, which opened up both the export and housing sectors to private initiative. In this situation, the demographic dividend (which had run its course in the urban areas) still provided a substantial reservoir of young workers available in the countryside, thus enabling rapid growth once demand-side conditions were in place.[7]

Second, China's emergence was thoroughly intertwined with the information technology (IT) revolution. On the one hand, IT directly facilitated China's rapid growth. Today, intensive use of IT in China is so pervasive that we take it for granted. However, China was a relatively late adopter of computer and communications technology. In the 1980s, the spread of the personal computer (PC) in China was slow. Incomes and wages were simply too low to support rapid PC adoption. As a result, the main phase of IT adoption came through mobile phones, beginning at the very end of the 1990s. Obviously urban dwellers adopted cell phones first, but China's migrants quickly began using them, too, which reduced information costs and uncertainty and facilitated the mass urban-to-rural migration that came after the turn of the century. Thus, the spread of IT through society after the end of the twentieth century must have contributed to rapid productivity growth and accelerated transformation. As far as I know, there are no technical studies of the precise impact, but it is reasonable to believe that IT hardware diffusion shows up in the rapid productivity growth that China marked after the late 1990s.[8]

At the same time, China's growth acceleration was intertwined with its emergence as a crucial base of IT hardware production during the phase of the IT production revolution that began in the late 1990s. The first phase of IT production growth had been dominated by Japanese corporations, which by 1990 were the clear leaders of the IT revolution, producing the best integrated circuits (chips), screens, and consumer electronics (to name just a few subsectors). But during the second phase of the IT revolution, a new model of radically open modular IT architecture gradually became dominant. Explosive progress in semiconductors and telecom (as well as internet) was centered in Silicon Valley, but it led quickly to the development of multinational networks that were founded on Sino-Taiwanese-American interactions. While Japanese firms tried to maintain their dominance by producing high-quality closed systems, they gradually fell behind the cheaper and more flexible hardware produced by (let's call them) "Sino-American" networks. When Japanese corporations also committed to a dominant, inside-Japan cell phone technology that never caught on globally, their position as the cutting-edge, leading global IT player came to an end. The center of technological dynamism shifted away from Japan to Sino-American networks.[9]

To be sure, the initial Chinese participation in the emerging system was quite passive, as only very low-skill, labor-intensive assembly was moved to China from Taiwan. But this was misleading, because new possibilities for upgrading quickly emerged (through copying, developing domestic suppliers, counterfeit [*shanzhai*] versions, etc.). Moreover, Taiwanese firms were actively and centrally involved in this restructuring from the beginning. After 2001, Taiwanese firms began to move essentially all their labor-intensive processes to the mainland. While they limited the transfer of the most advanced and sensitive intellectual property, the transfer of capabilities and knowledge to the mainland was still massive. Ironically, the radical openness of the Chinese system at this time with respect to high-technology investment contrasted sharply with Japanese policy, which was still influenced by the desire to maintain the full set of industrial capabilities in-house in the large corporation. More importantly, the Chinese hunger for high-tech investment succeeded in attracting a critical mass of incoming investment, consolidating China's place at the center of the IT revolution.

Thus, the IT revolution had a singularly concentrated impact in China, occurring almost entirely after the turn of the century and at extraordinary speed. IT technology increased the productivity of many economic processes (downstream). IT hardware became probably the most important component of the enormous expansion of Chinese exports that took place after 2003 (demand-side). Chinese start-ups opened up in close proximity to foreign-invested IT hardware producers, permitting whole new indigenous sectors to emerge (supply-side upgrading). This last effect is exemplified by Shenzhen, which utterly transformed itself from a low-tech export processing and real estate zone into a dynamic high-tech hub, based initially on cheap knockoffs of telecom equipment. Nobody really anticipated the magnitude of these effects.

Third, the restructuring of IT production networks described here was in some respects simply an especially concentrated version of a broader restructuring of the American model of the corporation. In a process sometimes referred to as the financialization of the corporation, U.S. companies across the board moved away from vertical integration and toward a different model of corporation that focused on core competences while outsourcing or off-shoring functions in which they did not have a competitive advantage. They sought to reduce the amount of capital on their balance sheets and push up profits and profit rates. As is broadly appreciated now, this produced a system of global production networks (GPNs) that increased their importance in global output and trade, particularly in the early years of the twenty-first century. By 2007, more than 20 percent of total global exports were intermediate stages in GPNs.[10]

This was not all China, but the overall development of GPNs is inseparable from China.[11] The dualistic trading regime China created in the 1990s allowed firms to import components and raw materials duty-free as long as they were manufactured into exports. These provisions were very friendly to GPNs, and more than half of China's exports were produced under them from 1996 through 2007. As China's trade commitments to the WTO kicked in, China became the location of choice for labor-intensive stages of GPNs. Excellent infrastructure and a light regulatory touch reinforced this advantage. In a related (but not identical) development, middle-man companies able to assist any individual produce anything in China sprang up. If you imagined a new toy or kitchen gadget, these companies could connect you to a Chinese company that could produce it and ship it to the United States at modest cost. You did not have to be a giant corporation to set up your own miniature version of a GPN.

These organizational changes again contributed to a faster-than-anticipated surge of growth in China after 2003. To be sure, WTO membership was partly responsible for this growth. But WTO membership alone is unlikely to have produced such enormous effects on China's exports in the absence of these organizational and technological changes. As a result, China's growth was more rapid, and its impact on the global system more abrupt, than otherwise would have been the case. In short, a combination of demographic, technological, and global corporate capitalism changes all contributed to China's sustained growth after the turn of the century and especially after 2004. Not having anticipated these changes, economists underestimated China's growth trajectory, even given their consistent optimism about China's overall growth prospects.

Fourth, these changes made China's impact on the rest of the world more powerful. Momentum is the product of mass and velocity. By 2003, China's economy was big and growing faster than anticipated. This unprecedented economic momentum made it harder for the rest of the world, including the United States, to adjust to the impact. However, adaptation was also more difficult because China's rise affected U.S. corporations very differently from the way it affected U.S. workers. Economists are big supporters of free trade because free trade produces efficiency gains that have the potential to make everyone better off. But economic theory is also very clear that free trade produces winners and losers, in predictable fashion. When an economy opens to trade, the scarce factor (relative to global averages) loses and the (relatively) abundant factor gains. For this reason, we expect the scarce factor in the United States—unskilled labor—to lose from open trade, while the abundant factors in the United States—capital and highly skilled labor—gain. This would be true under any scenario, and absorbing the entry of three hundred to four hundred million new unskilled workers from China (the mass again) was never going to be easy for the world economy. Given the presence of the accelerators identified

7.1 U.S. corporation after-tax profits as a share of GDP.

Source: U.S. Bureau of Economic Analysis, accessed through FRED, Saint Louis Federal Reserve Board, at https://fred.stlouisfed.org/graph/?g=1Pik.

in the first three points, the velocity was also great and the impact was inevitably even more difficult to absorb.

This impact was big and fast both for winners and for losers. U.S. corporations have gained mightily from the China effect. Not only has a new market opened up—served mostly by subsidiaries inside China—but overall production costs have gone down. One important result has been the significant increase in the share of U.S. corporate profits in American GDP, shown in Figure 7.1. Corporate profits made up 5.4 percent of GDP on average from 1981 through 2002. Corporate profits then began an extraordinarily rapid increase through 2005. Since 2006, and through the second quarter of 2019, U.S. corporate profits have averaged 9.6 percent of GDP. [12] Increased corporate profits led to a stock market boom, to the obvious benefit of the wealthier members of society. To be sure, this was not all due to China. Yet it is hard to imagine that it could have happened without China, and it is not accidental that the surge began around 2002–2003, just as China was integrating deeply into GPNs.

The abrupt adjustment was also evident for the losers, that is, American workers in labor-intensive manufacturing facilities. The important series of papers by Autor, Dorn, and Hanson has documented the negative impact of the rapid increase in imports from China, through 2007, on specific regions (commuting zones) in the United States.[13] These papers have been extremely influential not just because they document an effect with important policy implications for the United States, but because they tell us something about the nature of economies that challenges economists' normal assumptions. Economists normally assume that adjustment costs (friction) are modest and short term and can often be ignored. What Autor, Dorn, and Hanson showed was that adjustment costs were persistent and were still not overcome within the time period of the study (i.e., through 2007). For any given local economy, the negative competitive trade shock produced what might be described as a local mini-recession (my term, not theirs), so that the overall local downturn restricted or even reduced the pace at which labor could move into services and export-oriented manufacturing. Instead of adjusting to the trade shock, local economies were simply shocked. Obviously, this is partly a function of the speed and magnitude of the China trade shock, which was huge and unprecedented. The accelerators described earlier—combined with China's initial huge size— help explain why the shock to the U.S. economy was so difficult to manage.

Clearly, these shocks both contributed to the deterioration of overall income distribution in the United States and significantly worsened America's political climate. The increase in wealth was concentrated in the hands of the 1 percent, while the costs of adjustment fell disproportionately on localized economic clusters unfortunately specialized in labor-intensive manufacturing. Besides being undesirable in itself, this outcome has contributed to the growth of nativist and nationalist rhetoric and political forces in the United States.

Third Movement: Misunderstanding Policy Changes After 2003

China's economic condition was far better in 2003 than it had been a decade earlier, in 1993. Economists were very aware of this. Economic reforms had succeeded. Many of the fundamental obstacles had been surmounted. But Chinese society was experiencing an increase in uncertainty. State enterprise reform meant that the guarantee of permanent employment disappeared forever, and open unemployment remained high through 2002–2003. The collapse of the cooperative health care system in the countryside meant that catastrophic illness or other unforeseen events seemed more threatening than ever, and the SARS epidemic in 2004, although short-lived, contributed to this anxiety. Measures of Chinese happiness reached a low point around 2003.[14] The economists in their optimism had no way of understanding this broad social mood, and partly as a result, they miscalculated how policy would evolve from this crucial point. In short, there was a period when the short-term costs of reform were extremely evident, but the long-term benefits of improved productivity, increased employment, and faster growth were not yet evident.

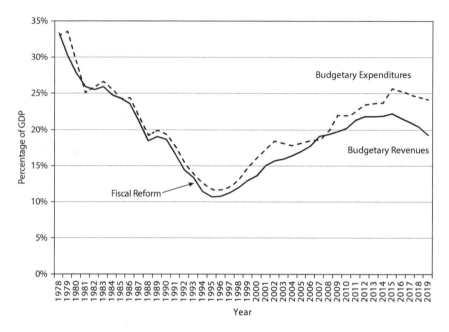

7.2 Budgetary revenues and expenditures as a percentage of GDP.

Source: National Bureau of Statistics, China. *China Statistical Abstract 2019*, p. 68; updated through Ministry of Finance, accessed at mof.gov.cn.

In particular, economists misunderstood the experience of declining state capacity followed by recovery. Economists generally agreed that China in the 1990s faced a crisis of state capacity because of the complete inadequacy of the fiscal and financial institutions inherited from the planned economy. The creation of new national institutions was therefore seen as a necessary and fundamental step in creating a market economy.[15] Therefore, when the new fiscal institutions began to work and revenues recovered, most economists regarded the problem as solved and, therefore, as an issue that was closed. Figure 7.2 shows the dramatic turnaround in budgetary revenues, which increased as a share of GDP every year for twenty years from 1995 to 2015. As a result, economists viewed fiscal reform (in particular) as a successful reform, one among a series of essential reforms, and assumed that its resolution would contribute to the general vindication and popularity of the market reform process. What almost nobody saw at the time was that fiscal reforms, having resolved the most immediate challenge that confronted the regime, would also remove the motivation for continued reform. That is, without the impetus provided by imminent crisis, the regime would steadily dial down its overall commitment to reform. This gradually became evident, but only after the regime carried

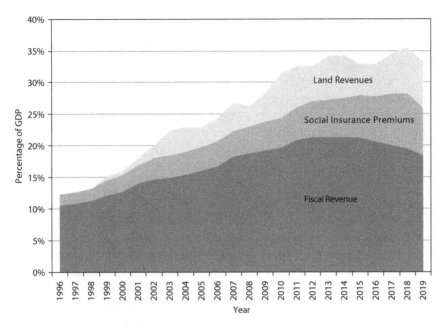

7.3 Total public revenues as a share of GDP.

Source: Barry Naughton, "Is China Socialist?" *Journal of Economic Perspectives* 31, no. 1 (Winter 2017): 1–23.

through its last real market-oriented reform, the restructuring of the state bank system. This reform—planned and designed in 2001–2002 in the waning years of the Zhu Rongji administration but implemented late in 2005–2006— achieved much but was in essence the final step of resolving the fiscal crisis of the previous decade

Nobody really predicted that China, having *stabilized* its budgetary revenues, would then step immediately onto a rapid expansion track and become a high-tax economy. In other words, China's fiscal capacity did not just recover from its precarious state in the mid-1990s, it grew well beyond that of an ordinary developing country. To see the magnitude of this growth, one has to include two additional revenue sources, which is done in Figure 7.3. China's social security system was introduced in the mid-1990s as a separate social insurance scheme, the revenues of which are not included in budgetary revenues. In essence, China adopted a high social insurance taxation regime in anticipation of the time when it would become an aging society, even though China will not enter the ranks of an aged society until around 2030. Most Chinese economists, and many outside economists, supported this prudent approach, hoping that China would accumulate social security reserves, avoiding the pitfalls of the pay as you go pension systems evident in the United States and many other developed countries. But the result was a continuing increase in taxation authority at a time when there was still a fairly limited growth in social insurance expenditures.[16] Separately, local government land revenues became a huge bonanza in the course of the 2000s decade, as sustained growth and the housing boom monetized the state's long-standing monopoly ownership of urban land. Together, these two factors added more than ten additional percentage points of GDP as revenues under the state's control.[17]

China thus became a strong state again. Multiple revenue streams were combined in state hands, and the government became rich. Of course, public revenue is not the only measure of state strength. The awesome power of the Chinese Communist Party to permeate all of the important institutions of the nation was intact. (Economists, like many others, if they thought about it at all, expected that permeation to become less ideological and at least partially institutionalized.) State ownership was maintained over the banking system, and therefore, direct and indirect influence over credit flows was maintained. As bank lending exploded in the stimulus program adopted in response to the 2008–2009 GFC, this financial resource exploded in size and became much more susceptible to policy steerage. The continuing presence of state-owned enterprises in key strategic positions further consolidated the government's position.

With money and personnel power once again concentrated in the hands of the political leadership, the fundamental questions confronting the leadership changed. With no way to observe the questions Chinese leaders face on a daily basis directly, we must try to deduce this from their actions. It appears that in China, after the early years of the Wen Jiabao administration, the fundamental question changed from "How do we reform our economy in order to succeed and grow?" to "How do we achieve great things?" Lampton has emphasized the need to "discern . . . the goals and objectives of leaders, the institutions that constrain or facilitate their activities, and the lenses through which key individuals and groups filter information."[18] In this respect, I believe that we economists increasingly missed the mark after about 2006 by failing to discern the shift in the objectives of leaders.

Overlooking this monumental change in leader and policy objectives was easy. Since China was still a middle-income country and average consumption levels were comparatively low, China faced serious problems, most obviously rebuilding and universalizing the social safety net and tackling pollution. These could easily be seen as part of the existing paradigm: reforms had achieved breakthroughs with marketization, and so the next (and complementary) step was to rebuild the social safety net. However, in retrospect, it was probably more accurate to see the shift as part of a broader shift to a more affirmative agenda: How do we accomplish great things? How should we spend the money we now have? In this respect, Wen Jiabao achieved quite a formidable list of accomplishments: rebuilding a public health system; spreading a (skimpy and bare bones) retirement system across the population; beginning a program of targeted industrial policy; buffering many sectors against the impact of WTO membership; and building China's military strength. To these must be added the prompt, decisive, and massive response to the GFC from November 2008. The record is remarkable, in many respects, but contrast this with Wen's record in terms of economic reform: no further financial reforms; no progress on capital account opening; a terrible record in terms of strengthening regulatory institutions; in sum, virtually nothing in terms of market-oriented economic reform.

While the actual outputs of the Chinese state were changing dramatically, most economists did not adjust their basic paradigms. Academic economists like myself and economists in international institutions and private firms pretty much continued to see China as a reforming economy, with pauses and uneven progress, but still fundamentally moving forward toward further reform. Moreover, we made enormous mental and practical accommodations to China based on this conception. For example, the International Monetary Fund quietly changed its criteria for a nation's currency to be included in the basket for special drawing rights, removing a hard requirement of convertibility on the capital account in order to recognize China's progress in internationalization of the renminbi.[19] It was very hard to change underlying views of China, forged over a multidecade period during which China had repeatedly returned to reform challenges, devised strategies, and successfully confronted the most important issues. Since China was, in Overholt's words, "digging itself out" faster than anyone else, how could we reconceptualize a country that was still making enormous economic and social progress but had simply lost interest in converging to a market economy of the type familiar to most of us?

To a certain extent, this failing must be linked with the type of personal interaction and firsthand information available to Western scholars. Foreign economists interacted regularly with Chinese economists who shared our paradigms. The Chinese economists generally expressed optimism about the possibility of further reforms and urged patience in dealing with the cyclical nature of Chinese policy making. They were and are extremely intelligent and highly articulate, and they remained standard-bearers for the conceptions of continuing market-oriented reform that they had successfully championed for more than a decade. Moreover, they were close to policy makers. They certainly were not the only influential advisers, but they seemed to retain the ear of policy makers and were in a good position to put their policy preferences through whenever political conditions changed a little. So Western scholars could easily neglect the fact that the policy batting average for this group of Chinese advisers was steadily declining. Unbeknownst to us, somehow, a different set of considerations, or a different set of advisers, with whom we foreigners did not interact, was becoming more influential with top policy makers.

As a result, Western economists as a group were slow to see the shift in the preferences of the Chinese government toward what I label as "steerage." Having resources, policy makers steadily sought to achieve new forms of control over the economy. Targeted sectors and projects were reinstated in the 2006 Medium to Long-Term Plan for the Development of Science and Technology, although initially at modest funding levels. The idea that state firms should retain control of certain strategic sectors was adopted in early 2006, although the regulatory principles underlying this shift were never published. Coal mines were nationalized as a way to address safety issues. All these changes occurred before the arrival of the GFC. But after the crisis, in discussing lessons learned, Wen Jiabao explicitly said, "At the same time as we keep our reforms oriented toward a market economy, let market forces play their basic role in allocating resources, and stimulate the market's vitality, we must make best use of the socialist system's advantages, which enable us to make decisions efficiently, organize effectively, and concentrate resources to accomplish large undertakings."[20]

In Wen's words, the advantages of the socialist system clearly refer to the ability of the central government to concentrate enormous financial resources and deploy them decisively. It is a fiscal feature, and only secondarily a political characteristic, and not at all a social or class-based characteristic of the system. In the wake of the perceived success of crisis management during the GFC, China rolled out explicit industrial policies, with real resources behind them, for the first time since the demise of the planning system. Strategic emerging industries were articulated in 2009 and baked into the subsequent five-year plans.[21] It is then a straight line from there to the policies that are at the center of international contention in today's world. The policies of Made in China 2025 and the Innovation-Driven Development Strategy were adopted in 2015 and 2016, respectively. They call for targeted interventions in specific industries, backed by very large government subsidies. Economists have been very slow to absorb this change of direction.

Economists thought there would be tweaks to the process of market-oriented reform, in line with China's gradualist strategy, and pauses to deal with changes in condition or capabilities. Because economists tend to bring a technocratic mindset to the policy process, we tended to see China's policy intellectuals as pragmatic, experimental, and adaptive. It was natural to be patient and wait for the extremely talented techno-pols to reassert their influence. Economists paid little or no attention to the fact that within the Communist Party there remained a strong and significant faction that was, at best, unenthusiastic about market-oriented reform, wanted a stronger and more nationalistic policy orientation, and was completely comfortable with a more overtly repressive political system if it achieved certain nationalistic goals. Jude Blanchette shows that these leftist voices remained a persistent, albeit muffled, presence throughout the reform era.[22] These troglodytes were around, but how could they possibly retain influence in the face of the intelligent and farsighted technocrats we knew? In fact, these conservative (or leftist) views have continuously reasserted themselves through the forty-year reform era. They dominated policy making for three years after the June 1989 Tiananmen events and tried to smother economic reform. In the mid-1990s, a strong, independent nationalist viewpoint achieved some prominence. At the turn of the century, Jiang Zemin was directly challenged by leftists who objected to his Three Represents policy of accepting capitalists into the Communist Party. It appeared then that Jiang swatted away the challenge, closing down the leftist media outlets, and proceeded to implement his policy preferences. It seemed so one-sided, yet in retrospect, it is clear that there was a continuing constituency for more hard-edged nationalistic policies that were less friendly to market-oriented reform. Clearly, this constituency existed both within the Communist Party and outside, in popular nationalism and independent leftist groups.

The existence of this group within the Communist Party was more important, however. To them, it was obvious from the beginning that successful economic reform would contribute to the legitimacy of the Communist Party and strengthen its hold on power. For most of us, this was not an immediate problem and did nothing to shape our research agendas. For myself, I thought not only that regime change was (obviously) not our business, nor within our capability or expertise, but also that the Communist Party's structure of governance would evolve with the demands of an increasingly complex and highly literate society to accommodate new interest groups in ways that depended on domestic dynamics. Moreover, there was enormous evidence that such a process of institutional adaptation was under way within the party, so the overall paradigm of constructive, evolutionary change remained in place.[23]

But we (I) did not reckon with the incredibly robust and comprehensive power of the Chinese Communist Party. In the first place, the party was able to control the flow of information so thoroughly that the basic interaction between economic success due to reform policy and public opinion was distorted and perhaps broken. Of course, this happens to some extent in every political system. Incumbents get to take credit when things go well and are blamed when things go poorly, and electorates are not very good at factoring in the time lags between difficult reforms and successful economic outcomes. But this has become far truer in China. By the time the Chinese economy entered its second takeoff after 2004, the name of Zhu Rongji no longer appeared in the press, and the link between Zhu's reforms and the rapid increase in living standards was never made. For most young people in China today, the name Zhao Ziyang means little or nothing; similarly, for them, China's prosperity today seems to show that the dimly remembered events at Tiananmen were a minor disturbance based on a misunderstanding. Thus, the fundamental feedback loop between the success of economic reform and an attitude of support for further opening and political and economic reforms—clearly in place in the 1980s—has largely been broken. Moreover, it has been broken by a sustained, comprehensive, and relentless propaganda undertaking of the Chinese Communist Party designed to deflect all economic success to the credit of the party.

Even more important than public opinion, however, is the linkage between the continuing multidimensional power of the Communist Party and the massive recovery of state capacity. Kenneth Jowitt has described the Soviet Communist Party as "nonbiodegradable," a term that seemed to lose relevance after the Soviet Party's unraveling.[24] Yet it seems quite relevant to China today. For all the incredible change in China and the quasi-institutionalization and professionalization of the governing cadre, the fundamental structures of the party are still 100 percent intact. The party regularly invests millions of man-hours in spreading information, aligning interests, and resolving problems, efforts that have real utility.[25] To be sure, these capabilities were a great resource to China as it confronted the myriad challenges of finding a feasible path to market-oriented reform. Party capabilities provided a backstop when things went wrong or markets weren't working, for example, being deployed with immediate effect during the GFC. Party structures also facilitated policy experimentation and at least reasonably effective incentive structures for local officials. When the state was underresourced, party institutions contributed enormously to China's ability to confront and solve problems. That seemed positive, so long as the overwhelming objective of policy makers was market-oriented transition.

The recovery of governmental capabilities in China in the wake of Zhu Rongji's reform success created an explosive new set of possibilities for the combination of a strong party and a rich state. Most fundamentally, it meant that market transition was no longer absolutely necessary. China became a posttransition political economy sometime in the mid-2000s. In a sense, we might say that even when the party was no longer needed to supplement the government, it still existed as a potent power resource. When the party-state began to be in a position to deploy hundreds of billions of dollars worth of resources on essentially discretionary objectives, the structures of the party were lying around ready to be mobilized and seized by an ambitious politician. Xi Jinping has created apparently new narratives of the greatness of China and the correct leadership of the Communist Party, but those narratives are obviously based on concepts and capabilities that were there all along. All that was needed was an ambitious leader to pick them up and divert them to new purposes and new goals of national greatness. At the end of the day, if you wield power and you don't need to reform, why should you?

Economists have failed rather spectacularly to think realistically about the goals Chinese leaders were trying to achieve. Our own commitment to market-oriented reform occluded our vision of other goals related to the economy. As a result, our understanding of the actual policy orientation of successive Chinese administrations has been correspondingly weak. Zhu Rongji, to be sure, was committed to market-oriented reform. While one might quibble with a few aspects of his vision, market-oriented reform was clearly a fundamental organizing objective of many of his policies. Since Zhu stepped down, no top Chinese leader has shared his vision. Do we understand what they are trying to achieve? Economists have been slow to raise, much less answer, this question.

This shortcoming affects how we analyze even the most basic trends in the Chinese economy. For example, it is very common to hear economists in many venues declare that China's economy is becoming more domestic oriented, more consumption oriented, and more service based. There are many reasons why these statements may be true. We observe that many economies go through structural phases of industrialization and then postindustrial service sector development (and China is now at this point). More specifically in East Asia, we observe that when eras of miracle growth end, investment and saving rates decline, opening up more space for consumption (and again, China is at this point). However, economists can frequently be heard saying (or implying) that Chinese government policy *fosters* consumption orientation and service sector development. Statements like this imply that in addition to underlying structural changes, the Chinese government is actually undertaking policy actions that accelerate changes toward (for example) consumption and service sector development. In such a case, it should be easy to identify the policy steps taken (such as cutting taxes to foster consumption), and it should be apparent that the structural changes anticipated are robustly and quickly apparent (compared to some notional structural benchmark).

In fact, neither are the policy steps evident nor is structural change especially pronounced. Figure 7.2 showed that China's budgetary revenues as a share of GDP did not begin to decline until 2015 (meaning that the overall tax burden was not reduced before that time). Even after 2015, Figure 7.3 shows that aggregate public revenues continued to increase until 2018. Indeed, it was not until the economy faced an uncomfortably sharp slowdown in 2019 that policy makers were finally willing to cut taxes on the population. China is only a little more consumption oriented and a little more service sector driven than it was a decade ago. What does this say about the actual policy orientation of Chinese leaders? What is the link between policy choices and structural outcomes?

These questions have been poorly addressed by economists because we have done a bad job in anticipating or understanding the potential policy trajectories in China. In part, this may be because economists are simply a lot better at tracing structural regularities and changes than they are at understanding policy and its impacts. More broadly, it seems to reflect a failure of imagination on the part of China economists. The benchmark for what is normal is drawn almost entirely from recent Chinese practice or, at best, from the neighboring East Asian economies, who provide such a positive model of economic development and change.

* * *

What have we learned, then? We have learned that the intellectual framework of reform and reformers was not sufficient to grasp the magnitude of what was happening in China. As an economist, I was naturally focused on market transition, on the pressing question of whether or not China would develop an adequate set of institutions to allow market forces to play a much stronger role, permit the productivity of the economy to increase dramatically, and in the process, absorb a huge amount of factors of production (especially labor) that might otherwise appear to be excess. The question, in other words, was whether reform would unlock enormous growth and diversification. While speaking for myself, I think my fellow economists, in academia and in government and international organizations, generally had the same orientation. From the beginning in 1978, this was the fundamental question that motivated all of our work, including all of my own, and probably through Nick Lardy's recent book *Markets Over Mao*.[26] In the past few years, however, and only in the past few years, does this fundamental question seem to have lost its absolute centrality. Thirty-five years is a long time for the market reform paradigm to have dominated the agenda of China economy research.

This is not to say that economists were wrong: on the contrary. What could be a better simple description of China's economic trajectory than the one sketched in the preceding paragraph? We believed that, and it came true. But we failed to see that China's remarkable commitment to market-oriented economic reform was to a certain extent inextricably interwoven with its status as a weak state. Reform began in 1977–1978 as Deng Xiaoping traveled abroad and proclaimed "backwardness must be acknowledged if it is to be overcome." Once reform succeeded and China again had a strong state, China's leaders began to behave in a very different fashion. That new behavioral pattern was far more destabilizing to global economic order than anything that had come before. Moreover, because China's ascension to strong state status occurred at an extraordinarily rapid pace—due to the four accelerators described in the Second Movement—global and national political systems had an extremely hard time adjusting to them.

China's financial resources *and* its ability to deploy those financial resources in targeted ways have both massively increased, thus creating a whole series of challenges to policy makers around the world. The slow uptake by economists of new paradigms about Chinese policy making has inadvertently contributed to initially slow and less effective responses to these new challenges. The WTO is an example. China's entry into the WTO was a triumph for the Chinese reform process and a political achievement of historic proportions for Premier Zhu Rongji. It was also a triumph for the development of global institutions. Moreover, the negotiators of China's WTO accession purposely demanded and achieved a set of China-specific commitments that were incorporated into China's accession agreement as a separate protocol. These included a radical transparency demand (all trade-related measures should be published in the Ministry of Commerce gazette), a commitment not to impose technology-transfer conditions on incoming foreign direct investment, and a promise that state-owned enterprises would operate purely according to commercial principles.[27] All these specific conditions were built into China's accession in recognition of specific challenges in China related to its unique system.

Most observers would agree that none of these three commitments has been achieved in practice. However, this outcome can be understood in two different ways. The WTO is primarily an organization set up to achieve trade liberalization and to regulate trading relationships so that countries can have greater confidence in opening up to trade. Seen in this way, the China-specific provisions do not necessarily appear to be of central importance. They can even be considered to be above and beyond what other countries were asked to do. In this sense, China's overall compliance with broad WTO provisions can be judged to be similar to that of other countries and thus okay.[28] This viewpoint is related to the economists' traditional stance: there is progress over the long term; remember how far they've come; now, let's rely on the possibility that domestic reformist forces will regain influence and push the marketization process further down the road. Yet this viewpoint is belied by other facts that support an alternative interpretation. In the first place, these provisions were specifically inserted into the accession agreement to deal with China's unique institutional features, so if they are not fulfilled, this represents a specific failure of the historic effort to achieve sufficient harmonization between China's institutions and global market institutions. By that standard, these provisions are not at all above and beyond and are instead basic safeguards for China's constructive participation in the WTO. In truth, China under Wen Jiabao responded to WTO membership with a systematic effort to reverse engineer WTO regulations and achieve the outcomes they wanted without running afoul of specific rules. For example, very large agricultural subsidies were created and dumped into the green box of permitted subsidy categories. This was part of a pattern of evasion that also incorporated the three China-specific provisions described earlier.

The framework in which we interpret China's lapses from WTO standards is of great importance. After all, China's overall record is not terrible, and many of the things we claim to have expected from China's WTO accession are in fact ex post reconstructions of high hopes and optimistic expectations for continued reforms. For example, the fact that China channels farm subsidies into less distortionary forms is, in one sense, exactly the purpose of the regulations. They were designed in the context of normal political systems to outlaw particularly pernicious forms of trade-distorting subsidy but allow other types of subsidy to go ahead. However, to an extent, China's actions represent the actions of a centralized political system purposely seizing on this distinction among subsidy types to increase the overall level of subsidization and thus broadly defeat the purpose of the basic objectives of the WTO and China's accession agreement. More broadly, since WTO entry, China seems to have pursued parochial economic interests with a heretofore rarely seen ferocity. China's approach only makes sense in the context of a dramatically changed policy orientation. That is, China's effort to buffer the impact of WTO membership would make no sense for a poor state that could not carry out, for example, an expensive agricultural subsidy regime. But it fits easily into a rich state that is seeking to limit interdependence, build national strength, and achieve other economic and strategic objectives. Economists have been extraordinarily slow to perceive this, and it has hampered our response to the China challenge.

The result has been an excessively polarized response to China's rise. The China economists who understand China's institutions well and have been optimistic about China's development have been slow to track or criticize the shift in China's policy framework. We have continued to treat China as a reforming and opening economy, when it is no longer clear that this is the case. Xi Jinping would no doubt be happy to have an economy that is highly efficient because it has reformed its institutions and allows him to work harmoniously through market forces to achieve his goals. But there is no evidence that efficient markets are part of his priority objectives; rather, they are at best subsidiary goals, or merely means to an end. Most critically, key reformist objectives are easily discarded by Xi if and when he deems that necessary, as he seeks to aggrandize the nation, the party, and himself.

This has left far too much scope to another camp of analysts who don't seem to actually know anything about China, who have never been particularly optimistic about China's development capability (or have portrayed China as being on the brink of economic collapse), and who have consistently seen China as a strategic threat. In David M. Lampton's words, "I see an understanding of China derived from big-power conflict theory to be in dangerous ascendance, not just in the United States, but in certain quarters of China as well."[29] We economists share a small part of the blame for this situation because we have not updated and communicated our portrayal of China's leadership objectives in a sufficiently effective fashion.

NOTES

1. The range of reactions is nicely captured in the article, and responses to it, by Kurt Campbell and Ely Ratner, "The China Reckoning: How Beijing Defied American Expectations," *Foreign Affairs* 97, no. 2 (March/April 2018): 60–70. See responses in Wang

Jisi et al., "Did America Get China Wrong? The Engagement Debate," *Foreign Affairs* 97, no. 4 (July/August 2018), https://www.foreignaffairs.com/articles/china/2018-06-14/did-america-get-china-wrong.

2. An edited volume that brings together the work of many American economists working on China is Loren Brandt and Thomas Rawski, eds., *China's Great Economic Transformation* (New York: Cambridge University Press, 2008). Other works reflecting a generally consistent approach include Nicholas Lardy, *Markets Over Mao* (Washington, DC: Peterson Institute, 2014); and Barry Naughton, *The Chinese Economy: Transitions and Growth*, rev. ed. (Cambridge, MA: MIT Press, 2018).

3. Dwight Perkins, *China: Asia's Next Economic Giant?* (Seattle: University of Washington Press, 1986), 57, 59–60, 71.

4. David Goodman and Gerald Segal, *China Deconstructs: Politics, Trade and Regionalism* (New York: Routledge, 1995).

5. Along the way, U.S. foreign policy aims were achieved: the creation of a U.S.-China condominium after the late 1970s isolated the Soviet Union and contributed to the collapse of the Soviet Union and the end of the Cold War.

6. For example, in 1996, I wrote that "GDP growth rates are likely to decline gradually to about 6 percent per year by 2015." Although that prediction turned out to be correct, I did not envision a growth *acceleration* in the intervening period of 2005–2010. Barry Naughton, "China's Emergence and Future as a Trading Nation," *Brookings Papers on Economic Activity* 2 (1996): 322.

7. Equally important, rapid growth required a high investment rate to allow the housing, transport, and employment of those millions. China had already achieved a stable high investment rate by the early 2000s.

8. For example, see Loren Brandt, Johannes Van Biesebroeck, and Yifan Zhang, "Creative Accounting or Creative Destruction? Firm-Level Productivity Growth in Chinese Manufacturing," *Journal of Development Economics* 97 (2012): 339–51.

9. This is not to deny the extraordinary technological capabilities of many Japanese firms to this day, but simply to point out that Japanese firms have retreated to very high-technology upstream segments where they retain a dominant position.

10. World Bank Group et al., *Global Value Chain Development Report 2017: Measuring and Analyzing the Impact of GVCs on Economic Development* (Washington, DC: International Bank for Reconstruction and Development/The World Bank, 2017), https://www.wto.org/english/res_e/booksp_e/gvcs_report_2017.pdf. See also Gary Gereffi and Karina Fernandez-Stark, *Global Value Chain Analysis: A Primer* (Durham, NC: Duke University Center on Globalization, Governance and Competitiveness, July 2016).

11. Similar trends are evident in the restructuring of the global auto industry, with German producers expanding with Poland-Czech-Slovak GPNs and U.S. producers expanding with North American Free Trade Agreement GPNs.

12. Data through FRED, Saint Louis Federal Reserve Board, "Corporate Profits After Tax (Without IVA and CCAdj)/Gross Domestic Product," https://fred.stlouisfed.org/graph/?g=1Pik. To be sure, corporate profits in the 1940s and late 1970s were higher than in the 1980s, surpassing 8 percent of GDP on occasion but overall averaging 6.6 percent from 1950 through 1980. Profits never made up 10 percent of GDP before 2005.

13. David Autor, David Dorn, and Gordon Hanson, "The China Syndrome: Local Labor Market Effects of Import Competition in the United States," *American Economic Review* 103, no. 6 (2013): 2121–68; David Autor, David Dorn, and Gordon Hanson, "When Work Disappears: Manufacturing Decline and the Falling Marriage-Market Value of Men,"

National Bureau of Economic Research Working Paper 23173, revised January 2018, https://economics.mit.edu/files/12736; and other papers.

14. Richard Easterlin, Fei Wang, and Shun Wang, "Growth and Happiness in China, 1990–2015," in *World Happiness Report*, eds. John Helliwell et al. (New York: Sustainable Development Solutions Network, 2017), 48–83.

15. Thus, almost no economists agreed with Yasheng Huang's argument that the 1990s represented a reversal of the grassroots entrepreneurialism of the 1980s. See Yasheng Huang, *Capitalism with Chinese Characteristics: Entrepreneurship and the State* (Cambridge: Cambridge University Press, 2008).

16. This is a much bigger and more complicated problem, primarily because China's social insurance provisions for covered workers are extremely generous, but only a small proportion of the workforce is fully covered. In Figure 7.3, contributions from the budget to the social insurance fund have been classified under social insurance premiums to avoid double counting.

17. Barry Naughton, "Is China Socialist?" *Journal of Economic Perspectives* 31, no. 1 (Winter 2017): 1–23.

18. David M. Lampton, *Following the Leader: Ruling China, from Deng Xiaoping to Xi Jinping* (Berkeley: University of California Press, 2014), 3.

19. This is, of course, the converse to the idea that China was asked to join an international system the rules of which it had not participated in making. An interesting essay should be written on the interaction of these two mutually inconsistent interpretations, both of which seem to be true.

20. Wen Jiabao, "Report on the Work of the Government (2010)," Third Session of the Eleventh National People's Congress, March 5, 2010, http://www.npc.gov.cn/englishnpc /Speeches/2010-03/19/content_1564308.htm.

21. Ling Chen and Barry Naughton, "An Institutionalized Policy-Making Mechanism: China's Return to Techno-industrial Policy," *Research Policy* 45 (2016): 2138–52.

22. Jude Blanchette, *China's New Red Guards: The Return of Radicalism and the Rebirth of Mao Zedong* (New York: Oxford University Press, 2019).

23. Barry Naughton, "Inside and Outside: The Modernized Hierarchy That Runs China," *Journal of Comparative Economics* 44, no. 2 (2016): 404–15.

24. Kenneth Jowitt, "Gorbachev: Bolshevik or Menshevik?" in *Developments in Soviet Politics*, eds. Stephen White, Alex Pravda, and Zvi Gitelman (London: Palgrave, 1990).

25. Daniel Koss, *Where the Party Rules: The Rank and File of China's Communist State* (New York: Cambridge University Press, 2018).

26. Nicholas Lardy, *Markets Over Mao* (Washington, DC: Peterson Institute, 2014). Lampton, with good reason, dates the beginning of the reform period to Deng's 1977 return to the Standing Committee. I retain 1978 as the start date here out of convention and because economists did not start working on reform until after the December 1978 Third Plenum.

27. World Trade Organization, "Accession of the People's Republic of China," November 10, 2001. This is the protocol that is considered a binding part of China's agreement to accede to the WTO. Available in Section V: Accession Package at https://www.wto.org /english/thewto_e/acc_e/a1_chine_e.htm.

28. Indeed, this is to some extent what the WTO Appellate Boards have de facto concluded. See Richard Steinberg, "The Impending Dejudicialization of the WTO Dispute Settlement System?" *Proceedings of the 112th Annual Meeting of the American Society of International Law* 112 (2018): 316–21.

29. Lampton, *Following the Leader*, 19.

PART III

ON THE GROUND, NONGOVERNMENTAL, PEOPLE-TO-PEOPLE COOPERATION

CHAPTER 8

STRATEGIC ADAPTATION

American Foundations, Religious Organizations, and NGOs in China

MARY BROWN BULLOCK

In 1966, the National Committee on U.S.-China Relations convened a group of prominent American citizens at New York's Hilton Hotel to explore the possibility of ending America's isolation from China. Included in the group were scions of an earlier period of American engagement in China, such as A. Doak Barnett and Lucian Pye, both sons of American missionaries in China, and John D. Rockefeller III, longtime trustee of both the China Medical Board and the Rockefeller Foundation. Barnett and Pye devoted their professional lives to the study of China, and Rockefeller created the Asia Society, which was designed to encourage cultural relations between the United States and Asia. Rockefeller called for a new perspective on China. "Our thinking about that great country has been dominated by fear," he said, "so much so that in the recent past many regarded it as virtually treasonable to even raise the question of rethinking China policy."[1]

But rethink China policy they did, charting a radical new beginning for cultural and diplomatic relations. This bipartisan conclave of leading American citizens was several years ahead of its government, testament to the significant role that nonstate actors and institutions would play in future relations with the still Middle Kingdom.

Several years later, in 1969, two profoundly pessimistic assessments of American engagement in earlier periods of Chinese history were published. Jonathan Spence's seminal book, *To Change China: Western Advisors in China, 1620 to 1960*, is a compelling chronicle of the apparently futile efforts by well-intentioned Westerners who devoted their lives to making a difference there.

James Thomson's *While China Faced West: American Reformers in Nationalist China, 1928–1937* was equally pessimistic. These sobering assessments, widely read and often remarked upon, gave American cultural organizations pause: Was any attempt to engage what was now Communist China really worthwhile?[2]

And yet, fifty years later, the cultural engagement between Americans and the People's Republic of China had become extraordinarily rich. Hundreds, if not thousands, of churches, foundations, and nongovernmental organizations (NGOs) had become intimately engaged with Chinese society. Writing while China was still closed, Spence and Thomson could not have predicted the enduring legacy of American missionaries, reformers, scientists, and educators. No, China did not become just like Kansas City, as some had envisioned, but Christianity did become a recognized religion in China, and the previous decades of trans-Pacific connections created a remembered pathway for the rapid cultural reengagement between the two countries.

Spence and Thomson, despite their pessimism, were nonetheless prescient in depicting the passion (some would say arrogance) of Americans attempting to change or reform China, regardless of regime. Such attitudes die hard and are with us still. Nonetheless, a special feature of the most recent half century of American engagement is the way in which American NGOs have adapted to the exigencies of working in the People's Republic. They were, for the most part, invited by Chinese counterpart institutions eager to take advantage of international assistance and enthusiastic about embracing for themselves the reform and opening era. As Norton Wheeler's study of American NGOs in China notes, this was an invited influence: "Chinese actors have variously tolerated, encouraged, and actively solicited the involvement of American institutions in the modernization of their nation. In many cases they have substantially shaped the agendas of resulting exchanges."[3]

American institutions proved to be nimble, persistent, and generally realistic in advancing their multiple agendas, whether religious, environmental, or legal, continually adapting their goals and operating styles to the vagaries of U.S.-China relations and to China's changing conditions. Their role and influence in representing American cultural and social values and the personal and institutional relationships established have defined an American presence in China that transcends the political and economic dimensions of the relationship. This in-depth engagement of such a pluralistic American community has enlarged the American China constituency, strengthened our understanding of Chinese society, nurtured China's civil society, and contributed to the social good of both countries.

That situation is now changing. China's transformation from the early twentieth-century sick man of Asia to a global economic and technological power carries with it the possibility that American philanthropy in China might soon become an oxymoron. The increasing capacity of China's own philanthropic and civil society, the advent of a more authoritarian regime, and the implementation of its recent Foreign NGO Law require a fundamental reorientation by all American foundations, religious organizations, and NGOs that have had a presence in China.

Beginnings

The United States and the People's Republic of China were officially estranged from the time of the Korean War until Richard Nixon's opening to China in 1972, but the 1966 creation of the nongovernmental National Committee on U.S.-China Relations and its sister organization, the Committee on Scholarly Communication with the People's Republic of China (CSCPRC),[4] heralded the beginning of changes in American attitudes toward China. While the advent of the Cultural Revolution in the same year precluded any significant activity, in 1971, ping-pong diplomacy, under the aegis of the National Committee, signaled a softening of rigid diplomatic positions. Following the Richard Nixon–Mao Zedong detente and the signing of the Shanghai Communiqué in 1972, China's door began to open.

Subsequently, both the National Committee and the CSCPRC were officially authorized to exchange delegation visits of academics and public citizens, and some American individuals and groups were also given limited access to China.[5] These introductory visits tantalized the American public, which was anxious to learn more. They also resulted in studies that updated American knowledge about China, suggesting areas of future exchange.[6] In China, as well, the demise of Mao and the overthrow of the Gang of Four in the mid-1970s ushered in a new era of more positive views of the United States. This introductory period of nongovernmental relations paved the way for the rapid escalation of ties after Jimmy Carter and Deng Xiaoping finalized the normalization agreement in January 1979.

Nothing better exemplifies China's changed view of America's historic influence than Deng Xiaoping's invitation to the Rockefeller Foundation during his visit to the United States in January 1979. To the Chinese Communist Party, John D. Rockefeller's Standard Oil Company and the Rockefeller Foundation had long epitomized American economic exploitation and cultural imperialism. Castigated as an enemy of the people and as a world organ for cultural aggression, opposition to the Rockefeller Foundation had gone hand in hand with the anti-Americanism of the 1950s and 1960s. But China's leaders were nonetheless well aware of the significant role the Rockefeller Foundation had played in Republican China in support of the natural, medical, and social sciences. As the upheavals of the Cultural Revolution began to wind down, the damage to China's intellectual infrastructure became painfully evident. China's new leaders were eager to benefit once again from American philanthropy, especially in building capacity in key knowledge institutions.

The change in sentiment toward the Rockefellers was first evident in 1973 when David Rockefeller, youngest son of John D. Rockefeller, became the first American banker to meet with Chinese premier Zhou Enlai. To David's surprise, his bank, Chase Manhattan, was selected as the first American bank to set up business in the People's Republic. In a long discursive session with David on U.S.-China relations, Zhou revealed how much he knew about American philanthropy and referenced the positive role of the Rockefeller Foundation in supporting China's science and medicine during the first half of the century.

Informal discussions between Chinese authorities and Rockefeller institutions continued in the 1970s, led by Rockefeller Foundation president John Knowles, who suggested to Zhou Enlai that "the Rockefeller Foundation can play a unique role in facilitating non-official cultural and scientific relations with the People's Republic of China to the mutual benefit of both the American and Chinese people."[7] China's appreciation of the Rockefeller overture was demonstrated when Deng Xiaoping paused to make a phone call to Knowles, who was then dying of cancer, during his 1979 American visit. With this call came Deng Xiaoping's blessing for a new era of Rockefeller engagement in China.

Soon nods were given to other American philanthropies that had previously worked in China. The China Medical Board, which had been funded by the Rockefeller Foundation as an independent foundation and had established and maintained Peking Union Medical College from 1915 to 1951, was invited back in 1980. Yale-China, which had begun its work in Changsha in 1901, primarily at Hunan Medical College, began short-term English language exchanges in 1979. Even organizations with explicit missionary backgrounds were invited back. In 1979, the Foundation for Theological Education in Southeast Asia was asked to assist in building a library collection for the Nanjing Theological Seminary, for which the foundation had been the original American sponsor. A year later, the United Board for Christian Higher Education in Asia, the mother institution of China's thirteen liberal arts colleges during the period of Republican China, was received by Hu Qiaomu, a devoted Marxist, party ideologue, and politburo member, in the Great Hall of the People. That an exchange agreement between the United Board and China's Ministry of Education was signed in his presence signaled China's growing openness to ties with American cultural institutions.

These American organizations with long roots in China were well aware of the decades of Chinese criticism of previous American cultural involvement there. Each of them strategically modified its approach to the new People's Republic of China. They did not endeavor to work exclusively with earlier partners. The Rockefeller Foundation did not set up a specific China program (as it had in the 1930s), but rather integrated China into its priority international programs in agricultural biotechnology and population sciences. The China Medical Board diversified its funding support to include not only the original Peking Union Medical College but also thirteen other medical universities. Yale-China continued to emphasize medicine but did not seek joint administration of the Hunan Medical College and later diversified its work to include other institutions. The Foundation for Theological Education in Southeast Asia worked closely with the officially designated China Christian Council. And the United Board for Christian Higher Education in Asia made clear that it did not seek a religious role or aim to reestablish relations with the previous liberal arts colleges, most of which had long since been modified and renamed. Instead, the United Board worked to enhance liberal arts education in multiple institutions.[8]

Joining these groups with historic ties to China was the Ford Foundation. While Ford had no previous role in China, the foundation had, for several decades, been the primary funder of China studies in the United States. Later, Ford also supported the early exchange programs of the National Committee on U.S.-China Relations and the CSCPRC. In 1979, anxious to formalize its programs in China, the Ford Foundation became the first American institution to sign an agreement with the Chinese Academy of Social Sciences for the promotion of individual and institutional exchange "in subjects that will contribute to the development of the four modernizations, to greater understanding by the world of China's development experience, and to the growth of common knowledge and understanding as a contribution to the peaceful resolution of international issues."[9]

A second, more recent institution, the Asia Foundation, also found an early seat at China's new philanthropic table. The Asia Foundation was created with U.S. government funding in the 1950s to strengthen American influence in the Asia-Pacific region. The goal was to block the Chinese Communist Party's efforts to expand its influence beyond the People's Republic of China. By the late 1970s, it had morphed into more of a development organization, supporting political and economic programs conductive to encouraging democratic governance. The Asia Foundation's entry into China was indirect. In 1979, it provided funds for an international computer science conference in Beijing, one of the first such meetings to be held there. Subsequent early Asia Foundation programs were in fields of foreign policy; administrative, legal, and economic reforms; and education. Ironically, for an organization initially established to counter Chinese influence in the Asia-Pacific region, the Asia Foundation now sought deep engagement with Chinese society.[10]

The initial activities of these and many more institutions began in 1979 and 1980. While all had sought contact after Nixon's opening in 1972, the door to China only opened wide with the normalization of diplomatic relations in 1979. Almost overnight, leading American cultural institutions seized every opportunity to gain entry to China. As a result of American enthusiasm and Chinese receptivity, the main contours of initial U.S. engagement were established then.

How can we understand the motivation and significance of these early non-governmental relations? Writing in 2002, Renee Yuen-Jan Hsia and Lynn T. White observed that:

> Since China's opening in the 1970s, foreign organizations have rushed into that country. The desire of contemporary Westerners to "rescue" China—which resembles the mentality of Europeans and colonialists from earlier centuries—is evident in the growing number of foreign entrants to the country.[11]

The characterization of "rescuing" China is more powerful than Jonathan Spence's description of "changing China" and evokes the long-standing desire of Americans not only to be involved in China's modernization but to shape it in ways compatible with American values.

This motivation was augmented not only by the desire of numerous foundations to return to China but also by the overall official structure of bilateral relations. In 1979, President Jimmy Carter had decreed that there would be no U.S. government development assistance programs for the communist country. American foundations stepped into the breach.

China's social and intellectual infrastructure, once heavily Marxist in its ideological orientation, was virtually crushed by the Cultural Revolution. Development assistance was part and parcel of the work of the Rockefeller Foundation, the Ford Foundation, the Asia Foundation, and the China Medical Board. Each was international in outreach and had developed institution-specific priorities. The Rockefeller Foundation, which had been the largest American donor to China in the Republican period, initiated fifteen- to twenty-year programs focused on developmental biology, plant sciences, and demography. The China Medical Board took responsibility for upgrading the medical faculties and libraries of the thirteen key medical universities, including its historic flagship, Peking Union Medical College. The Asia Foundation provided training for diplomats and books for China's libraries. The Ford Foundation focused on international relations, economics, and law. Over the decade-plus course of these programs, the cohort of young Chinese scholars who received international training through the Ford Foundation became the backbone of their professions in China and enriched American intellectual life as well. Many cite the Ford Foundation programs as the most consequential of American endeavors. Less visible but again strategically important were the programs initiated by the United Board for Christian Higher Education in Asia to strengthen China's humanities and social science faculties.[12] Between 1980 and 1990, more than five hundred Chinese scholars completed graduate degree programs in the humanities and social sciences outside China. Almost all of them returned home.[13]

Thus, in less than a decade, these and other independent American organizations and universities established close, ongoing working ties with China's policy and intellectual infrastructure in Beijing and in many provinces—in academies of science, social science, and engineering; the State Commission on Science and Technology; the Ministry of Justice; the Foreign Ministry; the Ministry of Health; and all the key universities and their institutes—just to note a few. Since all cooperating Chinese agencies were government sponsored, what evolved was a unique marriage between leading private American foundations and the Chinese government. While U.S. government agencies generally had a single counterpart in Beijing, the range of American foundation ties in China, operating on very small budgets, is striking. Ford, Rockefeller, and the China Medical Board were the largest donors, but only the Ford Foundation's budget ever exceeded $10 million a year (reaching $16 million in the late 1990s). In 1980s China, these funds—along with the international entrée provided—went a long way. Although their programs would change in the decades to come, these institutions continued to dominate U.S.-China cultural relations well into the twenty-first century.

Tiananmen 1989

The impact of Tiananmen on all aspects of U.S.-China relations cannot be overstated. In his thought-provoking book *China and the American Dream: A Moral Inquiry*, Richard Madsen describes how the Tiananmen massacre of June 1989 shattered the American Dream for China. The first decade of reengagement with China, he argues, "exceeded initial expectations on both sides and thereby generated new expectations too lofty to be fulfilled. . . . For many Americans the opening to China was a harbinger of the liberalization of the whole Communist world: finally 'they' were becoming like 'us.' "[14]

That perception changed with Tiananmen, with profound effects on official relations. Agreements between China and U.S. government agencies ranging from the National Institutes of Health to the U.S. Geological Service to Housing and Urban Development and the Department of Defense were halted.

Paradoxically, just when nongovernmental cultural relations might have been expected to shrink dramatically as well, the opposite occurred. Many American organizations openly decried the Chinese government's actions in Tiananmen. The United Board for Christian Higher Education in Asia raised a particularly strong protest, declaring:

> With many other friends of the Chinese people the United Board for Christian Higher Education in Asia deeply regrets the recent turn of events in China. We deplore the military action of June 4, killing unarmed civilians in the areas adjacent to Tiananmen Square. We are concerned for the future of higher education in China. . . . We are no longer confident that an academic environment open to the free exchange of ideas is possible in China.[15]

Nonetheless, the United Board continued its existing commitments while initially delaying the expansion of future ones.

Faced with isolation and censorship from many international bodies, the Chinese government encouraged the return of nongovernmental engagement. Even while Beijing was still under martial law, the government proclaimed that the situation had returned to normal and publicly welcomed international organizations to return. Thus, many foundations reaffirmed their ties to Chinese institutions. William Sawyer, the president of the China Medical Board, traveled to Beijing on June 6 to reassure Chinese medical institutions, especially hospitals that had treated the wounded on the night of June 4, that support from the China Medical Board would continue. Peter Geithner, the Ford Foundation's program director in China, persuaded the New York office that its programs in economics, law, international relations, and rural reconstruction should continue. In fact, Ford funding for China programs increased from $5.6 million in 1989 to $7 million in 1991.[16]

Not only did the international nongovernment sector soldier on, but it rapidly expanded in the 1990s, redoubling its efforts to be engaged with the Chinese people. The foundations introduced here all continued as many activities as possible. Many found new meaning in continuing to support Chinese individuals and institutions with which they had been associated earlier. What did change was that American nongovernmental institutions became more concerned about the absence of political and legal reform, including issues of human rights and the plight of Chinese dissidents. They also sought to move beyond support for key establishment institutions to areas and people underserved by the Chinese government. Changes in Chinese society, notably the advent of a new Chinese civil society, were key to providing new avenues for Americans to engage these more sensitive and political issues. The post-Tiananmen opportunity to work with China's growing civil society on issues related to health, poverty, women's issues, the environment, and legal reforms ushered in a new era in U.S.-China cultural relations.

Post-Tiananmen Engagement

Another major turning point in the evolution of the acceptance of civil society in China was the convocation of the Fourth World Conference on Women held by the UN in Beijing in May 1995, six years after Tiananmen. For days, China's capital city was filled with thousands of enthusiastic women representing women's groups and NGOs from around the world. For many of the Chinese women who participated, the conference was transformative. As Shawn Shieh notes:

> As part of this conference, an NGO forum on women played an important role
> in introducing the NGO concept to China. As the term NGO entered public

discourse, organizations established by women as well as other groups, and even GONGOs [government-organized nongovernmental organizations] such as the All-China Women's Federation began calling themselves NGOs. In the years following the UN Conference the political environment became increasingly hospitable to NGOs, and China saw significant increases in the number of international NGOs, GONGOs, and grassroots NGOs.[17]

The Chinese government had reason to be receptive to the work of NGOs. In the years after Tiananmen, the Chinese government was faced with a host of social and economic issues brought about, in part, by reform. The decline of socialist support networks, rapid economic development, and large-scale migration from rural areas to the cities created a shortage of social services of all kinds. The need to address these issues motivated the government to permit the rapid expansion of a variety of civil society organizations. In a country that was becoming increasingly pluralistic, communities and like-minded individuals banded together to form local grassroots groups to address issues not being adequately addressed by the government. Such groups grew in number from around 142,000 in 2000 to over a million in 2018. These NGOs are not, strictly speaking, entirely independent from the government. To be legal, all must register with an appropriate government agency that also exercises oversight of the NGO and vouches for its performance. A regulation limiting the number of NGOs in different fields (e.g., environment, poverty alleviation, education, people with disabilities, the elderly) to one at each level of government, from the central level down to the county, has severely restricted the number of NGOs with a national reach while allowing for a proliferation of NGOs at the grassroots level focused on local challenges and needs. Some of these grassroots organizations have also worked in areas of political sensitivity—from legal services to training minorities.

This proliferation of local-level NGOs also opened new avenues of cooperation for American NGOs. The growth in China's civil society was paralleled by an expansion of international NGOs in China. In his 2002 book *Internationalizing China*, David Zweig points out that Chinese regulations were relatively weak at that time and that many foreign entities were able to enter China and work with localities at all levels. "Linkage fever" was the name of the game. As Zweig describes it, "Chinese had long coveted foreign resources. What was new was that foreign NGO's arrived on the scene with millions of dollars for China's impoverished localities who were hungry for international assistance and that the central government acceded to their desire to work at the grassroots."[18]

In this new atmosphere, China's national and regional government organizations became more open to international collaboration, and American organizations were able to work not only with national-level institutions but with local grassroots organizations as well. Although numbers are not available, there was a veritable explosion of American local-level nongovernmental linkages with China.

To illustrate the range of American NGO involvement in China, we will look at one institution, the National Committee on U.S.-China Relations, and three sectors: religion, environment, and village elections. While quite different in nature, taken together, they give some sense of the pluralistic nature of American engagement in China.

The National Committee on U.S.-China Relations

In November 1989, five months after Tiananmen, the National Committee on U.S.-China Relations sent a nonofficial bipartisan delegation led by Barber Conable, a former Republican congressman and then president of the World Bank, and Robert McNamara, a former Democratic secretary of defense and former president of the World Bank, to meet with top Chinese political leaders, including the infamous Premier Li Peng. The purpose was both to express in the strongest possible terms the multiple ways in which the Tiananmen Incident had shattered the bilateral relationship and to explore paths to a new beginning.

Such an endeavor is typical of the nongovernmental umbrella role played by the National Committee on U.S.-China Relations. With a mission to promote mutual understanding between the two countries, the National Committee has consistently positioned itself as an independent organization with close ties to both the Chinese and American governments. While sometimes criticized as too much of an apologist for China, the National Committee has also striven for balance, thus enabling it to engage in topics and issues close to the political and economic marrow but with sufficient distance to be perceived as a neutral interlocutor. Since it first organized and hosted the visit of the Chinese ping-pong team to the United States in 1972, the National Committee has cultivated a wide range of senior contacts in many sectors in both countries. It is the go-to organization for both government and private groups looking for unofficial high-level dialogue or professional introductions.

The National Committee has played a singularly important role in introducing Chinese policy makers and professional groups at all levels to American society and vice versa. Exchanges of mayors, judges, lawyers, teachers, journalists, and foundation leaders have introduced these important communities to each other, and many have continued and expanded upon those initial connections. Similarly, the National Committee has been at the forefront of expanding the practical realms in which engagement occurs. The National Committee's promotion of cooperation in the environmental field is one such example. An early trilateral program with China and the USSR in the Ussuri River basin was one of the first in-depth environmental programs. Multiple exchanges in law and human rights introduced some of the key players in those communities to each other. In more recent years, Track II dialogues and multiple programs for a younger generation, discussed in the following paragraphs, have gained increasing importance.

Track II dialogues in security (since 1994), law and human rights (since 2009), and economics (since 2010) have provided yearly forums for Chinese and Americans to engage the critical issues facing the bilateral relationship. The continuity of these events has provided a reliable and safe space for frank discussion and sometimes produces policy recommendations. The most recent Track II dialogue on health care brought together experts from academia, think tanks, and industry to explore health-care issues related to both countries. The meeting resulted in a consensus agreement with recommendations for both countries, including multiple ways in which the health policy communities of both countries could work together. Areas of agreement illustrate the degree to which issues of medical care in the two countries are beginning to converge, for instance, on issues such as integrating medical care with nonmedical services that improve care and reduce costs; utilizing big data and information technology; reforming pay and delivery systems; and innovation of pharmaceuticals and medical devices.

Since the early twenty-first century, the National Committee has also focused attention and resources on the next generation of scholars and leaders in both countries. Its Young Leaders Forum has identified promising leaders in both countries and brought them together year after year in both China and the United States. The Public Intellectuals Program, launched in 2005, continues to identify groups of outstanding young American China scholars and introduce them to policy issues in both countries, including trips to China, Hong Kong, and Taiwan. The yearly Foreign Policy Colloquium brings Chinese graduate students studying in the United States to Washington to learn about domestic issues and the evolution of U.S.-China policy.

Similarly, the National Committee continues to engage the American public in understanding the complex bilateral relationship. Most notably, since 2006, it has sponsored what it calls the China Town Hall, which convenes yearly in one hundred American cities. Local groups organize programs around a featured live broadcast by distinguished bipartisan speakers, including former secretary of state Henry Kissinger, former ambassador to the United Nations Susan Rice, and former secretary of state Condoleezza Rice. The goal is to inspire a national conversation about China that provides Americans across the United States the opportunity to discuss issues in the relationship with leading experts.[19]

Religious Organizations

If the National Committee on U.S.-China relations represents the most visible NGO working with China, American religious organizations in China have operated almost beneath the radar. Religion can be sensitive in China.

The Chinese Communist Party continues to be ambivalent toward the role of the indigenous Christian church and can be suspicious of Chinese churches with foreign ties. Nonetheless, connections between religious groups in the United States and churches and religious organizations in China have found ways to flourish.

President Jimmy Carter can take considerable credit for having reopened the Chinese door to U.S.-based religious organizations, directly raising the question with Deng Xiaoping during his visit to the United States in January 1979. As Carter himself recounts:

> [Deng] reluctantly admitted that some good missionaries had come to China. However, he insisted that many of them had been there only to change the Oriental lifestyle to a Western pattern. I reminded him of all the hospitals and schools that had been established, and he said that many were still in existence. He was strongly opposed to any resumption of a foreign missionary program and said that the Chinese Christians agreed with him, but he listened carefully when I suggested that he should permit the unrestricted distribution of Bibles and let people have freedom of worship. He promised to look into it. (Later he acted favorably on both these suggestions.)[20]

Indeed, in the early years following normalization, Protestant and Catholic churches, Buddhist temples, and Muslim mosques that had been closed since the Cultural Revolution or before began to open once more. While the traditional Christian missionary was still not welcome and periodic persecutions of Chinese Christians continue, China's open door has included foreign access to, collaboration with, and funding for its own religious organizations.[21] The Christian presence in China and its American connections have become extensive and complex as different groups of American Christians have approached China with different theological and historical perspectives. The three most dominant groups, mainline Protestants, evangelical Protestants, and Catholics, have each initiated their own distinct programs.

American Catholic groups have worked primarily through the U.S.-China Catholic Association, which has operated in China since 1989. Sponsored by the Maryknolls, the Jesuits, and other Catholic orders, the association has a more or less unified approach to working in China. Aiming to promote fraternal ties, its focus has been on study tours to China, conferences on the Catholic Church in China, and numerous collaborative activities with Chinese Catholic groups, including training missions and seminars. Many of the Catholic activities in China are coordinated through Hong Kong and are more numerous than those of the Protestants, despite the relatively small number of Chinese Catholics. A recent agreement between the Chinese government and the papacy regarding the selection of Chinese bishops may facilitate reconciliation between the major Catholic groups in China whose growth has been far less than that of the Protestants.

Many mainline or liberal Protestant groups that had been active in China before 1949 decided that they should support China's establishment Protestants—those that have been given official permission to operate under the aegis of the China Christian Council and have agreed to the terms of the Three-Self Patriotic Movement, which requires China's churches to be self-governing, self-supporting, and self-propagating, requirements that effectively preclude foreign oversight of the Chinese church. Some evangelical organizations have felt that the China Christian Council is compromised by its government affiliation and thus have sought direct contact and support for churches operating outside of government control—the unregulated, often underground, so-called house churches. Richard Madsen describes the differing motivations of the mainline and evangelical Protestants: "For mainline churches the opening to China was an opportunity for reconciliation with a China already filled in some mysterious way with the presence of God. The evangelicals saw it as an opening for a new divinely mandated initiative into a godless territory." Put another way, mainline Protestants advocated a ministry of reconciliation, while evangelicals advocated a ministry of conversion.[22]

Both evangelical and mainline American groups have been able to develop contacts and collaboration with China's growing Protestant communities.[23] Many mainline groups developed direct contacts with the China Christian Council, initially led by the late bishop Ding Guangxun (K. H. Ting). Educated at St. John's University in Shanghai and later at Columbia University and Union Theological Seminary in the United States, Ding returned to China in the early 1950s. There, he became an early leader in China's Three-Self Patriotic Movement and, by the early 1980s, was the acknowledged leader of the Protestant Church in China. His experience in the United States made him uniquely able to communicate with American religious leaders, encouraging measured roles of engagement with China's churches.

One significant and welcome development advocated by Bishop Ding was the establishment in 1984 of the Amity Foundation, a faith-based social welfare organization designed to serve as a bridge for the Christian church and society. Amity is widely considered to be China's first NGO and was explicitly designed to work with international groups. During the 1980s, the Amity Foundation sponsored foreign teachers and developed what has now become the world's largest religious printing press, having printed more than 180 million Bibles—more than any other country (though most are said to be exported). Philip Wickeri, a representative from the U.S. Presbyterian Church and today a theologian based in Hong Kong, was assigned to the Amity Foundation in its early years and facilitated its ties with international religious organizations.

In recent years and especially since the death of Bishop Ding in 2012, the mainline Protestant connections to China have declined. Not only do these denominations face challenges in the United States, but many of the liberal American Protestant churches, some with active social agendas, do not easily relate to China's conservative pietistic church.

Despite the sensitivity of working with house churches, U.S. evangelical organizations have been able to develop extensive low-key ties with them, especially working through networks of house churches in Anhui and Henan Provinces, which have large groups of house churches. Until recently, it was estimated that over two hundred such American religious groups were active in China.

How do they work? Writing in 2015, Jonathan Tam and Reza Hasmath describe the ways in which eight religious NGOs, three of them American, were successfully operating in China. First, they "cooperated with local agents, fostering trust with the local state, and keeping a low profile." Second, they tapped into global linkages that provide both resources and an exchange of ideas. Finally, they responded to Chinese interest in bringing professionalism to the Chinese Christian community. Training of Chinese clergy has been a high priority, welcomed by government authorities because it maintains a measure of orthodoxy and prevents the rise of small, heterodox sects led by untrained but charismatic people.[24]

Training clergy has been the primary endeavor of the Foundation for Theological Education in Southeast Asia (FTESEA), the original Board of Founders of Nanjing Theological Seminary. When work in China was foreclosed in 1949, the foundation shifted attention to Southeast Asia but renewed its ties with the Nanjing Seminary (the preeminent Chinese Protestant seminary during the Republican period) and later with twenty-two other regional seminaries. The FTESEA provides books, building funds, and scholarships. Relatively few Chinese seminarians have come to the United States, but some U.S. seminaries are involved in training and exchange programs, especially Fuller Theological Seminary in California, which has taken the lead.

Of special note is the role that FTESEA has played in publishing two journals of Chinese theological writings—the *Nanjing Theological Review* and the *Chinese Theological Review*, edited by Janice Wickeri. Published in English and Chinese, these journals are designed to introduce Chinese Christian ideas, beliefs, and practices to a global Christian world. Its recent theme is both old and new: the sinicization of Christianity in China.

Sinicization is a term used frequently in the study of China's relations with the West and means to assimilate Western ideas or culture and make them Chinese. A 2018 article in *Chinese Theological Review* by Dr. Gao Feng, the president of both the Chinese Christian Council and the Nanjing Union Theological Seminary, explored the ongoing effort of the Chinese Protestant

Church to sinicize Christianity. Arguing that sinicization in no way requires that Christianity change its basic faith, he sees the implementation of the Three-Self principles as fundamental to successful sinicization. Chinese Christians must break through the idea of the "centrality of the Western Christian tradition" and "root themselves in the soil of Chinese culture," he argues, citing Xi Jinping's admonition that Chinese culture must penetrate every religion in China. Nonetheless, he still sees a sinicized Chinese church as founded on the original apostolic church of Christ. "Though the Chinese Protestant church is independent and self-run," he says, "it cannot divorce itself from reality. It must carry out the fundamental traditions of the church such that conferral of holy orders is our heritage from the apostles."[25]

The issue of sinicization is not a new one in China, nor has the issue been fully resolved. It dates back to early twentieth-century Chinese discourse on creating a Christian church led by Chinese and imbued with Chinese values. Today's movement is also directly linked to the Chinese Communist Party's ongoing effort to sinicize all religious groups, including Muslims and Tibetan Buddhists. One indication that the sinicization of Chinese Christians has not been fully implemented can be seen in the episodic attacks on Christian places of worship, such as the removal of crosses from steeples in Zhejiang Province.

The Environment

American interest in promoting environmental awareness in China emerged early as one of the primary foci of foundations and NGOs alike. The National Committee on U.S.-China Relations, the International Crane Foundation, and the Ford Foundation were three of the first American organizations to express an interest in the environment. The Rockefeller Brothers Fund, established by John D. Rockefeller Jr.'s sons as a foundation separate from the Rockefeller Foundation, had begun its work in China focusing on the arts and international relations. In the late 1980s, it turned its activities toward the environment and sustainability. Numerous other American environmental NGOs followed. By 2013, at least twenty-seven American environmental NGOs were operating in China.[26]

The first Chinese environmental NGO, Friends of Nature, was established in 1994 by Liang Congjie, one of China's leading public intellectuals and the grandson of the early Chinese reformer Liang Qichao. Friends of Nature was followed by a proliferation of other Chinese environmental NGOs. A study of twelve of China's most important environmental NGOs in 2000 noted that all were receiving funds and support from American and other international donors.

Two studies of the impact of international environmental NGOs emphasize the ways in which they have brought international norms and expertise to China's growing movement. The article by Wu Fengshi and Xu Yuan observes:

> Despite obstacles caused by both general politics and specific policies, the influence of American NGOs on environmental activism in China has been both evident and continuous. They achieve such influence mainly by supporting Chinese environmentalists and NGOs not only with financial resources, but more importantly expertise, information and knowledge and mentorship. Besides large foundations and NGOs such as the Ford Foundation and the Nature Conservancy, there are a few smaller organizations . . . even more proactive and innovative in allocating resources to the most needed local projects and incubating grassroots NGOs . . . in lesser developed regions.[27]

Jie Chen's article about the impacts on the green civil society in China credits the international environmental movement with introducing liberalizing norms into China and notes that international NGOs have consistently given priority to the role of the community in preserving the environment and have therefore also stressed the importance of participatory planning and governance. Of particular note is the support for and training of Chinese environmental activists who have learned how to use the language of global norms and environmental rhetoric—such as endangered species, biodiversity, greenhouse emissions, climate change, waste management, and energy—to advance their causes. Jie Chen believes that these norms have had a strong influence in shaping environmental practices.[28]

Examples from two American organizations, the Rockefeller Brothers Fund (RBF) and the Nature Conservancy, illustrate these points.

Beginning in the late 1980s, sustainable environmental stewardship emerged as the RBF's main mission, and by the late 1990s, South China had become the focus of RBF's philanthropic work in China. In explaining the choice of South China, RBF president Steven Heinz noted that because few international organizations worked there the RBF had South China to itself. The goal was seen as addressing "the links between the environment and human health; advancing sustainable approaches to meeting the region's energy needs; and strengthening community leadership in support of sustainable development."[29] With such an agenda, the RBF worked closely with environmental programs in several southern provinces, including Guangxi, Yunnan, and Guangdong, focusing on such issues as sustainable agriculture, pest management, and coastal management. Chinese counterparts included major government institutes such as the Yunnan Academy of Social Sciences as well as many local grassroots organizations.

As RBF staff worked in the nexus between official Chinese environmental organizations and fledgling grassroots organizations, they became strong advocates for Chinese civil society. The goal of strengthening community leadership had the political consequence of RBF support for grassroots NGOs with activist leaders who challenged government policies or sought new environmental programs. These grassroots NGOs needed resources and were often fragile. Grants were made to raise public awareness of such topics as official regulations and the impact of environmental degradation on health.

The Nature Conservancy took a more targeted approach to environmental challenges beginning with its work in the late 1990s in Yunnan with offices in Kunming and later in Lijiang. The first focus was on the watershed of four great rivers—the Mekong, the Yangtze, the Salween, and the Niu—in Yunnan Province. In collaboration with the Chinese government and Yunnan Province, the goal was to improve protection of what is considered China's most diverse biological region: "By supporting ecotourism development, the Yunnan Great Rivers Project hopes to encourage the conservation of the region's biodiversity and cultural heritage and provide a sustainable alternative income source for these isolated and fascinating local communities."[30] The strategy was through education and government regulations to improve and eventually expand the protected natural regions. Emphasis has also been placed on preserving local cultures and enabling minority groups to have a say in developing environmental policies. The Nature Conservancy's official motto states that "the organization is committed to empowering the community to have greater involvement in the conservation of their natural heritage. It claims that since most of the world's bio-diversity exists in areas inhabited by people, effective conservation cannot be achieved unless the people who live and rely on those lands are an integral part of the conservation process."[31]

Both the RBF and the Nature Conservancy have emphasized programs in training and management, sending study groups abroad and organizing workshops in project management and utilization of international standards. They and other American environmental NGOs have also expanded "horizontal networking and cooperation among Chinese activists themselves."[32] Encouraging such linkages across provinces is considered especially important, but politically sensitive, since these linkages can be interpreted by the government as potential political alliances. As noted earlier, the prevention of such alliances is one reason that government policy allows only one NGO of any type at each level of government.

Although American environmental projects earned considerable respect from government authorities, their engagement with local activist networks over time began to arouse government suspicions. As Wu Fengshi and Xu Yuan write, "Because some of the goals that these advocacy networks target are related to policy failures or state misbehavior, they have a tendency to mobilize the populace, instead of engaging in a dialogue with government agencies."[33]

Village Elections

One of the most surprising political opportunities that opened to American organizations in the late 1980s was the invitation to observe and provide advice as China began introducing competitive elections at the village level. With the dissolution of people's communes in the early 1980s, village leadership in many parts of the countryside began to deteriorate, as some village leaders abrogated their posts to go into business, some became corrupt, and others became dictatorial "local emperors." With so many local party leaders losing legitimacy, the central leadership became increasingly wary of a descent into chaos and even outright rebellion in rural areas. After considerable debate within the central leadership, the party, prodded by conservative party elder Peng Zhen, decided to introduce direct election of village committees in China's nearly one million villages. The relatively liberal Ministry of Civil Affairs, then under the direction of the open-minded and outward-looking Yan Mingfu, was charged with promoting the implementation of these elections. The ministry turned to several American organizations for guidance.[34]

Local staff at the Ford Foundation in Beijing were the first to observe a village election, and they introduced the voters to the notion of a secret ballot. In the early 1990s, the International Republican Institute (IRI), one of the four core institutes under the National Endowment for Democracy, was also invited to begin observing village elections. IRI gave advice and monitored some fifty elections over a period of several years. The Carter Center, which has the monitoring of elections worldwide as one of its primary activities, also began monitoring and assessing China's village elections, observing multiple elections each year from 1996 to 2005.[35]

Because they were learning largely about the technical aspects of elections (secret ballots, campaigning, voter registration, transparency, etc.), the Chinese government initially welcomed these interventions. Some international observers hoped that local elections would be the first step in China's movement toward democratic government. Several Chinese delegations came to the United States to witness the American electoral process. Shawn Shieh observed that the Chinese government initially

> had a supportive attitude towards this involvement because the village elections were positive for China's image in the world, but not so significant as to undermine the fundamental basis of China's political regime. By focusing on the more technical aspects, and not fundamental issues concerning the Chinese political regime, the INGOs were able to gain the trust and collaboration of the Chinese government in promoting participatory governance at the grassroots level.[36]

With changes of leadership at the Ministry of Civil Affairs, official enthusiasm for village elections began to wane along with previous enthusiasm for outside advice. While official reports touted the successful spread of village elections, questions remained about how democratic they really were, particularly because township leaders often intervened to choose the candidates. The advent of the color revolutions in Georgia in 2003, in the Ukraine in 2004, and in Kyrgyzstan in 2006 led to even greater wariness. The challenge to East European socialist governments from civil society groups, many supported by international organizations, was seen as a major cause of the downfall of those governments. Between 2005 and 2010, the Carter Center was not permitted to observe elections. A special exception was made in 2010 for an election in Yunnan Province, but that was the last such observation. The IRI had closed this facet of its China programs even earlier. These pullbacks were one of the signals that China was moving toward more restrictions of international NGOs.

New Challenges

The year 2008 was probably the apogee of American foundation and NGO activity and influence in China. By then, social and political change was coming from multiple directions. Alarmed by the color revolutions in East Europe and the Middle East where civil society had played such an important role, China's leaders became wary of foreign NGOs, especially those that were funding advocacy organizations. As Mark Sidel, a noted scholar of China's NGO community, put it:

> [T]he Chinese Communist Party and government are most concerned about oversight of two other kinds of groups: domestic advocacy organizations, and foreign nonprofit and philanthropic organizations operating in or providing assistance to China. In both cases, Party and government concern arises for political reasons—the Chinese state is concerned that advocacy organizations may build coalitions and alliances aimed at rapid political reform and political change and is concerned that at least a subset of foreign nonprofit and foundations groups are also engaged in activities aimed at political transformation.[37]

At the same time, the Beijing Olympics of 2008 symbolized China's coming out as a global power. Large-scale foreign assistance for knowledge infrastructure and social services was no longer needed. China's own philanthropy, stimulated by American models and fueled by successful entrepreneurs, had come to vastly outpace international support. Chinese civil society organizations, many inspired by international ones, were actively addressing charitable needs in local areas.

In the United States, the magnetic pull that first attracted American foundations had weakened. Small and relatively underfunded American organizations questioned what real difference they could make. China was no longer the neediest foreign country, and the United States faced social challenges of its own. The international focus of several large, bellwether foundations shifted away from China to parts of the world with more pressing development needs.

In the first decade of the new millennium, the Rockefeller Foundation ended almost a century of involvement in China, refocusing instead on the continent of Africa. The Ford Foundation had been the largest American donor in China, contributing $356 million from 1988 to 2015. In the early 2000s, the Ford Foundation began focusing its efforts on the issue of poverty alleviation, both domestically and internationally, retaining its presence in China but cutting its funding back sharply, with its annual budget for China decreasing from around $16 million in the late 1990s to $14 million in 2013 to around $11 million in 2018.[38]

Organizations that continued to focus on China revised their goals. With outlays of $6 to $7 million a year, the China Medical Board had long been the second largest American philanthropy operating in China. It was a grant-making organization with a focus on faculty and research development at China's major medical universities. By 2010, the China Medical Board was shifting toward programs that focused strategically on influencing China's medical policies toward health equity and facilitating collaboration with Southeast Asian partners.

In 2007, even as foundations and NGOs with longtime programs in China began to pull back, a new American actor, the Bill and Melinda Gates Foundation, arrived on the China scene. The programs of the Gates Foundation quickly dwarfed those of other American institutions. The initial mission of the Gates Foundation in China was primarily medical, focusing on tuberculosis, tobacco control, and HIV/AIDS. That original mission later expanded to include malaria and agricultural development and, more recently, global collaboration. The Gates Foundation works closely with Chinese government agencies, including the Ministries of Health, Commerce, and Agriculture, the National Natural Science Foundation of China, and many local corporations and institutes, expending some $50 million a year.[39]

The Foreign NGO LAW[40]

American civil society organizations began to face new challenges when China decided to implement a new law governing foreign NGOs. For the first three decades of engagement, the activities of foreign NGOs were not restricted by Chinese law, and the Chinese government exercised only loose oversight over the thousands of international organizations operating there. But as the government began responding to the burgeoning of China's own civil society with new regulations, it began to focus on the regulation of foreign organizations as well. Beginning in 2004, international organizations were encouraged to register officially by identifying a domestic supervisory organization and reporting to the Ministry of Civil Affairs. But by 2012, only eighteen organizations were actually registered.

By then, particularly with the advent of Xi Jinping's new administration, foreign organizations were aware that new regulations were coming, and early signs were that the requirements would be restrictive. The first troubling sign, following the alarms that were sounded in Beijing by Hong Kong's Occupy Central demonstrations in 2014, was that authority over international NGOs would be transferred from the more moderate and open Ministry of Civil Affairs to the Ministry of Public Security. Thus, the police were put in charge of civil society, bringing about what Mark Sidel, calls the "securitization" of foreign nonprofit management. A further troubling sign was the publication of the first draft of the NGO law in the spring of 2015. The law was far more restrictive than anticipated. Not only were foreign NGOs required to find professional supervisory units with overall authority resting with the Ministry of Public Security, but they "were to be guided by vague requirements and prohibitions . . . including requirements not to damage China's national security, unity and solidarity, China's interests, the public interest and the interests of other organizations."[41]

Although American NGOs generally operate independently from their government, the introduction of a new NGO law provided an occasion for which they sought governmental intervention. The U.S. Embassy in Beijing, the U.S. State Department, and President Obama himself weighed in on the importance of keeping the door open to American NGOs. The international outcry about the draft regulations resulted in some modifications. Most notably, assurance was given that academic exchanges and cooperation would not be adversely influenced and could continue as in the past. Assurances were also given that China was not closing its door to foreign NGO activity.

The law went into effect on January 1, 2017. The most important requirement is that all foreign NGOs that wish to register an office must secure the support of a government-approved ministry or institute that will serve as its professional supervisory unit. This unit, which serves as the NGO sponsor, reports to the Ministry of Public Security. Organizations without an office in China but planning various activities—a workshop or conference, for instance—are also required seek permission through a Chinese partner.

The experiences of two key American foundations described earlier—the Ford Foundation and the Asia Foundation—are illustrative of the effect of the law on major American NGOs. Both the Ford Foundation and the Asia Foundation had been operating offices in China for years, and both had supported programs in governance and law that could be seen as sensitive by Chinese authorities. Their portfolios were also multifaceted, making finding a single supervising sponsor difficult. Each mounted lobbying efforts with relevant Chinese authorities, testifying to the social good the foundation had rendered since normalization. The fact that hundreds of government officials had been involved in their training and overseas programs was particularly persuasive. Their efforts succeeded. By mid-2017, both organizations had been notified that the Chinese People's Association for Friendship with Foreign Countries had agreed to become the professional supervisory unit of both organizations.

Elizabeth Knup, the director of the Ford Foundation China office, describes how she successfully lobbied on behalf of Ford in China and what she learned in this process:

> First, I think proactiveness is key. Since January 1st 2017, my job everyday was to push the rock up the hill just a little bit. If I could do one thing every day—talk to somebody, go to a meeting, learning something. . . . Every single day—that was my goal. I think that if we hadn't demonstrated our positive desire then our Chinese stakeholders may not have understood our commitment to operating in China.
>
> Second, I think we need to have an openness to engage with government authorities, and I think this lesson is particularly applicable to ONGOs [overseas nongovernmental organizations] who are either not registered in China or don't know where to start. Government authorities are actually really helpful. They are surprisingly open, flexible and oriented to problem-solving. That's a really important transferrable lesson to take away. I've also learnt patience is a huge asset. Again, I think it is important to bring good faith to the process.[42]

By July 2018, seventy-eight American NGOs had been officially registered.[43] All were relatively large with established records in China. The largest group (twenty-three NGOs) were trade associations such as the American International Chamber of Commerce, Cotton USA, the International Copper Association, and the U.S.-China Business Council. The second largest group (eighteen NGOs) included those that had the environment as part of their portfolio, including the Nature Conservancy, Pacific Environment, the Natural Resources Defense Council, and the Wildlife Conservation Society. The third largest group (seventeen NGOs) were those focused on health including Orbis, the China Medical Board, Project Hope, Holt International, and the Gates Foundation.

Somewhat surprisingly, a number of American faith-based organizations have also been registered. These include the Go and Love Foundation operating in Yunnan, Blessing Hands operating in Guangxi, and the China Service Ventures and China-U.S. Volunteer Cooperation Service Society, both operating in Henan. These organizations provide charitable and humanitarian services for children, the elderly, and the indigent.

The Foreign NGO Law accelerated the decline in American work in legal affairs and social justice. Foundations with previously well-established law and governance programs had already begun phasing out their programs before the proclamation of the law. Funding for the Asia Foundation's long-standing program in administrative law ended in 2011, for instance, and the Ford Foundation's program in clinical legal education had been dropped because it no longer conformed to the Ford Foundation's overall mission.

The organizations that have not yet gained approval or decided not to apply for registration are generally those that work in legal services, legal aid, social justice, and human rights. These include the Soros Open Society Foundations, the IRI, and the National Endowment for Democracy, along with smaller NGOs working on human rights. The American Bar Association (ABA) is one example. Long active in China and funded by the U.S. Department of State and the U.S. Agency for International Development, the ABA worked in such areas as domestic violence, criminal justice, administrative law, transparent government, and LGBT visibility. Although discussions were held with high-level officials, the Ministry of Justice would not agree to serve as a professional supervisor. In March 2017, recognizing that the political climate was not conducive to their continuing activity in China, ABA announced:

In the wake of a new law threatening criminal prosecution of foreigners engaging in human and legal rights work in China, the ABA Rule of Law Initiative closed its Beijing office in December. China's detailed regulation of nongovernmental organizations, which went into effect Jan. 1, is the most comprehensive statutory crackdown on foreign influence among an increasing number of countries seeking greater control over civil society.[44]

The ABA moved its office to Hong Kong.[45] Thus, the robust, multidecade American role in promoting legal reform and advocating for social justice has, at least for the time being, ended.

More broadly, as Mark Sidel describes it, the Chinese government is clearly using the Foreign NGO Law to mold the nature of American engagement in China. Bureaucratic delays have resulted in the postponement or cancellation of previously active programs. As Sidel summarizes the impact of the Foreign NGO Law, "The initial 13 months of implementation show clearly that, in registering foreign NGO offices and foundations, China is distinctly favoring service provision and capacity building organizations and activities over advocacy and social justice groups and projects. . . . Foreign-based advocacy and social justice groups are already having a much more difficult time working in China and that will likely accelerate."[46]

Strategic Adaptation

During their four decades of work in an authoritarian country, American foundations, religious organizations, and NGOs have faced political, cultural, and institutional challenges. Looking at these activities as a whole and over time, one sees largely the positive nature of the engagement and the vibrant growth in society-to-society relations. Looking more closely, year by year and project by project, however, one is struck more by the many difficulties, often financial and bureaucratic but sometimes political, that the American NGO community has faced. That many have stayed the course is testament to the historic and continuing American passion for and commitment to hands-on participation in China's modernization. The continuing relationships with so many different partner organizations suggest that the Chinese are generally receptive, even enthusiastic, about their work. Indeed, Chinese organizations have often been the primary actors in American-sponsored projects—identifying their needs, suggesting modes of work, providing training, and smoothing away the political challenges.

But times have changed. How do we understand the relative success in earlier years and what might need to change for the future? The concept "strategic adaptation" suggests the ways in which many NGOs have learned to operate in China, ways in which they now hope will allow them to stay in China.[47] Among the ingredients for the successful strategic adaptation of American NGOs in China are the following:

1. A hybrid working style that engages local and national government organizations as well as grassroots organizations.

During the early period of renewed American engagement in China, from 1979 to 1989, most American foundations worked closely with government institutes, universities, and departments. When a pluralistic Chinese civil society began to blossom after 1995, both foundations and newly arrived international NGOs turned their attention to provincial-level and grassroots organizations, usually while still trying to maintain some national or regional government contacts.

This hybrid style of operation is being tested anew as all foreign NGOs must now be aligned with a professional supervisory unit that is responsible for approving their annual plans. Many are working with agencies with which they have had long-standing relationships. Both Conservation International and the Wildlife Conservation Society, for example, have been assigned to the State Forestry Administration, and the Environmental Defense Fund works under the aegis of the Ministry of Environmental Protection. While organizations with complex agendas generally face more difficulties finding an appropriate professional supervisory unit, the Chinese People's Association for Friendship with Foreign Countries has agreed to sponsor both the Ford Foundation and the Asia Foundation, both of which have multiple types of programs. Other international organizations with multiple agendas, however, have yet to identify a professional supervisory unit.

Elizabeth Knup's point about the need to engage with government authorities is important. While some have criticized American organizations for being too accommodating because of their ties to China's officialdom,[48] the reality has been and most likely will continue to be that some level of government approval will be necessary for any American NGO work in China. In fact, one of the most important impacts American NGOs have had in China is their influence on the Chinese government itself—witness all the training of Chinese government officials and the changing policies in law, environment, women's rights, AIDS, and social services, for instance.

2.   A focus on professionalization within their respective sectors.

One common element across many NGOs is the emphasis on training and professionalization. This is congruent with China's own desire to upgrade its human talent in all sectors. Especially important has been the American role in introducing global norms and building the capacity of the Chinese NGOs and foundations with which they have worked. This emphasis on training extends to the religious sector as well. With the rapid growth of Christianity in China and the paucity of seminaries and hence of well-trained pastors, much of the work of Protestant and Catholic groups has been to train Chinese clergy, usually locally but sometimes also internationally. One 2012 study concludes that "the government recognizes the need for both the Three-Self Patriotic Church and house churches to have improved theological training as a means of maintaining stability, preventing the rise of illegal cults, and creating good citizens."[49] With Xi Jinping's more restrictive policies toward Christian religious practices, however, these kinds of training opportunities have been markedly reduced.

3.   Policy experimentation at a local level.

Some international NGOs may be perceived as activist groups challenging government rules and regulations, but many of the most successful NGOs in China have also focused on developing model local programs and demonstration sites. This follows a longtime Chinese strategy of using demonstration sites to test and then perhaps adopt new policies. Noakes and Teets cite an NGO representative explaining that "we have worked with local partners to test new policies first in local pilot projects, adapt them to China's conditions, and then used the results to advocate successfully for policy adoption at the provincial and national levels."[50]

Many examples from the American experience illustrate this point. The Asia Foundation worked on improving civil laws with Henan Province, hoping that the changes would be successful and noticed by the national government. The Nature Conservancy's emphasis on education and improved regulation in demonstration sites, called social welfare protectorates, is another example.

4.   Selecting programs that are congruent with Chinese priorities.

The portfolio of American foundations and NGOs has evolved as China's interests and needs have changed. In the 1980s, revitalizing research and higher education provided a compelling and appropriate role for many foundations. In the 1990s and 2000s, China's own social agenda became more complex. Chinese civil society groups and American NGOs were able to work together nimbly at the local level to address such problems as poverty, women's empowerment, conservation, and health. During this period, the Chinese government was also making serious efforts to improve its social services and legal system. In keeping with their earlier focus on legal training and at the request of provincial departments and government agencies, the Ford Foundation and the Asia Foundation developed innovative programs.

The American agenda today is being diverted from engagement with those more cutting-edge political and social issues to areas in which China seeks international collaboration. Pressure is being exerted, directly and indirectly, to undertake work that focuses on U.S.-China relations or areas that would enhance China's international developmental role. The work of the Carter Center is a good example. When President Carter met with then vice president Xi Jinping in 2012 and expressed his hope that the village election agenda could continue, Xi gently reminded him that his great contribution had been the normalization of U.S.-China relations, suggesting that the Carter Center focus on programs related to that issue. Today, in programs with China's *Global Times*, the Carter Center is doing just that while at the same time pursuing efforts to link its own well-known public health program in Africa with China's medical programs there.

5. Supporting China's global linkages.

China's NGO community has matured so quickly that it now seeks its own international role in bringing Chinese ideas, relief, support, and technical assistance to Africa and Asia. But Chinese NGOs have little access to funds that would allow them to work internationally. Thus, they are beginning to partner with American foundations to undertake international programs. The Asia Foundation, which maintains eighteen offices in Asia, has long sought ways to link its work in China with its regional programs in Asia. When hundreds of local Chinese NGOs became involved in providing disaster relief following the devastating Sichuan earthquake of 2008, China was spurred to develop its own disaster relief programs. Recognizing a need, the Asia Foundation began training programs in disaster relief in China and then extended these to other parts of Asia. After the 2015 Nepal earthquake, Asia Foundation–trained Chinese relief teams were able to make a significant contribution. An Asia Foundation statement from 2017 reads:

> As China pursues the "Belt and Road Initiative" and regional development, the Foundation continues to utilize its technical expertise and well-established network in the U.S. and Asia to encourage China's constructive global engagement. We work closely with local partners to improve the understanding of China's development strategy, development assistance and responsible overseas investment, while strengthening the capacity of Chinese civil society organizations to tackle the intersection of these issues with disaster relief and assistance, environmental resilience, and gender equality.[51]

Other major institutions may follow. The Ford Foundation is considering a China in the World initiative, and the Rockefeller Foundation may reengage with China on topics of global governance.

While some of these ideas for assistance to an outward-bound China are laudatory, political caution is needed. China's growing dominance in some parts of the world is seen as threatening to local governments and societies. Enhancing China's soft power is not necessarily always in the interest of the United States.

6. Localization.

What is most likely in the future is that American NGOs in China will become more Chinese. A decade ago, there were no Chinese (citizens, China-born American Chinese, or U.S.-born Chinese) in leadership positions in American foundation or NGO offices in China, while the staffs included both Chinese and Americans. Now, not only are many offices in China led by Chinese citizens, but Chinese also dominate the programmatic staff as well. In the years ahead, the formal structures of some American foundations and NGOs in China may well change, as their missions continue through an organization that has become in essence Chinese. This would not necessarily spell the demise of American social influence but rather the next stage in strategic adaptation, a move away from donor-recipient relations to a more integrated collaboration between equals. This could be seen as the sinicization of foreign NGOs.

✳ ✳ ✳

The implementation of the Foreign NGO Law is in an early stage. It is still too early to predict the law's longer-term effect on American work in China. Similarly, it is still too early to comprehend how the recent downturn in the overall U.S.-China relationship will affect cooperation in the hitherto resilient nongovernmental sector or what changes might ensue under a new Biden administration. But a few preliminary conclusions can be drawn.

First, given China's increasing hostility to Western ideas under Xi Jinping, the fact that so many American social organizations still remain engaged with Chinese society is encouraging. The degree to which they will be permitted to implement their yearly plans remains unclear. The bureaucratic hurdles are numerous. Nonetheless, many are cautiously optimistic that they will be able to continue some form of their work in China.

Second, under the current, more authoritarian regime, the possibility that activist organizations hoping to address sensitive legal or social issues will be permitted to operate in China remains slim.

Third, Americans are still able to collaborate with a surprisingly large number of Chinese organizations.

At a time when some question the benefits of nearly half a century of U.S.-China engagement, it is well to consider the many ways in which American cultural engagement has influenced Chinese society. This includes, most notably, helping to build a Western-oriented intellectual infrastructure, engaging civil society at both the national and grassroots levels, and introducing global norms to fields ranging from the environment to health to law and human rights. American organizations have worked in all of China's provinces at both provincial and local levels. Their partners have spanned China's bureaucratic community, again demonstrating an unusual alliance between independent American institutions and the Chinese state. But they also worked in rural areas with local grassroots organizations, which are as close to real nongovernmental institutions as China may have. Tens of thousands of Americans have enthusiastically participated in China's social modernization. Close bonds and friendships have been created between citizens in both countries. Although work with China has often been frustrating, there is a sense of mission and purpose not dissimilar to that of the Western advisers profiled by Jonathan Spence.

This engagement linked key sectors of American society with Chinese society. It united Chinese and American people in tackling problems of poverty, health, clean water, and AIDS. The widest variety of American cultural and social values—from evangelical Protestantism to environmental activism to women's empowerment to criminal justice reform to community development—were transmitted in their work. Likewise, Americans working in China came to appreciate the rich spectrum of Chinese cultural traditions and societal engagement. Society-to-society linkages have proved flexible and adaptable to the political and social changes in China and, thus far, have prevailed through the most difficult ups and downs in the last half century of U.S.-China relations. The scale and depth of nearly fifty years of U.S.-China social engagement have left a mark on both countries that cannot easily be erased. Yes, the nature of our engagement will be different in the future, but its legacy will be found in the myriad of personal and institutional ties that will hopefully continue. These relationships have been the bedrock of U.S.-China relations.

Nonetheless, in this current era of increasing competition and often outright hostility between China and the United States, NGOs working in China are increasingly challenged, and many have simply withdrawn. David Lampton has declared the era of engagement to have ended and foresees a long period before the stars have sufficiently realigned for a new period of reengagement to begin. Several other contributors to this volume have also predicted a sustained period of strategic competition—and possibly worse. If history repeats itself, however, the remembered experiences of both Chinese and Americans who have worked together on common goals will be the starting point of any renewed engagement with a China that no longer looks to the United States for help, but as an equal partner in new complementary and cooperative endeavors.

NOTES

I have been affiliated with several of these organizations, am currently a trustee of the Asia Foundation, and was previously a trustee of the China Medical Board, the National Committee on U.S.-China Relations, the United Board for Christian Higher Education in Asia, and Yale-China.

1. Mary Brown Bullock, *The Oil Prince's Legacy: Rockefeller Philanthropy in China* (Stanford: Stanford University Press, 2011), 147.

2. Jonathan Spence, *To Change China: Western Advisors in China, 1620 to 1960* (Boston: Little, Brown, 1969); James C. Thomson, *While China Faced West: American Reformers in Nationalist China, 1928–1937* (Cambridge, MA: Harvard University Press, 1969).

3. Norton Wheeler, *The Role of American NGOs in China's Modernization: Invited Influence* (London: Routledge, 2013), 3.

4. In 1996, the name of the CSCPRC changed to the Committee on Scholarly Communication with China (CSCC).

5. For background on the National Committee, see Jan C. Berris, "The Evolution of Sino-American Exchanges: A View from the National Committee," www.ncuscr.org. For the CSCPRC, see Mary Brown Bullock, "Mission Accomplished: The Influence of the CSCPRC on Educational Relations with China," in *Bridging Minds Across the Pacific: U.S.-China Educational Exchanges, 1978–2003*, ed. Cheng Li (Lanham, MD: Lexington, 2005), 49–68.

6. See Leo Orleans, ed., *Science in Contemporary China* (Stanford, CA: Stanford University Press, 1980).

7. Bullock, *Oil Prince's Legacy*, 160. This is the source for all references to the Rockefellers and China.

8. See Mary Brown Bullock, *An American Transplant: The Rockefeller Foundation and Peking Union Medical College* (Berkeley: University of California Press, 1980), 161–73; on the United Board, see Paul Lauby, *Sailing on Winds of Change* (New York: United Board, 1996), 80–113; on Yale-China, see Nancy E. Chapman, *The Yale-China Association: A Centennial History* (Hong Kong: The Chinese University Press, 2001).

9. Zi Zhongyun, *The Destiny of Wealth: An Analysis of American Philanthropic Foundations from a Chinese Perspective* (Dayton, OH: The Kettering Foundation Press, 2007), 184.

10. Asia Foundation, *20 Years in China, Commemorative Report, 1999* (San Francisco: Asia Foundation, 1999).

11. Renee Yuen-Jan Hsia and Lynn T. White III, "Working amid Corporatism and Confusion: Foreign NGO's in China," *Non-Profit and Voluntary Sector Quarterly* 31 (2002): 330.

12. See Zi, *Destiny of Wealth*, 177–90.

13. Lauby, *Sailing on Winds of Change*, 97.

14. Richard Madsen, *China and the American Dream: A Moral Inquiry* (Berkeley: University of California Press, 1995), ix.

15. Lauby, *Sailing on Winds of Change*, 110.

16. Zi, *Destiny of Wealth*, 187.

17. Shawn Shieh, *The Roles and Challenges of International NGOs in China's Development* (Beijing: China Development Brief, Fall 2012), 9.

18. David Zweig, *Internationalizing China: Domestic Interests and Global Linkages* (Ithaca, NY: Cornell University Press, 2002), 262.

19. National Committee on U.S.-China Relations, "China Town Hall," https://www.ncuscr.org/program/china-town-hall.

20. Quoted in Madsen, *China and the American Dream*, 138.

21. This discussion on American religious organizations in China draws from interviews with Philip Wickeri, June 12, 2018; Brent Fulton, July 13, 2018, and Lester Ruiz, July 19, 2018.

22. Madsen, *China and the American Dream*, 140.

23. This is based on interviews with Philip Wickeri, June 12, 2018, and Brent Fulton, July 13, 2018.

24. Jonathan Tam and Reza Hasmath, "Navigating Uncertainty: The Survival Strategies of Religious NGOs in China," *Journal of Civil Society* 11, no. 3 (2015): 283–99.

25. Gao Feng, "Build Up the Chinese Protestant Church Through Sinicization," *Chinese Theological Review* 28 (March 23, 2018): 1–29.

26. These and other statistics on American environmental groups in China come from Wu Fengshi and Xu Yuan, "Sino-American Environmental Relations: The Potential of Trans-Societal Linkages," *Issues and Studies* 49, no. 3 (2013): 73–110.

27. Wu and Xu, "Sino-American Environmental Relations," 99.

28. Jie Chen, "Transnational Environmental Movement: Impacts on the Green Civil Society in China," *Journal of Contemporary China* 19, no. 65 (2010): 512.

29. Bullock, *Oil Prince's Legacy*, 197.

30. Northwest Yunnan Ecotourism Association, "Yunnan Great Rivers Project," www.northwestyunnan.com/project.htm.

31. Chen, "Transnational Environmental Movement," 516.

32. Chen, "Transnational Environmental Movement," 509.

33. Wu and Xu, "Sino-American Environmental Relations," 104.

34. Anne F. Thurston, *Muddling Toward Democracy: Political Change in Grassroots China* (Washington, DC: US Institute of Peace, August 1998).

35. Interview with Yawei Liu, June 1, 2018. I participated in a Carter Center village election survey in 1997.

36. Shieh, *Roles and Challenges of International NGOs*, 21.

37. Mark Sidel, "Managing the Foreign: The Drive to Securitize Foreign Nonprofit and Foundation Management in China," *Voluntas* 30 (2019): 664–77.

38. Interview with Elizabeth Knup, September 25, 2018.

39. Interview with Yinua Li, May 8, 2018, and with Kathleen Walsh and Rui Xi, July 30, 2018.

40. This discussion on the Foreign NGO Law is from the author's discussions with Joan Kaufman, Oma Lee, Katherine Wilhelm, Anthony Spires, Zhang Ye, and Mark Sidel.

41. Sidel, "Managing the Foreign," no pagination.

42. China Development Brief, "Our Registration Story: The Ford Foundation," August 21, 2017, https://mp.weixin.qq.com/s/Fv4407dcAwQqlix23SKiRw. Accessed July 23, 2018.

43. All data on registered NGOs comes from ChinaFile, "Registered Foreign NGO Representative Offices," China NGO Project, Asia Society, www.chinafile.com/ngo/registered-foreign-ngo-offices-map-full-screen#table. Interview with Jessica Batke, July 17, 2018.

44. Terry Carter, "ABA Closes Office in China While It Measures the Impact of New Restrictions on NGO Activities," *ABA Journal*, March 1, 2017, https://www.abajournal.com/magazine/article/aba_roli_china_rights_law/.

45. Interview with Oma Lee, July 24, 2018.

46. Sidel, "Managing the Foreign." Interview with Mark Sidel, August 8, 2018.

47. These concepts are adapted from Stephen Noakes and Jessica C. Teets, "Learning Under Authoritarianism: Strategic Adaptations Within International Foundations and NGOS in China," *Voluntas* 31 (2020): 1093–113.

48. For example, Shawn Shieh and Anthony Spires.

49. Tam and Hasmath, "Navigating Uncertainty," 296.

50. Noakes and Teets, "Learning Under Authoritarianism," 7.

51. Asia Foundation, *2017 Annual Report* (San Francisco: Asia Foundation, 2017), 9.

CHAPTER 9

U.S.-CHINA RELATIONS

A Public Health Perspective

YANZHONG HUANG

American involvement with the provision of health care in China can be traced to November 4, 1834, when Peter Parker, an American missionary, physician, and diplomat, founded China's first Western-style hospital, the Ophthalmic Hospital of Canton (Guangzhou). Three decades later, in 1866, the hospital became the site of China's first modern medical school.[1] By 1887, seventy-four missionary doctors, forty-one of them American, were working in China, where they appear in hindsight to have been more successful in the field of health than in fulfilling their religious missions.[2] In 1896, China-based missionaries from the Women's Board of the Methodist Episcopal Church sponsored two Chinese women, Kang Chen (known in English as Ida Kahn) and Shi Meiyu (known as Mary Stone) to study medicine at the University of Michigan. The two were the first Chinese women to become Western-trained physicians. Both returned to China in 1896 as missionary doctors, setting up training programs for nurses and establishing dispensaries and hospitals that treated thousands of women and children each year.[3]

Ten years later, the Yale Foreign Missionary Society (the predecessor of the Yale-China Association) launched the Xiangya (Yale-China) Hospital, the first Western medical hospital in Changsha, Hunan, which came to be known as the best hospital in southern China. In Sichuan Province, half of the thirty missionary hospitals were built by missionaries from the United States. By 1950, China had a total of 527 modern medical institutions, two-thirds of which were founded by foreign missionaries.[4]

This was no coincidence. The foreign missionary movement in the nineteenth and early twentieth centuries sought to promote Christianity by providing modern medical care and education to the Chinese people. American missionaries played a critical role in this process.

The American missionaries sent to improve the health of the Chinese people were later joined by other U.S.-based philanthropic organizations. In 1914, the Rockefeller Foundation, which soon became the largest American philanthropic donor to China, created the China Medical Board, which was charged with promoting the modernization of medical education and improving medical practices in China, as Mary Bullock describes in chapter 8 of this volume. Five years later, Peking Union Medical College (PUMC) opened its doors under the de facto directorship of Roger Greene, the resident director of the China Medical Board.[5] PUMC became the most elite medical college in China and had a profound impact on the nature of public health delivery and medical care there. In the 1920s and 1930s, PUMC professors and students pioneered the development of a three-tiered health-care network in Ding County, Hebei Province, with patients receiving rudimentary medical treatment at the village level, more advanced treatment in clinics at the level of the town, and still more advanced care in hospitals at the county level. These efforts laid the groundwork for the modern public health system that still exists in China today and inspired the use of barefoot doctors introduced by Mao in the 1960s.[6] In addition, the early twentieth century saw the increasing involvement of American pharmaceutical firms in China. The Indianapolis-based pharmaceutical company Eli Lilly opened its first overseas representative office in Shanghai in 1918.

With the communist takeover in 1949, American medical assistance to China fell victim to the hostility between the two nations. Foreign missionaries were viewed as part of a cultural invasion,[7] and some were condemned as drug dealers, spies, and running dogs of imperialism.[8] In the early 1950s, PUMC and other U.S.-sponsored medical schools and hospitals were nationalized, and health-related charitable organizations such as the China Medical Board were forced to leave. Public health–related exchanges thus came to a halt, not to resume for another three decades.

But the U.S.-built hospitals and schools continued to function, serving as silent reminders of American generosity and friendship in a bygone age. Indeed, they continue to function today, with their reputations for excellence intact. As Mary Bullock also recounts in her chapter, during his meeting with Chinese paramount leader Deng Xiaoping in January 1979, President Jimmy Carter pleaded for the return of missionaries. Deng refused, insisting that many of the missionaries had been there only to change the Oriental lifestyle to a Western pattern. After Carter reminded Deng of the hospitals and schools the missionaries had established, Deng agreed to consider permitting unrestricted distribution of Bibles and allowing Chinese people to have freedom of worship.[9]

Cooperative activities in the realm of health were among the first to be set up following the beginning of official bilateral exchanges in the 1970s. Cooperation in the field of health has been among the most successful aspects of the U.S.-China relationship over the past four decades, bringing considerable benefits to both sides. Only recently have new barriers to cooperation arisen, dampening and sometimes even reversing the gains of decades past.

What is the record of U.S.-China cooperation in the field of health? How have the vicissitudes of the overall Sino-American relationship affected bilateral cooperation in the area of health? To what extent does U.S.-China cooperation in the realm of health contribute to the dynamics of the broader U.S.-China relationship? To address these questions, this chapter examines the evolution of U.S.-China relations from a public health perspective over three stages—1971–2001, 2002–2016, and 2017 to present—focusing on government-to-government cooperation, the role of nongovernmental organizations (NGOs), and the growth and impact of pharmaceutical companies. For each stage, we explore the broader political and strategic context in which the cooperation took place and the accomplishments and challenges faced by each side.

1971–2001: Revival and Expansion of Cooperation

Health professionals were among the first Americans invited to visit China following the rapprochement of the early 1970s, and cooperation in the field of public health resumed shortly thereafter. In 1973, the biochemist and UCLA professor Emil Smith was appointed by President Richard Nixon to lead the first U.S. scientific delegation to China. As Milo Leavitt, then director of the National Institutes of Health (NIH) Fogarty International Center, noted, "For those who believe that the universal desire for health and relief from disease and suffering may be the strongest key to peace and international cooperation, it is significant and heartening to observe that physicians were among the first groups granted permission to visit the People's Republic of China."[10]

These visits gave U.S. health professionals and reporters a glimpse of China's public health-care system, including the policy process, the delivery of health-care services, and the use of a combination of Western and traditional Chinese medicines. The American public was given an introduction to traditional Chinese medicine in 1971 when the *New York Times* reporter James Reston published his personal account of being treated for pain with acupuncture following an emergency appendectomy in China.[11] The health policy process also drew the interest of such leading China scholars as Michel Oksenberg and David M. Lampton.[12] Lampton's work on the politics of medicine in China became essential reading in the field of China studies.

Some who were early visitors to China came to see the 1970s as China's golden years of health care. China had more professional health-care workers and hospital beds than virtually any other country close to its level of economic development.[13] The status of people's health had undergone remarkable improvement under the communist government. Official data suggest that between 1949 and 1975, China's infant mortality rate dropped from 20 per 1,000 live births to 7.32 per 1,000, while average life expectancy at birth increased from thirty-five to sixty-six years.[14] Much of this improvement can be attributed to the fact that after 1949 China had adopted a populist model of health care that emphasized equality and universalism and relied on social and political measures to promote disease prevention and health-care provision. The popularization in the countryside of barefoot doctors with basic medical training assured that rural babies were vaccinated and hundreds of millions of Chinese peasants had some rudimentary medical care.

Some early American visitors, seeing the Chinese model for the first time, thought it might offer an alternative to the Western approach that relies primarily on medical treatment by highly trained health professionals. Other observers were more cautious. Victor Sidel, who first visited in 1971, described himself as uncertain about how much the United States and other countries could learn from the Chinese experience.[15] Allen Dobson, who traveled to China with a George Washington University medical delegation in late 1979, recognized the unprecedented strength of the Chinese medical system, praising the accomplishments of mass campaigns in delivering inoculations and stamping out certain diseases and noting that medical care was vastly superior to what had existed before 1949. But he also found many aspects of the Chinese health-care delivery system lacking. Most traditional herbal medicines were ineffectual against infectious diseases. Medical equipment was often primitive and outdated. After decades without contact with Western doctors or access to Western medical books, and with the disruption of the health system during the Cultural Revolution, Chinese doctors had not been able to keep up with medical advances in other parts of the world.

Bilateral cooperation in the realm of health received a strong boost following the formal establishment of diplomatic relations between China and the United States in January 1979. In June of that year, the two countries signed a Protocol for Cooperation in the Science and Technology of Medicine and Public Health (the Health Protocol). The original Health Protocol was followed in 1980 by an ancillary agreement that identified major health issues slated for cooperative endeavors, including infectious diseases, mental health, reproductive health, and noncommunicable diseases such as cancer and cardiovascular disease. The nature of the cooperation included exchanges of specialists, coordination of scientific research projects, joint organization of seminars and conferences, and the exchange and provision of biological standards, reagents, and samples for laboratory tests and control.[16] American scientists conducted combined laboratory and lecture mini-courses in both Shanghai and Beijing, teaching participating Chinese scientists how to design experiments for testing hypotheses and developing new ones.[17] The U.S. NIH, America's leading agency responsible for biomedical and public health research, conducted numerous cooperative activities with China, supporting research on cancer and other health issues. Its Maryland-based Fogarty International Center served as an important training center for Chinese scientists. Many NIH-sponsored programs exposed Chinese scientists to new frontiers of basic health research. In 1982, the inaugural class of students from the China–United States Biochemistry and Molecular Biology Examination and Application (CUSBEA) program arrived in the United States. Created by Professor Ray Wu, a Chinese-born American biologist at Cornell University, the CUSBEA program alone enabled 422 students from mainland China to receive advanced training at ninety American universities and research institutes from 1982 to 1989. By 1989, somewhere between one thousand and three thousand Chinese students and scientists had been trained in biotechnology-related fields at American universities, and 125 Chinese scientists were working at NIH.[18]

In addition to U.S. government agencies, the 1980s and 1990s also saw American universities, NGOs, and the private sector become players in bilateral health cooperation. Health-related foreign philanthropic organizations began entering or returning to China, including the previously mentioned China Medical Board (1981), Project Hope (1983), the Ford Foundation (1988), and Smile Train (1999). As one of the largest grant-making organizations operating in China, the China Medical Board focused on providing funding to major Chinese medical universities and, later, promoting health equity and international health collaboration.[19] In 1988, Project Hope and the Shanghai municipal government agreed to establish Shanghai Children's Medical Center, which is now China's leading pediatric medical treatment facility and training center for health professionals learning the most advanced techniques in pediatric medicine.[20] In the 1990s, the Ford Foundation made reproductive health in China one of its funding priorities.

China's preoccupation with applied research also led to cooperation with American pharmaceutical companies through such means as contract research programs, joint ventures, wholly owned subsidiaries, and technology transfers.[21] In October 1982, Bristol-Myers Squibb entered the Chinese market to found Sino-American Shanghai Squibb Pharmaceutical, the first China-U.S. joint venture pharmaceutical firm. By the end of the 1990s, almost all the major U.S. pharmaceutical companies—Merck, Janssen (Johnson & Johnson), GlaxoSmithKline, Pfizer, Baxter International, and Abbott—had joint ventures with or offices in China.[22]

The benefits were largely one-sided during this initial stage of cooperation. With its modest research and development capability, China was the primary beneficiary of health-related academic exchanges. Despite the growth of contract research programs utilizing the skills of Chinese scientists, China's overall level of cooperation in commercial biotechnology remained low.[23] The asymmetric relationship constrained the scope of cooperation.

Underpinning the bilateral cooperation in the health sector during these years was the strategic cooperation to counterbalance the threat of the Soviet Union. Following the 1989 Tiananmen crackdown and the collapse of the Soviet Union in 1991, the nature of U.S.-China relations saw a dramatic shift. Absent the original strategic foundation for cooperation, new issues and concerns, such as human rights, came to the fore. Cooperation over health continued to grow in breadth and depth.

In September 1989, only months after the Tiananmen incident, Merck, the huge New Jersey–based pharmaceutical company, signed an agreement with China's Ministry of Health to transfer its hepatitis B vaccine technology to China. Under the break-even deal, China paid Merck $7 million, and Merck provided China with the full panoply of technology and equipment necessary for the production of the vaccine and trained Chinese personnel in quality control. The Merck–Ministry of Health deal is credited with having saved millions of lives. In the 1980s, more than 10 percent of the Chinese people were chronic carriers of the hepatitis B virus (HBV), which can cause cirrhosis, liver failure, and liver cancer. By 1994, when the technology transfer was complete, China had successfully manufactured its first batch of recombinant HBV vaccine. By 2002, the Chinese government was sufficiently confident in its ability to expand production and distribution of the vaccine that China's Expanded Programme on Immunization, run with World Health Organization (WHO) support, set a goal of reducing the level of HBV infections in Chinese children under five years old to less than 2 percent by 2012.

The program was remarkably successful. China succeeded in reducing the level of infection to under 1 percent by 2012. Between 1993 and 2018, at least five hundred million newborn infants were inoculated with the HBV vaccine.[24] Survey data in 2014 suggest that the vaccine prevented twenty-eight million chronic HBV infections and five million deaths from HBV complications.[25] While Merck surely had long-term market opportunities in China in mind when making their initial nonprofit decision to transfer vaccine-making capabilities to China,[26] their move also unintentionally projected U.S. soft power into China. Later, during a vaccine scandal in 2018, when hundreds of thousands of Chinese children were said to have received injections of substandard vaccines, a widely circulated story on China's social media lauded Merck for having transferred expertise and technology enabling the country to produce enough HBV vaccine to save millions of lives. Claiming that "Merck's contributions to China were more than 10,000 times those of [Norman] Bethune" (the Canadian doctor credited with saving the lives of many Communist Party members and

Chinese soldiers during World War II), the author called upon every Chinese person to be grateful to the American pharmaceutical firm. As Liang Xiaofeng, the deputy director of China's Center for Disease Control and Prevention (CDC), pointed out, "As a pharmaceutical firm, Merck could make high profit considering the number of the vaccine administered. Yet Merck chose to give the vaccine to China as a gift. It is an invaluable asset to Chinese people."[27]

2002–2016: The Golden Age of Cooperation

Jointly Fighting Infectious Diseases

In the 1980s and 1990s, a combination of agricultural decollectivization, fiscal and bureaucratic decentralization, and market-oriented reforms served to undermine the institutional and financial bases for China's programs related to health.[28] After the 1989 Tiananmen crisis and particularly following Deng Xiaoping's trip to southern China in 1992 to restart economic reforms, the regime came increasingly to rely on rapid economic growth to justify its legitimacy. Not only did the turn to performance-based legitimacy put the importance of public health on a backburner, but it also reinforced incentives for state actors to cover up major outbreaks of contagious disease. In the countryside, the return to household farming and the demise of communes removed the financial bases of major health-care institutions, such as cooperative health-care schemes and barefoot doctors (which were piggybacked onto the collective economy), leading to the collapse of the rural health-care system. In the cities, poor performance of state-owned enterprises (SOEs) and ensuing reform measures disrupted the provision of medical and health-care services that SOEs had previously provided their employees.

At the same time, globalization and China's integration into the global economy were facilitating the spread of pathogens. Beginning in the 1990s, China began to see the return or emergence of several major infectious diseases, and by the first decade of the twenty-first century, the country confronted a series of epidemics and pandemics, including acquired immunodeficiency syndrome (AIDS), tuberculosis (TB), severe acute respiratory syndrome (SARS), and avian flu. Confronting those challenges prompted major changes in how China, the United States, the United Nations, and most of the world viewed and managed issues of public health. Cooperation between China and the United States on issues of health expanded significantly, ranking high on the agendas of the highest-ranking leaders in both countries. As new health issues were addressed, the understanding of their implications also changed. Infectious diseases came to be seen not only as health issues but also as issues of national and international security. Furthermore, as China rose to meet its own infectious disease challenges, it also began to move from a recipient and beneficiary of international aid to being a donor and provider of international aid and ultimately came to assume a major role in the provision of pharmaceuticals.

AIDS

The first reported cases of AIDS in China were in the mid-1980s, but those patients had contracted the disease outside the country. The Chinese view of AIDS at the time was that it was a foreign disease and contrary to Chinese morality. China's health authorities were confident that an AIDS epidemic in China was unlikely. When the first indigenous HIV case was confirmed in 1989, the government did not act. Thus, the disease spread rapidly, morphing quickly from an illness that in the early 1990s had been restricted mainly to a small group of rural farmers who were infected with HIV from contaminated plasma donation equipment to one that infected intravenous drug users, sex workers, men who have sex with men, and finally the general population. Only in 2002 did China embark on a comprehensive nationwide survey that allowed a precise tally of HIV cases and turn to the United States for cooperation in meeting the challenge. In February 2002, President George W. Bush and President Jiang Zemin held an amicable meeting in the Great Hall of the People during which they discussed the importance of enhanced collaboration on HIV.[29] The two countries soon began working closely together to address China's looming HIV crisis. Nonetheless, by 2007, AIDS had become the deadliest infectious disease in China, affecting nearly one million people.[30]

SARS

However, it was the SARS crisis of 2002–2003 that served as the strongest catalyst forcing the Chinese government to fully recognize the potential seriousness of the AIDS epidemic, the danger of pandemics, and the need for international cooperation to address these and other infectious disease problems. Cover-up and inaction characterized the initial Chinese government response to SARS. The earliest case of the disease was discovered in mid-November 2002, but by early April 2003, the government authorities were still essentially in denial, sharing little information with the international community and barring international WHO experts from visiting Guangdong, the epicenter of the outbreak. The Chinese government's mishandling of the epidemic tarnished the country's international image and caused perhaps the most serious sociopolitical crisis since the Tiananmen crackdown in 1989. The virus—and the fear and panic associated with it—continued to spread, and international pressure built, together with growing international criticism of China's mishandling of the crisis. As Chinese leaders finally began to address the emergency in a more transparent and serious manner, they also came to a fuller understanding of the devastating impact that global spread of an infectious disease such as SARS could have. They saw, too, an urgent need for international cooperation that would have been difficult or impossible to achieve without the urgency and severity of the crisis. They accepted the U.S. offer of collaboration to improve China's capacity to address an acute pandemic.

Sobered by the mishaps surrounding its initial handling of SARS, the Chinese government also began to tackle its HIV/AIDS problems in a more transparent and aggressive manner.[31] Once the Chinese government recognized the potential for a serious AIDS epidemic in China, cooperation between the United States and China on issues of public health quickly expanded significantly. Two months after the end of the SARS crisis, U.S. Health and Human Services secretary Tommy Thompson visited China to forge a multiyear partnership with the Chinese Ministry of Health to develop a more robust public health infrastructure for responding to outbreaks of major diseases. He and Chinese health minister Zhang Wenkang signed a Memorandum of Understanding under which the U.S. NIH awarded the China CDC a five-year, $14.8 million grant to develop infrastructure to better characterize and monitor the spread of HIV. At the same time, the American embassy in Beijing acquired an attaché from the Department Health and Human Services charged with overseeing the American-funded programs in China.[32]

Based on the memorandum of understanding, the U.S. CDC's Global AIDS Program (GAP), in joint collaboration with the China CDC and the Chinese Ministry of Health, was launched in China in early 2003. The U.S. CDC assumed the task of helping to strengthen China's surveillance and laboratory capacities and promote evidence-based policy making.[33] The GAP joint collaboration program adopted a new and comprehensive strategy called "prevention for positives," which centered on increased surveillance of at-risk groups, and provided testing and follow-up care for those who tested positive. (The previous strategy had focused on promoting behavior modification and self-protection of at-risk populations through generalized health education and behavioral-based interventions.)[34] The policy of prevention for positives became the central component of China's national strategy on AIDS prevention and control and profoundly influenced China's approach in engaging at-risk groups and people living with HIV.

Health care continued to receive attention from the highest-level officials in both countries. President George W. Bush and President Hu Jintao met at the UN General Assembly in September 2005 to hammer out ten core principles of global pandemic response, a set of principles that were later supported by eighty-eight nations and agencies.[35] In 2006, all U.S. bilateral HIV programs with China were integrated into the President's Emergency Plan for AIDS Relief (PEPFAR), a governmental initiative to address the HIV pandemic that was coordinated by the Office of the U.S. Global AIDS Coordinator within the Department of State.[36] Under the Global AIDS Program (GAP), the U.S. CDC worked in close collaboration with the China CDC's Division for HIV/AIDS Prevention and Control, provided management and technical support in fifteen Chinese provinces, and helped Chinese health authorities establish three AIDS clinical training centers in rural areas, where three hundred government partners were trained. These partners are now providing antiretroviral therapy for fifty thousand patients in sixteen different provinces.[37]

Avian Flu H5N1

The outbreak of the H5N1 Avian flu in 2005 presented the Chinese government with a health crisis of a different nature. While AIDS is a slowly spreading epidemic of attrition due to the long incubation period between being infected with the disease and the actual onset of illness, the spread of a pandemic flu is considered an outbreak event that generates significant shocks over a very short period of time. Since 2005, the global spread of the highly pathogenic avian flu virus, especially the H5N1, H1N1, and H7N9 strains, has been considered a major threat to global health security. From April to June 2005, over six thousand migratory birds were found dead at Qinghai Lake in western China. The unprecedented die-off was followed by a fresh H5N1 outbreak of bird flu in China's Inner Mongolia, where twenty-six hundred birds died from the disease. Unlike most avian flus, which emerge briefly and are relatively localized, the H5N1 avian influenza spread widely among birds in Asia and had unusual staying power.[38] A report published by the National Academy of Science's Institute of Medicine called the H5N1 avian influenza in Asia "unprecedented in its scale, in its spread, and in the economic losses it has caused."[39] A 2005 study suggested it might be only a matter of time before H5N1 would adapt to humans and evolve into a 1918-type flu pandemic.[40]

A major concern of international health organizations addressing the global spread of H5N1 was whether health authorities in China, especially those at the local level, had the required laboratory and epidemiological capacity to detect, identify, and diagnose pandemic flu. Indeed, local-level authorities in China did not have such capacity. Local governments had few incentives to invest in disease control and prevention. Thus, in 2005, when chickens began to die in Heishan County in Liaoning Province and worried farmers sought help from provincial veterinarians, nearly two weeks passed before the H5N1 outbreak there was finally confirmed.[41] In Shaanxi Province, a vice governor was so frustrated that local cadres failed to implement the required H5N1 control and prevention measures that he chided them for "living off government money but doing nothing (*chi huangliang bu ganshi*)."[42]

Within the United States, the threat of a global pandemic became a political issue, uniting both parties. As then senators Barack Obama (Democrat, Illinois) and Richard Lugar (Republican, Indiana) wrote in the *New York Times*, "in an age when you can board planes in Bangkok or Hong Kong and arrive in Chicago, Indianapolis or New York in hours, we must face the reality that these exotic killer diseases are not isolated health problems half a world away, but direct and immediate threats to security and prosperity here at home."[43]

The United States and China worked closely together to solve China's local capacity problem and to stem the spread of the H5N1 avian influenza. The U.S. administration sought to include China in a variety of multilateral initiatives. In September 2005, President George W. Bush announced the International Partnership on Avian and Pandemic Influenza as an ongoing framework for U.S.-China cooperation. The inauguration of the Collaborative Program on Emerging and Re-emerging Infectious Diseases followed in October and led to the establishment of a CDC Global Disease Detection Center in China as part of its overall effort to expand the network of such centers around the world.[44] China's CDC center enabled public health agencies in both countries to collaborate to train field epidemiologists in China and to detect and effectively respond to outbreaks of disease. In November 2005, the U.S. Department of Health and Human Services and the Chinese Ministry of Health established a Joint Initiative on Avian Influenza, facilitating cooperation between U.S. and Chinese health and agricultural ministries on planning, detection, and vaccines.[45] Thus far, despite rare and sporadic human infections of the virus, H5N1 has not developed efficient human-to-human transmission.[46]

H1N1 Swine Flu

The 2009 H1N1 (swine flu) pandemic saw China and the United States further consolidate their cooperation in combating pandemic flu. Top leaders again got involved in health diplomacy. On May 6, 2009, when the swine flu was just spreading to the United States, Chinese president Hu Jintao personally called President Obama to discuss the spread of the virus, expressing his desire to maintain communication with the United States and other relevant parties, as well as to strengthen cooperation to deal jointly with the threat.[47] The swine flu was caused by a strain of H1N1 influenza virus that had never been encountered before and was first observed in April 2009 in Mexico. After early outbreaks in North America, the virus spread quickly around the world, including to China. By June, the WHO had pronounced the virus a full-blown pandemic. In November, the United States and China issued a joint statement pledging closer collaboration on H1N1 prevention, surveillance, reporting, and control.[48] Health authorities in both the United States and China exchanged technology and information to improve their core surveillance and response capacities, including monitoring the spread of flu and accelerating the development of a new vaccine. The United States provided China with virus samples and diagnostic kits, thus helping China become the first country to mass-produce an H1N1 vaccine. Chinese scientists, in turn, shared their method with the world, facilitating vaccine development efforts by pharmaceutical companies and American health agencies.[49] U.S. government scientists also assisted with on-site investigations of the pandemic flu in China, which involved providing laboratory diagnosis, identifying disease risk factors, and determining whether the virus had achieved human-to-human transmission.[50]

Thus, when China reported the outbreak of the H7N9 virus in eastern China in March 2013, prior collaboration between the United States and China enabled both sides to jointly combat the new outbreak more effectively. First reported in eastern China in March 2013, H7N9 was an influenza virus that the U.S. CDC labeled its greatest worry.[51] During the H7N9 outbreak, disease control agencies in both countries collaborated closely to share epidemiological data and conduct joint research on the virus.

Ebola

China and the United States were among the first countries to respond to the Ebola epidemic that broke out in western Africa in 2014, and for the first time, the two countries worked together to address a disease outbreak in a third country, thus taking their medical cooperation to a new level.

The Chinese response to the Ebola outbreak was, at the time, the country's largest overseas global health effort and included delivering medical supplies, dispatching medical and public health experts, and building laboratory and clinical facilities.[52] During the epidemic, staff from the U.S. CDC worked with staff at a Chinese mobile laboratory in Sierra Leone, which, according to Department of Health and Human Services Secretary Sylvia Burwell "played an important role in saving lives and turning the tide of the epidemic."[53] In addition to exchanging disease information and technical guidelines, Chinese military personnel also trained a Liberian engineering company that later assisted the U.S. Army in the construction of a new treatment center there. At the same time, the U.S. Air Force assisted the Chinese effort by providing large forklifts to unload the supplies that China had sent to Liberia.[54] In the fall of 2014, after a limited supply of an experimental anti-Ebola drug called ZMapp developed by American and Canadian scientists had quickly been exhausted, a small private Chinese company raced to produce the drug based on information in ZMapp's patent.[55] Within three months, the Chinese company had manufactured about

one hundred doses of a new drug labeled MIL77 that was believed to have successfully treated a British military nurse who was diagnosed with Ebola while
working in Sierra Leone in March 2015.[56]

The success of U.S.-China cooperation during the Ebola crisis provided strong
impetus for both countries to renew an agreement in June 2015, promoting still
closer cooperation, scientific discovery, capacity building, and exchange of information in the field of infectious diseases. As Vice Premier Liu Yandong said,
"China and the U.S. share more and more interests in maintaining global health
security and responding to emerging infectious diseases, and shoulder more and
more common responsibilities. Strengthening cooperation in the field of health
not only matters to the health of our two peoples but also has global implications."[57]

As the spread of infectious diseases became a global health issue, a new view
of infectious diseases began to emerge. Disease came to be seen not only as an
issue of health but also as an issue of national and international security. This
new view of epidemics and pandemics as issues of national and international
security began with the onset of the international AIDS crisis. On the U.S. side,
the destabilizing impact of AIDS and the potential devastating consequences
of a flu pandemic led the three administrations of Clinton, Bush, and Obama
to categorize infectious disease outbreaks not just as a health problem but as
a national security threat. As early as 1991, a classified U.S. intelligence report
titled "The Global AIDS Disaster" had described AIDS as a "time bomb" with
potentially severe economic, political, and military ramifications.[58] In 2000, a
report of the National Intelligence Council identified AIDS as one of its primary issues,[59] and National Security Advisor Sandy Berger declared deadly
infectious diseases a national security threat, pointing out that "a problem that
kills huge numbers, crosses borders, and threatens to destabilize whole regions
is the very definition of a national security threat."[60] Another National Intelligence Council report from 2002 identified China as one of the five countries
that could lead the next wave of AIDS.[61] In time, the prevention and control of
HIV and pandemic flu came to be integrated into the American foreign policy
agenda, as demonstrated in August 2010, when then secretary of state Hillary
Clinton declared that, "We invest in global health to protect our nation's security. . . . We need a comprehensive, effective global system for tracking health
data, monitoring threats, and coordinating responses."[62]

The United Nations was quick to embrace the concept of epidemic as security threat. In 2000, driven by concern about the security implications of AIDS,
the UN Security Council unanimously adopted U.S.-sponsored Resolution
1308, the first UN Security Council resolution on an issue of health. Resolution
1308 recognized the potential of an epidemic to pose a risk to stability and security and encouraged international cooperation in support of efforts to develop
effective long-term strategies to combat the disease.

Chinese leaders, too, came to view the possible outbreak of major epidemics
as tied to China's national and international security. In November 2003, the

Ministry of Foreign Affairs included HIV/AIDS as one of six nontraditional security threats.[63] Chinese leaders see the possibility of major outbreaks of infectious disease as potentially challenging the country's ability to move forward with economic development, maintain social and political stability, and protect national security.[64] China's leaders have agreed to support the Global Health Security Agenda, which was launched in February 2014 by the United States and is focused on bringing together nations from all over the world to address infectious disease threats and to elevate health security as a priority at the national leaders level.[65] Hence, both China and the United States came to view pandemics as a health, security, and foreign policy issue, and when China was hit by a series of pandemics, the United States played an important role in how those pandemics were addressed, leading to greater cooperation.

Medical cooperation between the United States and China during the first decades of the twenty-first century was not confined to infectious diseases. The U.S.-China Health Protocol was renewed twice, in November 2003 and April 2008. Under the revised protocol, bilateral health cooperation focused on disease prevention and control, supervision and regulation of health-related products, and health and biomedical research. In fiscal year 2004 alone, the U.S. Department of Health and Human Services funded more than $33 million for research and technical assistance to China, which included more than $28 million to the NIH for seven research grants and contracts and support for 469 Chinese scientists to participate in the Department of Health and Human Services visitors program.[66] In 2006, the Department of Health and Human Services and the Chinese Ministry of Health signed a memorandum of understanding on collaboration on biomedical research, technology, training, and personnel exchanges.[67] American and Chinese scientists continued to work together to combat both major infectious disease threats and noncommunicable diseases such as cancer. According to an internal NIH review, since 2010, the agency has provided annual grants of about $5 million for collaboration with China, with 20 percent going to cancer research. The joint projects have led to the publication of a number of high-impact papers on cancer.[68] By 2015, NIH had hosted more than seven hundred Chinese scientists in its Bethesda labs.[69]

The two sides have also cooperated to promote Greater China's participation in international health organizations. In June 2006, China nominated Margaret Chan, who had been Hong Kong's director of health during the 2003 SARS epidemic, to be the first Chinese candidate to run for the WHO's position of director-general. While Chan was not part of China's domestic political power structure or diplomatic missions, she was encouraged by a U.S. government official to meet with President Hu Jintao during a U.S.-China leadership summit.[70] U.S. support contributed to Chan's later election success. She served two five-year terms as head of the WHO, from 2006 to 2017.

Patterns of Cooperation

Cooperation between the two governments also became more institutionalized during the period from 2000 to 2010. In 2006, the presidents of China and the United States agreed to create a Strategic and Economic Dialogue (SED) to discuss long-term challenges facing the two countries. Under the SED, dialogues over health, food, and drug safety issues were handled by the U.S.-China Health Care Forum and involved the American Department of Health and Human Services, the Chinese Ministry of Health, and the Joint Commission on Commerce and Trade, which includes representatives from the U.S. Department of Commerce, the U.S. trade representative, and the Chinese vice premier responsible for trade.[71] In November 2008, amid the growing American concern about unsafe food products from China, China allowed the U.S. Food and Drug Administration to open its first overseas office in Beijing.[72] In June 2010, the two countries established the U.S.-China Health Care Forum to address bilateral commercial trade and policy issues relating to health. This forum, together with the preexisting annual U.S.-China Global Issues Forum, provided a platform for discussing broader public health concerns. Four years later, health became an important pillar of the annual U.S.-China Consultation on People-to-People Exchange that facilitated exchange among government agencies, medical schools, and institutions.

Medical cooperation between China and the United States was not confined to the two governments. Beginning in the early 2000s, American NGOs and other private sector actors also became actively involved with issues of health in China. In 2005, the Clinton Foundation forged a partnership with the U.S. CDC's GAP to establish a program in rural Linxin County, Anhui Province, training grassroots-level doctors in routine AIDS care and antiretroviral treatment. Meanwhile, the Clinton Foundation's China HIV/AIDS Initiative (CHAI) focused on improving the quality and accessibility of treatment for people living with HIV/AIDS. Operating from 2004 to 2011, CHAI was the largest international philanthropic program dedicated to treating AIDS.[73]

In 2006, the Gates Foundation also began working with the Chinese government on the prevention and control of HIV/AIDS and TB, as well as the control of tobacco use. Between 2006 and 2012, the Gates Foundation invested $50 million in scaling up HIV testing and intervention programs among at-risk groups (e.g., men who have sex with men) and provided care and treatment for people living with HIV/AIDS. Between 2009 and 2014, the Gates Foundation's partnership with Chinese health authorities included a $33 million research grant to pilot test innovative approaches to improve diagnosis and treatment of TB while reducing patient costs.[74] Chapter 8, by Mary Bullock, also discusses activities of the Gates Foundation and other NGO actors.

American-based NGOs have also played an important role in capacity building for health-related civil society in China. The Global Fund to Fight AIDS, Tuberculosis and Malaria, which is a partnership of governments, civil society, technical agencies, the private sector, and people affected by the three diseases and which once spent some $4 billion a year investing in programs to end those diseases, began working in China shortly before the SARS epidemic. Its funding guidelines require each country where it works to set up a Country Coordinating Mechanism (CCM) to govern the Global Fund–supported programs in that country. Each CCM is required to include representatives from government, the UN and donor agencies, NGOs, the private sector, faith-based communities, and people living with the three diseases.

In China, the Global Fund further required that the NGO representatives be elected by the NGO sector itself based on a democratic process developed by that sector. In the first round of China's CCM NGO elections, Jia Ping, a Beijing-based human rights lawyer focusing on AIDS, was declared the winner, but the procedures that led to his election victory were vociferously criticized by many participating NGOs. In response, Jia Ping offered to take the lead in organizing a new NGO election that would be fully democratic and transparent. While a visiting scholar in the United States, Jia Ping came into contact with the International Republican Institute, one of the core institutes of the National Endowment for Democracy, which offered to help monitor and observe the process, providing consultation as well. The election process lasted approximately seven months, from August 2006 to March 2007, and the result was an open, transparent, and independent election of an NGO representative and alternates to serve on China's CCM. This was the first time Beijing had allowed citizens who were not members of the Communist Party to organize a national, independent election and perhaps also the first time that representatives of so many different sectors of Chinese government and society came together around the same table as equals.[75] The joint efforts of American NGOs and Chinese civil society leaders also led to the establishment of NGO learning networks, where training sessions were conducted for community-based organizations working on AIDS prevention and control.

American private sector companies such as Merck also set up public health projects to help China fight infectious disease and promote health education. In 2005, Merck committed $30 million to support a partnership with the Chinese Ministry of Health to develop and implement a model joining together all aspects of AIDS prevention, patient care, treatment, and support. Introduced in Liangshan Yi Autonomous Prefecture in Sichuan Province, the public-private partnership sought to provide a range of interventions, including education, counseling, testing, harm reduction, and health services.[76] The Hopkins-Nanjing Center graduate Drew Thompson became the Beijing-based national director. Public-private partnerships were also pursued at the bilateral-sectoral level as when China and the United States founded the U.S.-China Health-care Cooperation Program (HCP) in January 2011 following a summit between American president Barack Obama and Chinese president Hu Jintao.

The HCP engages American government agencies (e.g., the Department of Health and Human Services and U.S. Trade and Development Agency [USTDA]) and China's Ministries of Health and Commerce, private sector organizations (e.g., AdvaMed, AmCham-China), and a dozen American health-care companies to improve health-care access in China. The health-care partnership began with a USTDA-funded exchange program for health professionals that included a series of visits to the United States by Chinese health-care officials and hospital managers. The visits encouraged the sharing of best practices between the United States and China and provided Chinese exposure to American medical technology.[77]

After 2010, China began to emerge not just as a recipient of American aid but as an indispensable partner in that cooperation. While the NIH provided $5 million annually for joint research projects with China, its counterpart in China began adding an additional $3 million annually.[78] In 2011, when the Global Fund announced that China's funding would end in 2014, Premier Wen Jiabao declared that China would rely on its own efforts.[79]

At the same time, China was becoming an international foreign aid donor, significantly increasing its investment in global health. Between 2004 and 2013, its health grants to Africa rose by almost 150 percent, from $1.54 billion during the five-year period from 2004 to 2008 to $3.8 billion during the five-year period from 2009 to 2013.[80] Throughout the 2000s, an increasingly robust pharmaceutical sector enabled Chinese pharmaceutical firms to set up subsidiaries and local distribution channels overseas. Since 2011, China has been pursuing an explicit policy mandate to develop its domestic pharmaceutical industries. During 2011–2015, the state invested a total of $1.1 billion in new drug development. China's ambition to become a global player in the pharmaceutical industry was abetted by a growing number of overseas returnees who had received training in health and life sciences in the United States.

The growing economic and trade links also highlight the key role China has played in the international pharmaceutical market. China has the largest number of registered drug manufacturers exporting drugs to the United States. The 2000 U.S.-China Fair Trade Agreement enabled U.S.-based multinational pharmaceutical firms to buy ingredients for critical drugs in China. With an annual output of one million tons of pharmaceutical ingredients, China is a world leader in global active pharmaceutical ingredient manufacturing and export.[81] Its ability to produce and supply active pharmaceutical ingredients is of critical importance to formulators in the United States. Moreover, more than five hundred contract research organizations in China are providing preclinical and clinical research services to multinational pharmaceutical companies, many of which are based in the United States. Unable to compete with Chinese companies on price, a number of established manufacturers in the United States and elsewhere have moved their operations to China. As a result, China is now the dominant global supplier of the essential ingredients to make penicillin and the largest exporter of the building blocks to make ciprofloxacin, an antidote to anthrax.[82] Indeed, China is now the world's leading source of antibiotics, including the main ingredient in vancomycin, a treatment of last resort against serious and multidrug-resistant infections.[83] The complementarity between the two countries' pharmaceutical industries opens doors for future cooperation in the development of vaccines and new drugs for addressing public health emergencies.

Interestingly, disputes over pharmaceutical-related intellectual property (IP) have not thus far been a major issue in U.S.-China economic relations. Driven by the need to join the WTO and attract foreign direct investment, China not only extended all patent coverage to twenty years but also agreed to U.S. demands on issues such as data exclusivity and patent linkage.[84] Furthermore, upon its entry into the WTO, China agreed to adhere to the Agreement on Trade-Related Aspects of Intellectual Property Rights (TRIPS), which sets standards for IP protection. TRIPS Article 31, in particular, places restrictions on compulsory licensing (i.e., a government authorizes a generic drug producer to produce a patented product or process without the consent of the patent owner). Implementation of this trade rule would not only significantly constrain China's ability to develop and export generic versions of patented drugs but also limit access to most effective medicines in China. Still, China has not used the flexibility offered in the WTO TRIPS agreement to take a more aggressive approach toward patent-related issues, despite an AIDS epidemic, an unprecedented crisis of non-communicable diseases, and a pharmaceutical industry capable of producing generic versions of most patented drugs sold in China. Thus far, there have been no successful applications for compulsory licensing of any patented drugs in China. The government even denied a Chinese manufacturer's application for producing a generic version of Tamiflu (an antiviral drug prescribed for influenza virus infections) during the 2009 H1N1 pandemic.

Rationale for Change

What explains the significant expansion of U.S.-China health cooperation in the twenty-first century, even in the absence of the strategic rationale that initially held the relationship together? One explanation is that health issues simply do not carry the same politically polarizing possibilities that underlie traditional security or human rights issues. Health, until very recently with the onset of the COVID-19 pandemic, has not been a politically polarizing topic. The fact that both countries want to promote the welfare of their citizens has tradition-ally allowed for relatively easy cooperation on health issues of mutual concern. Shared health concerns encourage both countries to work together jointly.

Another way of understanding that cooperation is through the lens of the new concept of health as an issue of both national and international security that began to develop in the 1990s. The health as security and health as foreign policy transformation has changed the substance and style of cooperation on health. Governments on both sides have recognized the importance of health in fulfilling the governance functions of foreign policy including secu-rity, economic well-being, international development, and human dignity.[85] During the 1990s, China also developed a new sense of accountability and commitment in its interactions with the outside world, which encouraged it to act as an internationally responsible state actively engaged in international affairs. The new identity prompted new thinking about the meaning of secu-rity and international cooperation. China unveiled a new security concept in 1996, the essence of which was to rise above one-sided security and seek common security through mutually beneficial cooperation.[86] As noted earlier, a December 2002 document from China's Ministry of Foreign Affairs further elaborated the new meaning of security, and formally included the need to incorporate non-traditional security (NTS) threats into China's strategy of national defense.[87] Although the government did not initially specify health as a non-traditional security threat, the release of a U.N. report "HIV/AIDS: China's Titanic Peril" earlier that year emphasized that HIV/AIDS is not just a public health problem, but also one that has significant social, economic, political, and security implications, which therefore demands the highest level of political attention.[88]

2017 to the Present: Cooperation Under Threat

Overall, until the end of the Obama administration, U.S.-China cooperation in the realm of health helped to stabilize other aspects of the bilateral relation-ship. The U.S. National Security Strategy unveiled by the Trump administration in December 2017 said little about international cooperation over health. The only allusion to partnerships in international health was about cooperation with other countries in the area of biosafety (i.e., ensuring that laboratories have in place safety and security measures for handling dangerous pathogens). Nonetheless, during the first year of the Trump presidency, bilateral cooper-ation in the realm of health not only survived but thrived. As Jordyn Dahl observed in April 2017, "Beijing and Washington have opposing views on nearly everything from North Korea's nuclear development program to trade and development in the South China Sea. But one area of collaboration is emerging as a potential bright spot in what has otherwise devolved into a tenuous bilateral relationship: global health."[89]

For example, in September 2017, Vice Premier Liu Yandong traveled to the United States to cochair the first round of the U.S.-China Social and Cultural Dialogue. Health cooperation was a critical component of the dialogue. As an outcome, both sides agreed to team up to launch cooperative programs to prevent and control major communicable diseases such as AIDS, promote exchanges between health personnel at various levels, and boost health research on noncommunicable diseases such as cardiovascular and cerebrovascular diseases as well as cancer. They also agreed to carry out joint public health programs in Sierra Leone, including vaccinations against HBV for newborns.[90]

U.S. government agencies also began working with their Chinese counterparts to reduce or eliminate the flow of illicit synthetic fentanyl and fentanyl precursor chemicals into the United States. Fentanyl was associated with more than 28,400 overdose deaths in the United States in 2017. After learning in August 2017 of a China-based supplier exporting fentanyl to the United States, the U.S. Department of Homeland Security's office in Guangzhou and the Chinese Narcotics Control Bureau began their first joint investigation, which led to the dismantling of the international supplier and stopped more than twenty million doses of the drug from reaching the United States.[91] During his visit to China in November 2017, President Trump brought up the issue with President Xi Jinping, and both sides agreed to cooperate on fighting narcotics crimes.[92]

Other partnerships were established in the non-government/private sphere. In 2017, the Gates Foundation partnered with the Beijing municipal government and Tsinghua University to jointly establish the Global Health Drug Discovery Institute. As the first research and development center of its kind in China, the institute focuses on major diseases faced by developing countries, including China. It leverages China's research and development capacities to promote international collaborations and enhance early drug development. The same year, the National Committee on U.S.-China Relations established a U.S.-China Track II Dialogue on Healthcare, which was devoted to examining the effectiveness of the health-care systems in China and the United States. Its recommendations included suggestions for better measuring and managing the delivery and efficiency of health care in the two countries.

In August 2018, despite their friction over trade and security issues, the two countries still convened a jointly organized regional armed forces health forum in Xi'an, which a top Chinese general described as "the first exchange between the Chinese and U.S. militaries on military health for the Asia-Pacific."[93]

Nonetheless, in contrast to the previous two presidential administrations where public health was consistently and clearly seen an important means of advancing a constructive relationship with China, the Trump administration's enthusiasm for pursing bilateral health cooperation seemed to have disappeared after only one year in office. The space for bilateral cooperation over health began to narrow. China has demonstrated its ambition to be an important innovator of pharmaceutical products. Its new Made in China 2025 policy released in 2015 identified pharmaceuticals and medical devices as one of the ten strategic industries that will receive state support to make Chinese firms the world leaders in global high-tech manufacturing. Because the policy directly challenges the U.S. dominance in high-tech industries, the Made in China 2025 policy became a primary target of Trump's trade war with China.[94]

Meanwhile, foreign pharmaceutical companies are facing increasing pressures to cooperate with the Chinese government's health-care reform and make their drugs more affordable to a majority of China's population.[95] In April 2018, the Chinese government unveiled measures that include authorizing the granting of compulsory licenses to enhance availability of innovative drugs.[96] In July, the box office hit Chinese movie *Dying to Survive* told the real-life story of a leukemia patient who was forced to smuggle cheaper generic drugs from India in order to save himself and others. The movie helped to generate new support for a government campaign to lower the price of cancer drugs sold by foreign pharmaceutical companies.[97] While the government efforts may quell domestic Chinese discontent over the price of drugs, the quest for lower drug prices could also lead to pharmaceutical IP issues becoming a prominent concern in U.S.-China economic relations.

Gary Cohn, chief economic advisor to President Trump from the time of his inauguration until April 2018, stressed the importance of cooperation when he reminded Trump, "If you're the Chinese and you want to really just destroy us, just stop sending us antibiotics." He argued with the president and Peter Navarro (director of the Office of Trade and Manufacturing Policy at the White House) on the absolute need to trade with China by invoking a Commerce Department study showing that China sold 97 percent of all antibiotics used in the United States.[98]

The tightening of political control in China also had an impact on bilateral health cooperation. In January 2017, the Chinese government began implementing the new Foreign NGO Law, which requires all overseas NGOs and nonprofit organizations to obtain a government sponsor and register officially with the police. The law has had a chilling effect on health-related foreign NGOs in China. Large, wealthy, and well-established foreign NGOs, such as the Rockefeller Brothers Fund, may continue to register and operate in China, but they may have to keep a low profile and exercise caution in their activities.[99] Chapter 8 in this volume describes the effect of the NGO law in considerable detail.

Perhaps more significantly, the heavy reliance of the United States on China for pharmaceutical ingredients and raw materials in making drugs raises a concern that China could use this dependence as a weapon in an increasingly fraught trade war.[100] This fear proved to be a real concern when a leading

Chinese economist suggested at a general meeting of the Chinese People's Political Consultative Conference in March 2019 that Beijing curb its exports of raw materials for vitamins and antibiotics as a countermeasure in the trade war with the United States.[101]

If the U.S.-China trade war continues, each side may also become more reluctant to share biological samples and other medical-related materials. In August 2018, a news report revealed that China had been withholding samples of the H7N9 virus from U.S. CDC labs for more than a year. Citing public health and national security reasons, China announced new regulations in June 2019 that would put checks on shipping human genetic materials abroad.[102] Refusal to share health-related information and materials not only undermines America's ability to protect its people's health but also jeopardizes global health security, the very core of U.S.-China health cooperation.

As of this writing, U.S.-China relations remain in a state of deterioration and the dialogues that used to take place on a fairly regular basis have not been revived. Indeed, the doors to social and cultural exchanges have been closing. According to the *Financial Times*, senior Trump advisor Stephen Miller once urged the president to deny student visas for all Chinese nationals.[103] While the proposal was not adopted, the fact that the idea was seriously discussed by policy makers points to a significant change in U.S. government policy toward academic exchange with China, as Robert Daly describes in more detail in chapter 10.

Years ago, John Thomson, a former U.S. diplomat who helped organize the first group visit by Chinese scholars in 1978, noted, "No matter how the U.S. domestic politics change, one wish has never changed, that is to conduct academic exchange with China, to exchange scholars and students. The U.S. believes that this is the best approach to strengthening mutual understanding."[104] Four decades after the establishment of diplomatic ties, the Trump administration showed little interest in scientific and technological engagement with China. Concerned about IP theft and industrial espionage, the U.S. government imposed tighter visa controls on Chinese students who study in any of the STEM fields—science, technology, engineering, and mathematics.[105]

The soured bilateral relationship reflects a growing distrust between the two nations. With China defined as a strategic competitor, U.S. government officials have publicly called for a whole of society approach to China, and health-related academic exchanges have been increasingly examined through the lens of security. In August 2018, Francis Collins, director of the NIH, sent approximately 180 letters to more than sixty U.S. institutions, warning that foreign entities were mounting "systematic programs to influence NIH researchers and peer reviewers."[106] Acting upon the NIH alert, Houston-based MD Anderson Cancer Center, the world's leading cancer research center, fired three ethnically Chinese scientists, all allegedly on the list of the Thousand Talents Plan, China's most prominent national talent recruitment program. In May 2019, Emory

University ousted two senior Chinese American biomedical researchers and closed their laboratory after the NIH expressed concern about their ties to China.[107] Investigations suggested that these scientists had broken NIH rules requiring their full disclosure of all sources of research funding.[108]

Although these incidents have been confined to a few individual actors and were not related to the overall NIH posture toward scientists of Chinese heritage, the timing of the investigation and severity of the punishment are worth noting. The ongoing economic Cold War between the United States and China has affected the U.S. health sector as well. In such a political atmosphere, aiding China's fight against cancer and other diseases seems to count as an un-American, even quasi-criminal activity.[109]

The tariffs on approximately $300 billion worth of Chinese products proposed by the Office of the U.S. Trade Representative in May 2019 excluded "pharmaceuticals, certain pharmaceutical inputs, and select medical goods."[110] However, the on-and-off of key products used by U.S. drugmakers from the trade tariff list has created uncertainties for U.S. biopharmaceutical companies.[111] Driven by increased manufacturing costs, they may switch to other countries, such as India, to procure active pharmaceutical ingredients. This, in turn, could result in higher prescription drug costs for American patients.[112]

In December 2019, a novel coronavirus was detected in Wuhan and soon evolved into a global pandemic. By mid-January 2021, Johns Hopkins University had reported more than 92 million cases of Covid-19 worldwide and close to 2 million deaths.[113] One would have hoped that the COVID-19 outbreak would play a role similar to what SARS once played in bringing the United States and China together to combat a common threat. In the beginning stage of the outbreak, the opportunities for cooperation seemed tremendous: The United States could have helped China investigate the origin and nature of the outbreak. China could have worked closely with the United States to minimize the disruption of the supply chain caused by the outbreak. The two countries could have mobilized their pharmaceutical capacities in a cooperative effort to develop, produce, and distribute a vaccine. These efforts would have cooled tensions and reinvigorated a relationship soured by the trade war and strategic rivalry.[114]

But that did not happen. Instead, the two countries descended into an acrimonious spat over the origin of the pandemic, China's handling of the outbreak, and China's relationship with the WHO. In the United States, the perception that China was the origin of a devastating pandemic, that it misled the world in sharing disease-related information, and that it tried to spin the outbreak to its advantage highlighted China's threat to global health security and galvanized support for a hard decoupling from China.[115] Meanwhile, China's ability to quickly contain the spread of the virus, the enormous upsurge of COVID-19 cases and deaths in the United States, and the crescendo of the Trump administration's charges against China reinforced the Chinese image of the United States as a diminishing and hostile power. In consequence, not only was the room for public health cooperation significantly constrained, but the overall relationship dropped to its lowest point since the 1970s.

* * *

Historically, cooperation between China and the United States on issues of health has been mutually beneficial and helped project U.S. soft power in China. Unlike U.S.-China military/security relations, cooperation in the realm of health was independent of the strategic foundations undergirding the relationship. Cooperation continued to grow in breadth and depth in the post–Cold War era. As both sides redefined security in light of the 2002–2003 SARS epidemic, shared health concerns challenged both countries to work together to address a wide array of global health issues, including HIV/AIDs, Public Health Emergencies of International Concern, and health-related developmental assistance. Meanwhile, cooperation expanded to include NGOs and the private sector. Growing economic links made cooperation and exchange in this area even more important. The cooperation generated its own self-sustaining dynamic, which not only contributed to the overall bilateral relationship but also helped improve global health security.

The recent downward spiral in U.S.-China relations, however, has threatened to derail U.S.-China bilateral cooperation over health, with the COVID-19 outbreak serving as a dramatic indication of how far Sino-American cooperation has deteriorated. Caught in the deepening economic and strategic tensions, cooperation over health has become a barometer of how dire the overall U.S.-China relationship has become. Abandoning the policy of positive engagement with China threatens to cause setbacks on every front of bilateral relations, including public health. Cooperation between China and the United States over issues of health has also become victim of the increasingly complex and troubled nature of the bilateral relationship. Joseph Biden's ascension to the presidency provides an opportunity to step back and take stock of how dangerous to the health of both countries continued hostilities could bring and to reset the relationship in a more positive direction of mutual benefit to the health and well-being of both China and the United States.

NOTES

1. Chi-Chao Chan, Melissa M. Liu, and James C. Tsai, "The First Western-Style Hospital in China," *Archives of Ophthalmology* 129, no. 6 (2011): 791–97, doi:10.1001/archophthalmol .2011.120.
2. Guangqiu Xu, *American Doctors in Canton: Modernization in China, 1835–1935* (New Brunswick, NJ: Transaction Publishers, 2011).

3. Connie A. Shemo, *The Chinese Medical Ministries of Kang Cheng and Shi Meiyu, 1872–1937: On a Cross-Cultural Frontier of Gender, Race, and Nation* (Bethlehem, PA: Lehigh University Press, 2011).

4. "Zhongguo lishishang you naxie jiaohui yiyuan?" [What are the religious hospitals in China's history?], *Zhihu*, November 13, 2017, https://www.zhihu.com/question/27939411; "1800–1950: Zhongguo de yiyuan doushi shei jianli de?" [1800–1950: Who built China's hospitals?], *Weibo*, April 28, 2017. https://www.weibo.com/p/230418a435ddd40102wti-u?from=page_100505_profile&wvr=6&mod=wenzhangmod.

5. Two Baptist ministers, Frederick Gates and Wallace Buttrick, played a crucial role in the launch of PUMC. See John Z. Bowers, "American Private Aid at Its Peak: Peking Union Medical College," in *Medicine and Society in China*, eds. John Bowers and Elizabeth Purcell (New York: Josiah Macy Jr. Foundation, 1974), 84–87.

6. Liming Lee, "The Current State of Public Health in China," *Annual Review of Public Health* 25, no. 1 (2004): 327–39, https://doi.org/10.1146/annurev.publhealth.25.101802.123116. See also http://blog.sina.com.cn/s/blog_14407d12b0102vtp5.html and chapter 8 in this volume by Mary Bullock.

7. Changsheng Gu, *Chuanjiaoshi yu jindai zhongguo* [Missionaries and modern China], (Shanghai, China: Shanghai renmin chubanshe [Shanghai People's Publishing House], 1981).

8. "Laihua chuanjiaoshi de chouxing" [The ugly dealings of missionaries in China], *Douban*, January 6, 2014, https://www.douban.com/group/topic/47853022/.

9. Richard Madsen, *China and the American Dream* (Berkeley: University of California Press, 1995), 138.

10. Joseph R. Quinn, ed., *Medicine and Public Health in the People's Republic of China* (Bethesda, MD: National Institutes of Health, 1973).

11. James Reston, "Now About My Operation in Peking," *New York Times*, July 26, 1971, https://www.nytimes.com/1971/07/26/archives/now-about-my-operation-in-peking-now-let-me-tell-you-about-my.html.

12. Michel Oksenberg, "The Chinese Policy Process and the Public Health Issue: An Arena Approach," *Studies in Comparative Communism* 7, no. 4 (Winter 1974): 375–408; David M. Lampton, *Health, Conflict, and the Chinese Political System* (Ann Arbor, MI: Center for Chinese Studies, University of Michigan, 1974); and David M. Lampton, *The Politics of Medicine in China: The Policy Process, 1949–1977* (Boulder, CO: Westview Press, 1977).

13. Martin King Whyte and William L. Parish, *Urban Life in Contemporary China* (Chicago: University of Chicago Press, 1984).

14. Yanzhong Huang, *Governing Health in Contemporary China* (New York: Routledge, 2013).

15. Victor W. Sidel, "Health Services in the People's Republic of China," in *Medicine and Society in China*, eds. John Bowers and Elizabeth Purcell (New York: Josiah Macy Jr. Foundation, 1974), 126.

16. "Science and Technology: Cooperation Between the United States and China," Hearings Before the Special Subcommittee on U.S. Trade with China of the Committee on Energy and Commerce, House of Representatives Ninety-Eighth Congress First Session, October 31–November 3, 1983, https://files.eric.ed.gov/fulltext/ED242517.pdf.

17. National Academy of Sciences Committee on Scholarly Communication with the People's Republic of China, Dean H. Hamer, and Shain-dow Kung, eds., *Biotechnology in China: Cooperation with the United States* (Washington, DC: National Academies Press, 1989), 9, https://www.ncbi.nlm.nih.gov/books/NBK236097/.

18. Xiaocheng Gu, "Ray Wu and the CUSBEA Program," *Science in China Series C: Life Sciences* 52, no. 2 (February 2009): 125–27.

19. See Mary Brown Bullock, *An American Transplant: The Rockefeller Foundation and Peking Union Medical College* (Berkeley: University of California Press, 1980), 161–73.

20. Project Hope, "Project HOPE and Shanghai Municipal Government Celebrate 10th Anniversary of Shanghai Children's Medical Center," May 31, 2008, http://donate .projecthope.org/site/PageServer?pagename=about_us_latest_Shanghai_Childrens _Medical_Center.

21. Hamer and Kung, *Biotechnology in China*.

22. "Kuaguo yaoqi jinru zhongguo douzai nayinian, zheli you daan" [In which years did multinational pharmaceutical companies enter China? Here are the answers], *Yiyao daibiao* [MRCLUB], July 29, 2017, http://wemr.club/companies/mnc-pharma-entering -chinese-market.html.

23. Hamer and Kung, *Biotechnology in China*.

24. "Luoyi·wajieluosi boshi de liwu: weile yige meiyou yigan de zhongguo" [Gift from Dr. Roy Vagelos: For a China without hepatitis B], *Wangyi xinwen* [NetEase News], April 6, 2018, http://news.163.com/18/0406/17/DENPP5U40001899N.html.

25. Cui Fuqiang et al., "Prevention of Chronic Hepatitis B After 3 Decades of Escalating Vaccination Policy, China," *Emerging Infectious Diseases* 23, no. 5 (2017): 765–72, https:// dx.doi.org/10.3201/eid2305.161477.

26. Reuters, "Merck Helping China Fight Hepatitis B Epidemic," *Journal of Commerce*, June 12, 1994, https://www.joc.com/merck-helping-china-fight-hepatitis-b-epidemic _19940612.html.

27. "Suoyou zhongguoren douyao ganxie de yaoshen: meiguo moke gongsi" [A god of drug every Chinese should thank: Merck & Co. from the United States], *Xinlang* [Sina], July 12, 2018, http://www.sina.com.cn/midpage/mobile/index.d.html?docID=h-fefkqq7783856&url=think.sina.cn/doc—ihfefkqq7783856.d.html.

28. Huang, *Governing Health in Contemporary China*.

29. J. Stephen Morrison and Bates Gill, *Averting a Full-Blown HIV/AIDS Epidemic in China: A Report of the CSIS HIV/AIDS Delegation to China, January 13–17, 2003* (Washington, DC: CSIS Press, February 2013), 10.

30. Malcolm Moore, "China Facing HIV 'Plague' as New Cases Leap 45 Per Cent," *Telegraph*, March 30, 2009, https://www.telegraph.co.uk/news/worldnews/asia/china/5075542/China -facing-HIV-plague-as-new-cases-leap-45-per-cent.html.

31. See Yanzhong Huang, "The Politics of China's SARS Crisis," *Harvard Asia Quarterly* 7, no. 4 (Fall 2003): 9–16.

32. Georgetown University Initiative for U.S.-China Dialogue, "U.S.-China Dialogue on Global Health Background Report," May 8, 2017, https://uschinadialogue.georgetown.edu /publications/u-s-china-dialogue-on-global-health-background-report.

33. Centers for Disease Control and Prevention, "Global HIV/AIDS: China," July 20, 2016, http://www.cdc.gov/globalaids/global-hiv-aids-at-cdc/countries/china/default.html.

34. Ray Yip, "International Philanthropic Engagement in Three Stages of China's Response to HIV/AIDS," in *Philanthropy for Health in China*, eds. Jennifer Ryan et al. (Bloomington, IN: Indiana University Press, 2014), 149.

35. Responding to the Threat of Global, Virulent Influenza: Hearing Before the Senate Committee on Foreign Relations, 109 Cong. 2 (2005) (testimony of Laurie A. Garrett, Senior Fellow for Global Health, Council on Foreign Relations).

36. Xiaoqing Lu and Bates Gill, *China's Response to HIV/AIDS and US-China Collaboration* (Washington, DC: Center for Strategic and International Studies, 2007), 6.

37. Georgetown University, "U.S.-China Dialogue." Since 2002, the U.S. CDC has also collaborated with the Chinese government to address tuberculosis.

38. World Health Organization, "Strengthening Pandemic Influenza Preparedness and Response," Report to Fifty-Eighth World Health Assembly, April 7, 2005, http://www.who.int/gb/ebwha/pdf_files/WHA58/A58_13-en.pdf.

39. Institute of Medicine, *The Threat of Pandemic Influenza: Are We Ready?* (Washington, DC: The National Academies Press, 2004), 12.

40. Jeffery K. Taubenberger et al., "Characterization of the 1918 Influenza Virus Polymerase Genes," *Nature* 437 (October 2005): 889–93.

41. *Nanfang dushibao* [Southern Metropolis Daily], Guangzhou, November 8, 2005.

42. *Huashang bao* [China Business News], November 18, 2005

43. Barack Obama and Richard Lugar, "Grounding a Pandemic," *New York Times*, June 6, 2005, https://www.nytimes.com/2005/06/06/opinion/grounding-a-pandemic.html.

44. Centers for Disease Control and Prevention, "Global Health Protection and Security," November 8, 2017, https://www.cdc.gov/globalhealth/healthprotection/gdd/china.html.

45. U.S. Department of State, "United States-China Joint Initiative on Avian Influenza," November 19, 2005, https://2001-2009.state.gov/r/pa/prs/ps/2005/57157.htm.

46. Centers for Disease Control and Prevention, "Highly Pathogenic Asian Avian Influenza A(H5N1) Virus," December 12, 2008, https://www.cdc.gov/flu/avianflu/h5n1-virus.htm.

47. "Hujintao tong aobama tonghua cheng yuan gongtong yingdui tiaozhan" [Hu Jintao and Obama called and shared willingness to jointly meet the challenge], *Xinlang* [Sina], May 6, 2009, http://news.sina.com.cn/c/2009-05-06/232117758961.shtml.

48. Office of the White House Press Secretary, "U.S.-China Joint Statement," November 17, 2009, https://www.hsdl.org/?view&did=31925.

49. Georgetown University, "U.S.-China Dialogue."

50. U.S. Department of State, "National Strategy for Pandemic Influenza Implementation Plan One Year Summary," May 2007, https://2001-2009.state.gov/g/avianflu/88567.htm.

51. Centers for Disease Control and Prevention, "Summary of Influenza Risk Assessment Tool (IRAT) Results," July 30, 2018, https://www.cdc.gov/flu/pandemic-resources/monitoring/irat-virus-summaries.htm.

52. Yanzhong Huang, "China's Response to the 2014 Ebola Outbreak in West Africa," *Global Challenges* 1, no. 2 (January 30, 2017), https://doi.org/10.1002/gch2.201600001.

53. Fogarty International Center, "US-China Renew Commitment to Global Health Security," *Global Health Matters Newsletter* 14, no. 4 (July and August 2015), https://www.fic.nih.gov/News/GlobalHealthMatters/july-august-2015/Pages/chinese-delegation.aspx.

54. China Internet New, "A Reporter Asked," http://www.china.com.cn/zhibo/zhuanti/ch-xinwen/2014-11/03/content_33955596.htm.

55. Sheri Fink, "A Chinese Ebola Drug Raises Hopes, and Rancor," *New York Times*, June 12, 2015, https://www.nytimes.com/2015/06/12/world/chinese-ebola-drug-brings-american-objections.html.

56. Nadia Khomami, "British Military Nurse Successfully Treated for Ebola," *Guardian*, March 27, 2015, https://www.theguardian.com/world/2015/mar/27/british-military-nurse-infected-with-ebola-has-been-discharged-from-hospital.

57. "Liuyandong chuxi zhongmei aibola ji quanqiu weisheng yantaohui" [Liu Yandong attended China-US Ebola and Global Health Safety Seminar], *Xinhuawang* [Xinhuanet], June 24, 2015, http://www.xinhuanet.com//politics/2015-06/24/c_127946636.htm.

58. U.S. Department of State, "The Global AIDS Disaster: Implications for the 1990s," 1992, https://www-cache.pbs.org/wgbh/pages/frontline/aids/docs/statedept.pdf.

59. John C. Gannon, "The Global Infectious Disease Threat and Its Implications for the United States," NIE 99-17D, National Intelligence Council, January 2000, https://www.dni.gov/files/documents/infectiousdiseases_2000.pdf.

60. Samuel R. Berger, "A Foreign Policy for the Global Age," *Foreign Affairs* 79, no. 6 (November–December, 2000): 22–39.

61. David F. Gordon, "The Next Wave of HIV/AIDS: Nigeria, Ethiopia, Russia, India, and China," National Intelligence Council, September 2002, https://fas.org/irp/nic/hiv-aids .html.

62. Hillary Clinton, "The Global Health Initiative: The Next Phase of American Leadership in Health Around the World" (speech, Johns Hopkins University's School of Advanced International Studies, Washington, DC, August 16, 2010), https://www.voltairenet.org /article166782.html.

63. Yizhou Wang, "Defining Non-traditional Security and Its Implications for China," Institute of World Economics and Politics, Chinese Academy of Social Sciences, 2005, http:// citeseerx.ist.psu.edu/viewdoc/download?doi=10.1.1.472.3779&rep=rep1&type=pdf. The other five nontraditional security threats aside from HIV/AIDS are listed as money trafficking, piracy, excessive poverty, refugees and immigrants, and environmental security.

64. Bei Tang and Yanzhong Huang, "Engagement in Global Health Governance Regimes," in *Sage Handbook on Contemporary China*, eds. Weiping Wu and Mark Frazier (New York: Sage, 2018).

65. Global Health Security Agenda, "About the GHSA," https://www.ghsagenda.org/about.

66. "U.S. Department of Health and Human Services," https://2001-2009.state.gov/documents /organization/96444.pdf.

67. In December 2010, the director of NIH and the president of the National Natural Science Foundation of China signed an implementation arrangement to develop the U.S.-China Program for Biomedical Research Cooperation, which aims to enhance cooperative biomedical research of benefit to both countries. National Institute of Allergy and Infectious Diseases, "US-China Collaborative Biomedical Research Program," https:// www.niaid.nih.gov/research/us-china-collaborative-biomedical-research-program.

68. Peter Waldman, "The U.S. Is Purging Chinese Cancer Researchers from Top Institutions," *Bloomberg Businessweek*, June 13, 2019, https://www.bloomberg.com/news/features /2019-06-13/the-u-s-is-purging-chinese-americans-from-top-cancer-research.

69. Fogarty International Center, "US-China Renew Commitment."

70. Author's communication with a Bush administration official, October 2, 2015.

71. See "Joint Communique on the Second Meeting of the U.S.-China Health Care Forum," May 22, 2007, http://www.export.gov/china/policyadd/Joint_Communique_HC.pdf.

72. Calum MacLeod, "FDA Opens Office in China," *USA Today*, Nov. 19, 2008. https:// usatoday30.usatoday.com/news/washington/2008-11-19-chinafda_N.htm.

73. Yip, "International Philanthropic Engagement," 150.

74. Bill and Melinda Gates Foundation, "Tackling Domestic Challenges," https://www .gatesfoundation.org/Where-We-Work/China-Office/Tackling-Domestic-Challenges . http://www.ngocn.net/news/80333.html

75. Yanzhong Huang and Jia Ping, "The Global Fund's China Legacy," International Institutions and Global Governance Program and Global Health Program, Council on Foreign Relations, March 31, 2014, https://www.cfr.org/report/global-funds-china-legacy.

76. Embassy of the People's Republic of China in the United States, "China and Merck Join to Fight the HIV/AIDS Epidemic in China," May 16, 2005, http://www.china-embassy .org/eng/zmgx/zmgx/Economic%20Cooperation%20&%20Trade/t195857.htm.

77. Paul Barr, "Trade Route," *Modern Healthcare*, March 7, 2011, http://www.modernhealthcare .com/article/20110307/MAGAZINE/110309989.

78. Waldman, "U.S. Is Purging."

79. Huang and Jia, "Global Fund's China Legacy."

80. Mohon Shajalal et al., "China's Engagement with Development Assistance for Health in Africa," *Global Health Research and Policy*, August 9, 2017, https://www.ncbi.nlm.nih.gov/pmc/articles/PMC5683463/.

81. "Woguo yuanliaoyao chanye fazhan xianzhuang, qvshi ji jiyu" [Development status, trends and opportunities of China's active pharmaceutical ingredient industry], *Jixianwang* [Xianjichina], March 11, 2019. https://www.xianjichina.com/news/details_102629.html.

82. Rosemary Gibson and Janardan Prasad Singh, *ChinaRx: Exposing the Risks of America's Dependence on China for Medicine* (Amherst, NY: Prometheus Books, 2018).

83. Steve Sternberg, "China's Lock on Drugs," *U.S. News & World Report*, May 8, 2018, https://www.usnews.com/news/best-countries/articles/2018-05-08/trumps-quest-for-lower-drug-prices-may-provoke-china-trade-war-experts-warn.

84. Data exclusivity refers to a practice whereby, for a fixed period of time, drug regulatory authorities do not allow generic drug manufacturers to use an originator's registration files to obtain a market authorization of their products. Patent linkage is a system or process by which drug regulatory authorities link drug marketing approval to the status of the patent(s) corresponding to the originator's product in order to ensure that no patent is being infringed before marketing approval for a new product is issued.

85. David P. Fidler, "Health as Foreign Policy: Harnessing Globalization for Health," *Health Promotion International* 21 (2006): 53–54.

86. Ministry of Foreign Affairs of the People's Republic of China, "China's Position Paper on the New Security Concept," July 31, 2002.

87. See Information Office of the State Council, "China's National Defense in 2002," December 9, 2002, http://www.china.org.cn/e-white/20021209/index.htm.

88. The *People's Daily* warned that if measures were not taken, the number of HIV cases could reach ten million by 2010, causing RMB7.7 trillion in economic losses. Yang Ruoqian, "Curbing AIDS Proliferation, No Time for China to Delay Any Longer," *People's Daily*, July 24, 2002, http://english.peopledaily.com.cn/200207/24/eng20020724_100289.shtml.

89. Jordyn Dahl, "How China Is on Course to Unseat U.S. as the Next Leader in Global Health," *Forbes*, April 26, 2017, https://www.forbes.com/sites/jordyndahl/2017/04/26/how-china-is-on-course-to-unseat-u-s-as-the-next-leader-in-global-heath/#136b8da1c467.

90. Xinhua, "China, U.S. Conclude Social, People-to-people Talks with Substantial Results," September 9, 2017, http://www.xinhuanet.com/english/2017-09/29/c_136649327.htm.

91. The Associated Press, "U.S., China Bust Fentanyl Drug Ring in First Ever Joint Investigation," *Global News*, August 30, 2018, https://globalnews.ca/news/4418315/fentanyl-drug-ring-bust-u-s-china-joint-investigation/.

92. Steven Jiang, "China Lectures the United States on Opioid Crisis," CNN, June 26, 2018, https://www.cnn.com/2018/06/25/asia/china-us-opioid-crisis-intl/index.html.

93. Reuters, "China-US Tensions Set Aside for Joint Military Forum on Health," *South China Morning Post*, September 17, 2018, https://www.scmp.com/news/china/diplomacy/article/2164505/china-us-tensions-set-aside-joint-military-forum-health.

94. Robert J. Samuelson, "Is the United States Losing the Trade War with China?" *Washington Post*, May 15, 2019, https://www.washingtonpost.com/opinions/is-the-united-states-losing-the-trade-war/2019/05/15/4495d808-7738-11e9-b7ae-390de4259661_story.html?utm_term=.b9953cab70b7.

95. Yanzhong Huang, "Three Take-Home Messages from China's Glaxo Verdict," *Forbes*, September 25, 2014, https://www.forbes.com/sites/yanzhonghuang/2014/09/25/three-take-home-messages-from-chinas-glaxo-verdict/#1f1071c78992; China Government Network, "Why Did Li Keqiang Visit This Foreign Anti-cancer Pharmaceutical Company When

He Visited Shanghai?" April 11, 2018, http://www.chinanews.com/gn/2018/04-11/8488243.shtml.

96. "China Announces New Initiatives to Level the Playing Field for Innovative and Generic Drugs," *Ropes & Gray*, April 17, 2018, https://www.ropesgray.com/en/newsroom/alerts/2018/04/China-Announces-New-Initiatives-to-Level-the-Playing-Field-for-Innovative-and-Generic-Drugs.

97. Nectar Gan and Alice Yan, "Why China's Premier Used Hit Movie 'Dying to Survive' to Push for Cheaper Cancer Drugs," *South China Morning Post*, July 26, 2018, https://www.scmp.com/news/china/policies-politics/article/2157019/why-chinas-premier-used-hit-movie-dying-survive-push.

98. Bob Woodward, *Fear: Trump in the Whitehouse* (New York: Simon & Schuster, 2018), 275

99. Interview with a Rockefeller Brothers Fund official, New York, January 2017.

100. Nandika Chand, "China Can Weaponize Prescription Drugs to Hit US in Trade War, Says Expert," *International Business Times*, June 1, 2019, https://www.ibtimes.com/china-can-weaponize-prescription-drugs-hit-us-trade-war-says-expert-2796920; Steve Sternberg, "China's Lock on Drugs."

101. Didi Tang, "China Threat to Halt US Antibiotics Supply," *Times*, March 1, 2019, https://www.thetimes.co.uk/article/china-threat-to-halt-us-antibiotics-supply-36tm2v2xp.

102. Brenda Goh, "China to Tighten Rules on Foreigners Using Genetic Material," Reuters, June 10, 2019, https://www.reuters.com/article/us-china-genes/china-to-tighten-rules-on-foreigners-using-genetic-material-idUSKCN1TB17N.

103. Demetri Sevastopulo and Tom Mitchell, "US Considered Ban on Student Visas for Chinese Nationals," *Financial Times*, October 2, 2018, https://www.ft.com/content/fc413158-c5f1-11e8-82bf-ab93d0a9b321.

104. Xin zhongguo shoupi wushier ming gongpai liuxue renyuan chuguo jishi" [Documenting the 52 government dispatched researchers from New China going abroad to study in the U.S.], *Zhongguo qingnian bao* [China Youth], December 7, 2011, http://news.sina.com.cn/c/sd/2011-12-07/103823590425.shtml.

105. Meng Jing, "For a Growing Number of Chinese Students, the Doors to America Are Closing," *South China Morning Post*, April 30, 2019, https://www.scmp.com/tech/article/3008128/growing-number-chinese-students-doors-america-are-closing.

106. Smiriti Mallapaty, "China Hides Identities of Top Scientific Recruits Amidst Growing US Scrutiny," *Nature Index*, October 22, 2018, https://www.natureindex.com/news-blog/china-hides-identities-of-top-scientific-recruits-amidst-growing-us-scrutiny.

107. David Malakoff, "Emory Ousts Two Chinese American Researchers After Investigation Into Foreign Ties," *Science Magazine*, May 23, 2019, https://www.sciencemag.org/news/2019/05/emory-ousts-two-chinese-american-researchers-after-investigation-foreign-ties.

108. Jeffrey Mervis, "NIH Probe of Foreign Ties Has Led to Undisclosed Firings—and Refunds from Institutions," *Science*, June 26, 2019, https://www.sciencemag.org/news/2019/06/nih-probe-foreign-ties-has-led-undisclosed-firings-and-refunds-institutions.

109. I thank Dr. Matthew Brown for bringing this to my attention.

110. Waldman, "U.S. Is Purging."

111. Bill Chappell, "U.S. Prepares Tariffs on Additional $300B Of Imported Chinese Goods," NPR, May 14, 2019, https://www.npr.org/2019/05/14/723162537/u-s-prepares-sanctions-on-another-300-billion-of-imported-chinese-goods.

112. "US China Trade War: end in sight but pharma must remain vigilant," SCAIR, March 4, 2019, https://supplychain-risk.com/2019/03/04/can-pharmaceuticals-sit-out-the-us-china-trade-war/.

113. Data from Johns Hopkins University Coronavirus Resource Center, January 14, 2021, https://coronavirus.jhu.edu/.

114. Yanzhong Huang, "The U.S. and China Could Cooperate to Defeat the Pandemic. Instead, Their Antagonism Makes Matters Worse," *Foreign Affairs*, March 24, 2020, https://www .foreignaffairs.com/articles/china/2020-03-24/us-and-china-could-cooperate-defeat -pandemic.

115. Andrew Michta, "We Need Hard Decoupling," *American Interest*, March 5, 2020, https:// www.the-american-interest.com/2020/03/05/we-need-hard-decoupling/.

CHAPTER 10

THINKERS. BUILDERS. SYMBOLS. SPIES? SINO-U.S. EDUCATIONAL RELATIONS IN THE ENGAGEMENT ERA

ROBERT DALY

Precursors, 1854–1949

The story of Sino-American higher educational relations from 1979 to 2020 is one of progress and frustration born of overlapping but often incompatible goals. Patterns of engagement over these four decades echoed those established during the century of scholarly interaction that preceded the founding of the People's Republic of China (PRC) in 1949. Parallels between the two periods make clear that whatever the benefits of overseas study and research may be for individual scholars and institutions, power imbalances between the United States and China have played a greater role than scholarly imperatives in shaping bilateral academic exchange. China's weakness and need to modernize and America's strength and desire to shepherd China's modernization have been the poorly synchronized twin engines of Sino-American higher educational interaction.

Yung Wing and the Chinese Educational Mission

The first Chinese to graduate from an American university, Yung Wing, returned to China after leaving Yale in 1854 and worked briefly with the Taiping rebels before being sent back to the United States in 1863 to purchase machinery for the Qing dynasty's military arsenal. Over the next ten years, Yung convinced the Qing government that China would be stronger if it sent young Chinese to the United States to master advanced technology.

Yung's Chinese Educational Mission (CEM) began in 1872, when 120 Chinese boys were sent to New England to study natural and military sciences and engineering, first in secondary schools and then in American universities and colleges. In 1881, China curtailed the program and brought the students home. The Qing government was concerned that the young men, some of whom had become Christians, taken up baseball, and courted American girls, were losing their Chineseness. China was also offended by the refusal of military academies at West Point and Annapolis to admit CEM students. Ten of the Chinese students refused to leave the United States. Those who returned were abused, for a period, as potential spies. Yung Wing died in 1912 after watching his Asian American children graduate from Yale.[1]

Boxer Indemnity Scholars

In 1906, twenty-five years after the failure of the CEM, Edmund James, president of the University of Illinois, wrote to President Theodore Roosevelt in support of training young Chinese in American universities:

> China is upon the verge of a revolution. . . . Every great nation in the world will inevitably be drawn into more or less intimate relations with this gigantic development. . . . The nation which succeeds in educating the young Chinese of the present generation will be the nation which for a given expenditure of effort will reap the largest possible returns in moral, intellectual, and commercial influence.[2]

Arguments like these convinced those in Washington to spend the portion of the indemnity that the Qing government overpaid to the United States following the 1900 Boxer Rebellion to educate Chinese students in American universities. As Michael Hunt has demonstrated, spending these funds on Chinese students was not purely altruistic.[3] It was also an attempt to advance American interests in Asia by building influence with China's elite youth. The program was forced on the Chinese side over its objections.

After the program was established in 1909, approximately thirteen hundred Chinese were educated in the United States under Boxer Indemnity scholarships.[4] China required that 80 percent of these students study engineering, mining, and communications technology. Many students later founded the modern scientific disciplines in China, including the nuclear physicist Dai Chuanzeng; the theoretical physicist Hu Ning; the mathematician Hua Luogeng, the father of modern Chinese astronomy Zhang Yuzhe; and Qian Xuesen, who helped develop China's nuclear weapons program.

The success of Boxer Indemnity students was not limited to what are now called STEM (science, technology, engineering, mathematics) fields, however. Alumni who returned to China and decided, with varying levels of enthusiasm, to support the Communists included the writer Bing Xin; the martyr and poet Wen Yiduo; the father of the modern study of Chinese philosophy, Feng Youlan; the father of modern Chinese architecture, Liang Sicheng; and his wife, the aesthete and intellectual Lin Huiyin. Other Boxer Indemnity returnees sided with the Guomindang after the outbreak of China's civil war, including General Sun Li-jen and the writer and diplomat Hu Shi. A third group spent most of their careers in the United States, including the Nobel Prize–winning physicist Yang Chen-Ning and P. C. Chang, a historian and diplomat who helped draft the UN Universal Declaration on Human Rights.

Boxer Indemnity scholars composed less than 40 percent of the roughly thirty-three thousand Chinese who studied in America between 1870 and 1949. During the same period, ten times that number studied in Japan. Future Communist Party leaders Deng Xiaoping and Zhou Enlai studied in France. Chinese women took advantage of overseas scholarships to pursue opportunities unavailable in China. The first Chinese woman to receive a degree in America was Jin Yunmei, who earned an MD from the Woman's Medical College of the New York Infirmary in 1885.[5] By 1911, there were at least fifty-two Chinese women studying in American universities.[6]

When the PRC was founded in 1949, approximately 5,600 Chinese were studying in America, most in engineering, medicine, or the natural sciences.[7] When the Korean War began in 1950, the United States, fearful that they would use their knowledge to strengthen the People's Liberation Army, banned these scholars from returning to the mainland, although thirteen hundred went back in 1956, following the Geneva Conference and Sino-American ambassadorial talks.

American Educators in China

Prior to 1949, American educational missionaries, together with European counterparts, Japanese academics, and pioneering Chinese, built many of the institutions that form the bedrock of the PRC's higher educational system today. The Presbyterian missionary John Leighton Stuart was instrumental in establishing an academy that became Zhejiang University. He later served as the first president of Yenching University, whose campus and departments were absorbed by Peking University after 1949. Tsinghua University, launched as a preparatory school for Boxer Indemnity students, was funded with Indemnity money. The Yale Foreign Missionary Society, set up in 1901, focused on medical education in Hunan Province. By the 1930s, sixteen Christian institutes of higher education, thirteen Protestant and three Catholic, were operating in China.[8] China's finest teaching hospital, Peking Union Medical College, funded by the Rockefeller Foundation with a curriculum modeled on that of the Johns Hopkins University School of Medicine,[9] was overseen by William Henry Welch, the dean of American medicine.

The Past as Prelude

The Chinese Communist Party's (CCP) 1949 victory closed the door on the promising first phase of Sino-American academic engagement. Thirty years of armed conflict and estrangement followed. Reviewing the Cold War experience in the 2020s might lead some Americans to ask whether higher educational cooperation before 1949 was a sucker's game. Didn't American universities strengthen a future adversary by training its nuclear physicists? In their promotion of human knowledge as an apolitical, global enterprise, did they not enable an adversary, and if so, were they guilty of something more serious than naiveté? Did America lose through early exchanges?

It may be that as the weaker, less developed nation China gained more from the first phase of academic interaction than the United States. It is far from clear, however, what metrics or time frame should be used to make such a judgment. For the United States, the great benefit of early academic engagement with China was the talent it brought to American shores. The Boxer Indemnity student Yang Chen-Ning, for example, was one of eight Chinese Americans to be honored as Nobel laureates as of 2020. But the benefits of academic integration cannot be measured only by the accomplishments of first-generation scholar-immigrants. Consider the case of Shu-Tian Li, who earned a PhD in engineering and economics from Cornell in 1926, returned to China for a twenty-five-year career as a scientist and university president, and then came back to the United States, where his economist daughter became the mother of Steven Chu, Nobel Prize winner and U.S. secretary of energy. Lin Huiyin, the Boxer Indemnity student mentioned earlier, became the aunt of one of the most original designers in America, Maya Lin, whose work includes the Vietnam Veterans Memorial in Washington, DC. The first generations of Chinese students in America have hundreds of thousands of American descendants. Their achievements, while impossible to capture statistically, make a clear anecdotal case that the United States would be worse off without the legacy of academic engagement with China before 1949.

Several themes in this review of pre-1949 Sino-American academic relations would reemerge after the establishment of diplomatic relations in 1979 and continue to shape American policy discussions today. These include the following:

- During both the pre-1949 and post-1979 phases of academic engagement, China gained knowledge of cutting-edge natural, applied, and social sciences from the United States, while the United States gained Chinese talent and interdisciplinary knowledge of China itself, which was a boon to American sinology but did not directly improve U.S. industrial or techno-logical capabilities.

- China articulates and pursues goals for educational relations clearly and con-sistently. The United States conducts its academic relations with China in a decentralized fashion through colleges, foundations, and scholars with a wide range of motives.
- The Chinese government has always worried that Chinese who studied in America might be influenced by corrosive American ideas, as evidenced by its treatment of returned CEM students. The United States has always had reservations about the reliability of Chinese students in America, which is why CEM students were not admitted to West Point and the U.S. Naval Acad-emy in Annapolis.
- Bilateral academic engagement is a whole-of-society affair. Scholars in both countries become not only classmates but colleagues, friends, neighbors, co-parishioners, and family members. Regardless of government policies, academic engagement, like engagement as a whole, is a complex, sprawling, amorphous dynamic that neither nation can fully control.
- The pre-1949 and post-1979 periods of academic engagement both ended amid a sense of relative American failure.

1979–1989: The Opening to Tiananmen

The United States and the PRC established diplomatic relations in 1979 to bal-ance against the Soviet Union. However, China's academic engagement with the United States had nothing to do with strategic triangles; its purpose was to develop China under the banner of the Four Modernizations.

The Four Modernizations were a guide for development proposed by Premier Zhou Enlai in 1963 and adopted as national policy in 1978 when Deng Xiaop-ing launched his reform program. The Four Modernizations were a blueprint for pulling even with developed countries in agriculture, industry, national defense, and science and technology by the early twenty-first century. It was not a secret scheme; the slogan appeared on billboards throughout China for over a decade. The United States did not oppose China's ambitions. The early scientific and academic programs of the Four Modernizations were carried out under the United Nations Development Programme and managed by an American.

Economic and technological policies under the Four Modernizations were the subject of a major report prepared for the U.S. Congress's Joint Economic Committee in 1982. The report summary, which ran to over six hundred pages, makes clear that American legislators understood from the beginning that "the measuring rod for China's modernization is no longer acquisition of the most advanced Western technology, but a judicious blend of foreign experience and *self-reliance* [emphasis added]," and that "after three decades of power . . . Chinese leaders aim to develop a modern, powerful, industrial state that would be capable of dealing on equal terms with the superpowers."[10] The main concerns of the report were not that China would draw even with the United States or threaten its interests but that China did not have enough hard currency to buy American weapons systems and that a slowdown in China's economy might hamper Americans' ability to profit from China's development. In his foreword to the report, Henry Reuss of Wisconsin concluded that, in reacting to the Four Modernizations, "Our own policies ought to be designed to foster China's efforts to achieve balanced economic development and to strengthen, not jeopardize, our relations."[11] The kind of alarm over China's go-it-alone instincts and acquisition of America technology that arose in response to Beijing's Indigenous Innovation program (2006) and Made in China 2025 goals (2015) played little role in U.S. policy during the 1980s.

Perhaps unwittingly, Reuss identified a conceptual and strategic divide that would plague U.S.-China relations over the next thirty-plus years and find them contemplating a new Cold War as this book went to press. He wrote:

> Joining the economic powers of the region and the world may be some time off for the People's Republic of China. China has launched modernization. The Western nations have adopted a policy of "normalization," accepting China into the global family of economies. Active and equal participation by China as an industrial nation in the world market is some years off.[12]

China's self-directed *modernization* and its *normalization* were not necessarily incompatible, but even in the 1980s, they were not the same project. Reuss made clear that normalization, conceived in the West as China's embrace of values and practices that would lead to its acceptance by the global community, was distinct from modernization, defined by China as improving the economic, technical, and material well-being of the Chinese people for their own sakes. As China's power grew over subsequent decades, the normalization and modernization conceptions of the purpose of Chinese reform increasingly came into conflict. In a 2018 interview, U.S. Secretary of State Michael Pompeo summarized the Trump administration's China policy as "a multipronged effort on behalf of all of the United States Government . . . to convince China to behave like a normal nation on commerce and with respect to the rules of international law."[13]

It was in order to modernize on China's terms, not to normalize by the standards of the West, that Deng Xiaoping began dispatching Chinese students to the United States in 1978. In discussing his plans with Americans, Deng did not mention the need to build mutual understanding but bragged that, "When our thousands of Chinese students abroad return home, you will see how China will transform itself."[14] Deng understood the risk of exposing Chinese to Western ideals, but the development imperative made the risk worth running. In October of 1986, in the face of opposition to his openness program, Deng declared that, "There are those who say we should not open our windows, because open windows let in flies and other insects. They want the windows to stay closed, so we all expire from lack of air. But we say, 'Open the windows, breathe the fresh air and at the same time fight the flies and insects.' "[15] Deng waved off the risks of a brain drain with characteristic confidence, noting that "even if half of those sent abroad do not return, there remains one half who return to help with the Four Modernizations."[16]

On the American side, goals for renewed academic relations were less explicit, but enthusiasm was high, as David M. Lampton and his colleagues at the Committee on Scholarly Communication with the People's Republic of China (CSCPRC) emphasized in their groundbreaking work, *A Relationship Restored: Trends in U.S.-China Educational Exchanges, 1978–1984*:

> Among people in both public and private life in the United States, there was a conscious recognition, or in some cases an intuitive sense, that the dramatic economic, social, and foreign policy experiments occurring in China would affect Americans. This sense of the importance of the current historical juncture in China has provided much of the impetus to the rapid growth in Sino-American academic exchange.[17]

Student Programs: The Chinese

In July of 1978, Frank Press, the White House science advisor, led the first delegation of American scientists to China in order to build "a relationship with China similar to those we have with other countries."[18] After a group of Chinese scientists made a reciprocal trip under the auspices of the National Science Foundation in October of 1978, the two nations announced their first formal exchange of students and scholars. Sixty federally funded Americans would conduct short-term studies in Chinese universities, while roughly six hundred Chinese would pursue degrees in the United States. In its report on the announcement, the *Washington Post* noted that "the Chinese have said they prefer studies in physical and biomedical sciences, engineering and applied technology, while U.S. scholars are expected to concentrate largely but not exclusively on social sciences, humanities, language and literature, archeology and art."[19] This was the exchange template whereby China would build its technological capabilities while the United States built its knowledge of China. It could hardly have been otherwise, as large numbers of scholars and access to the Middle Kingdom were all that a desperately poor China could offer the world's most developed nation in 1978.

From 1978 to 1989, over sixty-two thousand Chinese students pursued degrees in the United States, most at the graduate level.[20] A majority held J-1 visas, which required that they return to China two years after completing their studies. In keeping with China's modernization goals, over two-thirds worked in STEM fields.[21] The first generation of Chinese students studying abroad (*liuxuesheng*) was older than typical university students because only scholars trained before universities closed during the Cultural Revolution (1966–1976) had the academic background and English-language skills to study overseas.[22] Children of China's leaders also studied in America, thanks to the confluence of their parents' wish that they receive an elite, international education and the willingness of American universities to give scholarships to young Chinese who might become influential alumni. Deng Xiaoping's younger son studied physics at the University of Rochester from 1983 to 1990.[23] Jiang Zemin's son studied electrical engineering at Drexel University from 1986 to 1989.[24]

According to the 1978–1995 periodization used in Chinese statistics, approximately 15.4 percent of the Chinese who studied in America during this period returned to the PRC—well below the 50 percent envisioned by Deng.[25] Many *liuxuesheng* remained in the United States for the high salaries and freer lifestyles their families could enjoy there, but developments within China also shaped their decisions. They closely followed the Anti-Spiritual Pollution Campaign of 1983, in which CCP conservatives railed against the Western cultural infiltration that had accompanied Deng's reforms. China's premier, Zhao Ziyang, was embarrassed to have to answer questions about the campaign when he visited the United States that year.[26] In 1986, *liuxuesheng* were sympathetic when students at the University of Science and Technology of China in Hefei demonstrated to protest their "lack of power to nominate candidates for the National People's Congress."[27] As the protests spread, students across China cut classes, put up big-character posters, and burned copies of the *Beijing Daily*. The longer the protests continued, the more political they became. Student placards bore slogans like "Down with bureaucratism; return us to democracy" and "Long live democracy; down with autocracy."[28] After the demonstrations petered out in mid-January, Party General Secretary Hu Yaobang was forced to resign for his perceived coddling of students.[29] Four hundred eighty Chinese students in the United States signed an open letter opposing Hu's ouster, and one thousand more endorsed it anonymously. It was the first time Chinese had protested political developments on the mainland from American soil since the opening of China.[30]

This brief overview cannot capture the personal excitement, ambition, and goodwill that inspired many of the Chinese and Americans who lived through this period. Statistics incline readers to imagine the *liuxuesheng* as instances of a kind—as a subset of China's faceless masses—rather than as a diverse set of individuals. The confidence they demonstrated in leaving China, the difficulties they faced in a strange, competitive country, and the vicissitudes of the era in which they made their careers guaranteed that many would live new kinds of lives, and they did.

Gao Xiqing (高西庆) is a fitting poster boy for the era. After he graduated from the Duke University School of Law in 1986, Gao became the first Chinese citizen to pass the bar exam in New York State. In 1988, after two years on Wall Street, where he obtained the lingo of high finance and a hipster wardrobe, he returned to China to serve as director of public offerings and vice-chairman of the China Securities Regulatory Commission, as vice-chairman of the National Council for Social Security Fund, and as vice-chairman and president of the China Investment Corporation, where he managed $200 billion in state assets. Gao became an architect of China's leading financial regulatory agencies, including the Shanghai stock exchange, an advisor to Chinese leaders, and a bridge between the American and Chinese financial systems. In a 2008 interview with the *Atlantic*'s James Fallows, Gao said, "I have great admiration of American people. Creative, hard-working, trusting, and freedom-loving. But you have to have someone to tell you the truth. And then, start realizing it. And if you do it, just like what you did in the Second World War, then you'll be great again! If that happens, then of course—American power would still be there for at least as long as I am living. But many people are betting on the other side."[31]

Student Programs: The Americans

Attaining data on the exact numbers of Chinese students who have come to America since 1978, either cumulatively or in any given year, is difficult. Sound figures for American students and scholars in China are rarer still. According to statistics provided to the Association of International Educators by the Chinese State Education Commission, 6,600 American students went to China between 1979 and 1986 and 4,000 Americans taught there during the same period.[32] Also using Chinese data, David Lampton and his team concluded that from 1979 to 1983, "2,900 to 3,300 American students and scholars . . . traveled to China for what the Chinese government considers academic purposes."[33] American students in China have not been as widely studied as their Chinese counterparts in the United States, perhaps because the individual motives of the small number of Americans who visited China do not seem as significant as the policy decision of the world's largest country to send millions of youth overseas to modernize their nation. To overstate the disparity, but only a little, Americans in China studied abroad, whereas Chinese students in America changed history.

The number of Americans who have studied in China is paltry compared to the number of Chinese students in America. Even on a per capita basis, the number of Chinese students in the United States is 30 times greater than the number of American students in China. The experiences of Chinese and American students in each other's countries are different in kind as well as volume: most Chinese come to America to earn credentials that bolster their careers, while most Americans in China seek language study and cultural exposure, not academic credit. As late of 2011, only 8.3 percent of Americans studying in China were pursuing full degrees, according to the China Scholarship Council.[34]

As low as U.S. numbers were in comparison to China's, American interest in the academic opportunities afforded by the opening of China was strong. Institutions established before 1949, like Yale-China and Oberlin Shansi, resurrected their programs, and new institutions sprang up to meet and create demand. By 1984, American colleges and universities had established at least sixteen new language programs in China.[35] For-profit companies also saw opportunities. In 1982, Boston-based China Educational Tours (CET) worked with Wellesley College to set up its first Chinese-language center. By 1989, CET had trained eight hundred students at its Beijing and Harbin campuses.[36]

The most ambitious educational institution founded in response to the opening was the Johns Hopkins University–Nanjing University Center for Chinese and American Studies, or Hopkins-Nanjing Center (HNC), which began operations in Nanjing in 1986. The HNC was founded on the theory that U.S.-China relations were not so much a subject to be studied as a question that the two nations would have to work out together continually. Linguistic proficiency and cultural understanding were essential to the task. The HNC required that its Chinese and American students (third-country students would be added later) live together as roommates and conduct graduate-level studies in each other's languages. American students studied Chinese history, foreign policy, philosophy, and economy with Nanjing University faculty, with lectures, reading, research, writing, and class discussion conducted only in Mandarin. Their Chinese counterparts took American studies and economics courses in English with faculty hired by Johns Hopkins.

The program's great breakthrough was that all HNC students, Chinese and American, were guaranteed full academic freedom, including rights of discussion and inquiry, which had not previously been granted in the PRC. The HNC also featured China's first uncensored, open-stacks library. Any community member could borrow books that were banned in China and read them at leisure in their dorm rooms. In exchange for academic freedom, the Chinese side required that the HNC not become an evangelist for unrestricted research and debate. This meant that HNC students and faculty could not publish their work in China beyond HNC walls. In its early years, these rules made the HNC a bit of a cloister for academic freedom in China, but over time, it became a beacon.

The pioneering spirit of the first wave of American students was captured by Yale-China's Marc Salzman, who taught English and studied kung fu in Changsha from 1982 to 1984 and published a popular memoir, *Iron and Silk*, in

1986. A similar sense of wonder animated Peace Corps volunteer Peter Hessler's *River Town*, which recounted his two years in Sichuan, in 2001. While Salzman and Hessler deepened the U.S. understanding of China, their work suggests that, for most young Americans, study in China was more a voyage of discovery than an academic grind.

Scholarly Research

Students make the headlines in Sino-American educational relations, but much of the work of academic exchanges is done by volunteers or low-paid professionals whose activities have been too various, numerous, and low-key to merit mention in histories of academic exchange. There are no published statistics on the number of American English teachers, trainers, administrators, test prep coaches, educational consultants, tutors, and foreign experts of various stripes who have worked in China over the past decades. They hail from across the United States and range in age from twenty-two to ninety. China travelers read about their Friendship Awards in the *China Daily* and run into them in coffee shops in third-tier cities or in the gray apartments of Beijing's Friendship Hotel, where the State Administration of Foreign Experts Affairs is located and where many of these Americans lived in the 1980s and 1990s. Americans contributed to academic engagement not only in China but also in the United States, where host families, religious communities, language partners, and local governments and businesses welcomed Chinese students. A similarly vast assortment of Chinese citizen ambassadors and cultural guides helped American students to thrive in China. No survey of this sort would be complete without acknowledging the contributions these unsung volunteers have made to Sino-American academic cooperation.

The history of American scholars who conducted, or tried to conduct, research in China after 1979 is better understood. During the decades of Cold War estrangement, American sinologists studied Chinese in Taiwan and did their China watching from Hong Kong or points more distant. There was little chance of getting permission to visit China itself. The few who did get in could not escape their omnipresent handlers to conduct fieldwork or meet with ordinary Chinese. Polling, surveys, and free travel were forbidden to foreigners in Mao's China. Archives were closed. Data sets were either classified or nonexistent. The resulting state of China studies and China policy in the United States inspired screeds like that offered by Ramon Myers and Thomas Metzger:

> Between 1958 and 1970 nearly $41 million was poured into our institutions of higher education in support of Chinese studies. Has this investment paid off to produce high quality scholarship and a corps of reliable China experts? No. Few of the American-born scholars working on modern China have a strong

grasp of the Chinese language, or are able both to speak it well and to read works from different genres. Few avoid the misunderstandings that arise from restricting their training to a compartmentalized subfield.[37]

After the opening, American scholars were eager to make up for these deficiencies. Their work was still narrowly proscribed by the CCP, however, and they didn't know how to navigate the Chinese institutions with which they had to cooperate. Chinese universities, libraries, and archives were willing to work with Americans, within limits, but did not know how to accommodate them. The Committee on Scholarly Communication with the People's Republic of China (CSCPRC) stepped into this void and became indispensable to scholarly communities from both nations for over thirty years.

The CSCPRC had its roots in the 1960s, when the National Academy of Sciences convened humanists and natural and social scientists with a common interest in gaining access to China.[38] In partnership with the National Academy of Sciences, the Social Science Research Council, and the American Council of Learned Societies, CSCPRC began sending delegations to China and receiving delegations dispatched by Beijing after the Nixon visit in 1972. Through these exchanges, Americans were able to map the network of Chinese institutions capable of collaborating in the most promising fields for joint research, which included medical, agricultural, and earth sciences. As Mary Brown Bullock writes, China focused on

cutting-edge science and applied technology . . . [and] areas in which China was significantly underdeveloped but needed to advance, such as lasers and molecular biology. . . . American universities and U.S. government institutes, such as the National Institutes of Health and the U.S. Geological Survey, went out of their way to provide detailed and up-to-date briefings on American science to visiting Chinese delegations. American industry, from IBM to Exxon to Bell Labs, opened their doors to Chinese technical specialists.[39]

After 1979, China experts, social scientists, and humanities scholars were admitted to China in greater numbers, and CSCPRC kicked into high gear. Between 1979 and 1996, it sent over seven hundred American scholars to conduct research in China. Working with the American Embassy in Beijing, and later through its own China office, CSCPRC became an advocate for Americans who needed research access to archives or permission and geographic scope to conduct field studies. It also served as an advisor to China's Ministry of Education and the Chinese Academy of Sciences, which were often unsure of how to balance their security concerns and the research needs of U.S. academics. As the 1980s progressed, a growing number of bilateral university affiliations and U.S. government efforts, such as the Fulbright Program, meant that the CSCPRC was no longer the sole arbiter of scholarly relations between the United States and China, but the organization remained indispensable. Its long experience, understanding of Chinese bureaucracies, and expert staffs in Washington and Beijing made CSCPRC the most influential organization of its kind.

But its influence was limited. Ongoing tension between the U.S. goal of normalizing China and China's own modernization imperative was starkly depicted in the history of CSCPRC written by Mary Brown Bullock, who served as its director from 1977 to 1988:

> On the American side, the policy orientation [was] . . . to draw Chinese scientists into a broader international scientific arena. On the Chinese side, the selected topics, such as biotechnology, were in areas designated as priority science areas for China, and were designed to absorb and communicate as much new information as possible.[40]

The End of an Era

President Ronald Reagan summed up mutual hopes for Sino-American educational relations when he spoke at Fudan University in Shanghai on April 30, 1984:

> In the past few years, our two countries have enjoyed an explosion in the number of student exchanges. . . . More than 100 American colleges and universities now have educational exchanges with nearly as many Chinese institutions. . . . American students come to China to learn many things—how you monitor and predict earthquakes, how you've made such strides in researching the cause and treatment of cancer. We have much to learn from you in neurosurgery and in your use of herbs in medicine. And we welcome the chance to study your language, your history, and your society. . . . You, in turn, have shown that you're eager to learn, to come to American schools and study electronics and computer sciences, math and engineering, physics, management, and the humanities. We have much to share in these fields, and we're eager to benefit from your curiosity. . . . The scholars at all the universities in China and America have a great role to play in both our countries' futures. From your ranks will come the understanding and skill the world will require in decades to come.[41]

Mutual learning and joint growth were the themes of the era, despite the ideological divide between the two nations, which Reagan acknowledged. Chinese and American students—not corporations, political leaders, or celebrities—had become the primary symbol of what the United States and China might achieve together.

Those hopes were extinguished by the violence of June 4, 1989. Americans saw the young Chinese who had built their own Statue of Liberty on Tiananmen

Square mowed down by a government that seemed to suddenly reject the openness it had preached for eleven years. CCP leaders saw a Western-inspired riot that threatened to destroy the historic economic progress they had made since the opening. Academic relations built up over the previous decade fell apart in weeks. China suspended the Fulbright teaching and research fellowships. The Buffalo State School of Management closed a pioneering MBA program that had trained two hundred graduates at the Dalian University of Technology. The HNC remained open, but most American programs and students fled China. CET canceled its summer 1989 Beijing program, diverting students to Harbin and Taiwan. Its pre-1989 numbers would not recover for six years.

Many of the forty thousand Chinese students in the United States in 1989 supported the Tiananmen movement. After the killings, they demonstrated in front of China's embassy and consulates and called for democracy in China. Congress, wishing to protect the students from any political persecution they might face if forced to go home, passed H.R.2712, known as the Pelosi Bill, by 403 to 0 in the House and by voice vote in the Senate. The bill allowed all Chinese students to remain in the United States for up to four years regardless of when their visas expired and to attain permanent resident status without returning to China. In effect, the bill meant that any *liuxuesheng* who wished to could become an American citizen.

Beijing viewed H.R.2712 as a violation of America's 1987 agreements with China and as a cynical attempt to steal its talent. On November 30, 1989, President George H. W. Bush announced that he would veto the Pelosi Bill but took executive action that gave students "the same benefits" to "accomplish the laudable objectives of the Congress . . . while preserving my ability to manage foreign relations."[42] Following his executive action, most of the students who were supposed to return to China to help it modernize gave their talent to the United States instead.

1990–2007: Reform, Recovery, Complacency

In 1992, the presidential candidate Bill Clinton accused George H. W. Bush of "coddling dictators from Beijing to Baghdad." In 1998, as president, Clinton gave a speech to students and faculty at Peking University, which had been home to many Tiananmen protesters nine years earlier. He touched on human rights, but the thrust of his message was that China and the United States should master emerging technologies together to solve joint challenges and usher in a better future:

> I come here today to talk to you, the next generation of China's leaders, about the critical importance to your future of building a strong partnership between China and the United States. . . . Just three decades ago, China was virtually shut

off from the world. Now, China is a member of more than 1,000 international organizations. . . . Your social and economic transformation has been even more remarkable, moving from a closed command economic system to a driving, increasingly market-based and driven economy, generating two decades of unprecedented growth, giving people greater freedom to travel within and outside China, to vote in village elections, to own a home, choose a job, attend a better school. . . . From laptops to lasers, from microchips to megabytes, an information revolution is lighting the landscape of human knowledge, bringing us all closer together. . . . In the 21st century, your generation will have a remarkable opportunity to bring together the talents of our scientists, doctors, engineers into a shared quest for progress.[43]

The U.S.-China relationship had recovered from the shock of Tiananmen. After the massacre, Americans in China had rushed for the exits and China, a reviled nation shocked by the collapse of the Soviet Union and its own fragility, had hunkered down for a period in which domestic stability took precedence over development. But that period was brief. In 1992, Deng Xiaoping set China on its new course with a trip to the economically freewheeling south of his country. Declaring that "To get rich is glorious!" and "The case for development is unassailable!" he launched reforms that triggered an expansion of wealth unparalleled in human history. After the Tiananmen interregnum, it was again China's modernization—and American interest in profiting by it— that drove bilateral relations and academic engagement.

Higher educational relations developed steadily along predictable lines throughout this eighteen-year period. Bilateral channels for study and research became so diverse, numerous, and deeply intertwined with other aspects of the relationship—the growth of corporate and civil society ties in particular—that they were difficult to track amid the multifaceted comingling of American and Chinese civilizations. Political crises did not divert academic engagement from its established course, nor was the assumption that engagement was mutually beneficial often questioned, even as China's power grew.

Students

On June 9, 1989, Deng Xiaoping told generals responsible for enforcing martial law in Beijing that:

I have told foreign guests that during the last 10 years our biggest mistake was made in the field of education, primarily in ideological and political education, not just of students but of the people in general. We did not tell them enough about the need for hard struggle, about what China was like in the old days and what kind of a country it was to become. That was a serious error on our part.[44]

To correct this oversight, Chinese university freshmen were required to spend the summers before they matriculated at light-duty military boot camps, and the CCP general secretary, Jiang Zemin, instituted a Patriotic Education Campaign emphasizing China's Century of National Humiliation and the need for all Chinese to support the party as the sole guarantor of national salvation and development.[45]

These reforms and the suspicions of the United States they entailed did not greatly affect the flow of Chinese students to the United States. In fact, the years 1989–1994 saw the highest numbers of Chinese students in the United States since the opening, according to Chinese statistics[46] and Institute of International Education (IIE) Open Doors data.[47] According to the IIE, the number of Chinese students and scholars in the United States grew to 46,000 by 1994, 62,000 by 2003, and 80,000 by 2007. The upward trend was not halted by the Taiwan Strait Crisis of 1995, America's bombing of China's embassy in Belgrade in 1999, or the death of a Chinese pilot who flew his fighter jet into an American surveillance plane in international airspace off Hainan Island in 2001. China's leaders and young Chinese vented their rage at the United States in all of these instances, but that did not prevent Chinese students from lining up to take the TOEFL (Test of English as a Foreign Language) or apply for U.S. student visas in ever greater numbers.

Despite Washington's absorption of the forty thousand students in the United States in 1989, China was willing to let successive waves of its brightest youngsters study in America because its need for expertise was so great that it couldn't afford *not* to let them go. The top priority for China's leaders was the maintenance of the CCP's monopoly on power. In the 1990s, CCP legitimacy demanded high growth rates, and that, in turn, required ever higher amounts of technological, institutional, and, as the decade progressed, financial and legal expertise from overseas and from America in particular.

China had no other short-term solution than to encourage overseas study. But it also had a long-term strategy. The CCP used China's growing wealth to improve and expand China's higher educational system so that students could get the training they needed at home, on Chinese soil. The effort began in 1999 when Li Lanqing, vice-premier of the State Council, directed the Ministry of Education to revise its recruitment policies and enroll more students in China's universities. Admissions increased by nearly 50 percent in the first year, a growth rate that China would maintain for the next fifteen years as it founded new universities, built exurban campuses for existing schools, and, most problematically, trained sufficient numbers of qualified faculty.[48] Li Lanqing acknowledged that these reforms would damage educational quality in the short term but promised that the new policies would "(1) ease the immediate pressure of secondary school graduates on the labor market, (2) meet public demand for increased higher educational opportunity, and, most importantly, (3) accumulate human capital for future national development."[49] Although major questions of higher educational quality persist in China, the result of Li's strategy was that eight million students graduated from Chinese universities in 2017, ten times the number who earned degrees in 1997.[50] By 2016, China's undergraduate institutions produced nine times more STEM graduates than American universities.

As in the first decade of engagement, most Chinese scholars in America during this period were graduate students working in STEM fields, but a growing number went to the United States for master degrees in business and law and other degrees, and many Chinese students defied all established patterns. Yiyun Li came to the United States in 1996 to study immunology at the University of Iowa. After earning her master of science in 2000, she transferred to the storied Iowa Writers' Workshop and earned a master of fine arts for her English-language short stories. Her fiction has since appeared in the *New Yorker* and *Paris Review* and won the Frank O'Connor International Short Story Award and the Hemingway Foundation/PEN Award. *Granta* called her one of the best *American* (emphasis added) novelists under thirty-five. She has since won MacArthur and Guggenheim fellowships. This is not to suggest that all American-trained Chinese succeed—they don't—or that they always succeed in ways that benefit the United States. Eric X. Li, who took a degree at Berkeley and became famous for his TED talk challenging the proposition that development leads inexorably to democracy, returned to China to become an apologist for the CCP and active critic of the United States.[51] Wang Wen, who spent a year at the HNC, became one of China's most influential young nationalists, serving as deputy editor of the bombastic *Global Times* and then writing for Guanchazhe, a website funded by Eric Li.

At the turn of the century, as the size and number of Chinese universities expanded, so too did the variety of short-term academic and quasi-academic training opportunities open to Chinese in the United States and China. Hu Shuli, editor of *Caijing* and a 1982 graduate of Renmin University, spent a year as a Knight Journalism Fellow at Stanford in 1994 and earned an executive master of business administration through the Fordham University–Peking University program in Beijing in 2002. Former vice president Li Yuanchao was one of many Chinese leaders who received mid-career training at the Ash Center at Harvard's Kennedy School of Government, to which China sent senior cadres for leadership seminars beginning in 2002.[52] By 2012, the China Development Research Foundation had paid lavishly to send four thousand leaders for training at Harvard, Stanford, and other leading American universities.[53] Provincial and municipal cadre paid lower tuitions for training at public institutions, such as the University of Maryland College Park, which has designed public administration programs for over fifteen thousand party members since 2002.[54]

Chinese students changed as their country developed. If they came to America in the 1980s out of fascination and in the early 1990s out of desperation, those who made the trip between 1998 and 2007 acted primarily out of ambition. As China developed, young Chinese became more confident in their country's direction and more careerist in their approach to higher education. They had come to resemble their American counterparts in seeing themselves as educational consumers rather than as seekers of knowledge. For many Chinese, study in America was no longer seen as a life-transforming decision but as one good option among many.

American students were slow to return to China after Tiananmen. The country seemed less hospitable, and the joyous sense of adventure that had inspired Mark Salzman's generation had faded. CET's post-Tiananmen enrollments were so low that it was relieved to be purchased by Academic Travel Abroad (ATA) in 1994, after which its numbers began to recover. Between 1990 and 2010, ATA/CET trained 5,350 students at four China centers. HNC's enrollments did not plummet, but they also did not increase, as the HNC's founders had hoped. However, enrollments in Chinese-language programs in American colleges and universities climbed steadily through the 1990s, rising from 19,427 students in 1990 to 51,382 in 2006.[55] This trend gradually spurred American demand for study abroad programs in China. University partnerships and Chinese-language schools such as the Inter-University Program for Chinese Language Studies, Princeton in Beijing, and CIEE/College Study Abroad proliferated. The number of Americans earning college credit in China grew from two thousand in 1998 to twelve thousand in 2006.

These were anemic numbers. By the late 1990s, the success of Deng's reforms and China's importance for the United States and the rest of the world were manifest. China's wealth, geostrategic significance, and cultural heritage should have made it a major destination for Americans studying abroad. It was not. In 2001, fewer than 2 percent of Americans who earned college credit abroad did so in China. More Americans went to Ireland and Costa Rica.[56] The weakness of China's universities and its distance, authoritarianism, high cost, difficult language, and insular civilization were all factors in China's inability to attract U.S. students. It had also become apparent that young Americans who made a deep commitment to study Chinese would always be statistical outliers. Most students would rather hang out in the UK or Spain, where more fun could be had for less effort. Despite China's rapid development, there would be no tidal wave of American students.

Scholarly Research

After Tiananmen, students and scholars working in China under CSCPRC auspices left the country and the National Academy of Sciences suspended cooperation with China. But like American students, corporations, and tourists, scholars soon returned in greater numbers than before, and the CSCPRC reached the height of its influence as a gatekeeper organization for governmental, nongovernmental, and academic institutions that collaborated with China in the humanities and natural and social sciences. CSCPRC continued to update *China Bound: A Guide to Academic Life and Work in the PRC*, which was required reading for any academic in China.[57] However, as relations matured and a growing number of American universities, foundations, and nongovernmental organizations set up their own China offices, the need for a gatekeeper diminished. In 1996, CSCPRC closed its Washington office.

After CSCPRC closed shop, there was no institution with deep Chinese government connections and experience in the PRC and that could speak for U.S. academic interests when problems arose. The main recurrent issue for American researchers in China was their inconsistent access to Chinese archives. Changes in political winds, new personnel, opaque policies, and the seemingly random evolution and application of China's state secrets laws made it hard for foreign researchers to collect data in China. China denied American scholars access to information not only by putting archives off-limits but also by denying them visas. The danger of being refused admission to the nation at the core of their professional lives made some American scholars hesitant to criticize China, especially after the blacklisting of Andrew Nathan of Columbia University and Perry Link of Princeton became widely known.

Chinese scholars in the United States had an easier time of it. Many who had arrived in the early 1980s had become American citizens; been hired by American corporations, universities, or government laboratories; and started families. They founded professional associations such as the Society of Chinese American Professors and Scientists, which was established in 2003 at the University of Chicago and now has four hundred members in thirty states. They became not only tenured professors but faculty chairs and deans. In an attempt to lure some of them back to China, Jiang Zemin launched the Hundred Talents Program in 1998 that brought nearly eight hundred overseas scientists home over the next six years. According to James McGregor, however, "fewer than half had doctorates and almost none had tenured appointments abroad. . . . China was simply unable to bring back top talent due to uncertainty about academic freedom, the ability to conduct quality research, and weak IPR [intellectual property rights] protection."[58] It was a problem China would face again.

2008–2019: China Catches Up and the End of Engagement

The year 2008 was the first year in which educational relations were influenced as much by events in the United States as by conditions in China. The global financial crisis had two immediate and historic impacts on U.S.-China academic engagement. The first was that America's economic failure eroded assumptions about American competence that underlay Sino-American academic relations since the days of Yung Wing. Chinese began to doubt—at the personal and policy levels—that the United States still had wisdom worthy of study. It appeared that the world's strongest nation was in relative or absolute decline, as evidenced by both the U.S. recession and China's continuing rise. If China's modernization was nearing completion, there was little reason for China to continue to study at the feet of the United States and less reason for the United States to enable, or even wish for, China's continued economic and technological development.

The second impact of the recession was that American undergraduates who had previously paid high tuitions to attend U.S. public universities outside their home states chose instead to pay the lower costs of in-state study. The result was that most public universities, whose support from state budgets had declined over the preceding decades, saw tuition revenues plummet. They needed a new source of students to pay out-of-state tuition for four-year bachelor degrees. Recruiting higher numbers of Chinese undergraduates was an obvious solution. Young Chinese still wanted the prestige of an American degree, and many of their parents were rich enough to pay for the privilege. Study in the United States, moreover, freed Chinese teenagers from having to take China's high-stakes entrance exam, the *gaokao*, which would otherwise consume the energy and sap the pleasure from their teenage years.

They came to America in droves. From 2008 to 2018, the number of Chinese students in America soared from 98,245 to 350,755.[59] The ranks of Chinese undergraduates in America increased by 1,100 percent between 2006 and 2013, to over 110,000 students. America's leading public universities didn't need recruitment strategies for Chinese undergrads; they just had to decide how many to admit. At Georgia Tech, Chinese undergraduate applications rose from 33 in 2007 to 2,309 in 2014.[60] By the 2014–15 academic year, there were more Chinese undergraduates than graduate students in the United States.[61]

From 2008 to 2017, meanwhile, the number of American students in China fell by 15 percent, from 13,674 to 11,688—one twenty-eighth the number of Chinese in the United States. Edmund James's 1906 exhortation to Theodore Roosevelt, cited earlier in this chapter—that the "nation which succeeds in educating the young Chinese of the present generation will be the nation which for a given expenditure of effort will reap the largest possible returns in moral, intellectual, and commercial influence"—might still be read as prophetic in 2006, but it sounded more naïve and bombastic with each passing year. The disparity between the number of Chinese students in America and the number of Americans in China was no longer a sign of Chinese thirst for American wisdom or an index of U.S. soft power; it was evidence that the United States might be unprepared to compete with a risen China and that U.S. universities were too dependent on Chinese revenues.

Scholarly Research and Institutions

By 2008, U.S.-educated scholars of mainland Chinese origin were an established and essential presence on campuses throughout the United States and around the world. They had become valued pillars of the American higher educational and innovation systems but were in short supply in China itself. China's economic growth, the expansion of its universities, and policies such as the Indigenous Innovation program announced by Beijing in 2006 made the CCP as eager to bring its overseas talent back as the Qing dynasty had been after it established the Chinese Educational Mission in 1872.

Building on the experience of the earlier Hundred Talents Program, China established the Thousand Talents Program in 2008 to entice scientists to the PRC to pursue their research. High salaries, grand titles, cheap apartments, spousal employment, and new, well-equipped laboratories seemed like irresistible draws, but the program struggled to meet its goals. Over three thousand scholars returned to China in the first five years of the program, but few had PhDs and most came only for a summer term or a semester, while retaining their overseas academic appointments. Although the program had some success, the work of David Zweig and Huiyao Wang demonstrates that foreign-based Chinese scholars whose work is most often cited in peer-reviewed journals are least likely to return to China.[62]

Although American undergraduate enrollments in foreign language programs was declining, this period witnessed explosive growth in the number of international American campuses around the world and in China. Over 122 joint programs had been established by Chinese and American partner universities by August 2012.[63] New York University (NYU) opened its campus in Pudong, Shanghai, in 2012. Duke Kunshan admitted its first graduate students, most of whom were Chinese, in 2014 and its first undergraduates, many of them American, in 2018. Both schools claimed that they upheld American-style academic freedom within the PRC. In testimony before a subcommittee of the House Foreign Affairs Committee in 2015, NYU Shanghai's vice-chancellor stated that "we are vigilant in assuring that these principles of academic freedom are honored every day. . . . But if circumstances were to change and those principles were abrogated, NYU Shanghai would have to be closed down."[64] Duke Kunshan was equally emphatic in insisting that its students were free to discuss subjects that are forbidden on Chinese campuses, including the CCP's historical mistakes, freedom of the press, and universal values.[65]

Academic freedom was also guaranteed to American, Chinese, and third-country students at Schwarzman College, a one-year residential master's program created in 2016 by American financier Stephen A. Schwarzman.

2016 and Beyond: The End of Engagement and the Age of Rivalry

In May of 2015, China issued Made in China 2025, an industrial policy that spelled out China's ambitions for technological self-sufficiency and global leadership. The blueprint was intended to ensure that, within ten years, 70 percent of components in Chinese manufactures in key technological sectors would be of domestic origin. In Washington, the initiative was lumped together with China's Belt and Road Initiative infrastructure lending, talent re-recruitment programs, and rapid military buildup as evidence of a Chinese strategy to first develop a Sino-centric Asia and then replace the United States as the world's preeminent nation. Made in China 2025 might not have garnered the attention it did on Capitol Hill were it not for China's buildout of artificial islands in the South China Sea, its militarization of those islands, and its flaunting of the 2016 finding by the Permanent Court of Arbitration that Chinese territorial claims in the region had no legal merit. The South China Sea crisis crystallized an American consensus that U.S.-China relations had become high-stakes competition. U.S.-China higher educational relations would henceforth be politicized. The studies of *liuxuesheng* in America and the U.S. research trips of Chinese fellows and faculty now struck many Americans as elements of a Chinese plan for global dominance that were every bit as nefarious as intellectual property theft and espionage.

The 2017 U.S. National Security Strategy identified China as the greatest long-term security threat to the United States and highlighted American universities as vectors for the loss of strategically vital knowledge to the PRC:

> Competitors such as China steal U.S. intellectual property valued at hundreds of billions of dollars. . . . We must defend our National Security Innovation Base (NSIB) against competitors. The NSIB is the American network of knowledge, capabilities, and people—including academia, National Laboratories, and the private sector—that turns ideas into innovations, transforms discoveries into successful commercial products and companies, and protects and enhances the American way of life. . . . Protecting the NSIB requires a domestic and international response beyond the scope of any individual company, industry, university, or government agency. . . . Technologies that are part of most weapon systems often originate in diverse businesses as well as in universities and colleges. . . . Part of China's military modernization and economic expansion is due to its access to the U.S. innovation economy, including America's world-class universities.[66]

On February 13, 2018, at a Senate Select Committee on Intelligence hearing, Senator Marco Rubio of Florida asked the director of the FBI, Christopher Wray, for his views on "the counterintelligence risk posed to U.S. national security from Chinese students, particularly those in advanced programs in the sciences and mathematics." Wray answered:

> The use of nontraditional collectors, especially in the academic setting, whether it's professors, scientists, students, we see in almost every field office that the FBI has around the country. It's not just in major cities. It's in small ones as well. It's across basically every discipline. And I think the level of naïveté on the part of the academic sector about this creates its own issues. They're exploiting the very open research and development environment that we have. . . . So one of the things we're trying to do is view the China threat as not just a whole-of-government threat but a whole-of-society threat on their end, and I think it's going to take a whole-of-society response by us.[67]

Wray didn't spell out what whole-of-society threat meant, but one possible interpretation was that any Chinese coming to the United States should be viewed as potential agents of a hostile power, and most Chinese who came to the United States for extended stays were students.

The policy response was swift. In a reversal of a 2014 policy that permitted Chinese students to renew their visas once every five years, the Trump administration ordered American embassies and consulates to shorten the period during which large numbers of Chinese students could stay in the United States on a single visa. After the directive was issued, Chinese students in STEM fields related to Made in China 2025 targets had to be reinterviewed for new visas annually, back in China, at considerable cost and inconvenience.[68]

In only a few years, the United States had gone from welcoming large numbers of Chinese students as national assets and symbols of American soft power to viewing them as dangerous foreign agents. The attitude seemed to go all the way to the top. *Politico* reported that, at a private dinner for corporate leaders on August 7, 2018, President Trump told his guests that "almost every [Chinese] student that comes over to this country is a spy."[69] At the time, the roughly 350,000 Chinese students in American universities composed 30 percent of all foreign students in the country. They added $12 billion to the U.S. economy annually and earned 10 percent of all PhDs.[70] But the number of Chinese students applying for first-time student visas to the United States had begun to decline. In 2018, worried that accusations against Chinese students and the general deterioration of U.S.-China relations could cause a drop in enrollments and tuitions from the PRC, the University of Illinois at Urbana-Champaign insured itself against such losses. Taking out the first such policy in history, the University of Illinois business and engineering schools paid a broker $424,000 annually for three years to insure against a year-on-year 20 percent decline in Chinese students due to a trade war, visa restrictions, or other causes. The policy would pay the university up to $60 million dollars to indemnify such losses—an amount based on the two colleges' exposure to Chinese tuitions.[71]

The threat described by Christopher Wray comprised not only students but also American scholars and researchers of Chinese origin. In a 2017 speech that evoked a tradition of patriotic scholarship that went back to the Chinese Educational Mission, Chinese premier Li Keqiang said, "it is the duty of all people of Chinese descent to help achieve the investment, technological development, and trade goals of the People's Republic of China."[72] Beijing had created over two hundred talent re-recruitment projects to attract scientific expertise to the PRC, but after Li's speech, it was the Thousand Talents Program, which had been around for nearly ten years, that got the attention of Congress and American security agencies. The program was legal, but many of the American faculty who participated in it during summer vacations and sabbaticals neglected to inform U.S. employers of their Chinese appointments. Unreported double-dipping of this kind often violated conflict-of-interest or other disclosure policies of American departments or colleges.

In the newly hostile dispensation, Congress and the FBI saw concurrent Chinese and U.S. academic appointments as potential channels for the transmission of American intellectual property to China. A 2018 report by U.S. intelligence services estimated that 2,629 scientists had been lured back to China from the United States through the Thousand Talents Program alone. China had long acquired U.S. intellectual property through scholar-spies and other methods, but the focus on talent re-recruitment programs was new.

In 2018, congressional pressure and FBI warnings began to have an impact on policy at universities and national laboratories. On August 23, the director of the National Institutes of Health (NIH), Francis Collins, issued a "Statement on Protecting the Integrity of U.S. Biomedical Research" as guidance to all institutes that received NIH funding. Although he did not single out China, Collins noted that "three areas of concern have emerged: 1) failure by some researchers at NIH-funded institutions to disclose substantial contributions of resources from other organizations, including foreign governments; 2) diversion of intellectual property in grant applications or produced by NIH-supported biomedical research to other entities, including other countries; and 3) Sharing of confidential information by peer reviewers with others, including in some instances with foreign entities." NIH would therefore "identify robust methods to . . . improve accurate reporting of all sources of research support, financial interests, and affiliations . . . [and] mitigate the risk to intellectual property security."[73] The U.S. Department of Energy, a longtime leader in scientific cooperation with China, took a similar step in June of 2019 when it banned employees from working with the Thousand Talents Program.

A wave of arrests, firings, and accusations followed. In April of 2019, the University of Texas MD Anderson Cancer Center fired one researcher from China, and two others quit, in response to concerns put forth by the NIH. According to the *New York Times*, "the researchers failed to disclose international collaborators and . . . at least one confidential grant application was sent to a scientist in China in violation of federal policy."[74] In May, two Emory University neuroscientists, Li Xiaojiang and Li Shihua, were fired for failing to disclose research funding from China. Emory administrators confirmed that NIH director Francis Collins's warning had sparked their concerns.[75] In August of 2019, a University of Kansas researcher, Franklin Tao, was arrested for failure to disclose that he had signed a contract as a full-time Changjiang Scholar at Fuzhou University. He was charged not with espionage, but with program fraud. Perhaps the most alarming case was that of Charles Lieber, chair of the Department of Chemistry and Chemical Biology at Harvard, who was arrested in January of 2020 and charged with making fraudulent statements in connection with his Thousand Talents activities at a university in central China.

These cases, and growing government warnings about CCP influence throughout the United States,[76] led to accusations that America was engaged in racist persecution of Chinese American academics, an issue that dated back at least to the false accusations made against the Los Alamos nuclear physicist Wen Ho Lee in 1999. In April of 2019, the Committee of 100, a group of influential Chinese Americans from a range of professions, condemned "the racial profiling that has become increasingly common in the United States where Chinese Americans are being targeted as potential traitors, spies, and agents of foreign influence." The committee's statement referenced the Justice Department's failed prosecutions of Sherry Chen, an innocent hydrologist at the National Weather Service whose story was profiled on *60 Minutes*, and Xiaoxing Xi, a Temple University expert in superconductivity who was falsely accused.[77]

A backlash against broad suspicion of Chinese and Chinese American scholars gathered steam throughout 2019. While the Association of American Universities, the Association of Public and Land-Grant Universities, and the American Council of Education held numerous conferences at which FBI representatives described their security concerns to university leaders, a growing list of university presidents issued statements defending openness as essential to the U.S. innovation system. The leaders of Columbia, Yale, the University of Maryland, Johns Hopkins, the University of Chicago, the University of Michigan, Stanford, and others all made clear that they were committed to upholding national security and protecting classified research but would not police faculty, monitor students, or impede the global advancement of knowledge. Rafael Reif, the president of MIT, wrote:

> MIT has flourished, like the United States itself, because it has been a magnet for the world's finest talent. . . . I feel compelled to share my dismay about some

circumstances painfully relevant to our fellow MIT community members of Chinese descent. . . . As the US and China have struggled with rising tensions, the US government has raised serious concerns about incidents of alleged academic espionage conducted by individuals through what is widely understood as a systematic effort of the Chinese government to acquire high-tech IP. . . . Looking at cases across the nation, small numbers of researchers of Chinese background may indeed have acted in bad faith, but they are the exception and very far from the rule. Yet faculty members, post-docs, research staff and students tell me that, in their dealings with government agencies, they now feel unfairly scrutinized, stigmatized and on edge. . . . Such actions and policies have turned the volume all the way up on the message that the US is closing the door—that we no longer seek to be a magnet for the world's most driven and creative individuals.[78]

These arguments seemed to have an impact before COVID-19 and the 2020 presidential campaign threw U.S.-China relations into a free fall. In a June 2019 speech to the Education USA Forum, Assistant Secretary of State for Educational and Cultural Affairs Marie Royce declared that "the United States welcomes Chinese students" and revealed that "in 2019, only one ten thousandth of a percent . . . of student visa applicants from China have been refused" due to "the theft of intellectual property."[79] During an October 2019 press conference, President Trump remarked: "We're going to be very good to Chinese students. . . . We have the greatest university system in the world . . . and one of the reasons it's great is we have a lot of students from China. . . . They occupy a big space in our universities, and we want to keep it that way."[80]

It is tempting to read the Royce and Trump statements as a sign that, after the panic of 2017 and 2018, a balance might be struck between protecting American security and preserving academic openness. However, such hopes are premature. The U.S. government has yet to articulate a workable approach to U.S.-China higher educational relations in the era of rivalry. On November 18, 2019, a staff report titled "Threats to the U.S. Research Enterprise: China's Talent Recruitment Plans," released by the Senate Permanent Subcommittee on Investigations, offered a sober and sobering survey of China's efforts to obtain American intellectual property through cooperation with U.S. scholars. The report acknowledged that the global innovation system depends on the publication of research findings and on open universities, but also asked an essential question: Can the virtues of such a system be upheld when China uses its research to strengthen autocracy domestically and spread illiberal practices worldwide? The report concluded that the FBI, NIH, Department of Energy, and National Science Foundation had responded inadequately to Chinese talent re-recruitment programs and that "these failures continue to undermine the integrity of the American research enterprise and endanger our national security."[81] One month later, the National Defense Authorization Act (NDAA) of 2019 called on the White House Office of Science and Technology Policy and the National Academies of Science, Engineering, and Medicine to develop recommendations on how to preserve the openness and international character of American universities while protecting research with strong national security implications. The NDAA enjoyed strong support from the Association of American Universities and other national higher educational organizations.

From 1854 to 2016, higher educational relations between the United States and China were a tacit bargain through which China gained technical expertise and the United States gained talent. The deal worked for both sides despite mutual concerns about espionage and unwelcome influence. Now that the two nations are rivals and the balance of power is shifting toward China, the United States is asking whether the old arrangement still serves its interests.

It is a necessary question. During the Cold War, not even the most internationally minded American thought the United States should train Soviet scientists in nuclear physics. It is fair to ask whether the United States should provide Chinese scholars with advanced training in aeronautics now that the rivals are developing hypersonic weapons for possible use against each other.

U.S. policy makers face a paradox: America's greatest asset in its competition with China is its innovation system, but innovation depends on an open higher education system that would suffer without Chinese inputs. What risks and compromises are acceptable under these conditions? Can America safeguard its innovation system without telling Chinese scholars—arguably the world's biggest talent pool—that they are a despised class in the United States?

The American higher education system has supported China's modernization drive since the nineteenth century. It has supported China's reform and openness policies since 1979. Both epochal efforts were seen as essential to the well-being of the Chinese people and China's integration into global systems. America's cooperation with China toward these ends was seen as a humanitarian effort as well as a commercial opportunity. But modernization, reform, and openness are now properly understood as instrumental to the development of China's comprehensive national power. American interactions with China, including educational interactions, must be reevaluated based on sober judgement about the implications of Chinese power for American interests.

In 2015, David Lampton wrote that "the tipping point is near. The respective fears of Washington and Beijing are closer to outweighing hopes than at any time since normalization and, should this point be reached, impulses to threaten will gain ascendancy over impulses to cooperate."[82] That point has been reached. The fear Lampton warned of is compounded by fragility in China and chaos in the United States that cause both nations to overreact even to well-founded concerns.

The danger to higher education is acute. While campuses must raise their awareness of threats emanating from China, the list of demonstrable harms done to American security through higher educational cooperation with China is extremely short. Furthermore, those harms have not been weighed against the tremendous benefit—in every academic discipline, every profession, and every facet of our national life—that the United States has gained from the inflow of Chinese talent since the nineteenth century.

We are moving too fast. Careless assessments of strategic necessity are driving the United States and China toward a human tragedy. The citizens of the superpowers may be alienated from each other for decades. If that is allowed to happen, the global academic enterprise will be crippled, although that may not be the worst of our problems.

NOTES

1. For more on Yung Wing, see Ruthanne Lum McCunn, *Chinese American Portraits, 1828-1928* (San Francisco, CA: Chronicle, 1988); and Liel Leibovitz and Matthew I. Miller, *Fortunate Sons: The 120 Chinese Boys Who Came to America, Went to School, and Revolutionized an Ancient Civilization* (New York: Norton, 2012).

2. Edmund J. James, "The Sending of an Educational Mission to China," *School Journal* (March 31, 1906): 315.

3. Richard H. Werking, "The Boxer Indemnity Remission and the Hunt Thesis," *Diplomatic History* 2, no. 1 (January 1, 1978): 103–6, https://doi.org/10.1111/j.1467-7709.1978.tb00424.x.

4. Weili Ye, *Seeking Modernity in China's Name: Chinese Students in the United States* (Stanford, CA: Stanford University Press, 2001).

5. Weili Ye, "'Nü Liuxuesheng': The Story of American-Educated Chinese Women, 1880s-1920s," *Modern China* 20, no. 3 (1994): 315–46.

6. *Jiaoyu Zazhi* [Magazine on Education] 6 (1910): 50.

7. Yelong Han, "An Untold Story: American Policy Toward Chinese Students in the United States, 1949–1955," *Journal of American-East Asian Relations* 2, no. 1 (1993): 77–99.

8. Jessie Gregory Lutz, *China and the Christian Colleges, 1850–1950* (Ithaca, NY: Cornell University Press, 1971), 3.

9. Mary Brown Bullock, *An American Transplant: The Rockefeller Foundation and Peking Union Medical College* (Berkeley: University of California Press, 1980), 5.

10. John P. Hardt, "Summary," in *China Under the Four Modernizations. Part 1, Selected Papers Submitted to the Joint Economic Committee, Congress of the United States* (Washington, DC: U.S. Government Printing Office, August 13, 1982), 1–3.

11. Henry S. Reuss, "Forward," in *China Under the Four Modernizations, Selected Papers Submitted to the Joint Economic Committee, Congress of the United States* (Washington, DC: U.S. Government Printing Office, August 13, 1982), v–vi.

12. Reuss, "Forward."

13. U.S. Department of State, "Michael R. Pompeo Interview with Laura Ingraham of *The Laura Ingraham Show*," October 31, 2018, https://www.state.gov/interview-with-laura-ingraham-of-the-laura-ingraham-show/.

14. As quoted in Robert Lenzner, "The China Hand," *Forbes*, October 31, 2005, https://www.forbes.com/forbes/2005/1031/079.html?sh=2321ca6d2112.

15. George J. Church, "China: Old Wounds Deng Xiaoping," *Time*, January 6, 1986, 9.

16. Quoted in Cheng Li, "Introduction," in *Bridging Minds Across the Pacific: U.S.-China Educational Exchanges, 1978–2003*, ed. Cheng Li (Lanham, MD: Lexington, 2003), 3.

17. David M. Lampton, Joyce A. Madancy, and Kristen M. Williams, *A Relationship Restored: Trends in U.S.-China Educational Exchanges, 1978–1984* (Washington, DC: National Academy Press, 1986), 1.

18. Barbara J. Culliton, "China's 'Four Modernizations' Lead to Closer Sino-U.S. Science Ties," *Science* 201, no. 4355 (August 11, 1978): 512–13.

19. Culliton, "China's 'Four Modernizations.' "

20. Leo Orleans, *Chinese Students in America: Policies, Issues, and Numbers* (Washington, DC: National Academy Press, 1988), 88.

21. Lampton, Madancy, and Williams, *A Relationship Restored*, 37

22. Orleans, *Chinese Students in America*.

23. Seth Faison, "Condolence Calls Put Rare Light on Deng's Family," *New York Times*, February 22, 1997, https://www.nytimes.com/1997/02/22/world/condolence-calls-put -rare-light-on-deng-s-family.html.

24. Robert Strauss, "China Party Chief's Son Keeps Low Profile at a U.S. School," *New York Times*, July 2, 1989, https://www.nytimes.com/1989/07/02/world/china-party-chief-s-son -keeps-low-profile-at-a-us-school.html.

25. Cheng Li, "Coming Home to Teach," in *Bridging Minds Across the Pacific: U.S.-China Educational Exchanges, 1978–2003*, ed. Cheng Li (Lanham, MD: Lexington, 2003), 79.

26. Christopher Wren, "China Is Said to End a Campaign to Stop Spiritual Pollution," *New York Times*, January 24, 1984, https://www.nytimes.com/1984/01/24/world/china-is-said -to-end-a-campaign-to-stop-spiritual-pollution.html.

27. Julia Kwong, "The 1986 Student Demonstrations in China: A Democratic Movement?" *Asian Survey* 28, no. 9 (1988): 970–85, www.jstor.org/stable/2644802.

28. Kwong, "The 1986 Student Demonstrations," 973.

29. Alexander V. Pantsov and Steven I. Levine, *Deng Xiaoping: A Revolutionary Life* (Oxford: Oxford University Press, 2015), 401–2.

30. Nick Ravo, "Chinese Students Defend Open Letter," *New York Times*, January 26, 1987, https://www.nytimes.com/1987/01/26/world/chinese-students-defend-open-letter .html.

31. James Fallows, "Be Nice to the Countries That Lend You Money," *Atlantic*, December 2008, https://www.theatlantic.com/magazine/archive/2008/12/be-nice-to-the-countries-that -lend-you-money/307148/.

32. Linda A. Reed, *Education in the People's Republic of China and U.S.-China Educational Exchanges* (Washington, DC: National Association for Foreign Student Affairs, 1988), 100.

33. Lampton, Madancy, and Williams, *A Relationship Restored*, 53.

34. Raisa Belyavina, *U.S. Students in China: Meeting the Goals of the 100,000 Strong Initiative* (Washington, DC: Institute of International Education, January 2013), 20.

35. Lampton, Madancy, and Williams, *A Relationship Restored*, 244–46.

36. Mark Lenhart, "Building Chinese Language Programs in China: CET's Experience," in *The Field of Chinese Language Education in the U.S.*, ed. Vivian Ling (Lanham, MD: Routledge, 2018); and per e-mail correspondence with the author.

37. Ramon H. Myers and Thomas A. Metzger, "Sinological Shadows: The State of Modern China Studies in the U.S.," *Australian Journal of Chinese Affairs* 4 (July 1980): 1–34.

38. Mary Brown Bullock, "Mission Accomplished: The Influence of the CSCPRC on Education Relations with China," in *Bridging Minds Across the Pacific: U.S.-China Educational Exchanges, 1978–2003*, ed. Cheng Li (Lanham, MD: Lexington, 2003), 49–68.

39. Bullock, "Mission Accomplished," 53.

40. Bullock, 59.

41. Ronald Reagan, "Remarks at Fudan University in Shanghai, China," American Presidency Project, April 30, 1984, https://www.presidency.ucsb.edu/node/260718.

42. Kenneth J. Cooper, "Bush to Veto Bill Prolonging Students' Stays," *New York Times*, December 1, 1989.

43. "President Clinton's Beijing University Speech," BBC News, June 29, 1998, http://news.bbc.co.uk/2/hi/asia-pacific/122320.stm.

44. Quoted in Zheng Wang, "National Humiliation, History Education, and the Politics of Historical Memory: Patriotic Education Campaign in China," *International Studies Quarterly* 52, no. 4 (December 2008): 788.

45. Wang, "National Humiliation," 792.

46. Li Heng, "Growth of Chinese Students in the US Slows Down: Report," Chicago Consulate of the People's Republic of China, June 11, 2003, http://www.chinaconsulatechicago.org/eng/ywzn/jy/t40302.htm.

47. Compiled by Cheng Li for *Bridging Minds*, 78.

48. Katherine Stapleton, "Inside the World's Largest Higher Education Boom," *Conversation*, April 10, 2017, http://theconversation.com/inside-the-worlds-largest-higher-education-boom-74789.

49. Xiaoyan Wang and Jian Liu, "China's Higher Education Expansion and the Task of Economic Revitalization," *Higher Education* 62, no. 2 (August 2011): 213–29.

50. Stapleton, "World's Largest Higher Education Boom."

51. See, for example, his famous TED Talk: TED, "Eric X. Li: A Tale of Two Political Systems," July 1, 2013, video, https://www.youtube.com/watch?v=s0YjL9rZyRo.

52. See Ash Center for Democratic Governance and Innovation, "China Programs: Teaching," https://ash.harvard.edu/china-programs-executive-education.

53. William J. Dobson, "The East Is Crimson: Why Is Harvard Training the Next Generation of Chinese Communist Party Leaders?" *Slate*, May 23, 2012, http://www.slate.com/articles/news_and_politics/foreigners/2012/05/harvard_and_the_chinese_communist_party_top_chinese_officials_are_studying_at_elite_u_s_universities_in_large_numbers_.html.

54. See University of Maryland, Office of China Affairs, https://globalmaryland.umd.edu/offices/china.

55. Dennis Looney and Natalia Lusin, "Enrollments in Languages Other Than English in United States Institutions of Higher Education, Summer 2016 and Fall 2016: Preliminary Report," Modern Language Association, February 2018, https://www.mla.org/content/download/83540/2197676/2016-Enrollments-Short-Report.pdf.

56. Fei-ling Wang, "Balancing the Cross-Pacific Exchange," in *Bridging Minds Across the Pacific: U.S.-China Educational Exchanges, 1978–2003*, ed. Cheng Li (Lanham, MD: Lexington, 2003), 180.

57. Anne F. Thurston, Karen Turner-Gottschang, and Linda A. Reed, *China Bound: A Guide to Academic Life and Work in the PRC*, rev. ed. (Washington, DC: National Academy Press, 1994).

58. James McGregor, *China's Drive for "Indigenous Innovation": A Web of Industrial Policies, Global Regulatory Cooperation Project* (Washington, DC: U.S. Chamber of Commerce, July 28, 2010), 11.

59. Institute of International Education, "2017 Open Doors: Report on International Educational Exchange, China Fact Sheet," https://p.widencdn.net/ymtzur/Open-Doors-2017-Country-Sheets-China.

60. ICEF Monitor, "Chinese Enrolment in the US Shifting Increasingly to Undergraduate Studies," May 27, 2015, https://monitor.icef.com/2015/05/chinese-enrolment-in-the-us-shifting-increasingly-to-undergraduate-studies/.

61. See http://onsnetwork.org/uschineseundergrads/, quoting Institute of International Education Open Doors data.

62. David Zweig and Huiyao Wang, "Can China Bring Back the Best? The Communist Party Organizes China's Search for Talent," *China Quarterly* 215 (September 2003): 590–615.

63. Ministry of Education of the People's Republic of China, "List of China-Foreign Joint Higher Educational Programs," 2012, http://.crs.jsj.edu.cn/index.php/defaultindex/sort/1006.

64. NYU Shanghai, "Testimony of Jeffrey S. Lehman, Vice Chancellor of NYU Shanghai," June 25, 2015, https://shanghai.nyu.edu/sites/default/files/media/2015-6-25%20JSL%20Testimony%20Final.pdf.

65. Steve Inskeep, "Pushing for Academic Freedom in China," NPR, June 3, 2019, https://www.npr.org/2019/06/03/729191914/-a-foot-in-both-worlds-pushing-for-academic-freedom-in-China.

66. Donald J. Trump, *National Security Strategy of the United States of America* (Washington, DC: The White House, December 2017), https://www.whitehouse.gov/wp-content/uploads/2017/12/NSS-Final-12-18-2017-0905-2.pdf.

67. Elizabeth Redden, "The Chinese Student Threat?" Inside Higher Ed, February 15, 2018, https://www.insidehighered.com/news/2018/02/15/fbi-director-testifies-chinese-students-and-intelligence-threats.

68. Josh Lederman and Ted Bridis, "AP Sources: US to Impose Limits on Some Chinese visas," Associated Press, May 29, 2018, https://apnews.com/82a98fecee074bfb8373176obfbce515/AP-sources:-US-to-impose-limits-on-some-Chinese-visas.

69. Annie Karni, "Trump Rants Behind Closed Doors with CEOs," *Politico*, August 8, 2018, https://www.politico.com/story/2018/08/08/trump-executive-dinner-bedminster-china-766609.

70. Elizabeth Redden, "Did Trump Call Most Chinese Students Spies?" Inside Higher Ed, August 9, 2018, https://www.insidehighered.com/news/2018/08/09/politico-reports-trump-called-most-chinese-students-us-spies.

71. An insurance policy that seemed extreme in 2018 would seem essential to many universities in 2020 after the COVID-19 pandemic and a series of Chinese and American actions caused the bilateral relationship to deteriorate on every front. As of September 2020, it seemed possible that the bottom had fallen out of U.S.-China academic relations.

72. Jamil Anderlini, "The Dark Side of China's National Renewal," *Financial Times*, June 21 2017, https://www.ft.com/content/36oafba4-55d1-11e7-9fed-c19e2700005f.

73. National Institutes of Health, "Statement on Protecting the Integrity of U.S. Biomedical Research," August 23, 2018, https://www.nih.gov/about-nih/who-we-are/nih-director/statements/statement-protecting-integrity-us-biomedical-research.

74. Mihir Zaveri, "Wary of Chinese Espionage, Houston Cancer Center Chose to Fire 3 Scientists," *New York Times*, April 22, 2019, https://www.nytimes.com/2019/04/22/health/md-anderson-chinese-scientists.html.

75. Tara Law, "Emory University Fires 2 Neuroscientists Accused of Hiding Chinese Ties," *Time*, May 25, 2019, https://time.com/5596066/emory-fires-chinese-researchers.

76. See Larry Diamond, "China's Influence and American Interests: Promoting Constructive Vigilance," Hoover Institution, November 29, 2018, https://www.hoover.org/research/chinas-influence-american-interests-promoting-constructive-vigilance.

77. Committee of 100, "Committee of 100 Condemns Chinese American Racial Profiling," April 7, 2019, https://www.committee100.org/press_release/committee-of-100 -condemns-chinese-american-racial-profiling-2/.

78. MIT News Office, "Letter to the MIT Community: Immigration Is a Kind of Oxygen," June 25, 2019, http://news.mit.edu/2019/letter-community-immigration-is-oxygen-0625.

79. Bureau of Educational and Cultural Affairs, "Assistant Secretary Royce Remarks at the EdUSA Forum," July 30, 2019, https://eca.state.gov/highlight/assistant-secretary -royce-remarks-edusa-forum.

80. White House, "Remarks by President Trump and Vice Premier Liu He of the People's Republic of China in a Meeting," October 11, 2019, https://www.whitehouse.gov /briefings-statements/remarks-president-trump-vice-premier-liu-peoples-republic-china -meeting/.

81. U.S. Senate Permanent Subcommittee on Investigations, "Threats to the U.S. Research Enterprise: China's Talent Recruitment Plans," November 18, 2019, https://www.hsgac .senate.gov/imo/media/doc/2019-11-18%20PSI%20Staff%20Report%20-%20China's %20Talent%20Recruitment%20Plans%20Updated2.pdf.

82. David M. Lampton, "The Tipping Point: Can We Amplify What We Have in Common?" Center for International Relations and Sustainable Development, https://www .cirsd.org/en/horizons/horizons-summer-2015--issue-no4/the-tipping-point---can -we-amplify-what-we-have-in-common-.

PART IV

FAULT LINES, THREATS TO PEACE,
AND REFLECTIONS ON
THE FUTURE

CHAPTER 11

U.S.-CHINA MILITARY RELATIONS

From Enmity to Entente and Maybe Back Again

CHAS W. FREEMAN JR.

The history of American military interactions with China is both longer and more complex than many realize. The United States first projected military power to China and the Asia-Pacific in 1835, when President Andrew Jackson established an East India Squadron. This naval leap across the Pacific was a manifestation of an emerging sense of entitlement to a special role in world affairs consistent with Manifest Destiny, which posited America's God-given duty to remake the world in its image. The stated purpose of the squadron was to protect American citizens and their commercial interests in and around China, then the world's largest economy. Since then, Americans have sustained a continuous coercive military presence either in China or along its coasts, with only a brief reduction in force levels during the American Civil War of 1861–1865.

The United States was not a formal participant in the first and second Anglo-Chinese Opium Wars of 1839–1842 and 1856–1860. Nevertheless, the presence of the East India Squadron in Chinese waters enabled Americans to piggyback on British victories. Washington was able to gain the same concessions from the Chinese that the victorious British had, including extraterritorial rights in the five treaty ports.

The U.S. Navy and Marines in China

In July 1853, Commodore Matthew C. Perry, aboard the frigate USS *Susquehanna*, forced Japan to open its ports to American merchant vessels and traders.

Later, the *Susquehanna* steamed up the Yangtze River in China. This incursion inaugurated a regular Yangtze River Patrol that roamed up to fifteen hundred miles into the Chinese interior and was later incorporated in the U.S. Asiatic Fleet. Among its missions was upholding the U.S. Open Door policy in China. In August 1900, the U.S. Army's Fifteenth Infantry Regiment deployed to North China, where it took significant casualties in skirmishes with the remnants of the Boxers.

By the turn of the twentieth century, the China station was perhaps the most sought-after assignment in the U.S. Navy (and Marine Corps). Americans were above the law in China, and most hedonistic pleasures were readily and cheaply available. The often-cordial diplomatic relationship between the American and Chinese authorities contrasted with frequently violent anti-American protests and skirmishes with U.S. sailors and marines. U.S. naval patrols of the Yangtze continued until 1941, when Japan (which was then determinedly conquering China) put an end to them.

Few Americans have any memories of this history other than those derived from the 1966 film, *The Sand Pebbles*. But for Chinese, the American role as a fellow traveler of European imperialism in China is somewhere near the center of the Century of National Humiliation they suffered at the hands of foreign invaders. Neither the Republic of China (ROC) nor its successor in power on the Chinese mainland ever shared the common American view that U.S. involvement in China was disinterested or altruistic. Most in the United States viewed their country's enforcement of an Open Door policy in China with paternalistic pride, as having protected China against subdivision by imperialism. In contrast, most Chinese saw this as a successful effort by Americans to help themselves to whatever concessions and privileges other imperialists had bullied China into conceding.

Close Encounters with the Chinese Communist Party

Chinese ambivalence was not significantly altered either by U.S. support of the ROC during the last three years of its fourteen-year on-again, off-again war with invading forces from the Japanese Empire or by Washington's postwar aid in its effort to suppress the Chinese Communist Party (CCP). As the long civil war was coming to an end, CCP chairman Mao Zedong declared that with the establishment of the People's Republic of China (PRC), an opprobrious phase of history had ended and "the Chinese people [had] stood up."[1] There is every reason to believe that he had the U.S. role in the foreign subjugation of China very much in mind.

CCP hostility toward the United States had been stoked by vigorous, if not always acknowledged, American intelligence, military, economic, and political alignment and support for the CCP's Nationalist Party (or Kuomintang [KMT]) rival in the Chinese Civil War. Chiang Kai-shek's ROC, the ROC Army, and the Leninist Nationalist Party had been American entente partners (though mis-portrayed as allies) in World War II. As the CCP's military arm, the People's Liberation Army (PLA), vanquished the ROC Army and imposed CCP control in China. The PLA was at best unfriendly and at worst actively hostile to U.S. interests in China. Confrontations like the thirteen-month-long PLA siege of the American consulate general in Shenyang, the capital of present-day Liaoning Province, which began on November 20, 1948,[2] added to each side's sense of grievance.

The CCP Defeats the KMT

In December 1949, with logistical assistance from the United States, Chiang Kai-shek retreated to Taiwan, an island province of China annexed by Japan in 1895 and liberated from it in 1945. His retreat reduced him to the status of a warlord, albeit one with aspirations to re-conquer the entire country. The response of the United States to the CCP's victory in the Chinese Civil War was to withdraw completely from the Chinese mainland, wait to let the dust settle, and decline both to recognize the PRC and to break relations with the ROC.

After a review by the U.S. Joint Chiefs of Staff of the strategic significance of Taiwan that disparaged its importance, President Harry S. Truman announced on January 5, 1950, that the United States would not intervene to prevent Taiwan's conquest by the PLA.[3]

War in Korea

Washington's official posture of indifference to the fate of Taiwan and the U.S. policy of nonintervention in the Chinese Civil War both ended abruptly on June 25, 1950, when crack troops of the (North) Korean People's Army (KPA) charged over the thirty-eighth parallel dividing line between the Soviet-managed north and the U.S.-managed south in Korea. The North Koreans' objective was to unify their country by force. In the lead were battle-hardened Korean ethnic divisions of the PLA that had been repatriated to Korea after the CCP victory in the Chinese Civil War.

The United States perceived North Korea's attack not as an attempt by Koreans to restore the unity of their country but as a strategically inspired effort by the Sino-Soviet bloc to break out of U.S.-imposed containment. President Truman immediately ordered U.S. troops to assist in the defense of South Korea (the Republic of Korea [ROK]) against the North (the Democratic People's

Republic of Korea [DPRK]). On June 27, 1950, he directed the Seventh Fleet (the descendant of MacArthur's World War II naval strike force[4]) to prevent a wider communist breakout by imposing a suspension of the Chinese Civil War in the Taiwan Strait.[5] To accomplish this, he committed the United States to counter any PLA offensive against Taiwan, while demanding that Chiang Kai-shek cease all air and sea operations against the Chinese mainland.

The ROK defense against the DPRK did not go well. Seoul fell to the KPA on June 28. The United States sent troops from the U.S. occupation forces in Japan to help the ROK hold against the North Korean advance. The KPA decisively defeated these forces, inflicting crippling casualties. By August, ROK and U.S. forces were pinned down and fighting with their backs to the sea in a small area around Busan,[6] a port city on the southeast coast of the Korean Peninsula, apparently about to be overrun. But on September 15, U.S. and ROK Marines (followed closely by the U.S. Army's Seventh Infantry Division) made a brilliantly executed surprise landing far behind KPA lines at the coastal city of Incheon, near Seoul, just south of the thirty-eighth parallel.[7] The PRC warned that it would intervene if ROK and U.S. forces went on to cross that line and invade the DPRK. Neither General MacArthur nor Washington took Beijing's warnings seriously.

U.S. Combat with China

On October 7, 1950, ROK and continuously augmented U.S. forces began a rapid drive north of the thirty-eighth parallel, taking Pyongyang, the DPRK capital, on October 19. The same day, the first elements of a hastily formed, 270,000-man-strong Chinese People's Volunteer Army (CPVA) began crossing the Yalu River into Korea. On October 25, this force ambushed the advancing ROK and U.S. forces, achieving total surprise and inflicting significant casualties.

By November 25, the CPVA had established a sufficient presence in Korea to be able to launch an attack across the entire front. In the west, at the Battle of the Ch'ŏngch'ŏn River (清川江战役), it forced the U.S. Eighth Army into the longest retreat of any American unit in history. In the east, the seventeen-day-long Battle of Chosin Reservoir (长津湖战役) is remembered by both American and Chinese veterans as the most savage warfare they ever experienced. Despite appalling Chinese casualties, the battle boosted the pride of the newly established PRC. It had fielded the first Chinese army to succeed against a Western force since the First Opium War, more than a century before. For their part, the U.S. Marines consider the fighting retreat they were forced to conduct from the Chosin Reservoir to be a defining moment in the history of their corps.

Chinese and North Korean and U.S. and South Korean counteroffensives seesawed back and forth until, by the summer of 1951, the two sides reached a stalemate more or less along the thirty-eighth parallel—the original dividing line of the U.S. and Soviet spheres of influence on the peninsula.

Following a proposal by India and tedious negotiations amid ongoing warfare, the United States, KPA, and CPVA signed an armistice on July 27, 1953. The ROK Army did not sign, but the fighting ended, and the contending forces established a demilitarized zone (DMZ).

China withdrew the CPVA from the DPRK in 1958. The United States still garrisons the ROK. There has been no peace to replace the armistice.[8] The combatants are technically still in a state of war.

Ostracism, Containment, and Taiwan

The inauspicious battlefield introduction between the U.S. armed forces and the PLA quickly gelled into a relationship of active enmity. In the two decades that followed the truce in Korea, the U.S. and PRC armed forces had no contact besides unpleasantly contentious meetings of the Korean Military Armistice Commission in the DMZ at Panmunjom. Elsewhere, the two were engaged in overt or covert proxy battles in the continuing Chinese Civil War in the Taiwan Strait and on the borders of Tibet and Yunnan Province, as well as in support of the contending Vietnamese, Lao, and Cambodian forces in Indochina.

On May 1, 1951, as the Korean conflict slogged lethally on, a U.S. Military Assistance Advisory Group (MAAG) headed by a major general was assigned to the rump ROC on Taiwan. Its mission was to provide arms and military advice, to assist with training of the ROC Army, and later to implement a U.S.-ROC Mutual Defense Treaty. Concluded on December 2, 1954, the U.S.-ROC treaty was one of a series of treaties directed at containing the Sino-Soviet bloc. The ROC government in Taipei, with full U.S. support, continued to represent all of China in the United Nations and other international organizations. The United States imposed a total embargo on diplomatic and economic intercourse with the PRC, which controlled all of China other than Taiwan and a few islands in Zhejiang, Fujian, and Guangdong Provinces.

In February 1953, shortly after his inauguration, President Dwight D. Eisenhower bowed to anticommunist, pro-KMT sentiment in Congress and declared that the Seventh Fleet would no longer prevent Chiang Kai-shek from attempting a re-conquest of the China mainland. In August 1954, the ROC deployed seventy-three thousand troops to two strategically located islands across the Taiwan Strait in Fujian. Jinmen (Quemoy or Kinmen in English) blocks access to the mainland port city of Xiamen (Amoy). Mazu (Matsu) blocks the approaches to the provincial capital of Fuzhou. The PRC countered in September by shelling ROC installations on both Jinmen and Mazu and declaring that Taiwan must be liberated.

Washington responded by agreeing to conclude a mutual defense treaty with the ROC, which was signed on December 4, 1954. The United States warned that it was considering using nuclear weapons to defeat any PLA assault on Jinmen or Mazu.[9] The response of the CCP Politburo was to make the development of Chinese nuclear weapons a national priority.[10]

Thereafter, operational U.S. combat forces operating alongside the MAAG in Taipei were directed by a newly established U.S. Taiwan Defense Command (USTDC). USTDC reported directly to the commander in chief of the Pacific Command in Hawaii. By 1957, there were reportedly ten thousand official Americans present in Taiwan.

In 1958, despite the fact that Jinmen and Mazu were outside the scope of the mutual defense treaty, the United States responded to intense PLA shelling of these offshore islands by resupplying the ROC garrisons there. The United States equipped the ROC Air Force (ROCAF) with F-86 Sabre jets and Sidewinder missiles. The CIA helped the ROCAF fly frequent reconnaissance missions over the China mainland. The offshore island crisis became a major topic of debate in the 1960 presidential elections.

Eventually, the PRC and ROC came to a tacit arrangement in which they shelled each other's forces on alternate days.[11] This symbolic combat continued for twenty years until the PRC and the United States normalized relations and Beijing extended an olive branch to Taipei.

Entente Suddenly Replaces Enmity

Beginning in March 1969, China and the Soviet Union began a seven-month-long undeclared war along several sections of their enormously long border. On August 14 of that year, President Richard M. Nixon startled attendees at a meeting of his National Security Council (NSC) by declaring that the United States could not allow China to be smashed. By 1971, when Beijing displaced Taipei as the sole legal representative of (all of) China in the United Nations, Nixon had begun to convert U.S. policy from using Taiwan to contain the PRC to using the PRC to contain the Soviet Union. As part of this realignment, the United States facilitated China's purchase of technology for the Rolls-Royce Spey engine from Britain and, very likely, the propulsion plant for its initial Han class nuclear submarines from France as well.

In February 1972, Nixon visited the PRC, establishing de facto but not de jure relations. The Shanghai Communiqué was issued on February 28, 1972.[12] Nixon had expected to transfer diplomatic recognition from Taipei to Beijing during his second term as president but was forced from office in August

1974. His successor, Gerald R. Ford, lacked the political clout to accomplish the promised normalization. Ford's successor, James Earl (Jimmy) Carter Jr., who took office on January 20, 1977, accomplished the task.

On December 15, 1978, President Carter issued a joint communiqué that transferred Washington's previous recognition of the ROC as the sole legal government of China to the PRC, effective January 1, 1979.[13] The United States broke relations with Taipei, announced the withdrawal of all U.S. military forces and installations from Taiwan, and gave the one-year notice necessary to terminate the U.S.-ROC Mutual Defense Treaty in accordance with its terms.[14] In April 1979, American relationships with Taipei were put on a nominally unofficial basis, and both the MAAG and the USTDC were officially disbanded. Beijing responded to Washington's normalization of relations by setting aside its bellicose rhetoric toward Taiwan.[15] In its place, the CCP launched an effort to achieve the peaceful reunification of Taiwan with the mainland through economic integration, cultural rapprochement, and negotiation.[16]

To maintain the full range of cultural, commercial, and other unofficial relations with the people of Taiwan that the normalization communiqué permitted, the Carter administration submitted draft legislation to Congress, called the Taiwan Relations Act (TRA). Both houses of Congress accepted the body of the draft more or less without change but added a preamble declaring that U.S. policy was to make "available to Taiwan such defense articles and defense services in such quantity as may be necessary to enable Taiwan to maintain a sufficient self-defense capability." The TRA became law on April 10, 1979.[17] China's paramount leader, Deng Xiaoping, is reliably said to have seriously considered breaking relations with the United States over this amendment of the TRA. In the end, however, he accepted assurances from President Carter that the law would be administered in such a way as to be consistent with U.S. commitments to the PRC in the normalization communiqué.

Overt Defense Cooperation Unexpectedly Begins

With the establishment of diplomatic relations, embassies replaced the liaison offices the two countries had established in each other's capitals in 1973. By August of 1979, the U.S. embassy's marine guard detachment was in uniform.[18] The opening of the U.S. Defense Attaché Office (DAO) at the embassy added military-to-military relations to the diplomatic dialogue, trade, and people-to-people exchanges the two sides had authorized in the Shanghai Communiqué.[19]

Interaction between the two militaries was initially formal and standoffish rather than substantive. (Part of the reason was that the U.S.-ROC Mutual Defense Treaty was still in force.) But as the year ended, the Soviet Union unexpectedly mounted a blatant challenge to the security interests of both countries by invading Afghanistan.

The U.S. response to this invasion was an urgent visit to Beijing by Secretary of Defense Harold Brown to consult with the PLA. The visit, from January 5 to 11, 1980, was the first to the PRC by a secretary of defense. In remarks at his January 6 welcoming banquet in Beijing, Brown declared that the Soviet invasion of Afghanistan, on Christmas Eve 1979, had created circumstances in which "increased cooperation between China and the United States can be an important—and is a needed—element in the maintenance of global tranquility. . . . [Such] cooperation . . . should remind others that if they threaten the shared interests of the United States and China, we can respond with complementary actions in the field of defense as well as diplomacy."[20]

Brown's discussions with his Chinese counterparts formalized various aspects of U.S.-China defense cooperation, including defense dialogue; the transfer of U.S. dual-use technology, but not weapons, to the PLA[21]; and joint signals intelligence operations against Soviet forces and their missile development programs.[22] The latter replaced and augmented the capabilities of listening posts lost by the United States in January 1979, when the Islamic revolution in Iran overthrew the government of Shah Mohammed Reza Pahlavi. After Secretary Brown left Beijing, he quietly visited unidentified PLA units in the Xinjiang Autonomous Region in China's far west and Liaoning Province in the far northeast. These were areas of China adjacent, respectively, to Soviet weapons test ranges in central Asia and to Vladivostok, the headquarters of the Soviet Pacific Fleet, then commanding about one-third of Moscow's naval assets.

Shortly thereafter, the United States eased export controls for the sale to China of thirty types of nonlethal military support equipment, including advanced communications systems, trucks, helicopters, transport aircraft, and early warning radar.[23] When presented with this list, one of the deputy chiefs of the PLA, General Xu Xin (徐信), a hard-bitten soldier who had been wounded by U.S. forces in the Korean War[24] (and who was then in charge of foreign affairs and intelligence), wryly exclaimed, "Oh, I get it. You want us to be able to see the Soviets coming and then to be able to run away." The Chinese pressed for authorization to purchase lethal equipment.

In late May and early June 1980, Secretary Brown hosted a return visit to the United States by Vice-Premier Geng Biao (耿飚), accompanied by Liu Huaqing (刘华清), a deputy chief of the General Staff, whose focus was defense modernization. Liu became the visionary commander (some would say the father) of the PLA Navy (PLAN).

The delegation also included PLA Air Force (PLAAF) general Wang Hai (王海), the commander of the Guangzhou Military Region Air Force. Wang was a Korean War ace who had both shot down and been shot down by an American ace, General Charles A. Gabriel, then U.S. Air Force (USAF) chief of staff and the first fighter pilot to hold that position. Over dinner at the Pentagon, Generals Wang and Gabriel conducted an animated and increasingly warm exploration of their shared history. The two men eventually exchanged camera footage of each shooting down the other and came to consider each other friends, as former combatants often do.

In September 1980, after considerable internal debate in which U.S. Soviet specialists counseled against closer relations with China lest they trigger a Soviet overreaction, William Perry, the under secretary of defense for research and engineering, led a delegation to Beijing to discuss concrete programs of cooperation. Later that month, the PLA followed up with a visit to the United States to study the U.S. Army's logistics management system, including the U.S. Foreign Military Sales system. In October, the vice-minister of national defense, Xiao Ke (萧克), toured U.S. military academies and training facilities. In early December 1981, Robert Pirie, assistant secretary of defense for manpower, reserve affairs, and logistics, returned the Chinese logistics delegation's visit.[25]

These interactions worried Moscow, all the more because Sino-American cooperation now included the escalating provision of Saudi-financed Chinese arms and U.S. training for the indigenous resistance to the Soviet armed forces' occupation of Afghanistan (the mujahedeen).[26] The purpose of this assistance (called Operation Cyclone by the CIA, which managed it with the Pakistani military's Inter-Services Intelligence branch) was not just to put pressure on the Soviet Union but to raise the cost of its expansion beyond its borders and its occupation of a strategically located country, with a view, if possible, to forcing its withdrawal. The program began with $500,000 in 1979. By 1987, it had grown to $630 million annually.[27] China also had its own separate program of covert intervention against the Soviet presence in Afghanistan.

Thus, the Soviet invasion of Afghanistan had catalyzed the transformation of U.S.-China détente into increasingly robust entente.[28] Cooperation between China, Pakistan, Saudi Arabia, and the United States to assist the mujahedeen in countering the Soviet invaders considerably overachieved, ultimately playing a key role in bringing down the Soviet Union itself. (This assistance to an international coalition of jihads also inadvertently mid-wifed the birth of some of the Islamist resistance movements that ultimately attacked the United States on September 11, 2001, and that have infiltrated Xinjiang.)

Time Out for Taiwan Arms

The extent of U.S.-PRC military and intelligence cooperation against the Soviet Union was a revelation to President Ronald Reagan when he took office on January 20, 1981. An outspoken anticommunist, Reagan had campaigned on a pledge to restore official relations with Taipei and facilitate unrestricted arms sales to the anticommunist ROC regime. Once he understood the strategic leverage and concrete benefits the United States had gained through normalizing relations with China, however, he changed his mind.

As part of the U.S.-PRC normalization agreement,[29] Washington had undertaken to supply Taiwan only with carefully selected defensive weapons on a restrained basis.[30] This undertaking was an essential element enabling Beijing to finesse its disagreement with Washington over continuing arms sales to Taiwan. But Reagan remained determined to remove the constraints on such sales.

Jimmy Carter, Reagan's predecessor in office, had handed the new president a politically explosive issue by authorizing American companies to develop aircraft designed exclusively for export rather than for use by the USAF. Northrop Grumman responded with the F-20, a replacement for the Northrop Grumman F-5E, which was the mainstay of Taiwan's air force. Without a sale to Taiwan, Northrop Grumman could not hope to make a profit. Its competitor, General Dynamics (the manufacturer of the F-16), like the USAF, disliked the idea of an export-only fighter and wanted to sell its F-16, already in service in the USAF, to foreign customers. General Dynamics disingenuously offered an enfeebled version of the F-16 (the F-16/79) as its entry in the FX competition, confident that foreign purchasers would prefer it to the F-20 because they could later upgrade it to a fully capable F-16. General Dynamics calculated that dangling this possibility before potential buyers would kill any market for the F-20.

Neither of the competing aircraft had yet been built. One of them would create jobs in southern California; the other in Texas. Carter had not wanted to make a choice between them before the 1980 elections, given the political impact that any decision would have on voters in both states. For the same political reasons, Reagan also declined to choose an export aircraft. Instead, he declared that he would supply Taiwan with whichever version of the FX it chose. China made it clear that this would be unacceptable and would have grave consequences for U.S.-PRC relations.

Reagan's secretary of state, General Alexander M. Haig Jr.,[31] believed that U.S. willingness to sell weapons to the PRC might offset and overcome Chinese objections to an FX sale to Taiwan.[32] During a visit to Beijing in June 1981, Haig announced that the United States was lifting restrictions on the sale of lethal weaponry to China. The simultaneous disclosure of the existence of a joint electronic intelligence-gathering facility in western China underscored the strategic context of this policy change.[33] But the Chinese made it clear that they would not be interested in buying U.S. weapons unless the issue of continuing U.S. arms sales to Taiwan was settled to their satisfaction. By October, the PRC had signaled its willingness to downgrade relations with the United States over the issue.[34] China put diplomatic cooperation with the United States on hold.[35]

On January 11, 1982, relying on a Joint Chiefs of Staff study that discounted the importance of more capable interceptors like the FX to Taiwan's defense against the still-primitive PLAAF, the Reagan administration announced that it had decided not to sell Taiwan aircraft more advanced than the F-5Es already in its inventory. That same month, the U.S. embassy in Beijing began negotiations with the Chinese foreign ministry on the Taiwan arms sales issue. In May, Vice President George H. W. Bush traveled to Beijing to convey President Reagan's determination to find a modus vivendi on the issue, doing so directly to China's de facto leader, Deng Xiaoping. On August 17, 1982, the two sides issued a joint communiqué, their third, recording an interim modus vivendi.[36]

In this communiqué, China reaffirmed its determination to make best efforts to achieve reunification with Taiwan by peaceful means. The United States undertook, in parallel, to cap the quality and quantity of its arms sales to Taiwan and gradually to reduce them, with a view to an ultimate resolution of its differences with China on this issue. In effect, both sides returned to the essence of the understanding that had enabled them to agree to disagree during the normalization negotiations, but with the added promise that, as long as the PRC stuck to an emphasis on peaceful resolution of its differences with the authorities in Taiwan, U.S. arms sales to the island would decline.[37]

The imperative of sustaining a downward trend in U.S. arms sales to Taiwan put pressure on Beijing to find ways to clarify that it intended, if at all possible, to refrain from the use of force against the island. Over time, Taipei's military capabilities in relation to the PRC could be expected to decline, progressively shifting the military balance in the Taiwan Strait to Taipei's disadvantage.[38] The prospect of ever lessening access to U.S. weaponry put pressure on Taipei to explore alternatives to its traditional policy of military confrontation with the Chinese mainland. The United States offered clarifications and reassurance to Taipei that it would not accept further PRC restrictions on its sale of weapons to Taiwan, declining to advise Taipei on its policies toward the Chinese mainland and emphasizing that this was not for Americans to decide.[39]

Neither Washington nor Beijing was pleased by the concessions each had had to make to restore a working relationship between them, but both were relieved to have a chance to resume the previously positive trajectory. Gradually, this positive trajectory of relations was restored.

Strategic Cooperation

Secretary of State George Shultz, a seasoned public servant who had succeeded Haig just before the final touches were put on the August 17, 1982 communiqué, visited Beijing in February 1983 for talks on technology transfer and military cooperation, as well as global and regional geopolitical issues. Shultz was followed in May by Secretary of Commerce Malcolm Baldridge, who notified the Chinese that the United States had designated China as a friendly non-allied country, making it eligible to purchase advanced U.S. technology denied to the Soviet Union. (Previously, the two communist giants had been formally subject to nominally equivalent export controls.)

In late September, Secretary of Defense Caspar Weinberger visited Beijing. He emphasized the U.S. desire for continuing Chinese strategic cooperation against the Soviet Union and informed the PLA that the United States was prepared to sell them such defensive weapons systems as antitank and antiaircraft missiles, stressing that such sales would be limited by U.S. law, especially as related to the possible resale of weapons or technology to a third nation. The Chinese once again registered their dissatisfaction with continuing U.S. arms sales to Taiwan. The two sides announced that Premier Zhao Ziyang and President Reagan would exchange visits in early 1984, which they did in January and April, respectively.

China was then negotiating with the United Kingdom about the status of Hong Kong after the 1997 expiration of the British lease on the New Territories. On June 22–23, 1984, Deng Xiaoping met with a delegation of Hong Kong businessmen and women and proposed that the British colony's reunification with the rest of China take place under a formula of one country, two systems (一国两制).[40] Inasmuch as China could at any time take Hong Kong and Macau by force, this was reassuring to their inhabitants as well as the British. It pushed the Sino-British discussions forward. On December 19, 1984, the two sides were able to sign a joint declaration on the return of Hong Kong to Chinese sovereignty.

On June 12, 1984, the United States made China eligible for Foreign Military Sales. Shortly thereafter, Defense Minister Zhang Aiping arrived in Washington. On August 8, 1984, the Reagan administration notified Congress of the proposed sale of twenty-four S-70C2 helicopters—civilian derivatives of the Black Hawk military helicopter. After approval by the Coordinating Committee for Multilateral Export Controls, deliveries began in early October.[41] Also in August, John Lehmann became the first U.S. secretary of the navy to visit the PRC to discuss the modernization of PLAN antisubmarine warfare capabilities.

Other military sales and assistance programs soon followed. General Electric sold gas turbines to power Chinese destroyers. Between 1985 and 1987, the United States approved Foreign Military Sales cases to upgrade production of ammunition for the PLA's artillery and to modernize the fire control system in Shenyang J-8II fighters. It also sold AN/TPQ-37 artillery-locating radars and Mark-46 antisubmarine torpedoes to China.[42]

Bilateral military trade was not one way. In addition to the U.S. purchase of weapons for the Afghan mujahedeen under Operation Cyclone, China sold substantial quantities of Soviet-designed, Chinese-manufactured aircraft and other equipment to the United States for evaluation and use in aggressor squadrons training American pilots to counter Soviet armed forces and their armaments.[43] Ironically, while debate in Washington about military relations with China focused exclusively on U.S. transfers of weapons to the PLA, the United States was secretly purchasing and importing large quantities of armaments from the PLA and running a big deficit in military trade with China. (At the time, the civilian trade balance, which was then heavily in favor of the United States, was the subject of frequent Chinese complaint.)

In October 1986, Weinberger made a second visit to China, touring China's Xichang Space Launch Center in Sichuan and confirming arrangements for the first U.S. Navy vessel to call at a Chinese port. The ship visit took place from November 5 to 11, 1986, at the PLAN's North Sea Fleet's headquarters in Qingdao, Shandong. Two years later (September 5–11, 1988), Weinberger's successor, Frank Carlucci, became the first secretary of defense to visit the PLAN's East Sea Fleet's Wusong Naval Training Base in Shanghai.[44]

Carlucci conveyed Reagan's decision that, subject to congressional approval, the United States would allow U.S. companies to use China's Long March (长征) rockets to launch communications satellites into space. The first such launch took place on April 7, 1990.[45] By 1989, however, a series of events, which included the Tiananmen massacre, the fall of the Berlin Wall, and the emergence of democracy in previously authoritarian Taiwan, had reshaped global and regional geopolitics and ended Sino-American entente and, with it, the overt programs of military cooperation that had begun five years before.

U.S.-China Strategic Ties Lose Their Theme, Warmth, and Dialogue

On April 15, 1989, CCP general secretary Hu Yaobang (who had been deposed two years earlier for alleged bourgeois liberalism and weakness in handling countrywide student demonstrations) died of a heart attack. By April 17, thousands of student mourners had marched into Tiananmen Square. Five days later, on the eve of Hu's state funeral, the student presence in the square had grown to one hundred thousand, with demonstrators demanding liberalization of Chinese politics, more funding for education, and better pay for intellectuals. As the protests developed, the authorities veered back and forth between conciliatory and hard-line tactics, exposing deep divisions within the party leadership. The eyes of the entire world were upon the square on June 4, 1989, when PLA troops suppressed the protests with heavy loss of life in Beijing and in other cities where large demonstrations were also occurring. The widespread American illusion that China was evolving toward liberal democracy was shattered, and the U.S. relationship with China was drained of its warmth.

President George H. W. Bush immediately ordered sanctions against the Chinese government, including a ban on future arms shipments and military assistance, the cessation of high-level talks with Chinese officials, and a suspension of talks about nuclear cooperation. Bush hoped that these sanctions would be enough to express U.S. displeasure and anger over the events in Tiananmen Square. They were not. Over Bush's objections, the House of Representatives unanimously passed a new package of sanctions on June 29, including the proviso that the sanctions Bush had already proclaimed could not be lifted until there were assurances that China was making progress in the area of human rights. The new sanctions suspended talks and funds for the expansion of U.S.-Chinese trade and banned the export of police equipment to China.

The Berlin Wall came down in November 1989, marking the beginning of the end of the Soviet empire. The Soviet Union itself dissolved in 1991, with the Russian Federation emerging as an independent state bordering China. The demise of America's Soviet enemy nullified the strategic rationale for U.S. military cooperation with China. American exchanges and dialogue with the PLA ceased.

In 1990, facing both an increasingly hostile United States and the cost overruns that are all too typical of U.S. defense contractors, China terminated cooperation with the USAF on developing the J-8 and turned elsewhere for further assistance.[46] With Israeli help, the J-8 got a major upgrade, with a new multipulse Doppler radar, digital fire-control system, glass cockpit, in-flight refueling probe, a new engine, and new air-to-air missiles In June 1990, one of the Central Military Commission (CMC) vice-chairmen, General Liu Huaqing, traveled to Moscow to explore the resumption of sales of Russian weapons to China. In October of that year, no longer able to obtain spare parts for its U.S. heavy lift (Black Hawk–type) helicopters, China bought two dozen similar Mi-17 assault helicopters from Moscow—the first purchase of Soviet equipment it had made in decades.[47]

Amid strong domestic American opposition to the PRC after the Tiananmen massacre, the Bush administration could not sustain a working relationship with the Chinese leadership, still less with the PLA. In late 1992, with polls showing the presidential election too close to call, President Bush sought to appease voters in key states by authorizing major new weapons arms deals that would significantly increase employment in these states. One such transaction was a massive sale of F-16s (the largest single arms sale to that point in American history) to Taiwan. This broke the U.S. commitments in the August 17, 1982 communiqué (to which the United States nevertheless continued to give lip service), escalated military tensions in the Taiwan Strait (which had been on the wane), and emboldened some in Taiwan to step up exploration of the possibility that, shielded by the unilateral U.S. defense commitment laid out in the TRA, they might secure independence from China. Foreign Military Sales programs with the PRC continued for a while, but military-to-military contacts became focused on the legal and logistical issues involved in canceling such programs. The program cancellation process was essentially complete by William J. (Bill) Clinton's presidential inauguration on January 20, 1993.

Meanwhile, in the Gulf War of August 1990–February 1991, the United States won a stunning victory over the Iraqi Army, expelling it from Kuwait and cutting it back to a level of capabilities that its neighbor, Iran, could balance. U.S. military prestige rose to an all-time global high. The performance of high-tech U.S. forces against Iraq showed the PLA how relatively backward its capabilities were compared to major powers, spurring it to develop doctrine and reconfigure itself for what it ultimately came to call "winning *informationized* local wars." It also stepped up efforts to import advanced military technology.

Ideology and Ostracism in Command

Clinton had campaigned on a platform that was highly critical of those he condemned as "the butchers of Beijing." As president, he demanded that China improve its human rights record as a precondition for both foreign policy cooperation and most favored nation (MFN) status. This policy marked a break with the ideological truce inaugurated by the Shanghai Communiqué.[48] With no strategic consensus underlying U.S.-China relations and with all military intercourse halted, the two countries were increasingly politically estranged even as business between their companies blossomed into economic interdependence. The U.S.-PRC relationship no longer bore evidence of entente. It had become transactional, with cooperation taking place within an atmosphere of escalating wariness and distrust

The distrust was both demonstrated and aggravated when Washington, citing what turned out to be erroneous intelligence, ordered the U.S. Navy to detain a Chinese container ship, the *Yinhe* (银河 or *Milky Way*), in the Indian Ocean for a month, claiming—notwithstanding denials from the most senior levels of the Chinese government—that it was carrying materials used in manufacturing chemical weapons to Iran. In the final report on the incident, the United States agreed that there were no chemical weapons precursors aboard the *Yinhe* but refused to apologize because the United States had acted in good faith on intelligence.[49] Such high-handedness was humiliating to the Chinese leadership and injurious to the prospects for their cooperation on non-military matters of concern to the United States.

From the outset of the Clinton administration, the U.S. Treasury, Department of Commerce, and Department of Defense (DOD) had been privately skeptical about an approach to promoting human rights based on economic pressure, denunciation, and political ostracism, fearing that it not only would not succeed but also could preclude cooperation with China on various agendas within their remit. This skepticism seemed borne out as China stood its ground and rebuffed U.S. demands. In an attempt to make the policy succeed, the White House and the Department of State reluctantly yielded to the DOD's advocacy of U.S. reengagement with the PLA, hoping thereby to weaken the Chinese military's presumed opposition to accommodation of American demands.

A Resumption of Dialogue

In the first days of November 1993, I, as assistant secretary of defense for international security affairs, traveled to Beijing for an intense two-day round of meetings with the deputy director of the PLA General Staff, Lieutenant General Xu Huizi (徐惠滋); Defense Minister Chi Haotian (迟浩田); vice-chairman of the CMC, General Liu Huaqing (刘华清); and Vice Foreign Minister Liu Huaqiu (刘华秋). I did not accept Chinese assertions that the United States bore responsibility for the rift in bilateral military relations and insisted that repairing those relations was the responsibility of both sides. I rebutted Chinese criticism of U.S. arms sales to Taiwan, arguing that they had helped give Taipei the confidence to open a political dialogue with Beijing.

I pointed out that, in the absence of interaction between the two militaries, mutual ignorance could be expected to grow, buttressing suspicions that would in time produce a needlessly hostile relationship. Given the interest of both countries in the maintenance of a peaceful international environment, I argued, they should restore dialogue, reduce mutual misapprehensions, help prepare each other for cooperation in UN peacekeeping and disaster relief operations, and design and conduct exercises to gain the ability to conduct joint or parallel search and rescue, submarine rescue, counterterrorism, and antipiracy operations. China agreed to resume dialogue with the U.S. military but took the concrete proposals for bilateral cooperation the United States had advanced under study without implying that it would necessarily approve them.[50]

In May 1994, Clinton acknowledged that his attempt to link permanent normal trading status for China to changes in its human rights policies and practices had failed and declared the policy to have outlived its usefulness.[51] His administration turned from its former singular focus on the nature of China's domestic politico-legal system to the objective of integrating China into the U.S.-led global order. The aim was to stabilize that order and to facilitate China's eventual emergence as a cooperative partner for the United States in global governance. The attempt to renormalize defense dialogue and military exchanges was part of this effort. But it took place in a vastly different strategic and psychological context than when China and the United States faced a challenge to common interests from the Soviet Union.

Amid controversies over Chinese weapons sales to third countries and nuclear tests as well as continuing opposition from human rights advocates,

Secretary of Defense William Perry visited China from October 16 to 19, 1994, meeting in Beijing with the vice-chairman of the CMC, General Liu Huaqing, and Defense Minister Chi Haotian and traveling to Wuhan to meet with President Jiang Zemin (江泽民). He concluded his visit with a talk at the Stilwell Museum in Chongqing.

Political Limits on Collaboration Underscored

While in China, Perry also met with General Ding Henggao (丁衡高), then the director of the Commission for Science, Technology, and Industry for National Defense (国防科学技术工业委员会), for the inaugural meeting of a newly established U.S.-China Joint Defense Conversion Commission. China then assigned greater priority to the modernization of its agriculture, industry, and science and technology than to national defense. It was also engaged in an effort to redirect resources from military to civilian purposes and to shift factories from military to civilian production (军转民).

Perry reasoned that cooperating with the Chinese effort to demilitarize armaments factories would be in the U.S. interest and would also enable the U.S. armed forces to familiarize themselves with the PLA and its military-industrial base. The Chinese program was modeled on one already operating in post-communist Russia under the rubric of cooperative threat reduction. Although the program was obviously directed at collecting intelligence and developing American influence in the PLA, they nonetheless agreed.

Congressional reactions to Perry's proposal for American participation in defense conversion in China revealed the extent of opposition to a cooperative politico-military relationship with China. Opponents of Sino-American rapprochement successfully painted the program as one of concealed U.S. assistance to the Chinese military. In the first of a series of moves designed to limit peaceful cooperation between the U.S. armed forces and the PLA, the House and Senate passed legislation to prohibit it. The U.S.-China military relationship entered a new period of uncertainty, in a transactional mode, poised somewhere between cooperation and rivalry, but increasingly trending to the latter.

The pace and subject matter of exchanges of visits by ships and high-level defense and military officials provide convenient barometers by which to gauge the state of U.S.-China military relations. Strategy had little to do with the tit-for-tat approach both sides took to such visits. The fact was that neither side had much substantive business to transact. Each saw its travel to the other as justified more by opportunities for intelligence collection than for building institutional relationships. Visits by policy-level U.S. defense civilians, such as department secretaries, became rare.[52] Such visits promised few rewards and often provoked political criticism. Canceling ship visits seemed a relatively cost-free way of demonstrating displeasure with the attitude or actions of the other side.

Despite the frequent cancellation of port calls, including to Hong Kong, Joint Chiefs of Staff chairmen regularly alternated ceremonial visits with the chief of the PLA General Staff. Service chiefs continued to exchange visits but did so with frequent interruptions, as each side canceled or suspended them to underscore its objections to the policies and actions of the other (e.g., Taiwan arms sales, bilateral incidents, or retaliation for the cancellation of other scheduled visits). The July 1994 visit of Charles Larson, U.S. admiral and commander in chief of the Pacific Command, inaugurated a period in which interaction with the PLA was increasingly delegated to the U.S. Pacific Command. Larson's successors visited China almost annually.

Strate.gic Discomfort and the Beginning of an Arms Race

In the early 1990s, the strategic environment in Northeast Asia was undergoing momentous change. The DPRK had been decisively outclassed economically, politically, and militarily by the ROK. ROK advances enabled the commander, U.S. Forces Korea, to relinquish peacetime operational control over Korean forces to the ROK Army commander. The U.S. government continued frequently to express hope that there would be regime change in Pyongyang. China's developing relationship with the ROK had eclipsed its ties to the DPRK. Russia had been sidelined. The North Koreans launched an independent effort to develop nuclear weapons and delivery systems that could deter and counter their enemies, starting with U.S. bases in nearby Japan and then the United States itself. The United States responded by researching and developing a ballistic missile defense system.

Although the U.S. system was ostensibly aimed solely at North Korea, China had ample reason to believe that its nuclear deterrent could and would also be degraded by this system. Its apprehensions were dismissed rather than effectively addressed by the United States. The Chinese responded by redoubling efforts to develop multiple independently targetable reentry vehicles (MIRVs)[53] and hypersonic glide vehicles (HGVs) that would enable their intercontinental ballistic missiles (ICBMs) to overcome any U.S. ballistic missile defense (BMD).[54] Without China or the United States having intended this, the two fell into an arms race pitting PRC ICBMs against U.S. BMD interceptors.

An incident in October 1994 underscored the problems inherent in mutual unfamiliarity between U.S. and Chinese forces. Antisubmarine aircraft operating from the USS *Kitty Hawk* (an aircraft carrier) in the Yellow Sea discovered a PLAN submarine operating on the surface in international waters. "Following procedures that were routine when tracking Soviet submarines during the Cold War, [the U.S. aircraft] began to follow the submarine, dropping sono-buoys to gather acoustic signature information. The PLA was not amused and launched fighter aircraft." By the time they arrived, the U.S. aircraft were gone, but the PLA informed the U.S. Defense Attaché's Office in Beijing "that should this happen again China would attempt to shoot the U.S. aircraft down."[55]

Sino-Russian Relations Restored

Meanwhile, China and Russia moved from détente toward renewed military cooperation. In 1992, the long hiatus in significant Russian arms sales to China ended. In 1993, China bought its first Kilo-class diesel-electric submarines from Russia. In 1994, China and Russia agreed to mutual force reductions along their lengthy common frontier. In 1995, the PLAAF placed orders for SU-27 fighters (which it later successfully copied and marketed as the J-11). In early 1996, it gained a license to coproduce the SU-27 in China at the Shenyang Aircraft Corporation factory.

In 2001, the same year that China and Russia jointly launched the Shanghai Cooperation Organization (SCO),[56] the two countries concluded a China-Russia Treaty of Good-Neighborliness and Friendly Cooperation in which they agreed that they would consult if either of them was threatened by a third party. In 2003, they began a series of increasingly complex exercises designed to enable joint operations on land, in the air, and—since 2012—at sea. In 2004, they settled their last border dispute, replacing military confrontation with confidence-building measures.

Sino-American Relations Test Mutual Hostility

As Sino-Russian relations advanced, U.S.-China relations worsened. In 1995–1996, mutual suspicion gave way to active planning for war between the U.S. armed forces and their Chinese counterparts. The catalyst was the June 1995 visit to the United States of Lee Teng-hui (李登辉), the Taiwan-independence-leaning successor to Chiang Kai-shek's son, Chiang Ching-kuo (蔣經國), as president of the ROC (Taiwan).

Lee had funded the creation of an institute honoring himself at his U.S. alma mater, Cornell University, which then invited him to be its inaugural speaker. Secretary of State Warren Christopher assured PRC foreign minister Qian Qichen (钱其琛) that Lee would not receive a visa because issuing one would be inconsistent with [the U.S.'s] unofficial relationship [with Taiwan]. However, after a multimillion-dollar lobbying campaign organized by Taipei,

President Clinton capitulated to an overwhelming congressional demand that Lee be allowed to visit. He got his visa.

The PRC immediately withdrew its ambassador, Li Daoyu (李道豫), from Washington and launched a series of six shows of force in the form of exercises directed against Taiwan, beginning with the test-firing of missiles near Taiwan-held territory over July 21–26, 1995. More missiles were fired as part of August 15–25 naval exercises. To many, the Clinton administration seemed secretly pleased that Lee, who had humiliated Clinton by manipulating Congress to override him, was getting a bit of a comeuppance from the Chinese across the strait.

Washington did not react despite ample warning that the PRC planned continuing escalation of its military pressure on Taiwan, which included a finale that involved firing missiles at targets near or even in Taiwan's major ports of Keelung (基隆) and Kaohsiung (高雄) just before Taiwan's presidential election in March 1996. When Clinton met PRC president Jiang Zemin (江泽民) at the United Nations in New York on October 24, 1995, he failed to caution Jiang that, if the PLA went too far, the United States would feel obliged to mount a military response. In November, the PLA staged highly publicized amphibious landing exercises clearly aimed at Taiwan.

It took an alarmist story in the *New York Times*,[57] built around a garbled leak from an off-the-record meeting on January 4, 1996, in the White House Situation Room, to galvanize a hasty U.S. reaction to China's actions, which unfolded as foretold.[58] On March 8, 1996, the United States announced that it was dispatching the USS *Independence* aircraft carrier battle group (CVBG) to international waters near Taiwan. The next day, the PRC announced live-fire exercises to be conducted near Taiwan's Penghu Archipelago (澎湖群岛; the Pescadores) from March 12 to 20. On March 13, the PLA began firing missiles into the target boxes it had announced off Kaohsiung and Keelung. In response, the United States ordered the USS *Nimitz* CVBG to deploy to the Taiwan area from the Persian Gulf. A few days later, while offering assurances that it did not intend to invade Taiwan, Beijing announced a simulated amphibious assault planned for March 18–25.[59] Nothing further happened, as all sides backed away from confrontation.

The initial effect of Beijing's campaign had been to cause Lee Teng-hui to prepare a conciliatory draft inaugural address for use at his virtually inevitable inauguration.[60] The arrival of the U.S. Navy, apparently prepared to fight for Taiwan, changed his political calculus. Lee felt free to strike a defiant tone, and did.

In the end, the crisis led all three participants—Taipei, Washington, and Beijing—to mutually incompatible conclusions. Politicians in Taipei found reason to hope that they might be able to manipulate Americans into fighting for Taiwan's independence from China.[61] Political Washington imagined it had proven that shows of U.S. force would suffice to deter the PLA. The U.S. military was reminded that it might be called upon to defend Taiwan. Planning for this mission, which had been a low priority, now became the focus of much of the U.S. Pacific Command's routine war planning effort. Beijing inferred that there was hope of ending the Chinese Civil War either by maneuvering Taipei into negotiated reunification or, less desirably, by conquering it. And Beijing needed to be able to prevent U.S. power projection to the vicinity of Taiwan.[62] The PLA set about drawing up the long-term research, development, and acquisition plans needed to gain such capabilities.[63] As a stopgap measure, in December 1996, the PLAN placed an order for two Sovremenny-class destroyers, designed by the Soviet navy as carrier killers.

On July 1, 1997, Britain returned sovereignty over Hong Kong to China. The recovery of Hong Kong, and later Macau, placed pressure on the PRC leadership to set a schedule for reunification with Taiwan as well. U.S.-China tensions over Taiwan sharpened.

Yet, on January 17–21, 1998, U.S. secretary of defense William Cohen visited China. While in Beijing, Cohen signed the Military Maritime Consultative Agreement aimed at reducing the likelihood of miscalculation and accidents between U.S. Navy and PLAN forces operating at sea or in the air. This is the sort of agreement designed to temper the probability of conflict that one signs with an adversary, not a partner. Its signature symbolized the arrival of the U.S.-China military relationship in the western Pacific at a stage of strategic rivalry verging on adversarial.

The September 1998 visit of the CMC senior vice-chairman General Zhang Wannian (张万年) underscored the change. Reflecting the dissatisfaction of the chairman of the Joint Chiefs of Staff, General Shalikashvili, regarding the perceived lack of Chinese transparency during his May 1997 visit to China, Cohen denied Zhang access to various facilities he had hoped to tour. Meanwhile, China began to be studied as a serious potential adversary by government-affiliated think tanks in Washington.[64] At the Pentagon, China became the near-peer competitor of choice for purposes of war planning.

A Series of Stimuli to Chinese Defense Modernization: The Belgrade Bombing Incident

At around midnight on May 7, 1999, during the NATO bombing campaign in Serbia, the USAF struck the Chinese embassy in Belgrade with five precision-guided bombs, destroying much of the building, killing three communicators, and wounding twenty other Chinese embassy staff. The United States initially offered only a grudging apology, explaining that the bombing was an accident resulting from an obsolete map. No one in Beijing believed that the bombing was anything other than an act of war intended to humiliate China with a U.S. demonstration of irresistible military power. The American consulate at Chengdu was sacked by a mob. Angry Chinese protesters besieged the U.S. embassy in Beijing and consulates in Guangzhou, Shanghai, and Shenyang. The PRC suspended military interaction with the United States, pending receipt of a more satisfactory American response to its grievances.[65]

Meanwhile, arguments in Beijing about what to do about Taiwan continued. On July 9, 1999, the debate on both sides of the Taiwan Strait was decisively redirected by Lee Teng-hui's proclamation that Taiwan and the China mainland had become two states. That is, the Chinese civil war was in the past, and China was now officially divided into one state descended from the 1911 Revolution under Sun Yat-sen—the ROC—and another that was the product of the 1949 Communist Revolution under Mao Zedong—the PRC.[66] His two-state theory (两国论) was put forward on the Deutsche Welle,[67] presumably in the hope that the German experience of reunification, despite Cold War division into two states, would soften the impact of his repudiation of Chiang Kai-shek's and the PRC's insistence on one China.

Lee's statement was seen in Beijing as a de facto declaration of independence. The PRC suspended previously scheduled talks, as well as other dialogue channels with Taipei.[68] It also embarked on a frantic three-week search for military options to punish Taipei for its deviation from Chinese orthodoxy. The search turned up no feasible options, given existing PLA capabilities, serving to remind Beijing of its powerlessness.

In early August 1999, CCP leaders gathered at Beidaihe (北戴河), the Bohai Gulf beachside resort where informal, high-level policy consultations are an annual event. The main topic was what to do about Taiwan and its American backers. In the end, a compromise emerged, as the assembled leaders approved a classic "two-handed policy (两手政策) aimed at deterring independence and promoting reunification through a combination of political-economic enticement and military menace.

The CCP's United Front Work Department (中共中央统一战线工作部) and related state agencies (e.g., the Taiwan Affairs Office of the State Council [国务院台湾事务办公室]) were authorized to broaden and intensify efforts to deepen cross-strait engagement, build constituencies for cross-strait rapprochement, reduce opposition to reunification, and nurture a Taiwanese identity compatible with self-identification as Chinese. At the same time, the PLA General Staff was tasked with determining what would be required militarily to hold the United States at bay and bring Taiwan to heel, with a deadline of 2008 to meet the basic requirements for coercive reunification.

By the end of 1999, General Xu Huizi had produced a plan tied to just-in-time procurement of new equipment and technology, preceded by enough acquisitions to rotate troops through training in their use. His calculus was that modernization of Chinese weaponry would occur on an accelerating basis. Delayed procurement would ensure that there was time for research and development to perfect new systems before procuring them in bulk, that evolving capabilities could be concealed for as long as possible, that equipment was not acquired until it had been fully tested and developed, and that the burden of added defense spending on the central government budget would be minimized by deferring it until the Chinese grew large enough to bear it without strain.

The PLA's new fixation on the Taiwan target and meeting the initial 2008 deadline cured many of the ills of the previous approach to Chinese force modernization. China faced (and still faces) an extraordinarily complex variety of threats on its borders, many involving foreign forces with which it has previously been at war and that are more capable than the PLA.[69] Attempting to deal with all these threats simultaneously had produced force modernization plans that lacked focus, coherence, and funding and that responded more to entrenched service interests than to realistic future challenges. The concentration on Taiwan scenarios that included American intervention provided a clear direction for the remarkably rapid improvement of relevant Chinese military capabilities, especially those of the PLAN, PLAAF, and PLA Rocket Forces (PLARF; 解放军火箭军)[70] related to Taiwan contingencies.

Chinese defense budgets, which had been stagnant, now began to rise apace with the central government budget (i.e., at double-digit rates—faster even than the astonishingly rapid growth of China's GDP). In 2000, China's publicly announced defense budget was $14.6 billion at nominal dollar exchange rates. By 2018, it had grown to $175 billion. Economic growth offset these budget increases, keeping the defense burden low. Prior to 1999, defense spending averaged about 1.1 percent of GDP. In recent years, despite huge growth in absolute terms, it has been about 2 percent.[71] As American concern about Chinese defense modernization grew, Congress severely restricted a wide variety of military-to-military contacts that might create a national security risk due to an inappropriate exposure of U.S. activities relevant to war fighting.

In March 2000, Taiwan alarmed Beijing by electing pro-independence Democratic Progressive Party (民进党) candidate Chen Shui-bian (陈水扁) as president, ending fifty-five years of KMT rule. In July 2000, amid rising cross-strait tensions, Secretary of Defense Cohen traveled to Beijing, the first U.S. defense secretary to do so since the Belgrade embassy bombing. He was also the first not to visit any unit of the PLA. Cohen's counterpart, Chi Haotian, told him that the PRC was apprehensive about Chen Shui-bian but would reserve judgment. Chi protested U.S. pressure on Israel to cancel the $1 billion sale to the PLA of its Phalcon airborne early warning system, also registering objections to U.S. plans for ballistic missile defense.[72] For his part, Cohen complained about continuing transfers of Chinese anti-ship missiles to Iran.

Mutual Provocation Takes New Forms: The EP-3 Incident

In late summer 2000, a U.S. study of airborne intelligence collection requirements concluded that many flights against former targets in Russia were no longer necessary. This released flight time for lower priority targets. China was next on the list. Beijing soon observed a major increase in the frequency of EP-3 flights along its coasts and protested both in Beijing and in Hawaii at a December 2000 consultation with the United States on military maritime safety. But the Clinton administration was already well into the process of *fin de régime* disintegration, as policy-level officials left the government for more lucrative pursuits. China's concerns and their possible consequences went unaddressed at the policy level. Words not having sufficed to gain U.S. attention, the Chinese resorted to actions—aggressively intercepting U.S. reconnaissance flights.

When the George W. Bush administration took office in January 2001, it had no idea that the Chinese pilots provocatively harassing U.S. aircraft along their country's borders were reacting to a recent, sudden, unexplained increase in U.S. reconnaissance activities. But some of the administration's most senior officials had long posited Chinese hostility to the American presence in Asia and took Chinese behavior as confirmation of their presuppositions. In the absence of dialogue, aerial confrontations between Chinese and U.S. pilots off China's coasts intensified. Frustration on both sides grew into mutual exasperation. Each side levied accusations of unprofessional provocation against the other

On April 1, 2001, a midair collision downed a PLAN J-8 fighter, killing its pilot, Lieutenant Commander Wang Wei (王伟), and severely damaging a U.S. Navy EP-3 signals intelligence aircraft. The level of U.S.-PRC distrust had become such that each side immediately blamed the other for the accident.[73] The EP-3 made an unheralded emergency landing at a PLA air base at Lingshui (陵水), Hainan. The crew was interrogated, and the plane was held for eleven days but released when the United States sent a letter to the Chinese foreign minister saying that it was very sorry both about Wang's death and about having had to make an unauthorized landing at a Chinese base.

The Hainan Island EP-3 incident embittered both sides and brought military exchanges to a halt. The Pentagon deferred receiving the credentials of the new Chinese defense attaché, Major General Chen Xiaogong (陈小功), and declined to respond to a Chinese offer of post-9/11 support by facilitating a debriefing by him on Afghanistan, a subject on which he was uniquely knowledgeable.[74] Rumsfeld's DOD was, in effect, treating China as an enemy in a notable disconnect from other aspects of U.S.-China relations. The interdependence of the two economies was intensifying; cooperation in international fora was advancing; and tourist, cultural, and student exchange were expanding, even as military interactions became increasingly unfriendly.

9/11 and a Challenge from Taipei: Change the Subject

The slide toward overt Sino-American hostility was diverted by the terrorist attack on the United States on September 11, 2001 (9/11). The Bush administration saw an urgent need to clear the decks for action against al-Qaeda, the Taliban, other Islamist extremists, and Iraq and put its desire to pressure China on hold. In late October 2003, Secretary of Defense Donald Rumsfeld duly hosted a visit to the United States by the CMC chairman General Cao Gangchuan (曹刚川).

On August 2, 2002, cross-strait tensions rose to new levels when Chen Shui-bian attempted to reinvent Taiwan's international status, asserting that "Taiwan and China are each one country on each side [一边一国] of the Strait."[75] This was an explicit shift toward the one China, one Taiwan position that Beijing had always defined as a redline. Despite ferocious criticism of Chen's dangerous provocation, this time Beijing just doubled down on its military modernization plans. In September 2003, Chen announced a proposal to amend the ROC constitution and to address PRC pressure on Taiwan in a referendum. The United States became concerned that his pushing of the envelope in the Taiwan Strait would leave Beijing with no apparent alternative to the use of force against Taiwan. This led to recognition in both Beijing and Washington that the two had a common interest in reining in Chen's behavior.

On December 9, 2003, standing beside visiting PRC premier Wen Jiabao (温家宝) in Washington, President Bush delivered a blunt warning to Chen, saying "we oppose any unilateral decision, by either China or Taiwan, to change the status quo. . . . And the comments and actions made by the leader of Taiwan indicate that he may be willing to make decisions unilaterally to change the status quo—which we oppose."[76] Chen at first backed down. But after his reelection in March 2004, he proposed changing the legal status quo away from the previous one China consensus by adopting a new constitution for Taiwan.[77]

The PRC responded by drawing up the Anti-Secession Law. The new law, finally enacted on March 14, 2005, enshrined the essence of Jiang Zemin's Eight-Point Proposal.[78] It laid out topics for cross-strait negotiation but also stipulated contingencies that would require the Chinese government to use force against Taiwan, which included the following: (1) if Taiwan independence forces, under whatever name and method, accomplish the fact of Taiwan's separation from China; (2) if a major event occurs that would lead to Taiwan's separation from China; (3) or if all possibility of peaceful unification is lost.

A Great Leap Forward in the Taiwan Strait

Despite widespread consternation among U.S. China watchers and a resolution by the U.S. House of Representatives expressing grave concern, far from halting progress and the reduction of tensions in cross-strait relations, the passage of the Anti-Secession Law was followed by a major breakthrough in cross-strait relations. On April 26, 2005, KMT chairman Lien Chan (連戰) traveled to the PRC, visiting the Sun Yat-sen Mausoleum in Nanjing before meeting CCP General Secretary Hu Jintao (胡锦涛) in Beijing.[79] His visit reestablished a framework for party-to-party cooperation, which had ended nearly five decades before. The two party chiefs agreed on fifteen concrete programs for cross-strait interchange and cooperation.

The succeeding exchanges between the KMT and CCP culminated in an explosive growth of trade, travel, and investment between the two sides of the strait. The process of rapprochement that Lien began led to the progressive reduction of tensions and, ultimately, a decade later, on November 7, 2015, to a summit meeting in Singapore between KMT chairman and ROC president Ma Ying-jeou (馬英九) and CCP general secretary (concurrently PRC president and CMC chairman) Xi Jinping (习近平).

As tensions in the Taiwan Strait fell to an all-time low, the U.S. military became increasingly focused on wars in Afghanistan, Iraq, and Somalia and the possibility of war with Iran, rather than on China. Secretary of Defense Rumsfeld traveled to Beijing from October 18 to 20, 2005, where he met with the commander of the Second Artillery Force, General Jing Zhiyuan (靖志远), who reaffirmed China's no first use nuclear weapons policy.[80] In July 2006, Rumsfeld hosted a visit by CMC senior vice-chairman General Guo Boxiong (郭伯雄). The two sides agreed to hold a combined naval search and rescue exercise, thus implementing a proposal first put forward in November 1993.[81] The Chinese also agreed to a long-standing U.S. request for access to PLA archives with information on U.S. prisoners of war and missing in action in the Korean War.

In January 2007, China successfully tested an anti-satellite weapon, generating significant anxiety in the United States, given the heavy dependence of U.S. forces on satellite-supported command, control, communications, surveillance, reconnaissance, and intelligence. During Secretary of Defense Robert Gates's visit to Beijing that November, he complained about the Chinese program and the way in which the test had been conducted. Meanwhile, China's belated concern about the ability of the two sides to handle unexpected contingencies led it finally to respond to a long-standing U.S. proposal to establish a hotline with the Pentagon.

In March 2008, Chen Shui-bian was voted out of office. Over the next eight years, his KMT successor, Ma Ying-jeou, built on the KMT-CCP understandings reached during Lien Chan's 2005 visit to Beijing, achieving a remarkable reduction in cross-strait tensions and increase in cooperation. But the Chinese reaction to the outgoing Bush administration's final arms sales to Taiwan in October 2008 was an immediate suspension of most contacts with the U.S. military.

Trouble in the South and East China Seas

When Barack Obama assumed the presidency in January 2009, he soon had to deal with pushback from China on three issues: arms sales to Taiwan, U.S. naval and airborne reconnaissance activities along China's coasts, and the congressional ban on military contacts with the PLA. In March 2009, asserting that U.S. military reconnaissance activities in the two-hundred-nautical-mile exclusive economic zones (EEZs) established by the UN Convention on the Law of the Sea (UNCLOS) were illegal, the PLAN began to intercept and obstruct such activities.[82]

In part as a consequence of rising tensions between the U.S. Navy and PLAN (including Chinese objection to a U.S.-ROK military exercise in the Yellow Sea intended as a show of force against the DPRK), the United States and China found themselves on opposite sides. At an Association of Southeast Asian Nations (ASEAN) security dialogue in Hanoi on July 23, 2010, Secretary of State Clinton surprised and angered China by appearing to back Vietnam's effort to muster support from other Asian countries against Chinese claims in the South China Sea. Any subtlety in the American position was overwhelmed by the Chinese perception that the United States was adding South China Sea territorial disputes to the Taiwan issue as a new front in which to pursue military confrontation designed to contain China.

As this confrontation proceeded, China quietly dropped its argument that reconnaissance activities in EEZs were illegal. Despite its perception and assertion that such activities are politically provocative, China now carries out its own such activities off the U.S. territories of Guam and Hawaii. It has not sought to dislodge other claimants from the places they occupy in the South China Sea but has built island bastions atop barren islets and reefs and garrisoned them, establishing a radar picket and aerial patrol capability on the outer perimeter of the maritime approaches to China proper (from which the most recent invasions of China came).

The legal basis and extent of Chinese claims in the South China Sea remain unclear (and subject to negotiation with other claimants).[83] Neither China nor any other claimant has obstructed merchant shipping in or through the South China Sea. Two-thirds of that shipping is to or from Chinese ports. China's stake in keeping the sea lanes open is a key reason for its establishment of a permanent presence in the Spratly Islands. U.S. freedom of navigation operations (FONOPS) are unrelated to commerce, designed to challenge what the U.S. Navy regards as erroneous Chinese interpretations of the law of the sea and to demonstrate rights of military reconnaissance near Chinese-held territory. Thus far, their principal result has been to inspire an augmented PLAN presence in the South China Sea, including the accelerated placement of weaponry on fortified islands. U.S. Navy tensions with the

PLAN are now unprecedentedly high, as John Garver describes in chapter 3 of this volume.

Naval tensions in the East China Sea also increased after September 7, 2010, when a drunken and disorderly Chinese fishing captain was arrested after ramming a Japanese Coast Guard cutter trying to prevent him from fishing near the Senkaku Islands. These barren rocks in the East China Sea are claimed by China as part of Taiwan but have been administered by Japan since 1971. The legal proceedings against the fisherman were seen by China as a Japanese assertion of sovereignty, thus breaching a bilateral understanding from 1972 that neither side would force the other to address the issue. As the dispute unfolded, nationalist reactions on both sides caused a sharp deterioration in Sino-Japanese relations.

In these circumstances, the United States was compelled to reaffirm its long-standing position, to wit: while the United States has taken no position on sovereignty over the Senkaku Archipelago, it regards their defense as an American obligation under the U.S.-Japan Mutual Cooperation and Security Treaty and therefore defend Japan's continuing administration of them (against China). Since 2010, the Chinese and Japanese coast guards, navies, and air forces have carried out shows of force against each other. While they have been careful to avoid conflict, the emergence of an active dispute over the Senkaku Archipelago (called the Diaoyu Islands, or 钓鱼岛 in Chinese) is a potential *casus belli* between Japan and the United States on one side and China on the other.

Efforts to Improve the Atmosphere

In January 2011, as part of a Chinese effort to improve the less than ideal atmosphere for a prospective state visit by Hu Jintao in January 2012,[84] the PLA invited Secretary of Defense Gates for a second visit. Gates expressed appreciation for China's role in restraining North Korea, which, he stressed, was becoming a direct threat to the United States. In a belated Chinese demonstration of willingness to address U.S. proposals first made in November 1993, the two sides agreed to establish a working group to develop a framework for the conduct of exercises in maritime search and rescue, humanitarian assistance and disaster relief, counter-piracy, and counterterrorism operations.[85] Chinese defense minister General Liang Guanglie (梁光烈) did not agree to Gates's proposal to establish a strategic dialogue on nuclear weapons, missile defense, operations in space, and cybersecurity but took the idea under advisement.

In May and September 2012, Liang and Secretary of Defense Leon Panetta exchanged visits. Their discussions focused on the U.S. pivot (or rebalance) to Asia, a barely disguised U.S. move to constrain, if not contain, China's influence in its region. While in Beijing, Panetta signaled an intention to invite the PLAN to participate in the 2014 Rim of the Pacific Exercise (RIMPAC), a biennial Pacific-wide multinational naval exercise hosted by the U.S. Navy near Hawaii. The PLAN agreed and participated in 2014 and 2016.

Defense Minister Liang made another visit to Washington in August 2013. In return, Secretary of Defense Chuck Hagel traveled to Beijing in April 2014, where Hagel and Liang agreed to institutionalize an Asia-Pacific Security Dialogue that covered Korean issues and to launch an army-to-army dialogue. Hagel also invited the PLA to participate in a military medical drill in Hawaii after RIMPAC.

Turmoil and Trouble Over Taiwan, Trade, and Investment

In November 2016, Donald Trump was elected president on a platform that committed him to seek a radical adjustment of U.S. trade and investment relations with China. During the presidential transition, he exchanged a telephone call with Tsai Ing-wen, the cautiously pro-independence president in Taipei, raising questions about whether he might use the Taiwan issue to pressure China on trade or other issues. Once in office, he withdrew the United States from the Trans-Pacific Partnership (TPP), in effect discarding U.S. politico-economic engagement in East Asia in favor of reliance on military means to compete for regional influence with China.

Trump went out of his way to claim a personal relationship with Chinese president Xi Jinping, apparently calculating that such ties could mitigate his administration's confrontation with China on other matters and help enlist Beijing in support of U.S. objectives vis-à-vis the DPRK. By the spring of 2018, he had launched an all-out trade war against China, with huge collateral damage to other countries. A vision for how to leverage Chinese wealth and power to American advantage was nowhere apparent.

The trade war on which the two countries embarked has roots in both military rivalry and fear of economic eclipse. China, with its policy of building national strength through military-civilian fusion (军民融合), and the United States, with its concepts of a third offset and commercial off-the-shelf (COTS) procurement, are both engaged in exploiting commercial technology for military use.[86] The distinction between military and civilian technology is thus blurred, making virtually anything dual use.

After decades of disparaging China's ability to innovate and attributing its advances to the theft of foreign intellectual property, Americans are waking up to China's remarkable advances in science, technology, and engineering.[87] The Trump administration's National Security Strategy[88] and National Defense Strategy both deal with China as an adversary, alleging that both China and

Russia pose a threat to the rules-bound order of the Pax Americana and must be countered. New restrictions on investment in U.S. or Chinese technology companies are already drying up financial flows between the world's two largest economies.[89]

On the military front, in May 2018, the United States rescinded an invitation to the PLAN to participate in RIMPAC to express its unhappiness with Chinese military activities in the South China Sea (although it was not at all clear what specific activities the United States was protesting).[90] At the end of June 2018 (four years after the last such visit), Secretary of Defense James (Jim) Mattis flew to Beijing for a mutually respectful but unproductive discussion with Defense Minister Wei Fenghe (魏凤和). In addition to reviewing Sino-American differences over Taiwan, they discussed the South China Sea. When Mattis met with Xi Jinping, Xi remarked: "Not a single inch of the territory left behind by our ancestors must be lost, while we are not seeking to take any bit of what belongs to others."[91]

Straight talk between defense ministers, unaccompanied by any effort to identify opportunities for cooperation, is arguably better than the non-intercourse that has so often characterized the military relationship. Such unambitious, tactically oriented military dialogue, unguided by any strategic objective other than a desire for coexistence that avoids combat and the nuclear escalation it would risk, may be the best the two sides can hope for. But the United States might consider a return to its approach during the initial opening of strategic dialogue with the PRC in 1971–1973 when Washington asked Beijing to describe and explain its interests, listened carefully, and crafted a relationship responsive to Chinese interests as well as U.S. priorities.[92]

Conclusions and Prospects

Military interaction between China and the United States is now in its nineteenth decade. Certain patterns persist, reflecting disparities of power and ambition. Throughout this long period, the U.S.-China military relationship has been consistently asymmetric:

- U.S. armed forces have established garrisons in parts of China, patrolled its interior and coasts, and intervened in its civil war. China has never projected its power to the United States.
- All combat between U.S. and Chinese forces has been in or near China. No such combat has taken place in or near the United States.
- On several occasions, the United States has threatened to attack China, including with nuclear weapons. China has not reciprocated such threats, though it has made it clear that it would retaliate in kind.

- The United States has established alliances with China's neighbors in anticipation of war with it. China has not sought to do the same against the United States.
- American national security officials have rarely shown interest in Chinese perspectives or positions on international issues and disputes. They have concentrated instead on imposing Washington's views on the Chinese.[93]

Aside from the question of Taiwan (which is both an attractive, modernized Chinese society and a malignancy in terms of the U.S.-PRC relationship), Beijing and Washington have no concrete conflicts of interest that might lead to war. The issues dividing them have had more to do with status, pecking order, and face than with specific issues. As its power grows, remembering its past humiliations, China becomes ever more insistent on American respect and treatment as an equal in the management of the affairs of its region. The United States seeks to retain acknowledgment of its primacy in the Indo-Pacific, despite the emergence of an increasingly Sino-centric order there amid a balance of military power that is inexorably shifting toward China. The objectives of the two sides are not necessarily incompatible, but they have yet to be reconciled.

For nearly two centuries, the United States has been in China's face rather than the other way around. The past forty years, since the normalization of U.S. relations with the PRC in 1979, have not really changed this dynamic. Since 1979:

- Through a combination of perceived excellence at war fighting, intrusive actions, and threats to China's territorial integrity, the United States has been the driver of PLA doctrine, force structure, and weapons modernization.
- The United States has continued its military support of Taiwan against the PLA (i.e., its ongoing intervention in the still-unended Chinese Civil War). China has not taken sides in U.S. domestic political disputes or aided American dissident movements militarily.[94]
- The United States deploys its armed forces so as to underscore its unwillingness to accept the borders China claims with third countries (e.g., Japan, the Philippines, Vietnam). China has taken no position on U.S. territorial disputes with neighbors.
- No American soldier or official has been killed in an attack by the PLA, but Chinese diplomats and PLA officers have died at the hands of the U.S. military.[95]

China is now pushing back ever more firmly against American dominance. This (especially the PLAN's expanding presence in the South China Sea) is shifting the military balance in the western Pacific against the United States. The PLA's military modernization has given it capabilities that exceed those of the United States in some respects and others that the U.S. armed forces in some cases cannot effectively counter. The historical dynamic in which the United States acted, and China reacted, is being replaced by a more balanced interactive pattern in which China is shaping American policy and force structure almost as much as U.S. military power is shaping it.[96]

This raises the question that lies beneath the Golden Rule. As its power rises relative to that of the United States, will China begin to do to America what it perceives America to have done or to be doing to it? If so, the risk of armed conflict between the two countries will greatly increase. And the United States and China are poorly prepared to manage the evolving adversarial military relationship.

Despite forty years of engagement, China and the United States have not developed effective mechanisms for crisis management, escalation control, or even consultations on military contingencies in areas of common concern, such as the Korean Peninsula. The military relationship has varied between enmity, strategic cooperation, tactical interactions animated by mutual apprehension, and a dialogue in which neither side is dumb but we Americans are deaf and blind. The relationship now appears to be evolving from rivalry into active antagonism. Instead of the hopeful "new pattern of great power relations" proposed by Xi Jinping, the United States and China seem poised to enter a new cold war, or, perhaps more accurately, a new era of malicious coexistence amid a phony peace.[97]

NOTES

1. Mao Zedong, "The Chinese People Have Stood Up!," September 21, 1949, https://china.usc.edu/Mao-declares-founding-of-peoples-republic-of-china-chinese-people-have-stood-up.
2. See "A Hostage in Communist China, 1948-49," Association for Diplomatic Studies and Training, September 12, 2012, https://adst.org/2012/09/a-hostage-in-communist-china/.
3. Harry S. Truman, "Statement on Formosa," January 5, 1950, https://china.usc.edu/harry-s-truman-%e2%80%9cstatement-formosa%e2%80%9d-january-5-1950.
4. Established March 15, 1943, when the Brisbane, Australia–based Southwest Pacific Force was renamed.
5. Truman, "Statement on Formosa."
6. Sometimes spelled *Pusan*.
7. Lynn Montross, "The Inchon Landing: Victory Over Time and Tide," *The Marine Corps Gazette*, July 1951, http://www.koreanwar-educator.org/topics/branch_accounts/marine/p_inchon_landing.htm.
8. On April 27, 2018, the leaders of South and North Korea met at Panmunjom and pledged to replace the armistice with a peace treaty before the end of the year. China signaled its willingness to join such a treaty.
9. The PRC asserts that the United States has publicly or privately threatened to use nuclear weapons against it on at least six occasions.
10. China tested its first nuclear device on October 16, 1964.

11. Clandestine correspondence between Chiang Kai-shek and PRC premier Zhou Enlai of the PRC, facilitated by Soviet intermediaries, appears to have played a role in achieving this understanding.

12. "Shanghai Communiqué," Taiwan Documents Project, February 28, 1972, http://www.taiwandocuments.org/communique01.htm.

13. "Joint Communiqué on the Establishment of Diplomatic Relations," Taiwan Documents Project, January 1, 1979, http://www.taiwandocuments.org/communique02.htm.

14. Text of President Carter's statement can be found at http://www.presidency.ucsb.edu/ws/?pid=30309. Context is described at Office of the Historian, "China Policy," https://history.state.gov/milestones/1977-1980/china-policy.

15. "我们一定要解放台湾" (We will definitely liberate Taiwan).

16. Text of "Message to Compatriots in Taiwan" of January 1, 1979, can be found at http://www.china.org.cn/english/7943.htm. A statement of PRC policy was included as the fourth paragraph of the U.S.-China Joint Communiqué of August 17, 1982, recording a compromise on the contentious issue of continuing U.S. arms sales to Taiwan. Text available at "US–PRC Joint Communique, August 17, 1982," Wikisource, https://en.wikisource.org/wiki/US%E2%80%93PRC_Joint_Communique,_August_17,_1982. Context available at Office of the Historian, "The August 17, 1982 U.S.-China Communiqué on Arms Sales to Taiwan," https://history.state.gov/milestones/1981-1988/china-communique.

17. Taiwan Relations Act, Pub. L. No. 96-8, 93 Stat. 14 (1979).

18. The decision to put the marines in uniform, the author's first as chargé, drew a strong Chinese protest but was not reversed by Washington.

19. "Shanghai Communiqué."

20. Charles W. Freeman Jr., "The Process of Rapprochement: Achievements and Problems," in *Sino-American Normalization and Its Policy Implications*, eds. Gene T. Hsiao and Michael J. Witunski (Santa Barbara, CA: Praeger, 1983), 1–27.

21. The memorandum of the conversation at the meeting between Secretary of Defense Harold Brown and Vice-Premier Geng Biao, People's Republic of China, on January 7, 1980, can be found at David P. Nickles, ed., *Foreign Relations of the United States 1977–1980, Vol XIII, China* (Washington, DC: U.S. Government Printing Office, 2013), 1036. Available online at https://history.state.gov/historicaldocuments/frus1977-80v13/d290.

22. The intelligence relationship between the U.S. Central Intelligence Agency, National Security Agency, and the PLA Second and Third Departments and its subsequent evolution is outlined in the following United Press International report: John C. K. Daly, "Feature: U.S., China—Intel's Odd Couple," UPI, February 24, 2001, https://www.upi.com/Archives/2001/02/24/Feature-US-China-intels-odd-couple/6536982990800/.

23. U.S. Department of State, *Munitions Control Newsletter No. 81* (Washington, DC: U.S. Department of State, March 1980).

24. Hezi Jiang, "From China's Foe to Friend," *China Daily*, January 21, 2017, http://usa.chinadaily.com.cn/culture/2017-01/21/content_28015802.htm.

25. See "Two Years of U.S. China Relations—A Chronology of Events from January 1, 1979 Through December 29, 1980," in *Sino-American Normalization and Its Policy Implications*, eds. Gene T. Hsiao and Michael J. Witunski (Santa Barbara, CA: Praeger, 1983), 260–77.

26. Philip Taubman, "U.S. and China Forging Close Ties; Critics Fear That Pace Is Too Swift," *New York Times*, December 8, 1980.

27. Bruce Reidel, *What We Won: America's Secret War in Afghanistan, 1979–1989* (Washington, DC: Brookings Institution, 2014).

28. Détente is a relaxation of tensions that does not resolve the underlying causes of antagonism but that seeks to reduce the likelihood of conflict. Entente is a mutual undertaking,

based on the parties' recognition of shared interests despite differences, to pursue limited cooperation for limited purposes.

29. "Joint Communiqué," 1979.

30. U.S. Department of State, *Foreign Affairs Memorandum: Diplomatic Relations with the People's Republic of China and Future Relations with Taiwan* (Washington, DC: U.S. Department of State, December 1978), 4.

31. Haig had served as National Security Advisor Henry Kissinger's deputy and played a role in the rapprochement, accompanying President Nixon to Beijing and participating in the negotiation of the "Shanghai Communiqué" of February 28, 1972. Like Kissinger, he was an admirer of Chinese strategic thought and reasoning.

32. None of his advisers, including the author, who was then country director for the People's Republic of China and Mongolian affairs, agreed.

33. William R. Feeney, "Strategic Implications," in *Sino-American Normalization and Its Policy Implications*, eds. Gene T. Hsiao and Michael J. Witunski (Santa Barbara, CA: Praeger, 1983), 164.

34. See Leslie H. Gelb, "Arms for China and Taiwan: Twists in Diplomacy," *New York Times*, October 16, 1981, https://www.nytimes.com/1981/10/16/world/arms-for-china-and-taiwan -twists-in-diplomacy.html. (Some facts and dates in this story are inaccurate, but the gist is correct.)

35. Kerry B. Dumbaugh and Richard F. Grimmett, *U.S. Arms Sales to China*, CRS Report No. 85-138F (Washington, DC: Congressional Research Service, July 8, 1985.

36. "The August 17, 1982 U.S.-China Communiqué on Arms Sales to Taiwan," Office of the Historian, https://history.state.gov/milestones/1981-1988/china-communique. For a history of the communiqué's negotiations, see Chas W. Freeman Jr., "The 1981-82 Sino-American Taiwan Arms Sales Negotiations," August 19, 2019, https://chasfreeman.net/the-1981 -82-sino-american-taiwan-arms-sales-negotiations/.

37. The Taiwan Relations Act required that the U.S. executive branch assure a sufficient self-defense capability for Taiwan. The communiqué from August 17, 1982, implied that what was "sufficient" would be judged by weighing Beijing's intentions as expressed in policy as well as by consideration of the military balance in the Taiwan Strait alone.

38. See Chas W. Freeman Jr., "Diplomacy: A Rusting Tool of American Statecraft," February 2018, https://chasfreeman.net/diplomacy-a-rusting-tool-of-american-statecraft/. The opening of cross-strait negotiations in 1992 signaled the success of U.S. strategy of acting to facilitate a peaceful resolution of the Taiwan question—the issue of Taiwan's political relationship to the rest of China.

39. The "six assurances" were listed in congressional testimony by John H. Holdridge, assistant secretary of state for East Asian and Pacific affairs, who declared that, in negotiating the August 17, 1982, communiqué, the U.S. government (1) "did not agree to set a date certain for ending arms sales to Taiwan"; (2) foresaw "no mediation role for the United States between Taiwan and the PRC"; (3) would "not attempt to put pressure on Taiwan to enter into negotiations with the PRC"; (4) had not changed its "longstanding position on the issue of sovereignty over Taiwan"; (5) had "no plans to seek revisions to the Taiwan Relations Act"; and (6) the communiqué "should not be read to imply that [the United States had] agreed to engage in prior consultations with Beijing on arms sales to Taiwan." In 2016, these six assurances were endorsed by the House of Representatives in a nonbinding resolution. "H.Con.Res.88—114th Congress (2015-2016)," U.S. Congress, May 17, 2016, https://www.congress.gov/bill/114th-congress/house-concurrent-resolution/88/text.

40. Text of remarks can be found at "Deng Xiaoping on 'One Country, Two Systems,' " *China Daily*, June 22-23, 1984, http://www.chinadaily.com.cn/english/doc/2004-02/19

/content_307590.htm. Chapter 1, Article 5 of the basic law for the Special Administrative Region of Hong Kong passed by China's National People's Congress embodies "one country, two systems." It provides that "the socialist system and policies shall not be practiced in the Hong Kong Special Administrative Region, and the previous capitalist system and way of life shall remain unchanged for 50 years."

41. The Coordinating Committee for Multilateral Export Controls (CoCom) was established in the late 1940s, as the Cold War began. Its membership consisted of sixteen NATO countries plus Japan. CoCom ceased to function in 1994, following the dissolution of the Soviet Union.

42. Dumbaugh and Grimmett, *U.S. Arms Sales*, 16–22.

43. "USAF Aggressor Squadrons," Aces Flying High, February 25, 2015, https://acesflyinghigh .wordpress.com/2015/02/25/usaf-aggressor-squadrons/. See also the description of the overall Constant Peg program at the following sites: "4477th Test and Evaluation Squadron," Wikipedia, https://en.wikipedia.org/wiki/4477th_Test_and_Evaluation_Squadon; and "Constant Peg," GlobalSecurity.org, https://www.globalsecurity.org/military/systems /aircraft/constant-peg.htm.

44. Since then, many foreign visitors have toured this facility.

45. See https://en.wikipedia.org/wiki/lisst-of-Long/March/launches.

46. Jim Mann, "China Cancels U.S. Deal for Modernizin F-8 Jet, *Los Angeles Times*, May 15, 1990.

47. In the late 1990s, the PLAAF replaced the J-8 with the J-11, which is based on the RussianSukkoi Su-27. The J-8 is now considered obsolete but remains in limited service in the PL Navy Air Force.

48. The "Shanghai Communiqué" stated: "There are essential differences between China and the United States in their social systems and foreign policies. However, the two sides agreed that countries, regardless of their social systems, should conduct their relations on the principles of respect for the sovereignty and territorial integrity of all states, non-aggression against other states, non-interference in the internal affairs of other states, equality and mutual benefit, and peaceful coexistence. International disputes should be settled on this basis, without resorting to the use or threat of force. The United States and the People's Republic of China are prepared to apply these principles to their mutual relations."

49. See Robert Suettinger, *Beyond Tiananmen: The Politics of U.S.-China Relations 1989–2000* (Washington, DC: Brookings Institution Press, 2003), 174–77.

50. Jing-Dong Yuan, "Sino-US Military Relations Since Tiananmen: Restoration, Progress, and Pitfalls," *Parameters* 33, no. 1 (Spring 2003): 51–67. One reason for the PLA's hesitancy to exercise with the U.S. armed forces was apprehension that doing so would serve mainly to demonstrate the PLA's weaknesses and would therefore be more embarrassing than educational.

51. John M. Broder and Jim Mann, "Clinton Reverses His Policy, Renews China Trade Status," *Los Angeles Times*, May 27, 1994, http://articles.latimes.com/1994-05-27/news/mn -62877_1_human-rights. This ended a one-year period in which the virtually universal American hope that China would evolved toward an increasingly liberal domestic order became an organizing principle of policy rather than just a course advocated by human rights activists, critics of the U.S. opening to China, and members of the U.S. political elite disillusioned by the suppression of students and other demonstrators in Beijing's Tiananmen Square on June 4, 1989.

52. There has been no visit by a secretary of the U.S. Army or the USAF since 1989. Secretary of the Navy Richard Danzig went to China at the end of 1998; Ray Mabus did so at the end of 2009.

53. China had the technology to MIRV its ICBMs for quite a few years. The U.S. BMD program created the perceived need to do so. At the time, Geng was concurrently Secretary General of the CCP's Central Military Commission (CMC) and member of its Standing Committee.

54. Chinese scientists shared the skepticism of many of their American counerparts that the U.S. system would work but China felt impelled to apply worstt-case analysis to the issue. Liu Huaqing was commander of the PL Navy (PLAN), 1982–1988. His three-part development program for the PLAN called for it to be able to operate up to the "first island chain" (第一岛链), i.e. the area bounded by the Chinese mainland, Japan, the Philippines, Indonesia, and mainland Southeast Asia) by 2010, out to the "second island chain" ([第二岛链], i.e. from Honshu to the Bonin and Mariana Islands, Guam, Palau, to Irian Jaya) by 2020, and to develop as a globally competent force by 2040. The concept of island chains was first formulated by the U.S. Navy to describe Japan's strategic circumstances in World War II. Liu adapted it to describe China's defensive perimeters.

55. Paper prepared by Admiral (Ret.) Michael McDevitt for the National-Committee on Ameridan Foreign Policy (NCAFP) and Tsinghua University US-China Strategic Dialogue, November 14, 2010. Wang, like Gabriel, went on to become the first fighter pilot to head the PLA Air Force (PLAAF) from 1985 to 1992. In October 1985, when General Gabriel became the first USAF Chief of Staff to visit China, Wang served as jost. He did not himself visit the U.S. as PLAAF commander.

56. The SCO's purpose is cooperative security rather than military alliance. It aims to suppress the spread of Islamist terrorism and ethnic separatism, fill the vacuum left by the Soviet collapse, and provide a framework for cooperative management of Sino-Russian interactions in central Asia. Its initial members were China, Russia, Kazakhstan, Kyrgyzstan, Tajikistan, and Uzbekistan, with India and Pakistan recent additions. Currently, there are four SCO observers (Afghanistan, Belarus, Iran, and Mongolia), six dialogue partners (Armenia, Azerbaijan, Cambodia, Nepal, Sri Lanka, and Turkey), and three guests (the Association of Southeast Asian Nations [ASEAN], the Commonwealth of Independent States, and Turkmenistan).

57. Patrick E. Tyler, "As China Threatens Taiwan, It Makes Sure U.S. Listens," *New York Times*, January 24, 1996, https://www.nytimes.com/1996/01/24/world/as-china-threatens-taiwan-it-makes-sure-us-listens.html.

58. Personally interested as a result of long-standing involvement in U.S. handling of the Taiwan issue as an element in U.S.-China relations, I conducted my own investigation of the motives and plans of both sides in a self-financed visit to both Taipei and Beijing in mid-October 1995. I warned Beijing that, if it carried out its plans as I understood them, it would provoke a strong military response from the United States. After leaving the China mainland, I returned to Taipei to warn it that it should expect missiles to be fired at its doorstep just before its presidential elections.

Beijing said that it was confident in its own intelligence, which indicated that there would be no U.S. reaction. The Taiwan military took the warning seriously, but President Lee rejected it as unworthy of consideration. On my return to Washington, I warned the intelligence community and the Departments of State and Defense as well as the National Security Council staff of Beijing's plans as I understood them. I was dismissed as delusional. My urgent recommendation that, at his upcoming meeting with his Chinese counterpart, the president should warn Jiang Zemin that China's plans would evoke a U.S. military response was brushed aside.

In early January, before setting out on travels to India and the Middle East, I reiterated this warning to National Security Advisor Anthony Lake. Lake scoffed at the warning, declaring that, given the immense U.S. nuclear arsenal, the PRC would never dare to menace Taiwan by applying military pressure to it. In response, I informed him that, when I had made this same point to them, senior Chinese military officials had expressed confidence that the United States, which they said had threatened to use nuclear weapons against China on six previous occasions, would not dare to do so again, since China could now retaliate in kind against U.S. territory. They made it clear that they believed they had achieved effective immunity against U.S. nuclear black-mail because the United States could always be counted upon "to care more about Los Angeles than it did about Taipei." The latter point was leaked to the *New York Times* by two participants in the meeting (neither of whom had military or government experience) in such a way as to portray it as a Chinese threat to launch a nuclear attack on the United States, rather than as a Chinese expression of confidence in China's ability to deter a U.S. nuclear attack on it. Because the meeting was off-the-record and I was traveling abroad, I was not in a position to confirm, deny, or comment upon either the interpretation the media echo chamber had put on the anecdote or its entirely speculative attribution to Lieutenant General Xiong Guangkai (熊光楷), then deputy chief of the PLA General Staff.

59. Patrick E. Tyler, "China Signaling U.S. That It Will Not Invade Taiwan," *New York Times*, March 13, 1996, https://www.nytimes.com/1996/03/13/world/china-signaling-us-that-it -will-not-invade-taiwan.html.

60. This was privately reported to have been shared with mainland officials (but not with the United States).

61. For a portrait of the sources of Taiwan independence and Chinese nationalist views of Chinese on Taiwan and the mainland, see Chas W. Freeman Jr., *Interesting Times: China, America, and the Shifting Balance of Prestige* (Washington, DC: Just World, 2012), 83–102.

62. For an analysis of the conflicting conclusions of the parties and their implications, see Chas W. Freeman Jr., "Preventing War in the Taiwan Strait: Restraining Taiwan—and Beijing," *Foreign Affairs* 77, no. 4 (July–August 1998) 6–11, reprinted as "The Aftermath of the 1995–1996 Taiwan Crisis" in Chas W. Freeman Jr., "The Reemergence of the Tai-wan Problem," chap. 4 in *Interesting Times: China, America, and the Shifting Balance of Prestige* (Washington, DC: Just World, 2012), 122–141.

63. These capabilities are referred to in U.S. literature as anti-access/area denial (abbreviated A2/AD). PLA innovations include the deployment of ballistic missiles with terminal guidance that can strike moving targets (i.e., aircraft carriers) and long-range anti-ship cruise missiles that outrange U.S. equivalents.

64. For example, this was when the Center for Naval Analyses established its China Studies Center, now the premier institution analyzing politico-military matters relating to China.

65. On December 16, 1999, the United States formally apologized for the incident and paid $28 million in compensation to the Chinese government and $4.5 million to the families of those killed or injured. The intelligence officer found responsible for the error was dismissed. Six senior managers involved in it were reprimanded.

66. Lee's declaration was almost certainly stimulated by President Clinton's statement in Beijing on June 30, 1998, of U.S. policy on the Taiwan issue: "we don't support independence for Taiwan, or 'two Chinas,' or 'one Taiwan, one China,' and we don't believe that Taiwan should be a member in any organization for which statehood is a requirement." In August 1998, Lee had sponsored the formation of a team to "enhance ROC sovereignty and national status" headed by Tsai Ying-wen (蔡英文), an expert in

international law herself later elected president. The "two-state theory" was the product of this team's work. See Lee Teng-hui, " 'Two-State' Theory: Perceptions and Policy Change," http://www2.scu.edu.tw/politics/journal/doc/j294/4.pdf.

67. Germany's official broadcaster.

68. A visit to Taipei by Wang Daohan (汪道涵), the chair of Beijing's Association for Relations Across the Taiwan Strait (ARATS; 海峡两岸关系协会), and Ku Chen-fu (辜振甫), the chair of Taipei's Strait Exchange Foundation (SEF; 海峽交流基金會) had been set for October 1999 in a continuation of talks between the two begun in 1992.

69. China shares land borders with Vietnam, Laos, Myanmar, India, Bhutan, Nepal, Pakistan, Tajikistan, Kyrgyzstan, Kazakhstan, Russia, Mongolia, and Korea. It has disputed maritime frontiers with Vietnam, Malaysia, Indonesia, Brunei, the Philippines, and Japan. It must also deal with the threat from Taiwan and the U.S. forces protecting it.

70. Then called the PLA Second Artillery Corp, the PLARF became a separate military service within the PLA at the end of 2015.

71. By contrast, the U.S. Department of Defense budget alone is about 3.5 percent of GDP, while military expenditures in other departments' budgets (e.g., veterans' affairs, energy) bring the total to around 6 percent.

72. See P. R. Kumaraswamy, "Israel-China Relations and the Phalcon Controversy," *Middle East Policy* 12, no. 2 (Summer 2005): 93–103, https://www.mepc.org/journal/israel-china-relations-and-phalcon-controversy.

73. Neither side proposed either a coordinated search and rescue effort to recover Wang or a cooperative investigation of the incident. Both may have contributed to the collision. Wang was clearly flying dangerously close to the EP-3. On his third pass, he struck it or was struck by it. But the author has heard speculation from both American and Chinee sources that the pilot of the EP-3 was engaged in unsafe countermeasures, deliberately slowing to a speed below which Wang's J-8 could not sustain stable flight. This would have increased the risk of collision.

74. For a fuller description of the incident, see James Mulvenon, "Chen Xiaogong: A Political Biography," *China Leadership Monitor*, no. 22, https://www.hoover.org/sites/default/files/uploads/documents/CLM22JM.pdf.

75. "President Chen Delivers the Opening Address of the 29th Annual Meeting of the World Federation of Taiwanese Associations via Live Video Link," Office of the President, Republic of China (Taiwan), August 3, 2002, https://english.president.gov.tw/NEWS/490.

76. John King, "Blunt Bush Message for Taiwan," CNN, December 9, 2003, http://www.cnn.com/2003/ALLPOLITICS/12/09/bush.china.taiwan/.

77. In *Parity, Peace, and Win-Win: The Republic of China's Position on the "Special State-to-State Relationship"* (Taiwan, Taipei: Mainland Affairs Council, Executive Yuan, Republic of China, August 1, 1999), Lee Teng-hui's government had affirmed that "Taiwan and the Chinese mainland have always differed in their definition of 'one China.' Thus, in 1992, . . . the two sides eventually reached an agreement on 'one China,' with each side being entitled to its respective interpretation."

78. The Anti-Secession Law was an ironic mirror image of the U.S. Taiwan Relations Act of 1979. The text may be found at: "Anti-Secession Law (Full text)," Embassy of the People's Republic of China in the United States of America, March 15, 2005, http://www.china-embassy.org/eng/zt/999999999/t187406.htm.

79. Lien had served as foreign minister, premier, and vice president in Taiwan. He ran for president in 2000 but was not elected. Lien's political rival, James Soong (宋楚瑜), who had left the KMT to run against Lien as an independent in 2004, followed closely behind Lien, meeting with Hu Jintao in Beijing early in May.

80. Rumsfeld did not respond to the implied invitation to offer similar reassurances to the PRC. The issue of strategic deterrence has hardly been touched upon by the two sides and remains a dangerous weak point in U.S.-PRC military relations.

81. See discussion of the 1993 Freeman visit to Beijing earlier in the chapter.

82. The USS *Impeccable* is a U.S. Navy catamaran designed to collect intelligence on submarines with a towed sonar array. PLAN frigates and aircraft harassed it while it was in international waters south of Hainan Island collecting information on the approaches to the Chinese submarine base at Sanya, finally snagging its sonar array with a grappling hook. The United States protested and sent a destroyer to protect the *Impeccable*. See David Morgan, "U.S. Says Chinese Vessels Harassed Navy Ship," Reuters, March 9, 2009, https://www.reuters.com/article/us-usa-china-navy/u-s-says-chinese-vessels-harassed -navy-ship-idUSTRE52845A20090309.

83. China claims sovereignty over all land features in the South China Sea, as does Vietnam. A decision by an ad hoc tribunal convened under the United Nations Convention on the Law of the Sea at the request of the Philippines (but with U.S. backing) ruled that there were no "islands" in the South China Sea capable of generating EEZs. (See Permanent Court of Arbitration, "Press Release: The South China Sea Arbitration— The Republic of the Philippines v. The Peoples Republic of China," July 12, 2016, https://pca-cpa.org/wp-content/uploads/sites/175/2016/07/PH-CN-20160712-Pres -Release-No-11-English.pdf.) This finding does not invalidate China's claims to rocks there but does so with respect to reefs, on one of which China has built an artificial island. The finding awards the Philippines an EEZ beyond the territorial waters surrounding islands claimed and occupied by China and Vietnam. China refused to participate in the tribunal's proceedings and has ignored its findings as illegal. (See chapter 3 by John Garver in this volume for another discussion of issues surrounding the South China Sea.)

84. Things did not go well for Hu. See Chas W. Freeman Jr., "The Arabs Take a Chinese Wife: Sino-Arab Relations in the Decade to Come," May 7, 2006, https://chasfreeman.net /the-arabs-take-a-chinese-wife-sino-arab-relations-in-the-decade-to-come/.

85. These issues were overshadowed in the international media by a round of speculation (reflecting American egocentrism) that a test flight of a Chinese J-20 (歼-20) stealth air superiority fighter that took place while Gates was in Beijing was a sort of signal of one-upmanship directed at him. The evidence suggests that the timing was decided by the engineers in Chengdu responsible for developing the aircraft, without regard to political events in Beijing or elsewhere.

86. The case of ZTE Corporation was a particularly clear instance of this. Fined for having purloined the intellectual property of American companies, it was then put out of business to prevent it from engaging in espionage, a speculative charge without evidence and irrelevant to the original cause of its punishment. The company's closure cost seventy thousand Chinese jobs and an unknown number on the part of its U.S. suppliers. The Trump administration eventually backed off despite demagogic objections from members of the Senate and House of Representatives.

87. These aspects of China's competitiveness, as well as the basic contradictions afflicting U.S.-China relations, are discussed in Chas W. Freeman Jr., "The United States and China: Game of Superpowers," February 8, 2018, https://chasfreeman.net/the-united -states-and-china-game-of-superpowers/.

88. Donald J. Trump, *Nation Security Strategy of the United States* (Washington, DC: White House, December 2017), https://www.whitehouse.gov/wp-content/uploads/2017/12/NSS -Final-12-18-2017-0905.pdf; and Jim Mattis, "Summary of the 2018 National Defense

Strategy of the United States of America," Department of Defense, https://www.defense
.gov/Portals/1/Documents/pubs/2018-National-Defense-Strategy-Summary.pdf.

89. New restrictions resulted after passage of the Foreign Investment Risk Review Modernization Act of 2018.

90. The main legal issue at this point is China's use of straight baselines to delimit the territorial seas around the islands it claims and occupies in both the Paracel (西沙) and
Spratly (南沙) Islands. The United States insists that this is illegal under the UN Convention on the Law of the Sea.

91. Lolita C. Baldor and Christopher Bodeen, "Mattis, China Leaders Strike Positive
Tone Despite Tensions," AP News, June 27, 2018, https://apnews.com/article/2fd1a13f15
6c414ead855e1e14ffcaa3.

92. Complaints about China's lack of strategic transparency are embarrassing demonstrations of the failure of those who make them to pay attention to what Chinese write and
say about their strategy, which is a great deal, very little of which bears any resemblance
whatsoever to the mirror-imaging narratives that routinely prevail in official Washington. Repetition feeds further repetition until fantasies are taken as axioms. The likelihood that confidently asserted canards will be corrected is low. There is no political
spectacle more impressive than the Washington think-tank community wheeling, like
a shoal of fish, to align itself with the latest delusions of its government sponsors and
media predators. The intellectual lemmings of the press pick up the theme and march
with it, en masse, into the abyss where alternative facts reside, become fruitful, and
multiply.

93. The Chinese, following the logic of Sunzi (知己知彼百战百胜)—know yourself and
your opponent and you will win every battle—have devoted time and effort to understanding the United States and the American way of war. At present, Americans are
more likely to attribute views to the Chinese that fit U.S. stereotypes of what the Chinese must want—usually something that Americans think we would want if we were
Chinese rather than anything traceable to a reliable Chinese source. Sunzi did not live
to experience cable TV and social media, but had he done so, he would have pointed
out that replacing empirically derived situational awareness with gratifying political
fantasy and self-serving delusion is a sure path to needless carnage and defeat.

94. To the extent the United States treats Taiwan as a strategic asset, China can be counted
upon to treat it as a strategic liability and act accordingly.

95. In the Belgrade embassy bombing (1999) and the Hainan EP-3 incident (2001).

96. See Office of the Secretary of Defense, "Annual Report to Congress: Military and
Security Developments involving the People's Republic of China 2018," https://media
.defense.gov/2018/Aug/16/2001955282/-1/-1/1/2018-CHINA-MILITARY-POWER
-REPORT.PDF#page=5&zoom=auto,-257,67.

97. Carnegie–Tsinghua Center for Global Policy, "A New Type of Great Power Relations
Between China and the United States," July 6, 2013, https://carnegietsinghua.org/2013/07/06
/new-type-of-great-power-relations-between-china-and-united-states-event-4161.

CHAPTER 12

CHINA'S PERIPHERY

A Rift Zone in U.S.-China Relations

CARLA P. FREEMAN

A s Owen Lattimore, the great sinologist and expert on China's vast and complex border regions, observed, China's periphery has long been a geopolitical pivot area for great powers. In *Inner Asian Frontiers of China*, written soon after the Second World War when the international ascendancy of the United States put the spotlight on naval and air force capabilities as the source of international power, Lattimore drew attention to the continued importance of interactions between what he called "sovereignties" across frontiers to the balance of global economic and military power.[1] Today, the global consequence of the U.S. relationship with the People's Republic of China makes the broad dimensions of the bilateral relationship a natural focus of academic efforts to explain converging or conflicting interests between the two countries. Yet, for much of the history of relations between the United States and China, China's periphery, the zone in which China's borders—internationally recognized or unilaterally claimed—interact with the borders of other countries, has been a fulcrum of tensions between the two countries and has had geopolitical ramifications. This pattern has persisted throughout the past fifty years of U.S.-China relations, even when the two countries had strategic, economic, and transnational reasons for international cooperation. In short, China's periphery has been central, not peripheral, to U.S.-China relations. Through an examination of three cases, this chapter seeks to show why the periphery has been central and to derive lessons that may be useful in managing U.S.-China relations for international stability in the future.

Let me first clarify that I use the term *China's periphery* without any intention of suggesting that Asia's political geography does, or should, center on China. The United States has its own view of Asia's geography bounded by maritime, rather than continental, terms, as the designations it employs—Asia-Pacific, Pacific Rim, and Indo-Pacific—indicate. China's periphery, however, is a concept that encapsulates China's view of the geography along its borders as a buffer zone that is both sociocultural and strategic. As scholar Pitman Potter writes, the "periphery of China may be thought of as comprising those regions surrounding China proper that offer both shelter from and interaction with systems, cultures and peoples outside."[2] This buffer includes China's frontier regions, or *bianjiang* (边疆), which form the inner borderlands of China's modern state and that were once known as lying "beyond the pass" (*guanwai*, 关外), such as Manchuria, Mongolia, Tibet, and Xinjiang, and perhaps even Guizhou and Yunnan.[3] More expansively, the periphery may refer to China's "rim," or *zhoubian* (周边),[4] the countries in China's regional neighborhood. China's 2014 Foreign Affairs Work Conference, which laid the groundwork for a fresh diplomatic focus by China on neighboring countries, took the *zhoubian* or rimlands as its principal focus.

Beyond a buffering function for Chinese security and cultural integrity, China's periphery describes both an elastic strategic geography that expands and contracts in size with the ebb and flow of Chinese power and influence in Asia, as well as the geographies to which China attributes strategic importance. For example, the 2013 Science of Military Strategy (国防科技), which reflects the thinking of some of China's leading strategists, calls for moving China's first line of defense so that "China's borders and coasts are now viewed as interior lines in a conflict, not exterior ones."[5] As a zone determined by the scope of China's strategic interests, given China's expanding military, economic, and political clout, it is not surprising that many Chinese policy makers are increasingly expansive in their descriptions of China's periphery. As Renmin University scholar, Pang Zhongying (庞中英), observed in 2007, "China's periphery is such a vast area that it virtually covers the whole of Asia. China's fundamental interests lie in Asia."[6]

Pang's statement perfectly encapsulates why the U.S.-China relationship in China's periphery is strategically fraught. The United States has been a formidable global power for a century and, since the Second World War, has played a leading role in global security, with extensive economic and strategic interests in parts of Asia that overlap with China's periphery. As a world power, the United States has promoted global rules and norms compatible with its preferences; these, too, extend into Asia and thus into China's expansive periphery. In addition, America's identity as an international actor also includes promoting national ideals, which include the universality of human rights, including the right to political freedom and a democratic political order and, historically, free trade. There is an idealistic dimension to this aspect of American foreign policy. But it also reflects an important strategic perspective, one that scholar Michael J. Green describes as especially important to the United States in Asia, where Washington has sought to promote an "ideational balance of power" whereby "like-minded states reinforce American influence, access, and security."[7]

As a major presence in China's periphery, U.S. actions and policies have frequently run counter to many of China's preferences for the international environment in its near abroad. Indeed, American policy makers have generally thought it strategically and ideologically prudent to encourage states within China's periphery to formally or informally align with Washington or to maintain an orientation independent from China that enables them to either resist or reject Chinese influence.

U.S. policy in this regard took an extreme form during the Cold War, when the United States sought to expand the number of its allies and partners along China's periphery to support its anticommunist containment strategy. The United States had alliance relationships with Japan, the Philippines, Pakistan, South Korea, and Thailand and close security ties with Singapore. It had provided military assistance at various points in the decades after the People's Republic of China was established in 1949 to those countries, as well as to Indonesia and India. Washington also extended military support to Taiwan, which it recognized as the Republic of China until 1979, shielding it from military threats from Beijing as its ally from 1955 to 1979 and as its security partner since then. During the Cold War, Beijing saw the U.S. containment strategy as the encirclement of China by the U.S. military and Washington's prodemocracy foreign policy agenda as an existential threat.[8]

The sustained power projection of the United States into Asia through its "hub-and-spokes" alliance system of discrete security relationships with Australia, Japan, the Philippines, South Korea, and Thailand, as well as its many other security partnerships in the Indo-Pacific, increasingly complicates China's regional policy objectives. Like many great powers, Beijing seeks to use its economic and military capacity to maximize its national security and achieve its national interests in the region. Whereas Washington believes that it is responsibly promoting regional stability by responding to demand signals for U.S. political-military support from states along China's rim, Beijing sees neo-imperialist overreach and a U.S. desire to contain or encircle (*ezhi*, 遏制, or *weidu*, 围堵) China.[9]

China also strains against Washington's attempts to act as the global enforcer of international law, in some cases even at the risk of violent conflict. For example, Beijing has used its increasingly capable military to challenge unilateral freedom of navigation operations undertaken by U.S. naval vessels in the far western Pacific, which are meant to demonstrate established interpretations of the scope of a state's maritime jurisdiction under the international law of the sea. Beijing asserts that it has the right to restrict access by foreign navies to traverse its exclusive economic zone (EEZ).

In contrast, the United States contends that the law, both as customary law and as stipulated in the UN Convention on the Law of the Sea (UNCLOS), which the United States has not ratified, designates EEZs as high seas for naval and commercial shipping alike. Despite a bilateral code of conduct on unplanned air and naval encounters negotiated in 2014, risky encounters between the U.S. and Chinese navies in the Sea of Japan and South China Sea, as well as between military aircraft in airspace off the Chinese coast, occur with alarming frequency. Beijing sees the U.S. presence as destabilizing a region critical to China's economic, military, and energy security, whereas the United States sees its role as a stabilizing regional balancer and provider of maritime security and other global public goods.[10]

Similarly, China decries U.S. insistence that established interpretations of international law—those that reflect norms established by the United States and its Western allies—are the only legitimate interpretations. Beijing sees this defense of established norms as a defense of rules of the road serving Washington's interests and an element of a strategy of "constrainment" (*zhiyue*, 制约, or *qianzhi*, 牵制) meant to limit China's right as a major international power to influence global norms.[11] U.S. insistence that international law has a role in the disputes in the South China Sea is particularly grating for Beijing, not only because China and the Chinese people, who have been educated with maps and histories depicting the South China Sea as unequivocally Chinese, have no doubts about their sovereignty over its rocks, reefs, atolls, or islands, but also because they trace the failure to patrol these features by the Qing to the collapse of the *Pax Sinica* (盛世) in the region at the hands of the West.[12]

For Beijing, however, the most egregious U.S. challenge along its periphery is Washington's willingness to guard Taiwan's de facto independence, especially visible in the quasi-alliance relationship between Washington and Taipei, with which Beijing technically remains at war. Reunifying Taiwan with the mainland is core to the goal of reunifying all of the parts of China separated from China over the course of China's Century of National Humiliation. This goal remains central to the Chinese Communist Party (CCP) mission of national revival (*minzu zhenxing*, 民族振兴), which is fundamental to its political legitimacy. The idea is that without the CCP, China would not have overcome the division and weakness wrought by the imperial powers.[13] Developing military capabilities to retake the island by force in the face of Taiwan's security relationship with the United States has been a major driver of China's rapid defense modernization.[14]

In speaking about the U.S. role in forestalling the mainland's ability to restore control over the island, China frequently castigates U.S. interference (*ganshe*, 干涉) in China's internal affairs as undermining China's sovereignty and security interests.[15] But for Beijing, Taiwan is far from the sole example of U.S. interference. Beijing sees the United States as a persistent threat to its control over other culturally distinct regions where its sovereignty is otherwise unchallenged. David M. Lampton characterizes Beijing's view of these areas— Hong Kong, Tibet, and Xinjiang, as well as other border regions, such as Inner Mongolia—as "unreliable." They are "administratively and politically part of China, but not of China in ethnicity or spirit."[16] From Beijing's perspective, they are therefore vulnerable to the black hand of U.S. political manipulation aimed at encouraging separatism and/or political turmoil in China against its CCP-led political system and inhibiting its rise as a great power.

The three cases of U.S.-China relations in China's periphery addressed in this chapter are all sources of intense friction between Washington and Beijing at the time of writing. My first case study explores the 2016 decision by the Republic of Korea (ROK) to deploy the U.S. military's Terminal High Altitude Area Defense (THAAD) system, on the Korean Peninsula. Beijing remains deeply concerned about the U.S. military presence in South Korea, given its proximity to territory that, historically, has been the ingress for attacks on China. Among other strategic concerns, THAAD deployment to South Korea, a mere 710 miles from Beijing, is viewed by China as an effort by the United States to strengthen its capacity to defeat China in a war by adding new weapons and surveillance capabilities to the United States' forward-deployed arsenal. The United States protests that THAAD is solely directed at mitigating the ballistic missile threat posed by Pyongyang. For Beijing, however, there is no question that this addition of U.S. military capabilities to the peninsula seeks to weaken China's nuclear deterrent, specifically by enabling Washington to surveil China's nuclear facilities and monitor the boost phase of missiles directed at distant targets, such as the United States, thereby weakening China's second-strike nuclear capabilities. At the time of deployment, some observers drew parallels between THAAD and the 1962 Cuban Missile Crisis, including speculating that Beijing could launch preemptive strikes against THAAD.[17] China also interpreted the deployment as a maneuver to introduce strains in Beijing's steadily improving relations with Seoul to reinforce U.S.-ROK security ties and the American hub-and-spokes alliance system in the region.[18]

My second case study focuses on the Philippines arbitration initiated by Manila in 2013 under Annex VII of the UNCLOS contesting China's challenge to its territorial and other maritime claims in the South China Sea. The arbitration illustrates how China sees U.S. policy support for its ally and use of international law as constrainment. Washington considers its actions as appropriate given its ties to Manila. These links have been forged not only by a legacy of a half century as the occupying colonial power and Manila's military ally since 1951, but also by the importance of the United States as an economic partner and a primary source of foreign investment in the Philippines and by its deep cultural ties to the Philippines through its more than four million Filipino American citizens. For Beijing, however, Washington is an unwelcome antagonist in a bilateral sovereignty dispute that Beijing is convinced can be resolved absent third-party meddling. Underlying the contemporary dispute is China's own sense of its historical relationship to the Philippines, which includes tributary ties with Luzon dating to the Ming dynasty and a flourishing silk trade that gave rise to a Chinese trading community in Manila.[19]

My third case looks at the U.S.-China relationship in the context of Hong Kong's recent protests, beginning with the 2014 Occupy or Umbrella Movement through the time of writing in 2019–2020. The Hong Kong example shows how Washington's vocal support for the protests in the name of sustaining Hong Kong autonomy and way of life, including democratization and human rights, is perceived by Beijing as serving a U.S. objective of destabilizing or even fracturing (*fenhua*, 分化) China. For Beijing, Washington's vocal support for protestors and decision to revoke its preferential economic treatment of Hong Kong in reaction to Beijing's implementation in June 2020 of a new national security law for the territory has affirmed that U.S. interests in Hong Kong are principally geopolitical. For many in Washington, China's policies to curb Hong Kong's autonomy and suppress its democratic movement were emblematic of China's antipathy toward liberal political values and an affirmation that a globally powerful China posed a threat to democratic societies. However, in the context of broader U.S.-China strategic competition, the decision by the Trump administration to terminate Hong Kong's special customs status vis-à-vis the United States was also a way to close an important channel for high-technology imports that would otherwise fall within U.S. export controls.[20]

Hong Kong has figured importantly in the history of U.S. relations with Asia since it developed as a leading regional commercial and financial center under British rule following the First Opium War. Before U.S.-China rapprochement in the early 1970s, Hong Kong was a critical information-gathering post for the United States on developments on the Chinese mainland, as well as a base for CIA operatives.[21] Negotiations between Britain and China over Hong Kong's return to China in 1997 under the one country, two systems formula as a special administrative region took place amid a rapidly deepening and broadening U.S.-China economic relationship. The United States was not directly involved in the negotiations but used its relations with China and Britain to urge both countries to find a solution that supported the Hong Kong people's well-being.[22]

Before the 1997 handover, the U.S. Congress passed the 1992 United States–Hong Kong Policy Act. The act legislates regular reporting from the U.S. executive branch to Congress on such issues as the degree to which Hong Kong has maintained its autonomy from mainland China and the development of democratic institutions. Since the act was signed into law by President George

H. W. Bush, China has called it an example of U.S. interference as well as a demonstration of Washington's hegemonic insensitivity.[23] However, the act was not a major source of bilateral contention, in part, as Lampton observed two decades ago, because it offered benefits to Hong Kong, which was about to become an official part of China.[24] In 2020, China used similar language to describe U.S. policy actions initiated in response to Beijing's handling of protracted protests in Hong Kong in 2019–2020; however, it now also vowed retaliatory action.[25]

In all three examples, Washington's policies have reinforced the view in Beijing that the United States is unable to square its interests and objectives in the region with a regionally powerful China, and therefore, U.S. regional policy is fundamentally competitive with, if not directly hostile to, China. Washington, for its part, sees China's actions as manifestations of China's hostility to the U.S. presence in the region, as well as to the global rules and norms that have been the basis of the *Pax Americana* writ large.

The cases examined in this chapter, taken together, illustrate that, despite the fifty years of bilateral engagement and cooperation on hard and nontraditional security, deep economic ties, and growing flows of people, China's periphery has remained a geopolitical rift zone for the United States' relationship with China. American regional dominance forced China's compliance with U.S. preferences, but beneath the surface, deep strains persisted. As the three examples show, the periphery is replete with chronic fissures, each representing a fault line from which violent conflict could erupt. China's CCP leadership has made guiding China's rise to great power status, ensuring security along its borders, and restoring and assuring the integrity of Chinese territory fundamental objectives of its leadership. U.S. policies in China's periphery are perceived as seeking to constrain, encircle, and disrupt these Chinese ambitions and to undermine the CCP's legitimacy.

For Washington, however, many of China's actions seem designed to harm U.S. allies' interests, challenge established norms, and jeopardize the ability of the United States to project military force into eastern Asia, including by abrading U.S. alliance relationships—all cardinal affronts to a nation that "is, and will always be, a Pacific power."[26] The cases show how remarkable it is that the two countries have found modes of avoiding direct conflict even as, during the past five decades, some old fissures like Taiwan have widened and newer ones like the South China Sea have grown more acute. The cases also illustrate that this successful navigation was in no small part the result of the presence of leaders in smaller countries and other entities (or *third parties*, to use Lampton's term[27]) in China's periphery who have seen greater benefit from easing rather than inflaming frictions between the United States and China in the region. This has been fortuitous; it is not guaranteed.

The Threat of Encirclement: South Korea's Missile Defense

Seoul's July 2016 announcement that it had agreed to deploy a U.S. Terminal High Altitude Area Defense (THAAD) system on South Korean territory caused a near rupture in China-ROK relations. For Beijing, Seoul's decision to move ahead with the deployment in the face of Beijing's vehement objections was an act of treachery. China had come to see South Korea as good neighbor with which it had multifaceted ties, including as a trade and investment partner. The two countries' ties flowed naturally from their proximity and economic complementarity. Normalization between them in 1992 not only brought 30 percent annual growth in trade but was also accompanied by the resuscitation of cultural ties linked both to economic and education exchanges, as well as increased tourism and the penetration of Korean media into China. The two countries deliberately expanded cultural connections through a Chinese Cooperative Partnership for the Twenty-First Century, concluded in 1998.[28]

South Korea was also an emerging security partner for China in confronting mutual concerns about risks to regional security from both North Korea and a remilitarizing Japan. In 2014, Xi Jinping and then ROK president Park Geun-hye had met in Beijing on a visit described as a "trip of heart and trust" (*sim shin ji ryoe* in Korean or *xin xin zhi ru* [信心之旅] in Chinese) to forge a strategic cooperative partnership.[29] This marked a major breakthrough for China on the Korean Peninsula. South Korea seemed to have moved from seeing its relationship with China principally as a subset of its relationship with the United States to seeing China as a prospective partner in regional security, separate and apart from the U.S.-ROK alliance. For Beijing, the decision by Seoul to deploy THAAD, despite the system's role in increasing Washington's capacity to gather intelligence and enhance communications in conflict scenarios and thus to weaken China's nuclear deterrent, was an intolerable betrayal.[30]

Korean analysts emphasize that Seoul agreed to deploy THAAD with the sole intent of augmenting its ability to defend against a North Korean attack, with no plans to link it to a U.S.-led global missile defense network. However, according to some analysts, THAAD was also a move by Seoul to exercise an option to enhance its security that China opposed to assert its independence, even as the two countries grew strategically closer. As the South Korean scholar Hee Ok Lee put it, "Seoul needed to demonstrate that it would not permit China to exercise a veto over its right to deploy a system to defend its national security."[31] Previously, Seoul had said it would not join the U.S. missile defense program, referencing its high costs and South Korean plans to develop its own missile defense system.[32]

In 2014, Washington had begun to ratchet up pressure on Seoul to deploy THAAD over concerns about the threat posed by North Korea's medium- and intermediate-range missiles to American and South Korean troops on the peninsula, as well as to more distant targets, including U.S. bases in Japan. Some in Washington argued that Chinese deployment of Russian-made S-400 missile defense and antiaircraft systems on the Shandong Peninsula, which could potentially shield China from a limited North Korean missile attack, underscored the need for THAAD.[33] North Korea's fourth nuclear test in 2016 appeared to provide the impetus for Seoul to begin official consultation with the United States on THAAD deployment.

From the moment that Seoul appeared to seriously consider THAAD deployment, Beijing expressed its intense opposition. Senior officials made clear that China saw it as a disruption of the regional security balance and a threat to its security interests that would do little to protect against the North Korean threat. Beijing focused on the adjustability of the THAAD system's radar detection range, which would enable it to target China's strategic missile systems. These missile systems are important to Beijing's defense, particularly its coastal defense, and to Beijing's deterrence of Taiwanese independence.[34] In addition, Beijing anticipated that expected Russian countermeasures intended to defeat THAAD would also introduce further vulnerabilities to its own security.[35]

Beijing responded punitively against Seoul to the U.S.-ROK agreement on THAAD deployment. It suspended its high-level defense dialogue as well as a number of other official exchanges with South Korea and issued orders to cut the number of Chinese tourists to South Korea by 20 percent, which (in late 2017) represented an estimated economic loss of over US$15 billion in revenue to South Korea. Chinese authorities also encouraged a devastating consumer boycott and issued numerous citations for local codes violations of Lotte Group, a South Korean conglomerate that had owned the property purchased for THAAD construction and operated many shopping complexes in China.[36] By 2019, Lotte, which had had an estimated US$9.6 billion investment in China, had closed most of its stores and factories in China.[37] Appearances by Korean celebrities and popular Korean television shows aired in China also became casualties,[38] as did Korean automaker Hyundai, which saw its car sales in China drop dramatically.[39]

Beijing's officials also conveyed China's feelings about THAAD in language designed to make the strength of China's opposition clear to Seoul. Chinese Foreign Minister Wang Yi told his South Korean counterpart that the deployment would "directly damage the strategic security interests of China" and warned against using the specter of North Korea to take actions that "jeopardize China's legitimate rights and interests."[40] In an interview with Reuters soon after Seoul's announcement of the THAAD decision, Wang spoke more colorfully, likening THAAD deployment to a sword dance aimed at China with villainous intent.[41]

There is much to unpack in these statements about China's perceptions of its neighbors along its periphery and its relationship to the most historically close among them, including Wang's classical allusions—the sword dance is a reference to the *Shiji* (史记), or *Records of the Grand Historian* (94 BC), for example. A Chinese music video titled "No THAAD" that was shared on the social media account of the Chinese Communist Youth League and thus officially sanctioned, or perhaps even produced, is useful in illuminating the heart of the issue and illustrating why THAAD deployment kindled Beijing's ire and inflamed Chinese nationalist sentiment. The rap by the group CD Rev, sung in English and Chinese with Korean subtitles, begins in English with the line, "How many times do I have to warn you my lovely little neighbor boy? You don't really want that little toy. You know, big brother is annoyed." It then calls South Korea a "twenty-first-century colony." The rap continues ominously in English, "but I love you kid, you will get embraced," and then, in Chinese, "I also don't want to be reminded of the war between the two sides." It winds up with the question: "Why not choose us rather than Uncle Sam?"[42] The rap has it all: a reference to the Confucian hierarchy that once ordered regional relations in calling China "big brother," which also underscores the long history of Sino-Korean relations; it alludes to the Korean War that ended in stalemate between North and South Korea after China's entry into the conflict on the North Korean side; and it contains language to inflame popular Korean sensitivities about the sustained U.S. presence on its soil (a "twenty-first-century colony"). Seoul could not fail to understand that in deploying THAAD it was making a political choice to side with the United States against China.

After becoming president of South Korea in 2017, a victory that ended nearly a decade of conservative leadership in South Korea, Moon Jae-in moved swiftly to try to reset China-ROK relations on the basis of setting differences aside and finding common ground. Achieving progress required committing South Korea to three noes, stating that Seoul had no intention to (1) install additional THAAD batteries, (2) participate in a regional missile defense system, or (3) form a trilateral alliance with the United States and Japan.[43] In 2017, Moon also initiated an assessment of THAAD's environmental impact that effectively suspended installation of the THAAD battery component and, in 2019, announced South Korea was considering withdrawing from an intelligence-sharing agreement with Tokyo, against Washington's wishes.

Through its pushback against THAAD, China made clear to Seoul that it will not tolerate actions that it considers additional threats to its security along its periphery from the U.S.-ROK alliance. It has also made clear that, should the United States successfully pressure Seoul to remove THAAD from its current limbo or take steps that China sees as otherwise violating the three noes, there will be significant consequences. South Korea's history makes it deeply wary of becoming a locus for U.S.-China confrontation, and Seoul can be expected to do its utmost to minimize its own exposure. THAAD deployment could corrode rather than strengthen the U.S.-South Korea alliance, thereby weakening the United States' strategic position in Asia. For China, THAAD is an instrument of an American containment strategy against China, worth seeking to neuter by leveraging its influence over South Korea. This suggests that China sees little risk that South Korea or other regional neighbors will forego economic relations when they are the cost of failing to respond positively to its demands. For the United States, China's opposition to THAAD and use of economic coercion to compel South Korea to retreat from the system's deployment is itself a rationale for pressing forward with the deployment.

Shared concerns about the North Korean nuclear threat may mitigate the risk of THAAD itself becoming a flash point for U.S.-China conflict. However, the deployment of THAAD on the peninsula has become a litmus test for comparative U.S.-Chinese influence in the region. Thus, THAAD is the object of intense disagreement and intensifying mistrust between the United States and China on China's periphery.

Constraining Goliath: The Philippines Arbitration

In 2013, the Philippines took its decades-long dispute with China over maritime claims to the Spratly (*Nansha*, 南沙) Islands in the South China Sea to The Hague in a bid to invalidate the principal bases for China's claims to sovereignty and jurisdiction over South China Sea waters. The arbitration challenged China's claim of historic rights, as well as the classification of maritime features used by China as the basis for its maritime claims.[44] Manila hoped to turn the tide in its long-standing dispute with Beijing over the disputed territories, including Scarborough Shoal, as well as fifty other Spratly Island features called the Kalayaan Island Group, one of a number of disputes between China and its neighbors over islands, reefs, and atolls in the South China Sea. Manila has a limited military presence on nine of the Spratly features. The Permanent Court of Arbitration (PCA) ruling issued in 2016 was overwhelmingly favorable to the Philippines. Rodrigo Duterte, president of the Philippines since 2016, has pursued good relations with Beijing. During a 2019 meeting, he and President Xi affirmed that their relations rested upon their "centuries' old friendship" and the mutual "benefits" from cooperating.[45]

As of the fall of 2020, Beijing has occupied seven reefs in the Spratly Islands and has constructed military and maritime rescue facilities on a number of them. It has also asserted its administration of the Spratlys by assigning the islands to a Hainan provincial district. The Spratlys are significant not just for their resources, which include substantial energy deposits as well as minerals and living marine resources, but also for their strategic geography, which spans key maritime trade routes to Northeast Asia and makes them attractive as potential bases for both monitoring and controlling access to the South China Sea.

Although the arbitration did not itself resolve questions about the sovereignty of the maritime claims—and indeed could not, as UNCLOS does not include mechanisms to adjudicate sovereignty claims—for Washington, the arbitration process and its outcome were policy successes. Critically, the arbitral body found that in the Spratly chain there are no natural islands capable of sustaining human habitation and, thus, per Article 121 of UNCLOS, the islands do not generate the same maritime entitlements to an EEZ as other land territory.[46] The arbitration ruling also determined that China's nine-dash line claims, based on historic rights in the South China Sea, are incompatible with international law because "there was no evidence that China had historically exercised exclusive control over the waters or their resources."[47]

The arbitration unfolded against the backdrop of a series of Chinese policies aimed at asserting China claims. These policies not only included the construction of sophisticated military facilities on reclaimed reefs in the South China Sea but also the deployment of a heavily armed coast guard and fleets of state-backed, armed fishing boat maritime militias in disputed waters in order to drive off Filipino fishermen.[48] China's refusal to recognize the arbitration as a valid legal process and its ramping up of construction such as a new radar array on Spratly reefs supported an image of China as Goliath, using its far greater might to overwhelm the Filipino David, and buttressed U.S. condemnation of Chinese behavior in the region.[49]

Manila's position is that it has strong grounds for its territorial claims based on the principles of proximity, discovery, and effective occupation. It points to the use of its maritime claims as fishing grounds by Filipino fishermen since at least the Spanish colonial period. It also references the U.S. Navy's oceanographic surveys of the area in the 1950s, its use of the shoal in other defense-related activities, and its construction of a lighthouse on the shoal in the mid-1960s.[50] It notes that in 1946, soon after independence from the United States, Vice President and Foreign Secretary Elpidio Quirino mentioned the Spratlys as essential to the country's national security. In the 1950s, private citizens of the Philippines occupied some of the Spratlys' features, declaring them the Free Territory of Freedomland. Manila began to strengthen formal administrative control over the islands and reefs beginning in the 1970s. The government of Ferdinand Marcos renamed Freedomland "Kalayaan" (meaning freedom in Tagalog) and officially incorporated the territories into its closest province, Palawan.[51]

Beijing contends that it can document its dominion over the Spratlys to the second century BC and that the historical record also shows China's vigilant defense of the islands against would-be interlopers. It cites the Qing government's efforts to secure sovereignty over South China Sea islands after reports of a Japanese presence on one of them as more recent evidence of this vigilance. Beijing also points to China's protest in 1933 against the French occupation of nine Spratly islands and to at least one inspection tour of the islands under the Republic of China. In 1948, China's embattled Kuomintang government published an official atlas that showed an eleven-dash maritime boundary line enclosing most South China Sea features, the Spratlys and Taiwan among them, indicating the scope of China's claims in the waters.

In 1949, after the Communist government took power, China formally assigned the islands to an administrative authority in its new government. Under Premier Zhou Enlai, two of the dashes reaching into the Gulf of Tonkin were removed in order to placate Hanoi, resulting in what is today popularly known as the "nine-dash line." Since the 1970s, China has asserted its claims by deploying fishing fleets, sending officials on oceanographic vessels to the area, and constructing facilities on some of the features.[52] In the late 1980s, China began surveying the Spratlys and started building a permanent base on Fiery Cross Reef. In 1988, tensions between China and Vietnam, which then controlled more than twenty Spratly features, erupted in a bloody skirmish with casualties on the Vietnamese side.[53]

Ratification by China and the Philippines of the UNCLOS in 1992 and 1994, respectively, only added urgency to the two countries' territorial dispute and ratcheted up bilateral tensions. Under the UNCLOS, coastal states have the right to a two-hundred-nautical-mile EEZ within which they exercise exclusive jurisdiction over marine resources, including seabed mineral and hydrocarbon deposits. EEZs extend from coastal baselines, however. Only those islands that can naturally sustain human habitation are considered land with legal rights to such baselines. Where maritime features are concerned, the scope of a state's potential maritime rights that may be based on them thus depends on how they are categorized under the UNCLOS. For the Philippines, its status as an archipelagic state under the UNCLOS and its sovereignty over the Spratly islets and reefs confer sovereign jurisdiction over the islets' adjacent waters and their resources as internal or "archipelagic" waters. China, it should be noted, signed UNCLOS with a number of reservations germane to its dispute with the Philippines, including that it would effect through consultations its maritime boundaries with coastal states in its vicinity, and that it "[reaffirmed] its sovereignty over all its archipelagoes and islands as listed in Article 2 of the Law of the People's Republic of China on the Territorial Sea and Contiguous Zone which was promulgated on 25 February 1992."[54] Article 2 specifies that the "land territory of the People's Republic of China includes . . . Taiwan and all islands appertaining thereto," which comprise the Diaoyu, Penghu, Dongsha, Xisha, Zhongsha, and Nansha Islands, "as well as all the other islands belonging to the People's Republic of China."[55]

As bilateral tensions rose between Manila and Beijing in the 1990s, the two countries signed a bilateral code committing each other to peaceful conflict behavior and confidence building in the region, agreeing that any conflict between them shall be settled by the countries directly concerned. During the Asia-Pacific Economic Cooperation (APEC) meeting in late 1995, Chinese president Jiang and then Philippine president Ramos spoke about the possibility of jointly developing marine resources in contested areas. Although frictions between China and the Philippines intensified over the presence of Philippine marines on Second Thomas Shoal in 2002, the Gloria Macapagal Arroyo administration supported negotiation within the Association of Southeast Asian Nations (ASEAN) of a code of conduct on the South China Sea. The Philippines and China also engaged in confidence-building measures and supported joint exploration between a Chinese oil company and Philippine National Oil, an agreement joined by Vietnam in 2005.[56]

In 2008, however, President Arroyo signed into law the Philippine Baseline Bill (Republic Act No. 9522), a key step toward establishing the Philippines' maritime claims. The impetus for the bill was the May 2009 deadline for Manila and the other 128 states who became party to UNCLOS prior to May 1999 to file preliminary information concerning continental shelf claims. For the Philippines, this was important because international recognition of these claims could mean it could exercise exclusive rights over the estimated two hundred billion barrels of oil in its seabed, among other resources.[57] An oil field near the Spratlys is the source of approximately 15 percent of the Philippines' total national oil consumption.[58]

In May 2009, China responded to the Philippine Baseline Law and filings by other South China Sea claimants with the UN Commission on the Limits of the Continental Shelf (CLCS) by submitting a number of notes verbales for circulation to UN member countries. These notes verbales stated that China had "indisputable sovereignty over the islands in the South China Sea and the adjacent waters" as well as "sovereign rights and jurisdiction over the relevant waters as well as the seabed and subsoil thereof."[59] China's submission referenced an attached map that showed the nine-dash line around the islands and other maritime features in the South China Sea, a modified version of the Kuomintang's 1948 map.

Beijing's CLCS submission triggered a firestorm of speculation about its intentions. Observers in Washington and in the capitals of claimant states characterized the move as the de facto filing of a formal claim to virtually all of the South China Sea as a territorial or historic body of water. The submission, particularly following so soon on the heels of the *Impeccable* incident in which the Chinese navy harassed an American surveillance vessel in international waters in the South China Sea, affirmed for many in Washington that China posed a threat to freedom of navigation and overflight throughout the region.[60]

The level of attention that the Obama administration gave to the South China Sea disputes from 2010 to 2016 was unprecedented. Decades earlier, what some then called China's "southwest march" in the South China Sea had become a source of unease for Washington.[61] However, progress toward cooperative arrangements around energy development among claimants, including the Philippines and China, had largely confined American debates about China's intentions in the region to the defense arena.

New security net assessments examining military hardware and other strategic technology concluded that China was recalibrating its anti-access/area denial capabilities, which had previously focused on Taiwan Strait contingencies, to encompass other strategically significant maritime areas. The U.S. 2010 Quadrennial Defense Review noted that U.S. forces needed to be upgraded in order be able to maintain power projection in anti-access regions to "deter, defend against, and defeat aggression by potentially hostile nation states."[62]

There was a growing consensus in Washington that China's maritime claims in the South China Sea (as well as in the Sea of Japan/East Sea, where China and Japan dispute the sovereignty of the Senkaku/Diaoyu Islands; 钓鱼岛) posed a significant threat to U.S. strategic interests.

U.S. concerns increased in 2010 when Chinese officials began referring to the South China Sea as among China's *core interests*, a term that when applied previously to refer to geography had been used principally with reference to Taiwan and Tibet.[63] During the July 2010 ASEAN Regional Forum, Secretary of State Hillary Clinton offered a rejoinder, stating that the issue of open access to the South China Sea and legal solutions to maritime disputes were both a U.S. national interest and pivotal to regional security.[64] Clinton's remarks should be understood in the context of multiple factors. These include the *Impeccable* incident, China's CLCS submission, and an eagerness on the part of the United States to deepen defense ties with allies and partners in the region concerned about China's rise. These considerations also factored into the pivot to Asia framework that, beginning in 2011, would be applied to the cluster of U.S. policies aimed at demonstrating the growing strength of its economic and strategic commitment to Asia and restoring Washington's reputation in a region hard-hit by the global financial crisis. In 2011, Clinton would also affirm the strength of the U.S.-Philippines alliance from the deck of a U.S. warship in Manila Bay, referring to the South China Sea as the West Philippines Sea in her remarks calling for the peaceful resolution of maritime disputes between the Philippines and China.[65]

However, it was a series of incidents between China and the Philippines, including a 2011 confrontation in which a Chinese frigate fired at Philippine fishing vessels in a Spratly shoal, that led top U.S. officials to focus on Manila's dispute with Beijing. From the Obama administration's perspective, a failure to help its ally resist Chinese pressure (even if it did not take a stance on the question of sovereignty) would signify a de facto acceptance of China's forceful push for dominance in the South China Sea. This included what it perceived as Beijing's rejection of international law as an instrument for resolving international issues and China's effort to shift the regional political status quo. As the legal scholar Jacques DeLisle opined, were the United States to "acquiesce in China's assertion of rights (or dominance) . . . [it could] open the door to a revisionist Chinese agenda in international law that could reach well beyond the [South China Sea]."[66]

Manila initiated the arbitration, but sending the dispute to The Hague also served U.S. strategy. The international legal process offered a vehicle through which to challenge the legal bases for China's claims, without taking a direct stance on the sovereignty question. As the arbitration proceeded, the United States could strengthen its defense ties with the Philippines by expanding arms sales, restoring U.S. naval access to the former American base at Subic Bay, and increasing U.S.-Philippine naval exercises.[67] At the same time, it could use freedom of navigation operations to reinforce freedom of navigation under the UNCLOS and customary law, challenging the ambiguity inherent in China's nine-dash line.

For China, the Philippines' decision to pursue international arbitration was emblematic of the internationalization of a dispute Beijing felt could be stabilized, if not resolved, bilaterally. In its view, joint energy development, environmental management, and law enforcement offered ways forward to reduce tension and prevent conflict.

A set of no-holds-barred remarks on the arbitration decision to China's state media by State Councilor Yang Jiechi (杨洁篪) bear quoting extensively. In 2010, Yang famously remarked in an angry monologue in Hanoi following Secretary of State Clinton's remarks that freedom on the South China Sea was in the U.S. interest and that "China is a big country and other countries are small countries, and that's just a fact."[68]

In 2016 comments, Yang decries the arbitral process as political farce that was "staged under the cover of law and driven by a hidden agenda," calling its outcome a "so-called award" that "is illegal and invalid in every sense."[69] Yang attacks the Permanent Court of Arbitration as full of tricks, describing the then president of the International Tribunal for the Law of the Sea, Shunji Yanai, as a "right-wing Japanese intent on ridding Japan of post-war arrangements." Yang describes the South China Sea as "important to the Chinese people since ancient times . . . our heritage to which our forefathers devoted their wisdom and even lives. The Chinese government remains unwavering in its resolve to safeguard China's territorial sovereignty and maritime rights and interests in the South China Sea." On China's relations with the Philippines, Yang states that "China and the Philippines are close neighbors. . . . Our friendly exchanges date back over 1,000 years." He contends that the arbitration "goes against the common interests of the two countries and peoples" and threatens that it "is a major political obstacle to the improvement of bilateral relations." And, finally, Yang squarely assigns the blame for tensions between China and the Philippines over the territorial dispute to the United States, referencing countries outside the region that, "driven by their own agenda, have frequently intervened in the South China Sea issue under the pretext of upholding 'freedom of navigation' and 'maintaining regional peace,' leading to an escalation of tension. Such highly irresponsible moves have become the major source of risks that affect peace and stability in the South China Sea."[70]

Alongside the official reaction to the arbitral process that rejected China's claims of historic rights and its nine-dash line claims and documented violations by China of the UNCLOS,[71] Chinese citizens protested in front of Kentucky Fried Chicken outlets in cities across China. Demonstrators in Hebei held up a banner that read, "Boycott the U.S., Japan, South Korea and the Philippines. Love the Chinese people. What you eat is KFC. What is lost is the face of our ancestors."[72] In the Philippines, crowds celebrated, but the government's own response was cautious, with its foreign affairs secretary calling for "restraint" and "sobriety."[73]

Despite faint hope among the most sanguine observers that the arbitration might trigger constructive multilateral negotiations among claimants to South China Sea features, this did not occur. The Philippine president Rodrigo Duterte, who took office just weeks before the arbitration ruling, had described the process as futile and initially expressed a preference for bilateral dialogue to settle the dispute, also throwing doubt on his support for the Philippines-U.S. alliance.[74]

However, in the years since his election, Duterte appears to have found that his initial approach was out of sync with both popular sentiment and the preferences of the Philippine military. In July 2019, he reportedly called on the United States to declare war on China if Washington wanted China out of the region, indicating that he would provide support: "I want the whole seventh fleet of the armed forces of United States of America there. . . . When they enter the South China Sea, I will enter. I will ride with the American who goes there first. Then I will tell the Americans, OK, let's bomb everything."[75] Despite these comments, ahead of an August 2019 visit to China, Duterte downplayed a confrontation between Filipino fishermen and a Chinese vessel as well as reports that China had tested anti-ship ballistic missiles in waters disputed by the two sides. Moreover, while in Beijing in 2019, Duterte made clear that he would not hinge his country's bilateral relationship with Beijing on the arbitration ruling. Indeed, upon returning to Manila, Duterte conceded that he was running out of options to get Beijing to adhere to the arbitration decision.[76]

The United States has remained technically neutral on the question of sovereignty over the Spratlys and other features in the South China Sea. When it ruled the Philippines, the United States did not seek to assert control over these features. As the story of the Philippines' arbitration shows, however, it is the implicit challenge to freedom of navigation and, thus, also to the projection of naval power by the United States into the western Pacific posed by Beijing's assertion of its South China Sea claims that the United States has found intolerable. In contrast, China sees U.S. actions as intervening in a bilateral dispute in its near abroad and seeking, through what it perceives as an ambivalent ally, to use international law to constrain China's ability to secure its core interests and complicate its relations with its neighbors. U.S. policy initiatives led by Secretary of State Mike Pompeo, underway at the time of writing, which include declaring China's claims completely unlawful since they were rejected by the findings of the arbitral tribunal, have reinforced this view.[77]

Black Hands, Open Umbrellas: Hong Kong's Protests

In September 2014, the eruption of protests in habitually tranquil Hong Kong surprised authorities in Beijing with their scale and intensity. Protests that were similar in size had taken place in Hong Kong only twice before, once in the late 1960s against the British, ironically fomented by the CCP in the context of the Cultural Revolution then unfolding on the mainland, and then two decades later in 1989 in support of democracy on the mainland.[78] The catalyst for the 2014 protests in Hong Kong was the rejection by the Standing Committee of China's National People's Congress of proposed electoral reforms to allow universal suffrage in the 2017 elections for Hong Kong's chief executive. Beijing's proposed formula in response was that Hong Kong residents enjoy universal suffrage; however, they could only vote for a candidate from a roster screened and approved by mainland authorities.

In 2014, protestors in Hong Kong used civil disobedience to try to pressure Beijing to reconsider its decision on electoral rules, as well as to force the resignation of unpopular Chief Executive Leung Chun-ying (梁振英), who was widely perceived as corrupt and too close to Beijing. The 2014 demonstrations soon earned the moniker the "Umbrella Movement" because of the umbrellas carried by demonstrators to protect themselves from the pepper spray Hong Kong police used to disperse the largely peaceful crowds.

The 2014 protests continued for eleven weeks and marked the most significant effort up to that time to widen the political distance between Beijing and Hong Kong under the one country, two systems formula that had ended British rule over the island in 1997. That formula, enshrined in the Basic Law defining the relationship between Hong Kong and Beijing, had assured Hong Kong residents that they would not be subject to China's socialist governance and that Hong Kong's capitalist system and lifestyle could be sustained for fifty years.[79] Previous post-handover protests, such as those in 2003 against the Chinese government over its push for anti-subversion legislation, in 2012 against a plan by Beijing to introduce content to encourage patriotism toward China into Hong Kong textbooks, or in 2013 in support of universal suffrage, had been substantial in scale but short in duration.

Hong Kong's 2014 protests became the first in a series of large-scale, protracted political protests over the course of the next several years calling for changes to the political system in Hong Kong. In 2016, thousands of protestors rallied for Hong Kong independence and a Hong Kong republic after Hong Kong's electoral regulatory body barred several pro-independence candidates from competing in legislative elections. In 2019, mass demonstrations erupted that were initially triggered by popular anger over the Hong Kong government's proposed extradition bill (the Fugitive Offenders and Mutual Legal Assistance in Criminal Matters Legislation [Amendment] Bill) to legalize the extradition of suspected criminals to places with which Hong Kong does not have an extradition agreement, including the Chinese mainland. Opponents of the bill, which was eventually withdrawn, saw it as a threat to Hong Kong's autonomy. The anti–extradition bill demonstrations, which some estimates suggest drew millions to Hong Kong's streets, soon also included calls for democratic government as well as police reforms, responding to the heavy-handed tactics used by police against protestors.

In 2020, although the outbreak of the coronavirus pandemic led to a temporary reduction in large-scale rallies, some prodemocracy figures were arrested by Hong Kong police for their 2019 activities. New protests erupted after the announcement that the Standing Committee of the National People's Congress was drafting a national security law for Hong Kong to prevent, suppress, and punish acts deemed to be promoting secession, subversion, terrorism, or collusion with a foreign country or external elements to endanger national security related to Hong Kong. Provisions in Hong Kong's Basic Law, its de facto constitution, had led to local expectations that Hong Kong's Legislative Council would be the source of any national security legislation.[80]

Hong Kong's protests have presented a significant challenge for Beijing along multiple dimensions. They carry economic costs by disrupting commerce and damaging Hong Kong's image as a safe location for large-scale investments. Hong Kong is a leading source of investment and loans to the mainland, and many Chinese companies raise capital on the Hong Kong stock market. As a separate customs territory, Hong Kong enabled registered Chinese companies to avoid U.S. export controls and receive other favorable treatment.[81] (Mao Zedong notably chose to preserve Hong Kong's colonial status under Britain as a means of circumventing the U.S. blockade imposed on China after 1949.)[82] But beyond this, Hong Kong has been a potent political symbol for China. It remained a British colony for decades after the establishment of the People's Republic of China, and its reversion to China in 1997 was a triumph for CCP leadership—the peaceful restoration of Chinese territory lost to the British during what the Chinese recall as their Century of National Humiliation, which began with China's defeat by Britain in the First Opium War (1839–1842). The successful integration of Hong Kong into China has thus become a test of the CCP's commitment to restoring China's territorial integrity through peaceful reunification. Peaceful reunification is the pathway that Chinese leaders since Deng Xiaoping have emphasized as the preferred route to national reunification with Taiwan, although they have not ruled out the use of force.

Since the so-called handover of Hong Kong to China in 1997 based on a one country, two systems formula, China has sought to strengthen the one country side of the formula. It has done so by strengthening economic linkages and facilitating investment and trade between the two sides as well as through administrative connections. Infrastructure linkages have also been an important instrument. Beijing began incorporating Hong Kong into its national railway planning in 1993; today, there are extensive rail ties between Hong Kong, cities in the Chinese mainland, and Macau; a toll-free highway; and the thirty-mile-long Hong Kong–Zhuhai–Macau Bridge.[83] The high-speed rail terminal in Hong Kong locates mainland immigration checkpoints within Hong Kong.[84] Fostering a shared linguistic identity to encourage assimilation through an education policy that seeks to ensure the city's largely native Cantonese-speaking students all achieve spoken proficiency in Mandarin, with the long-term goal of adopting Mandarin as the language used in classes taught in Chinese, has been another dimension of Beijing's Hong Kong integration policy.[85]

The protests in Hong Kong reflected increasing dissatisfaction with many of these policies among many of the territory's residents. Material factors also contributed to a climate of local resistance to deepening integration with mainland China. Escalating housing costs in Hong Kong have meant skyrocketing costs for housing in a property market widely seen as controlled by the city's tycoons, de facto oligarchs whose status derives from political connections to Beijing. There is a psychological dimension as well: Hong Kong residents have moved from being a unique pivot point of Asia's economy to an economy on the periphery of the Chinese mainland. As Stephen Chiu and Tai-Lok Lui point out, Hong Kong was once a gateway from the mainland to the world, but over the past decades, it has found itself transformed into a gateway to the mainland.[86] But political grievances are what both ignited and sustained the repeated protests in Hong Kong amid growing popular concerns about the dilution of Hong Kong's administrative and political autonomy and Beijing's constraints on progress toward democratization of the territory's political system.

Beijing has portrayed the protests that have unfolded since 2014 as the work of the black hands of foreign interference, with U.S. agents as the lead actors. Beijing labels protest leaders as traitors who have helped foment unrest with foreign support. During the 2019 protests, Zhang Xiaoming (张晓明), director of the mainland's Hong Kong and Macau Affairs Office, discredited the demonstrations' local provenance by describing them as having "the clear characteristics of a color revolution."[87] In CCP-controlled media, such as the *Wen Wei Po* (文汇报), the United States is cast as the principal source of violent social unrest, with pro-independence forces from Taiwan identified as another set of black hands.[88] China has also specified certain U.S. officials as the behind the scenes black hand creating chaos. During the 2019 protests, for example, Chinese news outlets identified an American political counselor in the Hong Kong consulate as an expert in subversion.[89] Although American nongovernmental organizations (NGOs), like other foreign NGOs, had long operated with considerable autonomy in Hong Kong, in 2019, China imposed sanctions on Freedom House, Human Rights Watch, the International Republican Institute, and the National Endowment for Democracy, calling these groups anti-China plotters seeking to incite Hong Kong independence.[90]

The United States has responded to China's crackdown in Hong Kong with what might be called its nuclear option by ending the special status the United States had previously conferred on the territory. In accordance with the 1992 congressional mandate through the U.S.-Hong Kong Policy Act, the U.S. State Department has monitored and reported annually on the status of Hong Kong's autonomy under the one country, two systems framework. Its May 2020 report concluded, "China has shed any pretense that the people of Hong Kong enjoy the high degree of autonomy, democratic institutions, and civil liberties guaranteed to them by the Sino-British Joint Declaration and the Basic Law." On these grounds, U.S. secretary of state Mike Pompeo determined that Hong Kong's differential treatment under U.S. law should be revoked.[91] Following the June 2020 passage of the new National Security Law for Hong Kong by Beijing's legislature, on July 14, 2020, President Trump signed into law the Hong Kong Autonomy Act, building upon previous congressional legislation for the imposition of sanctions on foreign persons who have materially contributed to reducing Hong Kong's autonomy. The same day, the U.S. president also issued an executive order terminating preferential treatment for Hong Kong under U.S. law, directing that the city be treated like the rest of China in a number of critical areas, including immigration and export controls, and also suspending the bilateral agreement on extradition.[92]

Beijing's response to Hong Kong's protests made clear that its dream of Hong Kong's future was as a city fully integrated into China that retained a set of distinctive features reflecting Hong Kong's special history as center for international trade and finance. In stark contrast, Washington's response made it starkly apparent that its Hong Kong dream was for the territory to serve, to quote Pompeo from the "2020 Hong Kong Policy Act Report," as a "bastion of liberty and example of what China could aspire to become." In the report, the U.S. secretary of state also declares that the United States "stands with the people of Hong Kong" as they "struggle" against "the CCP's denial of the autonomy they were promised."[93] For Beijing, Washington's criticism of its political system and implied challenge to China's sovereign control over Hong Kong was salt in old wounds. For the United States, Beijing's draconian National Security

Legislation affirmed China's threat to other open societies in the region, most directly to Taiwan. By late summer 2020, the Trump administration had taken steps aimed at bolstering Taiwan's international stature and defense capabilities. Hong Kong was no longer simply a point of U.S.-China tension. It had become fuel for an increasingly combustible U.S.-China relationship.

Concluding Reflections

David M. Lampton's eulogy to U.S.-China engagement that concludes this volume dates the post-engagement era of U.S.-China relations to 2016. The three examples of U.S.-China interaction in China's periphery anatomized in this chapter all represent potentially dangerous rifts in the U.S.-China relationship representative of this shift. Around 2016, all became points of tension between the United States and China almost unprecedented in the nearly four decades since the two countries normalized ties. Each is an idiosyncratic issue in the bilateral relationship with unique dynamics. Simultaneously, each is also a manifestation of long-standing challenges for the two countries endemic to the admixture of China's preferences for managing security on its periphery and the global scope of U.S. security interests, including its alliance relationships in Asia and support for democratization. All three issues are now potential flash points, not because negotiated pathways toward equitable resolution are difficult to identify, but because they have taken on a symbolic significance as demonstration points for each country to assert its interests in an increasingly zero-sum contest.

As Lampton observes, the era of U.S.-China engagement was marked in Washington by a general policy of reassurance toward China, manifested in the growing breadth and depth of the relationship to include deepening economic interdependence, multifaceted government dialogues and people-to-people ties, and efforts to cooperate on global challenges. This has been replaced increasingly over the course of this decade by a U.S. strategy of deterrence against the rise of a China peer competitor and, during the Trump presidency, by a pursuit of economic and societal decoupling.

For China's part, there has been talk of self-reliance and growing international assertiveness in the face of rising tensions with the United States. During the era of engagement, Beijing saw strategic opportunity in the existing international and regional architecture. This included the U.S. alliance system in Asia that, at minimum, restrained Japan and other potential regional foes and fostered admittedly U.S.-promoted norms that nonetheless secured a relatively stable political and economic environment for China's rise. However, in the second decade of the twenty-first century, following the global financial crisis, China has seen its strategic interests better met by a more activist foreign policy.

Xi Jinping has called upon China to lead the reform of the global governance system.[94] China's 2019 defense white paper assigns China's military a global mission, addressing the "global significance of China's national defense" in a world in which an active international role for China's military is necessary for China's security.[95] On the economic front, beginning in 2018, Xi recalled Mao's calls for self-reliance development during the period of U.S. containment of China by repeatedly exhorting Chinese enterprises to achieve greater economic self-reliance in the development of advanced technology and innovation, later promoting a dual circulation economic model, with a goal of rebalancing the Chinese economy toward greater domestically driven demand.[96] These developments raise questions about how China may redefine its periphery today and in the future.

The three case studies described in this chapter lead to five principal conclusions. First, if the era of engagement in U.S.-China relations is over, then policy makers and policy experts alike should focus more attention on the historical lessons of preengagement interactions between the United States and China on the latter's periphery. When the two countries were enemies, China's periphery was often a zone for violent interactions between the two countries, which occasionally erupted into open war, including on the Korean Peninsula and in Vietnam. However, work by scholars such as M. Taylor Fravel shows that China is not prone to conflict on its periphery; rather, Beijing has engaged in a range of behaviors, from engaging in conflict to making substantial concessions depending upon its security concerns at the time.[97]

Second, as China's periphery becomes a more likely pivot for potential conflict and competition, the role of peripheral states and third parties is likely to take on an ever-larger role in U.S.-China relations. Two potential dynamics may be amplified by this shift. First, regional states with strategic significance in U.S.-China competition may seek to leverage this importance to play off the two powers for national gain. For example, at the time of writing, Philippine president Duterte appears to be experimenting with how he might use the Spratly dispute to garner benefits for the Philippines. In contrast, smaller states on China's periphery may also become more dependent on either the United States or China for their security, reducing their independence. Illustrating this dynamic is a burgeoning debate in South Korea's academic community on the risks and opportunities inherent in bandwagoning with China. In addition, the three cases discussed all demonstrate that the domestic politics of polities along China's periphery will increasingly internalize U.S.-China competition, with unpredictable political outcomes. This issue requires urgent analytical attention.

Third, at least to some degree, the cases analyzed in this chapter reflect a contest between the United States and China over partially incompatible visions for world order. In broad brush, the United States seeks to defend the international arrangements that it erected during its primacy. All three cases suggest, with the THAAD controversy doing so most clearly, that, in contrast, China's sense of international order has Confucian resonances in its implication that close relations, including geographic proximity and economic, political, and cultural links, signify recognition of China's preeminence.[98] Should this be seen as a largely rhetorical layer atop what is fundamentally nothing more than a normal assertion by a big power of its ability and right to shape its regional environment, reminiscent of Thucydides's Athenians at Melos? Or is it evidence of what scholars like David Kang have seen as a regional reordering led by China rooted in the hierarchical tradition of the tribute system?[99]

Fourth, both scholars and policy makers should remember that China's strategic periphery is an elastic concept. As it extends outward to the Arctic, the Indian Ocean, the Middle East, and beyond, how will the United States respond? Moreover, lessons from the dynamics of competition, confrontation, and cooperation on China's geographic periphery are also worth considering for their relevance to nonphysical and nonterrestrial domains. China's historical approach to security has included a focus on protecting inner China, or the *guannei* (关内), and the periphery has been the area in which China has sought to buffer its core interests through maintaining a degree of influence adequate to its security, including through the use of economic leverage (in the case of South Korea); physical force and the extraction of resources (as in the Spratlys); and tightening its political grip on Hong Kong by resisting pressure for political reform, squeezing space for social or political protest, and greatly fortifying its capabilities to repress challenges to its authority. In nonterritorial arenas, such as outer space or cyberspace, as China buffers itself against the exterior, what solutions will it mix together, and what conflicts will precipitate from them? How will China's new peripheries affect international relations in those domains? With respect to cyberspace, for example, China is developing surveillance capabilities that enable it to create a de facto cyberbuffer against outside influence on its intranet.[100]

Finally, what does this study suggest about potentially fertile approaches for the management of competition and strategic mistrust in the postengagement era? Above all, it reminds us that a deft reframing of the issues that are the source of tension will almost certainly be necessary. Chinese leaders reliably place peripheral issues in the context of core strategic interests such as territorial integrity and state sovereignty, and little compromise will be possible without either detaching peripheral disputes from these overarching concepts or situating compromises within them. Moreover, there is also the prospect that the resolution of some problems at the fringes of China's periphery may increasingly require the United States and China to cooperate with one another.

Finding these areas of constructive peripheral interaction—whether they be in transnational issue areas like climate change adaptation, economic efforts like development, or security affairs—may help policy makers in both countries shift the direction of the bilateral relationship toward engagement, even if only at the literal margins. Finally, all three cases discussed in this chapter illustrate that China's periphery is also a zone of self-interested third parties. The role of these actors has been critical in mitigating the potential escalation of the tensions between the United States and China that are playing out on their home turfs or in their immediate neighborhood.

Lee Kuan Yew once cautioned that as "China's development nears the point when it will have enough weight to elbow its way into the region, it will make a fateful decision—whether to be a hegemon, using its economic and military weight to create a sphere of influence, or to continue as a good international citizen."[101] This decision will pivot in large part on how China views its peripheries—as rift zones or as opportunities for constructive engagement—but also on where the United States chooses to challenge, cooperate with, and reach concessions with China. Peripheries may be at China's exteriors, but they are at the center of the future of U.S.-China relations.

NOTES

1. Owen Lattimore, *Inner Asian Frontiers of China* (Boston: Beacon, 1962), xx–xxii.
2. Pitman B. Potter, *Law, Policy, and Practice on China's Periphery: Selective Adaptation and Institutional Capacity* (Abingdon, UK: Routledge, 2010), 2.
3. James A. Millward, *Beyond the Pass: Economy, Ethnicity, and Empire in Qing Xinjiang, 1759–1864* (Stanford, CA: Stanford University Press, 1998), 3.
4. Michael D. Swaine, "Chinese Views and Commentary on Periphery Diplomacy," *China Leadership Monitor* 44 (Summer 2014): 43.
5. M. Taylor Fravel, "China's Changing Approach to Military Strategy: The Science of Military Strategy from 2001 and 2013," in *The Evolution of China's Military Strategy*, ed. Joe McReynolds (Washington, DC: Jamestown Foundation, 2016).
6. Pang Zhongying, "Transformation of China's Asia Policy: Challenges and Opportunities: A Personal View from China," 2007, http://library.fes.de/pdf-files/bueros/singapur/04601/2007-2/zhongying.pdf.
7. Michael J. Green, *By More Than Providence: Grand Strategy and American Power in the Asia Pacific Since 1783* (New York: Columbia University Press, 2017), 9.
8. "The Encirclement of China: *The People's Daily*, February 1, 1966," *Survival* 8, no. 4 (1966): 128–29.
9. Yong Deng, "Hegemon on the Offensive: Chinese Perspectives on U. S. Global Strategy," *Political Science Quarterly* 116, no. 3 (2001): 350.
10. Cary Huang, "China Takes Aim at the US for the First Time in Its Defence White Paper," *South China Morning Post*, August 7, 2019, https://www.scmp.com/comment/opinion/article/3021273/china-takes-aim-us-first-time-its-defence-white-paper.
11. Renato Cruz De Castro, "The Obama Administration's Strategic Rebalancing in Asia: from a Diplomatic to a Strategic Constrainment of an Emergent China?" in *The South China Sea: A Crucible of Regional Cooperation or Conflict-Making Sovereignty Claims?*, eds. C. J. Jenner and Tran Truong Thuy (Cambridge: Cambridge University Press, 2016), 42–58.

12. Stewart S. Johnson, "Understanding the World Order Contest in the South China Sea," *Journal of Conflict Studies* XIX, no. 2 (Fall 1999): 187–93.

13. Chen Jian, "Understanding the Logic of Beijing's Taiwan Policy," *Security Dialogue* 27, no. 4 (1996): 461.

14. David M. Lampton, "Xi Jinping and the National Security Commission: Policy Coordination and Political Power," *Journal of Contemporary China* 24, no. 95 (September 2015): 759–77.

15. "US Report 'Interfering' in China's Internal Affairs—FM," *China Daily*, May 27, 2008, http://www.chinadaily.com.cn/china/2007-05/28/content_881723.htm.

16. Lampton, "Xi Jinping," 764.

17. Simon Shen, "Will THAAD Row Lead to a Standoff Like the Cuban Missile Crisis?" Ejinsight, March 23, 2017, http://www.ejinsight.com/20170323-will-thaad-row-lead-to-a -standoff-like-the-cuban-missile-crisis/.

18. Ren Yuanzhe, "China's Policy Toward the Korean Peninsula," *PowerPoint*, June 13, 2016, https://www.stimson.org/event/chinas-policy-toward-the-korean-peninsula/.

19. Albert Chan, "Chinese-Philippine Relations in the Late Sixteenth Century and to 1603," *Philippine Studies* 26, no. 1/2 (1978): 51–52.

20. Brian C. H. Fong, "Hong Kong and the US-China New Cold War," *Diplomat*, May 16, 2019, https://thediplomat.com/2019/05/hong-kong-and-the-us-china-new-cold-war/.

21. Tai Ming Cheung, "Hong Kong's Strategic Importance Under Chinese Sovereignty," in *Chinese Security Policy and the Future of Asia: In China's Shadow* (Honolulu, HI: RAND Center for Asia Policy, 1996), 170–83.

22. "Hong Kong Returns to China, Part I," Association for Diplomatic Studies and Training, June 27, 2016, https://adst.org/2016/06/hong-kong-returns-to-china-part-i/.

23. Jonathan Mirsky, "Peking, Hong Kong, & the U.S.," ChinaFile, New York Review of Books China Archive, April 24, 1997, http://www.chinafile.com/library/nyrb-china-archive /peking-hong-kong-us.

24. David M. Lampton, "The Dilemma of Third Parties," in *Same Bed, Different Dreams: Managing U.S.–China Relations, 1989–2000* (Oakland: University of California Press, 2001), 147, 204–45.

25. Steven Lee Myers, "China Vows to Retaliate After Trump Signs Hong Kong Sanctions Bill," *New York Times*, July 15, 2020, https://www.nytimes.com/2020/07/15/world/asia/china -trump-hong-kong.html.

26. Barack Obama, "Remarks by President Obama at the University of Queensland," U.S. White House, November 15, 2014, https://obamawhitehouse.archives.gov/the-press-office /2014/11/15/remarks-president-obama-university-queensland.

27. Lampton, "Dilemma."

28. Yi Xiaoxiong, "Dynamics of China's South Korea Policy: Assertive Nationalism, Beijing's Changing Strategic Evaluation of the United States, and the North Korea Factor," *Asian Perspective* 24, no. 1 (2000): 79.

29. Jaeho Hwang, "The ROK's China Policy Under Park Geun-Hye: A New Model of ROK-PRC Relations," Brookings, June 2014, https://www.brookings.edu/research/the-roks -china-policy-under-park-geun hye-a-new-model-of-rok-prc-relations/.

30. Michael D. Swaine, "Chinese Views on South Korea's Deployment of THAAD," *China Leadership Monitor* 52 (Winter 2017), https://carnegieendowment.org/files/CLM52MS.pdf.

31. Hee Ok Lee, "THAAD: A Critical Litmus Test for South Korea-China Relations," 38 North, March 2, 2017, https://www.38north.org/2017/03/hleeo30217/.

32. Samuel Songhoon Lee, "Why Wouldn't S. Korea Want US Missile Defense?" CBS News, June 3, 2014, https://www.cbsnews.com/news/u-s-proposes-advanced-missile -defense-system-in-south-korea/.

33. Bruce W. Bennett, "Why THAAD Is Needed in Korea," RAND Corporation, August 7, 2017, https://www.rand.org/blog/2017/08/why-thaad-is-needed-in-korea.html.

34. Lee, "US Missile Defense."

35. Swaine, "South Korea's Deployment of THAAD."

36. Andy Zelleke and Brian Tilley, "In the Eye of a Geopolitical Storm: South Korea's Lotte Group, China and the U.S. THAAD Missile Defense System (A)," HBS Case Collection, December 2017, https://www.hbs.edu/faculty/Pages/item.aspx?num=53632.

37. "South Korea's Lotte Seeks to Exit China after Investing $9.6 Billion, as Thaad Fallout Ensues," Straits Times, March 13, 2019, https://www.straitstimes.com/asia/east-asia/south-koreas-lotte-seeks-to-exit-china-after-investing-96-billion.

38. Jeongseok Lee, "Back to Normal? The End of the THAAD Dispute Between China and South Korea," China Brief 17, no. 15 (November 22, 2017), https://jamestown.org/program/back-normal-end-thaad-dispute-china-south-korea/.

39. David Josef Volodzko, "China Wins Its War Against South Korea's US THAAD Missile Shield—Without Firing a Shot," South China Morning Post, November 18, 2017, https://www.scmp.com/week-asia/geopolitics/article/2120452/china-wins-its-war-against-south-koreas-us-thaad-missile.

40. Consulate-General of the People's Republic of China in Los Angeles, "Wang Yi Talks About US's Plan to Deploy THAAD Missile Defense System in ROK," February 13, 2016, https://www.fmprc.gov.cn/ce/cgla/eng/topnews/t1340525.htm.

41. Hee OK Lee, "THAAD"; Consulate-General of China, "Wang Yi Talks."

42. Liu Zhen, "THAAD? No Thanks, Say Officially Sanctioned Chinese Rappers," South China Morning Post, May 18, 2017, https://www.scmp.com/news/china/society/article/2094747/thaad-no-thanks-say-officially-sanctioned-chinese-rappers.

43. Lee, "Back to Normal?"

44. "The South China Sea Arbitration (The Republic of Philippines v. The People's Republic of China)," Permanent Court of Arbitration, https://pca-cpa.org/en/cases/7/.

45. Alexis Romero, "Duterte, Xi Stick to Opposing Stances on Arbitral Ruling," PhilStar Global, August 30, 2019, https://www.philstar.com/headlines/2019/08/30/1947670/duterte-xi-stick-opposing-stances-arbitral-ruling.

46. Natural islands can also be used to generate other maritime entitlements, including a territorial sea and continental shelf. See Article 121, UN Convention on the Law of the Sea, https://www.un.org/Depts/los/convention_agreements/texts/unclos/unclos_e.pdf.

47. Warwick Gullett, "The South China Sea Arbitration's Contribution to the Concept of Juridical Islands," Questions of International Law, February 28, 2018, http://www.qil-qdi.org/south-china-sea-arbitrations-contribution-concept-juridical-islands/.

48. Andrew S. Erickson and Conor M. Kennedy, "China's Maritime Militia," CA Corporation, March 7, 2016, https://www.cna.org/cna_files/pdf/Chinas-Maritime-Militia.pdf.

49. Amrutha Gayathi, "China-Philippines Standoff Likened to David Vs Goliath: Safety Alert Issued Over South China Sea Protests," International Business Times, May 11, 2012, https://www.ibtimes.com/china-philippines-standoff-likened-david-vs-goliath-safety-alert-issued-over-south-china-sea-697942.

50. Closely drawn from Bruce Elleman, Stephen Kotkin, and Clive Schofield, Beijing's Power and China's Borders: Twenty Neighbors in Asia (Armonk, NY: M.E. Sharpe, 2013), 240.

51. Bill Hayton, The South China Sea: The Struggle for Power in Asia (New Haven, CT: Yale University Press, 2014), 65–70.

52. Michael G. Gallagher, "China's Illusory Threat to the South China Sea," International Security 19, no. 1 (1994): 170.

53. Teh-Kuang Chang, "China's Claim of Sovereignty Over Spratly and Paracel Islands: A Historical and Legal Perspective," *Case Western Reserve Journal of International Law* 23, no. 3 (1991): 408.

54. United Nations Treaty Collection, "Chapter XXI: Law of the Sea, United Nations Convention on the Law of the Sea," December 10, 1982, https://treaties.un.org/Pages/ViewDetailsIII.aspx?src=TREATY&mtdsg_no=XXI-6&chapter=21&Temp=mtdsg3&clang=_en#EndDec.

55. "Law of the People's Republic of China on the Territorial Sea and the Contiguous Zone," Asian Legal Information Institute, February 25, 1992, http://www.asianlii.org/cn/legis/cen/laws/lotprocottsatcz739/.

56. Peter Kreuzer, "A Comparison of Malaysian and Philippine Responses to China in the South China Sea," *Chinese Journal of International Politics* 9, no. 3 (2016): 263.

57. Vera Files, "RP in Last Minute Scramble to Beat UN Deadline on Territorial Claim," GMA Network, March 24, 2008, https://www.gmanetwork.com/news/news/specialreports/86021/rp-in-last-minute-scramble-to-beat-un-deadline-on-territorial-claim/story/.

58. Ralph Jennings, "Oil Becoming Code for Sovereignty in Contested South China Sea," VOA News, November 23, 2016, https://www.voanews.com/east-asia-pacific/oil-becoming-code-sovereignty-contested-south-china-sea.

59. The United Nations, "Note Verbale," May 7, 2009, https://www.un.org/Depts/los/clcs_new/submissions_files/vnm37_09/chn_2009re_vnm.pdf.

60. Robert G. Beckman, "ASEAN and the South China Sea Dispute," in *Entering Uncharted Waters? ASEAN and the South China Sea*, ed. Pavin Chachavalpongpun (Singapore: ISEAS-Yusof Ishak Institute Singapore, 2014), 32–34.

61. Ross Marlay, "China, the Philippines, and the Spratly Islands," *Asian Affairs: An American Review* 23, no. 4 (1997): 195–210.

62. "What Is Anti-Access/Area Denial (A2/AD)?" Missile Defense Advocacy Alliance, August 24, 2018, https://missiledefenseadvocacy.org/missile-threat-and-proliferation/todays-missile-threat/china-anti-access-area-denial-coming-soon/.

63. Toshi Yoshihara and James R. Holmes, "Can China Defend a 'Core Interest' in the South China Sea?" *Washington Quarterly* 34, no. 2 (2011): 45–59.

64. "China Fears Hillary Clinton Far More Than It Does Donald Trump," CNBC, July 11, 2016, https://www.cnbc.com/2016/07/11/china-fears-hillary-clinton-focus-on-south-china-sea-human-rights-far-more-than-it-does-donald-trump.html.

65. Floyd Whaley, "Clinton Reaffirms Military Ties with the Philippines," *New York Times*, November 16, 2011, https://www.nytimes.com/2011/11/17/world/asia/clinton-reaffirms-military-ties-with-the-philippines.html.

66. Jacques DeLisle, "Political-Legal Implications of the July 2016 Arbitration Decision in the Philippines-PRC Case Concerning the South China Sea: The United States, China, and International Law," in *Asian Yearbook of International Law*, vol. 21, eds. Seokwoo Lee and Hee Eun Lee (Leiden, the Netherlands: Brill, 2017), 49–82.

67. Robert S. Ross, "US Grand Strategy, the Rise of China, and US National Security Strategy for East Asia," *Strategic Studies Quarterly* 7, no. 2 (2013): 20–40.

68. Josh Kurlantzick, "The Belligerents," *New Republic*, January 27, 2011, https://newrepublic.com/article/82211/china-foreign-policy.

69. MFA News, "Yang Jiechi Gives Interview to State Media on the So-Called Award by the Arbitral Tribunal for the South China Sea Arbitration," *South China Sea Issue*, July 15, 2016, https://www.fmprc.gov.cn/nanhai/eng/wjbxw_1/t1381740.htm.

70. MFA News, "Yang Jiechi Gives Interview."

71. Roncevert Ganan Almond, "Interview: The South China Sea Ruling," *Diplomat*, July 16, 2016, https://thediplomat.com/2016/07/interview-the-south-china-sea-ruling/.

72. Austin Ramzy, "KFC Targeted in Protests Over South China Sea," *New York Times*, July 19, 2016, https://www.nytimes.com/2016/07/20/world/asia/south-china-sea-protests-kfc.html.

73. Floyd Whaley, "After Victory at Sea, Reality Sets in for Philippines," *New York Times*, July 14, 2016, https://www.nytimes.com/2016/07/15/world/asia/philippines-south-china-sea.html.

74. Richard Javad Heydarian, "Philippines: Rodrigo Duterte's Pivot to China," Aljazeera, October 14, 2016, https://www.aljazeera.com/indepth/opinion/2016/10/philippines-rodrigo-duterte-pivot-china-161012062518615.html.

75. CNN Philippines Staff, "Duterte Dares US to Send 7th Fleet to South China Sea," CNN Philippines, July 9, 2019, https://www.cnnphilippines.com/news/2019/7/9/Rodrigo-Duterte-7th-Fleet-United-States.html.

76. Yuki Tsang, "Duterte Says He Allows Chinese Vessels to Fish in Philippine Waters to Prevent War," *South China Morning Post*, July 22, 2019, https://www.scmp.com/video/asia/3019799/duterte-says-he-allows-chinese-vessels-fish-philippine-waters-prevent-war.

77. See, for example, "Wang Yi: U.S. Is the Most Dangerous Factor Against Peace in South China Sea," CGTN, September 10, 2020, https://news.cgtn.com/news/2020-09-09/Wang-Yi-U-S-most-dangerous-factor-against-peace-of-South-China-Sea-TErNTlTLgI/index.html.

78. Ma Ngok, *Political Development in Hong Kong: State, Political Society, and Civil Society* (Hong Kong: Hong Kong University Press, 2007), 9.

79. Anastasia Yip, "Hong Kong and China: One Country, Two Systems, Two Identities," *Global Societies Journal* 3 (2015): 20–27; "The Basic Law of the Hong Kong Special Administrative Region of the People's Republic of China," July 2020, https://www.basiclaw.gov.hk/en/basiclawtext/images/basiclaw_full_text_en.pdf.

80. Lily Kuo, "Chinese Parliament Approves Controversial Hong Kong Security Law," *Guardian*, May 28, 2020, https://www.theguardian.com/world/2020/may/28/china-vote-npc-national-security-laws-hong-kong-us-protest.

81. Fong, "Hong Kong."

82. Fong.

83. Quan Hou and Si-Ming Li, *"Transport Infrastructure Development and Changing Spatial Accessibility in the Greater Pearl River Delta, China, 1990–2020," Journal of Transport Geography* 19, no. 6 (November 2011): 1350–60; Ng Kang-chung and Kanis Leung, "New Road Linking Hong Kong with Mainland China to Open This Month as Work on HK$33.7 Billion Border Crossing Enters Final Stages," *South China Morning Post*, May 17, 2019, https://www.scmp.com/news/hong-kong/transport/article/3010597/new-road-linking-hong-kong-mainland-china-open-month-work; "World's Longest Cross-Sea Bridge Opens, Integrating China's Greater Bay Area," Xinhua Headlines, October 23, 2018, http://www.xinhuanet.com/english/2018-10/23/c_137553194.htm.

84. Congressional-Executive Commission on China, *One Hundred Fifteenth Congress, Second Session: Annual Report* (Washington, DC: U.S. Government Publishing Office, 2018), 63, https://www.justice.gov/eoir/page/file/1106401/download; Alvin Cheung, "Will China Use Its Xinjiang 'Periphery Playbook' on Hong Kong & Taiwan?" *New Lens*, October 29, 2018, https://international.thenewslens.com/article/107047.

85. Juliana Liu, "Cantonese v Mandarin: When Hong Kong Languages Get Political," *South China Morning Post*, June 29, 2017, https://www.bbc.com/news/world-asia-china-40406429.

86. Stephen Chiu and Tai-Lok Lui, *Hong Kong: Becoming a Chinese Global City* (London: Routledge, 2009), 106–7.

87. Austin Ramzy and Tiffany May, "Chinese Official Warns Hong Kong Protesters Against 'Color Revolution,' " *New York Times*, August 7, 2019, https://www.nytimes.com/2019/08/07/world/asia/hong-kong-protests-china-violence.html.

88. Andrew Higgins, "China's Theory for Hong Kong Protests: Secret American Meddling," *New York Times*, August 8, 2019, https://www.nytimes.com/2019/08/08/world/asia/hong-kong-black-hand.html.

89. Higgins, "China's Theory for Hong Kong Protests."

90. Ministry of Foreign Affairs of the People's Republic of China, "Foreign Ministry Spokesperson Hua Chunying's Regular Press Conference," December 2, 2019, https://www.fmprc.gov.cn/mfa_eng/xwfw_665399/s2510_665401/t1720852.shtml.

91. U.S. Department of State, "2020 Hong Kong Policy Act Report," May 28, 2020, https://www.state.gov/2020-hong-kong-policy-act-report/.

92. White House, "The President's Executive Order on Hong Kong Normalization," July 14, 2020, https://www.whitehouse.gov/presidential-actions/presidents-executive-order-hong-kong-normalization/.

93. Department of State, "Policy Act Report."

94. "Xi Urges Breaking New Ground in Major Country Diplomacy with Chinese Characteristics," Xinhua, June 24, 2018, http://www.xinhuanet.com/english/2018-06/24/c_137276269.htm.

95. The State Council Information Office of the People's Republic of China, "Full Text of 2019 Defense White Paper: 'China's National Defense in the New Era' (English & Chinese Versions)," Xinhua, July 24, 2019, http://www.xinhuanet.com/english/2019-07/24/c_138253389.htm.

96. Gabriel Wildau, "China's Xi Jinping Revives Maoist Call for 'Self-Reliance,'" *Financial Times*, November 11, 2018, https://www.ft.com/content/63430718-e3cb-11e8-a6e5-792428919cee.

97. M. Taylor Fravel, *Strong Borders, Secure Nation: Cooperation and Conflict in China's Territorial Disputes* (Princeton, NJ: Princeton University Press, 2008).

98. Michael Swaine and Ashley Tellis observe that, "assertive policies in the case of China may be more likely" as a result of "the unique and long-standing Chinese experience of geopolitical primacy and the association of that primacy with good order, civilization, virtue, and justice," which "may make the pursuit of geopolitical centrality through assertive behavior once again attractive, even in the absence of a hierarchical Confucian world view." See Swaine and Tellis, *Interpreting China's Grand Strategy: Past, Present, and Future* (Santa Monica, CA: RAND Corporation, 2000), 231. See also Xue Li and Cheng Zhangxi, "What Might a Chinese World Order Look Like? Using the Ancient Concept of Li to Understand a Chinese Order," *Diplomat*, April 13, 2018, https://thediplomat.com/2018/04/what-might-a-chinese-world-order-look-like/.

99. David C. Kang, "Hierarchy and Legitimacy in International Systems: The Tribute System in Early Modern East Asia," *Security Studies* 19, no. 4 (2010): 591–622.

100. See Jack Stubbs, "China Hacked Asian Telecoms to Spy on Uighur Travelers, Sources Say," *Huffington Post*, September 5, 2019, https://www.huffpost.com/entry/chinese-hackers-uighur-asian-telecom_n_5d7136f4e4b0a606aa4f212e?yptr=yahoo.

101. Graham Allison and Robert Blackwill, "Interview: Lee Kuan Yew on the Future of U.S.-China Relations," *Atlantic*, March 5, 2013, https://www.theatlantic.com/china/archive/2013/03/interview-lee-kuan-yew-on-the-future-of-us-china-relations/273657/.

CHAPTER 13

FORTY-PLUS YEARS OF U.S.-CHINA DIPLOMACY

Realities and Recommendations

KENNETH LIEBERTHAL AND SUSAN THORNTON

The record of U.S.-China relations over the past forty years, as chronicled by the authors in this volume, is striking for its turbulence and vicissitudes. Time and again, unanticipated external events or domestic pressures from within threatened to derail relations and overwhelm the underlying logic of normalization.[1] Repeatedly returning U.S.-China relations to a constructive path required fortitude, restraint, experience in bilateral crisis management, and eventually, a deeper appreciation by both Chinese and American leaders of the other's ambitions and constraints.

Three Republicans (Ronald Reagan, George H. W. Bush and George W. Bush) and three Democrats (Jimmy Carter, Bill Clinton, and Barack Obama) have completed their terms as president since the United States and China reestablished diplomatic relations in 1979. While their political philosophies ranged broadly across the American political spectrum, most assumed their presidency as skeptics of China. But all eventually concluded that continued deepening of U.S.-China engagement was in America's interest.

Cold War concerns and strategic competition with the USSR provided the glue for U.S.-China relations through the Carter, Reagan, and George H. W. Bush presidencies. But additional motivations—such as bringing China into international institutions, providing advice and know-how to help lift several hundred million Chinese out of abject poverty, helping to develop legal expertise that would be important to China's economic development, and making educational opportunities in the United States available for a gradually growing number of Chinese students—increasingly took hold and developed their own supportive constituencies in both China and the United States. The importance of what was accomplished through expanding engagement can be better understood by considering the fact that during 1959–1976 China's educational system had been largely destroyed, its legal system had been dismantled, its economy had been severely disrupted, and civil violence and deprivation had taken an almost unfathomable toll on social trust and national cohesion. Successive American presidents rightly saw both a national interest and a moral imperative to help alleviate these enormous challenges. These American efforts took the form primarily of providing expertise and opportunities.

With the collapse of the USSR and the Soviet bloc and a renewed spurt of economic reform in China in the early 1990s, China's economy began to take on greater importance in Asia and more broadly. In the absence of a fundamentally security-focused strategic rationale, American goals in engaging with the People's Republic of China (PRC) increasingly put access to the growing Chinese market high on the list of priorities. During Bill Clinton's second term in office (1997–2001), the president sought to make China a major economic partner and to encourage policies that would make the PRC, in a term later coined by Robert Zoellick, a *responsible stakeholder* in the international system. Many other issues broadly associated with these goals concomitantly assumed more prominent places on the U.S.-China agenda.

In the years between 2000 and 2016, both the United States and China lent each other support at critical moments, such as in the wake of September 11 and in the throes of the global financial crisis in 2009–2010, as will be discussed in further detail later in this chapter. But with the PRC playing larger and more complex regional and global roles and the United States increasingly affected by partisan divides (exacerbated by the Great Recession) and seemingly endless conflicts in the Middle East, growing cooperation on several major issues and expanding economic interdependence in U.S.-China relations coexisted with increasing frictions and heightened distrust over each country's long-term intentions toward the other.

In sum, although U.S.-China relations have shifted focus over time and have repeatedly run into major problems and even crises, the relationship managed to sustain support (albeit with significant ups and downs) in both countries, even as the domestic politics on each side continued to shift and neither side ever felt completely content with the state of the relationship or the actions of the other side. From the Carter through the Obama presidencies, U.S.-China engagement repeatedly encountered challenges that threatened to set back ties and made additional progress daunting. How difficult navigating these crises proved to be depended on the impact of five factors that persisted across different administrations and through different phases of U.S.-China relations.

Five Constants Bedeviling U.S.-China Engagement

1. The Tendency of Domestic Politics in Both Countries to Reduce Mutual Trust

Strategists have a tendency to overlook the reality that in foreign policy as well as on domestic matters, most decisions by national leaders reflect more the pressures of domestic politics than the dictates of some grand strategy. In the United States, nearly every decision related to China policy has also had a domestic political dimension, a fact that has only become more prominent as the U.S.-China relationship has broadened and deepened over the years. The same has been true in Beijing.

In general, most policy makers in the United States do not sufficiently understand the political dynamics that constrain their counterparts in China and therefore do not know how seriously to take Chinese assertions that domestic political constraints can make reaching and implementing negotiated agreements difficult. Chinese officials also lack a sufficiently nuanced understanding of the American system to be able to differentiate gamesmanship by domestic opponents from strategies of deception by the White House to gain increased leverage in U.S.-China negotiations. For example, officials in Beijing typically have considerable difficulty parsing the intent or impact of congressional resolutions and legislation or threatened punitive actions or plans leaked to the media by domestic actors.

Simply stated, in the United States, information gushes forth from various sources, much of which is unreliable as a guide to official American intentions. The Chinese, by contrast, are extraordinarily nontransparent about their internal politics and decision-making. The political leadership in both countries fills in their uncertainties with the assumption that the other side is more disciplined, internally coordinated, and strategic than it really is. This way of connecting the dots often leads to severely unrealistic expectations and results in mistrust.

Domestic political pressures have also at times forced decisions that violated bilateral expectations and assurances. For example, in April 1999, Premier Zhu Rongji traveled to Washington to finalize and sign the U.S.-China Bilateral Accession Agreement for China's accession to the World Trade Organization (WTO).[2] President Clinton had been working hard to convince skeptics of the value of the deal for the United States, particularly those in his own party who worried about potential job losses as a result of China's entry into the WTO. In the end, one of Clinton's close advisors convinced him to postpone the signing until a few weeks after Premier Zhu's visit in order to make clear that he was not, as both Republican and Democratic critics had charged, willing to make too many concessions in his eagerness to have a high-profile signing event with Zhu in Washington.

But Zhu, on his side, had been pushing through major concessions in Beijing to get the agreement through and worried that his efforts would be undercut if Clinton failed to complete the agreement and sign it during his visit. Zhu's fears proved warranted. The failure to sign the agreement during his visit left him deeply wounded politically.

Zhu Rongji's political problems were further compounded when an official in the Clinton administration put a seventeen-page summary of commitments the Chinese side had made in the draft U.S.-China Bilateral Accession Agreement on the White House website a day before Zhu left Washington. PRC netizens and some officials in Beijing who spotted the text were highly critical of how far Zhu had gone toward meeting U.S. demands.[3] As a result, Zhu's standing in China was hurt, and the political headwinds faced by reformers in China grew stronger. On the U.S. side, when the critics in Congress and the business community saw the draft text, they castigated Clinton for not having signed the agreement during Zhu's visit—because the substance of the agreement was far better than they had anticipated. Clinton's bow to domestic political pressures thus proved extremely costly in both Washington and Beijing.

Then, on May 7, 1999, while tempers were still frayed and political motives still in question over the failure of Zhu's U.S. visit in early April, an American bombing mission misidentified the location of its authorized target and accidently bombed the Chinese embassy in Belgrade, extensively damaging the embassy and killing three Chinese. The Chinese did not believe the American explanation that the bombing was an accident and were suspicious that its embassy had been deliberately singled out.[4] But in reality, this tragic error resulted from a series of uncoordinated individual decisions and very low-probability coincidences in the planning and execution of the attack, none of which were intended to target the Chinese embassy. In a bow to domestic outrage at a crucial juncture in the bilateral relationship, Beijing allowed demonstrations directed against U.S. diplomatic missions in China to get out of hand, which resulted in the burning of the American consul general's residence in Chengdu and scenes of the American embassy in Beijing under siege by Chinese protestors.

Beijing demanded and received assurances from President Clinton that it would receive a full report on the bombing incident, and in subsequent weeks, the Chinese media incessantly demanded full accountability from Washington as quickly as possible. By late May, the official report of the American investigation was completed and ready to be given to the Chinese side. A White House official hand-delivered the report to the Chinese ambassador in Washington that evening. But when the ambassador saw the sealed manila envelope containing the report, he refused to accept it, peremptorily declaring it incomplete. When the White House official asked when the ambassador thought the report would be complete, the ambassador responded that mid-June would be about right. The sensitive tenth anniversary of the June 4, 1989, bloodshed in Beijing was approaching. It appeared to the American side that the Beijing leadership wanted to keep the focus of China's domestic media on China's outraged demands for a report on the Belgrade bombing incident until the tenth anniversary of the Tiananmen massacre had passed without disturbance.

The accidental bombing of the Chinese embassy in Belgrade also effectively further disrupted the effort to finalize the U.S.-China bilateral agreement for China's accession to the WTO. Negotiations only resumed in earnest months later, in early September 1999, when President Clinton met with President Jiang Zemin at the Asia-Pacific Economic Cooperation (APEC) leaders meeting in Auckland, New Zealand, where Jiang agreed to restart the final talks. The U.S.-China bilateral accession agreement deal was finally signed in November 1999 (although China's actual accession did not occur until December 2001).

George W. Bush entered the White House a China skeptic but over time found ways to balance short-term domestic political demands with longer-term U.S. interests in dealing with Beijing. The mini-crisis surrounding the Dalai Lama's visit to the United States to accept the U.S. Congressional Gold Medal, the country's highest civilian award, is one such example. The Dalai Lama is a highly revered religious figure who had frequently traveled to the United States and met with successive American presidents, which invariably incited apoplexy among Chinese officials. When the Dalai Lama traveled to Washington to receive his congressional award in October 2007, the Chinese government, not surprisingly, vociferously objected, putting on a full-court press to demand that the award ceremony be canceled and inveighing against President Bush's attending the ceremony or meeting the Dalai Lama.

But declining to attend a high-profile Congressional Gold Medal award ceremony would be politically impossible for any sitting U.S. president. President Bush's response to this conundrum was a compromise. He told Chinese president Hu Jintao that he had "good news and bad news" to convey and explained forthrightly that he was going to meet with the Dalai Lama in the context of the Congressional Gold Medal ceremony. But President Bush also told the Chinese leader that he was going attend the opening ceremonies for the Beijing Olympics and would bring his family. Bush thus registered grave U.S. concern about Tibet while also making clear his intention that Beijing's hosting of the Olympic Games would be a success. He kept those commitments even after unrest that erupted in Tibet in March 2008 was forcefully suppressed as the protests and demonstrations spread in the ensuing weeks.[5]

2. Complex and Opaque Policy Processes Exacerbate U.S.-China Mistrust

Policy making in the U.S. government generally breaks even modest initiatives into many concrete steps, each of which typically has its own history, constituency, sensitivities, and constraints. Effective staffing requires understanding what the president wants, what players may be affected, what the substantive issues are, what other issues and equities might be impacted, and how to communicate with relevant people in the international arena. The process requires a blend of political smarts, specific expertise, coordination among various players in the administration, and the use of trusted channels with other countries. No administration can manage this flawlessly, and the opportunities for mischief by dissenting participants are ubiquitous. In addition, in many issues related to the U.S.-China relationship, Congress plays a complex role that Beijing typically does not know how to interpret. Indeed, both governments have sprawling bureaucracies that are difficult to discipline, and both must take care to corral and tame people and institutions with competing specific agendas.

As a result of the complexity and opaqueness of the policy process in both countries, summit meetings between top leaders have played a particularly important role in U.S.-China relations. In both political systems, only the top leader has the comprehensive perspective and authority required to balance competing national and political priorities and interests and to set foreign policy for the agencies to carry out. The Chinese thus attach great importance to statements by the U.S. president and have been alarmed by administrations that seem to condone disruption or sudden changes and are continually unnerved by the tendency of American presidents to exhibit historical amnesia on issues like Taiwan.

Each government tends to distrust the stated concerns of the other side, regarding them as excuses or ploys to make unjustified gains. For example, the U.S. government often believes that Beijing is lying when it says that it is too difficult to get commitments implemented because of local resistance. But in fact, there are few issues in China that do not require an extended process of internal bargaining and consensus building with and among local officials to achieve effective implementation of national-level decisions.[6] The expression many local officials use to capture this reality is that "the center (national level) has its policies; we have our countermeasures."

Beijing commits a similar error. It assumes that the sprawling U.S. government is more strategic, disciplined, powerful, and tightly coordinated than is in practice the case. The American legal system and separation of powers are particularly vexing, it seems, for Chinese officials who, mirror imaging their own system, do not believe that powers are really separate and equal. This is particularly true regarding the U.S. Congress, which frequently promotes anti-China legislation that China then demands the executive branch to scuttle. It also suspects the U.S. government of hiding behind the independence of the judiciary when judgments unfavorable to China are rendered in U.S. courts.

Because of the mismatch in systems and lack of understanding of each other's policy process and operational limits on political power, each government at the highest levels fills in the blanks with assumptions about the essential nature and ambitions of the other. China has long believed that the U.S. government seeks to complicate, constrain, and possibly disrupt China's rise. U.S. attitudes have been more complicated but on balance assume that China's one-party, authoritarian political system has more internal discipline, coordination, and capability than it in fact possesses. And neither can understand why the other does not see its own key intentions more clearly, which each side believes that it has made very clear.

Given this complexity, in each successive U.S. administration, the Chinese have sought out one or two officials who they feel can provide reasonably reliable information on the U.S. administration's real goals and concerns—and who are themselves keeping a strategic eye on the overall scope of developments across the U.S.-China relationship. Often, the official they select has been the national security advisor, but on occasion, they have turned to others, such as Treasury Secretary Hank Paulson during the second term of George W. Bush.

3. Campaign Positions Rarely Survive the Realities of Actually Managing U.S.-China Relations

With the exception of George H. W. Bush, who had served as head of the U.S. Liaison Office in Beijing from 1974 to 1976[7] and as CIA director in 1976, incoming U.S. presidents since Gerald Ford have not had much background in foreign policy and have not given much serious thought to China or Asia before assuming office. Their presidential campaigns have focused mainly on domestic issues. No one has won the presidency, or any prior elective office, based on his foreign policy experience. Indeed, to the extent that successful presidential candidates have had any track record in U.S.-China relations, it was because they were critical of their predecessors' weak or soft positions on China during their election campaigns. As a result, each U.S. president since normalization of relations with China in 1979, regardless of political party or individual background, has started his tenure with a vague promise of a new China policy.

Thus, Jimmy Carter wanted to focus on China's human rights problems when he assumed the presidency in 1977, but for reasons both practical and principled, he was persuaded of the wisdom of proceeding with normalization. When President Carter hosted Chinese leader Deng Xiaoping in the Oval Office on January 29, 1979, Carter made the case for free movement of people and freedom of speech as core American principles. Deng reportedly responded with an offer to allow one million Chinese students to study in the United States. Carter appreciated both the importance of expanding individual options for Chinese citizens and the need to keep that objective within pragmatic boundaries. On most, but by no means all, other issues, Deng laid out important ways in which he envisaged China adopting policies that advanced the strategic interests of both China and the United States, including cooperation to keep tabs on and thwart Soviet expansionism and military developments. Deng's vision was realized, for example, when the United States and China cooperated in monitoring Soviet missile tests and, in the wake of the Soviet invasion of Afghanistan in 1979, when the two countries coordinated their responses and cooperated in providing weapons to the Afghan mujahedin.

Ronald Reagan, during his presidential election campaign, chided Carter for having normalized relations with the Chinese communists at the cost of recognizing Taiwan and suggested that he wanted to reintroduce some level of officiality into American relations with Taiwan, thus pushing the envelope on one of the key foundations of the U.S.-China normalization agreement. Upon assuming office, however, when President Reagan realized that China and the United States were cooperating to counter Soviet influence and that China, too, opposed the Soviet invasion of Afghanistan, he walked back his initial posture. Indeed, in June 1981, the Reagan administration announced a decision in principle to sell military hardware to China on a case-by-case basis and subsequently negotiated a joint communiqué issued on August 17, 1982, that artfully specified the principles for future U.S. defensive arms sales to Taiwan, an issue that had not been resolved in the U.S.-China normalization agreement in 1979 and, by the spring of 1982, threatened to unravel relations between the two countries.[8]

During his 1992 presidential campaign, Bill Clinton chastised George H. W. Bush for going easy on "the butchers of Beijing" in the wake of the June 4, 1989 bloody suppression of demonstrators in Beijing and elsewhere in China. In 1993, as president, Clinton officially conditioned the annual most favored nation renewal vote on trade with China on a significant improvement in Beijing's performance on human rights.[9] When Beijing essentially rejected Clinton's human rights benchmarks, Clinton relented on the grounds that a denial of most favored nation status would "drive us back to a period of mutual isolation and recrimination that would harm America's interests, not advance them." (He later argued to Chinese leader Jiang Zemin that China's stance on issues of human rights and religious freedom was putting China "on the wrong side of history.")[10]

George W. Bush was also a self-described China skeptic. His 2000 presidential campaign targeted, among other issues, questionable Chinese campaign contributions involving Al Gore, and he began his presidency with a vague commitment to be tougher on China. His vice president, Dick Cheney, was eager to move in that direction. But Bush subsequently recalibrated his views on China following a series of events that reordered his priorities. Two incidents were most important in changing his mind. The first was the April 2001 EP-3 incident in which a Chinese Navy J-811 interceptor fighter collided with a U.S. Navy EP-3 ARIES II signals intelligence aircraft off the coast of Hainan Island, killing the Chinese pilot and forcing the crippled EP-3 to land at a Chinese military airfield on Hainan.[11] The second was the September 11, 2001, terrorist attacks on the United States, which brought into sharp relief for Bush the high stakes in the China relationship. Bush quickly concluded that conflict with China was not in the interest of the United States and that accomplishing his priorities as president required a constructive relationship with China. By the end of his first term, he had even issued an unprecedented warning to President Chen Shui-bian, the pro-independence leader on Taiwan, who seemed to be attempting to force unilateral changes in the status quo of cross-strait relations.[12]

Barack Obama, in contrast to most of his predecessors, had thought about how to deal with China's rise and had some personal international, especially Asian, experience. But he also came into office with a skeptical view of China and worried that China was becoming emboldened to violate norms and agreements on international economic and security issues. The new president, however, was immediately confronted with a meltdown of the international financial system that had started in the United States. He knew Beijing's cooperation was key to his international strategy to staunch the cascading global financial hemorrhage. President Obama thus took concerted action to gain China's cooperation, including expanding the Strategic Dialogue framework that had been established under the Bush administration between Treasury Secretary Hank Paulsen and Chinese vice-premier Wang Qishan. Obama also promoted a shift from the G8 to the G20 (the PRC belonged to the latter but not the former) as the major focal point for coordination of global economic issues, thus ensuring China's participation in decision making. Following this, President Obama focused on eliciting resources and more constructive action from China to support the international system, much as George W. Bush before him had done.

4. Shocks to U.S.-China Relations from Exogenous or Unexpected Events

Thus, since 1979, most U.S. presidents' initial vague desire to toughen America's treatment of China gave way over time to more concrete and practical policy goals. But throughout the period of U.S.-China relations following normalization, unexpected events within China, between the United States and China, or completely outside of the bilateral relationship have had a significant impact on policy directions and created long-term consequences for the relationship. Often, presidents who came into office thinking one way about China were forced by such events to change their views or reorder their priorities. In some cases, for example, China was unexpectedly helpful in the event of an exogenous shock, and that help was both effective and appreciated. During the 1997–1998 Asian financial crisis, for example, China, at the urging of the United States, decided against devaluing the renminbi.[13] And immediately after news reached Beijing of the devastating September 11 terrorist attacks in New York and Washington, Jiang Zemin called President Bush and offered not only his condolences but also China's cooperation at the United Nations (UN) and elsewhere to mobilize support for American efforts to establish a broad coalition to remove the Taliban regime, destroy al-Qaeda, combat terrorist violence more broadly, and stop Iraq from obstructing UN-mandated inspections looking for hidden weapons of mass destruction.[14] In these and other cases, shocks altered the outlook of the U.S. and Chinese leaders about the potential in U.S.-China relations.

George H. W. Bush was the only president after 1979 to come into office eager to push U.S.-China relations forward, including in technological cooperation. Bush knew China well and initially believed, in those heady days of economic and possibly political opening, that opportunities for cooperation would be found on many fronts. But as soon became clear, greater political opening was not what China's leaders had in mind, especially given sharp internal disputes about growing problems of inflation and corruption and the directions that further reform should take. By 1989, those divisions within China's political elite had created space for large-scale demonstrations in Beijing and elsewhere, with protesters calling for more freedom of speech, an end to corruption, and movement toward democracy.

In early June, the Chinese authorities mercilessly suppressed the Tiananmen Square protests, killing hundreds, if not more. Less publicized suppressions of comparable demonstrations in dozens of cities across the country followed. In the wake of this bloodletting, Americans were outraged, favorability ratings of China dropped more precipitously than ever before recorded in the history of American polling, and Congress imposed blanket sanctions on technological cooperation. Bush tried to keep a channel open to China, but his more ambitious plans had to be shelved.

Two major financial shocks were also pivotal change points in the relationship. Most Americans do not recall the 1997 Asian financial crisis that affected most Asian economies and hit South Korea, Thailand, and Indonesia particularly hard. As the United States worked to put together stabilization packages with the International Monetary Fund (IMF), Washington worried that China might devalue the renminbi and thus imperil the efforts at stabilization. China was already a major exporter in 1997 and faced substantial losses by not devaluing. But China nonetheless agreed, with American urging, not to devalue its currency. This commitment, and the elevated consciousness of China's economic importance in the region, spurred acceleration of China's WTO accession negotiation with the United States.

The global financial crisis of 2008–2009 was an even more consequential financial shock. It not only ushered in a pivotal change in the power relationship between the United States and China, as China's financial sector was largely insulated from the crash, but also deeply tarnished China's confidence that the United States had mastered the know-how to create and sustain a modern economy in an era of globalization. China's economic growth recovered rapidly from the global financial crisis via a huge credit-fueled stimulus effort, and thereafter, Beijing became far less willing to accept specific advice on market reform and opening from the United States. This crisis also led to a decision to have the G20 replace the G8 as the major economic council of wealthy nations, the first de facto acknowledgement of a new global power structure in which the PRC was invited to play a major role.[15] The net result of these developments was that China's power position (both hard and soft) leapt ahead much faster than China's own leaders had previously anticipated and China's confidence that America uniquely understood how to develop and sustain a technologically dynamic, wealthy nation that could play a global leadership role sharply diminished.

5. All Presidents Have Evolved to Embrace Engagement

As noted earlier, all U.S. presidents who have come to office since the normalization of relations with China began their presidencies with the explicit intention of changing U.S. policy toward China. And yet, each eventually tacked back to a position that looked remarkably like his predecessor's—a mix of cooperation, cajoling, and censuring; pushing for progress in some areas, while hedging or resisting in others. Each president found that gratuitously worsening relations with China render a wide range of other international issues more difficult to manage. Nonetheless, moving U.S.-China relations significantly forward has never been easy in terms of domestic politics in either the United States or China.

After Ronald Reagan mocked President Carter's China approach and promised to improve ties with Taiwan during his presidential campaign, relations with China during the new Reagan administration got off to a bumpy start. They improved when in late spring 1981 President Reagan agreed to sell lethal military equipment to Beijing.[16] George H. W. Bush was uniquely poised to deepen cooperation with China but had to adjust to Tiananmen and was stymied by his reelection struggle. Bill Clinton entered the White House chiding Bush for coddling the "butchers of Beijing" but moderated his tone after the 1995–1996 Taiwan Strait Crisis, the 1996–1997 Asian financial crisis, and the growing economic interdependence between the United States and China. George W. Bush railed against Chinese funds allegedly illegally contributed to the Clinton-Gore political campaign.[17] However, he then moderated after September 11 and even put Taiwan's Chen Shui-bian on notice. President Obama was skeptical of China when he took office in 2009, but he needed Beijing to help stem the global financial crisis that had begun in 2008.

Looking back over the past forty years of U.S.-China relations, big ideas underlay Nixon's opening to China and China's opening to the world. The first was about furthering U.S. efforts to win the Cold War. The second was about cajoling China into becoming a responsible stakeholder in the global system and recognizing the benefits for both China and the United States from successfully doing so. China's determination to continue economic reform, even after the tragedy of Tiananmen made clear that fundamental political democratization was not on the horizon, tracked U.S. goals and interests sufficiently closely that, even without the strategic imperative of the Cold War, Washington could justify continued efforts to bring China into the international trading and financial system and into global institutions more broadly. These justifications were amplified by an American business community that was eager to tap the huge China market, particularly given the dizzying economic integration that was already happening in Asia. But President Clinton also asserted, in the wake of the Soviet Union's collapse, that economic liberalization and markets would likely, over time, reduce central political control in China as well. This was not the overriding objective of U.S. policy, as some now claim, but it did serve to ease political discomfort over prioritizing economic growth objectives in dealing with an authoritarian communist state.

Both the Chinese and American political systems, economies, and societies have experienced major changes over the past forty years. The changes in China have been substantially greater and more hotly contested than those in the United States. At every stage, some forces in each society have pushed back hard, decrying the shifting priorities and outcomes. Each political system includes both reformers and those who seek to undermine reforms, and neither system has had smooth sailing domestically as changes have at every stage produced losers as well as winners. And in both countries, U.S.-China relations have become embroiled in domestic political agendas that have added rancor to the relationship.[18]

Looking to the Future: Takeaways and Recommendations

Under the administration of Donald Trump, the American narrative on China swung from one of economic opportunity with deterrence to one that saw China as an existential threat. Many pundits asserted that the strategy of engagement with China was naïve and gave the PRC valuable resources with which to challenge and eventually erode American leadership in Asia and across the globe. That argument, however, is based on a false premise: that the core goal and therefore the key test of U.S. policy toward China since 1979 was the transformation of the PRC into a multiparty liberal democracy. It ignores the fundamental benefits for American national interests that the past forty years of engaging China have advanced. It also assumes that had the United States taken a more adversarial approach to China since the late 1970s, Asia would have somehow experienced greater peace and prosperity, China would have remained passive and its military capabilities would have stayed inconsequential, and the growing polarization and resulting dysfunction in U.S. domestic politics and serious miscalculations in U.S. foreign policy in the Middle East and elsewhere would not have impacted America's current challenges at home and abroad.

What did the United States gain from normalizing relations with the PRC in 1979 and pursuing a strategy of engagement across the terms of five U.S. presidents since? A short list follows:

- The end of the Cold War was accelerated (with a concomitant vast reduction in the threat of cataclysmic nuclear war).
- China was turned from a path of exporting revolution and standing outside of the U.S.-led international order to a path of pursuing economic development that prioritized participating in regional and global multilateral institutions and stressing international stability rather than revolutionary change.
- Unprecedented progress was achieved in directly and indirectly advancing the reduction of poverty in Asia (especially in the PRC) and globally.
- The salience and vibrancy of American alliances and partnerships were sustained by incentivizing moderation in China's behavior and creating conditions in which American allies and partners did not have to choose between siding with the United States or aligning with China.
- Militarily, as a result of the end of the Cold War and changing geopolitics that greatly reduced the chances of a major power war in Asia, the United States allowed major reductions in military expenditures. In 1984, the PRC also slashed its military budget by roughly 50 percent, based on Deng Xiaoping's assessment that China had a strategic opportunity to focus on economic development that would last for another three decades. China's military budget remains around 2 percent of its GDP, although with GDP rising at double-digit rates for most of the intervening years, the size of the military budget has increased apace.

More controversy attaches to the balance sheet of economic and social costs and benefits in the United States itself. Widening inequality in the distribution of wealth, wage stagnation, and the loss of manufacturing jobs with their associated benefits have caused enormous political and social repercussions in America, especially since the turn of the century. Now many in the United States explain these negative developments as primarily the consequences of *China's* policies and actions (e.g., China's state capitalist development model, theft of U.S. intellectual property, subsidies to state-owned enterprises and related industrial policies, and sharp limits on U.S. market access and investment opportunities in the PRC). Others attribute these developments more to failures in *U.S.* policies and actions (e.g., the politics of domestic tax and spending policies that did little to ameliorate growing inequality of wealth and opportunity; the impact of the digital revolution and related new technologies on the American economy, society, and politics; and the adoption of major changes in U.S. financial regulations). All these factors have in fact played significant roles, but assignment of relative blame has become closely integrated into arguments about the nature and terms of the relationship the United States should have with the PRC in the future.

While all recent presidents eventually became convinced that the U.S.-China relationship was too important to either abandon or mishandle, the current revisionist assessment of both the goals and the outcomes of the U.S. opening to China is skewing discussion of current U.S. policy options. Mistakenly concluding that engaging China has not served American interests spurs cartoonish and misguided narratives that tilt toward decoupling, containment, and confrontation. Resulting current predictions in Washington and among foreign policy circles about the future of the United States relationship with China are almost uniformly dire.

Although charting a specific path forward in the current charged environment is difficult, we nevertheless offer the following short summation of the takeaways from forty years of engagement with China and recommendations for how to manage U.S.-China relations so as to maximize medium- and long-term U.S. interests in a complex, globalized world.

Takeaways

It is unlikely that the U.S. presidents who will enter the White House in the future will know much more about China than their predecessors or that their assumptions about China will be more accurate. It is unlikely that they will be able to avoid crises, domestic political distractions, or problems with the policy process and miscommunication. On a more optimistic note, what might also remain unchanged is the fact that all American leaders, after initially entertaining sweeping changes to China policy, have come to grasp their limited maneuvering room and time horizon and hence have adjusted their goals.

To take advantage of China's many opportunities, push back effectively on the PRC's transgressions, and reduce the chances of accidents and disasters, the United States must have an organized and authoritatively controlled policy process to establish priorities; analyze options and their longer-term consequences; and disseminate, coordinate, and implement decisions. Nobody knows what the future holds, but we *do* know that unexpected events will occur, that technological changes are accelerating, and that resilience and crisis management systems are more important in today's world than ever before.

Domestic politics in both countries are currently working against smooth U.S.-China relations, and the likelihood of misunderstandings and mishaps is far too high. In addition, given that modern technologies are fast-evolving and difficult by nature for governments to regulate, future technological advances will likely outpace government policy and might well prove destabilizing. The need for the United States and China to work together to hammer out codes of conduct and responsibilities to ensure that all state actors are operating within the same guardrails will become increasingly important.

Since 2017, almost all regular Track I U.S.-China dialogues, including both civilian and military-to-military, have been either terminated or allowed to atrophy. But mechanisms for bilateral dialogue are valuable over time in building some measure of mutual understanding and trust, permitting potentially more wide-ranging explorations of hypotheticals, and allowing give-and-take beyond preset talking points on how a problem is perceived in each country and where the greatest concerns lie—and even how specific terms and phrases are understood (and misunderstood) by the two sides. Regular dialogue mechanisms are not the best means to negotiate an agreement, but they can make each side far better informed about the strategy and tactics most likely to be effective in getting to an agreement. Ending discussion of ongoing issues only increases the odds of critical misperceptions that in turn become grist for those on both sides who seek confrontation.

Recommendations for the United States

The United States, together with its partners and regional and global multilateral organizations, has over time contributed to opening China's economy and society, unleashing unprecedented global growth, bringing China into a rules-based order, and encouraging the PRC's growing willingness to become a contributor of public goods in, for example, development assistance, antipiracy operations, counterterrorism, nonproliferation, environmental protection, climate change, disease control, and peacekeeping. In virtually every one of these spheres, China's actions have been a mixed blessing. To regard Beijing's initiatives in all these areas as strategically pernicious and normatively hidebound does serious violence to the actual record and blindly reduces the space to work with the PRC to build on its capabilities, commitments, and sensibilities where these are needed to address some of the most consequential challenges confronting Americans now and through the remainder of the twenty-first century. It is very much in America's interests, therefore, to move from increasingly undifferentiated negative caricature toward more balanced realism in our discourse on and policies regarding China. This is an argument not for being softer but rather for being smarter.

With this in mind, recommendations for U.S. policy should keep in view four fundamental realities about the future:

- With land borders with fifteen countries and a very extensive coastline, a population of over 1.4 billion, and the second largest economy in the world, China will, for better or worse, remain a central factor in Asia's future.

- There is broad consensus in China, rooted in the country's deep history and its experiences over the past two hundred years, that the PRC should aim over the coming three decades to become a major power that is wealthy, strong, influential, and respected. These goals remain loosely defined but broadly posit that China should become one of the two or three countries of greatest consequence in the world and *the* country of greatest consequence in East and Southeast Asia and Oceania; that it should avoid the middle-income trap and become a high-income country (which requires that it also become a technologically innovative country with a consumption-driven economy and that it play a larger role in the regional and global economic and financial systems); that it develop a military that can protect the homeland, prevent the loss of any claimed territory, protect access to resources and markets, and deter the major threats from abroad; that it become more influential in shaping international rules and norms, in part by using China's position in major international organizations to shape definitions and rules (e.g., on sovereignty, standards, and human rights) to better reflect China's views; and that it gain international respect for the Chinese political system and for its approach to development, as well as for its core foreign policy principles and concepts.

Each of these goals poses potentially serious threats to American interests and values, and thus, neither Washington nor Beijing can count on friendly cooperation to be the major driver of future U.S.-China relations. But each of these goals can be pursued and operationally defined in terms more—or less—compatible with U.S. interests and values. Indeed, these basic goals long predate the past decade, and China has time and again been wracked by disputes over the best measures to achieve them and how to define success. There is again growing controversy not only abroad but also in China about the approaches China is currently taking.

- China's domestic developments, as well as its foreign policies, will have huge impacts on the Asian and global economies, financial systems, environmental and climate outcomes, disease exposures, technological developments and applications, and security challenges, among other issues. In every case, much of what China accomplishes will create difficult problems and strains.

- However, major Chinese failures in many of these areas can exact even greater costs on the region and beyond. Indeed, massive Chinese failures producing large-scale domestic unrest in China would almost certainly vastly destabilize Asia, provide fertile ground for transnational criminal organizations to grow and thrive, fundamentally worsen proliferation risks, generate migrant flows of unprecedented scale, lead to domestic and transborder armed conflicts as PRC national cohesion breaks down, and create space for a cascade of other problems that no country or multilateral organization in the region or globally would know how to manage satisfactorily.

In sum, although the United States and the international community have major, legitimate interests in modifying Chinese behavior in various domains, prioritizing decoupling from China and promoting across-the-board U.S.-China competition will exact enormous costs beyond those that at present are part of the policy considerations and broader debates in Washington. Our recommendations for U.S. policy take these complex, uncomfortable realities into account.

Specific Actions

Current political realities in the United States allow little prospect that the policy changes we recommend in the following section will be taken up in the immediate future in the directions we feel necessary. Therefore, we recommend that work now should focus especially on nongovernmental efforts to develop policy approaches that can be available as political space opens up (in both the United States and China). These approaches should be hammered out not only in discussions within the United States but also in international bilateral and multilateral Track II dialogues with relevant counterparts.

Drawing on lessons learned from the past forty years of U.S. relations with China, we have six recommendations that seek both to manage the risks inherent in China's ongoing rise and to enhance our ability, with China, to address the most critical problems faced by both countries.

Recommendations

Join What Is Now Called the Comprehensive and Progressive Agreement for Trans-Pacific Partnership

The Comprehensive and Progressive Agreement for Trans-Pacific Partnership (CPTPP), which came into effect in early 2019, is the world's third-largest trade agreement when measured by the aggregate GDP of its members.[19] The United States played a critical role in negotiating this multilateral agreement, whose broad objectives (from Washington's point of view) were to highlight the enduring commitment and major role the United States would play in the Asia-Pacific region for years to come; modernize existing trade provisions to cover significant parts of the goods and services that had become important in the past decade, especially concerning data storage rules, e-commerce, and other cyber-related high-tech goods and services; and create a high-quality trading platform that would be sufficiently important that it would attract additional countries to seek membership based on the scope and standards of the CPTPP. The PRC was excluded from the negotiations to form the Trans-Pacific Partnership (TPP; as the agreement had been initially named before the United States withdrew), but with the size and importance of this trading group, negotiating a future accession agreement with the PRC would provide strong leverage to promote standards and reforms in China's economy.

President Trump withdrew the United States from the TTP before it had been submitted for ratification by Congress. He has subsequently demanded bilateral negotiations with China and with American allies and partners around the world to modify previous trade agreements to America's advantage. His negotiating tactics and expansive use of national security claims to justify what otherwise would be considered violations of past American commitments have created major frictions and uncertainties throughout much of the international trade community.

Negotiations to join multilateral agreements have repeatedly proven important in strengthening economic reformers in China and promoting changes in the Chinese economic system itself. No agreement is ever an unmitigated success. Domestic politics and external developments are too unpredictable and contentious to assure smooth sailing. But the incentives for positive change and the politics of agreeing to those changes are far more positive when Beijing has sought to join important existing groupings than when it is confronted with tough demands by the United States in bilateral negotiations.

Withdrawing from the TPP has cost the United States credibility with the other eleven countries involved in the negotiations and left the United States seeking to achieve many of the same objectives with China without the added heft of having China's other largest trading partners already operating on the same basis. Now that the CPTPP has come into effect, quite a few other countries are considering applying for membership, and potential bridges are being built to put the CPTPP and the EU on the same footing.

In this context, it would not be surprising to see Beijing begin to explore negotiating entry into the CPTPP after a few years. Should Beijing join in the coming decade and the United States remain outside this agreement, Beijing, rather than the United States, would then be the dominant power in the major trading community in the Asia-Pacific (and possibly Europe). American entry would then have to meet demands shaped in part by Beijing, rather than the other way around. This is not in American interests in either the short or long term.

Reopen U.S.-China Bilateral Investment Treaty Negotiations

The Obama administration carried on prolonged negotiations with China to forge a bilateral investment treaty (BIT). These complex negotiations made major progress but were not completed in time to sign the BIT and submit it to Congress for ratification before the 2016 American presidential election. The Obama administration pursued these negotiations in order to establish rules that would remove most barriers to U.S. private sector direct investment in China, provide for equal treatment for U.S. and Chinese firms in the PRC, subject all sectors of the Chinese economy to the BIT rules except for those specifically designated as outside of the BIT (the so-called negative list[20]), and establish clear rules for treatment of state-owned enterprises, among other objectives. Fundamentally, the United States wanted to better protect intellectual property, allow majority or full U.S. ownership of firms in multiple sectors in China (including high value-added services, a space in which U.S. firms are especially competitive), and have far fuller access to the rapidly growing Chinese middle-class market.

A successful U.S.-China BIT would address many of the issues that the CPTPP does not cover. Completing both agreements and getting the U.S. Congress to ratify them were goals that proved too ambitious to achieve before Obama left office. Had they been pursued successfully by the new U.S. administration after it assumed office in 2017, they together would have put the United States in a strong position as it looked to America's economic future in the Asia-Pacific region and vis-à-vis China in particular. The Trump administration decided not to pursue the U.S.-China BIT. We recommend that the United States put this back on its agenda.

Reverse Withdrawal from the Paris Climate Agreement

We recommend that the United States reverse its withdrawal from the Paris Climate Agreement.[21] To have the government of the United States officially deny the reality of human contributions to climate change and adopt diplomatic, economic, and security policies that embody and promote that denial is extremely damaging to American interests. There are legitimate debates that must be pursued concerning the specifics of climate change, the most effective and efficient ways to mitigate and adapt to it, and the respective responsibilities of various countries and institutions to cope with it. However, the evidence of climate change, the science undergirding the models, the rapid acceleration of actual damage, and the increasingly short time lines to reduce the chances of irreversible and fundamental impacts on the natural world and future life make the present American position blatantly incompatible with a country that sees itself as a global scientific leader and norm setter.

The Paris Climate Agreement itself is too weak to galvanize the resources and action necessary to keep greenhouse gas emissions within tolerable limits. But the major powers shaped the Paris Agreement to gain global agreement and built in procedures to enhance national commitments at periodic intervals. U.S. withdrawal from the agreement enormously enhances the odds that catastrophic climate change will become a reality within decades. While the United States under Barack Obama played a leadership role in forging a global consensus to combat climate change, President Trump's withdrawal from the Paris Agreement and rejection of climate change as an issue amount in almost every way to a self-inflicted wound of startling proportions.

Reversing U.S. withdrawal from the Paris Climate Agreement would afford the United States an opportunity to achieve some important alterations in the agreement as an enticement for reentering it. We recommend, for example, that the United States require external monitoring and verification of greenhouse gas emission commitments and accomplishments of all major emitters. This measure would, among other benefits, strengthen the incentives of PRC officials at all levels to redouble efforts to control emissions and would also provide a better baseline upon which to base future projections and emissions targets.

Explore Cooperation with China on Clean Energy Research, Development, Testing, Evaluation, and Deployment

The United States and China have cooperated in myriad ways over several decades on clean energy research, development, testing, evaluation, and deployment, but the U.S. government currently is both abandoning support for clean energy efforts in general and increasingly regarding the PRC's efforts in this sphere as a national security challenge. Both countries have significant capabilities to advance the efficiency and availability of clean energy sources. But as the two largest economies in the world, the cost of developing and deploying breakthroughs in clean energy will become manageable only as each advance can be scaled up. In this sphere, adopting compatible standards in these two huge markets is critical to increasing the scale and reducing the cost of clean energy utilization.

There are significant issues regarding protection of intellectual property and the role of state subsidies in this sphere, even more than in most others. But where U.S.-China cooperation is feasible, the benefits to both sides (and to the global fight to mitigate greenhouse gas emissions) are potentially huge. In addition, in the absence of such cooperation and of major U.S. government support for clean energy development and deployment, China is likely to gain a decisive competitive edge as climate-related natural disasters put clean energy capabilities and products in very high demand.

In the Cyber Realm, Focus More Actively on Negotiating Agreements on Global Norms and Standards

The new digital world presents fundamental challenges that have no clear-cut solutions. This stems from three facts that are central to the dilemmas posed in the digital domain. First, the technological advances in various distinct spheres, such as artificial intelligence (AI), quantum computing, 5G, and virtual reality, are proceeding at a pace too fast for governments to understand or regulate effectively. Typically, by the time a government has addressed a problem and developed and adopted a law or regulation to govern it, the problem being addressed has itself changed to the point that the solution no longer effectively addresses the current reality.

Second, it has been the case for years and may well remain the case for many more years that no system is impenetrable by persistent, well-resourced hackers. In short, in the cyber world, offense trumps defense across the board, although this reality is rarely acknowledged or even understood by most officials and leaders of institutions.

And third, advances in AI, virtual reality, augmented reality, quantum computing, 5G networks, and the Internet of Things, along with the transition to digitization of increasing portions of our economies, entertainment, medical devices and health services, and so on, combine to put unprecedented and little-understood capabilities under the control of some companies, software engineers, and computer algorithms themselves. If all these developments were under the control of national governments, the opportunity for mischief would be very worrisome, but the capacity to reach truly effective agreements on limits and rules would be more feasible than is the current reality in the cyber world.

Perhaps of even greater consequence, the history of technological disruption is rife with examples of "Aha!" moments when capabilities developed for individual unrelated purposes can, if combined correctly, create a disruptive capability that nobody had previously anticipated. Present developments in the largely ungoverned realms of digital technology may well produce such "Aha!" disruptions within the coming decade. With many of the most dynamic developments in digital technologies taking place in the United States and China, each is understandably extremely worried about what the other can do both now and in the future.

There are no fully satisfactory solutions to the presented dilemmas. But the United States should devote far more attention to negotiating agreements on international norms (a digital Geneva Convention) and the standards for next-generation digital systems. China has been active in the standard-setting process, whereas the United States has paid it less attention. The standards are critically important for expanding sales into additional markets and can present major obstacles for new capabilities that are incompatible with already adopted applicable standards.

International norms in the digital realm are in a nascent stage, but on many issues (e.g., data storage and transfer regulations and sovereign controls over digital content and traffic), practices are in flux and are a major concern for governments, private companies, nongovernmental organizations and political activists, and financial institutions. In this as in many other arenas, serious dialogue to understand current concerns and the evolving impact of changing digital technologies to seek agreement on norms, where possible, is a worthwhile effort. The United States and China are not by any means the only significant participants in this arena, but U.S.-China consultations and consensus building could provide at least some impetus toward making the cyber realm less an arena of competition and conflict.

Nonetheless, when all is said and done, developments in the cyber realm are almost certain to grow as a driver of distrust between the United States and China. The recommendations we provide cannot solve this problem but seek to mitigate that distrust and its attendant dangers where possible. Given the ongoing rapid, multifaceted transformation of the cyber arena broadly defined and the continuing impossibility of guaranteeing the security of any system from penetration (i.e., the reality that in the hacking world offense trumps defense), it is not obvious that decoupling the networks and equipment of Chinese companies from those in Europe, the United States, and America's allies and partners around the world, even if possible, would necessarily produce a sustainable net increase in either China's or the United States' cybersecurity. Indeed, ongoing communications, joint research (e.g., in AI), and negotiations on norms and standards are arguably more likely to enhance the chances of more dynamic and less pernicious developments in the cyber realm.[22]

Resume and Expand U.S.-China Military-to-Military Dialogues

Military tensions between the United States and China have sharpened as the PRC's military capabilities have expanded; potential flash points have increased;

and the national security doctrines, deployments, and exercises of each military have enhanced the threat perceptions of the other. The growing tensions reflect significant changes on the ground as well as a growing perception of an increasingly zero-sum geostrategic rivalry. Against this background, since 2016, most U.S.-China military-to-military dialogues and related joint activities have decreased, and the contacts that remain have been primarily limited to the highest level within each military.

China has also undertaken a major reorganization of its military to transform it from having a primary mission of assuring domestic control to one that focuses on joint capabilities across military services organized around potential external theaters of conflict.[23] Especially in view of the resulting rapid changes in the command and control systems in the People's Liberation Army, the significant changes in doctrine in both militaries, and the enhanced deployments of both militaries in the first island chain, the potential importance of military-to-military dialogues at various levels has increased, not diminished. We recommend that the United States and PRC initiate discussions to determine the most useful military-to-military dialogues to either resurrect or develop, with the following three basic objectives:

- Develop additional agreed-upon procedures to follow when maritime incidents occur on the surface, below the surface, and in the air.
- Develop and exchange information regarding crisis management in each country in the event of accidents or incidents that could trigger escalatory responses.
- Regarding some specific issues, such as the possibility of conflict on the Korean Peninsula, initiate dialogues that clarify the personnel and communications to use in order to reduce the chances of direct U.S.-China military clashes.

The value to having Chinese and American military officers getting to know each other is that, as a result of such interactions, each side can gain a sense of the temperament, attitudes, and knowledge of their counterparts, which can be especially useful when a crisis erupts. Having agreed-upon protocols to reduce the likelihood of miscommunications or misperceptions during a tense situation greatly increases the probability of de-escalation rather than serious missteps that can trigger unwanted escalation. Especially during an escalating crisis, there is a tendency to assume that the other side must clearly understand one's own signals and to interpret the other side's signals in ways that fall into preconceived assumptions. And in both systems, crisis-induced distortions in internal communications and a stingier approach to sharing information increase the dangers.

Both the U.S. and Chinese militaries have experience in dealing with the other without compromising classified information. The value of dialogues and working out appropriate protocols for various types of incidents and situations far outweighs the potential risks of not doing so.

* * *

Forty plus years ago, the most populous country in the world, wracked by poverty and weakened by fanaticism and isolationism, began to join the international community, increasingly welcoming foreign businesses and know-how, becoming a strategic counter to Soviet aggression, and spurring decades of unprecedented domestic and global poverty reduction and prosperity. China's leaders provided the impetus for these initiatives, many of which required wrenching changes in China's society and political system, and the United States in its own interests saw the opportunity and supported the effort.

Neither the United States nor China approached these issues as naïve dreamers, and at many points, relations became fraught. But both sides recognized—across major changes in national leadership over forty years—that abandoning constructive bilateral engagement would leave both countries far worse off in economic and geostrategic terms. Today's level of interaction, not to mention the spectacular increases in global economic growth and four decades without a major war in Asia, would have been unachievable without the bold vision behind America's opening to China and behind China's opening to the world. This shared understanding was realized only through hard work, patience, and pragmatic determination on both sides.

The American and Chinese governments should recognize that restoration of U.S.-China relations in 1979 was a *necessary condition* for the ensuing four decades of economic growth and absence of major war. Looking forward, many of the most dangerous threats today, including climate change, terrorism, cyber war, nuclear proliferation, and pandemics, are inherently transnational and can be managed only if the United States and China find ways to cooperate or at least work along parallel lines. Each of these threats is likely to metastasize and become more intractable to the extent that the two countries instead regard each as an additional arena of zero-sum geopolitical competition and deterrence.

To be sure, there are important realities driving the current growing U.S.-China competition and rivalry. In this context, leaders and publics on both sides should not forget that managing the challenges outlined in this chapter effectively will require a significant modicum of U.S.-China cooperation. Unfortunately, popularized and misleading historical narratives that first caricature and then decry the goals and accomplishments of four-plus decades of U.S.-China diplomacy are reducing the political space for sustaining the necessary levels of cooperation even as both countries react to growing bilateral and multilateral frictions.

NOTES*

* Note that this chapter was completed before Joseph Biden assumed the presidency.
1. *Normalization* is the term of art for the establishment of full diplomatic relations between the PRC and the United States on January 1, 1979.
2. Every WTO member can negotiate a bilateral accession agreement that stipulates the terms it insists on to support a new applicant's accession to the WTO. In the case of China, the U.S.-China bilateral accession agreement addressed by far the broadest array of consequential issues and was seen by most of the other major members as covering more than 80 percent of the key issues for China to be accepted. Because the WTO operates by consensus, each bilateral accession agreement's terms are then rolled into the final overall terms for accession to the WTO.
3. See Paul Blustein, *Schism: China, America, and the Fracturing of the Global Trading System* (Waterloo, ON: Centre for International Governance Innovation, 2019), 40–42. Premier Zhu must have had Chinese Communist Party general secretary Jiang Zemin's support to accept those compromises, but it appears that the details were kept on very close hold and came as a surprise to many of the officials who had felt they should have had more input into these decisions.
4. The Chinese pointed to many aspects of the incident that fed their suspicion that the United States had deliberately targeted their embassy. In reality, though, the White House first learned of the attack when staff in the White House Situation Room saw a live report from the scene on CNN.
5. On the unrest and its suppression, see Robert Barnett, "The Tibet Protests of Spring 2008," *China Perspectives* 3 (2009): 6–23
6. Kenneth Lieberthal and David M. Lampton, eds., *Bureaucracy, Politics, and Decision Making in Post-Mao China* (Berkeley: University of California Press, 1992).
7. That is, as the de facto ambassador in Beijing before the two countries established full diplomatic relations.
8. An excellent, concise summary of the issues, challenges, and outcomes is available at U.S. Department of State, Office of the Historian, "The August 17, 1982 U.S.-China Communiqué on Arms Sales to Taiwan," https://history.state.gov/milestones/1981-1988/china-communique. For the text of the joint communiqué, see "U.S.-PRC Joint Communique, August 17, 1982," https://photos.state.gov/libraries/ait-taiwan/171414/ait-pages/817_e.pdf.
9. Most favored nation (MFN) status simply means that the country granted MFN will enjoy the same tariff treatment accorded to all other countries granted MFN. The United States and many other countries grant MFN to almost all countries with which they trade, and it typically does not require periodic renewal. In short, *not* having MFN status means that you have been singled out for discrimination. In the 1990s, the United States granted MFN to all but a very short list of countries. The WTO rules accord MFN to all countries who are in the WTO. The Clinton administration wanted to negotiate China's entry into the WTO, but the U.S. Congress had strong objections to anything that implied that China would receive exceptionally favorable tariff treatment. Clinton then got Congress to change the term *most favored nation* to the more accurate *permanent normal trade relations*, and in 2000, Congress voted to grant China that status. Without that change, when China entered the WTO in late 2001, all members of the WTO *except* the United States would have benefited from the concessions the United States had negotiated with China in its accession agreement.
10. "Summit in Washington; Clinton and Jiang in Their Own Words: Sharing a Broad Agenda," *New York Times*, October 30, 1997, A20.

11. "Hainan Island Incident," Wikipedia, https://en.wikipedia.org/wiki/Hainan_Island_incident.

12. When meeting with PRC premier Wen Jiabao in the Oval Office in December 2003, President Bush stated, "We oppose any unilateral decision by either China or Taiwan to change the *status quo*, and the comments and actions made by the leader of Taiwan indicate that he may be willing to make decisions unilaterally, to change the *status quo*, which we oppose." See Brian Knowlton, "Bush Warns Taiwan to Keep Status Quo: China Welcomes U.S. Stance," *New York Times*, December 10, 2003, https://www .nytimes.com/2003/12/10/news/bush-warns-taiwan-to-keep-status-quo-chinawelcomes -us-stance.html.

13. See further discussion later in the chapter.

14. Jacque deLisle, "9/11 and U.S.-China Relations," Foreign Policy Research Institute E-Notes, September 3, 2011, https://www.fpri.org/article/2011/09/911-and-u-s-china-relations/.

15. China was not a member of the G8.

16. Bernard Gwertzman, "U.S. Decides to Sell Weapons to China in Policy Reversal," *New York Times*, June 17, 1981, https://www.nytimes.com/1981/06/17/world/us-decides-to-sell -weapons-to-china-in-policy-reversal.html.

17. The history is summarized in: Andy Wright, "Trump Could Learn from Gore on How to Handle an Election Interference Scandal," Just Security, August 9, 2018, https://www .justsecurity.org/60200/trumps-unlearned-lessons-chinas-clinton-goreelection-interference/.

18. See, for example, Kenneth Lieberthal, "Domestic Forces and Sino-U.S. Relations," in *Living with China: U.S.-China Relations in the Twenty-First Century*, ed. Ezra Vogel (New York: W.W. Norton, 1997): 254–76.

19. Had the United States not withdrawn, the TPP (which became the CPTPP after President Trump withdrew the United States from it) would have increased the members' aggregate GDP from 13+ percent to nearly 30 percent of global GDP.

20. The PRC had previously operated on a positive list principle—that an agreement applied only to the sectors explicitly named in the agreement, with all other sectors excluded. Switching to a negative list principle marked a breakthrough in the BIT negotiations.

21. Although President Trump withdrew from the Paris Agreement in 2017, the United States will remain a formal member of the agreement until four years after the withdrawal decision. Therefore, until 2021, the U.S. government can reverse its withdrawal without requiring either formal renegotiation of accession to the agreement or any congressional action to approve this change.

22. The following resources provide a brief introduction to several of these issues: Anders Henriksen, "The End of the Road for the UN GGE Process: The Future Regulation of Cyberspace," *Journal of Cybersecurity* 5, no. 1 (2019): 1–9; Alex Grigsby, "The United Nations Doubles Its Workload on Cyber Norms, and Not Everyone Is Pleased," Council on Foreign Relations, November 15, 2018, https://www.cfr.org/blog/united-nations -doubles-its-workload-cyber-norms-and-not-everyone-pleased; and Melissa Hathaway, "Getting Beyond Norms," Centre for International Governance Innovation, April 20, 2017, https://www.cigionline.org/publications/getting-beyond-norms-when-violating -agreement-becomes-customary-practice.

23. Phillip C. Saunders et al., eds., *Chairman Xi Remakes the PLA: Assessing Chinese Military Reforms* (Washington, DC: National Defense University Press, 2019) provides a comprehensive analysis and assessment of the People's Liberation Army reforms, including their drivers, content, impact, and potential.

CHAPTER 14

━━━━

ENGAGEMENT WITH CHINA

A Eulogy and Reflections on a Gathering Storm

DAVID M. LAMPTON

> I speak not to disprove what Brutus spoke,
> But here I am to speak what I do know.
> You all did love him once, not without cause.
> What cause withholds you, then, to mourn for him?
> O judgment, thou art fled to brutish beasts,
> And men have lost their reason! Bear with me;
> My heart is in the coffin there with Caesar,
> And I must pause till it come back to me.
>
> —William Shakespeare, Mark Antony, funeral oration,
> *Julius Caesar*, Act 3, Scene II[1]

In the spirit of Mark Antony speaking at Caesar's funeral in William Shakespeare's telling, I have come to bury the U.S.-China engagement era as we came to know it in the forty-plus years since 1972. As in Antony's funeral oration, I will *praise* the deceased. Unlike Antony, I will do so plainly, unequivocally, and without apology or irony. After the praise, however, the living are nonetheless left with the core questions: What comes next? What is to be done?

In the postengagement era of U.S.-China relations, the character of the future interaction remains uncertain, although its direction is conflictual and profoundly contrary to the long-term, comprehensive interests of both nations and peoples. This trend is likely to persist because domestic politics in both countries increasingly are being driven by mutual security anxieties and the progressive alienation of constituencies in each nation that previously had been supportive of the relationship. The costs imposed by this trend will steadily mount until, in some indefinite future, more constructive and sober forces in each society have the opportunity, and perhaps the courage, to (re)assert themselves.

In the United States, the policies and sentiments of the two dominant political parties with respect to the People's Republic of China (PRC) are converging in many respects as we enter the third decade of the millennium. This convergence reflects a seismic downturn in American popular views of China, a downturn almost equally apparent in western Europe.[2]

Traditionally, the U.S.-China relationship operated as a sort of three-legged stool, with security, economics, and culture/diplomacy each constituting a leg. Until around 2010, when one leg of the stool had temporarily weakened, the others had the capacity to bear the weight and compensate. But after 2010, security concerns moved from serving as a supportive rationale for engagement and constructive relations to becoming a progressively more friction-laden consideration in each capital, as Thomas Fingar (chapter 2), Chas Freeman (chapter 11), John Garver (chapter 3), and Richard Madsen (chapter 5) explain in their respective contributions to this volume. As this occurred, the rationale for Beijing and Washington to sublimate other grievances was reduced because most societies privilege security over other concerns.

In Washington and Beijing, trade, finance, and educational relations have become increasingly entangled in security anxieties (see chapter 10 by Robert Daly in this volume), not to mention that each domain has itself become more friction laden in its own right. Each country's overall policies increasingly have alienated previously staunch supporters of the relationship in the other country. In the United States, Beijing's progressive alienation of major segments of the American business community is a case in point. Consequently, by 2016, the security, economic, and cultural/diplomatic legs of the three-legged stool of U.S.-China relations had all simultaneously become wobbly, something that had not occurred in the preceding nearly three decades. And then, beginning in the first quarter of 2020, the COVID-19 virus greatly magnified unfavorable views of China, with Beijing popularly seen as the origin of the epidemic, which it first sought to hide and downplay. Only later did the PRC grudgingly cooperate with the World Health Organization. Predictably, U.S. criticism of Beijing's initial COVID-19 response was seen as Washington's attempt to humiliate China and its people.

In America, this weakening of the foundational tripod for U.S.-China relations occurred against a background of deeply held popular views that the economic relationship was fundamentally unfair, lacking in reciprocity, and that prospects for more law-based, humane governance in China were receding.[3] The American business community saw economic reform in China as moving backward. (Chapter 6 in this volume, by Craig Allen, speaks directly to this issue, as does chapter 7 by Barry Naughton.) In Beijing, anxiety grew that America would never treat China as a coequal great power and was seeking to undermine regime stability—the 2011 pivot to Asia by the Obama administration and its refusal to accept the newly anointed Xi Jinping's call for a new type of major-power relationship became poster children for Beijing's understanding of underlying American purpose. This dark view was energized by a widespread view among Chinese that asserted that their country was now stronger and deserving of respect, if not a certain deference, and that U.S. decline (as viewed in Beijing) revealed in the global financial crisis required accommodation by Washington. In the United States, PRC bravado fueled American concerns that Beijing would test Washington's resolve. All this came to a head with the ascension to power in Washington and Beijing of Donald Trump and Xi Jinping, respectively. Both were populist leaders, and neither was invested in engagement to the degree that their predecessors had been. Both relied less on experts and technocrats, greatly centralizing their personal, strongman control instead.

This chapter is not focused on how America and China have reached the present juncture. Rather, among the questions considered here are: What are the indicators that the era of engagement with the PRC, as we have spoken of it for more than four decades, has ended in many significant respects? What were some of engagement's past gains, the likes of which will be diminished or foregone entirely as we move into a more friction-laden, less cooperative future? What have we learned about managing U.S.-China relations during that long, and in many respects productive, era that may assist in addressing upcoming challenges? And finally, how might the new postengagement period be similar to and different from the Cold War of the second half of the twentieth century (1946–1991)? The differences will be important.

The Demise of Engagement: From Reassurance to Deterrence

For purposes here, I define the engagement era as embracing the years circa 1971–2016. These decades were characterized by some essential continuities. A distinctive mode of interaction between the United States and China defined the era. A widely shared (though not universally accepted) set of attitudes, objectives, and policy predispositions prevailed in the United States. I treat this period as a unity to underscore the core features that endured for forty-five years—a comparatively long time as policy life spans go.

The era of engagement began with Richard Nixon's initial serious, albeit gradual, approach to Mao Zedong shortly after assuming the presidency in early 1969. The period ended as Donald Trump and Xi Jinping became their countries' respective paramount leaders. Despite the obvious and important differences among the eight U.S. presidential administrations (Richard Nixon, Gerald Ford, Jimmy Carter, Ronald Reagan, George H. W. Bush, Bill Clinton, George W. Bush, and Barack Obama) and four Beijing administrations (Mao Zedong, Deng Xiaoping, Jiang Zemin, and Hu Jintao), American and PRC modes of interaction with each other displayed essential continuity.

As Kenneth Lieberthal and Susan Thornton explain in their joint contribution to this volume (chapter 13), "Successive American presidents rightly saw both a national interest and moral imperative to help alleviate these enormous challenges [in post–Cultural Revolution China]." The challenges facing a Cultural Revolution–shattered China of the late 1960s and early 1970s included reducing poverty, rebuilding a savaged educational system, improving health care, and creating an international order in which Beijing perceived it had a positive stake. In short, the task for the United States was to be supportive of impulses toward more humane governance in China and to help create preconditions for peace.

Although the mutual objective of countering Soviet power initially brought the two sides together (discussed in detail in Thomas Fingar's contribution to this volume) and counterterrorism helped bind the two sides together later, throughout the engagement era, despite repeated instances of crisis and interrupted communication, engagement was rooted in the premise that *dialogue* was essential. In terms of interlocutors, the relationship continually broadened and deepened, moving from a supreme leader–centric pattern of interaction and dialogue with Richard Nixon (and Henry Kissinger) and Mao Zedong (and Zhou Enlai) to a progressively broadening *society-to-society interaction and dialogue* extending from Jimmy Carter and Deng Xiaoping onward, as Mary Bullock explains in chapter 8. At its core, engagement was a dialogue and intense interaction of an ever-growing number of elements of both societies at all levels.

The foundational thinking was that if the two sides built more robust mutual understanding and if the two societies and their economies, civil society organizations, and bureaucratic institutions became more intertwined, the relationship would become more stable, productive, and manageable. The more threads tying down the relationship like Gulliver, the more impediments there would be to systemic disruption. This expansion of economic, educational, and cultural intercourse dramatically enlarged the sectors, range of individuals, institutions, and government entities involved in the relationship in both nations, as almost every chapter in this volume attests, although the constraints on interaction were always greater in the PRC than in the United

States. Naturally, more actors within and between our societies meant more complexity and more points of friction, but the assumption was that this was a net addition to stability.

Despite periodic crises and bitter incidents (such as the 1989 Tiananmen bloodshed, the Taiwan Strait tensions of 1995 and 1996, the mistaken and lethal bombing of the Chinese embassy in Belgrade in 1999, and the fatal collision of a U.S. and a Chinese military aircraft off Hainan Island in 2001), neither side defined the other as its gravest national security problem, even though underlying strategic mistrust mounted. For a long period in the 1990s and into the 2000s, other developments such as the North Korean nuclear program and the global war on terror provided opportunities for limited U.S.-China security cooperation even as the underlying security rationale was eroding. As Thomas Fingar has put it in comments to this author, these developments allowed Beijing and Washington "to pretend" that the strategic relationship was healthier than it was. Equally important, throughout the new millennium, from 9/11 and the Afghanistan and Iraq wars on, Washington was preoccupied with areas outside East Asia.

As time progressed, both Beijing and Washington increasingly hedged their security bets as incidents multiplied and PRC military capacities grew. As the U.S. military became bogged down in central Asian and Middle Eastern quagmires, Beijing detected more than a whiff of U.S. decline. The global financial crisis of 2008–2009 greatly increased Beijing's perception of faltering American capacities, particularly given the PRC's ability to stoke its own domestic growth and weather the global trade and finance storm comparatively well. The confidence that began to grow in the PRC was buffered by its anxieties that Washington would become more belligerent as Beijing's power grew.

As for Washington, it anxiously looked out of the corner of its eyes as Chinese military, economic, and intellectual power grew with surprising speed. As Barry Naughton puts it in chapter 7 of this volume, "most economists (including myself) were simply unable to envision the vastness of the changes associated with China's emergence as an economic superpower" or to predict the speed of their occurrence. A U.S. view gradually but steadily took hold, based on mounting evidence, that Beijing had a conscious policy of illicitly acquiring intellectual property and of freezing the United States out of Chinese markets where American competitive advantage was greatest. China's most important effort in this regard was to use as a lure its enormous domestic market to gain essential technology transfer.

All these undertones aside, the emphasis in both nations' declarative policies and overall strategy throughout the engagement era was *reassurance rather than deterrence* and a focus on domestic economic goals facilitated by cooperative bilateral relations. In fact, the 2001 terrorist attacks against the United States gave U.S.-China security ties a temporary boost, as Lieberthal and Thornton describe in their joint chapter and as Chas Freeman explains in his contribution. Even as late as the end of the first decade of the twenty-first century, the global financial crisis underscored how important it was for Washington and Beijing to cooperate in their respective macroeconomic policies to maintain global growth and financial stability. Both sides viewed expanding bilateral economic ties as a substantial net plus for, and source of ballast in, the bilateral relationship, despite chronic problems such as the relentlessly rising U.S. merchandise trade deficit with China, exchange rates, market access, nontariff barriers, technology transfer, and intellectual property theft. Throughout this period, the idea of building security and prosperity through economic interdependence was the dominant concept. During the engagement period, the business community saw business problems, not strategic conflicts. Indeed, within the corporate business community, there was widespread support for normal trade relations with Beijing and for China's accession to the World Trade Organization, which occurred in 2001.

Although aspects of engagement era thinking came under increasing debate toward the ends of the Barack Obama and Hu Jintao administrations (with Beijing's assertive thrusts in the South China Sea and Washington's pivot to Asia [later dubbed the "rebalance"]), the dawn of the Trump-Xi era produced a dramatic alteration in the relationship. Interaction between the strongman leaders, each of whom was an unsettling departure from his predecessors, became a prominent feature of bilateral relations. More dominant senior leaders, each acting on the basis of *less* technocratic policy input from their respective bureaucracies and experts, are a prominent feature of the new era. Both Trump and Xi, as it worked out, were determined to play a more interventionist role in domestic and international economic affairs, having much less faith in the wisdom of markets or experts than their predecessors.

Degeneration of bilateral relations has proceeded on many fronts. The established pattern of broad and regular government-to-government, interagency dialogues, along with vigorous and relatively unconstrained nongovernmental organization (NGO) dialogues, has eroded considerably. Bilateral NGO interactions have declined conspicuously in frequency, scale, and significance, in part reflecting Beijing's January 2017 implementation of the Foreign NGO Law. Securing visas for one another's students, scholars, and think tankers has become progressively more arduous, and the fabric of academic and education ties has frayed, as Robert Daly and Andrew Mertha (chapter 4) note in their contributions to this volume. By mid-2019, scholars and business people moving between the two countries were becoming increasingly concerned, not only about gaining permission to travel, but about being harassed in a variety of ways (for example, at the border) if they moved between the two countries. What private sector dialogues have occurred often have proven vacuous, avoiding the very issues that most need to be addressed. The hunt for spies is well underway in both societies, and both seek to follow the money of the other's influence operations.[4]

The dynamics of deterrence and the reality of an arms race have overwhelmed serious attempts at reassurance through military-to-military exchanges and dialogue, with one indication being the use of the word *aggression* to describe Chinese behavior, rather than softer formulations such as *assertive foreign policy*. In both countries, the coercive instruments of statecraft are ascendant and those of diplomacy and cultural exchange in retreat. A good example of this is the U.S. Department of Defense's (DOD) policy to curtail some DOD funding for schools that continue taking PRC money for Confucius Institutes, with some members of Congress joining (indeed energizing) the chorus. In September 2019, the Office of Science and Technology Policy signaled the need for "federal government, research institutions, private companies, non-profit organizations, and law enforcement to come together to ensure the integrity and security of the American research enterprise in light of increasing threats."[5] In China, access to archives and field research opportunities for foreign scholars is narrowing. Commercial and financial ties are now a relationship-threatening bone of contention (see Craig Allen's contribution to this volume). As Washington and Beijing give reciprocity a bad name by engaging in tit-for-tat rounds of tariffs on each other's exports, the gigantic web of economic and commercial relations between the world's two largest economies is under political assault, with Washington pursuing decoupling and Beijing seeking self-reliance.[6]

As the relationship moved into the second half of 2019, China's exercise of power over Hong Kong (characterized by increasingly harsh pronouncements and local police activity) and Xinjiang ("reeducation" camps) became major bones of contention, as did increased pressure on Taiwan with the PRC's (unsuccessful) efforts to shape Taiwan's presidential election of 2020. In the face of months of turmoil in Hong Kong and China's efforts to curtail the movement for more autonomy there, in November 2019, the U.S. Congress passed, and President Trump signed, the Hong Kong Human Rights and Democracy Act. Beijing did not relent, instead arresting many in the older generation of Hong Kong democracy promoters early the following year and imposing a National Security Law that had extraterritorial reach to foreigners acting outside the borders of Hong Kong and the PRC. In August 2020, Washington sent its highest-level official to Taiwan since 1979, Health and Human Services Secretary Alex Azar, infuriating Beijing.

Beijing and Washington now each define the other as their principal external security challenge. President Trump has invoked national security to dislodge China from critical supply chains (e.g., Huawei, and an aborted attempt in the case of ZTE, with China retaliating in kind). China has literally excluded America's most competitive Internet firms (Google and Facebook, for example) from its enormous domestic market, even as China's comparable firms have made notable inroads in America and globally. President Xi summons the Maoist talisman of self-reliance in response to the anxiety of dependence on the United States, whether for food or for critical technologies.[7] In September 2018, *China Daily* carried a photo of Xi Jinping posing with a group of farm workers in a scene reminiscent of a famous tableau of Chairman Mao with peasants during the Cultural Revolution. The recent photo's caption told the reader: "President Xi Jinping underlined the importance of self-reliance in food security, the real economy and manufacturing . . . as the country faces rising unilateralism and trade protectionism internationally."[8] Washington and Beijing are energizing one another to adopt tougher security, mercantilist, and import-substitution policies while limiting intellectual exchange out of their respective fears of espionage and subversion. Four examples provide substance.

First, the Center for a New American Security, a Washington think tank cofounded by a Republican and a Democrat billing itself as "bold, innovative, bipartisan," has become a player in Washington discourse on China policy. One of the center's reports in mid-2019 accurately summed up the new, bipartisan national security view of the PRC in Washington: "The defense establishment is enjoying a period of bipartisan agreement on the need to prioritize strategic competition with China and Russia."[9] Another report from the same think tank by an adjunct fellow argued that "given advances in Chinese military innovation," there is a need for a multidimensional "competitive mobilization." Fearing that "future conflicts could start rapidly and without warning," the author argues for mobilization preparation, including expansion of the Selective Service System "to register not just men of 18 to 25 years, but to include Americans of all genders at least up to age 35."[10]

A second example, though promptly disavowed by the Department of State, is provided by Foggy Bottom's own then director of policy planning, who observed that this is "the first time that we will have a great power competitor that is not Caucasian."[11] This official articulated a racially tinged specter of a clash of civilizations to support Trump administration policy toward Beijing. Lest we think that only elements in Washington have steered into the dead end of racialism, in May 2014, Xi Jinping stated: "In the final analysis, let the people of Asia run the affairs of Asia, solve the problems of Asia and uphold the security of Asia."[12] Translation? "Asia for Asians."

In the United States, anxiety within the Chinese American community has mounted as its members fear that they could become targets of suspicion.[13] Reports of people of apparent Chinese ethnicity coming under physical and verbal assault have become increasingly frequent. The FBI called upon U.S. citizens to back a "whole-of-society response" to the threat of espionage and intellectual property theft by China.[14] In this regard, Beijing's policy of asserting that all persons of Chinese ethnicity living outside of the PRC (many or most of whom are citizens of other countries) have some diffuse obligation to help the motherland (China) has the presumably unintended effect of putting a target on the backs of all people of Chinese ethnicity living abroad. A former chief of CIA counterintelligence, James M. Olson, has written that while Russian intelligence often uses money as an inducement to recruit assets and Cuban intelligence appeals to ideology, PRC intelligence tends to employ ethnic solidarity.[15]

Third, U.S. policy during the engagement period eschewed promoting avowedly antiregime, anticommunist, ideologically charged, regime change–oriented rhetoric with respect to the PRC, preferring to talk about specific issues such as rule of law and human rights, global values and norms. There was an attempt to push ideological friction to the side while maintaining fidelity to American values. However, by June 2019, U.S. Secretary of State Pompeo was saying:

> Over the decades that followed [the violence at Tiananmen Square], the United States hoped that China's integration into the international system would lead to a more open, tolerant society. Those hopes have been dashed. . . . We salute the heroes of the Chinese people who bravely stood up thirty years ago in Tiananmen Square to demand their rights. Their exemplary courage has served as an inspiration to future generations calling for freedom and democracy around the world, beginning with the fall of the Berlin Wall and the end of communism in Eastern Europe in the months that followed.[16]

China's leaders view such statements as incitement to color revolution. Increasingly, Beijing sees Washington's black hands at work in encouraging destabilizing movements all around China's extensive and frequently unstable periphery—Hong Kong, Taiwan, Tibet, and Xinjiang (see chapter 12 by Carla Freeman in this volume). As one example, in this author's meeting with a Chinese diplomat in mid-2019, the diplomat protested that U.S. House of Representatives speaker Nancy Pelosi had recently said that the scene of millions of protestors in the streets of Hong Kong was a "beautiful sight to behold."

Washington has not been alone in ratcheting up the volume of the ideological sound track, as Mary Bullock notes in her chapter in this volume. One of the first Communist Party pronouncements of the new Xi era was the General Office of the Central Committee's Document Number Nine, which argued that the regime intended to augment its fight against external subversion and declared several ideas to be politically perilous, including constitutionalism, nihilism, civil society, universal values, and freedom of the press/media.[17] Shortly thereafter, Xi created a National Security Commission, a principal purpose of which was to coordinate the struggle against subversion by foreigners.[18] In other ideologically freighted areas, putting large numbers of Xinjiang Uighurs in reeducation camps and deploying available and developing technology to create what many construe to be an emerging surveillance state inevitably energized U.S. popular and governmental concern. A core feature of the PRC's 2016–2017 Foreign NGO Law was to transfer oversight of foreign NGOs from the Ministry of Civil Affairs to the Ministry of Public Security, a move that further increased apprehensions among domestic NGOs, as well as American and other foreign NGOs. American colleges and universities, research institutes, and NGOs shifted to a mode of constantly assessing the risk-reward ratio of their linkages with PRC counterparts.

Finally, echoing the Cultural Revolution phrase "the wind will not subside," the onset of the COVID-19 virus in China in late 2019 and its global spread thereafter fueled new, ideologically tinged critiques of the Chinese system for its poor transparency and initially grudging international cooperation, particularly with the United States. Mutual recriminations followed, with a few fringe figures in each country asserting (with no evidence) that the other had somehow unleashed the virus with intentionality.[19] Yanzhong Huang, in chapter 9 of this volume, details not only prior health cooperation but its recent deterioration. Indeed, by the spring of 2020, Beijing and Washington were both blaming the other for a slow response to the emerging pandemic that contributed to the virus's spread, with Washington withdrawing from the World Health Organization while Beijing was posturing as defender of multilateral cooperation to stem the spread of COVID-19. One of the first acts of the new Biden administration in 2021 was to rejoin the World Health Organization.

In short, the ideological conflict between the United States and China has intensified dramatically since the dawn of the Xi-Trump era. Recounting the progressive erosion of the engagement process, however, should not obscure that earlier era's many gains.

The Eulogy: The Goals and Accomplishments of Engagement

Goals. Given the downward turn of events just described, Beijing and Washington both have plenty of domestic critics of the engagement period. Policy inquests are ongoing in both countries. In both nations, there are widespread anxieties that something resembling a new Cold War lies ahead. On the U.S. side, perhaps the most often cited article early in the debate appeared in *Foreign Affairs* in spring 2018 and was written by two former U.S. officials of the Clinton-Obama era. In their analysis, Kurt Campbell and Ely Ratner laid down an inaccurate starting point for the U.S. inquest by attributing to engagement an overarching goal (making China just like America, democratic) that never was the central rationale for most of its architects and implementers during its forty-five-year run as U.S. policy. Campbell and Ratner wrote:

The United States has always had an outsize sense of its ability to determine China's course. . . . Washington now faces its most dynamic and formidable competition in modern history. Getting this challenge right will require doing away with hopeful thinking that has long characterized the United States approach to China. The Trump administration's first National Security Strategy took a step in the right direction by *interrogating* past assumptions in U.S. strategy.[20] [Italics added by editor]

And what did the National Security Strategy issued in December 2017 have to say?

China and Russia challenge American power, influence, and interests, attempting to erode American security and prosperity. They are determined to make economies less free and less fair, to grow their militaries, and to control information and data to repress their societies and expand their influence. . . . These competitions require the United States to rethink the policies of the past two decades—policies based on the assumption that engagement with rivals and their inclusion in international institutions and global commerce would turn them into benign actors and trustworthy partners. For the most part, this premise turned out to be false.[21]

The Campbell-Ratner thesis (and its antecedent Trump National Security Strategy) implicitly assumes that because the overall drift of PRC policy in the last decade or so has been unwelcome in the United States (and elsewhere), past policy either produced this turn of events or alternative policies adopted earlier could have lessened or averted these trends. As Thomas Christensen and Patricia Kim point out, because Campbell and Ratner "view the international order as by definition U.S.-led," any move Beijing makes to pursue its own interests is ipso facto revisionist, the behavior of a non–status quo power.[22]

In fact, during the eight previous U.S. presidential administrations of both parties, engagement was not pursued on the premise that Beijing would cease chasing its interests or would suddenly be governed in ways conforming to U.S. preferences. I can count on one hand the serious analysts of China who in the past three decades thought democracy (or anything remotely like it) was in the offing in the PRC.[23] One of the most thoughtful and data-based hopeful observers was Henry S. Rowen, who, in 1996, argued that China was liberalizing in the local election, media, and legal system realms and that very likely the PRC would begin the transition to stable democracy in about 2015. He anchored his optimism in what he argued was the high correlation between such transitions and per capita incomes of around US$7,000, which China was then nearing.[24] With China now approaching the $10,000 mark and political developments on the ground moving in the opposite direction, his optimism about an imminent transition was not borne out—at least yet.

Moreover, the Campbell-Ratner analysis fails to consider the threshold question of what preferable policy options were available earlier and what would have been the likely outcomes of following those alternative paths at prior decision points. What would have been the consequences of seeking to block the PRC at every turn early on? A more muscular U.S. response during preceding decades almost certainly would have produced a self-fulfilling prophecy of escalating conflict and would have garnered virtually no international support. Moreover, in the context of simultaneous, protracted, and large-scale conflicts entangling the United States in central Asia and the Middle East, along with conflicts and challenges in the heart of Europe since late in the 1990s, scarce U.S. leadership attention and national security resources had to be rationed. Additional tension with China simply has seemed undesirable and infeasible at prior decision points. A principal job of national leadership is to match resources to ambitions—to prioritize. Also not to be ignored, what would have been the opportunity costs of foregoing engagement's actual gains?

History is not over. All of the consequences of four-plus decades of engagement with the PRC are still playing out. Reform in the PRC and the process of engagement with the United States and the rest of the world have produced far more heterogeneous, pluralized, social and political structures in China than existed even two decades ago, much less at the time of Mao's death. In the PRC, sizeable chunks of the population, bureaucracy, and party now chafe under Xi's foreign and domestic policy directions because they have an interest in the changes reform, openness, and engagement previously achieved. We should appreciate the cumulative effects of modernization. I concur with the following observation from Andrew Nathan:

> The more China pursues wealth and power through domestic modernization and engagement with the global economy, the more students, intellectuals, and the rising middle class become unwilling to adhere to a 1950s-style ideological conformity. . . . But Xi's form of leadership creates its own dangers. Within the party, there is much private grumbling about the demand for loyalty to a vacuous ideology and what is in effect a ban on the discussion of policy. In the wider society, the intensity of control builds up psychological forces of resistance that could explode with considerable force if the regime ever falters, either in its performance or its will to power.[25]

Accomplishments of Engagement

There are many ways to tally the gains of the engagement period. Some accomplishments may appear modest while others seem weightier. The Lieberthal and Thornton and Fingar chapters address the many achievements in the strategic and foreign policy realms. Here, I focus on less frequently cited strides, not the oft-summoned contributions represented by engagement having (according to the World Bank) contributed to lifting 850 million people from poverty in China (1978–2019[26]) and having fueled a global economic expansion in which the PRC accounted for 33 percent of global growth by 2019.[27] I do not dwell on the absence of high-casualty wars on China's periphery (such as those that occurred in Korea and Vietnam in the 1950s, 1960s, and 1970s) that may have not occurred by virtue of cooperation with Beijing, nor do I dwell on the PRC's role in bringing the Soviet Union to its knees. Similarly, we will not discuss China's role in UN peacekeeping operations and its limited flexibility concerning the "right to protect" when it came to dealing with Sudan and other human rights problems in Africa. Also not emphasized here is the fact that constructive Sino-American relations made possible the creation of a relatively stable regional environment facilitating Taiwan's growth and democratization in the 1980s and thereafter, despite Washington switching formal diplomatic recognition from Taipei to Beijing in the late 1970s. It is hard to imagine that Taiwan would be democratic today if the Cold War tensions across the Taiwan Strait had persisted and the Nationalist Party (Kuomintang [KMT]) in Taiwan had an ongoing and demonstrable PRC threat as a rationale for continued martial law. Also, in Afghanistan, Beijing never set out to make the ongoing American intervention there more difficult directly or through its friend Pakistan; indeed, Beijing shares an American desire to stabilize the battered country.

Instead, I want to focus on what may seem to be smaller-aperture engagement gains, but ones carrying with them broad implications and stunning benefits in their own right. I do *not* attribute gains in each of the realms discussed exclusively to engagement. However, without that context, these strides would have taken longer to make, if they were made at all.

The realm of agriculture and food is a good example. Consider that in 1985 China lost over half of its fruits and vegetables between harvest and the dinner table. That loss rate now is likely in the 10 percent to 20 percent range overall, a remarkable 30 to 40 percent reduction in the loss rate for China's domestic supply of fruits and vegetables.[28] In the mid-1980s, the U.S. National Academy of Sciences and National Academy of Engineering, in cooperation with U.S. industry and land grant universities, worked with the Chinese Academy of Sciences and PRC industry to improve China's food supply chain, introducing aseptic packaging, cold storage, wholesaling systems, genetic modification of crops, and good handling and storage practices.[29] As a consequence, the Chinese people gained more varied, higher-quality, and more plentiful and affordable food to consume, and in the process, the PRC has become a large commercial market for American farmers and agribusiness. U.S. firms sold equipment, commodities, and agricultural inputs and boosted China's technological level, taking considerable pressure off the global food supply system.

Remarkably, the United States built such a stable and productive food relationship with the PRC that Beijing's leaders felt able to depend to a much greater extent on U.S. farm exports, something Mao never would have contemplated, viewing such dependence as a security issue given the United States' propensity to use food exports as a weapon. In the engagement period, the PRC became the United States' largest export market for agricultural products, and the nutritional status of the Chinese people climbed, dramatically so in the consumption of protein.[30] The UN World Food Program reports that "China alone accounts for almost two thirds of the total reduction in the number of undernourished people in developing regions since 1990."[31]

This kind of cooperation has now changed. Against the background of Xi Jinping's call for self-reliance and in the face of Washington's tariffs and Beijing's impulse to retaliate, U.S. soybean exports to China plummeted 98 percent from 2017 to 2018.[32] Current U.S.-China trade friction has taken a model of bilateral food and agriculture cooperation and turned it into a zone of friction and loss for both sides. The United States, as a result of Chinese retaliation in 2019, found itself facing reduced farm sales to the PRC, and a Republican nominally anti-subsidy administration in Washington resorted to massive subsidies to prop up farm sector revenues. The January 2020 phase one trade deal announced between Beijing and Washington has perhaps stabilized the U.S.-China food relationship, but the essential trust underpinning cooperation in this sensitive area took a great hit.

Air safety is another example of an area in which engagement era cooperation had very large payoffs for both countries. The U.S. Federal Aviation Administration (FAA) and the U.S. aerospace industry cooperated with the PRC to build one of the world's safest and fastest-growing airline industries. In an expanding aviation system, air traffic control and management are key. The United States and China cooperated to transform one of the world's most *un*safe air networks in the 1980s and 1990s (due to pilot errors, unreliable maintenance and erratic government oversight[33]) into an all-weather system with an air travel safety record at least equal to that of the United States.

> In the late 2000s, the fatal-accident rates of Chinese airlines were lower than those of airlines in Europe and the United States, even as Chinese carriers spent more and more hours in the sky. The culture of safety in China's skies did not come from centuries of Confucian culture and respect for authority. It came from a decisive intervention that overhauled China's aviation sector inside of a decade.[34]

The commercial and humanitarian impact of this cooperation was enormous. The Boeing Company now estimates that the PRC will be the top aircraft market worldwide by roughly 2023; that China will need 7,690 new planes through 2037; and that the PRC already accounts for 13 percent of Boeing's worldwide revenue.[35] Since August of 2010, Airfleets.net reports that there have been *no* fatal air accidents in China. By way of contrast, in 1990, 128 people died in air accidents and in 2002, 112 perished, with almost every year in this period witnessing loss of life.[36]

As in the case of agriculture, the bilateral trade conflict, ongoing since 2018, has also had a serious impact on the commercial aspect of aviation, a core field of long-standing U.S.-China cooperation. In 2017, aircraft and related parts was by far the single largest export category for the United States. Within this category, China was by far the largest importer. In 2018, Beijing placed *no* new orders with Boeing for aircraft.[37]

The U.S. auto industry and the broader issue of two-way foreign direct investment are other examples. In 2016, the McClatchy news service reported that about one hundred thousand Americans were working in Chinese-owned firms in the United States.[38] Detroit, a city that went bankrupt in July 2013 in the aftermath of the 2008 recession, saw more than one hundred Chinese firms invest in the auto parts industry there, thereby bringing more than a thousand jobs back to the beleaguered area.[39] In fiscal year 2017, General Motors sold almost 35 percent more vehicles in China than in the United States and more than 70 percent in the month of November.[40] Sales to China, rather than bailouts from Washington, account for GM's survival in the global financial downturn of 2008–2009. In Dayton, Ohio, Fuyao Glass America employs over two thousand workers and is the third-largest manufacturer and one of the top employers in the region.[41] Although trying to merge Chinese and American corporate and work cultures has not been easy, it appears this has been a net positive for Ohio and the Dayton region.[42]

Now, increasingly stringent rules and mechanisms are being implemented to limit Chinese investment in the United States. Chinese foreign direct investment into the United States fell about 40 percent in 2017 and fell a further 80 percent in 2018.[43] The Rhodium Group estimates that "Chinese investors abandoned deals worth more than $2.5 billion in the United States in 2018 due to unresolved CFIUS [Committee on Foreign Investment in the United States] concerns."[44] There are legitimate security apprehensions in Washington about some potential PRC acquisitions, but prudence can easily slide into counterproductive excess.

A final broad example of mutually beneficial engagement cooperation comes from the arena of international public health, an area of cooperation between China and America extending back to the first half of the nineteenth century. (For more on this, see this volume's chapters by Yanzhong Huang and Mary Bullock). In June 1979, the then U.S. Department of Health, Education, and Welfare (HEW) signed the Protocol for Cooperation in the Science and Technology of Medicine and Public Health, which provided the framework for subsequent cooperation between Chinese counterparts and HEW (later renamed the Department of Health and Human Services, or HHS), the U.S. National Institutes of Health (NIH), the Centers for Disease Control and Prevention (CDC), and other related government agencies.[45] Upon this foundation, health agencies in both countries subsequently cooperated on research, funding, and information sharing to manage successive international public health challenges of global gravity, including the HIV/AIDS crisis in the 1980s and 1990s, the SARS (severe acute respiratory syndrome) crisis of 2002–2003, the H5N1 (avian flu or bird flu) of 2003, the H1N1 (swine flu) epidemic with its epicenter in the United States and Mexico in 2009, and the 2014–2015 Ebola outbreak in West Africa. "In 2005, both governments [the U.S. and China] inaugurated a Collaborative Program on Emerging and Re-Emerging Infectious Diseases, which spurred the establishment of a CDC China Center,"[46] as Yanzhong Huang describes in his chapter.

Cumulatively, these medical and public health interactions, most particularly cooperation in the earlier H1N1 challenge:

> proved useful when a new strain of avian flu, H7N9, emerged in China in March 2013. This form of avian flu had a high [human] mortality rate of 30 percent. . . . China's internal reaction to the H7N9 outbreak prevented the virus from spreading much farther beyond mainland China other than a handful of cases in Hong Kong, Taiwan, and Malaysia. . . . Additionally, in October 2013, Chinese scientists developed a vaccine—the first flu vaccine developed entirely in China—and shared their method with the world, facilitating vaccine development efforts by the CDC and private pharmaceutical companies.[47]

Running parallel to this U.S.-China bilateral cooperation in international health, reduced cross-strait tensions between Beijing and Taipei (with KMT president Ma Ying-jeou in office) created the conditions in which Beijing suspended its (misguided) opposition to affording Taiwan "observer" status in the World Health Assembly (WHA). With the more recent rise in Sino-American and cross-strait tensions, in 2017, Beijing reverted to its very unfortunate posture of opposing even observer status for Taipei in the WHA. Indeed, with the global COVID-19 pandemic that started in late 2019, health cooperation between Washington and Beijing took a grievous hit and the story switched from health cooperation to health conflict. One immediate consequence of this friction was an increase in calls in the United States to dramatically and rapidly reduce American dependence on Chinese-manufactured pharmaceuticals.

More broadly, in this postengagement era, Sino-American cooperation in health care is becoming more controversial in the United States. In June 2019 hearings before the U.S. Senate Finance Committee concerning foreign nationals (particularly ethnic Chinese with actual or suspected connections to the

PRC) receiving NIH grants, Senator and Chairman Chuck Grassley (a Republican from Iowa) asked a witness, the biomedical engineer Joe Gray, "Does NIH conduct background checks, including of review for counterintelligence purposes, of PI's [principal investigators] prior to awarding a grant to their institution?" Gray answered:

> No, we do not . . . they are employees of their home institution. . . . I acknowledge there have been misuses of intellectual property and data and there needs to be vigorous enforcement of laws that punish countries and individuals who have committed such violations. . . . But the issue of imposing additional vetting is a difficult one. The process of doing this vetting stigmatizes the entire community that is being vetted and decreases their enthusiasm for coming to the United States to advance our science. I am worried that will diminish our own ability to innovate.[48]

The real issue at hand was, and remains, how far to go in collaborative research with scientists and scholars of PRC nationality and background. What are the costs and gains? What are the boundaries of decency necessary to avoid weaving a racial dragnet that impugns Chinese Americans as well as all scholars and researchers of Chinese ethnicity? And practically speaking, is it in American interests to alienate itself from the largest pool of brains in the world? As of this writing, the COVID-19 virus was spreading globally and the downturn in U.S.-China strategic and political relations was reflected in substantially less bilateral health cooperation than demonstrated in earlier disease outbreaks.

We also should weigh the strategic (security) gains of the engagement era in our overall calculus. For instance, in 2007, China played a constructive role in bringing some measure of peace to South Sudan, at least temporarily. Beijing also constructively contributed to the Joint Comprehensive Plan of Action (the nuclear agreement with Iran) in 2015, having disengaged from Tehran's nuclear programs about eighteen years earlier.[49] In late 2016, the PRC ratified the Paris Agreement on climate change.[50] If one believes that the management of transnational security issues requires multilateralism, then cooperation with the PRC on many issues of strategic, and in some cases existential, importance is essential. The admittedly sporadic, sometimes lukewarm, and often absent cooperation from Beijing regarding the North Korean nuclear issue also deserves mention. Of particular note in the nuclear area is the positive role Beijing played in the India-Pakistan Kargil Crisis of 1999, a conflict that had a nontrivial possibility of escalating to the nuclear level. Beijing exerted restraining pressure on Islamabad, something that Washington very much welcomed but could not itself apply.[51] Here we see an irony. Washington rightly worries about Beijing's intimacy with states such as Pakistan, Iran, and North Korea, but in times of crises involving these states, Washington often seeks to enlist the PRC in restraining those actors, something Beijing could not do if it had no sway with them.

Concisely, the balance sheet on engagement must include the diversified gains of the past forty-plus years in both societies and the resources and the potential lives not wasted in quagmire wars on China's periphery, an ever-present danger in U.S.-China relations, as Carla Freeman reminds us in her chapter. U.S.-China cooperation also provided the environment in which Asia (including Taiwan) made remarkable economic, social, and political progress. More recently, parallel and mutually reinforcing U.S.-China macroeconomic actions in 2008–2009 maintained sufficient levels of worldwide aggregate economic demand to address the biggest challenge, up to then, to worldwide growth since the 1930s—the global financial crisis. In addition, Sino-American educational cooperation (discussed in the chapters by Mary Bullock, Robert Daly, and Andrew Mertha) has similarly enhanced many fields in the hard sciences, social sciences, and humanities in general and China studies in particular. The approximately $15 billion in tuition and fees paid by Chinese students to U.S. institutions of higher education in 2016 is roughly equivalent to the size of annual U.S. soybean exports to China before the 2018–2019 U.S. export drought discussed earlier.[52]

Nonetheless, despite these gains, the deterioration in U.S.-China relations is proceeding rapidly in 2020. What is the character of the era into which both countries are headed? Is it likely to be a reasonable facsimile of the Cold War or something quite different? Does the engagement era suggest some lessons for the management of what lies ahead? How might we think about limiting the damage and maximizing gains in the period ahead, an era that almost certainly will be characterized by less reassurance, more deterrence, and comprehensive competition across the spaces of security, economics, ideology, and diplomacy? From the perspective of early 2021, and the incoming Biden administration, the process of making policy will be more fact based, professional, and multilateral in character but the underlying issues, trends, and dangers look unlikely to change any time soon.

A Second Cold War?

Ambassador Chas Freeman has called this postengagement era the "New World Disorder," an appellation that, for now, serves better than most. Whatever we call the new period into which we are entering, the context is quite different from the Cold War, as are at least some of the implications for future policy. The Cold War was a hierarchical system of two camps, with clear leaders and relatively tight alliance systems. There was virtually no economic interdependence between the planned and market-based economies. Current circumstances are considerably different.

In the late 1950s, 1960s, and 1970s, China's economy and society were in shambles. The Great Leap Forward and its aftermath of famine, followed by the Cultural Revolution, were two tragic and enormous developments in the post-1949 saga. At the start of the reform era, in per capita GDP terms, China was poorer than Haiti. During the Cold War, on average in the 1945–1979 period, the United States enjoyed a robust net national savings rate of 9.84 percent of GDP. By way of comparison, during the 1978–2016 period, the U.S. net national savings rate had dropped to closer to 2 percent. It was 2.9 percent in 2017. China's net national savings rate in 2017 was 20.32 percent of GDP. In the United States, between 1948 and 1978, growth in labor productivity averaged a very strong 7.75 percent; in the 1973–1978 period, it had declined to 3.99 percent, and thereafter, it grew still more slowly, expanding 1.99 percent in March 2019. Even under the strongly advantageous economic conditions that the United States enjoyed during the Cold War, however, America was fought to a standstill in Korea in the early 1950s, and with Beijing's considerable help, North Vietnam prevailed in the long struggle with the United States in the 1960s and 1970s. If Washington was unable to subdue China directly in the Korean War and indirectly in Vietnam, when U.S. national power was at its apogee and China's national strength near its nadir, it is hard to imagine how the current situation makes feasible any objective such as regional unilateral dominance (a goal articulated by some, as Richard Madsen explains in his chapter).[53]

Although interdependence is greater than in the Cold War and anything like decoupling would be a large blow to the two economies and all the suppliers involved in extensive value chains, it also is easy to overstate the interdependence that our two economies have thus far achieved. Americans run the risk of overstating their own economic leverage on the PRC. China has considerable capacity to resist American pressure and achieve its own objectives. According to economist Lawrence Lau, in 2018, 3.6 percent of Chinese GDP was involved in exports of goods to the United States. Because China contributes relatively modest value added to many of its exports, Lau tells us that "if all of Chinese exports of goods to the United States were halted, the reduction in Chinese GDP would amount to 2.4 percent, significant but still tolerable."[54] Lau also reports that U.S. goods exports to China constituted 0.58 percent of U.S. GDP in 2018. This relatively modest mutual interdependence implies that even with a prolonged and intense trade war, and granting that China would suffer comparatively more than the United States, both countries could move their economies forward while fighting each other, albeit with considerably less overall economic efficiency.

In the current age of globalization, competing economic interests among Washington and its allies with respect to the PRC have corroded alliance cohesion, as became apparent both when the United States failed (for the most part) to persuade its allies to eschew the Asian Infrastructure Investment Bank

(AIIB) and when it failed to get uniform allied support for not dealing with PRC telecom giant Huawei. China, with its huge domestic market as bait, has a capacity to play Washington and its allies off against each other in ways not possible during the Cold War embargo of the PRC. In the security realm in 2021, French President Macron was talking about the need for a far more independent EU security posture.

This suggests that alliance management for Washington may be much more challenging in the future than during the Cold War. Take the example of contemporary South Korea (ROK). In the Cold War, the PRC threatened the ROK, forcing Seoul into a high degree of dependence upon Washington. Today, many South Koreans, including the Moon Jae-in administration, see cooperation with Beijing as essential to their hopes for reunification, economic prosperity, and movement toward land connectivity with central Asia and Europe, which depends, in part, on transit through the PRC. All this notwithstanding, as Carla Freeman documents in her chapter, the ROK's defense commitments to Washington sometimes generate considerable heat with the PRC, as occurred in 2016 when Seoul agreed to deploy the U.S. Terminal High Altitude Area Defense (THAAD) missile defense system on Korean soil. Ultimately, however, Seoul agreed with Beijing to forego establishing further antiballistic missile sites in the ROK after initial, limited deployment.

In sum, a new Cold War would see America up against a stronger principal adversary than the Soviet Union ever was (with the important exception of nuclear weapons), and Washington might well have fewer unalloyed friends than it enjoyed in the Cold War. Much will depend on how adeptly Beijing drives wedges between the United States and its historic friends and allies. Washington might start by avoiding policies that aggressively alienate its own friends as it has been doing since early 2017. With the ascension of the Biden administration in 2021, Washington was seeking to do so—to what effect remains to be seen. Notable, too, is the fact that whereas in the first half of the engagement era, America was able to take advantage of the Sino-Soviet rift, Washington currently is pushing Beijing and Moscow into closer embrace.

How Is the Current Era Similar to the Cold War?

Nonetheless, the Cold War frame captures *some* important aspects of emerging reality along the lines stated in the Office of the U.S. Secretary of Defense's *Annual Report to Congress: Military and Security Developments Involving the People's Republic of China 2019*: "China's leaders increasingly see the United States as adopting a more confrontational approach in an attempt to contain China's rise."[55] Beijing can be forgiven such views when it reads calls for "the new containment" in the pages of such leading journals such as *Foreign*

Affairs,[56] coincidentally the journal that published George Kennan's initial call to containment in July 1947 under the "Mr. X" pseudonym.

Today, reminiscent of the Cold War, the United States and China are in a security dilemma, driven in part by technological change. When one side takes a step to increase its sense of security, the other feels less secure. This produces a cycle of action and reaction with no stable equilibrium. Washington and Beijing now are being carried along like flotsam on the river of technological action-reaction. The process is being animated by each side's belief that the other seeks military primacy and regional dominance. Each side, in part, seeks deterrence by excelling in developing the means to hold hostage the military and other assets of the other at the lowest possible exchange ratio. (The object being to destroy more than a dollar's worth of the opponent's assets with the expenditure of less than a dollar's worth of one's own resources.) For example, Beijing builds multi*million*-dollar terminally guided missiles and hypersonic missiles, each of which is capable of destroying multi*billion*-dollar U.S. aircraft carriers—a disadvantageous exchange ratio for Washington. Beijing has in the past few years dramatically increased its short- and medium-range missile capabilities, putting at risk both U.S. assets at sea and on America's Pacific territories, as well as on the territory of U.S. allies and friends in the Pacific. Washington is responding, and in the summer of 2019, it exited the Intermediate-Range Nuclear Forces Treaty (INF) with Moscow that heretofore limited Washington's ability to respond to Beijing's missile challenge in the Pacific.[57] It has also changed its war-fighting doctrine.

Similarly, both sides are developing cyber and space-based capabilities that can (relatively) cheaply interfere with the other's vastly more expensive civil and military systems on and off the battlefield. The boundaries of the future battlefield are blurring by the day. Beijing and Washington are developing, refining, and deploying drone air, undersea, and space craft, each small in size, relatively inexpensive, and capable of being amassed in great numbers—"swarms." These relatively inexpensive instruments can be used to surveil and attack the expensive systems of the other with little risk to the observer's or attacker's own personnel. These assets can be employed against civilian, as well as clearly military, targets. All this increases the dangers of miscalculation and sleepwalking into escalation.

To prevail in this upward arms spiral, technological innovation is essential, and China has been seeking to improve civil-military industry integration as a matter of national, strategic priority.[58] Each side's respective industrial policy, research, and educational capacities become key zones of contention and competition. Each nation endeavors to safeguard its own innovations and acquire the opponent's intellectual property through a combination of legitimate, illegitimate, and gray-area means. All this gives rise to, as Robert Daly points out in his chapter, questioning in the United States of whether the United States should now adopt a more strategic approach to educational relations with China.

As in Cold War deterrence theory, each side today judges the other's acquisitions and actions not by what the opposition actually *intends* to do, but rather what it *could* do in an uncertain future. And what it *could* do mutates into what it *would do*. *Possibilities* become *expectations* as the two military-industrial structures plod on.

Also, as with the Cold War, the current competition between the United States and China involves "salami" or gray-area tactics, the attempt by one side to make the maximum incremental gains at the expense of the other just below the threshold that will trigger drastic response(s).[59] This requires the defensive state to continually assess when a red line finally has been crossed. The uncertainty about the red line's exact location creates the ever-present danger that an accident or misjudgment in one or both capitals will spark unintended conflict between the two. In its 2019 report cited earlier, for example, the U.S. DOD said precisely that. Actions such as Beijing's gradual transformation of uninhabited rocks in the South China Sea into man-made, military platforms is one example, and using civilian fishing and other nonmilitary (e.g., Coast Guard and Fishery Enforcement) vessels to achieve fishery control and reinforce regional claims in various contested areas is another.

Beijing has felt similarly about Washington's close-in air and naval surface and subsurface surveillance along its coast for years. The United States' (and other countries') freedom of navigation operations (FONOPS) in the South and East China Seas are also included in the Chinese indictment.[60] Both Washington and Beijing see the other as habitually testing their resolve. Sooner or later an accident will happen, as occurred in the EP-3 incident near Hainan Island in April 2001. By mid-2020, Beijing was occasionally overflying the midline of the Taiwan Strait, forcing Taipei to scramble aircraft.

Current American and Chinese efforts to build, or maintain, a solar system of international multilateral institutions from which each seeks to draw succor and exclude the other will certainly remind veteran Cold War observers of the foundational realities of the U.S.-USSR conflict. Alice Ba has observed that this dynamic is becoming more prominent in U.S.-China relations.[61] Washington is seeking to build a constellation of multilateral regimes, trading blocs, and organizations supportive of its interests, norms, and values—structures in which the PRC does not figure prominently or at all. These include the Trans-Pacific Partnership (which President Trump declined to join and which became the Comprehensive and Progressive Agreement for Trans-Pacific Partnership, or CPTPP), the Free and Open Indo-Pacific initiative/strategy, the Quad (the United States, Japan, Australia, and India), the intelligence community's Five Eyes grouping, the Blue Dot Network, the Lower Mekong Initiative, and Washington's five bilateral security treaties (with Japan, South Korea, Thailand, the

Philippines, and Australia). For its part, Beijing is nurturing its own organizational cluster—the sixteen-nation free-trade Regional Comprehensive Economic Partnership (RCEP; consisting of the Association of Southeast Asian Nations [ASEAN] plus six other Asia-Pacific countries), the AIIB, the Belt and Road Initiative (BRI), the Xiangshan Security Forum, the Conference on Interaction and Confidence Building in Asia (CICA), the Shanghai Cooperation Organization (SCO), and others.

Furthermore, in a manner highly reminiscent of U.S.-Soviet practice, the United States and China operate in each other's political or geographic backyard, trying to loosen the bonds between the opposing power and its near neighbors, friends, and allies. So, for example, as relations now deteriorate between Washington and Beijing, the PRC seeks to shore up its ties with Cuba, Venezuela, and other countries in Latin America. Similarly, the more Washington anticipates friction with Beijing, the more ardent become its efforts to improve relations with Vietnam, Myanmar, India, Mongolia, and others, including Taipei, the latter being particularly sensitive in China's national interest calculations. Each power seeks to incentivize its generally smaller neighbors to carry its water, as Cambodia is often accused of doing for Beijing with respect to sensitive ASEAN decisions requiring consensus.

There also are what might be called the legacy issues along China's periphery, a subject Carla Freeman addresses in detail in her chapter. As in the Cold War, Beijing is prone to see an American black hand at work in Tibet, Xinjiang, Hong Kong, and Taiwan, particularly when there are problems of instability in these areas. The more numerous the demonstrations in Hong Kong (as in 2019), the fiercer the domestic resistance in Xinjiang to Beijing's heavy-handed rule, and the more intense the quest for autonomy on Taiwan, the more Beijing perceives Washington to be stirring the pot, trying to undermine the PRC's political cohesion and territorial integrity. In its waning days, the Trump administration took several steps in the arms sales and diplomatic areas to push the boundaries established by eight preceding US administrations with respect to Taiwan. In its opening days the Biden White House did not walk these efforts back.

And of course, Chinese repressive responses only serve to further energize American and other foreign sympathy for these societies and provide the impetus for a steady stream of expressions (and sometimes acts) of outrage or assistance to the underdog from the U.S. Congress and/or foreign NGOs. As demonstrations in Hong Kong gained intensity in fall 2019, for instance, Congress began expedited consideration of the Hong Kong Human Rights and Democracy Act, which was adopted in November 2019 (unanimously in the Senate and with only one dissenting vote in the House of Representatives) and immediately signed into law by President Trump. Subsequently, in March 2020, the Congress passed, and the president signed into law, the Taiwan Allies

International Protection and Enhancement Initiative (TAIPEI) Act.[62] These expressions and/or activities, in turn, further fuel Beijing's distrust, even if no actual U.S. support materializes. In the spring of 2020, there was a spike in open discussion in Communist Party and Internet venues of the feasibility of a quick, forceful reunification with Taiwan. While one can hope history will prove this just to have been unauthorized bluster or a deterrent warning, preemption and surprise are elements of Chinese doctrine that should cause concern.[63] Not taking its foot off the accelerator, in August 2020, the Trump administration sent the highest-level official to Taipei since 1979 and was debating other such moves. As of early 2021, the incoming Biden administration had not distanced itself from such efforts.

And finally, just as in the Cold War, the more small and medium powers see the competitive instincts of the two major powers, the more they seek to extract benefits for their affections—these are rental, not ownership, relationships, particularly now that Beijing has money. In a recent conversation, a senior U.S. DOD official spoke with contempt (and a bit of envy) about the "suitcases of money" Beijing lavishes on small nations.[64]

How Will the Period Ahead Be Different from the Cold War?

The most fundamental difference between the earlier Cold War era and the period of disorder into which we are proceeding is that the *magnitude* and *composition* of PRC power have expanded and changed rapidly, presenting an adjustment challenge to the American system. Even more importantly, the magnitude of the PRC's economic, diplomatic, and military power (with the exception of nuclear weapons) is greater, more varied, and more dynamic than anything the Soviet Union or Mao's China represented. For Mao Zedong, ideological power (revolution) and coercive power anchored in an enormous land army were Beijing's chief assets and the instruments of its external statecraft and internal governance. While not trivial (as Washington saw in Korea and Vietnam), these instruments were self-limiting. Maoist ideology had modest external appeal except among the destitute, and the rooting of Chinese military power in a defensively oriented land army limited the potential for direct power projection at any significant distance from the PRC, except for a small nuclear-tipped missile force bringing little beyond minimum deterrence.

As in the Cold War, each side's desire to maintain nuclear and other deterrence generates a cycle of acute action-reaction. Today, the action-reaction cycle is broadening into a race to acquire capabilities in sprawling new areas of technology in which there is no clear delineation between civil and military actors. Existential threats are multiplying beyond the nuclear realm to include the cyber sphere. Both nations are pursuing ways to increase force lethality by using robots and autonomous war-fighting devices. In each of these areas, civilian research has developed key aspects of these technologies, making the distinction between civil and military products and civil and military research arbitrary and challenging to regulate. This is energizing whole-of-system responses in both nations, which creates a stew of constructive competition, necessary vigilance, and fearmongering.

An example of what lies ahead can be found in a *New York Times* article from June 15, 2019, that noted allegations that the U.S. Cyber Command had attempted to embed malware in Russia's electrical grid. Earlier (in 2010–2012), it was widely and credibly reported that the United States and Israel had embedded malware in Tehran's nuclear program, disabling centrifuges and setting back its weapons development effort. This is only a foretaste of where the U.S.-China relationship could be headed unless both sides undertake serious strategic and arms limitations talks that produce constraints in which both sides have confidence.

The most striking difference between the eras of the Cold War and the future upon which we now are embarked has been the PRC's economic transformation. Beijing's economic strength has become its chief instrument of power, a fungible asset that can be converted into coercive and normative power to varied extents and at ever-greater distances from China's shores. The PRC economy grew at a rate of about 9-plus percent for four decades, before in recent years slowing to the still respectable 6 percent range in the period prior to COVID-19. In November 2013, "China surpassed the US as the world's leading trade partner, with 124 countries considering China their largest trading partner and only 76 having that relationship with the US. This was a major shift—in 2006, the United States was the largest trading partner for 127 countries, while China dominated among 70. Some historical American allies now consider China their top trading partner, including Australia and South Korea."[65] Thus, the PRC is rapidly becoming a competitive global player across a very much greater range of activities and localities than ever before. The Belt and Road Initiative (BRI) is an example.[66]

Nations are pulled in the direction of their economic interests, and China looms large in the external economic considerations of a growing number of societies. Assuming the PRC can maintain reasonably robust growth, Beijing will have increasing capacity to persuade both America's friends and its enemies in the future. In light of this, the United States needs to consolidate and strengthen its long-standing alliances, expand its range of friends, build coalitions, and, perhaps above all, strengthen its own economic and governance performance.

A Final Word

The careers of many of the authors in this volume have been bookended by the start and culmination of the engagement era as we came to know it. Among the questions that leaders, scholars, and commentators in the United States are asking themselves at the start of the third decade of the new millennium are the following: During that nearly half century of engagement, did the United States unwittingly nurture a comprehensive competitor and adversary? How should we evaluate the costs and gains of long-standing U.S. policy?

By my reckoning (conceding that there are no generally accepted accounting principles for this calculation), the gains have greatly exceeded the costs. Nonetheless, and irrespective of the fuzzy math of engagement's past pluses and minuses, the practical problem today is how to deal with the future we confront. As Lenin wondered aloud in 1902, fifteen years before the Bolshevik Revolution, "What is to be done?" My suggested framework for dealing with the new situation rests on several assertions: It is important to seize opportunities for cooperation when they present themselves. Conflicts and frictions between the United States and China are deep-rooted and long-lived. Domestic change in both societies is a prerequisite to durably moving in a better direction bilaterally, and America needs to get its own house in order. China, in Richard Madsen's words in this volume, will for the foreseeable future "combine a successful, dynamic economy with a repressive, authoritarian state." During the Trump era, both countries were governed by individual leaders and coalitions that made sustained, dramatic improvement in the bilateral situation impossible. Looking ahead in the Biden administration, much remains to be seen, but storm clouds gather. And finally, there is a role for deterrence in U.S. policy—coercive power does count. Although deterrence is based on threat, we have to achieve it without being provocative and while achieving a stable equilibrium at the lowest possible cost. This is a core challenge.

As it took twenty years for the political stars to align for Nixon and Mao to make their bold advance in the late 1960s and early 1970s, so the next favorable conjunction of the domestic stars in China and America may not come quickly. The Cold War itself reminds us that there is a tendency for such conflict to embed itself in institutions and habits of thinking that become ever more deeply entrenched. This leaves the current and upcoming generation of scholars, policy analysts, and leaders in both countries with a clear challenge— bridging what likely will be a very challenging, perhaps dangerous, interim and uncertain period between engagement's end and a more cooperative, stable future. We should set our sights on stopping or minimizing further deterioration and building the foundations for a new, cooperative, and reciprocal era when conditions are ripe.

Finally, effective policies require that we answer a deceptively simple question: What do we want? Beyond stability and security, Americans want, and should focus on, fair treatment or reciprocity. Granting that it is not always obvious what *fair* and *reciprocal* mean operationally, the basic principle should be *equal treatment* with respect *to equivalent undertakings*. During the era of engagement, it was both understandable and defensible that a China that at the start of its transformation was poorer than Haiti in per capita terms, had one-quarter of the world's population, and was not in most global institutions would initially be given special considerations. No longer can such considerable exceptionalism be justified. China has to admit it has grown up. America has to be willing to work on a basis of equality with the stronger China that has emerged.

NOTES

I hereby express my gratitude to Alicia R. Chen of Stanford University's Freeman Spogli Institute for both her research assistance and constructive comments on an earlier version of this manuscript. I also wish to thank my longtime friends and colleagues Thomas Fingar, Robert Kapp, Terry Lautz, and Anne F. Thurston, and the anonymous reviewers for Columbia University Press for their incisive comments on earlier drafts of this chapter. I also thank Zoe Balk for her data gathering on the U.S. Congress.

1. William Shakespeare, *Julius Caesar*, eds. Barbara A. Mowat and Paul Westine, updated ed., Folger Shakespeare Library (New York: Simon & Schuster Paperbacks, 2011), 125.
2. Dina Smeltz and Craig Kafura, "Do Republicans and Democrats Want a Cold War with China?," The Chicago Council on Global Affairs, October 2020, 5, https://www.thechicagocouncil.org/sites/default/files/2020-12/201013_china_brief_1.pdf; Laura Silver, Kat Devlin, and Christine Huang, "Unfavorable Views of China Reach Historic Highs in Many Countries," Pew Research Center, Global Attitudes and Trends, October 6, 2020, https://www.pewresearch.org/global/2020/10/06/unfavorable-views-of-china-reach-historic-highs-in-many-countries/.
3. In testimony before the U.S.-China Economic and Security Review Commission on March 31, 2016, I raised the "reciprocity" issue as a widespread and deeply felt American concern that Washington needed to put front and center as a core element of what I called a new policy of "reciprocal engagement." "One-Hundred and Fourteenth Congress, Second Session, March 31, 2016, 100–101," U.S.-China Economic and Security Review Commission, https://www.uscc.gov/sites/default/files/transcripts/March%2031%202016_Hearing%20Transcript_0.pdf.
4. Jeffrey Mervis, "Powerful U.S. Senator Calls for Vetting NIH Grantees on Foreign Influences," *Science*, June 6, 2019, https://www.sciencemag.org/news/2019/06/powerful-us-senator-calls-vetting-nih-grantees-hearing-foreign-influences. See also Larry Diamond and Orville Schell, *Chinese Influence and American Interests: Promoting Constructive Vigilance* (Stanford, CA: Hoover Institution Press, 2018); Jun Mai, "Be on Alert for External 'Hostile Forces', Chinese Security Chief Warns Cadres," *South China Morning Post*, June 21, 2019, https://www.scmp.com/news/china/politics/article/3015433/be-alert-external-hostile-forces-chinese-security-chief-warns.

5. Kevin K. Droegemeier, "Letter to the United States Research Community," Office of Science and Technology Policy, September 16, 2019, 2, https://www.whitehouse.gov/wp-content/uploads/2019/09/OSTP-letter-to-the-US-research-community-september-2019.pdf.

6. Xu Wei, "Xi Stresses Nation's Self-Reliance," *China Daily*, September 27, 2018, http://www.chinadaily.com.cn/a/201809/27/WS5babed9aa310c4cc775e8414.html.

7. Gabriel Wildau, "China's Xi Jinping Revives Maoist Call for 'Self-Reliance,' " *Financial Times*, November 11, 2019, https://www.ft.com/content/63430718-e3cb-11e8-a6e5-792428919cee. In May 2019, the U.S. Department of Commerce announced: "The Bureau of Industry and Security (BIS) amends the Export Administration Regulations (EAR) by adding Huawei Technologies Co., Ltd. (Huawei) to the Entity List. . . . BIS is also adding non-U.S. affiliates of Huawei to the Entity List because those affiliates pose a significant risk of involvement in activities contrary to the national security or foreign policy interests of the United States. . . . This final rule also adds to the Entity List sixty-eight non-U.S. affiliates of Huawei located in twenty-six destinations . . . [running from Belgium to Vietnam, ed.]." Industry and Security Bureau of the U.S. Department of Commerce, "Addition of Entities to the Entity List," *Federal Register*, May 21, 2019, https://www.federalregister.gov/documents/2019/05/21/2019-10616/addition-of-entities-to-the-entity-list.

8. Xu, "Xi Stresses Nation's Self-Reliance."

9. Susanna V. Blume, "Strategy to Ask: Analysis of the 2020 Defense Budget Request," Center for a New American Security, May 29, 2019, https://www.cnas.org/publications/reports/strategy-to-ask; for another example of Center for a New American Security propositions, see Robert O. Work and Greg Grant, "Beating the Americans at Their Own Game," Center for a New American Security, June 6, 2019, https://www.cnas.org/publications/reports/beating-the-americans-at-their-own-game.

10. Elsa B. Kania and Emma Moore, "The US Is Unprepared to Mobilize for Great Power Conflict," Defense One, July 21, 2019, https://www.defenseone.com/ideas/2019/07/us-unprepared-mobilize-great-power-conflict/158560/.

11. Steven Ward, "Because China Isn't 'Caucasian,' the U.S. Is Planning for a 'Clash of Civilizations.' That Could Be Dangerous," *Washington Post*, May 4, 2019, https://www.washingtonpost.com/politics/2019/05/04/because-china-isnt-caucasian-us-is-planning-clash-civilizations-that-could-be-dangerous/.

12. Xi Jinping, "New Approach for Asian Security Cooperation, May 21, 2014, Delivered at the Fourth Summit of the Conference on Interaction and Confidence-Building Measures in Asia," in *The Governance of China* (Beijing, China: Foreign Languages Press, 2014), 392.

13. One report from mainstream research and public education organizations is emblematic of the changing environment: Larry Diamond and Orville Schell, *Chinese Influence and American Interests: Promoting Constructive Vigilance* (Stanford, CA: The Hoover Institution Press, 2018).

14. In May 2019, FBI Director Christopher Wray said in an interview with the Council on Foreign Relations that China was stealing "its way up the ladder" and that "no country poses a broader, more severe intelligence collection threat than China. [It] has pioneered a societal approach to stealing innovation in any way it can from a wide array of businesses, universities, and organizations." Gordon Watts, "China's 'stealing its way up the economic ladder,' " *Asia Times*, May 1, 2019, https://www.asiatimes.com/2019/05/article/chinas-stealing-its-way-up-the-economic-ladder/.

15. James M. Olson, *To Catch a Spy: The Art of Counterintelligence* (Washington, DC: Georgetown University Press, 2019).

16. Michael R. Pompeo, "On the 30th Anniversary of Tiananmen Square, Press Statement," U.S. Department of State, June 3, 2019, https://www.state.gov/on-the-30th-anniversary -of-tiananmen-square/.

17. "Document 9: A ChinaFile Translation," ChinaFile, November 8, 2013, http://www.chinafile .com/document-9-chinafile-translation.

18. David M. Lampton, "Xi Jinping and the National Security Commission: Policy Coordination and Political Power," *Journal of Contemporary China* 24, no. 95 (2015): 759–77.

19. Juan Zhang, "Interview: David Mike Lampton on COVID-19: 'Decoupling' or 'Self-reliance' in U.S.-China Relations Are Dangerous Delusions," U.S.-China Perception Monitor, March 16, 2020, https://uscnpm.org/2020/03/16/david-mike-lampton-covid-19-demonstrates -that-decoupling-or-self-reliance-in-u-s-china-relations-are-dangerous-delusions/.

20. Kurt Campbell and Ely Ratner, "The China Reckoning: How Beijing Defied American Expectations," *Foreign Affairs* 97, no. 2 (March/April 2018): 60, 70.

21. Donald J. Trump, "National Security Strategy of the United States of America," The White House, December 2017, 2–3, https://www.whitehouse.gov/wp-content/uploads /2017/12/NSS-Final-12-18-2017-0905.pdf.

22. Thomas Christensen and Patricia Kim, "Don't Abandon Ship," in "Did America Get China Wrong? The Engagement Debate," *Foreign Affairs*, July/August 2018, https:// www.foreignaffairs.com/articles/china/2018-06-14/did-america-get-china-wrong.

23. One of the brashest statements of optimism was written by Bruce Gilley, *China's Democratic Future: How It Will Happen and Where It Will Lead* (New York: Columbia University Press, 2004).

24. Henry S. Rowen, "The Short March: China's Road to Democracy," *The National Interest*, September 1, 1996, https://nationalinterest.org/article/the-short-march-chinas-road-to -democracy-416.

25. Andrew J. Nathan, "The New Tiananmen Papers: The Secret Meeting That Changed China," *Foreign Affairs*, July/August 2019, https://www.foreignaffairs.com/articles/china /2019-05-30/new-tiananmen-papers.

26. World Bank, "The World Bank in China," https://www.worldbank.org/en/country/china /overview.

27. Jeff Desjardins, "The Economies Adding the Most to Global Growth in 2019," Visual Capitalist, March 15, 2019, https://www.visualcapitalist.com/economies-global-growth -2019/.China has, in turn, fueled growth in the rest of Asia. Together in 2019, China and "Other Asia" accounted for 63 percent of global growth, whereas the United States accounted for 11 percent.

28. Lisa Kitinoja and Adel A. Kader, *Measuring Postharvest Losses of Fresh Fruits and Vegetables in Developing Countries*, White Paper-15-02 (La Pine, OR: The Postharvest Education Foundation, September 2015).

29. U.S. National Academy of Sciences, *Postharvest Food Losses in Fruits and Vegetables* (Washington, DC: National Academy Press, 1986).

30. David M. Lampton, *Following the Leader: Ruling China, from Deng Xiaoping to Xi Jinping*, 2nd ed. (Oakland: University of California Press, 2019), 49, 142–47.

31. United Nations World Food Program, "10 Facts About Nutrition in China," https:// www.wfp.org/stories/10-facts-about-nutrition-china.

32. "The Soybean Tariff Issue in 5 Charts," *Proactive Advisor Magazine*, July 25, 2018, http:// proactiveadvisormagazine.com/soybean-tariff-issue/; see also Adriana Belmonte, "The

Incredible U.S.-to-China Soybean Nosedive, in One Chart," Yahoo Finance, November 19, 2018, https://finance.yahoo.com/news/incredible-u-s-china-soybean-nosedive-one -chart-161047194.html.

33. Andy Pasztor, "How China Turned Around a Dismal Air-Safety Record," *Wall Street Journal*, October 10, 2007, https://www.wsj.com/articles/SB119198005864354292. See also https://www.chinalawblog.com/2007/10/china_air_safety_damn_good.html.

34. Brandon Fuller, "China's Air Safety Overhaul," New York University, Marron Institute of Urban Management (blog), July 14, 2010, https://marroninstitute.nyu.edu/blog/chinas -air-safety-overhaul.

35. "Boeing's Bullish China Outlook Faces Trump's Trade War Headwind," *Bloomberg*, September 10, 2018, https://www.bloomberg.com/news/articles/2018-09-11/boeing-raises -china-forecast-but-trade-war-clouds-prospects.

36. "Accidents List for China," Airfleets.net, https://www.airfleets.net/crash/crash_country _China.htm.

37. Michael Sheetz, "Boeing Drags Down the Dow on Speculation China Could Single It Out in Trade War," CNBC, May 13, 2019, https://www.cnbc.com/2019/05/13/boeing-shares-fall-on -speculation-that-china-may-single-it-out-in-the-trade-war.html.

38. James Rosen, "About 100,000 in U.S. Now Work for Chinese Firms," McClatchy DC, May 27, 2016, https://www.mcclatchydc.com/news/politics-government/article80386057.html.

39. Melissa Anders, "See List of Chinese-Owned Companies in Michigan: Mostly Auto Parts, Mostly Detroit Area," MLive, September 4, 2013, https://www.mlive.com/business /index.ssf/2013/09/as_gov_snyder_tries_to_recruit.html.

40. "General Motors Company's Vehicle Sales by Key Country in FY 2017 (in 1,000 Units)," Statistica, February 2019, https://www.statista.com/statistics/304367/vehicle-sales-of-general -motors; and Wolf Richter, "GM's Business Is Booming in China," *Business Insider*, December 6, 2017, https://www.businessinsider.com/gms-business-is-booming-in-china-2017-12.

41. John Bush, "Fuyao to Expand Operations in Moraine," *Dayton Business Journal*, July 24, 2018, https://www.bizjournals.com/dayton/news/2018/07/24/fuyao-to-expand-operations -in-moraine.html.

42. For a subtle and balanced portrayal of the vagaries of establishing and growing this Chinese-invested glass factory in Ohio, see the Netflix documentary entitled *American Factory*, directed by Steven Bognar and Julia Reichert (Los Gatos, CA: Netflix, 2019).

43. Thilo Hanemann et al., "Two-Way Street: 2019 Update US-China Direct Investment Trends," Rhodium Group, May 8, 2019, https://rhg.com/research/two-way-street-2019 -update-us-china-direct-investment-trends/.

44. Hanemann et al., "Two-Way Street." CFIUS is a U.S. Treasury Department–led inter-agency body to assess and deny or approve foreign investments with security implica-tions. The CFIUS mandate has been broadening.

45. This author was on the trip in mid-1979 and witnessed the signing of this agreement by a delegation led by Secretary of Health, Education, and Welfare Joseph Califano.

46. Georgetown University Initiative for U.S.-China Dialogue, *U.S.-China Dialogue on Global Health: Background Report* (Washington, DC: Georgetown University, April 2017), 7.

47. Georgetown University, *U.S.-China Dialogue*, 8–9.

48. Mervis, "Powerful U.S. Senator"; Jeffrey Mervis, "U.S. Groups Urge Restraint in Investi-gating Academic Espionage by China," *Science*, August 12, 2019, https://www.sciencemag .org/news/2019/08/us-groups-urge-restraint-investigating-academic-espionage-china.

49. John Garver, "China and the Iran Nuclear Negotiations: Beijing's Mediation Effort," in *The Red Star and the Crescent, China and the Middle East*, ed. James Reardon-Anderson

(Washington, DC: Georgetown University Qatar, Oxford University Press, 2018), 123–48.

50. Subsequently the United States under the Trump administration withdrew from the Paris and Iran agreements. Trump's successor, Joe Biden, rejoined the Paris agreement at the start of his first term and expressed a desire to rejoin the Iran agreement with some modification.

51. Ashley J. Tellis, C. Christine Fair, and Jamison Jo Medby, *Limited Conflicts Under the Nuclear Umbrella: Indian and Pakistani Lessons from the Kargil Crisis* (Santa Monica, CA: RAND Corporation, 2001), 10. https://www.rand.org/pubs/monograph_reports/MR1450 .html. Also available in print form.

52. Marie Royce, "Assistant Secretary Royce Remarks at the EdUSA Forum: The U.S. Welcomes Chinese Students," July 30, 2019, https://eca.state.gov/highlight/assistant-secretary -royce-remarks-edusa-forum.

53. This assessment does not change even as one acknowledges the severe demographic, debt, and potential political instability challenges the PRC currently confronts and the fact that America is still growing fairly rapidly with a much bigger base to work from.

54. Lawrence J. Lau, "U.S.-China Trade and Economic Relations" (presentation, A Forum on U.S.-China Trade and Economic Relations: What Now? What Next?, Discovery Bay, Hong Kong, July 9, 2019).

55. Office of the Secretary of Defense, *Annual Report to Congress: Military and Security Developments Involving the People's Republic of China 2019* (Washington, DC: U.S. Department of Defense, 2019), 1. This report does *not* propose that the Chinese view is mistaken.

56. Michael Mandelbaum, "The New Containment: Handling Russia, China, and Iran," *Foreign Affairs* 98, no. 2 (March/April 2019): 123–31. Mandelbaum calls for a strategy of triple deterrence—Russia, China, and Iran.

57. David E. Sanger and Edward Wong, "U.S. Ends Cold War Missile Treaty, with Aim of Countering China," *New York Times*, August 1, 2019, https://www.nytimes.com /2019/08/01/world/asia/inf-missile-treaty.html. For an overview of growing space competiton, see William. J. Broad, "U.S. Counters Space Threat From China," *New York Times*, January 25, 2021, A1 & A17

58. See Eric Hagt's dissertation on civil-military integration entitled "China's Civil-Military Integration: National Strategy, Local Politics" (dissertation, Johns Hopkins University, 2019). Hagt argues that under Xi Jinping such civil-military integration has been elevated from a sectoral priority to an overarching national cross-sectoral priority and strategy.

59. Gui Yongtao and Li Boran, "Managing U.S.-China Gray Zone Competition and Mitigating Security Tensions in the Asia-Pacific Region," in *The U.S. and China in Asia: Mitigating Tensions and Enhancing Cooperation*, eds. David J. Bulman and Hu Ran (Washington, DC: PCI, 2019), 15–26.

60. The State Council Information Office of the PRC, Xinhua, *China's National Defense in the New Era* (Beijing, China: Foreign Languages Press, 2019).

61. Alice Ba, "U.S.-China Relations and Regional Institutions: Challenges and Paths Ahead," in *The U.S. and China in Asia: Mitigating Tensions and Enhancing Cooperation*, eds. David J. Bulman and Hu Ran (Washington, DC: PCI, 2019), 167–78.

62. David Lampton, "US' Taipei Act Is a Needless Provocation Aimed at China, Even if Unintended," *South China Morning Post*, April 14, 2020, https://www.scmp.com /comment/opinion/article/3079535/us-taipei-act-needless-provocation-aimed-china -even-if-unintended.

63. Minnie Chan, "China Tries to Calm 'Nationalist Fever' as Calls for Invasion of Taiwan Grow," *South China Morning Post*, May 10, 2020, https://www.scmp.com/news/china/politics/article/3083696/china-tries-calm-nationalist-fever-calls-invasion-taiwan-grow.

64. David M. Lampton, "Notes of Conversation with Senior U.S. Military Officer," July 12, 2019, 3.

65. "China Overtakes US as World's Largest Trading Country," RT, February 11, 2013, https://www.rt.com/business/china-us-largest-trading-country-908/.

66. David M. Lampton, Selina Ho, and Cheng-Chwee Kuik, *Rivers of Iron: Railroads and Chinese Power in Southeast Asia* (Oakland: University of California Press, 2020).

AFTERWORD

J oseph Biden assumed the presidency of the United States only weeks
before this volume went to press. He faces more vexing challenges,
foreign and domestic, than any president since Harry Truman in the
aftermath of World War II—a deadly pandemic, an economy in distress, a cit-
izenry divided along partisan lines, an international climate rife with tension.

The new president's first priority is to bring the deadly pandemic to an
end, so the economy can recover, people can go back to work, and children
can return to school.[1] He also seeks to repair the crumbling American polity.
Well before the pandemic began, Biden was calling attention to our stumbling
democracy. His goals include a revamping of the American educational system
so that a child's opportunity is not determined by zip code or race, enacting
reforms to address the inequities of the criminal justice system, and returning transparency, integrity, and accountability to government. Democracy, he
argues, depends on a strong middle class and a strong middle class depends on
economic security. To promote economic security, enormous, long-overdue
investments in infrastructure must also be made—in highways, bridges, railways, broadband, energy, and education.[2]

Biden's major foreign policy goal is to see the United States resume its leadership role in the world. America's capacity as world leader, he repeats like
a mantra, depends "not just on the example of our power but on the power
of our example."[3] Among his first acts as president were to rejoin both the
Paris climate accord and the World Health Organization (WHO). He wants
to reinstate Taiwan as a member of the WHO.[4] He plans a new coalition of the
world's democracies, beginning with a global Summit for Democracy aimed

at renewing the shared spirit and purpose of the free world in the face of new challenges. He sees a triumvirate of challenges: climate change, the renewed threat of nuclear war, and disruptive technologies.[5] To those who criticize his foreign policy as a relic of Cold War thinking, he promises that many of the country's historic partnerships will be re-imagined in a new light. Relations with our longtime allies, alienated by an administration that has treated friends as enemies and dictators as friends, will take time to repair.

His decades-long tenure on the Senate Foreign Relations Committee has given Biden more foreign policy experience than any other incoming president in history, including George H. W. Bush, who had served as head of the American Liaison Office in Beijing from 1974 to 1976. Biden visited some sixty countries while a senator, meeting some 150 leaders. He values expertise and relies on a seasoned team of foreign policy advisors, many of whom worked with him during the Obama administration. He promises to rebuild the State Department, decimated under Trump by the loss of some thousand experienced experts.

Biden's interactions with China span more than forty years. His first trip outside the United States took him to Taiwan, and he first visited China in 1979 as part of the first congressional delegation to China after the establishment of the People's Republic thirty years before. His concern with human rights in China dates at least to 1989, when the violent suppression of peaceful protesters in Beijing brought the human rights issue to the center of American consciousness. Believing that China (and other Asian countries) needs access to objective news reporting and a better understanding of Western democracies, he proposed an American-run news broadcasting station directed at Asia. Radio Free Asia, established in 1996 and still in operation today, was the result. He supported China's entry into the World Trade Organization and, together with Barack Obama, publicly welcomed China's economic rise.[6] A photograph taken in 2001 shows a smiling Joseph Biden in a rural village outside Beijing bending down to shake hands with a little nine-year-old boy. According to one recent story, the boy, now grown, remembers that Biden joked that maybe he could one day become the leader of China.[7]

In 2011 and 2012, Vice President Biden met with Xi Jinping eight times, for a total of about twenty-five hours, hoping to understand what kind of leader Xi was likely to become. He also hosted Xi Jinping's visit to the United States in 2012. Initially impressed and mistaking Xi for a reformer, Biden's admiration for the new Chinese leader soon began to wane. During the presidential campaign, he referred to Xi as a thug, and promised to get tough on China.[8] Indeed, early signs are that the promise is real. A get-tough China policy is perhaps the only commonality between this president and the last.[9] But Biden's international experience, fact-based decision-making style, and willingness to compromise suggest that his management of the U.S.-China relationship will be considerably less conflictual than it was under Donald Trump. Biden is more likely to seek to steady the relationship by finding issues on which to cooperate while remaining resolute on issues where the two sides disagree.

Two areas where greater cooperation between the United States and China is both imperative and possible are climate change and health. Biden sees climate change as the greatest long-term threat to the planet and knows that success in addressing the issue requires international cooperation. China is by far the world's largest polluter. Its emissions are greater than the United States and the European Union combined, largely because of its extensive reliance on coal. But it is also the largest consumer and producer of solar and wind energy. As a member of the Paris agreement, China is committed to accomplishing the goal of limiting global warming to less than two degrees centigrade above preindustrial levels by the end of the century and expects its emissions to peak by 2030 or earlier. The United States might have much to learn from China's experience with solar and wind energy.

The ongoing pandemic also points to the absolute necessity of international cooperation in areas of health, a case made in this volume by Yanzhong Huang, whose expertise has informed many of the press reports on China's handling of the pandemic. Both the United States and China squandered any early chance for cooperation on the pandemic. The United States blamed China for the virus, labeling it the "China virus." The Chinese initially covered up the outbreak, silencing experts who were trying to publish the truth, and then sold faulty medical devices and protective equipment abroad. Biden's ascension to the presidency and his overriding concern with ending the pandemic in the United States ought to provide an occasion for the two countries to revive at least come measure of their earlier cooperative health endeavors.

Another area of possible cooperation is on the issue of nuclear weapons in North Korea and Iran. China shares some of the American concern over the possible production of nuclear weapons in these countries and has considerably more leverage over them than the United States.

But frictions will continue. China will remain, as Graham Allison describes it, the most perplexing international challenge to the United States in its 244-year history.[10] China's ongoing human rights violations will remain a source of friction with the Biden administration, which has taken early note of two current human rights issues there. The first is the situation in the Xinjiang Autonomous Region in China's far west, where as many as a million Muslim Uighurs have been incarcerated in reeducation camps where they are often forced to renounce their Muslim religion, compelled to speak Mandarin Chinese, and may be trained in a trade. The second is the abrogation by Beijing of significant aspects of the one country, two systems formula whereby Hong Kong was returned to China in 1997. China's interference in Hong Kong's relatively democratic political arrangements continues to grow, as does the anger and desperation of growing numbers of the Hong Kong population.

Finally, China's recent provocations of Taiwan, including fighter jets crossing the midline of the Taiwan Strait and random firing across the island's shores, could quickly throw the U.S.-China relationship off track. Many China specialists believe that the only disagreement between the two countries that could lead to real war is the issue of Taiwan.[11] The issues of Hong Kong and Taiwan are intimately linked. Since the remnants of Chiang Kai-shek's forces fled to Taiwan in 1949 and established the Republic of China, the island has become a successful, well-functioning, lively democracy with a thriving economy, advanced standard of living, and an increasingly independent identity. But the government of the People's Republic of China still claims Taiwan as its own and has never renounced the possibility of using force to take it. Every move against Hong Kong's independence is a reminder to the people of Taiwan that they could be next. The United States retains a policy of strategic ambiguity on the question of its possible response to China taking the island by force. But, like China, the United States has not renounced the use of force should China take the step.

In short, the strains between China and the United States will not disappear with Biden's assumption of the presidency. The disagreements are tangible and potentially dangerous. But the expertise and experience of the incoming president and his determination to re-staff the State Department and to rely on seasoned expertise suggest that the relationship will be better and more rationally managed, allowing the two countries to find issues on which they can cooperate alongside the existing inevitable conflicts. The world might be a marginally safer, if still troubled, place.

NOTES

1. See Alex Ward, "Joe Biden's Plan to Fix the World," Vox, August 18, 2020, https://www.vox.com/2020/8/18/21334630/joe-biden-foreign-policy-explainer.
2. Joseph R. Biden Jr., "Why America Must Lead Again," Foreign Affairs, March/April 2020, 65–68.
3. Biden, "Why America Must Lead Again," 65.
4. Simone McCarthy, "US Under Biden Set to Stay in WHO," South China Morning Post, November 9, 2020, https://www.scmp.com/news/china/diplomacy/article/3109068/us-under-biden-set-stay-who-experts-say-health-body-needs.
5. Biden, "Why America Must Lead Again"; Ward, "Joe Biden's Plan to Fix the World."
6. See Edward Wong, Michael Crowley, and Ana Swanson, "Joe Biden's China Journey," New York Times, September 6, 2020, https://www.nytimes.com/2020/09/06/us/politics/biden-china-html/.
7. "Joe Biden: Chinese Villagers Remember President-Elect's 2001 Visit," South China Morning Post/Agence France Presse, November 11, 2020.
8. Julian E. Barnes, Lara Jakes, and Jennifer Steinhauer, "In Confirmation Hearings, Biden Aides Indicate Tough Approach on China," New York Times, January 24, 2021.
9. Barnes et al., "In Confirmation Hearings, Biden Aides Indicate Tough Approach on "China.
10. Graham Allison, "Grave New World," Foreign Policy, January 15, 2021.
11. Nicholas Kristoff, "Biden's Nightmare May Be China," New York Times, January 31, 2021.

ACKNOWLEDGMENTS

O ur deepest debt of gratitude is to David M. (Mike) Lampton, both for his contribution to this book and his lifetime service to the China field as a whole. In early 2018, when Mike announced that he would soon be retiring from the Johns Hopkins University's School of Advanced International Studies (SAIS), where he had been Hyman Professor and director of China Studies for some twenty years and had also served as dean of faculty, his colleagues wanted to find an appropriate way to honor him. This book is the result.

The idea for a book came from Dr. Carla Freeman, the director of the Foreign Policy Institute at SAIS and Madelyn Ross, the associate director of China Studies. Mike would not countenance the possibility of a Festschrift. If there were to be a book, it would have to be a serious scholarly endeavor, a contribution to the field of China studies. My colleagues invited me to serve as editor.

The effort began with a conference titled "Five Decades of U.S. Engagement with China: What Have We Learned?" held in Racine, Wisconsin, on November 3–5, 2018, at the Johnson Foundation's Wingspread Conference Center. The Wingspread Conference Center, noted for its idyllic rambling grounds and Frank Lloyd Wright architecture, has served as the site of many high-level U.S.-China conferences and dialogues over some fifty years. By holding the conference at Wingspread, we wanted to acknowledge and draw inspiration from that past. The conference assembled together a remarkable group of China specialists from academia, nongovernmental organizations, and public service, many of whom were on the verge of retirement, others of whom were at the height of their careers. The conference also served to pass the symbolic baton from one generation of China specialists to the next. Most of the chapters in this volume began as presentations at that gathering. The Johnson Foundation's facilities and skilled staff helped make the conference a decided success.

The depth of experience of the China specialists who have contributed to this volume gives the content a rarely matched level of credibility and gravitas. Although the contributors approach China from different perspectives and surely do not see eye to eye on everything, their understanding of and experience with China is profound. Moreover, in the midst of this increasingly polarized world, they tend not toward extremes but to a reasonable, evidence-based, balanced point of view. We thank them for their superb contributions to this volume.

Many individuals and organizations played important roles in bringing the book to fruition. Staff at the Johns Hopkins University's Development Office, particularly Hugh Sullivan and Jonathan Henry, are to be thanked for their success in raising funds for the endeavor. We especially appreciate the generosity of Geraldine Kunstadter and Pete Nickerson, who have been stalwart friends and supporters of many undertakings critical to the China field over many years. The support of the Ford Foundation was also important to this effort, as for so many others in the China field over the past six decades. In particular, we thank the Ford Foundation's China representative, Elizabeth Knup, for her important support.

Many other colleagues at SAIS exerted themselves to make this overall effort possible, most importantly Zhaojin Ji, program coordinator of China Studies at SAIS and Professor Andrew Mertha, director of China Studies. Andrew Mertha and Carla Freeman contributed chapters to the volume, and Madelyn Ross helped with both editing and logistics. For their help, too, many thanks. As the China studies program at SAIS moves to incorporate the numerous, multifaceted, internationally based China oriented programs tied to the Johns Hopkins University into a single global research center of contemporary China, this book is expected to serve as an early example of what kind of work the new research center can be expected to produce.

Outside of SAIS, the comments and suggestions of two anonymous reviewers provided inspiring and useful comments and suggestions, and Stephen Wesley at Columbia University Press has been a most gracious, supportive, and constructive editor. We thank, also, the press's copy editors for their painstaking and meticulous attention to detail. We are especially pleased that the book appears under the imprimatur of the Columbia University Press series in honor of Nancy Bernkopf Tucker and Warren I. Cohen, exemplars of the field from whom we all have learned and who we have respected and admired. And finally, I extend special thanks to Peter W. Bernstein, my long-standing agent, without whose efforts the book could not have been published.

CONTRIBUTORS

ANNE F. THURSTON began teaching in the China Studies program at the Johns Hopkins University's School of Advanced International Studies in 1999 and became a senior research professor when she set up the Grassroots China Initiative working with NGOs in China. She began her teaching career at Fordham University and went on to serve as staff for the China programs at the Social Science Research Council. She has received fellowships from the MacArthur Foundation, the U.S. Institute of Peace, the Woodrow Wilson International Center for Scholars, the National Endowment for Humanities, and the Rockefeller Foundation. She is, most recently, a coauthor with Gyalo Thondup, the older brother of the Dalai Lama, of *The Noodle Maker of Kalimpong* (Public Affairs, 2015). Her books and monographs include *Enemies of the People: The Ordeal of China's Intellectuals During the Great Cultural Revolution* (Knopf, 1987 and Harvard University Press, 1988); *The Private Life of Chairman Mao* (Random House, 1994), written with Mao Zedong's personal physician; *A Chinese Odyssey: The Life and Times of a Chinese Dissident* (Scribner's, 1991); *Muddling Toward Democracy: Political Change in Grass Roots China* (U.S. Institute of Peace, 1998); and a revision of *China Bound: A Guide to Academic Life in the People's Republic of China* (National Academies Press, 1994). She writes for both academic and popular journals and holds a PhD in political science from the University of California, Berkeley.

CRAIG ALLEN is currently president of the U.S.-China Business Council (USCBC), a private, nonpartisan, nonprofit organization representing over two hundred American companies doing business with China. Prior to joining USCBC, Allen had a distinguished career in public service, beginning in 1985 at the Department of Commerce's International

Trade Administration (ITA) and serving as an international economist in ITA's China office. In 1988, Allen became director of the American Trade Center under the American Institute in Taiwan and returned to the U.S. embassy in Beijing as commercial attaché in 1992. After serving in the American embassy in Tokyo and at the National Center for APEC in Seattle, Craig returned again to the American embassy in Beijing as the senior commercial officer and later became deputy assistant secretary for Asia at the U.S. Department of Commerce's ITA. He served as the U.S. ambassador to Brunei Darussalam from 2014 until July 2018, when he became president of the USCBC. He received his BA from the University of Michigan in political science and Asian studies in 1979. He received a master of science in foreign service from Georgetown University in 1985.

MARY BROWN BULLOCK is president emerita of Agnes Scott College. She was the director of the Committee on Scholarly Communication with the People's Republic of China (CSCPRC) at the time both diplomatic and academic relations with China were reestablished and later served as director of the Asia programs of the Woodrow Wilson International Center for Scholars. She has served on the boards of the Asia Foundation, the Council on Foreign Relations, the National Committee on U.S.-China Relations, and the China Medical Board of New York and is currently executive vice-chancellor of the Duke Kunshan University. She is author of *An American Transplant: The Rockefeller Foundation and Peking Union Medical College*. She holds an MA and PhD in Chinese history from Stanford University.

ROBERT DALY has been the director of the Kissinger Institute on China and the United States at the Woodrow Wilson Center since August 2013. He began work in U.S.-China relations as a diplomat, serving as cultural exchanges officer at the U.S. embassy in Beijing in the late 1980s and early 1990s. After leaving the Foreign Service, he taught Chinese at Cornell University; worked on television and theater projects in China as a host, actor, and writer; and helped produce Chinese-language versions of *Sesame Street* and other Children's Television Workshop programs. He later served as American director of the Johns Hopkins University–Nanjing University Center for Chinese and American Studies in Nanjing. Daly has testified before Congress on U.S.-China relations and has lectured at scores of Chinese and American institutions, including the Smithsonian Institution, the East-West Center, the Asia Society, and the National Committee on U.S.-China Relations. He lived in China for eleven years and has interpreted for both Chinese and American leaders, including Jiang Zemin, Li Yuanchao, Jimmy Carter, and Henry Kissinger.

THOMAS FINGAR is a Shorenstein APARC Fellow in the Freeman Spogli Institute for International Studies at Stanford University. He was the inaugural Oksenberg-Rohlen Distinguished Fellow in 2010–2015 and the Payne Distinguished Lecturer at Stanford in 2009. From 2005 through 2008, he served as the first deputy director of National Intelligence for Analysis and, concurrently, as chairman of the National Intelligence Council. Dr. Fingar served previously as assistant secretary of the State Department's

Bureau of Intelligence and Research (2000–2001 and 2004–2005), principal deputy assistant secretary (2001–2003), deputy assistant secretary for analysis (1994–2000), director of the Office of Analysis for East Asia and the Pacific (1989–1994), and chief of the China Division (1986–1989). Between 1975 and 1986, he held a number of positions at Stanford University, including senior research associate in the Center for International Security and Arms Control. Dr. Fingar is a graduate of Cornell University (BA in government and history, 1968) and Stanford University (MA, 1969 and PhD, 1977, both in political science). His most recent books are *Reducing Uncertainty: Intelligence Analysis and National Security* (Stanford University Press, 2011); *The New Great Game: China and South and Central Asia in the Era of Reform*, editor (Stanford, 2016); *Uneasy Partnerships: China and Japan, the Koreas, and Russia in the Era of Reform*, editor (Stanford, 2017); and *Fateful Decisions: Choices That Will Shape China's Future* (edited with Jean Oi, Stanford, 2020).

CARLA P. FREEMAN is currently associate research professor of China Studies and director of the Foreign Policy Institute at Johns Hopkins University's School of Advanced International Studies (SAIS). In 2020, she served as the chair of U.S.-China Relations at the Library of Congress. Her research focuses on the links between domestic and foreign policy in China and addresses China's regional and environmental policies, nontraditional security challenges, and role in global governance. She has edited books on relations between China and North Korea and on China's role in the developing world and has authored numerous articles for academic publications, including articles on the Asian Infrastructure Investment Bank for *Global Policy* and on China's interactions with parts of the global commons for the *China Quarterly*. A forthcoming study of China and global public goods will appear in the *British Journal of Politics and International Relations* and is the topic of her current book project. Carla Freeman regularly consults with government and nonprofit organizations and has been a fellow at the U.S. Institute of Peace, Harvard's Fairbank Center, and the Chinese Academy of Social Sciences. She did her undergraduate studies at Yale and earned an MA in international economics and China studies and a PhD in international relations from the Johns Hopkins SAIS.

CHAS W. FREEMAN JR. is currently a senior fellow at Brown University's Watson Institute for International and Public Affairs and was the principal American interpreter during President Nixon's path-breaking 1972 visit to Beijing. He served as assistant secretary of defense for international security affairs from 1993 to 1994, ambassador to Saudi Arabia from 1989 to 1992, principal deputy assistant secretary of state for African affairs from 1986 to 1989, and chargé d'affaires at Bangkok from 1984 to 1986 and Beijing from 1981 to 1984. He served as vice chair of the Atlantic Council from 1996 to 2008; cochair of the U.S.-China Policy Foundation from 1996 to 2009; and president of the Middle East Policy Council from 1997 to 2009. He is the editor of the *Encyclopedia Britannica* article on diplomacy and the author of *America's Continuing Misadventures in the Middle East*; *Interesting Times: China, America, and the Shifting Balance of Prestige*; *America's Misadventures in the Middle East*;

The Diplomat's Dictionary; and *Arts of Power: Statecraft and Diplomacy.* Chas Freeman speaks frequently to educational and policy-related institutions throughout the United States. A compendium of his speeches is available at chasfreeman.net.

JOHN W. GARVER is emeritus professor in the Sam Nunn School of International Affairs at the Georgia Institute of Technology where he taught for thirty years, during which he also led summer student programs on China's and East Asian development and conducted extensive field investigation in China's provinces and multiple East Asian countries. He served for many years on the editorial boards of *China Quarterly, Journal of Contemporary China, Issues and Studies,* and *Asian Security* and is a member of the National Committee on U.S.-China Relations. He has testified before U.S. congressional committees and consulted with the State Department and other executive agencies. He served in the U.S. military from 1969 to 1970.

Garver's research focuses on China's foreign relations, a topic on which he has published eleven books and over a hundred journal articles and book chapters. He is a well-recognized, leading scholar on China's foreign relations. His most recent book, a culmination of his life's work and the first comprehensive history of China's foreign relations, is *China's Quest: The History of the Foreign Relations of the People's Republic of China* (Oxford University Press, 2018). Other books include *Chinese-Soviet Relations, 1937–1945* (Oxford University Press, 1988); *Protracted Contest: China-Indian Rivalry in the Twentieth Century, Face Off: China, the United States, and Taiwan's Democratization,* and *China and Iran: Ancient Partners in a Post-Imperial World* (University of Washington Press, 2001, 1997, and 2006, respectively); *The Sino-American Alliance: Nationalist China and American Cold War Strategy in Asia* (M.E. Sharpe, 1997); *Foreign Relations of the People's Republic of China* (Prentice Hall, 1993); and *China's Decision for Rapprochement with the United States* (Westview, 1982).

YANZHONG HUANG is professor and director of global health studies at Seton Hall University's School of Diplomacy and International Relations, where he developed the first academic concentration among U.S. professional schools of international affairs explicitly addressing the security and foreign policy aspects of health issues. He is also a senior fellow for global health at the Council on Foreign Relations, directing the Global Health Governance roundtable series and codirecting the China and Global Governance project. He founded *Global Health Governance: The Scholarly Journal for the New Health Security Paradigm.* Huang has written extensively on China and global health and published numerous reports and book chapters, including articles in *Survival, Foreign Affairs, Public Health, Bioterrorism and Biosecurity,* and *Journal of Contemporary China,* as well as op-ed pieces in the *New York Times, International Herald Tribune, YaleGlobal,* and *South China Morning Post.* In 2006, he coauthored the first scholarly article systematically examining China's soft power. He is the author of *Governing Health in Contemporary China.* He has testified before congressional committees and regularly consults and speaks on global health issues and China. He is a member of the Council on Foreign Relations and the

National Committee on U.S.-China Relations. He has taught at Barnard College, Columbia University, and Tsinghua University. He obtained his BA and MA degrees in international politics from Fudan University and his PhD in political science from the University of Chicago.

DAVID M. LAMPTON is currently senior research fellow in the Foreign Policy Institute of the Johns Hopkins University's School of Advanced International Studies (SAIS) and was Oksenberg-Rohlen Fellow at Stanford University's Asia-Pacific Research Center in 2019–2020. He is Hyman Professor and director of China Studies emeritus at SAIS, where he also served as dean of faculty. Lampton received his BA, MA, and PhD at Stanford and began his academic career at the Ohio State University. He went on to serve as president of the National Committee on U.S.-China Relations and chairman of the Asia Foundation. His last book, *Following the Leader: Ruling China, from Deng Xiaoping to Xi Jinping*, initially published in 2014, was reissued with a new preface in 2019. His other books include *Same Bed, Different Dreams: Managing U.S.-China Relations, 1989–2000* (University of California Press, 2001); *The Three Faces of Chinese Power: Might, Money, and Minds* (University of California Press, 2008); and *The Making of Chinese Foreign and Security Policy*, editor (Stanford University Press, 2001). His newest book with Selina Ho and Cheng-Chwee Kuik, *Rivers of Iron: Railroads and Chinese Power in Southeast Asia* (University of California Press, 2020), is based on field research in nine countries and focuses on Beijing's effort to build high-speed and other rail lines from South China to Singapore.

KENNETH LIEBERTHAL is senior fellow emeritus in foreign policy at the Brookings Institution, where he served as director of the John L. Thornton China Center from 2009 to 2012 and senior fellow in foreign policy from 2009 to 2016. He is also professor emeritus at the University of Michigan. Dr. Lieberthal served as special assistant to the president for national security affairs and senior director for Asia on the National Security Council from 1998 to 2000. He has authored or edited twenty-four books and monographs and authored some seventy-five articles and chapters in books. Recent books and monographs include *Bending History: Barack Obama's Foreign Policy*, with Martin Indyk and Michael O'Hanlon; *Addressing U.S.-China Strategic Distrust*, with Wang Jisi; *Cybersecurity and US-China Relations*, with Peter Singer; *Managing the China Challenge: How to Achieve Corporate Success in the People's Republic*, and *Governing China: From Revolution Through Reform*, which continues to be widely used in university courses on Chinese politics. Dr. Lieberthal serves on a number of editorial and nonprofit boards and advisory committees.

RICHARD MADSEN is distinguished research professor and director of the Fudan–University of California Center on Contemporary China at the University of California, San Diego. He is a coauthor (with Robert Bellah et al.) of *The Good Society* and *Habits of the Heart*, which received the Los Angeles Times Book Award and was jury nominated for the Pulitzer Prize. He has authored or coauthored eight books on China, including

Morality and Power in a Chinese Village, for which he received the C. Wright Mills Award; *China and the American Dream; China's Catholics: Tragedy and Hope in an Emerging Civil Society;* and *Democracy's Dharma: Religious Renaissance and Political Development in Taiwan.* His most recent publication, coedited with Becky Yang Hsu, is *The Chinese Pursuit of Happiness: Anxieties, Hopes, and Moral Tensions in Everyday Life.*

ANDREW MERTHA is George and Sadie Hyman Professor of China Studies and director of the SAIS China Studies Program and formerly a professor of government at Cornell University and an assistant professor of political science at Washington University. Mertha specializes in Chinese bureaucratic politics, political institutions, and the domestic and foreign policy process, and his specialization has recently broadened to include Cambodia. His books include *The Politics of Piracy: Intellectual Property in Contemporary China* (2005); *China's Water Warriors: Citizen Action and Policy Change* (2008); and *Brothers in Arms: Chinese Aid to the Khmer Rouge, 1975–1979* (2014). His articles have appeared in such journals as *China Quarterly, Comparative Politics, International Organization,* and *Issues and Studies,* and he has contributed chapters to several edited volumes. His edited volume, *Svay: A Khmer Village in Cambodia,* authored by May Ebihara with an introduction by Judy Ledgerwood, was published in 2018. Mertha has testified before the U.S.-China Economic and Security Review Commission; briefed the Congressional-Executive Commission on China; and accompanied a U.S. congressional staff delegation to Beijing, Xinjiang, and Shanghai to discuss issues of terrorism and narcotics trafficking. He has appeared on National Public Radio, the British Broadcasting Corporation, and Voice of America and is often quoted by the press.

BARRY NAUGHTON is the So Kwanlok Professor at the School of Global Policy and Strategy, University of California, San Diego. Naughton's work on the Chinese economy focuses on market transition, industry and technology, foreign trade, and political economy. His first book, *Growing Out of the Plan,* won the Ohira Prize in 1996. A new edition of his comprehensive and readable overview text, *The Chinese Economy: Adaptation and Growth,* was published in 2018, and the Chinese translation was published in 2020. Naughton is currently working on Chinese industrial policy. He did his dissertation research in China in 1982 and received his PhD in economics from Yale University in 1986.

SUSAN A. THORNTON is a retired senior U.S. diplomat with almost thirty years of experience with the U.S. State Department in Eurasia and East Asia. She is currently a senior fellow and research scholar at the Yale University Law School Paul Tsai China Center, director of the Forum on Asia-Pacific Security at the National Committee on American Foreign Policy, and a nonresident fellow at the Brookings Institution. Until July 2018, Thornton was acting assistant secretary for East Asian and Pacific affairs at the Department of State and led East Asia policy making amid crises with North Korea, escalating trade tensions with China, and a fast-changing international environment. In previous State Department roles, she worked on U.S. policy toward China, Korea, and the former Soviet Union and served in leadership positions at U.S. embassies in central Asia, Russia, the Caucasus, and China. Thornton received her MA in international relations from the Johns Hopkins SAIS and her BA from Bowdoin College in economics and Russian. She serves on several nonprofit boards and speaks Mandarin and Russian. She was one of the organizers of the July 2019 open letter to the president published in the *Washington Post*, titled "China Is Not an Enemy."

INDEX

Page numbers in *italics* represent figures or tables.

CPSIA information can be obtained
at www.ICGtesting.com
Printed in the USA
JSHW062356291222
35500JS00002B/77

9 780231 201292